S0-AIA-945

NURSING ADMINISTRATION HANDBOOK

Third Edition

Editorial Advisory Board

Barbara J. Brown, RN, EdD, FAAN
Editor
Nursing Administration Quarterly

Beverly Henry, RN, PhD, FAAN
Professor and Head
Department of Administration
    Studies in Nursing
College of Nursing
The University of Illinois at Chicago
Chicago, Illinois

Loucine M.D. Huckabay, RN, PhD, FAAN
Professor of Nursing
California State University, Long Beach
Department of Nursing
Long Beach, California

Lucie S. Kelly, RN, PhD, FAAN
Professor Emeritus
Schools of Public Health and Nursing
Columbia University
New York, New York

Vi Kunkle, RN, MS
Clinical Faculty, College of Nursing
University of Illinois at Chicago
University of Illinois Hospital and Clinic
Chicago, Illinois

Norma M. Lang, RN, MSN, PhD
Dean, School of Nursing
University of Pennsylvania
Philadelphia, Pennsylvania

Barbara A. Mark, RN, PhD
Associate Professor, Chair,
    Nursing Department
Medical College of Virginia/VCU
Richmond, Virginia

Norman Metzger
Professor
Mount Sinai School of Medicine
New York, New York

Russell C. Swansburg, RN, PhD, CNAA
Lecturer
Incarnate Word College
San Antonio, Texas

RT89
N765
1992

NURSING ADMINISTRATION HANDBOOK

Third Edition

Edited by
Howard S. Rowland
and
Beatrice L. Rowland

DISCARDED
URI LIBRARY

AN ASPEN PUBLICATION®
Aspen Publishers, Inc.
Gaithersburg, Maryland
1992

Library of Congress Cataloging-in-Publication Data

Nursing administration handbook / [edited by] Howard S. Rowland,
Beatrice L. Rowland. — 3rd Ed.
p. cm.
Includes index.
ISBN: 0-8342-0304-9
1. Nursing services—Administration. I. Rowland, Howard S. II. Rowland, Beatrice L.
[DNLM: 1. Nursing, Supervisory—handbooks. WY 39 N9737]
RT89.N765 1992
362.1'73'068—dc20
DNLM/DLC
for Library of Congress
92-6968
CIP

Copyright © 1992 by Aspen Publishers, Inc.
All rights reserved.

Aspen Publishers, Inc., grants permission for photocopying for limited personal or internal
use. This consent does not extend to other kinds of copying, such as copying for general
distribution, for advertising or promotional purposes, for creating new collective works, or for
resale. For information, address Aspen Publishers, Inc., Permissions Department,
200 Orchard Ridge Drive, Suite 200, Gaithersburg, Maryland 20878.

Editorial Services: Barbara Priest

Library of Congress Catalog Card Number: 92-6968
ISBN: 0-8342-0304-9

Printed in the United States of America

1 2 3 4 5

Table of Contents

Preface

In the last five years, the nursing administrator has been confronted by a wide range of new developments in the health care industry, developments that affect critical areas of management, including finance and costing, risk management, strategic planning, quality assurance, marketing, and information management, to name just a few. Each of these areas undergoing change has had a direct impact on nursing and now requires dramatic adjustments in management techniques, policies, and procedures within the nursing department.

The *Nursing Administration Handbook* has had a long history as a proven problem-solving tool for use in all areas of administration. It has also become the leading text used in nursing administration courses throughout the nation. As a result, we feel it is essential that the book be periodically updated to assure readers that they are getting the most current and authoritative information.

With this in mind, we have reviewed the entire book from cover to cover and thoroughly revised every chapter. Much of the new information, as well as many of the suggestions for changes and additions to the text, has come from prominent nursing administrators working in the field and from educators familiar with the most current and successful nursing administration practices.

Because of the wealth of new material that has been included, we particularly commend the fol-lowing chapters as worthy of close attention: Chapter 11 (*Ethics*), Chapter 14 (*Computers and Information Management*), Chapter 21 (*Quality Assurance*), and Chapter 22 (*Risk Management*). These contain vital information for the nurse administrator who wants his or her department to remain in the vanguard throughout the 1990s.

In addition, fresh insights regarding management techniques and innovative state-of-the art management approaches required that major new sections be introduced in most of the chapters. For example, Chapter 12 (*Fiscal Management*) has been thoroughly revised to accommodate the new emphasis on costing in delivery of care by the nursing service. Chapter 32 (*Troubled Employees*) now includes guidelines for dealing with impaired or addicted nurses. Chapter 23 (*Supplies and Equipment*) contains an important section on new technology and provides an orderly procedure for making decisions about high-tech equipment. Chapter 18 (*Staff Adjustment Techniques*) offers proven procedures for handling layoffs, a responsibility faced by more and more nurse executives. Chapter 13 (*Patient Care*) now includes a vital discussion of alternatives in delivery of care. Chapter 27 (*Communications*) offers sound practices for maximizing relations with physicians, board members, and the community. And Chapter 20 (*Productivity*) offers new and proven techniques and approaches for improving productivity in specific areas of responsibility.

Finally, because of recommendations from both nursing administrators and nurse educators, we have introduced three totally new chapters. Chapter 19 (*Operational Reviews*) provides detailed methods and guidelines for assessing and evaluating the operations of the overall department and individual units. Chapter 37 (*New Developments and Directions for Nursing Service*) focuses on many of the new thrusts in nursing, such as product line management and marketing. Chapter 38 (*Grant Programs and Research*) presents distinct approaches for getting funds for innovative programs and provides guidance on how to encourage research activities within the nursing service.

The additions and changes mentioned above indicate the extent of the new material in this third edition of the *Nursing Administration Handbook*. We trust this guide will satisfy many of your immediate needs and will suggest pertinent answers to your most pressing administrative problems. However, we recognize our own limitations, particularly with respect to local requirements. For this reason, we urge you to write us regarding omissions or lapses, and if you have better materials or can suggest where or from whom they can be obtained, we would be more than grateful to hear from you. This book is under constant revision, and we continue to depend upon our readers as our most important source of authoritative and current information.

Howard S. Rowland
Beatrice L. Rowland

Part I

Management

Chapter 1

Leadership

OVERVIEW

The roles and responsibilities of today's nurse administrator are more complex than those of counterparts a century or even a decade ago.

In the past decade alone, forces such as prospective payment systems, cost containment, increased competition, corporate mergers, and alternative care delivery systems have converged upon health care organizations. The current health care system is characterized by sicker patients, specialized personnel, expensive technology, increasing regulation, and shorter lengths of hospital stay. In a climate of uncertainty, rapid change, and a national shortage of nurses, the challenge to the nurse administrator to ensure the delivery of quality nursing care is greater than ever.

The contemporary nurse executive must be able to relate to higher corporate management, to colleagues in other settings and other professional groups, to the community and consumers, to nursing and ancillary personnel, and to clients within the hosital and home settings. Today's top nurse executive sets the pace for a wide variety of management activities, including the determination of appropriate rewards and incentives for staff, the design of the structure for the work of professional nurses, the establishment of systems to measure and ensure the quality of care, long-range strategic planning, negotiation

with other departments, and responses to external regulating bodies. Furthermore, the nurse executive must perform all management activities while monitoring the pulse of clinical nursing practice. Although today's top nurse executive needs to be prepared for multiple roles, his or her chief responsibility remains the management of an environment that facilitates nursing practice.*

Attributes for Excellence in Nursing Leadership**

Excellent executive nursing leadership is vital to the survival of health care agencies in the current turbulent environment. Nurse executives play a critical role in determining the vision for hospital departments and in setting the climate for changing practice. It is thus crucial to iden-

---

*Source: Joanne Comi McClosky, Diane Gardner, Marion Johnson, and Meridean Maas, "What Is the Study of Nursing Service Administration?" *Journal of Professional Nursing*, vol. 4, no. 2, © 1988 American Association of Colleges of Nursing.

**Source: Janne Dunham and Elaine Fisher, "Nurse Executive Profile of Excellent Nursing Leadership," *Nursing Administration Quarterly*, vol. 13, no. 2, © 1989 Aspen Publishers, Inc.

tify and define the leadership role of the nurse executive. One long-range study, completed between 1986 and 1989, examined excellent nurse executives' leadership styles. Nurse administrators with a reputation for excellence were selected for in-depth interviews on the characteristics of leadership in nursing. The following discussion identifies the primary themes that emerged from the ideas and concepts and practices of the executives interviewed.

Nurse executives identify excellent nursing *leadership* with universal leadership skills. Excellent leadership attributes include administrative competence with adequate educational background, business skills, and clinical expertise combined with a global understanding of leadership principles.

Nurse executives deviate from this general leadership description when they emphasize nursing's responsibility to influence the practice environment. They stress the importance of creating an environment in which the professional nurse can participate at both the organizational and the professional level. This emphasis on nursing practice exists because people come to the hospital for patient care. As one executive stated, "The primary role of any nursing administrator is to facilitate clinical practice at the bedside level."

Another aspect of excellent nursing leadership is the integration of nursing into the overall organizational effort. The effective nurse executive is a *team player* who receives interdisciplinary respect and cooperation. Team players contribute to and ultimately determine the success or failure of the organization.

Negotiation skills are another must for the excellent nurse leader. The leader appreciates the difference between negotiation and compromise. The idea becomes "give some to get some," because "winning a battle might mean losing the war." Such executives are not afraid of losing or withdrawing from a battle. They preferred to reframe "battles" as team efforts aimed at a mutually agreed-upon outcome.

Excellent nurse executives serve as *ambassadors* representing nursing in its relations with the medical staff, the board, hospital administrators, and the public. They have the ability to "translate the patient care needs into a language

that the people of the power tables understand and appreciate."

Excellent leaders have *strong value systems*. The following qualities were identified: honesty, fairness, integrity, trust, and caring, accompanied by a drive for quality and excellence. These leaders are willing to take a stand on issues and remain true to their convictions. Nurse executives consistently *model* these values with the expectation that staff will emulate these values when caring for patients.

Excellent nursing leaders are *creative*, have a *vision* of what can be accomplished, and are *risk takers*. Their vision is dynamic. They have good ideas and are open to new ideas from others.

Excellent nursing leaders are *charismatic*. They challenge, interest, and excite people about the vision, so that staff members also become committed to accomplishing the vision. The executives' vision surpasses that shared with staff members. The part of the vision shared with staff members stretches them, yet not so much that they think the vision is not possible.

Executive leadership involves *constant communication*, both written and verbal, combined with strong interpersonal skills. Part of the effectiveness of top nurse executives' communication stems from a commitment to being direct as well as from an ability to ask the right questions. Knowing when to say, or not to say, something and knowing when to listen are considered very important. Executives use their vision to structure *goals* and set the direction.

Empowerment occurs when the vision and direction are clear. The leaders empower staff members by motivating them to make the vision a reality.

Empowerment requires recognizing staff potential and unleashing that potential to accomplish the vision. It involves turning "control over to nursing staff leaders while at the same time helping to guide the direction and create the environment." "Excellent nursing leadership is orchestrating your professional practice climate in such a way that the system moves effectively in the caring of patients and is cost-effective, yet your hand is hardly noticed."

Executives agree on the importance of recognizing excellence in others. Leadership "is not always being in front and having a whole army of followers.'' Although there is a place for leaders, leaders without an army of excellent people to support their efforts are not going to achieve what they are employed to achieve. There was agreement that power comes from below, not above.

Selection of *excellent staff* is a key factor. Excellent leaders teach and train staff, often serving as role models, *mentors*, and facilitators. Excellent leadership is being visible to staff and establishing relationships with them.

Excellent nurse leaders are decision makers. They have a well-developed sense of timing in addition to the ability and confidence to make immediate decisions, wait for outcomes, and persevere when necessary. They know when to make decisions, when to delay them, and when to let others make them.

Excellent nurse leaders *constantly grow and learn*. They learn by listening to those around them, staying current, challenging themselves continuously, and learning from their own mistakes and the mistakes of others.

There was consensus that excellent nursing leaders have well-developed *business skills*, including an understanding of finance and budgeting (i.e., knowing the bottom line), resource management, long- and short-range planning, systems analysis, and personnel management.

Excellent nurse leaders are involved outside the hospital in professional organizations or in influencing governmental policy. This involvement is intraorganizational and broad based.

LEADERSHIP STYLE

Factors Affecting Leadership Style*

The leadership style adopted by the manager depends a great deal on factors such as (1) the importance of the results, (2) the nature of the work, (3) the characteristics of the workers, and (4) the personal characteristics of the manager.

Source: Jonathan S. Rakich, Beaufort B. Longest, and Thomas R. O'Donovan, *Managing Health Care Organizations*, W.B. Saunders Co., © 1977. Reprinted by permission of CBS College Publishing.

If work activity must be performed immediately, perhaps under disaster or crisis conditions, the health care manager may have to adopt a style from the autocratic end of the continuum. At other times, when work need not be done immediately, another style, perhaps consultative or participative, may be used.

The type of work being performed by subordinates can influence which style is most appropriate. If it is routine clerical work and must have a specific sequence flow, the manager may be more consultative than democratic in determining how and when the work activity will be performed. However, if the work is creative and flexible and other departments do not rely on its timely completion, the manager may be able to adopt a participative or democratic style. Certainly, the manager of the billing or accounts receivable department will adopt a different leadership style than the manager of a medical research department.

The subordinates' characteristics—their training, education, motivation, and experience—can influence the leadership style adopted by the manager. This factor is closely related to the type of work, since personnel skills tend to correspond closely with the work required. If the subordinates are skilled professionals, the manager may seek their opinions more readily (consultative or participative style) in determining how and when the work is to be performed. If they are unskilled, not necessarily dependable, or inexperienced, the manager may have to make most of the decisions. Furthermore, there are some employees who, because of their value systems or previous experiences, will not accept decision-making responsibility if it is offered.

Finally, the personal characteristics of the manager can affect the leader authority style adopted. Some individuals, by reason of their personality traits, previous experiences, values, and cultural background, function better under one style or another and may find it difficult to change with the situation. No one style is appropriate at all times. Which style is correct can only be answered after an evaluation of the situation, including the work environment, what is to be done, the nature of the employees, the personality of the manager, and the organizational climate.

Styles

Various terms such as "autocratic" and "democratic" have been attached to the decision-making behavior vis-à-vis the manager and the subordinates. These labels are traditionally called "styles of leader decision authority" and can be displayed on a continuum. In addition, terms such as "employee-centered" and "work-centered" have been used to describe various supervisory styles used by managers in overseeing work activity. Rather than nodes on a continuum, they represent opposite ways in which managers interact with subordinates.

Autocratic

In the continuum of leader authority presented in Figure 1-1, the "autocratic" end represents the manager who makes decisions and announces them to the group. The use of the autocratic style means that the manager has made a decision pertaining to what the purpose of the group activity is, how the group activity is to be structured, and who is to be assigned to what specific tasks. The total interacting relationship and the work setting have been decided by the manager. The role of subordinates is to carry out orders without having any opportunity to materially alter the decisions that have been made. The manager provides little opportunity for a subordinate to participate in making decisions.

In health care settings, we seldom see the pure form of the autocratic leader decision authority style exercised by administrative personnel. It is often the physician who adopts this style as the individual responsible for the activities required for patient care. Out of necessity, the physician must make decisions that no one else can. Consequently, he or she will make decisions and announce them to other personnel, such as nurses and technicians, who will be expected to carry out the activities without deviation.

Consultative

The "consultative" style appears to the right of "autocratic." In this situation, the manager "sells" the decision or presents ideas and invites questions from subordinates, or both. Specifically, the manager makes decisions concerning the work activity to be carried out, its purpose, how it is to be done, when, and by whom and attempts to sell the subordinates on the decisions. The manager may recognize the possibility of some resistance and invite questions; however, unless overwhelming reasons cause a change in the decisions made, they stand.

Participative

If the manager presents a tentative decision that is subject to change or presents the problem to the subordinates, gets suggestions, and then makes the decision, we are dealing with a "participative" style. The manager identifies the purposes, the problems, and the means by which the activities should be carried out; presents a tentative decision already made or seeks subordinate opinion; and then makes the decision. In this instance, the "area of decision freedom for subordinates" is much greater and the "use of authority by the manager" is much smaller than with the autocratic and consultative styles.

Participative management is a very powerful motivator in enabling employees to have some measure of influence and control over work-related activities. The work group can influence the decisions made concerning work activities and their purpose.

Democratic

Within a "democratic" style the manager defines the limits of the situation and the problem to be solved and asks the group to make decisions. The subordinates have a relatively large "area of decision freedom," as indicated in Figure 1-1. The boundaries of activity are set by the manager, who permits the group to make decisions within those limits. For example, a nurse supervisor might allow only RNs to give medication but might permit them to decide among themselves who will give the medication and who will perform other tasks that must be done.

Laissez-faire

The term "laissez-faire" was originally coined for the doctrine that government should not interfere with commerce. It is sometimes called "free rein." Under such leadership, sub-

Figure 1-1 Continuum of Leader Decision-making Authority

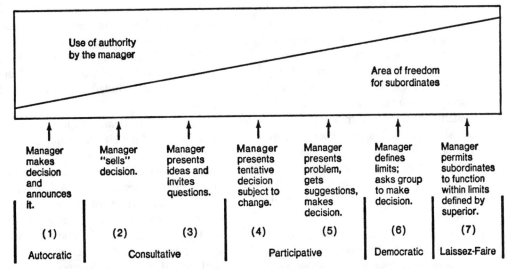

Source: Reprinted by permission of the *Harvard Business Review*. An exhibit from "How to Choose a Leadership Pattern" by Robert Tannenbaum and Warren H. Schmidt (May/June 1973). Copyright © 1973 by the President and Fellows of Harvard College; all rights reserved.

ordinates are permitted to function within the limits set by the manager's own superior. There is no interference within the group by the manager, who, although participating in the decision making, attempts to do so with no more influence than any other member of the group. The subordinates basically have complete freedom in making decisions, with minimum participation by the manager. The manager is merely a figurehead. This style of leader decision authority is rarely found in health care organizations.

NEGOTIATING A NEW ADMINISTRATIVE POSITION*

The strategies that could help a newly appointed chief nursing officer include the following:

- *First, establish your agenda*. While the expectations are high, establish a philoso-

phy that can be narrowed down to a phrase or two that you can use over and over and to which you can return when the time comes to be firm. Some phrase that succinctly captures what is important to you helps your staff have something about which to get excited.

- *Decide on your objectives and share them symbolically*. A few well-chosen strategies are better than diffusing your agenda in many different directions. A new logo to announce a nursing model or offering a special class at the facility helps you send a serious message in time-efficient ways.

- *Develop positive coalitions quickly*. As much as is possible, begin to network with your staff, professional colleagues, and other executives. An easy method is to determine the areas of conflict that a predecessor may have had and target those as opportunities. Be clear about your objectives in developing the coalitions; you still don't know enough about the culture to make good decisions this early in the game.

- *Maintain the old symbols as much as possible*. Even apparently innocuous systems can be symbolic, and care should be taken

Source: Judeth N. Javorek, "What Ronald Reagan Has To Do with Making It in a New Position," *Nursing Management*, vol. 21, no. 9, September 1990. Reprinted with permission.

not to disassemble any structure whose purpose or history makes it important.

- *Maximize the use of personal charisma to reach your constituents, but don't rely on it.* It is possible to use charisma in our profession, but you must demonstrate regard and respect for the established layers. Allowing staff access to you via conferences and regular bulletins helps to underpin your philosophy. Allowing staff nurse access via an open door is fraught with difficulty no matter how attractive the prospect may appear, and initially open-door access should be reserved for formal structures like exit interviews.

- *Use your supporters to get your message out.* You will need all the support you can get in the opening days of your tenure, and you should use every opportunity for good publicity and every photo opportunity. Making rounds on the weekends and assisting in minor ways on the units are all means by which "institutional legends" are born. You should be careful to be consistent with your general philosophy; otherwise the mixed messages you will send can confuse your agenda and disgruntle your budding cheerleaders.

- *Know the institutional legacy.* A new incumbent needs to know that there often is a legacy of bad feeling—the only variables may be the degree of intensity and the significance. Interviewing, asking questions, and seeking feedback may help ferret out the problem and help you begin to incorporate the appropriate people into your network. These techniques also help you to develop information about opposition to your plans and assist you in planning a response.

- *Optimism and an upbeat attitude are winners.* An air of enthusiasm and interest and exploration is satisfying to staff who have undergone the loss of leadership and are looking to be included in a meaningful future.

- *Use the theory of small wins to consolidate your agenda.* Publicize the gains that you and your staff have made. Pay attention to the impact of recognizing the hard work that contributed to your success. Acknowledging staff who have published or earned a degree or have been selected for office says a lot about what you value and helps your staff understand that the future is created with small steps and successes. Keep reminding them that their actions directly reflect your agenda, and reward them consistently and often.

- *Understand that you are creating a legacy for someone else.* It is difficult to consider your ultimate successor as you plough through each day, but you will leave a better prepared staff when the time comes to move on if you do not create, even inadvertently, a personal cult. Another way of benefiting the next administration is to plan appropriately for succession or, at the very least, provide for candid and supportive career planning for the senior staff who must prepare for a new vision and a new agenda.

- *Provide equal measures of task and people orientation.* It has been determined conclusively that people look to their leaders to deliver equally on the task and the people continuum.

Chapter 2

The Role and Characteristics of Management

DIFFERENTIATING MANAGERS FROM EXECUTIVES*

As the layers of nursing administration have proliferated with the changing structure of health care facilities, a distinction has evolved between the concepts of managers and executives. This contrast is largely the result of basic entrepreneurial activities, the growth of large-scale hospital chains, the separation of ownership and control, the development of strategic management theory, and the differentiation of operational responsibilities from key leadership responsibilities.

Management implies a dynamic and proactive approach to running operations. It suggests that managers are concerned not only with achieving efficient operations but also with ensuring that effective performance is attained. The manager will react to resource allocations in an organization by negotiating, arguing, politicking, or other means to acquire a larger allotment. Pressures on the organization are resolved by adjusting the current process and structure of service delivery for immediate resolutions. The man-

ager may also be actively involved in defining a vision of which goals and objectives the program, department, or organization will pursue.

The primary feature that differentiates managers from executives is the extent of their authority to formulate organizational vision. Managers hold a limited strategic vision for their program, department, or organization because they are extremely involved in controlling current operations. They have restricted time, freedom, and prerogative to determine where an organization is headed over the long run. On the other hand, executives are more interested in forming a strategic vision of where a program, department, division, or organization is headed and in elucidating the conceptual steps that are required to arrive at that point. As a result, executives have an expanded vision for the organization.

Managers are oriented toward current operations. Consequently, their effort is directed to operations management or fine-tuning of operations. This is generally reflected in a short-run outlook in planning. Goals and objectives are primarily set for a period that is consistent with the current budgeting cycle. The culmination of this operations orientation is a limited vision of where an organization is headed. Less effort is devoted to conceptualizing which direction the organization should pursue because so much effort is given to how the organization is currently performing.

*Source: Judith F. Garner, Howard L. Smith, and Neill F. Piland, *Strategic Nursing Management: Power and Responsibility in a New Era,* Aspen Publishers, Inc., © 1990.

Executives are normally oriented toward both current operations and long-run strategy. They attend to operations to make certain that efficiency and effectiveness goals are achieved. They do not overly dwell on current operations, however; that is a responsibility for managers.

Executives maintain an outlook of the long run. Their planning horizon is seldom less than one year. They concern themselves with events outside the organization and the manner in which those events might be detrimental to operations. The result is an expanded vision of the direction in which the organization is headed. Executives temper this vision with a healthy awareness of internal operations. The abilities and limitations of the organization are well analyzed. Therefore, executives avoid moving too quickly or ambitiously and thereby endangering fiscal solvency, competitive posture, and the general essence of the organization. Executives define the organization and determine what the organization will become many years hence.

FUNCTIONS OF MANAGEMENT

Overview*

The duties common to all managers are most often referred to as functions of management. They include planning, organizing, directing, coordinating, and controlling. (See also Table 2-1.)

Planning

The planning process is largely one of forecasting and decision making. Forecasting provides the manager with information and messages about the future. By combining the forecast with other data related to the past and present, a manager can then select those courses that appear to be most appropriate in terms of forecasting conditions. Yet, while a manager can be assisted in the planning process by various staff groups, it should be noted by each

*Source: Gene Newport, *Tools of Managing,* © 1972. Addison–Wesley, Reading, Massachusetts. Pp. 7–9. Reprinted with permission.

manager that the ultimate responsibility for planning rests with him or her alone.

Since planning is always future-oriented, it can be further characterized as the process whereby the management of an organization bridges the time span between where it is at present and where it wants to be at some point in the future. In doing so, planning involves the choice of objectives along with the policies, strategies, programs, procedures, and rules that are necessary for their accomplishment. In this sense, planning directs our thinking toward *what* we expect to do, *why* it will be done, *where* it will be done, *when* we expect to do it, *how* it will be done, and *who* is going to do it.

Organizing

Basically, the purpose of organizing is to establish a chain of command and a division of labor. To accomplish these ends, organizing involves the identification of duties to be performed; a grouping of these duties to indicate division, unit, section, or departmental arrangements; and an assignment of authority according to the line, staff, or functional relationships that will exist between individual jobs and total organizational units.

The steps outlined above can, of course, be applied either to the initial design of an organizational structure or to the maintenance of the structure once it has been established. In each case, the process is indispensable, since it combines human and material resources into an orderly and systematic arrangement that provides the basic ingredients necessary for a coordination of effort.

Directing

While planning can determine what will be done, organizing can combine the necessary resources for doing the job, coordinating can maintain harmony among the resources, and controlling can monitor performance, it is direction that initiates and maintains action toward desired objectives. Direction is, therefore, closely interrelated with leadership, in that a manager's style of leadership is determined by the manner in which he or she exercises authority in the direction of subordinates.

Table 2-1 Summary of Managerial Roles

Role	Description	Identifiable Activities
Interpersonal		
Figurehead	Symbolic head; obliged to perform a number of routine duties of a legal or social nature	Ceremony, status requests, solicitations
Leader	Responsible for the motivation and activation of subordinates; responsible for staffing, training, and associated duties	Virtually all managerial activities involving subordinates
Liaison	Maintains self-development network of outside contacts and informers who provide favors and information	Interdepartmental relations and other activities involving outsiders
Informational		
Monitor	Seeks and receives wide variety of special information (much of it current) to develop thorough understanding of organization and environment; emerges as nerve center of internal and external information on the organization	Handling all contacts categorized as concerned primarily with receiving information (e.g., periodical news, observational tours)
Disseminator	Transmits information received from outsiders or from other subordinates to members of the organization; some information factual, some involving interpretation and integration of diverse value positions of organizational influencers	Forwarding mail into organization for information purposes, verbal contacts involving information flow to subordinates (e.g., review sessions, instant communication flows)
Spokesman	Transmits information to outsiders on organization's plans, policies, actions, results, etc.; serves as expert on organization's industry	Department meetings; handling contacts involving transmission of information to outsiders
Decisional		
Entrepreneur	Searches organization and its environment for opportunities and initiates "improvement projects" to bring about change; supervises design of certain projects as well	Strategy and review sessions involving initiation or design of improvement projects
Disturbance Handler	Responsible for corrective action when organization faces important, unexpected disturbances	Strategy and review sessions involving disturbances and crises
Resource Allocator	Responsible for the allocation of organizational resources of all kinds—in effect the making or approval of all significant organizational decisions	Scheduling; requests for authorization; any activity involving budgeting and the programming of subordinates' work
Negotiator	Responsible for representing the organization at major negotiations	Negotiation

Source: From *The Nature of Managerial Work* by Henry Mintzberg (pp. 92–93). Copyright © 1973 by Henry Mintzberg. Reprinted with permission of Harper & Row Publishers, Inc.

Success in carrying out this function depends on many factors. Among the most important are delegation, communication, training, and motivation. Through delegation, subordinates receive the authority required for the fulfillment of their responsibilities. Communication provides individuals with the information needed in performing their jobs and allows for feedback of results related to their performance. Training is involved with the initial orientation of employees in addition to the continued direction of learning once they are on the job. Finally, motivation is concerned with assisting individuals in satisfying their needs in such a way that they continue to exhibit behavior that is consistent with their potential.

Coordinating

A coordination of effort involves the synchronization of activities toward established goals. If all employees are given the right to do a job in their own way, each is usually guided by his or her own ideas of what should be done. And even though these individuals may be quite willing to cooperate, the end result could well be a waste of time, effort, and money, since there is no meaningful direction to guide their efforts. Consequently, coordination is required and becomes a major responsibility of all managers.

To reiterate, coordination is different from cooperation. While the latter may arise spontaneously among the members of a group, coordination occurs only through effective lead-ership. As with a tug-of-war, the manager can make a great contribution by learning when and how to let go of the rope, so to speak, in order to call the cadence that causes the team to pull together. In this sense, coordination is the means of concentrating and applying cooperative effort to accomplish a task with economy and effectiveness. Therefore, it becomes the very essence of management and results from good planning, organizing, directing, and controlling.

Controlling

The purpose of control is to see that actual performance corresponds to that which is called for in various plans. All managers exercise control by (1) knowing or establishing the standards that relate to a particular course of action; (2) measuring actual performance against the standards; and (3) correcting deviations from standards, when necessary.

Leadership is also essential to control, since inanimate objects are really not controlled in the strict sense. People operate machines, use equipment, follow procedures, and, in fact, bring an organization to life. Thus control focuses on the direction of human behavior, but leadership is needed to cause persons to perform in a desired manner.

Each of the functions and activities identified here is performed by every *professional* manager at every level. The differences are ones of magnitude and frequency. Figure 2-1 shows the variation in the percentage of effort devoted to

Figure 2-1 Proportion of Management Effort Devoted To Planning, Organizing, Directing, Staffing, and Controlling

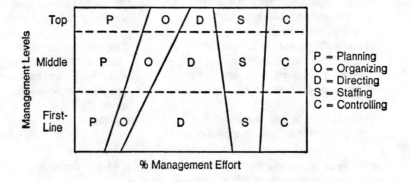

each of the five functions at three levels of management.

As is readily apparent from the illustration, the biggest variation in proportionate effort is in the directing function. The closer the manager is to production activity, the larger is the proportion of effort likely to be devoted to the directing function. Conversely, the further away from production the manager gets, the less time and effort should be devoted to directing and the more attention should be given to the other functions. Obviously, the actual mix of the various functions will not be as smooth as in the illustration, and it will be influenced by other factors as well. Nevertheless, the marked change in the mix as a manager proceeds up the management ladder is inescapable. Therefore, a highly successful first-line supervisor will not necessarily make a good middle manager. Nor, on the other hand, will a middle manager who possesses the necessary skills to perform effectively at that level be a guaranteed success as a first-line supervisor.

THE CREATIVE EXECUTIVE*

To start with, the creative executive has more energy, is more impulsive, and is more responsible to emotions and feelings than the less creative manager. Creative executives can generate large numbers of ideas rapidly, choose and investigate a wide variety of approaches to problems, discard one frame of reference for another, change approaches, and adapt quickly to new developments.

Less creative colleagues often suffer from "hardening of the categories," which is a lack of flexibility that often results from overfamiliarity with objects or ideas. Really creative executives allow their thoughts to mill about without categorizing.

Source: Reprinted, by permission of the publisher, from "Are You a Creative Executive?" by Eugene Raudsepp, *Management Review,* February 1978, © 1978 by AMACOM, a division of American Management Associations. All rights reserved.

Youthful Curiosity

Creativity is contingent upon how much of our innate curiosity and youthful sense of wonder has remained intact. Unfortunately, these attributes are educated out of most of us by the pressures of conformity and conservatism. Very few adults retain them, but the creative executive holds on to an intense curiosity about everything. An interested, expectant, responsive attitude toward life keeps the creative mind well stocked with all kinds of information that can be drawn on when engaged in creative activity. Creative executives are not content just to see how something works, but they delve into the whys, the cause-and-effect relationships, of what they perceive. Their curiosity is not centered just on their own fields; their spectrum of interest embraces disparate areas and generates spontaneous enthusiasm toward almost any puzzling problem.

Originality and Openness

Originality in thought is another trait of the creative executive. He or she can think of unusual solutions and can see remote relationships between phenomena. Such persons are likely to perceive the unexpected, the novel, and the fresh in everything they encounter.

The creative individual's openness to unusual ideas sometimes extends to the point of gullibility. Such managers are usually quite ready to entertain bizarre or crackpot ideas and frequently play around with them seriously before discarding them. New perspectives, new concepts, and venturesome ideas offer an endless source of mental exercise.

Sensitivity to Problems

The creative executive not only finds fresh approaches to problems, but also detects problems. The ability to see need areas or to be aware of the odd or promising allows this manager to note gaps in his or her department's organization or services.

Such executives can also see opportunities in situations that less sensitive managers might overlook. They are acutely aware of people's needs and of the unrealized potential of their staff. Always interested in improving upon existing products or situations, these managers are like the Socratic philosopher with a "thorn in his flesh"—perpetually disturbed by something. For the creative executive, there is hardly a situation free of problems; this happy state of dissatisfaction keeps his or her problem-orientation constantly alive.

Confidence To Dare

Daring to transcend accepted patterns of thinking and to stick to convictions in the face of possible discouragement or censure is very necessary in creative work. Rare indeed, however, is the established creative executive, and even rarer the novice who can maintain complete detachment from criticism.

Self-confidence is an important attribute that can be developed only through experience and exercise. It has been said that nothing breeds success like success, and this is probably true; buy the corollary that failure breeds failure need not also be true. Though fear of making a mistake is a devastating emotional block to creativity, executives should realize that progress is made through failure as well as through success.

Since most executives' career orientations are governed by the premise of success, the specter of failure looms large. In the risk-taking enterprise of creativity and innovation, however, failures do occur. Failure should be regarded as a situation from which new or improved ideas may arise. In reality, the greatest failure is not to attempt a new idea at all.

The fear of failure prevents many executives from daring anything really creative, especially when the element of risk taking is considerable. So the young executive needs encouragement and recognition in order to develop the confidence that he or she will eventually come through, no matter how many failures there are.

High Motivation vs. "Success"

Some executives, however, blunt their effectiveness by excessive motivation or the desire to succeed too quickly. The overmotivated executive may narrow his or her field of observation, looking for and using only clues that provide a quick solution to a problem. This person frequently passes up leads to novel or better solutions by picking the first workable solution rather than considering alternatives.

Overmotivation can also result in excessively ambitious goals. Some executives want to tackle only very big and complex problems. Failure to solve such complex problems successfully can undermine confidence to tackle problems well within their capabilities.

A lack of persistence or a feeling of flagging interest is often a signal to get away from a problem and relax for a while. Many creative executives turn to another problem because they find they function best when involved in several undertakings simultaneously, each at a different stage and each affording the chance to "relax" when necessary.

During the creative process, however, the creative executive maintains an uninterrupted rapport with the "proposals" that emerge from the subconscious as he or she forms them into something that makes daylight sense. This requires great self-discipline.

Toying with Ideas

There is often a seemingly light side to the creative executive's involvement in work. The executive may seem to be lost in an irresponsible play of ideas, relationships, and concepts, which he or she shapes into all kinds of ostensibly incongruous combinations. However, this apparently purposeless exercise strengthens and, at the same time, loosens the "muscles" of imagination. It enables the person to come up with more unique solutions to problems.

Creative executives have often found that playful sketching and shaping of ideas helps them come upon really valuable ones. Furthermore, this toying serves to get them in a proper mood to start ideas flowing. These quasi-serious exercises relax the ever-present critical and conservative orientation of the conscious. By putting this watchful censor to sleep, they can set the stage for the emergence of novel ideas and solutions.

Tolerance of Ambiguity and Complexity

One reason for the lack of creative ideas among many executives is their strong preference for predictability and order. Many immediately reject ideas that either do not fit into an established pattern or are too elusive for immediate comprehension and categorization.

On the other hand, creative executives can tolerate a high degree of ambiguity. They are actually suspicious of any pat explanations and have developed a healthy respect for groping around and for the unknown during the creative process. Creative persons can perceive a variety of possibilities and are able to simultaneously consider and balance different, even conflicting and contradictory frames of reference and concepts.

Selectivity

Likewise, creative executives differ from the less creative or noncreative in the quality they show in the selection of elements when confronting a problem. They are able to choose more fundamental aspects and cast the superfluous aside. In creative problem solving, it is, as a rule, not necessarily the executive who is highly fluent with the problem who shows the highest degree of creativity. Whether fluent in thinking or not, the executive who can grasp the heart of the matter frequently shows the highest degree of creativity. In creative thinking, it is quality that counts, not necessarily the quantity of ideas.

Creative Memory

The subconscious is a storehouse of facts, observations, impressions, and other memories. While the creative executive's mind is always richly stocked with these memories, this does not in itself indicate creativity. As a matter of fact, a prodigious memory can act as a deterrent to creativity.

What makes memory creative is the dynamic mobility of the components. Where the uncreative memory files its data and impressions within neat and independent cubicles, the creative memory's boundaries are permeable. All kinds of related and unrelated data and ideas can always be cross-indexed and interrelated.

The creative mind is continuously rearranging, pruning, discarding, relating, and refining these data and ideas. In such a permeably structured memory, there is the ever-present possibility for new configurations and combinations.

Creativity requires exact, recallable observations and discriminating use of the senses. Try this simple test: In the margin of this page, draw the face of your watch—without first looking at it.

This test illustrates the effect of overfamiliarity. We look at our watches so often we cease "seeing" them. That's what happens when behaviors become automatic and when we take objects too much for granted.

Incubation

There comes a time when thinking becomes clogged, when errors pile up, and when no significant insights about a particular problem occur. At this point, the creative executive stops working on that problem and turns to something entirely different. According to Dr. A. Schlien of the University of Chiciago, "Although he has confidence in his ability, the creative individual also has an attitude of respect for the problem and admits the limits of his conscious power in forcing the problem to solution. At some point, called 'incubation' by many who have reported the process, he treats the problem as if it has a life of its own, which will, in its time and in its relation to his subliminal or autonomous thought processes, come to solution."

The creative executive also likes to contemplate, reflect, meditate, or just "chew the mental cud." During these periods the executive often gets some of his or her best ideas.

A Creativity Checklist

The creative executive has distinct characteristics that set him or her apart from less creative colleagues. There are many gradations of attributes and skill levels among creative persons, but all such executives have some measure of these characteristics in common. The creative executive:

_____Is willing to give up immediate gain or comfort to reach long-range goals.

_____Is determined to finish work even under conditions of frustration.

_____Has a great amount of energy, which is channeled into productive effort.

_____Perseveres despite obstacles and opposition.

_____Has the ability to examine his or her own ideas objectively.

_____Has great initiative.

_____Is irritated by the status quo and refuses to be restricted by habit and environment.

_____Has many hobbies, skills, and interests.

_____Can open up to experiences and abandon defenses.

_____Feels he or she has untapped potentials.

_____Criticizes him- or herself more than others do.

_____Is not afraid to ask questions that show ignorance.

_____Likes ventures involving calculated risks.

_____Believes, even after repeated failures, that he or she can solve a problem.

_____Has the confidence to meet new problems, find out new things, and do original things.

_____Is willing to stand alone if integrity demands it.

_____Does not blame others or make excuses for errors or failures.

_____Competes with self rather than others.

_____Has neither fear nor resentment toward authority and is nonauthoritarian.

_____Is open and direct with people and respects their rights.

_____Wants to examine things from another's viewpoint.

_____Knows how to give inspiration and encouragement.

_____Is governed by inner stimulus rather than outer command and has a rising level of aspiration.

_____Gets the greatest pleasures from creative activities.

_____Believes that fantasy and daydreaming are not a waste of time.

_____Has an inherent desire and respect for perfection.

_____Wants to integrate utility with the aesthetic.

_____Moves toward solutions using intuition.

_____Knows that getting stuck on a problem is frequently a result of asking the wrong question.

_____Is alert to new perspectives and knows that much depends on the angle from which a problem is seen.

_____Is willing to listen to every suggestion, but judges for him- or herself.

_____Always has more problems and work than time to deal with them.

Source: Reprinted, by permission of the publisher, from "Are You a Creative Executive?" by Eugene Raudsepp, *Management Review*, February 1978, © 1978 by AMACOM, a division of American Management Associations. All rights reserved.

Some managers tackle problems with a dogged effort. Although commendable, keeping busy without time for relaxation or change of activity frequently serves as an effective barrier to novel solutions. The executive who knows when persistence with a recalcitrant problem begins to result in diminishing returns, and who then drops it for a while, frequently finds that, on returning to it, a fresh approach comes with greater ease.

There is a popular but fallacious notion that the creative individual relies on effortless insight and unforced spontaneity. True creativity requires a great deal of self-discipline and old-fashioned effort.

The majority of creative executives do not know the meaning of an eight-hour workday. Their preoccupation with problems is incessant. Creativity, in whatever field, is generated by hard thinking, prolonged reflection, and concentrated hard work. But creative persons have their moments of joy when ideas start flowing after a disrupting hitch.

Frequently, however, the intense struggle with problems is useless. But these efforts, futile as they seem to be, are not necessarily wasted, because they activate the subconscious processes of cerebration and incubation. Without preparatory work, the subconscious can be notoriously unproductive.

Whatever the field, creation is a product of hard thinking, prolonged reflection, and concentrated toil. There is a continuous assimilation of data and observations, a continuing pondering on the causes of regularly met difficulties, and a sorting out of hunches and ideas that flash across the firmament of consciousness.

Creative executives develop a retrospective awareness of when they have solved problems creatively. They take note of the methods that have succeeded and failed. They try to learn "why" by retracing as far as possible the routes followed and those avoided.

Creative individuals schedule their creative thinking periods for times when they have their most favorable mental set for producing ideas. They are aware of their personal rhythms of output. By keeping a record of their most creative periods during a day, they can establish a pattern and plan ahead, reserving peak periods for concentration, contemplation, and uninhibited thinking and using the less productive times for reading or routine tasks. But even without a time sheet of productive periods, the creative executive develops a sensitivity to moods that promise good returns—and knows when these moods are approaching.

NURSE MANAGER CHARACTERISTICS*

Based on the critical decision areas for nurse managers (see Table 2-2) requisite competen-

---

Source: Tables 2-2 to 2-5 are from Maryann F. Fralic and Andrea O'Connor, "A Management Progression System for Nurse Administrators, Part I," *The Journal of Nursing Administration*, April 1983. Reprinted with permission of J.B. Lippincott Company.

cies related to three basic skill areas—conceptual, human, and technical—have been identified (see Tables 2-3, 2-4 and 2-5).

A Set of Self-Evaluation Tools*

Leadership

Of all management skills, leadership is most highly valued—and most difficult to define. Of course, a good leader may be easy enough to identify: "His people will do anything he asks of them." "She knows how to make her group pull together."

But even when we watch good leaders in action, we find it difficult to pinpoint exactly *what* they do and *how* they do it. Nevertheless, while there's a lot about leadership we don't know, some insightful checkpoints can provide a rough rule of thumb measure of this crucial skill. Try the quiz that follows, sticking reasonably close to your own experience. Mark each item true (T) or false (F).

1. I do a good job of getting my people to cooperate in achieving goals.
2. My people don't hesitate to bring their really tough work problems to me.
3. When the heat's on, I can get my people to go full steam without any gripes from them.
4. When I'm not around to supervise personally, my subordinates go on working pretty much as usual.
5. I have a good record of helping individuals improve their job performance.
6. I have never had a justified complaint about showing favoritism.
7. I can usually get people to accept changes, even if they have to make a big adjustment.
8. In case of an argument or controversy involving other departments, I back up my people when I know they are right.
9. I have relatively little trouble in getting my people to level with me.

Source: From *The Executive Deskbook*, 2nd edition, by Auren Uris, © 1970, 1979, by Litton Educational Publishing Inc. Reprinted by permission of Van Nostrand Reinhold Company.

Table 2-2 Critical Decision Areas for Nurse Managers

I. *Environmental Interface*
   A. External Environment
      1. The Organization
         a) The Overall Organization
         b) Intradivision
            (1) Manpower Supply
            (2) The Contemporary Worker
            (3) Technology
            (4) Institutional History
         c) Interdepartment
            (1) The Contemporary Worker
            (2) Technology
            (3) Institutional History
         d) Medical Staff
            (1) The Contemporary Physician
            (2) Patient Care
            (3) Research
            (4) Technology
            (5) Institutional History
      2. The Government
         a) Accrediting, Regulatory, and
            Legal Bodies
         b) Political Relations
         c) Economic Forces
      3. The Profession
         a) Professional Nursing Practice
            Issues
         b) Nursing Education Systems
         c) Student Relationships
      4. The Society
         a) Health Care Trends and Issues
            (1) General Population
                Demographics
            (2) Societal and Economic
                Forces
            (3) Emerging Technologies
         b) Public Relations
            (1) Community Relations
            (2) Societal and Economic
                Forces
   B. Mission, Purpose, and Goals
      1. Organizational
      2. Divisional
      3. Unit Level
         a) Philosophy
         b) Objectives

II. *Organizational Design*
   A. Work
      1. Analysis:
         a) Patient Care, Research Support

B. People
   1. Type
      a) Preparation
      b) Knowledge
      c) Capability
      d) Tenure
   2. Numbers
   3. Mix
C. Structure
   1. Division of Work
   2. Allocation of Decision Making
   3. Design of Variable Approaches for
      Varying Degrees of Uncertainty
      a) Imitative
      b) Innovative
D. Coordination
   1. What Requires Coordination
   2. How Is It Best Coordinated
   3. Intersystem Dependencies
      a) Interunit
      b) Nonnursing Support Systems
      c) Medical Care Systems
      d) Research Systems

III. *Managerial Strategies*
   A. Formal Managerial Technologies
      1. Standards of Care
      2. Quality of Care Indexes
      3. Audits
      4. Position Descriptions
      5. Performance Appraisal
      6. Reward System
      7. Educational System
      8. Scheduling/Assignments
      9. Procedures
      10. Planning Technologies
      11. Research
      12. Committees
      13. Policies
      14. Work Rules
      15. Budgetary Processes
      16. Information Systems
   B. Informal Managerial Processes
      1. Power
      2. Status
      3. Influence
      4. Leadership
      5. Committees
      6. Allocation of Informal Rewards
      7. Relationships
         a) Unit Level RN/MD
         b) Staff
         c) Peer Collaboration

Table 2-3 Competencies Reflecting Conceptual Skills

Analyze the work to be done.

—Identify discrete elements of the work.
—Identify optimal sequences for work processes.
—Establish priorities.
—Assess the degree of uncertainty inherent in the work and surrounding the work.

Formulate goals.

—Define the unit's purpose and objectives.
—Define mutual expectations of staff and manager regarding unit goals.
—Establish directions for the unit through priority setting.

Assess resources.

—Consider time, space, materials, equipment, finances, and people as available resources.
—Evaluate available resources in terms of strengths, weaknesses, and limitations in a systematic, businesslike manner.
—Maintain objectivity.

Predict outcomes.

—Identify and interpret recurrent patterns of organizational events, considering both people and systems.
—Make rough correlations regarding the probable impact of variables on organizational events.

Plan for the future.

—Formulate a vision for the future of the unit, service, and/or organization.
—Develop and communicate a long-range plan against which results can be measured.
—Develop short-term strategies to achieve the long-range plan.
—Effect a marketing plan designed to facilitate the long-range plan.
—Retain a practical view of possible means of shaping and responding to future eventualities.

Clarify relationships of the unit to the larger organization's parts and whole.

—Articulate goals and functions of the organization, service, and their units.
—Retain a perspective on organizational goals and functions.
—Achieve congruence between unit, service, and organizational purposes and objectives.

Maintain a professional identity.

—Identify standards of professional nursing practice.
—Foster the growth and development of the profession.
—Recognize the social responsibilities imposed by one's professional identity.
—Facilitate the education of nursing students.

Maintain an awareness of societal trends.

—Recognize the social climate in which health care is delivered.
—Recognize the political constraints within which the health care delivery system operates.
—Recognize trends in health and illness that may impact health care delivery.
—Recognize existing and emerging technologies that may impact health care delivery.
—Recognize the nature of the contemporary worker.
—Recognize the nature of the contemporary health care professional.

Table 2-4 Competencies Reflecting Human Skills

Communicate clearly and dispassionately with peers, colleagues, subordinates, and superiors.

—Foster open communication through clear expression and receptive listening.
—Explain the rationale for one's decisions and requests.
—Explore reasons for another's position on an issue.
—Deal with anger and frustration in a direct and constructive manner.
—Demonstrate sensitivity and insight regarding the perceptions and reactions of others.

Facilitate communication between staff and others in the organization.

—Obtain, process, and disseminate information essential to job performance.
—Represent staff in contexts external to the unit.
—Build networks by establishing relationships with appropriate people inside and outside the organization.

Establish a climate of mutual trust and respect.

—Maintain a predictable leadership style.
—Maintain credibility.
—Maintain confidentiality.
—Maintain integrity.
—Deal with staff in a fair and just manner.
—Act as advocate for staff.

Work harmoniously with peers, colleagues, subordinates, and superiors.

—Collaborate with others to achieve goals.
—Act interdependently as necessary.

Foster an innovative and motivating work environment.

—Initiate, stimulate, and facilitate change.
—Provide meaningful, productive work.
—Provide learning opportunities to enhance employees' personal and professional growth.

Act assertively to achieve goals.

Use power, status, and influence appropriately to achieve goals.

Promote group work to solve problems and achieve goals.

—Promote the participation of others in group processes.
—Participate in group processes.
—Promote the solidarity and growth of groups over time.

Facilitate the management of an employee's personal or professional crisis.

Manage conflict.

—Assess the characteristics of conflicting parties and situations.
—Structure the environment in which the conflict is addressed.
—Intervene to ameliorate or eliminate the cause of a conflict.
—Mediate a conflict using appropriate strategies.

Perform under varying degrees of stress.

Objectively analyze and respond to others' critique of one's performance.

Assume responsibility for one's personal and professional growth.

Act as a patient advocate.

Table 2-5 Competencies Reflecting Technical Skills

Nursing Practice Technology

Maintain professional-technical competence in an area of nursing practice.

Achieve goals of direct patient care.

Act as a patient advocate.

Support family members.

Support the goals of biomedical research.

Demonstrate knowledge of purposes, procedures, and processes of biomedical research.

Management Technology

Organize, direct, and control operations essential to goal achievement.
   —Assume responsibility for decision making within one's scope of control.
   —Exert authority.
   —Perform effectively in ambiguous situations.
   —Plan and implement political strategies to achieve both short-term and long-term goals.
   —Influence the acceptance of one's decisions.
   —Take calculated risks.
   —Assume accountability for one's decisions.

Select a leadership style appropriate to the work, the workers, and the situation.

Obtain, process, and disseminate information essential to job performance.
   —Systematically scan relevant information resources.
   —Select relevant information.
   —Use appropriate information resources in planning.
   —Identify priorities.
   —Organize information meaningfully.
   —Present information effectively using oral and/or written communication processes.

Solve or mitigate problems.
   —Assess the nature of a problem.
   —Identify appropriate means for solving a problem.
   —Involve others in the use of problem-solving processes.
   —Persevere in the search for a solution.

Initiate, stimulate, and facilitate change.
   —Effect a planned change.
   —Anticipate change.
   —Support the change initiatives of others.
   —Respond flexibly to a changing environment.

Develop systems for the conduct of work.
   —Coordinate the optimal use of organizational resources.
   —Delegate appropriately.
   —Manage time effectively.
   —Use available technologies.

continued

Table 2-5 *continued*

Manage resources.

—Consider time, space, materials, equipment, finances, and people as potential resources.
—Document the need for resources.
—Conduct interviews with prospective personnel.
—Obtain necessary resources.
—Function with limited resources.
—Allocate resources.
—Account for resource utilization.
—Use budgetary processes.
—Use fiscal systems for financial analysis, forecasting, and monitoring.

Provide learning opportunities to enhance employees' personal and professional growth.

—Identify present and potential learning needs of staff.
—Identify and mobilize educational resources.
—Use role modeling to teach others.
—Control the physical and interpersonal climate for learning.

Evaluate the performance of employees.

—Base expectations for performance on knowledge of competent patient care.
—Base expectations for performance on knowledge of the demands of research on patient care requirements.
—Clarify expectations for performance and the rationale for expected behaviors.
—Base evaluation on objective analysis of relevant behaviors.
—Communicate evaluation of performance and related decisions in an objective and supportive manner.
—Use praise and constructive criticism appropriately.
—Document performance evaluation in writing.
—Apply civil service and PHS procedures and criteria in rating performance.
—Develop mutual plans for improving performance, including a mechanism to evaluate progress toward goals.
—Use appropriate formal and informal rewards.
—Stimulate improved performance.
—Maintain confidentiality.

---

10. I use encouragement often.
11. My subordinates seem to take criticism from me and respond constructively.
12. I find it easy to get volunteers.
13. I make a special effort to be fair in assigning tasks equitably.
14. My people feel I'm readily available for assistance as they need it.
15. I am proud of my staff and don't hesitate to show it.

Scoring: Give yourself 10 points for each item marked true, then rate yourself on the scale below.

130 to 150—You're an outstanding leader, a combination of Solomon and Caesar.

100 to 120—You're good, with only a slight case of Achilles' heel.

Under 100—You're not sure of your leadership ability, and this results in job headaches.

If you're dissatisfied with your score, go back over all the questions. Each one highlights a major opportunity for leadership performance. Questions you answered incorrectly are prime areas for improvement.

Your Decision-Making Practices

Your decision-making success depends on how well you can evaluate or compare alternative solutions to your problems, despite time pressure and insufficient data.

1. Do you avoid leaving yourself left high and dry because of failure to decide on a course of action *in time*?
2. Similarly, do you avoid making decisions *before* you have to, and later receive information that would have changed your actions?
3. In developing alternative courses of action to given problems, do you make use of the experience and knowledge of
   a. your superior?
   b. colleagues?
   c. professional sources of know-how?
   d. your subordinates?
4. In evaluating the advantages and disadvantages of alternatives do you
   a. list the pros and cons of each possibility in writing (at least for critical decisions)?
   b. check the opinions of experts or people with relevant experience?
   c. try to quantify as many factors as possible, to make comparisons easier and more meaningful?
5. In your final selection of a course of action, do you consider the possibility of combining the favorable aspects of two or more alternatives?
6. In analyzing decisions that misfired, was the reason
   a. a misunderstanding of the objectives you were trying to achieve?
   b. a miscalculation of the difficulties of the situation?
   c. an overestimation of the abilities of your subordinates?
   d. an underestimation of their abilities?
   e. a failure to keep up with new developments affecting your decision?

Problem-Solving

Unsolved problems are stones in the road of progress. The executive administrator is confronted by an unending parade of problems day in, day out. Are you able to keep the stones out of the road? As an indication:

1. Do you go looking for problems in order to account for
   a. plans that haven't jelled?
   b. unanticipated developments?
   c. unexpected behavior on the part of your staff?
2. Do you agree that a problem generally holds the clue to its solution?
3. When you're faced by a problem, do you automatically
   a. start digging out the relevant facts?
   b. mentally line up the people who can help solve the problem?
   c. try to approach the situation on a logical, systematic basis?
4. Do you motivate the problem-solving activities of your subordinates by communicating to them the excitement and challenge of facing up to a tough problem?
5. Do you give your unconscious a chance to work on your problems by generating mental input—focusing on the circumstances and facts of the difficulty, thinking about the problem, and not trying to think through to a solution, leaving that to your unconscious mind?
6. As a starter for creative problem solving, do you examine and challenge the assumptions you may have about the circumstances of the problem as well as the possible solution?

Planning

The ability to study cause and effect, to see short-range difficulties in the light of long-range goals, is a key to overall executive accomplishment.

1. Do you review objectives periodically so that your planning can be updated?
2. Do you take advantage of group brainpower by permitting subordinates to participate in planning procedures?
3. Would you benefit by formalizing your planning procedures, that is, allocating specific time periods to planning activities?
4. Do you use the basic "tools" of planning—calendar, pencil, paper, charts, graphs, pertinent records of past performance, and so on?
5. Is your planning flexible enough to meet changing conditions—higher standards, shorter deadlines, and so on?

6. Are your planning methods organized well enough for you to be able to explain them to someone else?
7. Do you try to develop the skills of your subordinates as an aid to achieving your most ambitious plans?
8. Do you devote "training time" to helping your subordinates plan their activities?
9. Are you planning the activity of any subordinate who should be on his or her own?
10. Are any of your subordinates performing planning functions that you should be doing?
11. Do you ask your superior for enough information to make your planning sufficiently long range?
12. Do you consult your superior to get suggestions on your planning activities, including suggestions on objectives, resources, methods, and evaluation of results?

Order-Giving Review

How good is your command of the order-giving process?

1. Before giving orders, do you
   a. clarify the end results you're after?
   b. prethink the moves required to meet objectives?
   c. decide on the right people to do the job?
   d. help make needed resources available to them?
2. In giving orders or instructions, do you
   a. suit the type of order to the individual: a direct order for the beginner, "result-wanted" order for the veteran, etc.?
   b. indicate, wherever necessary, the additional information (data, reference material) the staff will need to finish the job?
   c. try to put into your instructions the challenge that will create the strongest motivation for the individual?
   d. provide written instructions and other "support" material, as needed?
3. In setting goals for subordinates' activities, do you
   a. let them join in a discussion of the relevance and importance of goals?
   b. permit those with initiative enough leeway to exercise it?
   c. give those who lack self-confidence the opportunity to check back with you as often as will be helpful?
4. To aim at better teamwork, do you
   a. give your group the opportunity, where possible, to share in planning operations?
   b. keep group goals clearly in view at all times?

NURSE POWER

Overview*

Power has multiple meanings and frequently negative connotations. It is used here to mean the ability to get and use whatever resources are needed to achieve nursing goals.

Organizational power refers to the power that exists within hospitals and other health care institutions. This kind of power is in the decision-making process of organizations. It is organizational power that nurses need to influence the conditions of nursing work.

In addition, individuals have *personal power* derived from the decisions they make on a daily basis about how they are going to organize their lives. Political scientists refer to an individual's sense of political efficacy—that is, the individual's feeling that he or she can influence events through personal effort. A sense of political efficacy becomes a self-fulfilling prophecy. If individuals believe that they make a difference and can influence events in their lives, they are likely to participate actively in trying to get what they want. This participation will make them feel more powerful even if it is not all that successful. However, the opposite is equally true. If individuals believe themselves powerless to influence events and therefore do not even try, they are going to feel even more powerless.

Source: Jennie Larsen, "Nurse Power for the 1980s," *Nursing Administration Quarterly*, vol. 6, no. 4, © 1982 Aspen Publishers, Inc.

Sources of Power and Influence

Where does power come from? Writers and researchers seem to agree that the major sources of power and influence are as follows:

- *reward power*—power to reward behavior, give positive opportunities, or remove negative effects
- *coercive power*—the ability to impose penalties for nonconformity
- *legitimate power*—power based on the internalized norms, beliefs, roles, and values of those being influenced
- *referent power*—power based on identifying with other people who have power
- *expert power*—power that derives from the knowledge, abilities, and credibility of the person exerting influence
- *informational power*—power arising from the ability and opportunities of an individual to gain and share valuable information (e.g., access to and influence on organizational gossip can be a valuable resource)

Power holders usually have a combination of these sources of power. But having power is not in itself sufficient to make an individual powerful—his or her sources of power must be used as resources to achieve desired goals. Nursing has and always has had power; the problem lies in the use, nonuse, or misuse of this power.

Powerful Leaders

One factor that clearly distinguishes good leaders from bad, effective leaders from ineffective, and liked leaders from disliked ones is the ability to mobilize organizational resources to make things happen.

The assignment of formal organizational authority does not necessarily ensure access to power in the organization. For example, how much power does a nursing supervisor really have in the typical hospital? How much power does he or she have to hire and fire, make budget decisions, grant staff development opportunities, or redesign nursing jobs?

Nursing supervisors need organizational power to back up nursing demands and decisions and ensure the confidence and loyalty of staff nurses.

Organizational power is derived from having influence at the decision-making levels of the organization, from having informal connections with sponsors and peers, and from having a visible high-status position. People are quite knowledgeable about who has power in the organization and who does not. When asked, organizational members will often state they prefer to work with managers who can get things done.

Powerful nursing leaders tend to generate high group morale primarily because of their ability to get things done. Powerful nursing leaders are mobile and aid in the advancement of their staff nurses. These leaders tend to adopt participatory management styles in which they share information with the staff nurses, delegate responsibility, and are flexible about organizational rules.

Power in the Hospital Environment*

In 1988 a special commission of the Health and Human Services conducted an inspection of a large hospital sample to determine the extent to which nurses participate in hospital decision making through representation on hospital governing bodies and key committees. The visibility and voting power of chief nursing officers (CNOs) were compared to those of the CEO and other hospital management positions. It was estimated that one-third of CNOs attend governing body meetings regularly and another one-third attend when invited. Fewer than 2 percent of all CNOs vote. While CNOs seldom vote on governing bodies, they do not appear to have been singled out for exclusion from governing body deliberations, because, except for CEOs, very few other hospital management officials are voting members. Chief nursing officers are seldom represented on the two hospital committees where business and financial matters are discussed—executive and finance—but do partici-

---

*Source: *Nurse Participation in Hospital Decision Making: Potential Impact on the Nursing Shortage,* Office of the Inspector General, Office of Analysis and Inspections, Department of Health and Human Services, October 1988.

pate in substantial proportions on the planning committee. Not surprisingly, there is also a high degree of representation on committees that have traditionally dealt with patient care issues, which have always been nursing's primary concern.

Generally, the status, autonomy, and span of control of today's CNOs appear to be greater than in years past. The majority are at the vice-presidential level in the hospital organization and report directly to the CEO. Half supervise nonnursing as well as nursing services, and the majority are paid as much as or more than their organizational counterparts. CNOs control nursing budgets and the hiring and firing of nursing staff. In large hospitals, these powers have been further delegated to the unit level. The improvements in status of CNOs may reflect hospitals' increased awareness of the critical role of nursing, but they may also be the result of the efforts of a more sophisticated, better educated and better organized nursing profession. The majority of nurse administrators feel that input into patient care and management decisions results in a sense of control in the workplace and a stake in the success and well-being of the organization.

Finally, the survey reported that the majority of CNOs report directly to CEOs, which allows them to occupy a significant position on the institution's executive management team.

*Fitting into the Executive Team**

The chief nurse officer (CNO) position has evolved from the traditional director of nursing position responsible for maintaining the functioning of a more simply defined single department to a nurse executive position responsible for managing many facets of patient services. More than any other member of the executive management team, the CNO must be acutely aware of both clinical and managerial demands, acutely aware of the politics of power in the institution, and acutely wary of getting caught in power struggles.

The CNO's broad scope of responsibility and interface with all areas of hospital operations

makes the CNO the CEO's prime resource. At first appraisal, the CNO seems to occupy a paradoxical position, maintaining independence and integrity while at the same time representing the CEO and personifying the CEO's goals and philosophy. Clearly, acknowledgment of a shared philosophy eliminates the paradox. The foundation of the relationship of the CEO and the CNO is, however, more than shared goals; it is the ability of two personalities to connect in a way that feels balanced and brings about positive results.

The mutually supportive relationship between the CEO and the CNO can be enhanced by keeping in mind these practical suggestions:

- Detect potential problems and resolve them yourself whenever possible, while always keeping the CEO informed. Be aware that your decisions and actions reflect directly on the CEO.
- Be conscious of your visibility. In your interface with so many hospital departments and in leading your own, you are under the scrutiny of the entire institution and are representing the CEO.
- Maintain professional networks both in nursing, in other health care–related organizations, and in the community. You serve as a vital link and may be the first to know about both current and future issues, trends, and problems.
- Foster and maintain a positive and active relationship with the medical staff. In addition to being a liaison between physicians and administration, you must establish a collegial working relationship with the medical staff leadership. Without this, the CEO will be thrust into the peacekeeper role, which will not be appreciated.
- When presenting a proposal or suggestion, give the CEO the opportunity to review material in advance. Keep in mind that the CEO is everyone's boss and must consider the impact on the entire institution. Put yourself in the CEO's position.
- Offer the CEO options; no one likes being boxed in. Particularly when presenting alternatives for resolving a problem or con-

Source: Lenore M. Appenzeller, ''The CNO-CEO Relationship,'' *Aspen's Advisor for Nurse Executives,* vol. 3, no. 6, © 1988 Aspen Publishers, Inc.

flict, stubbornness, ultimata, and lack of flexibility are counter-productive.

- Give the CEO the opportunity to change his or her mind. Allow for graceful adaptation, changes of opinion, and room to negotiate.
- Do not avoid responsibility. You may have to "take the heat" for others' decisions as well as your own. You are a member of a management team and must support its decisions.

Strategies for Influencing Staff*

Among the influence strategies that effectively channel the elements of the leader's power into productive results are these:

- Obtaining and sharing accurate information. In many situations, a leader is able to influence others primarily because of access to accurate information and the ability to communicate it effectively to followers.
- Demonstrating expertise. The degree to which a leader is perceived as having special knowledge or skill is an important factor in influencing others. An expert's opinion is more influential than that of a majority of the group.
- Using legitimate authority in effective ways. Legitimacy is based on norms and expectations held by group members.
- Encouraging subordinates to identify with the leader. A subordinate either has or wants a feeling of oneness with the leader. Such identification comes from a feeling of knowing the leader, sharing common goals and values, and being able to talk with him or her. The leader's communication skills are an important aspect of this strategy.
- Using rewards and punishments effectively. Basic to coercion is the perception by one or more persons that another person is able to mediate rewards for them. If both

"sides" do not agree about what constitutes a reward, however, the strategy is weak. If what the supervisor thinks of as rewards is not perceived by the staff as such, the rewards will not be effective means of influence.

- Understanding how to manipulate cues affecting a decision. This can involve the manipulation (withholding) of information to promote ignorance, for example. This strategy restricts the number and range of perceived alternatives, affects the quality of a decision, and affects the values and abilities of the decision maker.
- Effectively controlling the work environment. Agendas are an important type of environmental control. The agenda for a meeting or a listing of decision priorities provides an important control on the influence of others.

Buffering*

The concept of leadership buffering is easily understood by examining Figure 2-2. In this model, a leader buffers his or her subordinates by protecting them from various forces and pressures in the health care environment; this allows them to achieve improved departmental and organizational outcomes.

The nursing leader interested in improving team, departmental, or work-unit effectiveness should give special attention to the diversity of pressures causing the need for buffering. Nursing leaders may be too busy with traditional work demands—completion of their own nursing tasks, administrative tasks, and supervision activities—to justify a broader definition of nursing leadership. Effective leaders, however, delegate their more routine administrative and nursing duties to subordinates, thus allowing much greater concentration on the art of leadership.

---

*Source: Claudette G. Varricchio, "The Process of Influencing Decisions," *Nursing Administration Quarterly,* vol. 6, no. 2, © 1982 Aspen Publishers, Inc.

*Source: Howard L. Smith and Nancy Wint Mitry, "Nursing Leadership: A Buffering Perspective," *Nursing Administration Quarterly,* vol. 8, no. 3, © 1984 Aspen Publishers, Inc.

Figure 2-2 The Buffering Process

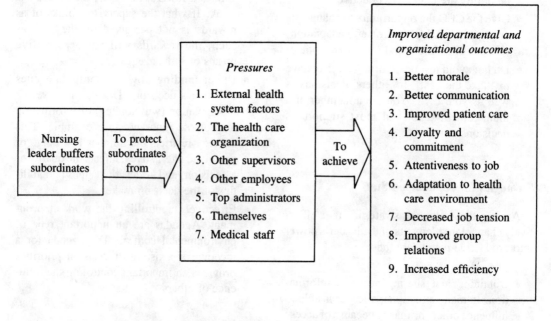

Source: Howard L. Smith and Nancy Wint Mitry, ''Nursing Leadership: A Buffering Perspective,'' *Nursing Administration Quarterly*, vol. 8, no. 3, © 1984 Aspen Publishers, Inc.

Chapter 3

Planning, Directing, and Controlling

PLANNING

The Nature of Planning*

The function of planning incorporates both strategic and tactical planning. *Strategic planning* involves determining the direction in which an organization should be headed. *Tactical planning* involves allocating resources that enable an organization to reach strategic objectives.

Second, plans are primarily mechanisms for guiding organizational efforts. The real test of planning is the ability to direct efforts on a daily basis, that is, to move from the abstract to the implemented. It is not enough just to create plans. They must be articulated and then put into action. Once the action occurs, control should be implemented to ascertain whether performance targets have actually been achieved. For a comprehensive plan to work effectively each step must receive equal attention, and the cycle must be completed (i.e., from planning to implementation and then to control) before returning to planning. It should also be remembered that planning, to be effective, should not occur just at the top echelons. It should be implemented throughout an organization (see Figure 3-1).

Source: Judith F. Garner, Howard L. Smith, and Neill F. Pilard, *Strategic Nursing Management: Power and Responsibility in a New Era*, Aspen Publishers, Inc., © 1990.

Third, planning is a continual process that moves from setting the mission to setting operational objectives.

Fourth, values and expectations often determine what missions and strategies are adopted.

Figure 3-1 Prerequisite for Effective Planning.

In many health care organizations, the short run is the immediate fiscal period. Intermediate plans cover one to two years. Long-run plans fall in the three to five year range. Variances in health care markets, the general economy, public regulation, patient preferences, industry structure, social climate, societal values, competition, and related factors tend to shorten the time frame of planning. Nonetheless, it is useful for health care organizations to extrapolate their efforts to five to ten years in the future.

Finally, reviewing and evaluating plans support control. Planning does not occur in a vacuum. Accomplishments or failures are ultimately analyzed, and the information gained thereby is used to revise plans where necessary.

Phases*

The different phases of the planning process are interdependent and continuous; they frequently overlap in time and are often not discrete. Several of these phases have been separated and are discussed as though a plan is totally developed and then implemented. This is not meant to convey the idea that planning always takes place in rigid and sequential steps. Viewed in phases, the planning process consists of

1. seeking common purposes and objectives
2. identifying issues and concerns
3. determining organizational structure for planning
4. selecting participants (and hiring staff if necessary)
5. collecting and analyzing data
6. assessing needs and resources
7. developing recommendations
8. developing the plan of action
9. implementing the plan of action
10. evaluating and reviewing progress in implementing and in continuous planning

No one phase of planning is more important than another. Each has significance for bringing about the actions needed to solve nursing problems.

Framework for Organizing

To design and create a planning mechanism adapted to your department's conditions and needs, you must

- assess planning experience and readiness for planning

---

*Source: Planning for Nursing Needs and Resources, National Institutes of Health, DHHS, 1972.

- outline the perimeters of nursing concerns and required actions and set the objectives of planning
- pinpoint data and information needs and availability
- determine what special studies or surveys may be required
- consider and understand the so-called power structure in the area affected
- decide what tasks must be undertaken to assess needs and resources and to reach planning objectives
- identify leaders and select participants for functional tasks
- determine staff requirements
- set a tentative timetable
- estimate budgetary requirements

Determining Objectives

The nursing concerns requiring assessment by planning groups should first be identified. Then a study outline should be completed for each concern. The outline should list influential factors, information needed for assessment, sources for data, and any required special studies.

The completed study outline provides a basis for determining planning procedures and the course to be followed. The planning techniques, data requirements, and need for special surveys and studies will, in turn, influence staff and budgetary requirements.

Other concerns or aspects of issues and problems requiring analysis and study will emerge as planners begin to seek solutions to particular nursing problems.

Collecting Data

Using Existing Data. The use of data from existing sources presents few problems and precludes elaborate, time-consuming data collection. Use of these data involves the following: (1) identifying their sources; (2) assessing their relevance, timeliness, and accuracy; (3) abstracting the data from the original sources for use in the planning documents in a way that would be most meaningful to the planning group; and (4) analyzing the meaning and implications of the data in terms of the planning objectives.

Conducting Special Studies. It is difficult to anticipate the kinds of special studies that may have to be undertaken for a specific planning activity. The studies that are needed will depend upon the nature of the problems encountered in the planning process as well as the status of available data.

To mention but a few, special studies have been conducted in the following areas:

- utilization of nursing personnel
- nurse staffing
- patient need for services
- turnover of nursing personnel
- job and career satisfaction and incentives
- salaries and fringe benefits
- processes of recruitment for nursing
- nature of nursing school applicants and applicant experience
- cost of nursing services
- inactive nurses

Methods of Collecting Original Data. Questionnaires, interviews, and observation are used to collect original data. Any one or all of these methods may be employed to gather data on the same subject.

Questionnaire. Administering a questionnaire, perhaps the most widely used method for original data collection, is the simplest type of data-collecting method. It is also less expensive and time-consuming than other methods. Questionnaires are used to elicit data on the following: (1) *objective facts*, such as the number of facilities and services available and the number of personnel employed; (2) *behavioral variables* that may be of interest to planning groups, such as kinds of nursing activities performed; (3) *evaluations*, such as feelings about the quality of patient care; and (4) *specified events*, such as the time spent by nurses on clerical activities.

Interview. Interviews are used when questionnaires cannot provide the depth of response required. The unstructured interview permits probing into the responses solicited to verify

meaning and to obtain in-depth data. The highly structured interview allows for the collection of standardized data and information and for probing to clarify and broaden responses.

Observations. Observation is used for studies in which evaluation is the primary objective or where the data required are complex, are difficult to obtain, and need considerable interpretation. Such studies would include, for example, evaluating the activities of personnel or the quality of their performance. Data are recorded in the form of an evaluative rating of what is being observed, a narrative description of what was seen, or entries on a checklist. The use of this method requires considerable control over the observation to ensure reliability.

Developing the Plan of Action

When recommendations have been formulated and priorities have been determined, they are then incorporated into a definitive plan for meeting nursing needs. In developing the plan, attention is given to the following:

- specifying goals, objectives, and policies for carrying out recommendations and suggested programs
- phasing activities so that resolution of problems requiring immediate action leads to actions and measures for attaining long-range goals
- indicating the individuals to carry out each recommendation
- specifying a time span for achieving specific objectives or steps in the plan
- providing methods for evaluating progress in meeting objectives

The plan of action should build upon existing services and manpower resources. The diversity of needs, resources, and existing patterns of education and service must be dealt with.

In developing the plan, problems to be encountered in its phasing must be considered (e.g., resistance to the introduction of new concepts). Measures to surmount potential obstacles must be worked out in advance and integrated into the plan.

Goals

The plan could

- designate the type and kinds of new or existing nursing service programs
- set priorities for the expansion, improvement, or development of nursing service programs
- prescribe administrative reorganization or new organizational mechanisms required so that the available manpower can be utilized with the greatest efficiency and economy
- prescribe utilization patterns for each type of nurse in varying work situations
- establish the boundaries of nursing responsibilities in relation to other health disciplines and overall health effort and health needs
- define new roles for nursing personnel and patterns of service for meeting health care requirements
- recommend measures to improve job satisfaction and employment and career incentives that contribute to the quality of nursing service, such as the following:
  —personnel policies, practices, and procedures
  —working conditions
  —in-service and continuing education
  —on-the-job training
  —salaries and fringe benefits
- set priorities for the expansion and development of nursing in-service education programs by type of program to meet the specific demands of the hospital, and also prescribe target dates for achievement of specific aspects of the plan
- recommend broad measures to support the plan and its goals, such as the following:
  —utilization of resources from educational programs
  —recruitment activities and programs
  —measures contributing to improvement in career incentives

Evaluation

A plan is good or generally acceptable if it

- is in line with a clearly stated objective
- indicates the procedural method for putting the plan into action
- can be communicated effectively (allowing for appropriate dissemination methods)
- is operational, professionally sound, and economically feasible
- represents an integrated whole and not an isolated entity
- allows for alternate courses of action as changes occur and opportunities for new approaches arise
- wisely utilizes human talents, abilities, and skills to their maximum potential and makes judicious use of material resources in order to improve patient care and educate the nursing staff

CHANGE AND INNOVATION

Change

The primary goal of nursing service administration is the facilitation of effective and efficient nursing services for people. To work toward this goal in an increasingly complex and changing health field, the director of nursing must employ modern management theory and practices in planning, directing, facilitating, coordinating, and evaluating nursing services.

Evaluating nursing programs, then using the results for implementing changes as well as for long-range planning, ranks as a high priority for successful administration. Management by objectives, systems analysis, change process, and other management techniques should be incorporated into the daily functions of nursing service administrators. In implementing needed changes in nursing, the focus of administration cannot be limited to the day-to-day operations of the institution.

Too frequently, busy nurse executives find themselves resorting to a crisis intervention approach, dealing with the immediate problems and devoting little attention to long-range resolution and/or prevention. Of all the leadership positions in the nursing field, the director of nursing is in the most strategic position to effect needed innovations in nursing. It is imperative nursing administrators expand their scope to take a more active leadership role in long-range goal definition and broad program planning for health care.*

*Types**

If one were to attempt to characterize the nature of change, three types of change could be identified. *Structural change* affects the organizational process, such as alterations in authority charts, budget procedures, or rules and regulations. *Technological change* affects the physical environment and work practices or systems. *People-oriented change* affects the performance and conduct of employees, such as the introduction of different training schemes, appraisal systems, sets of standards, or promotional devices.

*Phases**

Kurt Lewin identified three phases of change—unfreezing, moving, and refreezing.

Unfreezing is the development of a need to change through problem awareness. Even if a problem has been identified, a person must believe there can be an improvement before he or she is willing to change. Coercion has been used for unfreezing. Removing a person from the source of his or her old attitudes to a new environment, punishment and humiliation for undesirable attitudes, and rewards for desirable attitudes affect change.

Moving is working toward change by identifying the problem or the need to change, exploring the alternatives, defining goals and objectives, planning how to accomplish the goals, and implementing the plan for change.

Refreezing is the integration of the change into one's personality and the consequent stabilization of change. Frequently personnel use old behaviors after change efforts cease. Related changes in neighboring systems, momentum to perpetuate the change, and structural alterations

---

*Source: G. Matsunaga, "Nurse Administrator Must Be Chief Initiator of Change," *The American Nurse*, April 1975. Reprinted with permission of the American Nurses' Association.

which support the procedural change are stabilizing factors.

Implementation

Change doesn't simply happen; it is brought about by forces within the organization. There are various organizational approaches used to introduce change.[1] At one extreme is the *unilateral* approach, in which authoritative decisions are made at the top of the power structure and handed downward. At the other extreme is the *delegated* approach, in which subordinate levels hold the responsibility for new solutions to identified problems. In between is the *shared power* approach, the most successful means of arranging change, in which higher-level authority interacts with lower-level decision groups. Each of these approaches takes several forms.

I. Unilateral Approach

- *By decree.* An impersonal announcement handed down by the top echelon, a "one-way" declaration of intention usually phrased in a memo, policy statement, or lecture. The assumption is that automatic compliance with authority will produce changed behavior and anticipated improvements.

- *By replacement.* A singling out of strategically located key positions to be filled more effectively by new personnel. This is a device used when the decree approach is insufficient, but it rests on the same assumptions that upper authority control and mandate are necessary to bring about change at the bottom organizational rungs.

- *By structure.* A relatively formal mechanism for change that relies on a redesign of the organizational pattern, with the assumption that the creation of new or different slots will result in improved performance. If the arrangement is not adjusted to the informal authority lines evident in current practices, it will be ineffective, becoming merely an exercise in logic on paper.

---

[1]L.E. Greiner, "Patterns of Organization Change," *Harvard Business Review*, May-June 1967, pp. 119–122.

II. Shared Power

- *By group decision making.* A two-phase approach where upper-authority identifies the problem but subordinates debate and select the most appropriate solution for stimulating change. The assumption is that participation in the change decision increases support and commitment.
- *By group problem solving.* The two functions of problem identification and solution are faced by the subordinate discussion group in recognition of their practical experience and knowledge of the issue at hand.

III. Delegated Power

- *By case discussion.* A generalized discussion of a situation aimed at developing problem-solving skills which can then be applied by personnel to carry out changes.
- *By sensitivity sessions.* A psychologically oriented method which doesn't deal with task-oriented problems or changes but instead places emphasis on social or interpersonal processes. Led by a professional trainer, the members of the group develop self-awareness and insight into the attitudes of others. This increased understanding is expected to lead to informal and self-initiated change. Customarily used for top management, the method has been used in nursing services (e.g., by an entire staff of an individual unit).

Guidelines for Implementing Change*

Ralph Besse, a highly successful chief executive, has ten conditions under which change can be made *more* acceptable. In general, change is more acceptable

1. when it is understood than when it is not
2. when it does not threaten security than when it does

3. when those affected have helped to create it than when it has been externally imposed
4. when it results from an application of previously established impersonal principles than it is when it is dictated by personal order
5. when it follows a series of successful changes than it is when it follows a series of failures
6. when it is inaugurated after prior change has been assimilated than when it is inaugurated during the confusion of other major change
7. if it has been planned than if it is experimental
8. with people new on the job than with people old on the job
9. with people who share in the benefits of change than with those who do not
10. if the organization has been trained to plan for improvement than if the organization is accustomed to static procedures.

Guidelines for Implementing Innovations*

Identification of strengths and areas needing improvement provides a data base around which changes can be made. The plan of systematic evaluation should provide direction and valuable information. Avoid the attitude of "change for change's sake."

Develop a master plan with target dates for time of accomplishment of different aspects. This is your blueprint. The job, when looked at as a whole, may appear overwhelming. Break it down into small pieces that can be handled. Recognize that the timetable may have to be revised.

Ensure staff involvement. People tend to support what they help plan. The size of your staff will cause your approach to vary. If you have a staff of 20, you can use approaches that would not work with a staff of 200.

Source: R. Besse, "Company Planning Must Be Planned," *Dun's Review and Modern Industry*, vol. 69, no. 4, April 1957, pp. 62–63.

Source: D. Shumaker, "Change Theory and Instructional Innovation," *Instructional Innovations*, National League for Nursing, Pub. No. 16-1687, 1977. Reprinted with permission.

Define the constraints under which you must operate. These may be in terms of money, time, skill of staff, equipment, and clinical facilities.

Identify and analyze the choices, for there is more than one way to get to an objective.

Consider all the ramifications of the change. Innovations that are helpful in one area may have undesirable side effects in other areas.

Plan for evaluation. Have you ever noticed that in most books evaluation is often the last chapter? We even list it as the last step in the nursing process. It should start at the beginning of your process and continue throughout.

Perhaps the most important point: Make failure acceptable. Risk taking is associated with change, and this can be anxiety producing. Not succeeding should not become degrading to individuals.

When working with staff, bring out hidden agendas so that real issues can be handled. Remember, one of the factors for promoting change is not threatening the autonomy and security of individuals.

When deadlocks occur, brainstorm and try to identify alternatives. Try not to vote in this kind of situation.

Try not to have a "final" or "set" decision in a small group that will result in defensiveness when recommendations are presented to the total group and suggestions are offered, for it is likely they will be. Label materials "Draft 1, 2, 3" or "Working Copy." This helps develop the mental set that decisions can be changed. They are not carved in stone.

The final guideline pertains to maintaining a perspective. Remember, there's nothing like a little experience to upset a theory.

CONTROLLING

Overview*

Controlling is the management function in which performance is measured and corrective

---

Source: Joan G. Liebler, Ruth E. Levine, and Hyman L. Dervitz, *Management Principles for Health Professionals*, Aspen Publishers, Inc., © 1983.

Transition Tactics

Resisters should become "targets" of the administrator's strategy for making the effective change. The administrator should take the following steps:

- Allow targets to ventilate their fears, concerns, insecurities, and grief in an environment that treats these feelings as legitimate.
- Focus targets' attention on the future, not the past.
- Reward those who are supportive of the change and apply pressure to those who are resistant.
- Assign roles, tasks, and responsibilities so targets feel they are involved and exercising influence.
- Provide targets with the logistic, economic, and political resources needed to achieve what you asked of them.
- Identify anchors who targets can trust and who will remain constant and provide stability.
- Provide targets with training in how to understand their own reactions, as well as the reactions of others, to the change process.

Source: Donna Richards Sheridan, "In the Business Literature," *Aspen's Advisor for Nurse Executives*, vol. 6, no. 2, Aspen Publishers, Inc., © 1990.

---

action is taken to ensure the accomplishment of organizational goals. It is the policing operation in management, although the manager seeks to create a positive climate so that the process of control is accepted as part of routine activity. Controlling is also a forward-looking process in that the manager seeks to anticipate deviation and prevent it.

The manager initiates the control function during the planning phase, when possible deviation is anticipated and policies are developed to help ensure uniformity of practice.

Close supervision and a tight leadership style reflect an aspect of control. Through rewards and positive sanctions, the manager seeks to motivate workers to conform, thus limiting the amount of control that must be imposed. Finally, the manager develops specific control tools, such as inspections, visible control charts, work counts, special reports, and audits.

The Basic Control Process

The control process involves three phases that are cyclic: establishing standards, measuring performance, and correcting deviation. In the first step, the specific units of measure that delineate acceptable work are determined. Basic standards may be stated as staff hours allowed per activity, speed and time limits, quantity that must be produced, and number of errors or rejects permitted. The second step in the control process, measuring performance, involves comparing the work (i.e., the service provided) against the standard. Employee evaluation is one aspect of this measurement.

Studies of consumer/client satisfaction are key elements when services are involved. Finally, if necessary, remedial action is taken, including retraining employees.

Note: For further discussions of control methods see Chapters 12, 20, and 34.

Characteristics of Adequate Controls

Several features are necessary to ensure the adequacy of control processes and tools:

- *Timeliness*. The control device should reflect deviations from the standard promptly and at an early stage, so there is only a small time lag between detection and the beginning of corrective action.
- *Economy*. If possible, control devices should involve routine, normal processes rather than the special inspection routines at additional cost. The control devices must be worth their cost.
- *Comprehensiveness*. The controls should be directed at the basic phases of the work rather than the later levels or steps in the process.
- *Specificity and appropriateness*. The control process should reflect the nature of the

activity. Proper quality of care inspection methods, for example, differ from a financial audit.
- *Objectivity*. The processes should be grounded in fact, and standards should be known and verifiable.
- *Responsibility*. Controls should reflect the authority-responsibility pattern. As far as possible, the worker and the immediate supervisor should be involved in the monitoring and correction process.
- *Understandability*. Control devices, charts, graphs, and reports that are complicated or cumbersome will not be used readily.

Tools of Control

Certain tools of control may be combined with the planning process. Management by objectives, the budget, the Gantt chart, and the PERT network are examples of tools used both for planning and controlling. The flow chart, the flow process chart, the work distribution chart, and work sampling (see Chaper 20) all may be used in planning workflow or assessing a proposed change in plan or procedure. They also may be adapted for specific control use, such as when the flow chart is employed to audit the way in which work is done, as compared to the original plan.

Specific, quantifiable output measures may be recorded and monitored through a variety of visible control charts. In addition to these specific tools, the manager exercises control through the assessment and limitation of conflict, through the communication process, and through active monitoring of employees.

How To Control*

Money, Material, and People

Essentially, a supervisor controls three entities or a combination of them: money, material, and people. Each, however, is handled dif-

---

*Source: Nancy Diekelmann and Martin Broadwell, *The New Hospital Supervisor*, Addison-Wesley Publishing Company, Inc., © 1977. Pp. 57–74. Reprinted with permission.

ferently, each takes a separate skill. Money and material are usually more constant and easier to budget. Money will buy just so much, and you have just so much money, so you must decide what to do with what you have.

But people aren't that easy to budget (control); no two are alike and each person may show different qualities from one time to the next. That's what makes a person an individual. When you start to budget (control) people, you must consider that they work at a different speed in the morning than in the afternoon, and with a different attitude on Monday than on Friday, or on evenings than on nights.

Often, you may try to control without a plan, which means you're doing some guesswork with your controlling. For example, when you decide in the middle of a project that it's taking too many supplies and too much time, and *then* start to "control," very likely you didn't have a pre-set plan to begin with.

A rule of thumb—really more of a guide—is that when you need to take drastic action with people, materials, or money, either the planning or the controlling stage broke down. In general, controlling consists of (1) determining standards, (2) measuring results against standards, and (3) taking remedial action as necessary.

Determining Standards

In determining standards, look for answers to some basic questions: Who sets the standards, and how will you know they are the standards? Your plan may or may not specify how far you can stray from the standards without courting trouble. You must have this information; you cannot hope to control without it.

And you need to know who will measure the results of your work and who will see the results of those measurements. Is there a quality-control person (such as a systems engineer or an infection-control officer) who reports to higher management? Or has someone on your own staff been given partial responsibility for watching quality?

Of utmost importance is what will be measured and why it particularly is being measured. Are you getting valid information or just watching a meaningless figure?

Sometimes you can overreact to situations, too. Your superior tells you to watch out for certain problems or expenditures, and you set up a control system much more complicated than you need. Long after the crisis is past, you're still filling out forms and sending reports up the line. Once forms and reports come into being, getting rid of them is next to impossible. *Start them only under extreme need!*

What are some items that can be measured? Obviously, you want to measure output of services. How long did it take? How much did it cost? What was the final quality?

Then you need to look closely at expenses. When you measure them, you must measure all of them. Are you taking into account everything that's being charged to the particular job? Are you including staff help, hidden costs that eventually will need to be shown?

Using Resources

You must also account for the use of resources. Again, this means people, time, and money—but here you're measuring efficient use. Are you doing a good job of matching people and jobs? Remember, a job done well isn't necessarily proof of good supervision. You must consider who's doing the job. If your people are capable of doing much more because of experience, education, training, or talent, you can't be too proud that they've done the job well. Your aim is to match ability with job requirements as closely as possible, then let the people grow out of their jobs as they develop. As a supervisor, you must constantly measure—at least in your mind—both how well the employee matches the job and whether he or she has outgrown it.

This is also true for other resources. Are you really getting the most out of overtime? Are you doing jobs that could be left undone or eliminated altogether, then using overtime for essential things? Sometimes you can trap yourself this way, spending valuable time on unimportant chores, forcing yourself into overtime. Or you might use people on nonessential assignments when they could be working on more worthwhile projects. You can have everyone pitch in and help when admissions are very heavy. But if this means you neglect other work that will put you behind schedule or cost you time and money later on, you've made a bad decision.

Using the Budget

The budget is perhaps the oldest and best control device you have. It gives you something to measure your progress by and something at which to aim. As you compare yourself constantly with the budget, you're also getting feedback on where you can expect to be at the end of the budget period.

Here are a few basic points of reference on budgets. First, a budget is put together to let the administration know just how much money is needed and where it can best be spent. Good budget planning takes local needs into account, and good budget designers solicit help from all levels in determining the best use of funds.

The trouble starts when each level becomes unrealistic about its needs. With each unit adding just a little extra, a little cushion here or there, the total budget becomes bloated. Either the demand is too big or the hospital must look for more money than it really needs. When this happens, someone at the top usually starts to whittle the figure, and everyone gets hurt.

Don't include in your budget anything you can't substantiate; sooner or later, you'll have to account for what you requested. If your figures won't stand the test, not only will the budget be cut, but your reputation as a supervisor will suffer.

Measuring Results

Once you've determined the standards by which you're to control, you must measure the results against those standards. Sometimes this is routine—a simple matter of seeing how many patients were treated, and so forth, then reporting the obvious results by whatever method is provided.

All evaluating isn't that obvious or that easy, however. In some situations, so many contributing factors are involved that you aren't quite sure just what the results mean.

One of the best avenues open to you is the process known as sampling. There's nothing complicated about it. It's simply a means of looking at large or complicated services and obtaining reliable results without taking a measurement on *every* detail and *every* person involved in that effort. Instead, you take a small, average sample and use its results to represent the entire operation. Or take one complete case or instance out of several, assuming that the rest are like this one.

You can look for ways of getting true samples regularly: Check the employee absentee list occasionally and notice if certain persons or a constant number are absent regularly. Spot-check three or four days in a row and notice how much time the employees are taking for break or when they're coming back from lunch. Look at patient complaints once a week for several weeks and find out what's causing trouble. These are good indicators of how well you're doing and a good means of controlling.

When sampling won't help in measuring results, and the measuring seems too difficult to do on the whole operation, you may choose to look for a substitute measurement. Thus, you can examine something like absenteeism or tardiness and get a good idea of the group's morale. High turnover may be a good substitute measurement of the extent of available job enrichment and training. A look at previous records may be a good measure of motivation or employee morale in the work unit, providing other things are equal. The substitute measurement may be a tangible means of measuring intangibles such as attitudes, job satisfaction, morale, and so forth.

Taking Remedial Action

Controlling would be useless if it didn't include the final facet of control: taking remedial action when required. When measuring processes show that things are running smoothly, you should be a good enough supervisor to recognize it and leave things alone. But when results show that a situation is getting out of hand or that you should be doing better, you should step in and take action.

You may not be the one literally to take action, but you might instigate it by reporting to the right person. If you've found a problem on the unit, ask yourself who should know about it. The obvious answer is: Someone who can do something about it. Whether the problem is overtime, a union grievance, or whatever, telling the right person as soon as possible may ward off a much more serious problem later on.

However, it's better to solve the problem yourself than to pass it on to someone else. This means you must have the authority to take the necessary remedial action. It also means you may need to repeat the entire planning, organizing, and directing functions. If that's what the remedial action requires, that's what you, the good supervisor, should do.

Systems Engineering

*Activities**

Health systems engineers (frequently referred to as industrial or management engineers) are employed by hospitals and other health care institutions to study facility design and utilization, information flow, personnel utilization, and the degree to which performance objectives are being met, in the expectation that they will be of aid in reducing costs and improving the quality of and access to care.

Eleven activities summarize the majority of services provided by systems engineers:

1. The analysis, design, and improvement of work systems, work centers, and work methods.
2. The establishment of work standards for determining staffing patterns, personnel utilization, and costs.
3. The development of job descriptions, job evaluation plans, merit rating procedures, and employee motivation plans.
4. The design of physical facilities, layout and arrangement, floor space utilization, material flow, and traffic patterns.
5. The installation of systems for production control, inventory control, and quality control in the storing, handling, processing, and using of materials and supplies.

6. The economic analysis of alternative combinations of personnel, materials, and equipment, and the development of models to optimize such combinations.
7. The simplification of paperwork and the design of forms.
8. The improvement of organizational structure, authority-responsibility relationships, and patterns of communications.
9. The development of data processing procedures and management reports in order to establish information systems for managerial control on a continuing basis.
10. The generation of technical information, the forecasting of future needs and demands, and the conversion of relevant information into a form useful in managerial and administrative decision making.
11. The performance of general staff work for the administrator for his use in policy determination, fiscal budgeting, building plans, and public relations.[1]

*Analysis**

Operations Analysis. This function is described as making a thorough analysis of an operation by dissecting it into its component parts or elements. Each part or element then is considered separately, and the study of an operation becomes a series of fairly simple problems. Systems engineers have found from experience that few established methods cannot be improved if examined sufficiently.

Process Analysis. Another term for a similar evaluation is *process analysis*. It is described as "the act of studying the process used for producing a product for the purpose of developing the lowest-cost, most efficient process which will yield products of acceptable quality." Applied to health care, the end result of a process should

---

[1]Harold E. Smalley, *Hospital Management Engineering,* Prentice-Hall, Inc., Englewood Cliffs, N.J., © 1982, p. 397. Copyright © Harold E. Smalley. Reprinted by permission of the author.

*Source: David F. Johannides, *Cost Containment through Systems Engineering,* Aspen Publishers, Inc., © 1979.

---

*Source: David F. Johannides, *Cost Containment through Systems Engineering,* Aspen Publishers, Inc., © 1979.

result in better health, although objective measurement may be difficult. When a current process is evaluated to find ways of improving it, the analysis usually is made with the aid of one or more types of process charts. The process chart is a convenient way to show the relations among operations, the steps of a process, and such factors as distance moved, working and idle time, cost, operations performed, and time standards. It permits the quick perception of a problem so that improvement can be undertaken in a logical sequence.

Systems Analysis. Another evaluation term is *systems analysis.* A system is defined as a network of interrelated operations joined together to perform an activity. In a sense, it is a broader application of the operation analysis definition, with key elements reviewed for their negative or positive impact on the decision points of the system.

Systems analysis requires ten steps in which the systems engineer must

1. define the problem
2. prepare an outline of the systems study
3. obtain general background information on the areas to be studied
4. understand the interactions between the areas being studied
5. understand the existing system
6. define the system requirements
7. design the new system
8. prepare economic cost comparisons
9. sell the new system to management
10. provide implementation, follow-up, and re-evaluation[1]

In addition to this process, an effective system should produce the following important results:

1. the right information furnished to the right people, at the right time, and at the right cost
2. a decrease in uncertainty and improvement of decision quality

3. an increased capacity to process present and future volumes of work
4. an ability to perform profitable work that was previously impossible
5. increased productivity of employees and capital, and reduced costs[1]

To achieve these results, one step is all-important—the design of the new system. Here the information developed earlier is combined into a synchronized approach to desired goals. It requires the recognition that alternative configurations may offer success in varying degrees, which must be assessed. It is a practical process that is limited by the availability of such resources as time, money, and personnel. It remains a key instrument for implementing decisions.

*Systems Theory**

The systems model is made up of four basic components: inputs, throughputs or processes, outputs, and feedback (Figure 3-2). The overall environment also must be considered.

Inputs. A systematic review of inputs for a health care organization or one of its departments could include:

- characteristics of clients: average length of stay, diagnostic categories, payment status
- federal and state laws concerning employers: collective bargaining legislation, the Occupational Safety and Health Act, workers' compensation, Civil Rights Act
- multiple goals: patient care, teaching, research

Throughputs (Withinputs). Throughputs are the structures or processes by which inputs are converted to outputs. Physical plant, workflow, methods and procedures, and hours of work are throughputs. Throughputs are analyzed by work sampling, work simplification, methods improvement, staffing patterns, and physical

---

[1]John M. Fitzgerald and Ardra F. Fitzgerald, *Fundamentals of Systems Analysis,* John Wiley & Sons, © 1973. Reprinted with permission.

[1]Ibid.

*Source: Joan G. Liebler, Ruth E. Levine, and Hyman L. Dervitz, *Management Principles for Health Professionals,* Aspen Publishers, Inc., © 1983.

Figure 3-2 Basic Systems Model

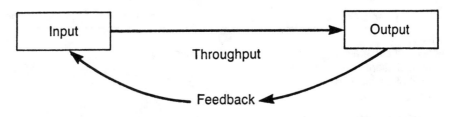

layout analysis. For example, a chief of service cannot control patient arrivals for walk-in service in a clinic; this input is imposed on the system. The policies and procedures for processing walk-in patients, however, constitute a cluster of throughputs that can be determined by the manager.

Outputs. Outputs are the goods and services that the organization (or subdivision or unit) must produce. These outputs may be routine, frequent, predictable, and somewhat easy to identify.

Some outputs for health care institutions are

- processing of specified laboratory tests within ten hours of receipt of specimen
- retrieval of patient medical record from permanent file within seven minutes of receipt of request
- 100 percent follow-up on all patients who fail to keep appointments

Feedback. Changes in the input mix must be anticipated. In order to respond to these changes, managers need feedback on the acceptability and adequacy of the outputs. It is through the feedback process that inputs, and even throughputs, are adjusted to produce new outputs. The communication network and control processes are the usual sources of organized feedback. The management by objectives process, short interval scheduling, and Program Evaluation Review Technique (PERT) networks constitute specific management tools of planning and controlling that include structured, factual feedback.

If there is an absence of planned feedback, if the communication process is not sufficiently developed to permit safe and acceptable avenues for feedback, or if the feedback is ignored, feedback will occur spontaneously. In this case, it tends to take a negative form, such as a client outburst of anger, a precipitous lawsuit, a wildcat strike, a consumer boycott, or an epidemic.

Closed Systems vs. Open Systems. Systems may be classified as either closed or open. An ideal closed system is complete within itself. No new inputs are received, and there is no change in the components; there is no output of energy in any of its forms (e.g., information or material). Few, if any, response or adaptation systems are needed because such a system is isolated from external forces in its environment and internal change is self-adjusting.

Organizations have been viewed as closed systems, that is, the emphasis has been placed on the study of functions and structure within the organization without consideration of its environment and the consequent effect of environmental change on its processes.

An open system is in a constant state of flux. Inputs are received and outputs produced. There is input and output of both matter and energy, continual adaptation to the environment, and, usually, an increase of order and complexity with differentiation of parts over time.

Classic functions of a manager, which are carried out in the distinct, unique environment of a given organization, are reflected in the systems approach. Table 3-1 summarizes this interrelationship.

Management by Objectives*

There are three distinct phases in the MBO cycle: the planning phase, the performance

---

*Source: Ibid.

Table 3-1   Relationship of Classic Management Functions and Systems Concepts

Systems Concept	Predominant Management Function
Input analysis	
Identification of constraints	Planning
Assessment of client characteristics	
Assessment of physical space	
Budget allocation analysis	
Throughput determination	
Development of policies, procedures, methods	Planning and controlling
Development of detailed departmental layout	
Specification of staffing pattern	Staffing
Methods of worker productivity enhancement	Controlling, leadership, and motivation
Output analysis	
Goal formulation	Planning
Statement of objectives	
Development of management by objectives plan	Planning and controlling
Feedback mechanisms	
Development of feedback processes	Controlling, communicating, and resolving conflict
Adjustment of inputs and outputs in light of feedback	Renewing planning cycle
Adjustment of internal throughputs	

review phase, and the feedback phase leading to a new planning phase. Table 3-2 summarizes the MBO cycle in terms of each phase, key activities for the phase, and the participants involved in each phase.

Planning

Selection of objectives is the basic activity on which the MBO process is built, and it must be given careful attention. A guiding principle for the choice of objectives is the rule of the critical few, also referred to as the Pareto principle. In essence, this concept reflects the probability that most of the key results will be generated by only a few of the activities, while most of the activities will generate only a few of the key results.

Performance Objectives. In the MBO process, the performance objectives developed are essentially operational goals or objectives. The objectives that are determined for an MBO sequence should be distinguished by three characteristics:

1. *Specificity.* Each objective should include a plan that shows the work to be done, the time frame within which it is to be accomplished, and a clear designation of the individual who is to accomplish the work.
2. *Measurability.* Each objective, as far as possible, should have quantifiable indicators for the measurement of work accomplished. If an activity cannot be quantified, qualitative factors should be developed.
3. *Attainability.* Each objective should be realistic; it should be possible to carry out the activity within the time frame established.

Performance objectives have much in common with operational goals, which will be discussed here briefly in conjunction with their use in management by objectives.

Operational Goals. In addition to the formal statements of objectives and desired functional statements of performance, a manager may wish to develop operational, or working, goals for internal department use only. Operational goals

Table 3-2 Summary of MBO Cycle

Phase	Key Activities	Participants
Planning	Identifies and defines key organizational goals	Manager
	Identifies and defines key departmental goals that stem from overall goals	
	Identifies and defines performance measures (operational goals) for employees	
	Formulates and proposes goals for specific job	Subordinate
	Formulates and proposes measures for specific job	
	Participate in management conferences	Manager and subordinates
	Achieve joint agreement on individual objectives and individual performance	
	Set up timetable for periodic meetings for performance review	
Performance review	Continue to participate in periodic management conferences	Manager and subordinates
	Adjust and refine objectives based on feedback, new constraints, and new inputs	
	Eliminate inappropriate goals	
	Readjust timetable as needed	
	Maintain ongoing comparison of proposed timetable and actual performance through use of control monitoring devices, such as visible control charts	
Feedback to new planning stage	Reviews overall organizational and departmental goals for the next planning period, such as the next fiscal year	Manager

are also highly specific, measurable, and attainable; they must be sufficiently concrete to relate the overall goals and objectives to specific actions.

Operational goals may be seen as temporary measures that take into account the reality of changing, usually difficult, work situations. They reflect the impact of a high turnover rate, absenteeism, employees in a trainee status, physical renovation of the work area, or temporary emergency situations. Operational goals may become progressively more refined as progress is achieved in certain areas.

Performance Review

The performance objectives determined in the MBO conference must be fair, based on all known relevant conditions, adjusted to the individual's capability, and adjusted to the specific constraints of the work situation. The objectives themselves do not vary from one performance

meeting to another, but the points to be measured are subject to change because of variations in conditions during work cycles.

The purpose of performance review is not only to monitor the performance, but also to make adjustments as indicated by the situation. Successful use of MBO includes the allowance for a margin of error, that is, planning for mistakes and accepting the human factor. This planning for contingencies gives realism to the objectives and is helpful in enhancing employee acceptance of the process.

Feedback

There are several, even many, management conferences to formulate the original plans, to adjust these plans during the performance review phase, and to obtain the necessary feedback. During the management conferences between workers and managers, specific planning takes place:

1. Appropriate objectives are identified through mutual agreement.
2. Time periods for achieving the objectives are established.
3. Responsibility in terms of results is defined.
4. Revision and adjustments are made periodically.

Formats for MBO Plan

The format for writing a detailed MBO plan varies; managers develop a format to suit their own needs unless a specific format is imposed by a higher authority in the organization. Regardless of what format is used, certain information should be included routinely in the MBO plan:

- department
- unit or subdivision
- overall objectives and the derived operational objectives
- the period covered in the MBO cycle
- key participants
- workflow factors and special constraints
- identification of training needs
- methods of evaluation to be used
- detailed time plan

MEETINGS*

Meetings are the mainstay of managers and their major headache. No manager can function without meetings to provide direction and to process issues for revealing areas that require direction and resolution.

Types of Meetings

Information Meetings

The information meeting is held simply for the transfer of information. You have something to pass along to your employees or others and you choose to do this with a meeting rather than by

some other means. The basic purpose of any information meeting is to transfer information to the group, and in this setting the leader may do most or all of the talking. Although there are usually questions and discussion for the sake of clarification, the transfer of information is essentially one-way communication.

Discussion Meetings

The objective of a discussion meeting is to gain agreement on something through the exchange of information, ideas, and opinions. The essence of the discussion meeting is interchange; the exchange of information must be established between and among all participants.

Directed Discussion. A directed discussion meeting may be appropriate when a conclusion, solution, or decision is evident. The conclusion has already been determined; yet it is not simply being relayed to the group as straight information. It is the leader's objective to gain the participants' acceptance of the solution. In effect, a directed discussion is a "sales pitch."

Problem-solving Discussion. This type of meeting is held when a problem exists and a solution or decision must be determined by the group. Although the answer determined by joint action may well turn out to be based on the ideas of a single participant, at the outset it is apparent only that there is a problem with which several parties could reasonably be concerned.

Exploratory Discussion. The purpose of an exploratory discussion meeting is to gain information on which you or others may eventually base a decision. The objective is not to develop a specific solution or recommendation but rather to generate and develop ideas and information for others (perhaps yourself, but possibly your boss or some other manager) who must make the decision.

The Staff Meeting

The staff meeting may be an information meeting, a discussion meeting, or both. A staff meeting is usually held for the purpose of communication among the members of a group. Staff members may report on the status of their activities, and thus each may be required to

*Source: Charles R. McConnell, *The Effective Health Care Supervisor*, ed 2, Aspen Publishers, Inc., © 1988.

effect the one-way transfer of information to others. This meeting form is also used to solve problems, sell ideas, and explore issues, and, depending on the business at hand, it may take on any or all of the three forms of the discussion meeting.

Determining the Need for a Meeting

While the conduct of meetings serves an administrative function, many meetings unfortunately are largely a waste of time because they lack clear purpose or are poorly led. Some meetings are a total waste of time and resources—they should not be held at all. Meetings are costly relative to other ways of doing business. They are not necessarily costly in the sense of out-of-pocket expenditures; their cost is reckoned largely in terms of the expenditure of unrecoverable time or lost productivity. What would these people have been doing had they not been involved in a meeting?

In defense of meetings, it is necessary to point out that meetings often represent the best available technique for arriving at joint conclusions and determining joint actions. As such, meetings are essential to consultative and participative leadership styles. Joint decisions and actions take longer to arrive at than do unilateral decisions and edicts, since two-way communication, including discussion and feedback, requires more time than so-called one-way communication. However, the extra time spent in meetings can represent a small price to pay for the benefits afforded by an honest, open, participative leadership style (see "Committee Meetings" below).

In determining the need for a meeting, an administrator should consider the following:

- How many people are involved? If very few, perhaps you can use the telephone, letters, or memos.
- Will a meeting save time? Often a problem can be solved by a memorandum or report, but if an exchange of ideas is needed, then a meeting may avoid a seemingly endless series of other contacts.
- Should everyone get the same story? Perhaps the issue is complex or technically

involved, calling for different levels of participation by both medical and nonmedical personnel. Perhaps there are policy issues to be considered, suggesting that certain matters be taken up at a policymaking level before they can be dealt with generally.

EFFECTIVE USE OF COMMITTEES*

The productivity of a nursing unit, department, or division is greatly enhanced if groups are used efficiently. The nurse manager needs to know how to select and structure groups for work projects, and he or she needs to be able to run the meetings of groups effectively. Every nurse manager should carefully scrutinize the use of committees and other groups in the organization.

The nurse manager must be aware of the limitations of committees. Many projects are better assigned to a single individual or a two-person team than to a "bulkier" committee. Projects that require complex research and planning are better planned by a single individual, who can become familiar with and sensitive to each aspect of the project.

In addition, no committee should be used to supplant the authority and responsibility of line managers. Committees are not designed to handle most day-to-day decisions. Indeed, the dilution of individual responsibility within committees makes them easy places to avoid decision making. Committees are better suited to handling the larger issues, such as major policy changes or long-term plans.

Types of Committees*

The following types of groups serve specific functions.

Standing committees are permanently assigned to make decisions or handle problems related to a specific area of concern. These committees are of long duration, often having mem-

*Source: Barbara Stevens Barnum and Catherine O. Mallard, *Essentials of Nursing Management*, Aspen Publishers, Inc., © 1989.

bers who rotate off and on at periodic intervals. The concerns addressed by standing committees are those that will need continual monitoring over the lifetime of the organization. Most standing committees in nursing are located at the divisional rather than the departmental or unit level, but different organizations build committees on different levels.

A *design group* (or task force) is an ad hoc committee created to handle a specific problem or task and then dissolved once its task is completed. Major ad hoc committees that handle complex assignments are often termed design groups or task forces. Membership on such a committee is typically earned by virtue of expertise related to the committee's assignment. The goal of the design group is to utilize the organization's best talents for a particular problem.

Groups based on organizational position and function exist in most nursing divisions. A head-nurse group or a steering committee of nurse managers is an example. In determining whether such groups should be formally designated, the nurse executive needs to evaluate the desirability of providing a vehicle for group cohesion and power. Most nurse executives find it useful to create an administrative council to facilitate communication and participative management. These position-based groups typically monitor and respond to the changing work environment. They tend to be responsive to immediate administrative problems of diverse kinds and to grease the wheels of day-to-day operations.

Interdivisional committees combine nursing with nonnursing divisions, departments, groups, or individuals. These groups result when (1) coordination of goals and activities is necessary, such as between service and education or among members of a health team working toward a common goal, and (2) recurrent problems arise because of conflicting goals or systems, such as those that may occur between nursing and the dietary or laundry department.

Making a Committee Productive*

The first consideration is to establish the degree of power delegated to the group. It is

Source: Ibid.

important that the group be given enough authority to fulfill its objectives. The nurse manager may give a committee power to recommend or power to decide. He or she may give a committee one standing level of power or may give it power options relevant to specific issues and assignments. When the nurse manager chooses to adjust the power level for different assignments, it is important that the committee members clearly understand their powers in each case.

The committee should be viewed primarily as a means of getting work done, not as a means of meeting status needs, as a popularity contest, or as an exercise in the democratic process. There is no logic in appointing a member to a committee if one can predict that the person will not contribute to the committee's objectives. Managers must also be cautious about overuse of the same reliable people on numerous committees. When such participants become a select group, to the exclusion of others, an obstructive "we-they" syndrome may occur.

A committee should consist of the smallest number of persons who can meet the committee's objectives. To appoint more is to misuse human resources. Committee membership can be controlled on large projects by designating a small stable nucleus of members and giving them the option to call in others as needed at various stages of the project.

Often a committee is unproductive because it does not really need to exist, as when its objectives are either not attainable or not relevant at the particular time. When the objectives of a committee are judged to be valid but the committee is still unproductive, it may be trying to do the job with the wrong people. A committee leader without appropriate skills may be the problem. A second possibility is an incompatible membership (i.e., incompatible with regard to the objectives of the committee, not necessarily incompatable with one another).

Periodic status reports are useful to the nurse manager because they let him or her know the direction, rate of progress, and general productivity of the committee. The nurse manager can then calculate any needed redirection, support, or alteration in its membership. The requirement of periodic status reports (as opposed to mere minutes) also pressures committee members to attend to original goals and to evaluate progress toward those goals.

What Makes Committees Work?

Committees work when they are formally organized, have assigned jobs to do, have a leader, keep written records of their deliberations for future reference, and know results are expected. Committees fail when they are not wisely constituted, when their purpose is vague or is lost sight of, when members are not well oriented and are not convinced that the results will be worth the effort, when they meet only for the sake of meeting, or when the preparation for their meetings is inadequate.

Checklist*

1. *Purpose.* The charge to the committee should be clearly defined, and its responsibilities, duties, and objectives should be spelled out. The choice of chairperson and members and the willingness of individuals to serve largely depend on the committee's purpose.

2. *Need.* Is the committee the best technique for accomplishing the purpose that has been defined? If so, should a new committee be formed or can an existing committee do the job? Or would a conference of one or two sessions do it just as well?

3. *Functions.* What kind of committee is this going to be? Is it to be administrative, assigned a definite action responsibility such as that for the development of policies and procedures? Or is it to be advisory, set up to explore, to communicate, and to coordinate?

4. *Organization.* How many members will it have, and how will they and the chairperson be selected and appointed? Will there be ex officio members and will they have votes? To whom will the committee report? How often will it meet? Who will call special meetings? Who should receive copies of the minutes? Will the

committee spend money, and how much? Who will be responsible for arrangements, agenda, and call notices?

5. *Selecting the Leader.* First, would the prospective leader be optimistic about the committee's task? The leader's attitudes have a very definite influence on the group.

Second, would the prospective leader be able to organize the committee into a tightly knit task-oriented group? A clue as to whether a potential leader would be able to organize the group efficiently might be found by looking at the employee's daily work patterns. An employee who is conscientious, organized, and efficient would probably bring those same patterns to the committee.

Third, would the prospective leader be able to ask pertinent questions and to listen and comprehend the answers which are received?

6. *Committee Members.* A sensitive administrator will carefully select individuals who can comfortably work with other individuals. The following questions might be asked of potential committee members. If the answer is yes to most of these questions, the chances are good that he or she will be a productive member of the group.

- Has this individual worked on committees before? If yes, was his or her input constructive?
- In general, does the individual relate well to his or her peers within the hospital?
- When there is conflict, can this individual look at the underlying causes of the problem?
- Does this individual think critically?
- Can this individual look past his or her interests in order to examine all sides of an issue?

7. *Feedback.* When an administrator lets a committee know that he or she is pleased with the work which they are doing, gives suggestions on how they could do their work better, and is available as a resource person, he or she is providing a healthy impetus for the committee.

An administrator cannot afford to set up committees and let them flounder. He or she must

---

*Source: Items 5 through 8 are adapted from Robert Veninga, ''Applying Hospital Control to Hospital Committees,'' *Hospital Topics,* June 1974. Adapted with permission.

keep track of what is going on within the committees and give encouragement and support.

8. *Committee Recommendations*. Taking the suggestions of the committee seriously does not necessarily mean always agreeing to what a committee has recommended. It does mean, however, that the administrator will carefully look at the suggestions, meet with the committee to understand the logic behind the recommendations, and then respond to the output of the committee.

How To Get More from Committee Meetings*

Before

1. Explore alternatives to meeting.
   a. A decision by the responsible party often eliminates the need for group action.
   b. Postpone the meeting. Consolidate the agenda with that of a later meeting.
   c. Cancel the meeting. Ask yourself, "Is this meeting necessary?"
   d. Send a representative. This gives a subordinate experience and saves you time.
2. Limit your attendance. Attend only for the time needed to make your contribution.
3. Keep the participants to a minimum. Only those needed should attend.
4. Choose an appropriate time. The necessary facts and people should be available.
5. Choose an appropriate place. Accessibility of location, availability of equipment, size of the room, and so forth are all important.
6. Define the purpose clearly in your own mind before calling the meeting.
7. Distribute the agenda in advance. This helps the participants prepare—or at least forewarns them.

8. Compute the cost per minute of meeting by figuring the total salaries per minute, adding perhaps 35 percent for fringes. Assess the cost of starting late and of the time allocated to the topics on the agenda.
9. Time-limit the meeting and the agenda. Allocate a time to each subject proportional to its relative importance.

During

10. Start on time. Give warning; then do it. There is no substitute.
11. Assign timekeeping and minutes responsibilities. Keep posted on the time remaining and the amount behind schedule if any.
12. Hold a stand-up meeting if appropriate. This speeds deliberations. Try it on drop-in visitors.
13. Start with and stick to the agenda. "We're here to. . . . The purpose of this meeting is. . . . The next point to be decided is. . . ."
14. Control interruptions. Allow interruptions for emergency purposes only.
15. Accomplish your purpose. What was the specific purpose of the meeting—to analyze a problem, to generate creative alternatives, to arrive at a decision, to inform, to coordinate? *Was it accomplished?*
16. Restate conclusions and assignments to ensure agreement and to provide reinforcement or a reminder.
17. End on time. Adjourn the meeting as scheduled so that participants can manage their own time. Placing the most important items at the start of the agenda ensures that only the least important will be left unfinished.
18. Use a meeting evaluation checklist as an occasional spot check. Questions should be answered by each participant before leaving. Was the purpose of the meeting clear? Was the agenda received in advance? Were any materials essential for preparation also received in advance? Did the meeting start on time? If not, why not? Was the agenda followed adequately

---

*Source: Reprinted, by permission of the publisher, from *The Time Trap*, R. Alex Mackenzie, © 1972 by AMACOM, a division of American Management Associations, pp. 110–112. All rights reserved.

or was the meeting allowed to wander from it unnecessarily? Was the purpose achieved? Were assignments and deadlines fixed where appropriate? Of the total meeting time, what percentage was not effectively utilized? Why? The evaluations, unsigned, should be collected for the chairperson's immediate review.

After

19. Expedite the preparation of the minutes. Concise minutes should be completed and distributed within 24 hours if possible or 48 hours at the outside. Minutes are a reminder and a useful followup tool, as shown in the next suggestion.
20. Ensure that progress reports are made and decisions executed. Provide followup to ensure the implementation of decisions and checks on progress where warranted. Uncompleted actions should be listed under "Unfinished Business" on the next meeting's agenda.
21. Make a committee inventory. Survey all committees, investigating whether their objectives have been achieved and, if not, when they can be expected to be. Abolish those that have accomplished their intended purpose.

Groupthink*

Most of us know that obvious factors, such as embarrassment and fear of reprisal, tend to restrict free expression of ideas in groups. However, other more subtle restrictive factors, such as high regard for unanimity sought by members of groups, also are at work.

The danger is not that each will fail to reveal his or her strong objections to a proposal, but that each will think the proposal is a good one without even attempting to carry out a critical scru-

tiny that could reveal grounds for strong objections.

As a group becomes excessively close knit groupthink develops. The process is characterized by a marked decrease in the exchange of potentially conflicting data and by an unwillingness to conscientiously examine such data when they surface.

Groupthink Symptoms

1. Illusion of unanimity regarding the viewpoint held by the majority in the group and an emphasis on team play.
2. A view of the opposition as generally inept, incompetent, and incapable of countering effectively any action by the group, no matter how risky the decision or how high the odds are against the plan of action succeeding.
3. Self-censorship of group members in which overt disagreements are avoided, facts that might reduce support for the emerging majority view are suppressed, faulty assumptions are not questioned, and personal doubts are suppressed in the form of group harmony.
4. A shared feeling of unassailability marked by a high degree of esprit de corps, by implicit faith in the wisdom of the group, and by an inordinate optimism that disposes members to take excessive risks.

Preventing Groupthink

1. *Leader Encouragement.* The leader should encourage free expression of minority viewpoints, do all he or she can to protect individuals who are attacked, and create opportunities for them to clarify their views.

2. *Diversity of Viewpoints.* Attempt to structure the group so that there are different viewpoints. Diverse input will tend to point out nonobvious risks, drawbacks, and advantages that might not have been considered by a more homogeneous group.

3. *Legitimized Disagreement.* Voicing objections and doubts should not be subordinated to fears about "rocking the boat" or reluctance to "blow the whistle." Each member should take on the additional role of a critical

Source: Reprinted, by permission of the publisher, from "Groupthink: When Too Many Heads Spoil the Decision," C.W. Von Bergen, Jr., and R.J. Kirk, *Management Review*, March 1978, © 1978 by AMACOM, a division of American Management Associations. All rights reserved.

evaluator and should be encouraged by the leader and other members to air reservations.

4. *Advantages and Disadvantages of Each Solution*. The group should try to explore the merits and demerits of each alternative. This process of listing the sides of a question forces discussion to oscillate from one side of the issue to the other. As a result, the positive and negative aspects of each strategy are brought out into the open and may become the foundation for a new idea with all its merits and few of its weaknesses.

Brainstorming*

Brainstorming is a technique that can be used to generate a wide variety of ideas on almost any subject. It can be used to identify problems, programmatic actions, or alternative strategies. The emphasis in brainstorming is on the quantity of ideas, not necessarily on their quality. From the many ideas, some useful ones are sure to emerge.

The Structure

The following nine rules or conditions permit the brainstorming process to operate in an optimum manner:

1. Everyone should know and understand the issue.
2. No one should be permitted to criticize the ideas of another panel member.
3. Creative and free thought should be encouraged.
4. Tagging one's ideas to another's should be encouraged.
5. Panel members should help other members to express their ideas.
6. No one should be permitted to challenge another person's ideas.
7. The obvious ideas should be given as much attention as the less obvious or creative ones.

8. All members should have a chance to discuss their ideas.
9. The largest number of ideas that can be produced in the shortest time period should be the goal.

USING CONSULTANTS*

A consultant is a "sometime thing" in a hospital, entering only on invitation, and usually for a stated purpose. The consultant has the advantage of objectivity, but the limitation of being an outsider. Little may be known prior to the visit of the history, the traditions, the personalities, or the problems contributing to the institution's profile. How these gaps in knowledge are bridged is critical to the consultant's success.

There are many valid reasons for using a consultant in nursing services. An expert in a particular area can share information; examine a system and evaluate its structure and outcomes; and advise on the modifications which appear to be indicated. Educational consultants can advise on the in-service education program, emphasizing the processes which are essential to an understanding of the system and its values.

Consultants may survey the total organization or a single department. They may review decisions or programs to comment on the rationale or conceptual problems. A consultant may be particularly helpful in identifying solutions to problems requiring the particular expertise the consultant has.

There are also some situations not amenable to consultation. A consultant is no substitute for a prepared nursing service administrator. The consultant can only provide some additional options for the administrator to consider in making management decisions. Occasional consultation cannot prepare incumbent administrators for positions for which they lack academic and professional experience. Neither can a consultant continually confront and advise on poor deci-

---

Source: Herbert H. Hyman, *Implementing Institutional Objectives: A Guide for Hospital Planners*, Aspen Publishers, Inc., © 1983.

Source: Cynthia Kinsella, "Consultant's Role Must Be Clearly Defined," *The American Nurse*, April 1975. Reprinted with permission of the American Nurses' Association.

sions which have been made by the incumbent without affecting the institution's support of that individual.

A consultant's purpose should be determined by the needs of the organization and the expressed willingness to undertake change by those in key management roles.

Areas of Administrative Inquiry

There are five areas of inquiry important for a nursing service administration consultant to understand: a sense of mission, a sense of climate, a sense of structure, a sense of program, and a sense of outcomes.

Sense of Mission. It is important to determine what each institution's decision makers see as the institution's mission and the contribution they expect of nursing service in accomplishing that mission. In attempting to compare and contrast these perceptions, an opportunity may come to identify implicit congruence or contradictions. There may also be deviations from the statement of purpose for the institution or nursing service. When key people view the mission differently, the consultant must be sensitive to all of the implications.

Sense of Climate. It is important to understand and appreciate the social community of the hospital and be able to characterize the interprofessional and interdepartmental relationships. Who speaks to whom? How? About what? Why? What is the feeling that prevails? Is it any different in the nursing service than in the hospital as a whole?

What is the climate? Is it authoritarian or collegial? Friendly or antagonistic? Professional or labor oriented? Depending on the assumptions made about the working climate, readiness for changes within the nursing service can be projected and the timing for change can be planned.

Sense of Structure. While organizational charts have their own message to convey, seldom do they depict power structure, communications systems, or management style. A consultant needs information about the mechanisms which exist for policy formulation, program development, and problem solving. Is the

director of nursing privy to the councils which serve these purposes?

What is the nursing service director's position in the bureaucratic structure? How does the director perceive that role in the hierarchy? Are title and status consonant? Is the institution administration-oriented, physician-dominated, or patient-centered? In making recommendations, it is important to consider the center of power and ways of achieving support for necessary change.

It is also important to develop a sense of structure as it exists within the nursing service. What is the authority pattern, the communication system, the staffing plan within nursing? What has been the value system at work in developing these structures? Is nursing viewed as a hospital department or a clinical service? What is the basis for such a classification? Where does the clinical leadership reside?

Sense of Program. What is the program of care provided for patients? Is it illness-oriented and confined to the four walls of the hospital? Does it extend to the community, and, if so, how are prevention and rehabilitation included? Where do the responsibility and the accountability for patient care decisions lie? How is care monitored? What mechanisms exist to help the practicing nurse achieve clinical excellence in practice? What is the reward system?

The nursing program must be reviewed in terms of the mission of the institution, the medical care provided, and the population served.

Sense of Outcomes. The objectives of the nursing service should be reflected in program activities. It is imperative for a consultant to understand the means used to measure achievement of outcomes sought.

The sophistication of the quality assurance program in nursing provides a very important signal, essential to any program focused on the nursing service.

Just as in physical diagnosis, when the physician or nurse seeks signs and symptoms which evidence disease processes, the consultant has the chance to "treat" an organization and perhaps "revive" it, based on careful diagnosis and appropriate prescription.

Guidelines*

Paid Consultants

- Define your problem clearly.
- Consider cost.
- Interview prospects; look for skill, objectivity, responsibility.
- Get references from persons whose judgment you trust.
- Do not be unnecessarily impressed by credentials.
- Review any published work.
- Spell out responsibilities of both the agency and the consultant.
- Inform staff and Board.
- Retain your authority in working with consultants.
- Listen to, monitor, and analyze consultant findings.
- Be prepared to make decisions throughout process.
- Terminate if work is unsatisfactory.

Volunteer Consultants

- Recruit experts with talents appropriate to need; managers in private industry, university faculty, health professionals.
- Be aware of political climate in your choice of expert.
- Call upon those that you know have done a good job.

*Source: Health Manpower Planning Process, DHHS, Pub. No. (HRA) 76-14013, 1976.

- Approach formally through organization channels to allow the expert more ease in making commitment.
- Allow the expert sufficient time within own busy schedule.
- Offer some form of recognition for help received.
- Keep in mind that your responsibility and judgment must prevail.

Finding a Consultant*

Some consultants are employed by firms specializing in consultation to nursing or offering a broader range of services. Some are self-employed, either full or part-time, and may hold other jobs as well. There are few practical opportunities for these consultants and firms to publicize their services widely to the specific persons who might use them. Thus, when a nursing administrator needs advice from outside his or her agency to assist with a problem or project, it is often difficult to find the consultant best suited for the job.

The *Journal of Nursing Administration* publishes each year in the August issue a directory of consultants to nursing administration. Information regarding size of the organization, time in operation, areas of expertise, and fee structure is provided. The directory includes the names of over 350 independent consultants and consulting firms. The listing is grouped according to 37 areas of expertise.

*Source: "JONA's Semiannual Directory of Consultants to Nursing Administration," *Journal of Nursing Administration*, February 1984. Reprinted with permission.

Chapter 4

Problem Solving and Decision Making

PROBLEM SOLVING*

Following is a list of conditions that may indicate a problem that needs further study.

Problem Indicators

Backlog of unfinished work in any operation.

Delays and interruptions in the performance of a function or service.

Overtime which is needed repeatedly in the carrying out of an activity.

Waste of effort, equipment, material, personnel, time, or space.

Complaints from patients, personnel, or visitors.

Costs of the function appear to be unduly high.

Absenteeism or *turnover* occurring continually in any hospital area.

Loss or *damage* of hospital supplies or equipment; also injury to employees and others.

Congestion or *disorderliness* of a work area involving one or more individuals.

Excessive time being devoted to an activity in proportion to the actual end result.

Location of an object in an out-of-the-way place.

Fatigue due to walking, bending, reaching, or other nonproductive or tiresome work motions.

Selecting a Problem for Study

As a first step in the process of selecting a problem for study, attempt to develop a complete listing of all work situations which may offer improvement possibilities. This listing should be kept current by adding to it any newly identified problem situations as they come to mind.

Then establish an order of study priority with respect to the various work problems which have been identified. In ranking the relative importance of each of the listed problems, certain factors should be considered in making a decision. Some of these relevant factors are listed below in the form of questions which should, of course, be adapted to the needs of the specific problem situation involved.

1. Which problem situation is causing the most difficulty?
2. How soon must a solution be found to the problem situation?

---

*Source: Except where noted, Addison C. Bennett, *Methods Improvement in Hospitals*, J.B. Lippincott, © 1964. Reprinted with permission.

3. Is the problem situation in question really the one to be solved, or is it simply a part of a still larger problem which requires study?

4. What is the status of the job in question? Is it temporary in nature? If not, what will be the future demands?

5. Is the timing for study appropriate from the standpoint of employee turnover, absenteeism, work demands, and personalities presently involved in the job situation?

6. Is there a good chance of achieving success in the way of improvement?

7. How soon can discernible results be attained? What may be the extent and the nature of the benefits to be achieved?

8. How long has it been since any changes were introduced on the job in question? What were the experiences with these changes?

9. What are the attitudes of personnel toward the existing process or procedure? How much employee resistance or resentment may be anticipated?

10. Are there any management policies or professional requirements that might limit changes in the existing situation?

11. Are there any management plans presently underway that might either eliminate the problem situation or have some effect on the nature of the problem?

Analyzing and Solving Problems

Following is a questionnaire that provides a procedure for analyzing and solving problems.

*Problem Analysis and Strategy Planning Questionnaire**

1. What is the difficulty, the concern, the problem?
   - Who sees it as a problem?
   - Who is affected by it?

---

*Source: Power: Use It or Lose It, National League for Nursing, Pub. No. 52-1675, 1977. Reprinted with permission.

Figure 4-1 Problem Analysis and Strategy Planning

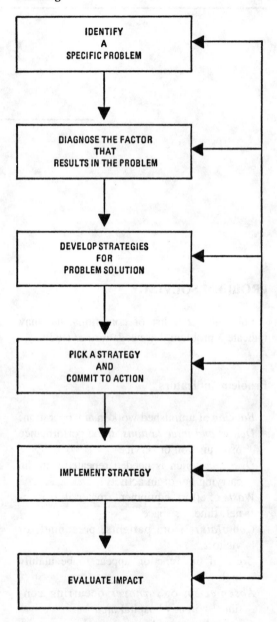

- How are they affected?
- What significant events or typical incidents illustrate the problem?
- To what extent are there differences in goals toward which individuals or groups are working in this situation?

2. Identify the various values (assumptions, beliefs, or feelings that serve as criteria by which goals are determined) of the total organization, any groups, and the individual persons involved.
3. Identify the various norms (i.e., behavior patterns highly valued or discouraged) of the total organization and any groups.
4. Identify the various individuals and groups which influence (i.e., have power and/or status) the decisions and behavior of the total organization, groups, and individuals.
5. Identify the various sanctions (i.e., punishments and rewards) by which norms are maintained in groups or the total organization.
6. Identify your roles (i.e., positions and functions) in the situation. What other roles seem important in the situation? As you refer to other people, explain the relationships between you and them.
7. Identify the various patterns of communication (i.e., who talks to whom, formally and informally). You may wish to diagram this.
8. Identify the various steps (i.e.,. defining, clarifying, developing alternatives, etc.) and categories by which the group makes decisions.
9. Identify the various actions that relevant groups take which help the organization maintain its identity and separateness.
10. Identify the means by which groups maintain linkage (communication) with other groups.
11. In reviewing your diagnosis, now what seem to be the underlying problems?
12. Which elements or processes seem to be most critical to the problem?
13. List what you have tried to do about the problem within the past six months. (Include as specifically as possible the goals and strategy which informed your actions, as well as the effects of the actions.)
14. What do you think you might try to do about the problem within the next six months? List as many specific actions as

you can, and your anticipation of their effect on relevant organization elements and processes. You may wish to review your next strategy and consider such questions as:
   a. What are the self-interest groups involved in your concern?
   b. Who sanctions efforts in the problem area?
   c. Whose ideas are normally accepted in this area?
   d. Who gets things done in this area?
   e. What tactics will spread your concern and mobilize support for it?
   f. On what goals and objectives are you operating?
   g. How will you identify and organize resources?
   h. What further strategies seem relevant?

PARTICIPATORY PROBLEM SOLVING: QUALITY CIRCLES*

A quality circle is generally defined as a group of people (usually between 4 and 15) who work in the same or similar area who voluntarily meet on a regular basis to identify, assess and solve problems in their area of work.

The three most often mentioned management objectives of quality circles are (1) to improve patient care quality in the hospital, (2) to improve productivity and (3) to improve employee motivation and morale. Other objectives may include the following: to instill cost containment awareness in employees, to encourage and utilize employee creativity, to help employees develop into managers, and to help employees grow professionally and personally.

The objectives that top management will have for quality circles will differ from the objectives of the employees who choose to participate in the circles. Management and employee objectives should be complementary but not necessarily identical for a quality circle program to succeed.

Source: James E. Orlikoff, "Quality Circles in the Hospital Setting," *Topics in Health Record Management*, vol. 3, no. 4, © 1983 Aspen Publishers, Inc.

Characteristics

For a quality circle program to succeed, the following characteristics must be present:

- Participation in the circles must be voluntary.
- Management must be supportive of the program (by allowing circles to meet on company time, by officially recognizing the activities and results of circles, and by allocating resources to support the program). Training in problem-solving methods, group process techniques, data gathering and data analysis must be a fundamental component of the program.
- Quality circle members must work together as a team.
- The program must have a people-building, not a people-exploiting, orientation.
- Circle members must work to *solve* problems, not just to identify them.
- Each circle must have the right to select its own problem for study and resolution.

Quality Circle Program Organization

A quality circle program should not be imposed on employees by being presented as a new organizational structure. Rather, such a program should be integrated into the existing organizational structure of the organization. The quality circle program will, however, have an independent organizational infrastructure consisting of a steering committee, a facilitator, a leader, circle members, a problem-solving process and management presentation.

The Quality Circle Steering Committee. The steering committee is the body that directs the overall quality circle program. The members of the committee should include representatives of the medical staff and of the major departments of the organization. The committee

- develops the overall objectives of the quality circle program
- develops a plan to implement the program (beginning with a pilot program)

- develops an informational and promotional campaign for the program
- develops a description of the job and qualifications of the facilitator
- chooses a facilitator
- determines whom the facilitator reports to
- determines how quality circles will interface with other hospital systems (such as suggestion and reward programs, employee development programs and such hospital functions as quality assurance)
- determines the financial support for the program
- identifies areas where quality circles can be pilot tested
- establishes implementation dates for the pilot circles
- establishes some type of measures for the pilot and the entire program
- determines how often and for how long the circles will meet
- establishes a reward and recognition program for circles

The Facilitator. The facilitator will be the person directly responsible for guiding and coordinating the activities of the circles throughout the hospital. The facilitator will at a minimum perform two general functions: (1) train all circle leaders and (2) act as process observer and technical assistant to the circles. The facilitator acts as the bridge between all the circles and coordinates the circle activities with the rest of the hospital.

Specifically, the facilitator trains circle leaders and acts as a resource in the areas of group process techniques; group problem-solving techniques; data gathering, statistical analysis, and data display techniques; and management presentations.

The Leader. Generally, the leader for each quality circle is the supervisor of the employees who are the circle members. In this way, the circle fits into the existing organizational structure of the institution and will therefore be more likely to be accepted by all involved in the quality circle program.

The Members. The members of any given circle are employees in the same area or department who volunteer to participate in the circle. They may drop out of the circle if they desire, and other employees who did not choose to volunteer at first may do so later. Eight is the optimum number of members per circle. There should be no more than 14 members.

The Problem-solving Process. Each circle should follow these steps:

1. The members identify a list of problems in their area.
2. The members select one problem for study.
3. The circle analyzes the problem (the circle may call in internal experts to give them technical assistance in analyzing the problem).
4. The circle presents its findings and recommended solutions to management.
5. Management reviews the circle's presentation and decides whether or not to implement the circle's suggestion.
6. Based on management's decision, the circle implements the action designed to correct the problem.

Management Presentation. Using charts, graphs, and other visual aids, the circle members present their analysis to management. This procedure is viewed as being intrinsically rewarding to circle members and is an opportunity for management to communicate enthusiasm and support to the members for their activities and accomplishments.

DECISIONS

The Scope of Nurse Executive Decision Making*

The Joint Commission on Accreditation of Healthcare Organizations' (Joint Commission)

---

*Source: Carole H. Patterson, "New Joint Commission Standards for 1991 Require R.N. Decision Making," *Nursing Administration Quarterly*, vol. 15, no. 4, © 1991 Aspen Publishers, Inc.

nursing standards are designed to help health care organizations focus on improving the quality of care through key activities that directly affect care. A number of the standards address collaborative and decision-making functions required of registered nurses and the hospital's nurse executive. The specific standards are listed in Table 4-1.

On a hospitalwide basis, the nurse executive is expected to participate along with leaders from the governing body, management, medical staff, and clinical areas in the *hospital's decision-making structure and processes* (NC 5). That collaboration is focused on the leadership group's ability to work together in order to foster continuous improvement in the hospital's patient care structures and processes. When the nurse executive does not participate "at the table" where decisions are made, the hospital loses the wealth of nursing knowledge and experience in patient care.

Specific requirements in the new standards relative to the nurse executive's responsibilities include the authority to establish nursing practice standards throughout the hospital (NC 3.1.1) and the monitoring, assessment, and improvement in the quality of patient care provided by nursing staff members (NC 5.3 and NC 6.1). In addition, the nurse executive is required to develop the nursing budget (NC 5.2.1) in collaboration with other nursing leaders. By functioning at the leadership levels of the hospital (NC 5 and NC 5.4), the nurse executive can appropriately plan for and support nursing practice through the hospital's budget planning, strategic planning, policy development, and quality monitoring and improvement activities.

Leadership theory is built on data gathering and decision making. Effective leaders know their people and the processes they have available to them and what they need to further the objectives of the group. These standards for nursing care foster both the decision making required to support the professional practice and decision making of registered nurses while also addressing the leadership responsibilities of the nurse executive who leads and works with the nursing staff of the hospital. The theory states that the communication and collaboration

Table 4-1 Joint Commission Requirements

The following standards outline the nurse executive's decision-making and participation responsibilities.

The nurse executive and other nursing leaders participate with leaders from the governing body, management, medical staff and clinical areas in the hospital's decision-making structures and processes. [NC 5]

If the hospital utilizes a decentralized organizational structure, there is an identified nurse leader at the executive level to provide authority and accountability for, and coordination of, the nurse executive functions. [NC 5.1.1]

The nurse executive has the authority and responsibility for establishing standards of nursing practice. [NC 3.1.1]

The nurse executive and other nursing leaders participate with leaders from the governing body, management, medical staff, and clinical areas in planning, promoting, and conducting hospital-wide quality monitoring and improvement activities. [NC 5.3]

The nurse executive is responsible for implementing the monitoring and evaluation process. [NC 6.1]

The nurse executive develops the nursing budget in collaboration with other nursing leaders and other hospital personnel. [NC 5.2.1]

The nurse executive and other nursing leaders are responsible for developing, implementing, and evaluating programs to promote the recruitment, retention, development, and continuing education of nursing staff members. [NC 5.4]

The nurse executive and other nursing leaders participate in developing and implementing mechanisms for collaboration between nursing staff members, physicians, and other clinical practitioners. [NC 5.3.2]

The nurse executive, or a designee(s), participates in evaluating, selecting and integrating health care technology and information management systems that support patient care needs and the efficient utilization of nursing resources. [NC 5.5]

---

between and among nurses and members of other clinical groups are the necessary first steps in achieving the positive work environments hospitals need to recruit and retain the best professionals (NC 5.4). When such an environment exists, improvement in both patient care outcomes and the morale and job satisfaction of the staff automatically occur.

Finally, the nurse executive or a designee is required to "sit at the table" when health care technology and management information systems that support patient care needs are evaluated, selected, and integrated into the hospital. Such technology and information-management decisions need to include the perspective of the nursing staff because of the potential impact on the efficient utilization of nursing resources in terms of both time and numbers. The nurse exec-

utive's decision making in these areas will help focus the discussions and resultant decisions on patient care issues in order to assist the hospital in maximizing its scarce monetary resources.

Decision Making*

Decision making is choosing options that are directed toward the resolution of organizational problems and the achievement of organizational goals.

The purpose of decision making within the health care organization is the coordination of

---

Source: Kathleen Kerrigan, "Decision Making in Today's Complex Environment," *Nursing Administration Quarterly*, vol. 15, no. 4, © 1991 Aspen Publishers, Inc.

goals and objectives of its members to deliver optimal patient care while controlling cost. The nurse manager, as a decision maker, has a vital role to play in bringing to fruition the achievement of these organizational goals and objectives.

Certain attributes are essential for the decision maker to make effective and efficient decisions. First, the nurse manager must have the freedom to make the decision in question. This requires the necessary power and knowledge to select the decision. Second, the manager must have the capacity and ability to make a wise decision. This requires sound judgment, deliberation, objectivity, and experience. Finally, the manager must have the will, motivation, and commitment to choose. This requires volition, a conscious activity of the will to make a decision. These qualifications are essential for the nurse manager, since decisions impact upon others and may encompass life-and-death situations.

Some subtle obstacles to rational and objective decision making include biases or prejudices, ignorance, time and financial constraints, resistance to change, unclear goals and objectives, and the fear of risk taking. The nurse manager must make a conscious effort to be constantly attuned to these influences in order to make intelligent and objective decisions. There are a series of steps to guide the decision-making process.*

Types of Decisions**

1. *Considered Decisions.* Considered decisions are usually those of great magnitude—that is, they tend to be complicated and call for considerable reflection. In addition to a lot of personal thought, they require interaction with others, because the perceptions and ideas of

other people often provide multiple alternatives that help in approaching the problem situation.

In seeking this kind of help, we ask associates for their opinions, we sound out their feelings, we identify what they know about the subject.

Obviously, a considered decision requires time—time to find alternatives, to seek other opinions, to get dissent, to determine implementation problems. Incorporating these elements in a decision-making situation leads to appropriate decisions that can be implemented with minimum trouble and maximum probability of success.

2. *Operational Decisions.* Operational decisions are those we make practically every day. Some of these decisions, in fact, may be made at approximately the same time each day, and they may prevent problems as well as solve them.

From a management development point of view, operational decisions give subordinates an excellent opportunity to practice decision making. A subordinate for instance, may draw up a needs plan. After the projections are verified and discussed between manager and subordinate, the decision is implemented.

Subordinates can eventually make decisions by themselves. Periodic reviews and later discussions reinforce good decisions and reveal areas in which other directions might have been appropriate.

3. *Swallow-hard Decisions.* Swallow-hard decisions are ones that are often personally uncomfortable to make because they may result in discomfort or uneasiness for subordinates or others. These can be generally classified as decisions impacting interpersonal relationship—that is, decisions affecting relationships among people in an organization. But although this kind of decision makes us feel uncomfortable, it is a kind of decision that is necessary—the kind that managers are paid to make.

Consider a decision on changing the way employees are scheduled. Say that a manager's boss looks at the schedule and decides that scheduling should be done in a different manner. Because of the subordinate manager's personal knowledge of the organization and its people, he may feel that this new approach would be disastrous to morale.

Source: Kathleen Kerrigan, "Decision Making in Today's Complex Environment," *Nursing Administration Quarterly*, vol. 15, no. 4, © 1991 Aspen Publishers, Inc.

**Source*: Reprinted, by permission of the publisher, from "How To Make Different Kinds of Decisions," Peter G. Kirby, *Supervisory Management*, February 1979, © by AMACOM, a division of American Management Association. All rights reserved.

A swallow-hard decision is called for. As subordinate in the boss-subordinate relationship, the manager has the obligation to tell his boss that the new plan is not a good one and to give specific reasons why. If his opinions and ideas are then rejected, the manager again has the obligation to swallow hard and carry out the decision as outlined by his boss.

4. *Ten-second Decisions*. Ten-second decisions are ones we make during daily operation. They are the decisions that bring our operation together, keep it ready, alive, and running well. The overriding factor in a ten-second decision is the pressure to make it quickly.

Before we make a ten-second decision, we must first determine whether the situation really requires one. Basically, we are asking, "I know this person wants the answer now—but is the answer potentially of such a consequence that I should delay answering the request?" Too many times the precedents we set—and the rules and guidelines we inherit—result from ten-second decisions that perhaps should have been considered or operational decisions.

Second, if we do decide to make a ten-second decision, then we should determine the major objective of that decision. Before we leap in and "solve the problem," we should first determine what we are trying to accomplish.

Third, once we have identified our objectives, we must determine what alternatives are available.

Fourth, once we have considered alternatives, the last question concerns implications. That is, what could go wrong in the future if we pursue a given course of action?

Consider these four areas when responding to problem situations that require quick decisions. If we do this automatically, we can shift from making snap decisions to making sound ten-second decisions.

Process*

The basic method for making a decision involves a sequence of six steps:

*Source: The Executive Deskbook, 2nd edition, by Auren Uris, © 1970, 1979, by Litton Educational Publishing Inc. Reprinted by permission of Van Nostrand Reinhold Company.

1. *Analyze and Identify the Situation*. You first clarify the situation you're trying to resolve. Sometimes this step is simple. For example, there may be a vacancy on your staff. You want to promote one of several possible subordinates into the spot. You have to make a decision; choose among them.

However, some situations may not be clear-cut: A department in your jurisdiction is doing poorly. Before you can make a remedial decision, you have to take into consideration the circumstances, find out *what's* wrong and *why* it's wrong, in order to proceed.

2. *Develop Alternatives*. In every decision-requiring circumstance, there are at least two possible actions, for example, taking action or not taking action. In most cases there are more. For instance: in filling a vacancy on a leadership level one might

- leave it unfilled
- hire from the outside
- promote the person who is most familiar with the duties of the open job
- set up some kind of test which will make it possible for you to grade the qualifications of applicants for the job
- ask for volunteers

3. *Compare Alternatives*. There are few cases where the nurse executive is lucky enough to have one alternative that represents the likelihood of 100% satisfaction. Usually each alternative has advantages and disadvantages. An alternative that you might prefer may be too costly, or you may lack the manpower to carry it out. Where the decision is crucial, take the time to actually write out the advantages and disadvantages of each alternative.

4. *Rate the Risk*. One of the differences between decision making and problem solving is that a proper solution to a problem is sure-fire, if it is indeed the right solution. You're practically sure of getting the results desired.

But in decision making, the usual situation is one in which every alternative you're considering includes an uncertainty factor. Since you seldom have total information about the situation you are dealing with, you can never be sure that the decision you make will be completely satisfactory.

Accordingly, in considering alternatives, it is important to rate the degree of risk each one involves. Obviously, this must be an estimate. Yet this approximation should be a part of the considerations that lead you to select the most desirable alternative.

In rating the risk, you may use percentages or any other rating system you prefer: grading from 1–10, using the academic A–F rating, and so on.

5. *Select the Best Alternative.* If the previous steps have been done carefully, it is possible that the most likely alternative becomes self-evident. But there are other possibilities.

- No alternative is desirable. The riskiness of all alternatives, for example, may properly persuade you not to take any action, because no move you can think of at the time promises to be successful.
- Merge two or more alternatives. In some cases you may find that while no single alternative provides the averages you want, combining elements of two or more provides you with the most likely plan.
- The "resources factor" may swing your decision. Alternative A may have more advantages than Alternative B. However, in carrying out Alternative B, you may have a piece of equipment that promises to save the day. Or, and this element is often crucial, you may have a subordinate of outstanding skill that will make Alternative B a much better bet because of his or her availability for this move.

While it's wise to gather information and check facts, get expert opinion and project the possibilities into the future. There will still remain some uncertainty in your attempt to pinpoint the best move. This uncertainty element can never be completely eliminated, and the usual practice is for the nurse executive to select between two otherwise "even" alternatives by hunch or intuition. Don't underestimate the importance of your feeling. Veteran nurse executives consider intuition a standard part of decision making and use it when facts, logic, or systematic considerations are unavailable.

6. *Get into Gear.* After a decision has been made, it must be made operative. You, or a subordinate, must take on the assignment of getting the people, resources, and so on, involved in putting the decision to work.

It may seem like an unnecessary emphasis to make this final point at all. But the fact is that many a decision, made even after days or weeks of effort, fails to produce results; or the decision is followed up in such a weak fashion that despite its many excellences only mediocre results are achieved.

In short, a decision implemented with energy and conviction can make a sizable difference in the outcome. For example, the manner in which a decision is communicated to the people who will be affected by it is, in itself, an important factor. And the manner in which the assignments represented by the decision are given to the people that are to carry out the plan is a major aspect of its effectiveness.

Quantitative Decision Tools*

There are several techniques or aids the nurse manager can utilize in making more competent and effective decisions. These are known as quantitative decision tools.

Two tools that the nurse manager can use are the Payoff Table and the Decision Tree. These tools assist the manager in overcoming personal preferences or biases in order to arrive at an impartial and objective decision.

The *Payoff Table* aims at a statistical decision by establishing a methodical approach for choosing an action. Probabilities are assigned to various possible outcomes. The payoff is the key component in selecting an option (see Figure 4-2).

The *Decision Tree* (see Table 4-2) represents a graphic visualization of goals, available alternatives, and outcome probabilities.

Source: Kathleen Kerrigan, "Decision Making in Today's Complex Environment," *Nursing Administration Quarterly*, vol. 15, no. 4, © 1991 Aspen Publishers, Inc.

Figure 4-2 The Payoff Table

Results

		180 (.6)	200 (.4)
Alternatives	180	1 $9	2 $24
	200	3 $10	4 $10

Expected costs if 180 are ordered:
$9 (.6) + $24 (.4) =
$5.40 + $9.60 = $15.00

Expected costs if 200 are ordered:
$10 (.6) + $10 (.4) =
$6.00 + $4.00 = $10.00

Explanation: The chart above depicts data from an outpatient department of a large hospital where paper gowns are used. It is determined that on a weekly basis, there is a 60 percent probability that 180 gowns will be used and a 40 percent probability that 200 gowns will be used. Costs are assigned to each of these alternatives. The cost of 180 gowns is $9.00. The cost of 200 gowns is $10.00. If there were a shortage of gowns, a special order would entail an extra cost of $15.00. Thus, if 180 gowns are available and the amount used during the week is 180 the cost is $9. If 180 gowns are available but 200 gowns are needed, the cost will be $24 ($9 for available gowns plus $15 for the special order). If 200 gowns are available and 180 are used the cost is $10. If 200 gowns are available and used the cost is $10.

Decision: Alternative 4 appears to be the least costly option while providing a sufficient number of gowns.

Source: Kathleen Kerrigan, "Decision Making in Today's Complex Environment," *Nursing Administration Quarterly*, vol. 15, no. 4, © 1991 Aspen Publishers, Inc.

Table 4-2 The Decision Tree

Objective of decision	Alternative/action	Probability	Expected outcome
Adequate staffing with wisest expenditure of money	1. Hire FT R.N. $16/hr	a. Increased patient load (.7) (will have to pay) $16 × .7 = $11.20	$16.00 adequate staffing
		b. same patient load (.3) $16 × .3 = $4.80	
	2. Pay OT $24/hr	a. Increased patient load (.7) (will have to pay) $24 × .7 = $16.80	$16.80 adequate staffing
		b. same patient load (.3) (will not have to pay)	
	3. Hire per diem R.N. $20/hr	a. Increased patient load (.7) (will have to pay) $20 × .7 = $14.00	$14.00 adequate staffing, least cost
		b. same patient load (.3) (will not have to pay)	

Explanation: This chart shows data from an intensive care nursery in which it is predicted that during the fiscal year 1991 patient census will increase. There is a 70 percent probability that the patient load will grow and a 30 percent probability that it will remain the same. The goal of the unit is to provide adequate staffing of nurses while controlling cost. Salary for a full-time (FT) registered nurse (R.N.) is $33,280 or $16 per hour. Overtime (OT) cost is $24 per hour, while per diem R.N. cost is $20 per hour.

Decision: Alternative 3 appears to be the least costly option while providing adequate staffing.

Source: Kathleen Kerrigan, "Decision Making in Today's Complex Environment," *Nursing Administration Quarterly*, vol. 15, no. 4, © 1991 Aspen Publishers, Inc.

AFTER THE DECISION*

Recognizing Uncertainty

The nurse executive has two recourses after she has made her decision.

Test Run

In some cases it's possible to try out the decision short of full implementation. For example, a nursing director has decided to adopt a new scheduling procedure throughout her department. She makes a trial run of the procedure and tests it out in a single unit. If she's satisfied with the results, she goes all out. If not, she can rethink her decision.

Flexibility

It is possible to develop a decision with "branching" steps. For example an executive says, "Let's use training method A with a group of 10 people, and training method B with another 10. Then we can compare results, and adopt the method that works best for all our new aides."

Implementation

"Not *what* you do, but the *way* you do it," holds the secret of a successful outcome in decision making. This is the opinion of a veteran executive decision maker who has seen both in her own experience and that of colleagues the crucial role played by implementation in determining the outcome of decisions.

There are several basic considerations to be made in implementing a decision.

Commitment. Once a course of action has been decided, others involved must be willing to put aside all hesitations, partial commitments to other courses of action, and so on. You have made a decision. You must move ahead on the decided course without further hesitations or doubts.

Announcement. In some cases this element is minor. But in others the way in which a decision is revealed to a staff can make a difference in its acceptance and its viability. When a decision is stated with resolution, confidence, and optimism, its chances of success are considerably increased, as compared to a reaction of doubt, hesitation, gloom, and pessimism.

Personnel. Who gets to do what in putting a decision to work is often a crucial factor. Some alternatives can simply not be adopted because the people to develop them are not available.

In considering the personnel aspect of implementing a decision, think of it not only in terms of quantity, but in terms of quality. You may have enough people to do a job but ascertain that they have the skills, experience, initiative, and so on, to achieve assigned objectives.

And more and more, nurse executives are learning to use small groups rather than individuals in personnel assignment in some situations. Ask yourself "Would a team of two or three be better for a given assignment than a single individual?"

Time. Exactly when to start a plan, what deadlines to set, what pace to adopt, must be clearly spelled out. An undertaking started prematurely may suffer just as much as one started too late. On the question of pace, you must consider whether a particular project should get "crash" treatment or may be spaced over time. Considerations may involve the state of mind of a work group. For example: you may want to announce an exciting new program in the fall, when people are psychologically "ready to buckle down," rather than during the summer doldrums.

Responsibility. You may want to stand at the helm to make sure that the implementation of the decision remains on course. Or you may want to delegate this responsibility. If you make the latter move, the individual you select and the manner in which you hand out the assignment may be crucial.

There's a big difference in the motivating effect of "Jan, there's a little project I'd like you to take over for a few weeks," and "Jan, there's an important responsibility I've decided to turn

---

Source: The Executive Deskbook, 2nd edition, by Auren Uris, © 1970, 1979, by Litton Educational Publishing Inc. Reprinted by permission of Van Nostrand Reinhold Company.

over to you, and the outcome of it so important that it can make a considerable difference in the futures of both of us.''

When Decisions Go Sour

Nurse executives—using one method or another—somehow manage to make decisions. But only a small percentage of decision makers know how to proceed when a decision goes wrong. And remember, even the most carefully considered, well-planned decision can turn sour. Five positive moves may save the day.

Recognizing. This move is a "must" prelude to all the others. Clear-headed, honest recognition of the fact that, on this particular decision, you have come up with a clinker. It may not be your fault at all. Other people, other forces, other events may be wholly or partially responsible. But whatever the cause, there is nothing to be gained by clinging to a losing situation. Executives who don't—or won't—recognize the inevitable, who are determined to make a decision work, to stick it out come what may, are only compounding wrong. *Your* lead: to accept the losses, analyze the causes, try to recoup what you can.

Reversing. Many a decision is the result of a multi-step process. From Step A to Step B to Step C . . . and on and on till the final stage is reached. Somewhere along the line you may have tripped. Can you, after thinking things out, retrace your steps to the point where the misstep occurred? Backtrack from E to B, for instance? Then revising B, begin a subsequent series of

steps, this time in the right direction? If so, you're halfway home.

Replacing. There will be times when you have a decision that looks great—on paper. You've followed all the proper procedures, made all the right moves, said all the right things. Then, in execution, up pops a weak link. And trouble. Does this mean that your idea is not workable? Not at all.

The weak link should be replaced, the decision can look good again—on paper and in execution.

Revising. In some instances, of course, a decision-turned-bad can't be remedied by simply replacing or retracing. Accordingly, major surgery is called for, a complete revision of the original plan. Now's the time to ask yourself, "Do I have an alternative? Is there a workable Plan B that I can substitute for unworkable Plan A?" Undoubtedly, in arriving at Plan A you had considered other ways, other means of achieving your objective. Can one, or a combination of these, with additions, subtractions, amendments, successfully serve your purpose? Possibly it can.

This stage, incidentally, may call for consultations up, down, and along the line.

Reviewing. Results are the proof of the decision-making pudding. When they go wrong, analyzing when, why, how can teach you a great deal. About your own decision-making ability. About techniques that need sharpening. About pitfalls to be avoided. About planning, performance, people. Failure often triggers more knowledge than success.

Chapter 5

Delegation, Time Management, and Stress

USING SUBORDINATE LEADERS*

Providing Assistance

How your subordinate leaders perform is a reflection of your own leadership.

You may find it relatively easier to modify your subordinates' leadership situations than your own, once you determine the types of situations in which they perform best. You are in an excellent position to counsel them on the types of leadership situations in which they appear to perform well. You are able to give them not only guidance, but also tangible assistance by modifying their leadership situation. If you desire, you can work with them to analyze their situation and determine what is best for them.

There are many different ways in which you can help match your subordinate leaders' job situation with their abilities. You can assign the leader to harmonious or to more conflicting groups, and gradually change the composition of the group to make it more harmonious or more challenging as a problem in personnel administration. You can assign to one leader highly structured tasks, or give highly detailed and specific instructions on how the task is accomplished. You can assign to another leader the

problems and tasks which are naturally more vague and nebulous, or you can give your instructions in a less specific manner and imply that the leader and his or her group are to develop their own procedures in dealing with the problem.

You can shore up the leader's authority by providing a great deal of support and backing, by ensuring that all the organizational information is channeled through the leader, and by extending greater authority to reward and punish or by letting everyone know that you will almost certainly accept the leader's recommendations.

You can give leaders close emotional support by making yourself available to them for guidance and advice, by being as nonthreatening as possible, and by giving them assurance that you stand behind them. Alternatively, you can take a more aloof evaluative stance, implying that subordinate leaders are on their own and that it is up to them to find the right methods and to develop the appropriate policies to deal with their problems. While this latter way of dealing with your subordinate leaders might appear cold, certain types of leaders are better able to perform in this type of climate than in a warmer, more accepting atmosphere. There are also leaders who prefer this type of relationship with their boss. Different types of people perform better under different sorts of control, and we should not automatically assume that our preference is shared by all.

---

*Source: Fred Fiedler et al., *Improving Leadership Effectiveness*, John Wiley & Sons, Inc., © 1976. Reprinted with permission.

Selection and Placement

You can also modify the leadership situation of your subordinate managers by selection and placement, that is, the proper assignment of your subordinates to a leadership situation in which they are most likely to perform well.

Knowing the personality of your subordinates and the nature of the task, you can select the leader who will excel at the beginning or the type of leader who will gradually mature into a great performer.

You may require that certain leaders obtain intensive training, knowing that others may perform just as well with little or no training (remembering that all leaders must have minimum qualifications in order to be considered for a leadership position).

You should ensure that leaders are either placed in a position in which they can perform well or that the situation is modified so that their leadership potential is used to the fullest.

Consider the options which are open to you in selecting subordinate leaders for maximum performance. If you opt for long-range performance, the recommendations which might guide your procedures are indicated in Table 5-1. The general rule is that you wish to keep task-motivated leaders in high-control and low-control situations or get them there as soon as possible, and relationship-motivated leaders in moderate-control situations or get them there as soon as possible.

DELEGATION

How to Delegate*

Generally, you should consider delegating as much of your technical task authority as possible. Even some of the routine portions of a few of your managerial tasks can be delegated. For example, you can delegate much of the numerical work involved in preparing a budget as long as you maintain final decision-making authority over the complete budget.

Determine the specific authority you will have to provide the person to whom you delegate an

activity. Plan also on defining the limits of that authority. In all cases the authority given should be consistent with the responsibility assigned.

Select and Organize the Task

The first thing to do is to take time to make a list of duties you perform that could reasonably be delegated. Some managerial activities lend themselves to partial delegation. For instance, you may obtain staff input and assistance in planning, scheduling, budgeting, purchasing, and other such activities, but the authority to approve, recommend, or implement still calls for the exercise of your supervisory authority.

However, if you consider each workday for a period of weeks, noting down each such task whenever one occurs, you may be surprised at the significant amount of work falling into the category of tasks that can be delegated. Preparing routine reports, answering routine correspondence, preparing service schedules, serving on certain committees, and many other activities may present themselves as candidates for delegation. List them all and rank them according to two criteria: the amount of your time they require and their importance to the institution. In short, establish a priority order of tasks for delegation.

Do not, however, attempt to delegate all these nonmanagerial duties at once.

Pick *one* task to begin with, preferably that which either is of most importance to the institution or takes the largest part of your time, or both. You should plan on delegating a single function, or as much of one as possible, to a single person and thus avoid the situation in which a function is so broken up that no one person is able to develop a sense of the whole job. Also, in considering activities to delegate, concentrate on ongoing functions, on jobs that regularly recur. There is little to be gained by delegating a one-shot activity if you can do it faster and better by yourself.

Select the Appropriate Person

Pick the employee you will delegate to by matching the qualifications of available employees with the requirements of the task to be delegated. Beware of either overdelegating or underdelegating. When you overdelegate, the employee to whom you give a task is clearly not ready to handle it. While a modest amount of

---

*Source: Charles R. McConnell, *The Effective Health Care Supervisor*, ed 2, Aspen Publishers, Inc., © 1988

Table 5-1 Guide for Assigning Subordinate Leaders

If the situation for the experienced leader is:	The situation for the inexperienced leader is:	If the leader is:	To obtain best long-range performance, proceed as follows:	To obtain best short-run performance, proceed as follows:
High control	Moderate control	Task-motivated	Train leader Structure task Increase position power Support leader	If possible, do not select If selected, train Structure task Provide position power
		Relationship-motivated	Do not increase leader control Rotate eventually	Select if possible Do not train Keep task structure low
Moderate control	Low control	Task-motivated	Do not increase leader control	Select if possible Do not train or structure task more than necessary
		Relationship-motivated	Train leader Structure task Support leader Increase position power to move situation to moderate as quickly as possible	If possible, do not select If selected, train intensively, support, structure task
Low control	Very low control	Task-motivated	Support leader Structure task	Select if possible
		Relationship-motivated	Increase position power Train leader	Do not select

Explanation of Terms

Kinds of Leadership Styles

1. *Relationship-motivated*: concerned with maintaining good interpersonal relations, sometimes even to the point of letting the task suffer.

2. *Task-motivated*: emphasis on task performance. These leaders are the no-nonsense people who tend to work best from guidelines and specific directions.

Kinds of Leadership Situations

1. *High-control* situations allow the leader a great deal of control and influence and a predictable environment in which to direct the work of others.

2. *Moderate-control* situations present mixed problems—either good relations with subordinates but an unstructured task and low position power, or the reverse.

3. *Low-control* situations offer the leader relatively low control and influence, where the group does not support the leader and neither the task nor his position power gives him or her much influence.

challenge is certainly desirable, too much challenge can be overwhelming to the employee. Overdelegation frequently leads to an employee's failure in a first attempt at handling increased responsibility, a harsh beginning that is not easily overcome. On the other hand, underdelegation—assigning a task to an employee who is overqualified and can obviously handle it with the greatest of ease—can be fully as damaging. Underdelegation is a waste of an employee's capabilities and often results in that employee's boredom and stagnation. Ideally, delegation should provide a modest amount of challenge, a modest but recognizable opportunity for growth, and the opportunity for diversification and expanded usefulness. Also, the employee must be able to see the importance of the delegated task.

You must also be reasonably convinced that the employee you have in mind has the time available to handle the delegated task. Even if person and task are properly matched, you can create a hardship by assigning more work to someone who is already fully occupied.

Instruct and Motivate the Person

One of the most common errors in delegation is turning an employee loose on a task with inadequate preparation. It is at this point that the pressure of time can set the stage for delegation failure. If the task you are delegating is one you have previously done yourself, and very often this is the case, there may be few instructions, procedures, or guidelines existing in writing. It may be that the only available instructions are those in your mind. In gathering the information you need to turn over a job, it may be necessary for you to put those instructions in writing as well as prepare to personally teach the employee how to do the job.

When you are completely ready to turn a task over to an employee, you should be able to provide satisfactory answers to the following questions:

- Am I prepared to give the reasons for the task, fully explaining why it is important and why it must be done?
- Am I giving the employee sufficient authority to accomplish the results I require?
- Are all the details of the assignment completely clear in my mind?
- If necessary, can I adapt all the instructions and procedural details to the level of the employee's knowledge and understanding?
- Does the assignment include sufficient growth opportunity to appropriately motivate the employee?
- Does the employee have the training, experience, and skills necessary to accomplish the task?

- Are the instructions or procedures sufficiently involved that they should be put in writing?

Assuming you can answer the foregoing questions satisfactorily, turning a task over to an employee then becomes a critical exercise in two-way communication. When meeting to make the actual assignment, encourage the employee to ask questions. If questions are not readily forthcoming, ask the employee to restate your instructions. Whenever possible, demonstrate those parts of the activity that lend themselves to demonstration and have the employee perform those operations to your satisfaction.

Last in the process of turning over a task, but extremely important, is the necessity for you and the employee to achieve agreement on the results you expect.

Maintain Reasonable Control

Control of delegation is largely a matter of communication between supervisor and employee. The frequency and intensity of this communication will depend significantly on your assessment of the individual. You should know your employees well enough to be able to judge who needs what degree of control and assistance. Overcontrol can destroy the effects of delegation. The employee will not develop a sense of responsibility, and you may remain as actively concerned with the task as though you had never delegated it at all. Undercontrol is also hazardous in that the employee may drift significantly in unproductive directions or perhaps make costly or time-consuming errors that you could have helped to avoid.

Set reasonable deadlines for task completion, or for the completion of portions of the task, and prepare to follow up as those deadlines arrive. Give the employee plenty of time to do the job, including, if possible, extra time for contingencies. However, when a deadline arrives and you have not been presented with results, take the initiative and go to the employee. If you let only a few deadlines slide by unmentioned, some employees will automatically adapt to this pattern of behavior and assume that the deadlines you impose are unimportant. On the other hand, if you make it a habit to always follow up on deadlines, your employees will pick up on this pattern and expect you to look for timely results.

Throughout the entire delegation process, try to avoid being a crutch for the employee. Regardless of how much guidance and assistance you are called on to provide, try to avoid solving problems for your employees. Rather, focus on showing your employees *how to solve* their own problems.

In most instances of delegation failure, the responsibility rests with the supervisor, not with the employee.

Assess Your Performance

To keep failures to a minimum, you should regularly assess your performance with the following questions:

- Did I assign a task only to take it away before the employee could truly demonstrate any competence at the task?
- Did I maintain too much or too little control?
- Did I split up an activity such that no single person with some authority could develop a sense for the whole?
- Was I overly severe with an employee who made a mistake?
- Am I giving proper credit to the employee for getting the job done?
- Am I keeping the more interesting tasks for myself, delegating only the mundane or unchallenging activities?
- Have I slacked off in my own work as I delegated certain activities away, or have I used the time saved to increase my emphasis on managerial activities?

Where and When To Delegate*

Here are five areas to consider for delegation:

1. *Routine Tasks*. Screening mail, preliminary interviewing of job applicants, handling minor scheduling problems—activities like these may be parceled out to subordinates when you're not inclined to do them yourself.

2. *Tasks for Which You Don't Have Time*. There's another group of activities, not necessarily routine, but of comparatively low priority. When you have time for these, you prefer to do them yourself. But when more urgent matters occupy your attention, these may be passed along to a capable subordinate.

3. *Problem-Solving*. Some executives properly turn over a problem situation to a subordinate. This is usually of a low or medium priority area; and actually there may be one (or more) of your subordinates with a particular knowledge or skill in the area that qualifies him or her to take on the task. In addition, he or she will be motivated to give it special attention, since it will represent a challenge.

4. *Change in Your Own Job Emphasis*. For the average executive, job content changes over the years, slowly in some cases, rapidly in others. As executives become aware of these changes in emphasis, they understand that new elements in their activity require more of their time. To "make" the time, the executive must, as a practical matter, delegate "old" aspects of his or her responsibility to subordinates.

5. *Capability Building*. Last but not least, delegation may be used to increase the capability of individual subordinates and your staff as a group. Properly managed, delegation becomes the means by which you train and develop the skills of subordinates.

When Not To Delegate

Just as there are situations for which delegation is a solution, there are circumstances which make it inadvisable.

Delegation can cause trouble if the wrong duties are handed over. Some of your responsibilities are yours for keeps:

- *The power to discipline*. This is the backbone of executive authority.
- *Responsibility for maintaining morale*. You may call upon others to help carry out

---

*Source: From *The Executive Deskbook*, 2nd edition, by Auren Uris, © 1970, 1979, by Litton Educational Publishing, Inc. Reprinted by permission of Van Nostrand Reinhold Company.

assignments that will improve morale. You cannot ask anybody else to maintain it.

- *Overall control.* No matter how extensive are the delegations, ultimate responsibility for final performance rests on your shoulders.
- *The hot potato.* Don't ever make the mistake of passing one along, just to take yourself off the spot.

Some jobs must be retained. It's best to hang on to them if:

- *The jobs that are too technical.* Staff scheduling or annual budgeting may be routine to you—but completely beyond a subordinate's skill.
- *The duty involves a trust or confidence.* For instance, handling confidential department information or dealing with the personal affairs of one of your staff.

Staff Building*

Greater efficiency isn't the only motive for delegating a part of your job. Enlargement of a subordinate's job can give three other important results:

1. *It develops a sense of responsibility.* You may wish to make an assignment purely in the interest of increasing the subordinates ability and value to your activity as a whole.
2. *It increases general understanding.* For instance, the best way to stress the importance of patient relations for one of your assignments might be to ask the subordinate to take over answering patient complaints.
3. *It increases job satisfaction.* Some subordinates thrive on varied assignments; their interest in the job increases along with its responsibility. Delegation of challenging projects helps maintain a subordinate's effectiveness as a team member.

Used in these ways, delegation is another means of getting cooperation, of increasing ability and motivation.

Barriers to Delegation*

Barriers in the Delegator

1. Preference for operating oneself
2. Demand that everyone "know all the details"
3. "I can do it better myself" fallacy
4. Lack of experience in the job or in delegating
5. Insecurity
6. Fear of being disliked
7. Refusal to allow mistakes
8. Lack of confidence in subordinates
9. Perfectionism, leading to overcontrol
10. Lack of organizational skill in balancing workloads
11. Failure to delegate authority commensurate with responsibility
12. Uncertainty over tasks and inability to explain
13. Disinclination to develop subordinates
14. Failure to establish effective controls and to follow up

Barriers in the Delegatee

1. Lack of experience
2. Lack of competence
3. Avoidance of responsibility
4. Overdependence on the boss
5. Disorganization
6. Overload of work
7. Immersion in trivia

Barriers in the Situation

1. One-man-show policy
2. No toleration of mistakes
3. Criticality of decisions

Source: Ibid.

Source: Reprinted by permission of the publisher, from *The Time Trap*, by R. Alec Mackenzie, pp. 133–134, © 1972 by AMACOM, a division of American Management Associations, New York. All rights reserved.

4. Urgency, leaving no time to explain (crisis management)
5. Confusion in responsibilities and authority
6. Understaffing

One theorist says the most difficult part of learning to delegate is learning to accommodate differences. It is easy to accept the idea that people are not the same; it is much harder to accept its application. There can be immense variations not only in the quality and quantity of work performed but also in the ways it is done. The manager must be prepared to accept and live with the subordinates' methods and decisions. It may be a very big order, but the manager cannot reap the benefits of delegation unless he or she is willing to accept the risks. Delegation is a calculated risk and we must expect that over time the gains will offset the losses.

TIME MANAGEMENT*

Most people think their time problems are external, that they are caused by the telephone, meetings, visitors, and delayed information or decisions.

In almost all cases, it is possible to influence, if not control, externally generated time problems. More difficult to identify, as well as to manage, are the internally generated time wasters: procrastination and indecision, lack of self-discipline, the inability to say no, the inability to delegate, or the tendency to fight fires, to act without thinking, and to jump from task to task without finishing any of them.

Time is a constant that cannot be altered. The clock cannot be slowed down or speeded up. Thus we cannot manage time itself. We can only manage our activities with respect to time.

The same skills are needed as those used in managing others—the abilities to plan, organize, delegate, direct, and control. Time management is simply self-management. It is

Source: E.B. Schwartz and R.A. Mackenzie, "Time Management Strategy for Women," *Management Review*, September 1977. Reprinted with permission of the author.

impossible to be effective in any position without controlling one's time effectively.

Paradoxes in Time Management

Open-door Paradox. By leaving a door open in hope of improving communication, managers tend to increase the wrong kind of communication, that of a trivial or socializing nature. This multiplies interruptions and distracts them from more important tasks. The "open door" was originally intended to mean "accessible," not physically open.

Planning Paradox. Managers often fail to plan because of the time required, thus failing to recognize that effective planning saves time in the end and achieves better results.

Tyranny-of-the-Urgent Paradox. Managers tend to respond to the urgent rather than the important matters. Thus long-range priorities are neglected, thereby ensuring future crises.

Crisis Paradox. Managers tend to over-respond to crises, thereby making them worse.

Meeting Paradox. By waiting for latecomers before starting a meeting, we penalize those who came on time and reward those who came late. So next time those who were on time will come late, and those who were late will come later.

Delegation Paradox. A manager tends not to delegate to inexperienced subordinates due to their lack of confidence. Yet subordinates can win the manager's confidence only by gaining the experience that only comes through delegated authority.

Cluttered-Desk Paradox. Managers leave things on their desks so they won't forget them. Then they either get lost or, as intended, attract attention every time they are seen, thus providing continual distractions from whatever the manager should be doing.

Long-Hours Paradox. The longer hours managers work, the more fatigued they become and the longer they assume they have to complete tasks. For both reasons they slow down, necessitating still longer hours.

Activity-vs.-Results Paradox. Managers tend to confuse activity with results, motion with accomplishment. Thus, as they gradually lose sight of their real objectives, they concentrate increasingly on staying busy. Finally, their objective becomes to stay busy, and they have become confirmed "workaholics."

Efficiency vs. Effectiveness. Managers tend to confuse efficiency with effectiveness. They will be more concerned about doing the job right than doing the right job. No matter how efficiently a job is done, if it is the wrong job, it will not be effective.

Paradox of Time. No one has enough, yet everyone has all there is.

Planning

As mentioned before, a paradox of time is that if we take time to plan, we will have more time. An hour of effective planning can save three to four hours in execution and produce better results. Managers who spend 10 to 15 minutes at the end of the day reviewing the things that did not get done, looking at new developments, and planning how best to achieve maximum results the next day will easily save an hour and get better results on that day.

Planning answers basic questions: Where am I now? Where do I want to be? How do I achieve this? The first question calls for an assessment of the present situation, the second involves setting goals, and the last requires an outline for action.

Audit: Where Am I Now? To plan more efficient use of time, you must first determine how you use it now, how it should be used, and how to schedule its proper use.

Most people are unaware of exactly how they spend their time. Practically every serious study of managers' use of time stresses the surprise of most managers when they discover where their time is really going. Yet, unless we know, we cannot choose among alternative ways to use it.

Time Log. Probably the simplest and most accurate way to find out where your time goes is to keep a time log. You must log daily activities against a time segment (say, each 15-minute interval) and account for the time used. The object is to locate a trend or pattern in daily activities.

A time log is a "self-help" tool, a way to look closely at the day, at how you really spend your time. It aids both in planning time and in delegating tasks to others.

Time Analysis. One week is usually long enough to log your time. Job priorities should then be compared with what you actually do. Can nonessential work be spotted? Unnecessary meetings? People who should not have been seen? Time spent on things that do not relate to goals? Problem areas?

Analysis of the data from the time log confirms some of our time wasters and makes us aware of others we did not suspect we had. It can also help us measure our progress in solving these time wasters by showing us how much time we saved each day and how results have improved. It can be used continuously to signal deviations from plans and therefore encourage immediate correction.

Goal: Where I Want To Be. How can good use of time be made without goals and priorities? Defining goals, an overall direction—professionally and personally—is crucial. Goals for your life, the year, and the day should be set. "What do I expect to accomplish today?" "What are the most important things to get done at home and at the office?" Put them in writing. A goal or plan that is not written down is a dream.

Plan: How To Achieve This. Once goals are established, a plan is needed to reach them. It commits us to "making it happen" rather than to letting things happen and then reacting to crises. At the end of each workday, prepare a list of what must be done at the office on the following day. Do the same thing in the evening for the home. A list not only ensures against forgetting but also leaves the mind free for important matters. The palest ink is better than the best memory.

Assign Priorities. Time management experts tell us again and again that most people waste 80 percent of their time on unimportant things. The 80/20 law says the 80 percent of value comes from 20 percent of the things we do. Of ten tasks, for example, two yield 80 percent of the valued results. For effective time management, the key is to find these two, label them top priority, and *do* them. On a busy day, the remaining eight can probably be postponed without real harm.

Doing the most important things first is valuable when emergencies interrupt our day. If the highest priorities have been accomplished, we are free to respond to the crises.

In assigning priorities, you must ask: How does that task relate to my goals and objectives? What is the immediacy of the task? Is it really that important? Why am I doing it? What am I doing that should not be done at all? Could others do it? What is the nature of the task (for example, can it be combined with anything else)?

In setting priorities for paperwork, group it into three categories: Priority One (most important, handle at once); Priority Two (less urgent, do when you get to it); and Priority Three (low priority, keep it just in case someone asks; throw away when the drawer is full). By setting priorities, you can distinguish "most important" tasks from the "most urgent," perhaps eliminating a tendency to operate by crisis.

Delegation

Delegation extends results from *what one can do* to *what one can control*. Moreover, it develops subordinates' initiative, skill, and confidence. A manager needs to devote more time to training and motivating people than to doing the technical work. To accomplish this, activities and tasks should be delegated to the lowest practicable level. (See the section on "Delegation" earlier in this chapter.)

Action

The plan must be put into action. Many people know what they want and how to accomplish it, but they procrastinate. Take your plan for the day and then start with the most important thing you need to do. The first hour sets the style for the rest of the day.

In fact, discretionary time—time you can really control—generally comes only in fragments later on. Most of us have only a half hour to two hours a day of discretionary time. This time should be invested on the most important things. At least what doesn't get done will be less significant and less important.

Give Total Attention to Each Task. If you do not have time to do it right, when will you have time to do it over? Highly successful people concentrate on whomever they are talking to or whatever they are doing. Sincere total attention, as well as being a timesaver, is also great human relations.

Complete Each Task the First Time. Get all needed data before you start writing a report or speech. Arrange to work without interruptions and finish the job in one session if at all possible. Make it a rule to try to handle each piece of paper only once.

Make it a practice, too, to be brief, to the point, and understood. Words saved are time saved. Learn to speak up and shut up. Also, learn to listen skillfully. Studies indicate people lose more than two-thirds of what they hear immediately after they hear it.

Be Considerate of Other People's Time. Organize to cut down on frequency of visits. When you must see someone, phone for an appointment. Efficient people rarely see you unless they have important things to discuss. Usually, several items are saved for a single conversation. This saves time for you and for them.

Minimize Meetings. Call a meeting only when it is more efficient than the telephone. Send an agenda before the meeting to each person who will attend and keep the discussion limited to the necessary points. Whenever those involved are not aware of the agenda prior to the meeting, time will be wasted in orientation.

Set a specific time limit for the meeting and keep it. An announced starting and ending time allows for those involved to plan the balance of their day. And do not attend meetings that are not absolutely necessary; instead, ask for a copy of the minutes.

Use Telephone Timesavers. Prior to important calls, outline the basic points that must be made during the conversation. Then, when you make the call, identify yourself and move immediately into the business of the call.

Eliminate Unproductive Reading. Read reports and other documents once and act or reply at once. Read less essential material when you need a break, have a break, or are traveling.

Close Your Door When You Have Jobs That Must Be Completed. Too many interruptions? Close the door. Don't take telephone calls. Get the work done.

The average manager is interrupted every eight minutes all day long. Successful control on interruptions is essential.

Follow up on the Day's Work. Control also means follow-up, adjusting the plan, time schedule, and performance in terms of objectives and conditions. At the end of the day analyze what tasks were not completed. Track and eliminate time-killers. Did you spend too much time on the phone? Were tasks left undone because you did not want to do them and therefore managed to postpone them? Give them top priority on the next day's list and do them.

Some people, believing they work better under pressure, procrastinate until forced into action. Do they really work better under pressure or just faster and less effectively?

Some Strategies*

There are numerous suggestions for saving time. The following are brief recommendations on using time to one's own advantage. Although it is not possible to put all of these into effect immediately, *now* is the time to start.

- *Eliminate paper.* Do not allow it to accumulate. The best advice regarding paper control is to pick it up once and dispatch it.

*Source: Victor J. Morano, "Time Management: From Victim to Victor," *The Health Care Supervisor*, vol. 3, no. 1, © 1984 Aspen Publishers, Inc.

Assign it to someone else, make a decision, give it to one's secretary, or use the "round file."

- *Conduct regular staff meetings.* Establish a set time, day, and place for regular meetings. Say it once to 20 people rather than say it 20 times to each individual.
- *Block your time.* Some projects demand uninterrupted time. Plan and prepare for these by setting aside a block of time to complete the task. In some institutions a quiet hour is observed. During this time telephone calls, visits, and interruptions of any kind are not permitted for those people involved. The results have proven to be most rewarding.
- *Take time to train.* The time spent in effectively training one's staff pays great dividends in both time saved and increased productivity. This ties in with proper delegation.
- *Relinquish ownership.* A common time trap indigenous to supervisors is accepting problems that are not theirs. Determine who owns the problem and graciously return it to its rightful owner. Also, involving employees in the art of problem solving will help them to grow.
- *Simply say no.* The victor of time management does not try to be all things to all people. Persons who attempt to do this end up being nothing to themselves. Learn the fine art of saying no. Refuse to accept those things that are not one's responsibility or that one cannot handle at that time.
- *Plan your emergencies.* Despite the apparent contradiction in terms, it is possible to carefully plan one's time so that marginal emergencies are controlled. For the supervisor who schedules and plans ahead, it is possible to expect the unexpected. Most health care supervisors are able to predict the time of day, week, month, or year when their workload increases. One can anticipate when budgets are due, when reports need to be submitted, and so on. Many emergencies are somewhat predictable and supervisors can plan the time to deal with them.

- *Be complete.* A real and insidious time robber occurs without one being aware of it. It is work that is left unfinished: the stopping and getting back into the project again, working at an uneven pace that shifts from slow to frantic, and the missing of deadlines. To combat this time robber, one must be complete and finish fully what is initiated. Work should be accomplished at a reasonable and controlled pace. Deadlines should be set and met.

- *Get away.* Minivacations are a strong deterrent to time anxiety. These are selected brief interludes during the course of the day to "get away from it all." Selected means that these minivacations should be scheduled at specific times. What one does during the five- or ten-minute respite is up to the individual. The only restrictions are that it not be work-related, and that it be something one enjoys. It may be a brisk walk around the block, listening to one's favorite music, reading poetry, or whatever. A minivacation is to be taken daily, perhaps once in the morning and again in the afternoon. It will help to reduce stress and revitalize a person so that he or she may continue to take charge of time.

COPING WITH STRESS*

Most nursing administrators and supervisors have long recognized the stress-laden nature of their jobs. In addition to having adverse effects on the person's biophysiological and psychological systems, stress decreases efficiency, morale, and work performance, ultimately affecting patient care and management.

There are two main types of human beings: *racehorses*, who thrive on stress and are happy only with a vigorous, fast-paced life style, and *turtles*, who in order to be content and happy require peace and quiet and a tranquil environment. A quiet and peaceful life would frustrate and bore most racehorses.

To summarize, in order for nurse-leaders to cope with the job-related stresses or, for that matter, any form of stress, they should do or acquire the following behaviors:

1. Determine whether they are racehorses or turtles, and live their lives accordingly.
2. Set realistic goals and aim to achieve them.
3. Practice altruistic egoism—looking out for oneself by being useful to others.
4. Adopt a set of attitudes that
   a. views change as a challenge rather than a threat;
   b. portrays commitment to whatever one is doing;
   c. makes one feel in control over the environment and the job.
5. Cultivate a social support system; have a rewarding life outside of work—with family members, spouses, other such social groups as club and church memberships, friends, and relatives.
6. Acquire knowledge about the stress-producing situation. One should not be afraid to investigate the problem. As one becomes more knowledgeable about the stress-producing situation, one will gain more power and control over it and over the environment.

*Source: Loucine M.D. Huckabay, "Stress and Leadership: A Coping Mechanism," *Nursing Administration Quarterly*, vol. 8, no. 3, © 1984 Aspen Publishers, Inc.

Resilience to stress is an acquired behavior, and all administrators should make an effort to learn it.

Part II

The Working Environment

Chapter 6

Improving Facilities

NEW FACILITY DESIGN*

When facilities are to be newly designed or redesigned, usually a health facilities planning committee is created.

Typical health facilities planning committees are composed of representatives from administration, medical staff, and nursing staff. Medical representatives are frequently influential senior members who have previously been involved in planning and operating particular medical services. When a representative from nursing is included, often he or she is an administrator. If possible both the administrative and the clinical points of view should be represented. Also nurses with previous experience and proven ability in organizing projects which involved collaboration with other health professionals and community persons would be appropriate choices.

Stages in Construction of New Patient Care Facilities**

There are several discrete stages in facilities building. The nurse executive will want to be involved at each phase.

Long-Range Planning: The goals and needs of the community and the organization itself are considered, and future needs are projected. This part of the planning involves both long-range goal setting and the gathering of much demographic and other data to support the legitimacy of those goals.

Marketing Plan: The institution that hopes to put up new buildings also must deal with the community. Does the community wish for the proposed facility? Are there groups that will contest the operation? Good relations with a community often make the difference between a building plan progressing smoothly or meeting unsurmountable obstacles. Once an institution has determined that it wants to build, a good marketing plan usually is the next step—selling the notion to all potential interest groups.

Design of Facilities: First block schematics are drawn, simply to show how major areas to be built will relate to each other, both horizontally and vertically. In an actual block drawing, the scale would be indicated. When dealing with block schematics, the nurse executive must be careful to note the common pathways by which patients flow from one department to another.

Single-Line Sketches: Single-line sketches are composed for all areas to be constructed. Actual space constraints such as internal columns, elevators, and corridors are drawn to

---

*Source: Department of Health and Human Services.

**Source: Barbara J. Stevens, *The Nurse as Executive*, ed 3, Aspen Publishers, Inc., © 1985.

scale, and rooms are designed with beds and room equipment also drawn to scale. Entrances and exits are indicated in the single-line drawings. The finished single-line drawings reveal the configuration of each unit, the size and shape of planned spaces, and the functional relationships (horizontal and vertical connections) between planned units.

Design Development Drawings: These drawings include such things as structural, mechanical, electrical systems, as well as any built-in equipment. By the time the architects reach this stage of development, they are very hesitant to make changes, and changes will cost significant amounts of money for the organization.

Development of Blueprints: Refinements of the design development drawings.

Building Phase: By then it usually is too late for any changes unless a catastrophic error is discovered. Indeed, if a major error is discovered at this late date, it means that the executive did not give enough attention to the project at an earlier stage.

Nursing Service Input

The planning process for designing and building new facilities can involve nursing service input in each of its six stages: need and feasibility studies, programming, architecture and engineering, equipping, construction, and the operations changeover.

Need and Feasibility Studies. The views of nursing administrators may be significant on questions dealing with such subjects as shared services, educational facilities, research, interdepartmental relationships, and suggested priorities as to short-range, intermediate, and long-range needs.

Programming. Emphasis is on specific departmental needs—each department head should develop a list of "needs" and some order of priority which can be integrated into the total plan.

Architecture and Engineering. Nursing administrators can play an important role in reviewing the rough architectural drawings before they go to blueprints. They can make suggestions about the location and type of items such as sterilizers, furnishings, desks and telephones, elevators, patient room lights, lavatories, doors, and medical gas outlets. They can also explain how new nursing procedures that they would like to introduce might influence design elements.

Equipment. A major contribution can be made in the selection of new equipment by the nursing administrator. He or she has the distinct advantage of direct experience with everything from scalpels and flow meters to typewriters and nurse call units. Long in advance the nursing administrator should make a list of recommended equipment and supplies and be prepared to defend his or her choices. Manufacturers must be given sufficient time to meet required delivery dates.

Construction. During construction the nurse administrator can begin personnel planning. It should take account of the many new procedures that will be introduced in the new facilities. The nursing administrator might ask that a mock-up of the new patient room be built—one that is fully operational. In this way, not only can placement of fixtures such as outlets and lights and performance of equipment be evaluated but the nursing staff can become familiar with the new facilities before the changeover. Later the room could be used permanently as an in-service teaching environment.

Opening and Changeover. A smooth changeover can take more than a year of planning. Some of the factors to be considered are: preparation of new nursing procedures, orienting personnel to the new equipment and facilities, planning for patient comfort during the changeover days, and anticipating malfunctions during the transitions.

Checklist. With these stages of the design or redesign of facilities in mind, here are some questions that the nursing administrator planning for new facilities might seek answers to:

• What, where, how, when, and why functions are to be performed?

- What functional spaces and dimensions are required?
- What fixed equipment is required?
- What environmental conditions are required?
- What workloads and workflows are entailed?
- What staffing complements and patterns are needed?
- What portable equipment will be needed for a properly functioning department?
- What communication and transport networks are involved?
- What intramural and extramural relationships are to be accommodated?
- What provisions should be made for possible future changes?

Nursing Services Facilities Design

Within the nursing services department, activities can be analyzed as to three functions:

Administration. This supports the activity of a department. It consists of offices, files, and reception areas.

Functioning Area. This is the prime reason for the department's existence. It occupies the greatest amount of space within a department.

Ancillary. The people who operate the department require convenience space, such as a rest area, personal hygiene facilities, and a place to eat. Lockers and showers may also be necessary.

Facilities specifically assigned for use by the nursing services department consist of office space for the director and assistant director of nursing services, nursing stations on each of the patient areas and units that enable the nursing personnel and the medical staff to conduct activities associated with patient care, utility rooms which are in most cases adjacent to the nursing stations and used for storage of needed supplies and portable equipment, linen closets for storage of laundry items, and on two floors small conference rooms seating four to six people and used for medical consultations. Equipment and furnishings are much the same in each of the nursing stations and consist basically of

charting desks, patient charts, medicine preparation tables and cabinets, and a minimum of paging and communication equipment. There is some portable equipment such as resuscitators, chest respirators, and irrigation apparatus charged to the department.

ARCHITECTURAL CONCERNS

Overview

During the planning phases for building or renovating a nursing unit, the nurse executive will need to consider the proposed architecture as it relates to (1) flow patterns for patients, staff, and visitors, (2) security needs, (3) the facilities' proximity needs, (4) movement of equipment and supplies, (5) placement of nursing offices and managerial space as they relate to the space of other key managers, and (6) patients' convenience in use of the facilities.

*Basic Plans for Patient Units**

A particular item of interest to a nurse executive in planning a new facility may be the design of patient care units. The oldest and least satisfactory design is the single corridor design, in which patient rooms as well as nurses' stations, treatment rooms, and other service areas all are rooms off the same long hall. Obviously, such a long-hall construction calls for many more manhours spent walking than needed with more compact designs. (See Figure 6-1 for illustration. Here and in subsequent design illustrations the dark areas indicate nurses' stations and other staff work areas.)

In the double corridor design (Figure 6-1), patient rooms branch off halls located on both sides of a central core containing the work areas of the unit. Advocates of this design claim walking time is cut nearly by half, compared to time required for a single corridor with the same number of patient rooms. Some nurses are uncomfortable with the fact that this design cuts down visibility of hall activities because only one-half of the floor can be seen at any one time.

Source: Barbara J. Stevens, *The Nurse as Executive*, ed 3, Aspen Publishers, Inc., © 1985.

Figure 6-1   Patient Unit Design

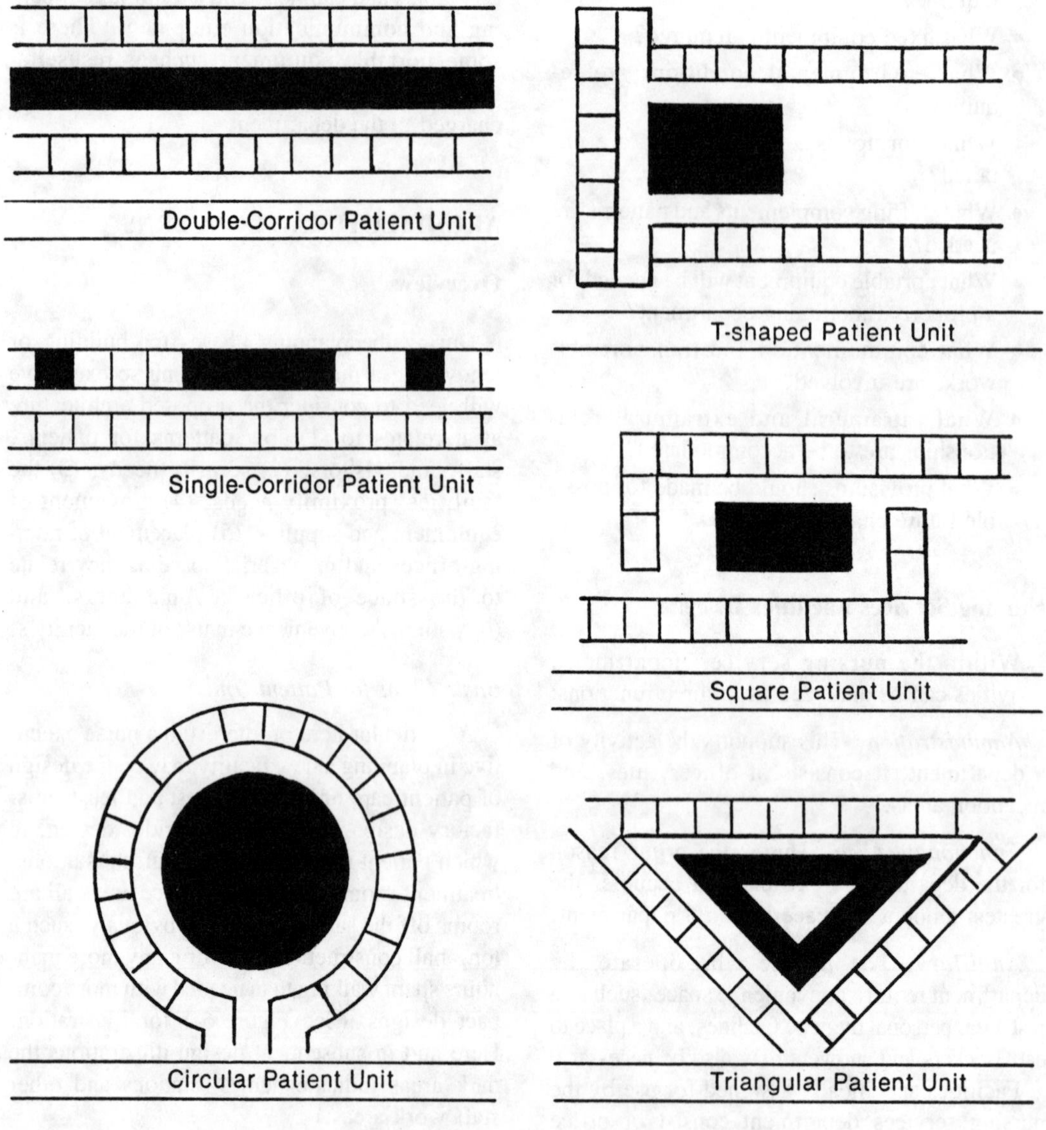

Double-Corridor Patient Unit

Single-Corridor Patient Unit

T-shaped Patient Unit

Square Patient Unit

Circular Patient Unit

Triangular Patient Unit

Dark areas indicate nurses' stations and other staff work areas.

Each variation in unit design has both advantages and limitations. The square, triangle, and circle designs usually simplify the nursing logistics but tend to waste space by having more central work area than really is necessary (see Figure 6-1). T-shaped units attempt to solve this problem while still shortening the length of any given corridor. Typically the nurse executive prefers smaller units than does the architect or perhaps his or her boss, who is looking more for

economy than for convenience and ease in the provision of nursing care.

*Patient Rooms**

Most rooms are semiprivate or multibed accommodations, with two, three, four, or even

Source: I. Donald Snook, Jr., *Hospitals: What They Are and How They Work,* ed 2, [pp. 78–9] Aspen Publishers, Inc., © 1992.

up to six beds in one room. More recently, there has been a trend toward the private or single-bed accommodation.

Whether the patient rooms are private or multi-accommodations, they will vary in size. It has been suggested that the minimum size for a private room should be not less than 125 square feet, with a minimum width of at least 12 feet, 6 inches. As to the two-bed accommodation, a minimum of 160 square feet is usually provided, with the beds separated by cubicle curtains. For a four-bed room, the minimum is generally considered to be 320 square feet. The hospital bed is generally 86 inches long, 36 inches wide, about 27 inches from the floor, and can be varied electrically or mechanically into different positions.

Guidelines for Nursing Services Administrative Office Space*

The nursing services administrative offices generate moderate to heavy traffic. A central location, convenient to the executive unit in the administrative block, is appropriate.

Reception Area

This area functions as a reception and waiting area for visitors to the unit and controls traffic to and from the secretarial and clerical work area and the offices of the various officials. This area is not routinely required in the nursing services administration unit of a 100-bed hospital. There it is usually satisfactory for visitors to enter the secretarial and clerical work area directly from the administrative corridor, with one of the secretaries functioning as a receptionist as an additional duty.

Office of Director of Nursing
(Director and up to Six Visitors)

Total area required:
  100 beds—169 square feet.
  300 beds—223 square feet.
  500 beds—223 square feet.

———
*Source: *Administrative Services and Facilities for Hospitals*, DHHS, 1972.

Assistant Directors of Nursing

  100 beds—Four assistant directors of nursing services (one for days, one for evenings, one for nights, and one for relief duty), and three visitors: 192 square feet.
  300 beds—Five assistant directors of nursing services (one for days, two for evenings, and two for nights), and four visitors: 192 square feet.
  500 beds—Six assistant directors of nursing services (two for days, two for evenings, and two for nights), and four visitors: 296 square feet.

Nursing Education Director

If there is a nursing education department, the nursing education director's office may be located either in this department or in the nursing services administration unit.

In general, offices for assistant nursing education directors and/or instructors, as well as classroom facilities, will be remotely located with respect to the administrative block.

Secretarial and Clerical Work Area

This area provides administrative secretarial and clerical support for the nursing services administration unit. For the 100-bed hospital, it also provides for initial reception and control of visitors.

This area also provides for visitor traffic to and from the adjacent offices and conference room.

Estimated Requirements

  100 beds—Secretary, reception secretary, and waiting area for three visitors: 287 square feet.
  300 beds—Three secretaries: 444 square feet.
  500 beds—Three secretaries and one clerk typist: 544 square feet.

Conference Room

This room provides a limited area for conducting meetings, group discussions, and conferences involving the administrative, educational, and supervisory personnel responsible for the hospital's nursing services program. These meetings are frequent and vital to an adequate program of nursing services and nursing education.

Toilet and Locker Room

This area provides toilet facilities for personnel of the nursing services administration unit and dressing space for administrative personnel of the unit to put on uniforms.

Total area required:
  100 beds—80 square feet.
  300 beds—108 square feet.
  500 beds—108 square feet.

Storage Room

This area provides storage space for inactive files, including secured files, and short-term inventory office supplies. Space allocated ranges from 40 to 88 square feet.

Chapter 7

Organization

A PRIMER ON ORGANIZATION*

Overview

Organizing is the process of grouping the necessary responsibilities and activities into workable units, determining the lines of authority and communication, and developing patterns of coordination. It is the conscious development of role structures of superior and subordinate, line and staff. The organizational process stems from the underlying premises associated with formal institutions: that there should be a common goal toward which work effort is directed, that the goal is spelled out in detailed plans, that there is need for clear authority-responsibility relationships, that power and authority factors need to be reconciled so individual interactions within the organization are productive and goal directed, that conflict is inevitable but may be reduced through clarity of organizational relationship, that individual needs must be reconciled with and subordinated to the organizational needs, that unity of command must prevail, and that authority must be delegated.

---

*Source: Except where noted, material in this section is from Joan Gratto Liebler, *Managing Health Records*, Aspen Publishers, Inc., © 1980

Hierarchical Organization

Hierarchy refers to the arrangement of individuals into a graded series of superiors and subordinates. A pyramidal shaped organization tends to result from the development of hierarchy (Figure 7-1).

Individual workers are placed in a specific authority relationship to a superior whose authority can be traced from the next level of authority on up to the top level of the hierarchy. This flow of authority and responsibility constitutes a distinct chain of command, also referred to as the scalar principle: the chain of direct authority from superior to subordinate. A companion expectation is that unity of command will prevail. Unity of command is the uninterrupted line of authority from superior to subordinate so that each individual reports to one, and only one, superior. A clear chain of command shows who reports to whom, who is responsible for the actions of an individual, who has authority over the worker.

The authority delegation given to any individual must be equal to the responsibility assigned. This principle of parity—that responsibility cannot be greater than the authority given—ensures that the individual given an assignment can carry it out without provoking conflict over the person's right and duty to do so.

Figure 7-1 Pyramid-shaped Organization

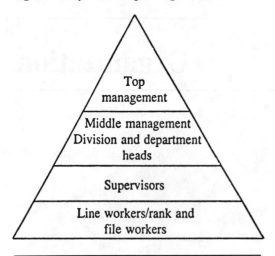

At the same time, no managers can so completely delegate authority that they themselves have no responsibility. This is stated in the principle of the absoluteness of responsibility: that authority may (and must) be delegated, but ultimate responsibility is retained. The superior who delegates authority ultimately remains responsible for the actions of the subordinate. It is from this same concept that the manager receives the right to exercise the necessary controls and retains the required accountability.

Participatory Management*

In contrast, there are writers and practitioners of management who believe that a less hierarchical, more flexible structure which promotes greater participation in decision making is a preferable way to run an organization. This group, representing the "behavioral" approach, are the proponents of the "participatory" management style.

The "bureaucratic" design of hierarchical organization, based on centralized authority and

*Source: S.J. Hurka, "A Mix of Organizational Models," Dimensions in Health Service, Journal of the Canadian Hospital Association, April 1978. Reprinted with permission of the author.

highly specified procedures and control, is the appropriate management style in departments performing routine activities. In contrast, where the tasks are complex and are performed by highly skilled professional employees, a "participatory" decision-making structure may be more appropriate. In such departments the work relationships among employees are based on knowledge rather than on administrative authority.

Hospitals have traditionally developed around the classical pyramidal form of organization. This design is appropriate if the organization is a part of a stable environment and performs relatively simple and predictable tasks. This may have been appropriate given the environment of the early hospitals.

Present-day health care agencies have to cope with a more dynamic and complex environment. The increasing demand for well-trained specialists, along with the advances in health care technology, to mention a few changes in the environment of the modern hospital, is similar to the experiences faced by other organizations in the public and private sectors. These organizations seem to be moving quickly toward other organizational models.

Dual Pyramid of Organization

Health care institutions are also characterized by a dual pyramid of organization because of the traditional relationship of the medical staff to the administrative component. The ultimate authority and responsibility is vested in the governing board. That board, in accordance with the stipulations of licensure and accrediting agencies, appoints a chief executive officer (administrator) and a chief of medical staff, resulting in two lines of authority. The chief executive officer is charged with the responsibility of effectively managing the administrative components of the institution. This administrative official in turn delegates authority to each department head in the administrative component. In this sense, there is a typical pyramidal organization, with a unified chain of command within the administrative units.

A second organizational pyramid results from this organization of the medical staff into clinical services, with each having a chief of service who reports to the chief of staff.

Although all authority flows from the governing board, there are two distinct chains of command, one in the administrative sector and one in the medical staff sector. In matters of direct patient care, the physician exercises professional authority; thus, a particular employee (such as a nurse) may be subject to more than one line of authority.

Line and Staff Relationships

The original usage of the term ''staff'' evolved in the military. The military developed the staff assistant pattern as a means of relieving commanders of details that could be handled by others. The concept of the ''assistant to'' is the sense in which the term was used, and this assistant was an extension of line authority. The staff assistant or specialist provides advice and counsel or technical support to the line manager, who has the right to command others to act.

The essence of line authority is this direct chain of command or line from the top level of authority through each successive level of the organization. A manager with line authority has direct authority and responsibility for the work of a unit, while a staff assistant provides advice, counsel, or technical support that may be accepted, altered, or rejected by the line officer.

Organizational Charts

An organizational chart is an attempt to depict through a schematic drawing the formal organizational relationships of people and departments. It identifies channels of communication, levels of accountability, and areas of responsibility.

It can be used for planning, policy making, instituting organizational change, evaluating strengths and weaknesses of present structures, showing relationships with other departments and agencies.

It can facilitate the identification of flaws in organization such as

- confused lines of authority
- overlap and duplication of functions
- dual reporting relationships
- overextended spans of management
- lack of intermediate supervisory levels
- excessive levels of supervision
- gaps in functions

It can be used as an instructional tool in orienting new employees or familiarizing interested parties with the department's structure and operation. Many have found the chart a more effective tool for representing the department's organizational structure than a written description. (See Figure 7-2.)

Limitations

However, there are certain limitations inherent in the rather static structure presented by the organizational chart, including the following:

- Only formal lines of authority and communication are shown.
- Important lines of informal communication and significant informal relationships cannot be shown.
- The chart may become obsolete easily if not updated—at least once a year, and more frequently if there is a major change in organizational pattern.
- There is a tendency to confuse authority relationships with status: Individuals higher up in the organization as depicted in the chart may be perceived as having authority over individuals lower on the chart.

Traditional Organization*

Figure 7-2 is an example of a traditional organizational chart. It shows which individuals report to whom and which individuals have

Source: Elizabeth N. Lewis and Patricia V. Carini, *Nurse Staffing and Patient Classification: Strategies for Success*, Aspen Publishers, Inc., © 1983.

Figure 7-2 Traditional Organizational Chart Showing Performance Accountability

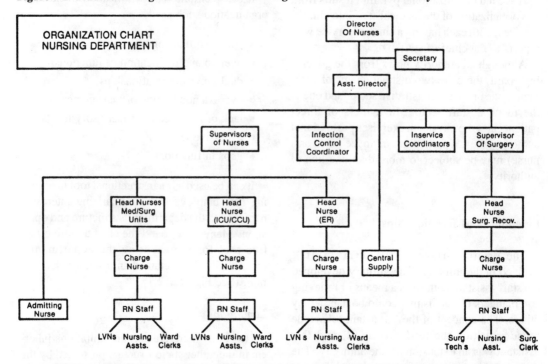

responsibility for other members of the department, such as LVNs, nurse's aides, and ward clerks. Although it is necessary to show performance accountability and it is a fact of nursing administration that people report to other people, the traditional model separates individuals of the group by the clearly spelled-out supervisor-subordinate relationship.

NURSING DEPARTMENT ORGANIZATION

Overview*

The nursing services department is organized in a pyramid fashion very much like the hospital as a whole. The primary responsibility rests with the director of the nursing services department, referred to as the director of nurses (DON) or vice-president of nursing.

Directors are usually selected because of their management abilities; they are often registered nurses with advanced degrees (sometimes in the specific discipline of nursing services administration). Often, the director has one or two assistant directors to aid in the management of the department. The title of supervisor is frequently given to the position held by a registered nurse who supervises or directs the activities of two or more nursing units. The supervisor may manage and direct the many nursing service activities during the evenings, nights, or weekends; thus, the titles of night supervisor, weekend supervisor, or day supervisor are often applied. If a hospital has a nursing school, the director of nursing is often responsible for both the nursing services and the nursing school. Or the nursing school may have its own director who reports to the director of nurses. If there is no school of nursing, the training function of the nursing department is usually assigned to an assistant director who is responsible for the education, orientation, and continuing in-service education of all employees in the department of nursing.

*Source: I. Donald Snook, *Hospitals: What They Are and How They Work*, ed 2, Aspen Publishers, Inc., © 1992.

The nursing services department is also organized along geographical lines. Each of the nursing service responsibilities for patient care is decentralized to a specific location in the hospital called a nursing unit or patient care unit. Certain responsibilities and functions to operate a nursing unit are assigned to a head nurse. A head nurse or nurse manager supervises the personnel in a patient care unit. This person is accountable for the quality of the nursing care on the unit, controls the supplies, and schedules the staff. Usually the head nurse has a series of staff nurses. The staff nurses are assigned specific responsibilities for the nursing care of patients on the nursing unit.

Line or Staff Role for the Nursing Director?*

Figure 7-3 illustrates the difference between the director's role in line and staff models.

The major difference between the two models is that the nursing director in the staff model is no

Source: Robert R. Tacey, "The Nursing Director's Role," *Nursing Administration Quarterly*, Aspen Publishers, Inc., vol. 3, no. 2, © 1979 Aspen Publishers, Inc.

longer in charge of services to patients, but rather serves the organization itself. In this capacity, the nursing director advises the chief executive officer and the program heads, develops curriculum and staff, consults and advises nursing personnel, defines nursing policies and standards, rates nursing program heads, assists in professional recruitment and selection, and conducts community liaison.

The most common problem for nursing directors in the staff model is a lack of power. The chief and the program leaders have the option to confer power to the nursing director for a necessary task. For the most part, however, the director must rely on influence and professional respect within the facility to accomplish anything. The role becomes uncomfortable for people who are used to wielding power and having an immediate impact on a program.

The Nursing Unit

As noted earlier, the nursing care of the hospital is organized in a decentralized fashion into patient care units or nursing units. The size of nursing units varies. They can be very small, with 8- to 10-bed units for specialized care, or they can be large, with 60- to 70-bed units.

Figure 7-3 Comparison of Nursing Director's Role in Line and Staff Models

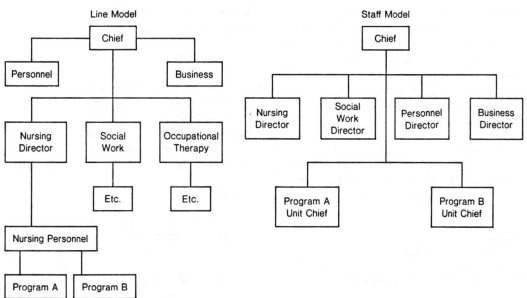

Perhaps the most common size is between 20 and 40 beds per unit.

Specialized Nursing Units*

The special nursing units in the nursing services department usually include medical, surgical, pediatric, obstetric, and psychiatric. In addition to the overall responsibilities and functions of nursing services, the units also carry more specific responsibilities and functions of patient care, varying with each nursing unit. The establishment and execution of educational programs for staff and student nurses may also be functions of these special nursing units.

Medical and Surgical. Nursing care is provided in medical and surgical units in accordance with the physician's instructions and recognized techniques and procedures. While medical conditions are not easily divided into distinct categories, medical nursing is considered a specialty in that normal and abnormal reactions or symptoms of diagnosed diseases must be recognized and reported. The patient with a stroke or a cardiac condition requires a much different type of nursing from that given the patient with an ulcer or diabetes. Surgical patients also require special preoperative and postoperative care.

Pediatrics. This service embraces the care of children. Care of the newborn is usually in a separate unit located in the obstetric unit. The activities of the pediatric unit require understanding of the unique needs, fears, and behavior of children, which is reflected in the type and degree of nursing care given. Where illnesses require protracted convalescence, educational and occupational therapy become concerns of the nursing service. Relationships with parents pose further important responsibilities.

Obstetrics. Prenatal care, observation, and comfort of patients in labor, delivery room assistance, and care of mothers after delivery, as well as nursing care of newborns, are important responsibilities of this unit. Obstetric nurses

assist in instructing new mothers in postnatal care and care of the newborn. Care of the newborn, particularly the premature, requires special nursing skills dictated by their unique requirements.

Psychiatric. While most emotionally disturbed patients are treated in specialized hospitals, the general hospital also recognizes a responsibility and provides facilities for the mentally ill. Nursing care of the mentally ill requires a knowledge of their various behavior patterns and how to cope with them. Techniques must be learned for dealing with all types of problem behavior, so that skilled, therapeutic care is given to such patients.

Operating Room. This unit has primary responsibility for comforting patients in the O.R.; maintaining aseptic techniques; scheduling all operations in cooperation with surgeons; and determining that adequate personnel, space, and equipment are available. Nursing personnel assist the surgeon during operations and are part of the surgical team. Preparation for operations includes sterilization of instruments and equipment; cleaning up after operations is also part of the unit's responsibility.

Recovery Room. In many hospitals, the recovery room unit is an adjunct responsibility of the operating room unit. Special nursing attention must be given patients after an operation until they have completely recovered from the effects of anesthesia.

Emergency Room. This unit is responsible for emergency care, and for arrangements to admit the patient to the hospital, if necessary. The unit completes required records; makes reports to police and safety and health agencies; handles matters of payment and notification of relatives; and refers patients to other services within the hospital or community, as needed.

Special Care Units*

The sophisticated modern hospital may have a variety of special care facilities to manage and to

---

*Source: Job Descriptions and Organizational Analysis for Hospitals and Related Health Service, U.S. Training and Employment Service, U.S. Department of Commerce, 1970.

*Source: I. Donald Snook, Hospitals: What They Are and How They Work, ed 2, Aspen Publishers, Inc., © 1992.

maintain patients with special illnesses and injuries. These facilities may include intensive care units for medicine and surgery, special cardiac care units, hemodialysis or renal dialysis centers, inpatient psychiatric units, inpatient alcoholic and drug addiction units, pediatric units, and skilled nursing facilities for long-term care.

Intensive Care Units. The most common type of special care unit in the hospital is the medical/surgical intensive care unit (ICU). The purpose of ICUs is to manage the critically ill patient who is in a precarious clinical status and requires "eagle eye" supervision. The ICUs handle both surgical and medical cases. ICU cases could be patients in shock, stroke victims, or persons with heart failures, serious infections, respiratory distress, and so forth.

By marshalling the hospital's resources in one geographical area, it is much easier and efficient to provide high-quality care. Not only are sophisticated equipment and instrumentation available in ICUs, but a highly concentrated nursing staff is also used. These nurses may have completed critical care training at the hospital or elsewhere.

Coronary Care Units. Today, nearly all the hospitals in America have CCU capacities. The CCUs do for cardiac patients what the ICUs do for severe medical and surgical patients.

For both ICUs and CCUs, it is usual to have a medical director assigned either full-time, part-time, or on a rotating basis to manage the units medically. Individual attending physicians manage their own patients. However, because there is a medical director, the attending physicians have to relinquish some of the old concept of total and complete control over their patients and realize that their care is a shared responsibility in these two intensive care units.

The nurse's role in these units is critical. The nurses should be intelligent observers, and they must be able to interpret changes in a patient. Under critical circumstances, they might have to diagnose and even treat the patient. One of the prime objectives of the CCU is to detect early signs of impending cardiac disaster so that it can be treated before cardiac arrest takes place.

Neonatal ICU. A special offshoot of the ICUs is the neonatal intensive care unit, which specializes in the management of critical health problems in the newborn. Caring for the critically ill newborn requires a specially trained nurse and physician. The neonatal intensive care units have had great success in the handling of premature infants, giving them a new lease on life.

DECENTRALIZING A NURSING DEPARTMENT

Decentralization of control and decision making is one way to promote autonomy in a nursing department. The result of decentralization can be a more open philosophy among nursing leaders and elimination of the frequent unrest in the traditional hospital structure, where power, authority, and accountability were centered at the top of the nursing department. Under decentralization power and the authority for decision making and change exist with the individuals most closely concerned with the decision or the change.*

Qualities Needed to Decentralize a Nursing Department*

For decentralization to develop in a nursing department, a number of qualities must exist.

A Desire To Decentralize. There must be an enthusiastic desire on the part of nursing managers to decentralize. Since decentralization brings about increased decision making at the unit level, nursing managers need to feel comfortable in making independent decisions.

Goals and Objectives Defined. Unit coordinators (head nurses) and supervisors must clearly define the goals and objectives of their unit to their unit staff.

Leadership. There must be strong leadership abilities in the key management individuals, i.e., the head nurses, unit coordinators, and supervisors in the nursing department. The nurs-

---

Source: Elizabeth N. Lewis and Patricia V. Carini, *Nurse Staffing and Patient Classification: Strategies for Success*, Aspen Publishers, Inc., © 1983.

ing administration must look clearly at the mix of the staff in each unit as well as the capabilities of the members of the staff when selecting the unit coordinator (head nurse) or supervisor of that unit. Individuals respond differently to different leadership styles. Different styles of leadership are appropriate for different management settings.

Guidance by Nursing Administration. Nursing administrators should hold regular, scheduled, informal meetings with individual members of the middle management team as well as group meetings. Nursing administrators need to communicate to the nursing middle managers their own understanding of decentralization concepts and also their expectations of the decentralization process.

Advantages of Decentralization*

The advantages of decentralization seem to outweigh the disadvantages. Decentralization increases morale and promotes interpersonal relationships. When people have a voice in governance, they feel more important and are more willing to contribute. Increased motivation provides a feeling of individuality and freedom that encourages creativity and commits the individual to making the system successful. Decentralization fosters informality and democracy in management and brings decision making closer to the action. Thus decisions may be more effective because people who know the situation and have to implement the decisions are the ones who make them. Because managers do not have to wait for the approval of their superiors, flexibility is increased and reaction time is decreased. Fewer people have to exchange information. Consequently, communications are swift and effective. Coordination improves, especially for services, and operations that are minor to the total production receive more adequate attention. Plans can be tried out on an experimental

basis in one unit, modified, and proven before being used in other units. Risks of losses of personnel or facilities are dispersed.

Decentralization helps determine accountability. It makes weak management visible through semi-independent and often competitive divisions. Operating on the premise that people learn by doing, decentralization develops managers by allowing them to manage. A management pool can be developed that thereby eases the problem of succession. There is usually less conflict between top management and divisions. Decentralization releases top management from the burden of daily administration, freeing them for long-range planning, goal and policy development, and systems integration.

Disadvantages*

Several problems can also result from decentralization. An organization may not be large enough to merit decentralization, or it may be difficult to divide the organization into self-contained operating units. Top administrators may not desire decentralization. They may feel it would decrease their status, or they may question the abilities of people to whom they could delegate. They may feel that most people prefer to be dependent upon others and do not want decision-making responsibility. An increased awareness of division consciousness and a decrease in company consciousness may develop. Divisions may become individualized and competitive to the extent that they sacrifice the overall objectives for short-range profitability and work against the best interests of the whole organization. Because of conflicts between divisions, it may be difficult to obtain a majority vote, and compromises may result. If the majority vote is delayed, it may come too late to be effective.

Decentralization involves increased costs. It requires more managers and larger staffs. There may be underutilization of managers. Divisions

---

Source: Ann Marriner, *Guide to Nursing Management*, 2nd edition, The C.V. Mosby Co., © 1984. Reprinted with permission.

Source: Ann Marriner, *Guide to Nursing Management*, 2nd edition, The C.V. Mosby Co., © 1984. Reprinted with permission.

may not adequately use the specialists housed at headquarters. Functions are likely to be duplicated between divisions and headquarters. Because decentralization develops managers, there are novice managers in the system who will make mistakes. Division managers may not inform top management of their problems. There are problems with control and nonuniform policies. Some restrictions on autonomy remain. Even with decentralization, top management remains responsible for long-range objectives and goals, broad policies, selection of key executives, and approval of major capital expenditures.

Decentralization Using a Nursing Administrative Committee*

The nursing administrative committee can be used to discuss projects and plans, interpret state or Joint Commission requirements for nursing, and develop solutions, examining the potential effects of the solutions or decisions on patient care. Attendance at meetings can be open to all nursing managers. Among their concerns might be subjects such as cost-effectiveness, work productivity, and motivational aspects that can lead to job satisfaction. Through small working groups, projects and methods of improvement often are developed and then presented to the entire nursing administrative committee for further discussion and final approval. The committee may provide necessary feedback of information to allow for further improvement of a project.

The individuals selected for the ad hoc committees are usually determined by the nature of the problem, project, policy, or procedure; individuals may volunteer or be appointed to serve. This can allow members of the administrative committee to work on a variety of projects in the department with peers who offer a different focus. Time frames and project deadlines are assigned to each working group project.

Restructuring the Nursing Supervisor's Role*

The role of the nursing supervisor, whatever the official title, is often the most ill-defined role in the hospital hierarchy. Inability to clarify the role has led many organizations to eliminate the position and to give the head nurse more authority. Often when the supervisor appears, the head nurse reacts as though a "foreigner" has invaded his or her territory.

Most of the recent attempts to alter the supervisor's role have been designed to soften the competitive response to this position. The title has been changed to that of coordinator, and job descriptions have been altered to define the nursing supervisor as a "resource person." Nevertheless, attempts to change the image of the supervisor have minimal effect if the position retains line authority over the head nurse. Such alterations in image do not change the essential problem inherent in the supervisor's role. The problem, simply defined, is that the commonly assigned supervisory tasks are merely extensions of the head nurse's responsibilities rather than discrete, separate functions. The supervisory level must have a job function that is different from that of an extended head nurse.

One possibility for restructuring the supervisor's role is to analyze the nursing management components and to assign each supervisor to the management of a specific component. For example, suppose a hospital has 15 units (15 head nurses) and 3 supervisors. The director might decide, on the basis of their number, to divide tasks into the following areas: (1) evaluation and improvement of patient care, (2) staffing and regulation of personnel, and (3) administrative processes and nursing systems. Each supervisor then would be responsible for guiding and directing his or her assigned specialty in each of the 15 units. With this chance to specialize, it is likely that each supervisor could become expert in his or her particular field.

Source: Elizabeth N. Lewis and Patricia V. Carini, *Nurse Staffing and Patient Classification: Strategies for Success*, Aspen Publishers, Inc., © 1983.

Source: B. Stevens, "The Problems in Nursing's Middle Management," *Journal of Nursing Administration*, September-October 1972. Reprinted with permission.

The psychological advantage to this scheme merits examination. The head nurse is less likely to react negatively to the supervisor who has only a partial interest in the head nurse's "territory," thereby making it easier for him or her to accept each supervisor in the "expert" role and to take advantage of the guidance offered.

The system of divided function must be carefully structured, for it infringes on the time-worn principle that each person should have to report to only one boss. Actually, this principle is broken every day without major incident. For example, the nurse director is responsible not only to his or her immediate boss but also to the personnel director for upholding any contracts or policies of the personnel department. This division of authority causes no problems. The nurse director is quite capable of differentiating what is "owed" to the personnel director and what is not within the scope of the director's authority. Clearly the head nurse cannot be responsible to three supervisors who may give incompatible orders, but he or she can be responsible to each supervisor within a clearly defined and delimited scope of activities.

This system can work well if each supervisor has a clear understanding of his or her function and insists that problems outside his or her range be referred to the proper supervisor. For example, with the theoretical division of function between three supervisors, job descriptions may be framed as follows.

Supervisor A (Coordinator of Patient Care Services)

1. Directs and implements patient care evaluation tools
   a. Nursing chart audit
   b. Nursing quality control
   c. Patient interview systems
2. Evaluates nursing care plans
   a. Checks nursing care plans for patients needing complex care
   b. Checks nursing care plans on other patients on a periodic basis
   c. Makes rounds on selected patients
   d. Suggests care improvements to head nurses

3. Daily follows the care progression of patients who are critical or require complex nursing care
4. Serves as a resource person and expert in nursing care
   a. Is available to head nurse at his or her request to assist in solving care problems
   b. Is available to head nurse at his or her request to set up care plans for complex patients
   c. Periodically assists in team conference focusing on patient care problems
5. Participates in patient care research
   a. Helps head nurse identify needed areas of research
   b. Assists head nurse in constructing research test systems
   c. Assists in implementing and evaluating patient care research
6. Coordinates care problems as needed with physicians and allied health groups

Supervisor B (Coordinator of Nursing Personnel and Staffing)

1. Directs and implements policies for hiring, promoting, transferring, and discharging personnel
   a. Coordinates vacancies with personnel department
   b. Arranges with head nurse for interviews for hiring, evaluating, and discharging personnel
   c. Assists the head nurse in developing interviewing skills
2. Evaluates daily staffing patterns
   a. Uses patient rating systems to evaluate staffing needs
   b. Confers with head nurse concerning needed changes in daily staffing
   c. Assigns float staff personnel
   d. Plans for evening and night staffing needs
3. Analyzes and recommends permanent staffing patterns
   a. Researches staffing needs
   b. Determines levels of nursing skill required

4. Serves as arbitrator for personnel grievances and problems that cannot be settled at the head nurse level
5. Coordinates all payroll data
6. Serves as an assignment expert for the head nurse
   a. Teaches head nurse and team leaders appropriate means of developing team assignments
   b. Periodically evaluates staff assignments
   c. Makes recommendations to head nurse for improvements in assignment patterns
   d. Researches new concepts and patterns in assigning and staffing
   e. Assists head nurse in constructing, implementing, and evaluating new models for assignments
   f. Periodically evaluates staff responses to their assignments

Supervisor C (Coordinator of Nursing Systems)

1. Evaluates systems by which care is delivered and recommends appropriate changes
   a. Examines daily routines of care, such as bath schedules, medicine distribution, and linen changes
   b. Evaluates emergency routines, such as cardiopulmonary resuscitation and disaster plans
   c. Examines accepted nursing procedures
2. Evaluates forms that record nursing data
   a. Chart forms
   b. Kardex forms
   c. Forms for staff assignments and notices
   d. Forms for patient data such as bedside signs and intake and output sheets
   e. Interdepartmental communication forms
3. Maintains expert and up-to-date knowledge of nursing and hospital policies
   a. Serves to communicate policy changes
   b. Serves as a resource to head nurse in policy issues
4. Coordinates nursing policies with others
   a. Communicates among nursing units

   b. Communicates with other hospital divisions and individuals
   c. Participates in formulating policies that involve nursing plus other divisions
5. Serves as an expert resource in applying management techniques to nursing function

No two hospitals would be likely to make the same division of tasks. Job divisions would depend on many factors: number of units, number of supervisors, abilities of supervisors, nursing objectives, to name a few.

In addition to giving each supervisor a job unlike that of the head nurse, the proposed system offers the director other advantages. Since the job division requires close coordination, the director has a real purpose for staff meetings with supervisors. Too often meetings between the director and supervisors evolve into meaningless recitals of patient admissions, discharges, and deaths. With the proposed system, immediate in-house patient data are not the only focus, and proper attention can be given to relating patient data to delivery systems and policies. Thus staff meetings can become dynamic problem-solving, decision-making sessions rather than being simply informational in nature.

As a second alternative, it would be possible to create a functional unit larger than the patient ward. For example, suppose a supervisor manages three wards and a common basis for action can be identified in spite of the differentiated functions of the wards. Possibly all wards serve surgical patients or perhaps they serve geriatric patients. If a unifying factor can be identified, it can guide the establishment of common goals and needs of the wards. The unity could be of a broad nature and still serve the purpose.

The supervisor might then begin to wield the separate wards into a single functional team. The supervisor could hold staff meetings with the head nurses to set common goals or to try common projects. Any transferring of personnel to meet daily variations in patient numbers and needs among these wards could be managed cooperatively rather than reaching outside the new functional unit. Indeed, the head nurses could plan a methodical interchange of personnel so that each employee is properly oriented to the other two wards and to their special equipment and patient care needs. Necessary staff relocations then would not cause the usual employee protest and resistance, since workers would be prepared for such interchange.

If an assistant head nurse role does not exist in the institution, the head nurses could also orient themselves to their related wards in order to be available as resource persons during their coworkers' days off.

With this proposed structure, the job of the supervisor is clearly differentiated from that of the head nurse. The supervisor has a territory of his or her own, the larger (combined) unit. The supervisor functions within the larger unit as a whole rather than interfering in the everyday function of the head nurse; helps the unit evolve group goals and long-range objectives and no longer attempts to usurp the day-to-day head nurse functions; maintains a broader objective and serves to coordinate the activities of the new functional unit; and now meets head nurse needs through the staff meetings more often than in individual conferences.

Using Clinical Supervisors*

Allegheny General is a 700-bed private voluntary hospital in the metropolitan setting of Pittsburgh. Under its decentralized nursing service system (Figure 7-4), each major clinical nursing specialty has become a division, for example, Division of Medical-Surgical Nursing, Division of Obstetric-Pediatric Nursing, Emergency-Ambulatory Services, Operating-Recovery Room Services, and Inservice Education. The individual divisions function with a high degree of autonomy under the direction of a division head and with the coordinated efforts of clinical coordinators and clinical supervisors.

Just as each major clinical specialty becomes a division, each patient care area becomes a unit under the direction of a clinical supervisor. The units may vary in patient census and patient care

*Source: D.M. Stitely, "The Role of the Division Head in a Decentralized Nursing Service System," *Nursing Clinics of North America*, June 1973. Reprinted with permission.

complexity. Therefore, the management aspects will differ from unit to unit in material as well as personnel needs. The clinical supervisor, as the first-level management person, must establish and maintain quotas for supplies and equipment through the Department of Materials Management for automatic delivery service. Other duties are the preparation of personnel time schedules, evaluation of personnel work performance, and the initiation of personnel disciplinary action. The clinical supervisor is expected to make the day-by-day operational decisions that are specific to the individual unit. However, a most important element of these administrative duties is the sharing of information related to the management and operation of each and every unit with the division head. Thus, the lines of administrative responsibility are clinical supervisor to division head to the department head.

Clinical Responsibilities

The clinical advantage of a decentralized system is that the key figures in each division are clinically proficient. For example, the division head of medical-surgical nursing must be prepared educationally and with experience in the care of adult patients, while a maternal-child health background is essential for the division head of obstetrics and pediatrics. Another advantage of this system is the ability to utilize a clinical expert who has no administrative responsibilities, that is, the clinical coordinator. This person has the responsibility and the authority to make nursing decisions related to direct patient care. The clinical coordinator may function as a specialist with direct relationships to the patients and families, as a consultant to all staff members for improving nursing arts and skills, and as an evaluator of clinical nursing practice. Thus, the clinical lines of the organizational chart will follow from the clinical supervisor on each patient care unit, to the clinical coordinator in an area of expertise, to the division head, and to the department head.

The Division Head

Since the division head has the responsibility and authority for both the management operations and the clinical practice within the specific

Figure 7-4 Decentralized Nursing Service — Clinical Supervisors

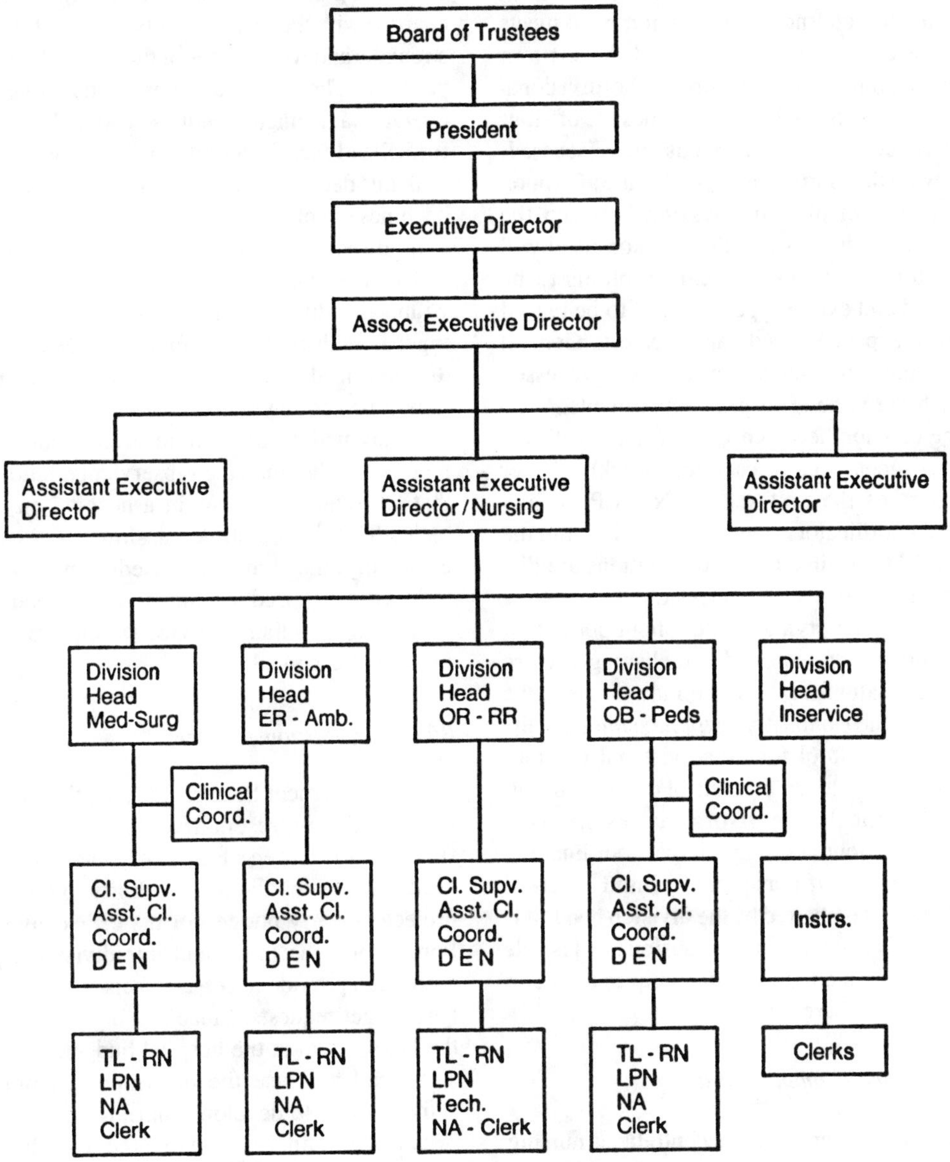

```
                         ┌─────────────────────┐
                         │   Board of Trustees  │
                         └─────────────────────┘
                                    │
                         ┌─────────────────────┐
                         │      President       │
                         └─────────────────────┘
                                    │
                         ┌─────────────────────┐
                         │  Executive Director  │
                         └─────────────────────┘
                                    │
                      ┌──────────────────────────┐
                      │ Assoc. Executive Director │
                      └──────────────────────────┘
                                    │
        ┌───────────────────────────┼──────────────────────────────┐
┌──────────────────┐   ┌──────────────────────┐   ┌──────────────────┐
│ Assistant        │   │ Assistant Executive  │   │ Assistant        │
│ Executive        │   │ Director / Nursing   │   │ Executive        │
│ Director         │   │                      │   │ Director         │
└──────────────────┘   └──────────────────────┘   └──────────────────┘
                                    │
   ┌─────────┬───────────┬─────────┼──────────┬───────────┐
┌────────┐ ┌────────┐ ┌────────┐ ┌────────┐ ┌────────┐
│Division│ │Division│ │Division│ │Division│ │Division│
│Head    │ │Head    │ │Head    │ │Head    │ │Head    │
│Med-Surg│ │ER - Amb.│ │OR - RR │ │OB - Peds│ │Inservice│
└────────┘ └────────┘ └────────┘ └────────┘ └────────┘
```

Division Head Med-Surg	Division Head ER - Amb.	Division Head OR - RR	Division Head OB - Peds	Division Head Inservice
	Clinical Coord.		Clinical Coord.	
Cl. Supv. Asst. Cl. Coord. D E N	Cl. Supv. Asst. Cl. Coord. D E N	Cl. Supv. Asst. Cl. Coord. D E N	Cl. Supv. Asst. Cl. Coord. D E N	Instrs.
TL - RN LPN NA Clerk	TL - RN LPN NA Clerk	TL - RN LPN Tech. NA - Clerk	TL - RN LPN NA Clerk	Clerks

division, methods must be established to receive unit input, refer information through proper hospital channels, take appropriate action, and respond to personnel. The division head is in the thick of a communication system which must connect all levels of nursing personnel with top hospital management and top management with all nursing personnel. How does one individual meet these obligations? The first step is to establish a means of communicating within the individual division.

Intradivisional Communication

Of course, daily one-to-one contact between people is the most direct method of sharing information. However, this is impossible where patients and personnel are numbered in the hundreds. Daily reports and weekly rounds will permit the average unit problems to be solved. Each morning and afternoon the division head meets with the clinical coordinators and the off-tour assistant clinical coordinators at the divisional intershift reports. During these times the off-tour patients and operational needs are discussed. Following the morning and prior to the afternoon report, a brief planning session between the clinical coordinators and the division head will allow for immediate clinical problems to be reviewed and extra supportive staff to be placed where the patient needs are greatest. General management problems may also be processed through the various hospital departments.

The division head schedules rounds with the clinical supervisors of each unit weekly. Other members of the unit staff, RNs, LPNs, and clinical coordinators, are encouraged to join the rounds. At this time the unit operations are discussed and patients are reviewed.

Although reports and rounds are important for receiving information and establishing a close working relationship between individuals at the unit level, the *monthly operational council* is the most effective tool for intradivisional communication. The council consists of clinical coordinators, clinical supervisors, representatives from the off-tour assistant clinical coordinators, and the registered nurse and licensed practical nurse staff. It is chaired by the division head. It is through this council that the division head is able to activate problem-solving techniques in a democratic atmosphere.

Interdivisional Communication

The second step in the decentralized nursing service communication system is a mechanism through which all division heads and the department head can effectively utilize the divisional input for planning patient care and operational management programs. Many nursing practice procedures and allied health care services are shared by all divisions. Therefore, a close interdivisional relationship must be developed. The Executive Council of Nursing is the method most often used for communication. The participating members are the division heads and the clinical coordinators, and the council is chaired by the department head. This group is charged with the responsibility of identifying the strengths and weaknesses of the care delivered to patients. The information from the divisions' operational council meetings is pooled and more formalized fact-finding programs are generated.

In this decentralized system, the division head becomes the primary participant on the planning committees involving a specific clinical specialty area. Since the lines of communication within the divisions are so direct, the nursing input is realistic from a functional aspect. The division head is also in the advantageous position of promoting nursing to a peer relationship with the medical and administrative committee members rather than the subservient relationship that so frequently exists in a hospital environment. This is sometimes a slow process, but eventually, the clinical knowledge and managerial skills required of the division head in a decentralized nursing service system are recognized and accepted.

Budgetary Responsibilities

The department head rather than the division head is the representative to the executive finance committee. However, each division head is delegated the responsibility to prepare a projected yearly budget for his or her division. Fortunately, the inter- and intradivisional programs can provide necessary facts to justify certain budget requests. Since nursing personnel is the largest item in the hospital budget, the division head will use the information from the activity study to develop a staffing pattern.

The division head also meets with each clinical coordinator and clinical supervisor to determine the major equipment needs. A written justification for additional hypothermia units, pacemakers, or other major items must accompany the request. The routine operational items are also adjusted. The division head makes an estimate of the operational costs by reviewing the expenditures for two previous years.

The final step in the budgetary procedure is to submit the total projected divisional costs with the justifications of the department head.

Using a Shared Governance Structure*

Shared governance is a decentralized approach which allows nurses to retain influence about decisions that affect their practice, work environment, professional development and personal fulfillment. An essential underlying belief is that, given the opportunity, environment, and framework, registered nurses will make appropriate and meaningful judgments in providing care and enacting their role as professionals. This organizational structure also requires practitioners to assume higher levels of accountability for patient care, clinical practice, and professional activities. By building on peer relations, governance can augment the professional practice model of a department of nursing by minimizing the isolation a primary nursing system causes. Also, it enhances the staff's ability to take more responsibility and accountability for themselves and their peers. Its council structure fosters teamwork (see Figure 7-5), thus allowing staff nurses a more active role in developing and implementing systems designed to achieve patient care outcomes and develop professional nursing practice.

Bylaws to Support the Governance Model**

One mechanism for building and supporting a professional governance model is bylaws, or simply rules that govern the internal affairs of an organization. Bylaws applied to any nursing structure should be congruent with the philosophy and goals of the corporate organization, but they should not remove the nursing professional's obligation to set standards of practice and monitor compliance and quality within a defined practice arena.

Source: Laura Caramanica and Sara Rosenbecker, "A Pilot Unit Approach to Shared Governance," *Nursing Management*, vol. 22, no. 1, January 1991. Reprinted with permission.

**Source*: Kathryn J. McDonagh, "Nursing Bylaws: A Blueprint for a Professional Governance Model," *Aspen's Advisor for Nurse Executives*, vol. 3, no. 9, © 1988 Aspen Publishers, Inc.

> **Nursing Bylaws—Key Components**
>
> - Philosophy of the professional nursing organization
> - Definition of nursing
> - Governance functions of the professional nursing organization
> - Role of the professional nurse
> - Professional nurse staff membership
> - Credentials review process
> - Description of the governance structure
> - Discipline, appeals, and parallel levels processes
> - Bylaw review and revision process

The most important purpose of nursing bylaws in a shared governance structure is to legitimize the professional governance model of the nursing organization. Bylaws that are adopted by the professional organization and approved within the corporate structure comprise a governance model that will carry the necessary and legitimate authority to carry out its business. The existance of bylaws also means that the governance structure transcends individuals and does not dissolve as new leaders or executives enter the organization.

The bylaws should also describe the process of appointment to the professional nursing organization, including the process of applying for nursing staff privileges, the credentials necessary for membership, and the conditions and duration of the appointment. Further, the bylaws could delineate how the nursing staff will organize, integrate, manage, and evaluate the delivery of nursing care services. A description of how the nursing councils and committees operate and where the accountability for decision making rests could also be outlined.

Review of the nursing bylaws by the nursing coordinating council assists the governance structure in balancing the power and relationships among nursing councils and serves as an ongoing self-assessment and improvement process.

Figure 7-5 Sample Decision Tree for Shared Governance

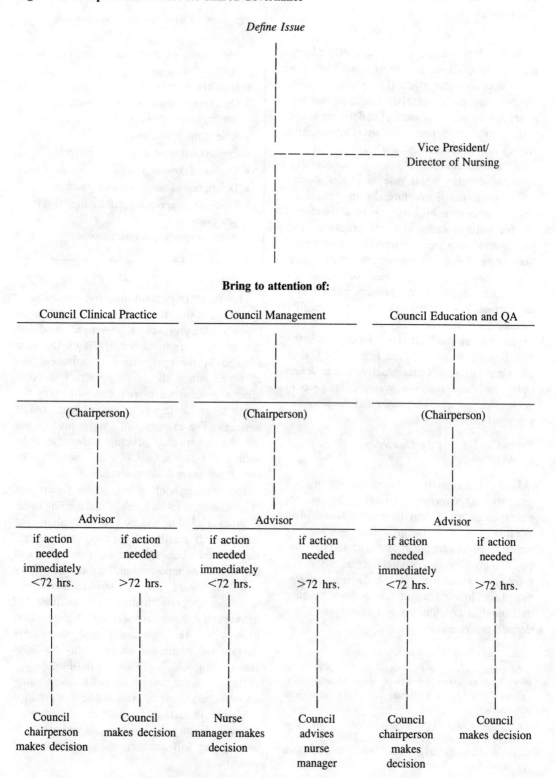

Key: Directing Issues to the Appropriate Council

Check to see whether the issue is listed within the scope of the council before reporting it.

The Council for Clinical Practice
—Clinical standards of nursing practice such as concerns about patient care
—Issues around role and responsibilities of the registered nurse
—Policies regarding nursing practice and resultant nursing care
—Peer review—evaluations
—Clinical ladder program
—Nursing standards

The Council for Education and Quality Assurance
—Nursing inservices/continuing education
—Preceptors
—Orientation
—Maintaining care plans, policies, procedures, care conferences

—Revision of nursing procedures
—Joint Commission review preparation/meeting standards of
—Incident reports

The Council for Nursing Management
—Hiring/interviewing
—Staff conflicts
—Time requests/scheduling
—Policymaking
—Nurse licensure

Nurse Manager
—Allocation of fiscal resources, including budgetary, operational, capital, and contingent financial resources essential to the practice of nursing in the pain/rehab program
—Time cards
—Policymaking <72 hours
—Back up for all of the above council activities

Source: Laura Caramanica and Sara Rosenbecker, "A Pilot Unit Approach to Shared Governance," *Nursing Management*, vol. 22, no. 1, January 1991. Reprinted with permission.

MULTIHOSPITAL SYSTEMS*

The U.S. health service industry, particularly the hospital sector, is in the middle of a wide-scale, serious debate about how health care institutions should be structured and managed. Cost constraints, reimbursement strategies, tax policy, and the continuing rapid changes evolving in medical technologies lead many observers to question the viability of the single, free-standing, separately managed hospital. Some people question the viability of single small hospitals but recognize that a wide range of organizational strategies exist to help the needed and necessary hospital which finds it difficult to cope in today's harsh marketplace.

---
*Source: Except where noted, the material in this section is reprinted from Montague Brown, "Systems Development: Trends, Issues and Implications," *Health Care Management Review*, vol. 4, no. 1, © 1979 Aspen Publishers, Inc.

Types of Integration

Horizontal integration refers to the addition of organizations or services of the same type (e.g., one hospital acquiring another hospital).

Vertical integration occurs when the organization decides to engage in a new enterprise or new services, such as a substance abuse clinic, a long-term care unit, or a psychiatric program.

Are U.S. health services, particulary hospitals, moving toward a more integrated system? Is the performance of the more integrated hospital and health services superior to that of less well integrated single units? Is there potential for further improvements in performance in the more integrated multiunit hospital system and for the formation of other such organizations? The general answer to these questions seems to be yes.

Multiunit Organizations under Single Management

Multiunit organization development has been stimulated by a variety of factors. Satellite hospitals have allowed existing organizations to follow physicians and patients to the suburbs. Mergers often bring together organizations that are short on capital, serve overlapping markets, and face pressures for program expansion or elaboration. Increasingly, hospitals and multiunit systems have decided that economies of scale are sufficient to justify their going into new markets or joining with others to ensure sufficient size to deal both with exploding costs of technological demands and with the politics of regional planning.

Some communities, mostly those with small hospitals, have chosen to lease their operation to an outside organization, thus retaining the long-term option of regaining total operational control. Still others have retained ownership and control while hiring larger multiunit systems to supply the key management teams for the operation.

Researchers have identified a number of factors associated with proprietary hospital systems: savings in construction, volume purchasing, the ability to afford specialized management talent, standardization of supplies and equipment, and sufficient breadth and diversity to attract capital.

Others point out benefits in cost-effectiveness, comprehensiveness of care, availability of care, organization and management, and acceptance of voluntary not-for-profit systems. The evidence suggests that not-for-profit multiple unit systems are more efficient than similar units operating independently. Specifically, reports of multiunit systems effectiveness show:

- slower growth in case cost
- lower levels of average case cost
- lower price levels
- slower growth in prices
- higher outputs
- comparable services with other hospitals

- lower average lengths of stay (suggesting stronger management—tighter control of medical practice patterns)
- higher wage rates but not high labor costs
- slower growth in labor hours per case.

Organizational Arrangements for Systems Integration

A variety of organizational arrangements are being developed to facilitate systems integration. Among these are shared services, condominiums, consortia, mergers, regional multiunit hospital systems, and national chains.

Shared Services. Sharing involves two or more organizations joining together to produce and/or use the same service for the member institutions. This ranges from the joint use of computers, laundries, and laboratories to purchasing and specialized clinical services. A variety of organizational arrangements have been developed to handle shared services among organizations, including new corporations, existing hospital associations, contractual agreements among institutions, and the outright sale of services from one (usually large) institution to others in need of the service.

Condominium Hospitals. In a private condominium, multiple owners have unique and shared space. For the individual, having a condominium allows one to retain social control over one's personal space while sharing the ownership and use of common space and services. The same holds true for commercial condominiums. In Texas, the Texas Medical Center (TMC) hosts 23 separate organizations sharing grounds, power, parking, buildings, services, and a multitude of other things.

Consortia. Consortia of hospitals, often including medical schools, are membership organizations with full-time staff devoted to joint planning and programming. The consortia seek to get agreement on which institution should specialize in each major clinical service. This will help to limit major investment to fewer institutions and to improve utilization patterns and thus may help to ensure efficient and quality services.

Mergers. Some of the early consortia have contributed to the complete merger of some or all of the institutions involved.

Regional Multiunit Systems. A regional multiunit health care organization can share physicians and provide different levels of care to the same or overlapping patient populations. These regional systems most resemble the classical regional health care system. More organizations aspire to this type of configuration than succeed, but the bulk of the interest in multiunit systems in this country applies to this configuration.

National Chains. National chains refer to the ownership and management of more than one hospital with none or few of the owned hospitals having any medical staff or patient populations in common. Investor-owned chains represent the fastest growing sector of the industry, with chains owning, operating, or managing about 11 percent of the industry and more than 55 percent of the investor-owned sector. Religious orders and church-related chains constitute the other most important sector of the group. The religious chains have been around for some time. What is changing among these groups, however, is that they are adopting the corporate management approaches of the investor-owned chains.

Multihospital System Benefits*

- Centralization of administrative and support services, thereby securing economies of scale through specialization and reducing unit costs by the shared application of advanced technology.
- Greater management capability to cope with internal problems and weaknesses as well as with the external environment.
- Larger capital bases providing additional financial stability.

- A central focus for assigning priority to financially realistic program and resource decisions.
- An opportunity to bring medical staffs into a rational management structure that recognizes the need for their input in key management activities such as planning and evaluation.

Dealing with Mergers*

Mergers directly affect some 25 to 50 percent of the work force. Because of low initial commitment to the merger, employees move instinctively to protect themselves by deliberately resisting alterations in their work patterns. While turnover rises, morale drops—and with that, productivity, competitive advantage, revenues, and profits deteriorate as well.

Essentially, the role of the nurse manager is to cope with the instinctive resistance or withdrawal and to channel workers' efforts into forming new work patterns—and new relationships which the workers will eventually see as profitable not only to the enterprise but also to themselves. Managerial power is best exerted in persuading staff members that change is not only inevitable, but also presents safer or broader options than they had before.

To determine just where they stand at the onset, nurse managers need to assess carefully the compatibility of the merging organizations. Traditional hierarchies create niches whose deeply invested stakeholders heavily resist any changes which would alter their relationships and scopes of operational authority.

Furthermore, every organization follows its own aging and learning cycles which may bring "generational" conflicts to merging processes. If each organization is at some different stage of learning or maturity, attention must focus on evolving toward common ground. A clear picture of the present situation enables managers to

Source: James Reynolds and Ann E. Stunden, "The Organization of Not-for-Profit Hospital Systems," *Health Care Management Review*, vol. 3, no. 3, © 1978 Aspen Publishers, Inc.

Source: Eva L. Fine, "Community Hospital Merger: The Challenge to Nursing Management," *Nursing Management*, vol. 20, no. 12, December 1989. Reprinted with permission.

reshape the organization in a sequence of activities which will dispel the influence of anxiety and uncertainty while it builds a larger sense of competence, control, and commitment.

Priority I: Establish a common knowledge base. Nurse administrators need to introduce useful information on a realistic timetable with definite goals. Employees immediately need a clear, honest picture of why the merger is taking place, e.g., to increase market base, to diversify service offerings, or to strengthen purchasing power. Making the plans for reorganization quickly available is also a crucial step to turning everyone toward the desired direction. Therefore, nurse managers should arrange for exchange visits and meet to review one another's philosophy, standards of care, and goals, as well as policies and procedures in delivering care. Early, visible interest in pursuing common concerns signals to subordinates and superiors alike nurse managers' determination to prevent diffficulties now rather than cure them later on. This is the time to learn the other hospital's "personality" and to plan resolution of cultural mismatches.

As planning progresses, adopt a "plan, announce, act" pattern. Anticipate what staff areas are hardest hit and spend time accordingly. As soon as possible, inform and provide for those employees who will lose their present jobs. Mix employees as much as possible at all levels in the newly combined organization to eliminate "we/they" attitudes.

Priority II: Encourage a collaborative attitude. Effective collaboration develops from visible, persistant gestures of mutual respect and from open, direct communications. A good place to concentrate early is upon blending the competencies of like staff members in the merging constituencies. How merged departments and unit managers handle job descriptions, staffing ratios, acuity systems, pay, and benefits profoundly influences the attitudes merged staff members will develop toward one another.

Priority III: Stabilize individual behavior. Comparing performance evaluations before and after mergers helps identify self-protective behaviors or those which indicate declining commitment. Concentrate on preventing or quickly resolving power struggles as well as on reassuring staff members who are considering leaving before giving the new regime a fair chance.

Priority IV: Develop new group identities and loyalties. Nurse managers of merging institutions should realize they have a relatively rare opportunity to strengthen nursing's position in the system as a whole—but only if they present a united front at corporate levels of decision and activity. Early joint activities between nursing departments and units can help establish positive networks, identify a common leadership group, and gather staff support for it. Sponsoring a community health fair or conducting a common research program helps draw groups together without threatening personal "turf."

In pursuing these priorities, nurse managers are, in effect, "unfreezing" old patterns and attitudes as painlessly as possible by introducing new information, challenges, and opportunities which put prevailing corporate cultures in a different light.

Chapter 8

Nursing Service Jobs

NURSING MANAGEMENT

Nurse administrators have many titles, among which the most frequently used are director of nursing or chief nurse (top management); associate or assistant director of nursing and/or staff development or assistant chief nurse (middle management); day, evening, or night supervisor (middle management); and head nurse (first-line management). Other newer titles designated for the top nursing management person, particularly in the large health care institutions, are vice-president for nursing, vice-president for patient care, or assistant administrator for nursing.

Following are brief descriptions of the nursing management jobs within the hospital, followed by descriptions of the staff jobs within the nursing service.*

Nursing Service Director

Job Duties. Organizes and administers the department of nursing.

Source: Except where noted, descriptions of supervisory nurses are adapted from *Job Descriptions and Organizational Analysis for Hospitals and Related Services*, U.S. Training and Employment Service, Department of Labor, 1971.

Establishes objectives for the department of nursing and the organizational structure for achieving these objectives. Interprets and puts into effect administrative policies established by the governing authority. Assists in preparing and administering budget for the department. Selects and recommends appointment of nursing staff.

Directs and delegates management of professional and ancillary nursing personnel. Plans and conducts conferences and discussions with administrative and professional nursing staff to encourage participation in formulating departmental policies and procedures, promote initiative, solve problems, and interpret new policies and procedures. Coordinates activities of various nursing units, promoting and maintaining harmonious relationships among nursing personnel and with medical staff, patients, and public. Plans and directs orientation and in-service training programs for professional and nonprofessional nursing staff. Analyzes and evaluates nursing and related services rendered to improve quality of patient care and plan better utilization of staff time and activities. Participates in community educational health programs.

Education, Training, and Experience. A baccalaureate degree in nursing is a minimum requirement, with a master's degree preferable.

Current licensure by state board of nursing is a necessity. Five years administrative experience as a director, assistant director, or supervisor of nursing services required.

*Specific Qualifications.** What follows are the qualifications which were defined as important for the administrator of nursing in a recent NLN publication under three categories: an experienced nurse, a management colleague, and an educator.

1. Experienced Nurse Role. The administrator of nursing must be a nurse who:

- Understands both patient care and nurses; has demonstrated stature in the nursing profession; has had some influence in the nursing field; has kept abreast of changes in the profession.
- Plans for the department; establishes goals and directions for that department and helps the hospital establish its own goals; ensures that nursing has proper influence on the total institutional goals and that nursing goals and directions complement and support the total.
- Has integrity and can be relied on to speak frankly and not waste time playing games; is respected for his or her opinions.
- Is a leader who can measure, evaluate, act, motivate, and deal with people; can calculate trouble in advance and steady the organization; excludes unnecessary interference in the internal operations of the department by being a strong and effective manager.
- Is an interpreter for nursing and the hospital, both intramurally and extramurally; speaks for quality and can motivate people in general; understands elements of human behavior.
- Thinks independently; is knowledgeable in the field and willing to draw upon that knowledge to establish a position; can say no and then find a productive alternative.

Source: The Role of the Director of Nursing Service, National League for Nursing, Pub. No. 20-1646, 1977. Reprinted with permission.

(Policies and procedures, organizational charts and regulations are not substitutes for thinking. The nursing administrator must properly proportion rules, hardware, and talent to gain the most effective means of achieving the best in total patient care.)

- Is a member of the management team with a business mind and attitude; is able to delegate responsibility so that available resources are utilized; keeps decision making close to the patient and thus responds to patient needs and not professional resentment; demonstrates warmth and concern for people as individuals and has an interest in total patient care; above all, has a sense of humor and is able to supply a light touch when the going gets rough.

2. Management Colleague Role. The position of nursing director is a top administrative one and an extension of the administrator or chief executive officer. It would not be enough for a potential candidate to be simply interested in nursing management. This management colleague should be able to meet certain considerations, such as:

- Being qualified through having some management training and preferably a master's degree, plus a demonstrable ability to cope with management responsibilities.
- Having the ability to perform as a management representative. This colleague must represent management, which means having direct access to the administrator, the medical staff, and the trustees; being able to sit down with the doctors and plan problem-solving techniques with them; being multi-department-oriented and a constructive change agent to move ideas forward in the organization.
- Having knowledge of volunteers and their respect to help them channel their energies in the most effective, productive way possible to the benefit of the hospital and patients.
- Having knowledge of community health needs and a willingness to become a working member of the community and help plan community health.

- Being an organizer; a planner of strategies; one who keeps an eye on the objectives and functions of the organization and develops resources to achieve such goals through planning, idea development, and clear perspectives.
- Having knowledge of budgets. A person in a management capacity must use all the tools for management, and one of the tasks of the nurse executive is to understand and participate in the budget process. This person must recognize that the budget is a tool used to get things done; it is not just something that interferes with nursing opportunities. One who can put budget pieces together correctly and stand accountable for personal actions as well as for the actions of others under his or her jurisdiction; one who understands the control mechanism and has the attitude and the ability to apply it; one who understands economics in the field (the key to survival of the hospital department), who understands that competition does not necessarily reduce the price of care. In fact, it is just the opposite. The oversupply of facilities, underutilization, increases the cost of care. Perhaps one of the most important considerations in the process of budgeting is to be able to relate dollars to quality.
- Having knowledge of the role the government plays in health care and its effect on that care. Regulatory processes, in a large measure, are aimed directly at doctors. The government has learned that the best strategy is to use the hospitals to apply restraints and restrictions on the medical profession, a devious and divisive process. Top-level management must be able to cope with the regulatory process, sometimes anticipating problems and planning defenses in advance.
- Being knowledgeable about labor relations; someone who understands labor relations and the techniques of dealing with people; one who can handle professional pressures when conflicts develop. For example, when union activity is presented under the umbrella of professional organization, there is a problem when the organization

says one thing and the employer another. This creates a tremendous pressure within the hospital and situations will occur that must be handled diplomatically but firmly.

3. Educator Role. The staff member in charge of education must be:

- Someone able to understand the balance between education and practice; to know what is necessary in the area of personnel education as required by the employer to ensure the best possible patient care; and to be able to correlate hospital needs with educational requirements.
- Someone who can provide input into educational programs for the hospital and bring new ideas into the organization concerning education.
- Someone with adequate information on educational laws and who knows how they apply in the state as well as nationally.
- Someone able to demonstrate self-improvement and have the ability to motivate others to higher levels of performance through better educational opportunities.

Assistant Nursing Service Director

Job Duties. Assists in organizing and administering the department of nursing; assumes responsibilities delegated by the nursing service director.

Conducts conferences and discussions with personnel to encourage participation in formulating departmental policies, promote initiative, solve problems, and present new policies and procedures.

Analyzes nursing and auxiliary services to improve quality of patient care and to obtain maximum utilization of staff time and abilities. Coordinates activities of the nursing service units to achieve and maintain efficient and competent nursing service and to promote and maintain harmonious relationships among personnel supervised, medical staff, patients, and others. Assists in establishing lines of authority and responsibility and defining the duties of nursing service personnel, consistent with good administrative techniques, to ensure that department objectives are accomplished.

Assists in review and evaluation of budget requests against current and projected needs of nursing service.

Interviews applicants and recommends appointment of staff personnel, outlining their duties, scope of authority, and responsibilities. Participates in establishing and administering orientation and in-service training programs for both professional and nonprofessional personnel. Ensures proper and economical use of equipment, supplies, and facilities for maintaining patient care. Maintains personnel and other records, and directs maintenance of patient care records.

Cooperates with medical staff performing research projects or studies as they affect nursing. Works with other agencies and groups in the community to promote the growth and broaden knowledge and skills of professional staff and improve quality of hospital services.

Education, Training, and Experience. Graduation from an accredited school of nursing with bachelor's degree preferred, and master's degree desirable. Current licensure by state board of nursing required, and demonstrated administrative ability.

Experience in a supervisory capacity, with demonstrated executive ability and leadership.

Qualifications. The role of an assistant director of nursing is filled with numerous administrative and clinical responsibilities. To be prepared, an assistant director might well hold an MSN degree and be backed up by one year of experience in management and two years in clinical service. Additional workshops or courses in management topics should provide support in handling labor relations, problem solving, and planning. On the personal level, the assistant director should be purposeful but not rigid, assertive but not overly-aggressive, articulate about own views but not deaf to the opinions of others.

Skills and Responsibilities. Leadership skills in decision making, problem solving, and interpersonal relations are involved in the daily contacts of working with head nurses on the unit.

Assistance is given, on an individual or group level, for setting objectives, structuring plans, handling complaints, and finding solutions. Administrative skills are called for in the performance of several functions. The assistant director is concerned with budgeting; helping the head nurse to document, justify, and submit requests for positions; and evaluating head nurse performance. He or she is concerned with staff development, identifying staff instructional requirements to the in-service department and suggesting or teaching new programs. He or she is also concerned with committee participation, serving on the nursing service administration council and in a representational capacity on his or her clinical units' committees; specialty interest committees; departmentwide committees, such as the committee on quality assurance; and interdepartmental committees.

The maintenance of quality patient care in the units under their supervision is a major responsibility of assistant directors. For some assistant directors the objective is demonstrated practically, by periodically working the unit floor to become acquainted with staff members as working partners and to act as models in the giving of proper care. Others increase communication contacts during the normal course of duties; they show a heightened involvement in short-term crises and long-term projects. Still others concern themselves with technical improvements, streamlining systems, altering forms, clarifying procedures, and implementing standards.

Supervisor Nurse

Job Duties. Supervises and coordinates activities of nursing personnel engaged in specific nursing services, such as obstetrics, pediatrics, or surgery, or for two or more patient care units; also assigned to such areas as the operating room, the outpatient department, the recovery room, and special or intensive care units.

Participates with the director of nursing in the development and implementation of the philosophy and objectives for nursing service.

Supervises head nurses in carrying out their responsibilities in the management of nursing care. Evaluates performance of head nurses and nursing care as a whole and suggests modifications. Inspects unit areas to verify that patient needs are met.

Participates in planning work of own units and coordinates activities with other patient care units and with those of related departments.

Consults with head nurses on specific nursing problems and interpretation of hospital policies. Supervises maintenance of personnel and nursing records.

Plans and organizes orientation and in-service training for unit staff members and participates in guidance and educational programs. Interviews prescreened applicants and makes recommendations for employing or for terminating personnel. Assists the director of nursing service in formulating unit budget. Engages in studies and investigations related to improving nursing care.

The supervisor nurse is usually known by name of nursing section to which assigned or in which she has specialized, such as Supervisor Nurse, Medical-Surgical or Supervisor Nurse, Pediatrics. Specialized duties will be required by the specialized section.

Job Duties of Evening or Night Supervisor. Supervises and coordinates activities of nursing personnel on evening or night tour to maintain continuity for around-the-clock nursing care.

Visits nursing units to oversee nursing care and to ascertain condition of patients. Advises and assists nurses in administering new or unusual treatments. Gives advice for treatments, medications, and narcotics, in accordance with medical staff policies, in absence of physician. Arranges for emergency operations and reallocates personnel during emergencies. Admits or delegates admissions of new patients. Arranges for services of private-duty nurses. Determines necessity of calling physician. May perform some bedside nursing services.

Delegates preparation of reports covering such items as critically ill patients, new admissions, discharges or deaths, emergency situations encountered, and private-duty nurses employed. Informs supervisory personnel on ensuing tour of duty of patients' condition and hospital services rendered during work period.

Education, Training, and Experience. Graduation from an accredited school of nursing and current licensure by state board of nursing. Advanced education desirable. Experience as a head nurse, with demonstrated administrative, supervisory, and teaching abilities.

Specific Qualifications. The beginning supervisor should:

- Have at least five years experience as a head nurse.
- Be intelligent, capable of learning readily and of retaining the knowledge.
- Be able to convey knowledge to others in an understanding and interesting way.
- Be tolerant and understanding.
- Be objective.
- Be able, when necessary, to show authority without being too demanding and without losing the respect of subordinates.
- Have self-confidence and be able to gain the confidence of others.
- Have good physical and mental health.
- Be able to promote good public relations.
- Keep up with new trends in nursing and be able to convey this information to others.
- Be able to do new procedures and to use new equipment (as well as older methods) and to instruct others with clarity.
- Maintain interest in good nursing care.
- Know administrative regulations of the general hospital and how they apply to self and coworkers.
- Give support where needed and a helping hand at times.
- Set the climate for cooperation between coworkers and shifts for a smooth-running institution.[1]

Head Nurse

Head nurses direct and supervise nursing staff in provision of nursing care and ensure the avail-

_____
[1]Betty J. Robinson, "Supervision As I See It," *Supervisor Nurse*, October 1974.

ability of support services which facilitate this care. The first-line nurse administrator serves as a resource to staff, interpreting philosophy, goals, standards, policies, and procedures. The head nurse participates in varying degrees in policy formation and decision making with other members of nursing administration. These administrators are the vital link between nursing management and the staff that delivers care to the client. Head nurses are responsible for delivering care that is therapeutically effective and safe as well as cost-effective. They accomplish this by effective utilization of resources through the administrative process. Usually a head nurse is responsible for a nursing unit.[1]

Activities that received the most votes by head nurses as most representative of their responsibilities were identified in one survey:[2]

- Supervises and coordinates all patient care on the unit, including communication with physicians.
- Assumes 24-hour responsibility for the unit.
- Confronts and resolves conflicts involving staff, physicians, patients, and personnel.
- Schedules daily activities of the unit, including assignment planning, scheduled meal and break time, and conferences.
- Provides feedback to each employee on a planned basis, including a yearly observation.
- Meets regularly with nursing administration for feedback and problem solving.
- Aids in the implementation of new policies and procedures.
- Implements, evaluates, and revises plans to meet unit goals.

Education, Training, and Experience. Graduation from an accredited school of nursing and current licensure by state board of nursing. Advanced preparation in the clinical specialty, ward management, principles of supervision, and teaching is preferred.

Experience as a professional nurse, with demonstrated administrative and supervisory potential.

CLINICAL NURSE SPECIALIST

Overview*

Clinical nurse specialists have master's degrees and clinical preparation in a subspecialty such as cardiovascular care, pulmonary care, critical care, or adult health care. Traditionally, the position of clinical nurse specialist has been a staff position rather than a line position. As a staff position, clinical nurse specialists have acquired authority by their professional knowledge, experience, and expertise. They do not have authority over other personnel, as one does in a line position.

A clinical nurse specialist is often responsible to the director of nursing or a division director. In institutions where there is more than one clinical nurse specialist, a different organizational structure may be appropriate.

For example, although the clinical nurse specialist may be responsible to the director of the critical care division and spends a majority of time in activities specifically for the division, this organizational structure does not restrict the clinical nurse specialist to only critical care division activities. Specialists may (upon request) conduct programs related to their specialty in other divisions, contribute to departmentwide projects, or participate on committees within the school of nursing.

Graduate programs that prepare clinical nurse specialists have identified five role components: clinician, consultant, administrator, teacher, and researcher. The functional role of the clinical nurse specialist is greatly dependent on the individual and the employment situation.

Teacher. It seems that the majority of clinical specialists spend most of their time in some form

[1]Committee to Renew Roles, Responsibilities, and Qualifications of Nursing Administrators, "Roles, Responsibilities, and Qualifications for Nurse Administrators," American Nurses' Association, 1978.

[2]Linda Dixon Stahl, Janice Johnson Querin, Ellen B. Rudy, and Mary Ann Crawford, "Head Nurses' Activities and Supervisors' Expectations: The Research," *Journal of Nursing Administration*, June 1983. Reprinted with permission.

*Source: Arlene N. Hayne and Zeila W. Bailey, *Nursing Administration of Critical Care*, Aspen Publishers, Inc., © 1982.

of education involving either staff or patients. Often the staff development department is understaffed, overworked, or not able to meet the specific needs of the critical care nurses. For example, the clinical nurse specialist is particularly beneficial in a critical care division in planning and implementing education programs for the staff. Because of the nature of critical care units, nurses working in these areas have a greater depth of knowledge and skill in a particular subspecialty. These nurses therefore have knowledge and clinical educational needs that require the advance knowledge and preparation of a clinical nurse specialist. The clinical nurse specialist with education or experience in cardiovascular or pulmonary nursing should be able to make the transition to critical care clinical specialist with little difficulty.

Clinician. The clinician role component has been implemented in different ways by clinical nurse specialists over the past ten years. Some maintain a case load of patients in direct care relationships. The rationale for this approach is to serve as a role model to staff. In reality, often a small group of patients receive high-quality but expensive care, because the influence of the clinical nurse specialist is limited in this matter. The clinical nurse specialist functioning in this manner can lead to staff nurse resentment and nurse administrator frustration. The times when the expert skills are desirable in direct patient care are: for meeting the specific needs of a patient, for evaluating patient care, for teaching or research purposes, or for furthering specialist knowledge and skills.

The clinical nurse specialist does serve as role model and clinical teacher. Being available and having a rapport with staff nurses results in the practitioner consulting with the clinical nurse specialist. This can facilitate growth in the staff in assessment and problem solving related to patient care. In this way the clinical nurse specialist is a catalyst for broad systems' change, which results in higher quality of care to the critical care patients. It is not the goal of the clinical nurse specialist to be a ''super'' nurse but to assist in the development of super nurses. The specialist is continually analyzing health care practices to identify areas where change may improve patient care.

Consultant. To be effective as consultants, clinical nurse specialists must establish themselves as approachable experts. They develop a rapport with nursing staff and other departments and are consulted by physicians, nurse leaders in the organization, as well as the staff. They may also serve as consultants for other hospitals.

Researcher. The researcher component is emphasized in the graduate program and implemented by clinical nurse specialists in a variety of ways that are determined by the needs of the institution. Often this is informal rather than formal research.

Administrator. The administrator role is at times implemented by utilizing a line position; however, these individuals have an administrative component in a staff position. Clinical nurse specialists are responsible for setting goals and objectives. They work with the leaders in the division to facilitate accomplishing unit and division goals. They participate on committees and serve as chairpersons on organization committees. They contribute to the evaluation process of staff through a patient care coordinator. They are involved in the decision-making process of the organization, including the development of policies and procedures that affect the quality of patient care.

Qualifications for CNS Title*

Clinical Nurse Specialist is the job title usually reserved for nurses who have earned a master's degree in nursing and have become highly skilled clinicians (see Table 8-1 for certification designations for clinical and other nurse specialists). Nevertheless, through experience, the nurse clinician title may be awarded to nurses who demonstrate a high degree of clinical acumen with or without advanced academic preparation. For example, the qualifications may read:

1. Has a Bachelor of Science in Nursing *or* certification in area of clinical expertise *or* Master of Science in Nursing with no post-

Source: Julianne Morath, ''Putting Leaders, Consultants, and Teachers On the Line,'' *Nursing Management*, January 1983. Reprinted with permission.

Table 8–1 Nurse Specialty Certification Designations

If your specialty area is:	Your designation will be:
Community Health Nurse Adult Nurse Practitioner Family Nurse Practitioner School Nurse Practitioner Gerontological Nurse Gerontological Nurse Practitioner Maternal and Child Health Nurse Child and Adolescent Nurse Pediatric Nurse Practitioner High-Risk Perinatal Nurse Medical-Surgical Nurse Psychiatric and Mental Health Nurse	R.N., C.—Registered Nurse, Certified

Clinical Specialist in Medical-Surgical Nursing
Clinical Specialist in Adult Psychiatric and
    Mental Health Nursing
Clinical Specialist in Child and Adolescent
    Psychiatric and Mental Health Nursing
	R.N., C.S.—Registered Nurse, Certified
	Specialist

Nursing Administration	R.N., C.N.A.—Registered Nurse, Certified in Nursing Administration
Nursing Administration, Advanced	R.N., C.N.A.A.—Registered Nurse, Certified in Nursing Administration, Advanced

Source: *The Measure of Distinction among Professionals: Certification Catalog,* American Nurses' Association, © 1985. Reprinted with permission.

master's clinical experience *or* other demonstrated recognition of clinical expertise.

2. Five years experience in clinical nursing with at least two of these five years in area of clinical expertise (exception—MSN with no post-master's clinical experience).
3. Has the ability to establish and maintain good interpersonal relationships and communications.
4. Demonstrates the ability to accept and implement change.
5. Has consultative ability and skills.
6. Has teaching ability and skills.
7. Has an attitude of clinical inquiry.
8. Shows evidence of continuing professional growth; membership in a professional nursing organization is desirable.
9. Is able to work flexible hours as needed.

This, of course, can be adapted to any nursing department. It is possible that a master's-pre-

pared nurse may not be available in every community, but probably every hospital has nurses who excel in providing care and demonstrating leadership among their colleagues. Those valued characteristics can be described in behavioral terms and serve as position criteria, thereby outlining performance levels for staff to aspire to and to be recognized when they are achieved.

OTHER NURSE SPECIALISTS*

Clinical Coordinator, Nursing Service

The major responsibilities of this position are directly to the director of the department of nursing.

_____

Source: Russell C. Swansburg, *Management of Patient Care Services,* C.V. Mosby Co., © 1976. Reprinted with permission of the author.

- Coordinates activities with all hospital services and families in providing for the patients' total needs; directly supervises charge nurses of inpatient units.
- Makes walk-through rounds and observes all patients—visits all seriously ill, very seriously ill, and other patients reported on the 24-hour report.
- Assists in providing adequate staffing for all inpatient units.
- Serves as advisor and resource person for nursing personnel on duty as needed.
- Advises committees as designated by the chairperson of the department of nursing.
- Performs weekly rounds using checklist:
  a. Sees that medications are secure and that pouring of medications is done at time due.
  b. Checks ward alcoholic and narcotic register book.
  c. Reviews list of nurses proficient in intravenous medication administration.
  d. Checks biologicals:
     —Checks documentation of temperature of refrigeration unit.
     —Checks to see that thermometer is present.
     —Checks discarding of outdated drugs.
     —Checks dating of open vials.
- Performs PRN checklist:
  a. Checks admission schedules; coordinates with admission and discharge clerk on bed availability.
  b. Reviews time schedules every two weeks as submitted.
  c. Coordinates scheduling of personnel for courses and programs such as race relations.
  d. Reviews nursing licenses: registration number, state, expiration date.

Charge Nurse—Clinics

General Therapy Clinic

- Assesses and identifies patients' health problems and needs.
- Assists with or initiates emergency lifesaving procedures.

- Provides health teaching for patients and families.
- Assists with research related to the improvement of the delivery of health care services.

Surgical Clinic

- Plans, organizes, directs, coordinates, and evaluates all nursing functions in the surgical specialty clinics.
- Screens patients and refers them to appropriate physicians, clinical specialists, or hospital departments.
- Identifies patients' nursing care needs and problems and practices nursing to meet established goals.
- Maintains accurate records of nursing assessments, plans, and care.
- Is self-directing in practice; makes professional judgments, counsels and teaches patients, families, and coworkers.

Obstetrical-Gynecological Clinic

- Directs and coordinates all nursing activities in the obstetrical-gynecological clinic.
- Provides health services, which include health education, maintenance, prevention, and early case finding.
- Plays an important role in interpretation of treatment, making diagnostic reports, giving emergency care, taking patients' histories, and initiating charts.

Superintendent of the Department of Nursing—Outpatient Clinics

The major responsibilities of this position are to the chairperson of the department of nursing.

- Assigns nursing technician personnel and provides adequate staffing of all outpatient clinics.
- Supervises all nursing technicians assigned to the outpatient clinics where there are no charge nurses.

- Inspects clinics daily and identifies the necessity for rotation of personnel in general therapy clinic and emergency room, for training, and for adjusting schedules to provide for competent patient care at all times.
- Keeps supervisors informed of special abilities of technicians or other pertinent items of special interest.

Charge Nurse—Anesthesia

- Supervises, directs, and controls the staffing assignments of nurse anesthetists to ensure 24-hour daily coverage.
- Maintains adequate levels of drugs, anesthetic agents, and supplies used in the treatment of patients.
- Assists in the anesthesia training of dental and surgical interns and residents.
- Is supervised directly by the chief of the anesthesiology service.

Charge Nurse—Central Sterile Supply

- Manages central nursing sterile supply service, including the management of personnel over a 24-hour period.
- Plans, directs, and coordinates all activities relating to the procurement, processing, storage, and distribution of supplies and equipment needed to give patient care efficiently and safely.

EDUCATIONAL POSITIONS*

Director of Staff Development
(In-service–Education Coordinator)

Job Duties. Plans, develops, and directs program of education for all hospital nursing service personnel, and coordinates staff development with nursing service program.

Develops, schedules, and directs orientation program for professional and auxiliary nursing

---

*Source: Job Descriptions and Organizational Analysis for Hospitals and Related Health Services, U.S. Training and Employment Service, Department of Labor, 1971.

service personnel. Develops instructional materials to assist new personnel in becoming oriented to hospital operational techniques. If not scheduled by personnel department, schedules hospital tours and addresses by administrative staff to acquaint new personnel with overall operation and interrelationship of hospital services. Determines effectiveness of orientation materials and procedures through practice sessions. Sets up demonstrations of nursing service equipment to acquaint hospital staff with new equipment and make them more familiar with established equipment.

Plans, coordinates, and conducts regular and special in-service training sessions for hospital nursing staff to acquaint them with new procedures and policies and new trends and developments in patient care techniques and to provide opportunity for individual members to develop to their full potential.

Keeps current on latest developments by attending professional seminars and institutes and reading professional journals. Assists supervisors and head nurses in planning and implementing staff development programs in their units. Keeps bulletin boards current by listing information on seminars and institutes and promotes appropriate staff attendance at these professional meetings. Plans training sessions for supervisory staff members.

May participate with committees in writing and maintaining policy and procedure manuals and nursing service forms. Reviews suggestions submitted by nursing service staff for changes or clarification in policies and procedures.

Writes annual reports on activities and prepares plans for future activities. Prepares budget requests.

Education, Training, and Experience. Graduation from an accredited school of nursing and current licensure by state board of nursing; graduation from a recognized college or university with specialization in education; bachelor's degree required. Experience as head nurse, supervisor nurse, or nurse educator.

It would be a positive advantage for the director of staff development to have had professional experiences that would encompass clinical, teaching, and supervisory practice within a large active nursing service organization. It is important that the director be "service minded" and familiar with the needs and problems of service personnel. The director should have a broad and thorough knowledge of nursing skills that would enable him or her to appraise the quality of nursing care being given as well as to assess the abilities enabling an individual nursing practitioner to meet the expectations of a specific job.

Nurse Educator

Job Duties. Plans, coordinates, and carries out educational programs (theoretical and practical aspects of nursing) to train ancillary nursing personnel.

Prepares and issues trainee manuals (which describe duties and responsibilities of nursing assistants) to be used as training guides. Familiarizes new employees with physical layout of hospital and hospital policies and procedures, organizational structure, hospital etiquette, and employee benefits. Plans educational program and schedules classes in basic patient care procedures, such as bedmaking, blood-pressure and temperature taking, and feeding of patients. Teaches nursing aides and orderlies nursing procedures by demonstration in classrooms and clinical units and by lectures in classrooms, using such aids as motion pictures, charts, and slides. Observes trainees in practical application of procedures. Secures cooperation of supervisors and head nurses to assist in teaching their specialty; coordinates training with all nursing service units to maintain consistency in practice and establish relationships, to give scope to the educational program, and to point out variations of duties required by different units and on different shifts.

Prepares, administers, and scores examinations to determine trainees' suitability for the job. Makes recommendations to nursing service regarding placement of trainees according to test scores and practical application performance. Evaluates trainees' progress following training period and submits report to nursing service for further processing. Conducts meetings with trainees and with supervisors to discuss problems and ideas for improving nursing service training program.

Education, Training, and Experience. Graduation from an accredited school of nursing and current licensure by state board of nursing; advanced training in teaching methods and supervision.

One year's experience as head nurse or supervisor nurse.

Nursing Instructor: In-service

Job Duties. Plans, directs, and coordinates in-service orientation and educational program for professional nursing personnel.

Assists director of staff development in planning and carrying out program of staff development. Confers with director of staff development to schedule training programs for professional nurses already on the staff, according to departmental work requirements. Lectures to nurses and demonstrates improved methods of nursing service. Lectures and demonstrates procedures, using motion pictures, charts, and slides.

Orients new staff members and provides in-service refresher training for professional nurses returning to hospital nursing service.

Instructs volunteer workers in routine procedures such as aseptic practice and blood-pressure and temperature taking.

Education, Training, and Experience. Graduation from an accredited school of nursing and current licensure by state board of nursing; advanced training in teaching methods and supervision.

One year's experience as head nurse or supervisor nurse.

STAFF POSITIONS*

Expanded Role Nurses**

Initially, an expanded role for nurses referred to the assumption of responsibilities previously

---

*Source: Except where noted, all job descriptions in this section are from *Job Descriptions and Organizational Analysis for Hospitals and Related Health Services*, U.S. Training and Employment Service, Department of Labor, 1971.

**Source: Adapted from Hedy Freyone Mechanic, "Redefining the Expanded Role," *Nursing Outlook*, vol. 36, no. 6, November-December 1988.

associated with medical practice: obtaining health histories, performing physical examinations, ordering laboratory studies, making referrals, and the medical management of patients, including prescribing medications. Nurses from varying entry-level educational backgrounds were prepared for the expanded role through postbasic continuing education programs consisting of six to nine months of classroom work and clinical practice. Nurses practicing in the expanded role worked under medical supervision and medical authority. Today, however, the scope of contemporary nursing practice has made aspects of the original model obsolete.

A main feature of the original model of the expanded role was health assessment, which included performing physical examinations and obtaining health histories. Today, physical examination is taught in virtually every baccalaureate nursing program in the United States. Whatever the practice area, data collection using skills in physical examination and health history has become the cornerstone of nursing process and the first essential step in the professional standards of practice.

These skills can now be considered part of the "core" of practice or "common practice." Similarly, other activities, such as monitoring the course of an illness, interpreting laboratory or screening data, health teaching, counseling, initiating referrals, listening to and distinguishing normal from abnormal lung sounds, or administering prescribed IV medications, can all be considered established or "common" areas of practice and within the scope of practice. All of the myriad activities associated with a nurse's role constitute established and legally authorized areas within a nurse's scope of practice; however, nurses who do not possess the necessary knowledge and skills should not perform these activities.

Because of shared bodies of knowledge and practice skills, some areas of practice interface or overlap with other disciplines. Examples of this are health teaching and counseling, anticipatory guidance, and emotional support. Activities arising from shared bodies of knowledge require no protocols, special authority, or interdisciplinary supervision.

There are situations, however, in which an area of overlapping practice clearly belongs in the domain of one profession. When nurses perform activities previously considered to be exclusively within the medical domain, this constitutes practice within the extended role. For example, during emergency situations critical care nurses are permitted to defibrillate patients.

New Model for Defining the Expanded Role

A nurse practices in the expanded role in three ways. First, both in health promotion and protection and during episodes of illness, nurses view clients and their health concerns from an integrated multisystem perspective and intervene from this perspective in assuming primary care responsibility. Second, they maintain a collegial and collaborative relationship with other health team members. Third, acting with autonomy and authority, nurses assume full accountability for their actions. Collegiality extends beyond relating on a first-name basis or consulting with each other on case management. It centers on recognizing each other's authority and autonomy over practice. By licensing an individual, society establishes that both the individual and the profession are responsible and accountable for all aspects of their practice, including all acts of omission or commission. Accountability can be fostered in the practice setting through intra- and interdisciplinary peer review.

Generalist and Specialist Practice in the Expanded Role

The central prerequisite is educational preparation. Nurses cannot practice in expanded roles if they hold narrow conceptualizations and understanding of the health issues confronting clients or if they perceive intervention primarily within a disease-oriented framework.

Generalist practice in the expanded role must begin at the baccalaureate level to meet the demands of the role. Similarly, advanced practice within a multisystem framework, with adjunct skills for practice in the extended role, requires in-depth theoretical knowledge, advanced clinical skills, and expertise that is attainable only through clinical specialization at the master's level.

Distinguishing between practice in the expanded role and advanced practice as a specialist also raises the issues of licensure and credentialing. If the expanded role requires educational preparation attainable only at the baccalaureate level, then licensing examinations and licensure must reflect this.

Redefining the expanded role with concomitant changes in licensure and credentialing has implications for reimbursement. As currently structured, certification and third-party reimbursement requirements limit direct access to insurance carriers to nurses certified as "nurse practitioners" who are practicing in "expanded roles." In contrast, regardless of educational preparation, knowledge level, degree of clinical expertise, or certification achievements, clinical nurse specialists and nurse generalists with certified advanced competencies are ineligible for direct reimbursement. In effect, the current narrow and restrictive definition of the expanded role limits nurses' potential for third-party reimbursement to a select few. A redefinition of the expanded role and a restructuring of credentialing mechanisms that demonstrate advanced competencies at both the generalist and the specialist level could potentially increase direct reimbursement opportunities for nurses.

Staff Nurse

Job Duties. Renders professional nursing care to patients within an assigned unit of a hospital, in support of medical care as directed by medical staff and pursuant to objectives and policies of the hospital.

Performs nursing techniques for the comfort and well-being of the patient. Prepares equipment and assists physician during treatments and examinations of patients. Administers prescribed medications, orally and by injections; provides treatments using therapeutic equipment; observes patients' reactions to medications and treatments; observes progress of intravenous infusions and subcutaneous infiltrations; changes or assists physician in changing dressings and cleaning wounds or incisions; takes temperature, pulse, respiration rate, blood pressure, and heart beat to detect deviations from normal and gauge progress of patient, following

physician's orders and approved nursing care plan. Observes, records, and reports to supervisor or physician patients' condition and reaction to drugs, treatments, and significant incidents.

Maintains patients' medical records on nursing observations and actions taken, such as medications and treatments given, reactions, tests, intake and emission of liquids and solids, temperature, pulse, and respiration rate. Records nursing needs of patients on nursing care plan to ensure continuity of care.

Observes emotional stability of patients, expresses interest in their progress, and prepares them for continuing care after discharge. Explains procedures and treatments ordered to gain patients' cooperation and allay apprehension.

Rotates on day, evening, and night tours of duty and may be asked to rotate among various clinical and nursing services of institution. Each service will have specialized duties, and staff nurse may be known by the section to which assigned, such as Staff Nurse, Obstetrics or Staff Nurse, Pediatrics. May serve as a team leader for a group of personnel rendering nursing care to a number of patients.

Assists in planning, supervising, and instructing licensed practical nurses, nursing aides, orderlies, and students. Demonstrates nursing techniques and procedures, and assists nonprofessional nursing care personnel in rendering nursing care in unit.

May assist with operations and deliveries by preparing rooms; sterilizing instruments, equipment, and supplies; and handing them, in order of use, to surgeon or other medical specialist.

Education, Training, and Experience. Graduation from an accredited school of nursing and current licensure by state board of nursing.

Orientation training in specific unit only; no experience required beyond that obtained in school of nursing.

Licensed Practical Nurse/Licensed Vocational Nurse

Job Duties. Performs a wide variety of patient care activities and accommodative services for assigned hospital patients, as directed by the head nurse and/or team leader (see Table 8-2).

Performs assigned nursing procedures for the comfort and well-being of patients, such as assisting in admission of new patients, bathing and feeding patients, making beds, helping patients into and out of bed. Takes patients' temperature, blood pressure, pulse, and respiration, and records results on patients' charts. Collects specimens, such as sputum and urine, in containers, labels containers, and sends to laboratory for analysis. Dresses wounds, adminis-

ters prescribed procedures, such as enemas, douches, alcohol rubs, and massages. Applies compresses, ice bags, and hot water bottles. Observes patients for reaction to drugs, treatment, cyanosis, weak pulse, excessive respiratory rate, or any other unusual condition, and reports adverse reactions to head nurse or staff nurse. Administers specified medication, and notes time and amount on patients' charts. Assembles and uses such equipment as catheters, tracheotomy tubes, and oxygen supplies. Drapes or gowns patients for various types

---

Table 8-2 LPN/LVN Competencies

NAPNES has developed a statement on entry level competencies for practical/vocational nurses. This statement was approved by the Board of Directors in August 1980.

Competencies of licensed practical/vocational nurses who have progressed beyond the entry level will depend on motivation, clinical experiences, and continuing education and should be assessed on an individual basis.

1. Assessment
   Uses basic communication skills in a structured care setting.
   Obtains specific information from patients through goal-directed interviews.
   Participates in the identification of physical, emotional, spiritual, cultural, and overt learning needs of patients by collecting appropriate data.
   Analyzes data collected in relation to patients' pathophysiology.

2. Planning
   Determines priorities and plans nursing care accordingly.
   Formulates and/or collaborates in developing written nursing care plans.
   Participates in developing preventive or long-term health plans for patients and/or families.

3. Implementation
   Protects the rights and dignity of patients and families.
   Utilizes basic communication skills in a structured care setting.
   Safely performs therapeutic and preventive nursing procedures, incorporating fundamental biological and psychological principles in giving individualized care.

Observes patients and communicates significant findings to the health care team.
Does incidental teaching and supports and reinforces the teaching plan for a specific patient and/or family.

4. Evaluation
   Evaluates, with guidance if necessary, the care given and makes necessary adjustments.
   Records evaluations of the results of nursing actions.
   Identifies own strengths and weaknesses and seeks assistance for improvement of performance.

5. Professional Responsibilities
   Recognizes the LP/VN's role in the health care delivery system and articulates that role with those of other health care team members.
   Maintains accountability for own nursing practice within ethical and legal framework.
   Serves as a patient advocate.
   Accepts role in maintaining and developing standards of practice in providing patient care.
   Participates in nursing organizations.
   Seeks further growth through educational opportunities.

Source: "What Should Practical Nurses Be Able To Do," *Journal of Practical Nursing*, November-December, 1980. Reprinted with permission.

of examinations. Assists patients to walk about unit as permitted, or transports patients by wheelchair to various departments. Records food and fluid intake and emission. Sterilizes equipment and supplies, using germicides, sterilizer, or autoclave. Answers patients' call signals, and assists staff nurse or physician in advanced medical treatments. Assists in the care of deceased persons.

May specialize in work of a particular patient care unit and be known by the name of that unit, such as Licensed Practical Nurse, Recovery Room or Licensed Practical Nurse, Psychiatrics.

May be required to work rotating shifts.

Education, Training, and Experience. High school graduation plus graduation from a recognized one-year practical nurse program. Must pass state board of nursing licensing examination.

Nursing Aide (Nurse Aide, Nursing Assistant)

Job Duties. performs various patient care activities and related nonprofessional services necessary in caring for the personal needs and comfort of patients.

Answers signal lights and bells to determine patients' needs. Bathes, dresses, and undresses patients and assists with personal hygiene to increase their comfort and well-being. May serve and collect food trays, feed patients requiring help, and provide between-meal nourishment and fresh drinking water, when indicated. Transports patients to treatment units, using wheelchair or wheeled carriage, or helps them to walk. Drapes patients for examinations and treatments; remains with patients, performing such duties as holding instruments and adjusting lights. Takes and records temperature, pulse, respiration rate, and food intake and output, as directed. May apply ice bags and hot water bottles. Gives alcohol rubs. Reports all unusual conditions or reactions to nurse in charge. May assemble equipment and supplies in preparation for various diagnostic or treatment procedures performed by physicians or nurses.

Tidies patients' rooms and cares for flowers. Changes bed linen, runs errands, directs visitors,

and answers telephone. Collects charts, records, and reports, delivers them to authorized personnel. Collects and bags soiled linen and stores clean linen. May clean, sterilize, store, and prepare treatment trays and other supplies used in the unit. May be known by unit or section of hospital to which assigned, such as Nursing Aide, Psychiatric or Nursing Aide, Nursery, where special duties required by patients are performed.

May be required to work rotating shifts.

Education, Training, and Experience. High school graduation preferred.

Hospital-conducted on-the-job training programs. To work in some departments, additional training is given.

Orderly (Nursing Assistant, Male)

Job Duties. Assists nursing service personnel by performing a variety of duties for patients (usually male) and certain heavy duties in the care of the physically or mentally ill and the mentally retarded.

Performs same job duties as nursing aide.

Education, Training, and Experience. High school graduation preferred.

Hospital-conducted on-the-job training programs. For work in some departments, additional training is given.

The Patient Care Technician*

The patient care technician (PCT) has been conceived of as a nonlicensed individual to perform repetitive technical tasks. The position is designed to double the hands of the RN and extend his or her ability to meet patients' needs. The PCT works under the direct supervision of an RN, and the two function as a team for a

---

*Source: Marjorie Splaine Wiggins, Judith M. Farias, and Judith R. Miller, "The Role of the Patient Care Technician at the New England Deaconess Hospital," in *Patient Care Delivery Models*, Gloria Gilbert Mayer, Mary Jane Madden, and Eunice Lawrenz, eds., Aspen Publishers, Inc., © 1990.

group of assigned patients. The PCT can perform multiple technical tasks, but the nurse is still fully responsible and accountable for the patients' care. For example, the PCT may perform simple to moderately complex dressing changes, but the nurse is required to observe and assess the status of each patient's wound and initiate appropriate interventions. The assignment of the task has the potential of saving hundreds of RN hours on a unit that has a high surgical census and numerous dressing changes. Other tasks performed by the PCT include tube feedings, ostomy care, catheterization, removal of skin staples, and basic hygiene measures. Each task delegated to the PCT by the RN is reviewed for appropriateness before the task is assigned.

In addition to technical tasks, the PCT assists patients with activities of daily living and performs all the jobs related to patient care that were previously carried out by the nursing assistant. The addition of new skills and training at the PCT level has in essence provided the nursing assistant with an opportunity for advancement.

The RN must be made aware that the full responsibility for the nursing care of the patient remains with him or her and may not be delegated to a nonnurse. With the exception of recording vital signs and limited flow sheet documentation of activities of daily living and tasks performed, the RN is responsible for documenting all nursing observations, care delivered, and responses to interventions in the patient's medical record.

NONNURSING JOBS*

Some nursing administrators have sought relief from responsibilities that fall outside of direct patient care by inserting a nonnursing person into the nursing service organizational structure—the unit supervisor. The unit supervisor is intended to provide administrative direction in the patient unit while the nursing staff retain full control over patient care.

---

*Source: Job Descriptions and Organizational Analysis for Hospitals and Related Health Services, U.S. Training and Employment Service, Department of Labor, 1971.

Unit Supervisor

Job Duties. Supervises and coordinates administrative management functions for one or more patient care units.

Supervises clerical staff and ensures accomplishment of administrative functions on a 24-hour basis by scheduling working hours and arranging for coverage of nursing care unit by nonnursing personnel. Performs personnel-management tasks by orienting and training new personnel. Evaluates performance of assigned workers by checking for quality and quantity.

Inventories and stores patients' personal effects either within the unit or in the hospital vault.

Establishes and maintains an adequate inventory of drugs and supplies for that unit.

Coordinates with other departments such as housekeeping and maintenance to maintain a unit that is hygienically safe and functional. Checks for cleanliness of the unit and reports discrepancies to the appropriate supervisor. Performs daily maintenance inspection, and through proper channels initiates minor facility improvement projects.

Maintains close contact with medical and surgical reservations in regard to admissions, transfers, discharges, and other services. Serves as liaison between the specific patient care unit and other departments. Reviews special tests at the end of shift.

Ensures that the medical record is completed in accordance with the standards of the Joint Commission on Accreditation of Healthcare Organizations. Ensures hospital compliance with Medicare requirements insofar as certification and related administrative matters are concerned. Checks charts of patients scheduled for surgery or other special procedures to verify completeness of orders of consent, preparation orders, and lab results and for necessary signatures.

Greets, directs, and gives nonprofessional factual information to patients, visitors, and personnel from other departments.

Participates in projects, surveys, and other information-gathering activities approved by hospital management.

Education, Training, and Experience. One year of college or equivalent.

A minimum of one year's supervisory experience.

On-the-job training in coordinating nonnursing services for the assigned nursing units.

Unit Clerk (Floor Clerk, Nursing Station Assistant)

Job Duties. Performs general clerical duties by preparing, compiling, and maintaining records in a hospital nursing unit.

Records name of patient, address, and name of attending physician on medical record forms. Copies information, such as patients' temperature, pulse rate, and blood pressure, from nurses' records. Writes requisitions for laboratory tests and procedures such as basal metabolism, X-ray, EKG, blood examinations, and urinalysis. Under supervision, plots temperature, pulse rate, and other data on appropriate graph charts. Copies and computes other data, as directed, and enters on patients' charts. May record diet instructions. Keeps file of medical records on patients in unit. Routes charts when patients are transferred or dismissed, following specified procedures. May compile census of patients.

Keeps record of absences and hours worked by unit personnel. Types various records, schedules, and reports and delivers them to appropriate office. May maintain records of special monetary charges to patients and forward them to the business office. May verify stock supplies on unit and prepare requisitions to maintain established inventories. Dispatches messages to other departments or to persons in other departments and makes appointments for patient services in other departments as requested by nursing staff. Makes posthospitalization appointments with patients' physicians. Delivers mail, newspapers, and flowers to patients.

Education, Training, and Experience. High school graduation or equivalent, including courses in English, typing, spelling, and arithmetic, or high school graduation supplemented by commercial school course in subjects indicated.

No previous experience is required.

On-the-job training in practices and procedures of the hospital and certain medical terminology.

VOLUNTEERS

Many hospitals are the grateful recipients of donated labor, to the extent that more and more hospitals deem it necessary to hire paid directors to coordinate and develop in-service volunteer programs.

There has, however, been a shift in the nature of the manpower resources and the focus of auxiliary groups. The traditional volunteer, the unemployed woman with leisure time and "giving" impulses, now seeks a sense of personal fulfillment and the opportunity to update skills in preparation for entry into the job market. In her place is an abundant supply of persons who receive volunteer-release time from large corporations, teenagers, and the retired, referrals from vocational schools and courts, and persons who themselves have been recipients of volunteer services.

Auxiliaries, freed from the management of volunteer programs by paid directors, are now transferring their attention to larger issues, asserting influence on community relations, legislation, and educational affairs. Auxiliaries are forming study committees, tracking the progress of health-related legislation, organizing appropriate letterwriting campaigns to state representatives, and arranging talk sessions between hospital personnel and congressional representatives. An alert administrator will recognize this development and make use of this group as hospital advocates.

Organizing a Volunteer Service

In organizing a volunteer service in the nursing department, AHA recommends applying the basic principles of management:[1]

- Spell out the objectives of the service. What is the service expected to accomplish?

---

[1] "Practical Approaches to Nursing Service Administration," American Hospital Association, Fall 1965.

Major objectives might be to assist in direct nursing care of patients, or to provide a "visitor" service, or to assist with indirect patient care services. Objectives provide direction and a means of measuring success. To be effective, objectives should be formulated and accepted by both volunteers and the nursing service.

- Utilize a director of volunteers. Either a hospital staff member or a volunteer should be selected by the director of nursing to hold major "charge" responsibilities: to assist in recruiting and in maintaining a competent, satisfied volunteer staff. The role involves participation in policymaking, interpretation of regulations, orientation of new volunteers, schedule formation, and recordkeeping. Reports and recommendations are made to the director of nursing.

- Establish clear lines of authority. The volunteer should know to whom he or she is responsible and from whom he or she receives directions. This is usually the head nurse on the unit where the volunteer is assigned. However, the volunteer "in charge" is the coordinator of the service and is the person held accountable by the director of nursing for maintaining overall policies. To illustrate, if the policy of no-access to medical records is violated by the volunteer who is recording information at the request of the head nurse, the director of volunteers is obligated to take action.

- Determine the place of the volunteer in the organization of the unit. In some cases, assigning a volunteer to participate in conferences and become an integral part of a nursing team has been successful. In other situations, giving the volunteer specific assignments that serve more than one team has proved satisfactory. There is no one right method because many factors influence the way nursing is organized in a patient care unit. The important consideration is how the volunteer can be integrated into the existing pattern so that he or she will feel useful and needed and the nurses will be convinced that his or her service will benefit patients.

Functions of Volunteers

The functions of volunteers in the nursing department obviously relate to the objectives established for the service. In determining the functions of a volunteer service, keep in mind the following:

- It is the responsibility of the department of nursing to determine those functions which volunteers may perform.

- Head nurses and supervisors who are responsible for directing volunteers should participate in making decisions concerning functions. Disagreements on this fundamental issue could jeopardize the program itself.

- Differences among nursing units require adaptations. The volunteer is likely to perform different services in a surgical unit than in a pediatric or outpatient unit. Common functions and adaptations should be agreed upon and accepted as a total program.

- A written statement outlining the program should be given to all volunteers and should be available in the units where they work. In some hospitals, general policies, regulations, and other pertinent information about nursing service are included in this statement.

Chapter 9

Nursing Service Standards and Policies

NURSING SERVICE STANDARDS

Nursing service standards created by the various professional organizations and governmental agencies concerned with quality health care can be of immense value to the director of nursing by serving as a framework for departmental evaluations. The difficulty is in deciding which set of standards to use—though in some instances there is no choice. State and city regulations or the "voluntary" criteria linked to an accreditation process, as with the Joint Commission on Accreditation of Healthcare Organizations, are often backed by sanctions, legal or otherwise. The standards most often referred to by nursing administrators are those of the American Nurses' Association (ANA).

There are, however, an ever-increasing number of nursing specialty organizations that have been busy formulating practice standards in their area of expertise. A partial list of organizations who may be consulted for standards includes the American Association of Critical Care Nurses, American Association of Nurse Anesthetists, American Nephrology Nurses' Association, American Radiological Nurses Association, Association for Practitioners in Infection Control, Association of Operating Room Nurses, Inc., Association of Rehabilitation Nurses, Intravenous Nurses Society, Nursing Association of the American College of Ob-

stetrics and Gynecology, National Association of Neonatal Nurses, National Association of Orthopaedic Nurses, National Nurses Society on Addictions, Oncology Nursing Society, and Society of Gastroenterology Nurses and Associates, Inc.

The function of established standards is to supply professionally desirable norms against which the department's performance can be viewed. Once areas for improvement have been identified, the criteria continue to serve in setting directions for corrective action. The process is not complete until the decisions for improvement are transformed into a plan of action and implemented. And even later, at the time of reassessment, the original data collected can be used as a baseline for measuring progress against the standards.

ANA Standards for Nursing Services

According to the ANA, a profession must seek control of its practice in order to guarantee the quality of service to the public. Behind that guarantee are the standards of the profession that provide that the guarantee will be met. The ANA's Congress of Nursing Practice has been concerned with the development of nursing practice standards since the early 1970s, when the basic *Standards of Nursing Practice* and *Stand-*

ards of Medical Surgical Nursing Practice came out. In the last decade alone, the following standards related to hospital nursing practice were published: *Cardiovascular Nursing* (1981), *Perioperative* (1981), *Psychiatric-Mental Health* (1982), *Maternal-Child Health* (1983), *Child and Adolescent Psychiatric and Mental Health* (1985), *Rehabilitation Nursing* (1986), *Community Health Nursing* (1986), *Home Health* (1986), *Gerontological Nursing* (1987), *Hospice Nursing* (1987), *Oncology* (1987), *Practice for the Primary Health Care Nurse* (1987), and *Addictions Nursing Practice* (1988).

Following are the ANA standards for organized nursing services in hospitals, community health agencies, nursing homes, industry, schools, ambulatory services, and related health care organizations.

ANA Standards for Organized Nursing Services*

Standard I—The division of nursing has a philosophy and structure that ensure the delivery of high quality nursing care and provide means for resolving nursing practice issues throughout the health care organization.

Standard II—The division of nursing is administered by a qualified nurse executive who is a member of corporate administration.

Standard III—Policies and practices of the division of nursing provide for equality and continuity of nursing services that recognize cultural, economic, and social differences among patients of the health care organization.

Standard IV—The division of nursing ensures that the nursing process is used to design and provide nursing care to meet the individual needs of patients/clients in the context of their families.

Standard V—The division of nursing provides an environment that ensures the effectiveness of nursing practice.

Standard VI—The division of nursing ensures the development of educational programs to support the delivery of high quality nursing care.

Standard VII—The division of nursing initiates, utilizes, and participates in research studies or projects for the improvement of patient care.

Hospital Accreditation and Standards*

Health care professionals have always regarded evaluation as a necessary precursor to improvement. They have further recognized that evaluation must be based on well-developed standards and criteria—measures that allow self-assessment of current performance and provide guidance in attaining higher quality care. Voluntary accreditation of hospitals is a tangible reflection of this professional commitment.

Joint Commission Standards

The bedrock of the Joint Commission's accreditation process is its standards. Consisting of statements of measurable, quality-related expectations, the standards have continued to evolve over the years. A new edition of the *Accreditation Manual for Hospitals*, for example, is published each August. The standards are currently organized to reflect the responsibilities of a hospital's major organizational units in the performance of key quality-related processes. These activities engage governing bodies, managers, practitioners, and support staff, and they range from ongoing, objective evaluation and improvement in patient care to detection and control of infections. They also include assessment of individual clinical competence, accurate and timely recording of important patient care information, management of potentially dangerous material and equipment, and attention to the physical safety of the hospital environment.

Each of the standards has been subjected to a rigorous consensus-building process. These standards describe activities that, if performed well, should increase the probability that

---

*Source: *Standards for Organized Nursing Services*, American Nurses' Association, ANA Pub. No. NS-1, 1982. Reprinted with permission.

*Source: Joint Commission on Accreditation of Healthcare Organizations, *1986–1988 Hospital Accreditation Statistics*, © 1990 by the Joint Commission on Accreditation of Healthcare Organizations. Reprinted with permission.

patients will receive the maximum benefit that health care has to offer. Compliance with these standards does not, however, guarantee excellent or even acceptable care for any individual patient. It is also unreasonable to view a hospital that does not comply with any single standard or that exhibits unsatisfactory compliance with several standards as being unable to provide good, even exceptional, care to an individual patient. However, since outcomes are directly linked to structures and processes, compliance with Joint Commission standards that describe proven methods of providing quality care may increase the potential that a hospital will perform well.

It is also important to emphasize that Joint Commission standards are often intended to stimulate the hospital field to higher levels of performance in the interest of improved quality. Today, a hospital's willingness to adhere to national accreditation standards and to subject itself to rigorous evaluation reflects a substantial organizational commitment to quality.

Summary of Joint Commission Accreditation Standards for Nursing Services*

A nursing administrator's role is to understand the requirements, to communicate them, and to make certain the staff is in compliance with them.

Nursing Process. The standards require that the nursing assessment, planning, intervention, and evaluation provide individualized, goal-directed nursing care for all patients. Each patient's nursing needs are to be assessed by a registered nurse at the time of admission. Goals for treatment are to be set mutually with the patient and family, whenever possible, and are to be realistic, measurable, and consistent with the therapy prescribed by the responsible medical practitioner. The standards specify the required nursing documentation that is necessary to adequately reflect the status of the patient, as well as the need for documentation to be pertinent and concise.

A plan of care, reflecting current standards of nursing practice, is developed by a registered nurse, and is documented. It is revised as the needs of the patient change.

---

*Source: Ibid.

Coping with Standards

As a nursing administrator, you have two major functions: to know and understand Joint Commission requirements and be to sure your unit is in compliance with all of the standards. You should

1. Obtain a copy of the current Joint Commission requirements. Read the sections on nursing, quality assurance, and any other section cross-referenced under nursing in the index (also read special care units if applicable to you).
2. Based on Joint Commission requirements, develop a checklist to use at least monthly on head nurse rounds (or delegate to staff to do regularly; you do random checks).
3. Be sure your survey includes:

   - staffing and assignment requirements
   - nursing process documentation requirements
   - nursing care documentation requirements
   - education and training program requirements
   - policy and procedure requirements
   - quality assurance requirements

Source: Donna R. Sheridan, Jean E. Bronstein, and Duane D. Walker, *The New Nurse Manager: A Guide to Management Development*, Aspen Publishers, Inc., © 1984.

Nurse Licensure. All registered nurses, and other nursing personnel as required, must have a valid, current license at all times when they are providing care to patients.

The standards also provide that there be a mechanism to follow up on temporary licenses.

Nursing Direction and Staffing. The hospital must establish appropriate policies and procedures addressing the provision of nursing services. The standards provide that the nursing department/service be administered by a qualified registered nurse with appropriate education, experience, licensure, and demonstrated ability in nursing practice and administration.

There are also requirements for supervision of nursing care as well as for the qualifications of nursing personnel in the emergency, rehabilitation, surgical, anesthesia services, and special care units.

The standards outline the process the hospital must use to determine the appropriate levels of staffing required to meet the nursing needs of patients.

Monitoring and Evaluation of Nursing Services. These standards require that there be an ongoing, planned, and systematic process in place to monitor and evaluate the quality and appropriateness of patient care delivered by the nursing department/service.

The monitoring and evaluation should encompass all major clinical activities of the department. There should be routine collection of information about important aspects of care provided. The data should be periodically assessed, using clinically valid, objective criteria that reflect current knowledge and clinical experience. The standards provide that through ongoing monitoring, when opportunities to improve care or problems are identified, the staff must take action to address these issues and evaluate the effectiveness of the action. This process is the principal component of the quality assurance program of the hospital relating to nursing care.

NURSING SERVICE POLICIES

Policy Development*

There are three general areas in nursing that require policy formulation: (1) areas in which confusion about the locus of responsibility might result in neglect or malperformance of an act necessary to a patient's welfare; (2) areas pertaining to the protection of patients' and families' rights, e.g, right to privacy, property rights; and (3) areas involving matters of personnel management and welfare.

It is not necessary that policies always provide detailed directions for action on every issue.

---

*Source: M.M. Cantor, "Policies . . . Guidelines for Action," *Journal of Nursing Administration,* May-June 1972. Reprinted with permission.

Perhaps, for some issues, *specification of where the responsibility resides is the most pertinent consideration.*

Occasionally one hears that a policy is "just a guideline, not a rule calling for rigid enforcement." The implication seems to be that one can choose to follow a different course, that the policy is simply a suggestion. This might at least in part be reasonable at certain levels of functioning, but at others such an approach could generate chaos, particularly when the very reason for the existence of such policies may be to avoid the possibility of individual choice of action. The extent to which a policy will not be followed to the letter or might even be ignored entirely will likely depend on the difficulty of its implementation and the degree to which individuals are led to believe that departmental policies do not constitute mandatory matters.

If a policy is developed with attention to its feasibility within the actual setting, there should be little occasion for individuals to deviate from or ignore it. If the persons who have the information needed to make decisions in individual situations are given appropriate degrees of latitude, and those who are not equipped to deviate are given clear directions to follow explicitly, little difficulty should be experienced in maintaining strict implementation of policy.

Setting the expectation that a policy must be followed and holding to that expectation are essential for effective use of policies. If a policy is deemed necessary to achieve a particular purpose, then one ought to assume that it should be followed. If it appears not to matter whether or not individuals follow it, then one might well question the need for it.

There could be several reasons why a policy is not or cannot be implemented. If a policy fails to take into account the constraints within a situation then one can expect that it will not be implementable. A policy which requires isolation of individuals with wound infections would not be implemented on an area in which there exist no such accommodations. A policy which requires that only a registered nurse shall perform certain functions, when in fact registered nurses are not always available, is doomed from the beginning. The decision to change the policy to allow for discrepancies in the situation as opposed to modifying the situation so that the policy can be implemented is a serious one. One must be careful not to assume that, because a policy is not currently being implemented, the policy should necessarily be changed. If the situation is such that the policy as it stands is not implemented and that serious consequences might occur as a result, it would appear that the situation must be changed to ensure that the policy is followed.

The criteria by which one can judge the appropriateness of departmental policies have to do with the degree to which they facilitate the achievement of the goals of the department. Policies that do this will probably show the following characteristics:

1. The purposes of the policies can be stated in terms of the effects to be achieved as a result of their formulation and implementation.
2. The expected consequences of the policies can be shown to be instrumental in achieving the objectives of the department.
3. The content of the policies is directly related to their stated purposes and reflects the due consideration given to relevant factors in their formulation.
4. The amount of direction included is based on the level characterizing the position in which the implementation must occur.

Nursing Service: Mission, Philosophy, and Objectives*

Purpose or Mission

Each institution exists for a specific purpose or mission and to fulfill a specific social function. For health care institutions this means health care services to maintain health, cure illness, and allay pain and suffering.

Defining mission or purpose allows nursing to be managed for performance. It describes what it will be and what it should be. It describes the constituencies to be satisfied. It is the professional nurse manager's commitment to a specific definition of purpose or mission.

*Source: Russell C. Swansburg, *Management of Patient Care Services*, The C.V. Mosby Co., 1976. Reprinted with permission of the author.

Philosophy

Philosophy describes vision, what the nursing service manager sees the nursing service as and what he or she believes it to be. The written statement of philosophy explains the beliefs that determine how the mission or purpose is achieved; it gives direction to achieving purpose. Philosophy is abstract, and, with the mission or purpose statement, it sets the character and tone of service.

Objectives

Objectives are concrete and specific statements of the goals that the nurse manager of the department of nursing plans to accomplish. They are action commitments through which the mission or purpose will be achieved and the philosophy or beliefs sustained. They are used to establish priorities. They should be stated in terms of results to be achieved and should focus on the production of health care services to clients.

Objectives are similar to the philosophy of the department of nursing because both support the mission or purpose: Philosophy states beliefs and values, and objectives state specific and measurable goals to be accomplished. Both must be functional and useful—alive.

Areas for Objectives. Objectives are the fundamental strategy of nursing, since they are the end product of all nursing activities. They must be capable of being converted into specific targets and specific assignments so that nurses will know what they have to do to accomplish them. Objectives become the basis and motivation for the nursing work necessary to accomplish them and for measuring nursing achievement.

Management must balance objectives. Some will be short range, with their accomplishment in easy view or reach. Others will be long range, and some may even be in the "hope to be accomplished" target date timetable. The budget is the mechanical expression of setting and balancing objectives.

In nursing all objectives should be performance objectives. They should provide for existing nursing services for existing patient groups. They should provide for abandonment of unneeded and outmoded nursing services and health care products. They should provide for new nursing services and health care products for existing patients. They should provide for new groups of patients, for the distributive organization, and for standards of nursing service and performance.

Objectives are the basis for work and assignments. They determine the organizational structure, the key activities, and the allocation of people to tasks. Objectives make the work of nursing such that it is clear and unambiguous, the results are measurable, there are deadlines to be met, and there is a specific assignment of accountability. They give direction and make commitments that mobilize the resources and energies of nursing for the making of the future. Objectives are needed for the department and all wards or units. They should be changed as necessary, particularly when there is a change in mission or purpose or when they are no longer functional.

NURSING SERVICE POLICY MANUAL

Setting up a policy manual for the nursing service, and keeping it current, involves a lot of work, but the result is well worth the time and effort involved. Writing and organizing it require concentrated thought, and the result is usually clearer, more realistic policies. Since departmental policies must reflect the policies of the hospital the carefully thought out manual defines the scope of departmental responsibility within the hospital. The manual becomes a tool for orienting staff, a reference when unexpected problems arise, a foundation on which to develop administrative procedures, and a firm basis for discussion when differences occur. Conflicts and issues are easier to settle in terms of policy than in terms of personalities; the basis of the conflict becomes the point of discussion and not who is to blame for it.

Setting up a Policy Manual

Some manuals contain a combination of policies and administrative procedures. Others are limited to policies only. When the two are mixed, it is often difficult to be sure what is policy and what is procedure, and the manual may become bulky with lengthy instructions and sample forms. But whatever will work best for the individual department should be included.

Here are a few suggestions from AHA to keep in mind when writing policies and organizing them into a manual:

1. Use concise, simple language; keep it easy to understand and next to impossible to misunderstand.
2. Remember that policies are guides for making decisions about what to do, so keep them realistic and be sure they truly reflect the objectives of the department.
3. Organize the manual as simply as possible, so it will be easy to use. Give thought to indexing, to dating entries, and to the need for keeping it up to date. Provide for incorporating policy changes into the manual.
4. Plan for periodic review of policies, and set up a timetable for such review.
5. In reviewing, evaluate effectiveness and workability; review experiences of personnel in carrying out the policies; and verify that policies are being followed.
6. Be objective about changes; don't let policies become sacred.
7. When changes are made, provide for informing all personnel.[1]

Checklist for a General Nursing Service Policy Manual*

The suggested checklist in Table 9-1 is intended as a guide in developing nursing service policies. Though it can scarcely be all-inclusive, it is an indication of the type of material that should be included in a policy manual.

A similar manual should be prepared for each clinical unit which would include those items pertinent to that area.

---

[1]"Practical Approaches to Nursing Service," *AHA*, vol. 1, no. 1, Summer 1962.

Source: Sister Jean Marie Braun, S.C.S.C., "A Checklist for Nursing Service Policy Manual," The Catholic Health Association. Reprinted with permission.

Table 9-1 Checklist for a General Nursing Service Policy Manual

Part I. Internal Nursing Service

I. Accidents
A. Care
1. Who
a. Patients
b. Personnel
c. Visitors
2. Where
3. Whose responsibility
B. Reporting
1. Forms
a. Number of copies
b. Who fills out
c. Who receives
2. Oral
a. Who
b. What office
c. Telephone number
C. Precautions to prevent

II. Admissions
A. Receiving patients
1. Information obtained
2. Instructions given
B. Notifying
1. Intern
2. Doctor
3. Other departments

III. Autopsies
A. Obtaining permission
1. By whom
2. From whom—
relationship
3. Witness
B. Arrangement
1. By whom
2. Use of morgue

IV. Breakage
A. Classification
B. Responsibility
C. Reporting

V. Bulletin boards
A. Location
B. Posting of information
1. What
2. Who
C. Removing information

VI. Communicable diseases
A. Types accepted
B. Where placed
C. Cared for by whom
D. Reporting
E. Immunization of
personnel
F. Isolation techniques
1. Concurrent
disinfection
2. Terminal disinfection
3. Gowning and
masking
4. Disposal
a. Food
b. Linen
c. Waste
G. Visiting

VII. Complaints
A. How handled
1. Type
a. Patient
b. Personnel
c. Visitors
2. Kind
a. Routine
b. Emergency
B. Action taken
1. By whom
2. When

VIII. Consents
A. Obtaining
1. By whom
2. From whom
a. Husband and wife
b. Parents
c. Emancipated
minors
3. For what
a. Legal responsibility
b. State regulations
4. Witness
B. Filing

IX. Consultations
A. List of required
B. List of appropriate

X. Deaths
A. Notifying
1. Who
a. Doctor
b. Family
2. By whom
B. Care and identification
of body
C. Care of personal
belongings
D. Death certificate
1. Making out
2. Signing

XI. Discharge
A. Time
B. Notifications
C. Checking of clothes
and valuables
D. Accompaniment of
patient

XII. Doctors
A. Relationship with
B. What to do if they
cannot be contacted

XIII. Doctor's orders
A. Automatic stop orders
B. Cancellations—surgery
cancels all previous
orders
C. Telephone
D. Verbal

XIV. Documents, legal
A. Types
B. Notary public
1. When necessary
2. Where obtained
C. Who may witness

XV. Emergency
A. Definition
B. Use of available beds
C. No available beds

XVI. Elevator service
A. Where
B. Who

continues

Table 9-1 *continued*

XVII. Equipment and supplies
A. List
1. Expendable
2. Nonexpendable
B. Care
C. Lending
D. Repairing
E. Requesting

XVIII. Fire regulations; evacuation; disaster
A. Drills
1. Frequency
2. Plan
a. Who in charge
b. Departmental instructions
B. Prevention
1. Hazards
2. Extinguishers
a. Location
b. Use

XIX. Funeral directors
A. Notification
1. By whom
2. How selected
B. Release of body

XX. Flowers
A. Delivery
1. To hospital
a. When
b. Where
2. To patient

XXI. Interns and residents
A. Relationship with
B. Notification of
1. When
2. Where

XXII. Information
A. Nature of hospital information
B. Publication
1. When
2. What
3. By whom

4. To whom
a. Press
1) Name
2) Telephone number
b. Police
1) Station
2) Telephone number
c. Relatives

XXIII. Linen
A. Distribution
B. Requesting
C. Damaged

XXIV. Lost and found
A. Where kept
B. How long
C. Whose
1. Patients
2. Personnel
3. Visitors
D. Whose responsibility

XXV. Meetings
A. Frequency
B. Purpose
C. Types
D. Members
E. Minutes

XXVI. Mentally ill
A. Admission
B. Notification
C. Restraints
D. Supervision
E. Transfer

XXVII. Messenger service
A. Who served
B. By whom
C. Where
D. When

XXVIII. Night watchman
A. Services
B. How contacted

XXIX. Nursing care
A. Borderline functions
1. Administration and preparation

a. Intravenous fluids
b. Blood transfusions
c. Removing sutures
d. Applying traction
e. Acute cardiac care
f. Other
B. Charting
1. Forms used
2. Red and blue ink
3. Things to note
C. Daily assignments
1. By whom
2. Where
3. When
D. Dentures
1. Identification
2. Responsibility
E. Emergency drug supply
1. Contents
2. Responsibility
3. Location
F. Ice water
1. Where obtained
2. Who allowed
G. Kardex
1. Use
2. Sample form
H. Lights out regulations
I. Medications
1. Card system
a. Color
b. Responsibility
c. Checking
2. Errors
a. Correction
b. Reporting
J. Oxygen
1. When given without an order
2. Storage of equipment
3. Care of equipment
K. Property of patient
1. Responsibility
2. Placement

continues

Table 9-1 *continued*

XXX. Patients
- A. Relationship to
- B. Booklet of privileges
  - 1. Activity
  - 2. Postal service
  - 3. Questionnaires
  - 4. Radios and televisions
    - a. Renting
    - b. Time limit
    - c. Use in wards
  - 5. Smoking
  - 6. Telephones
  - 7. Tipping
  - 8. Visiting

XXXI. Photography
- A. Requesting
- B. Consent
- C. Ownership

XXXII. Private duty nurses
- A. Cancellation
- B. Engaging
- C. Obligations to hospital
  - 1. Reporting
  - 2. Following regulations
- D. Supervision
- E. Evaluation
- F. Remuneration

XXXIII. Reasonable and due care
- A. Definition
- B. Explanation
- C. Legal implications

XXXIV. Release from responsibility
- A. Abortions
- B. Discharges without order
- C. Use of electric pads
- D. Valuables

XXXV. Reports
- A. Forms
  - 1. Number
  - 2. Where kept
  - 3. Where sent
  - 4. Types
- B. Responsibility

XXXVI. Reporting
- A. On and off duty
  - 1. Information given
  - 2. Who present
- B. Leaving unit
  - 1. When
  - 2. To whom

XXXVII. Restraints
- A. When applied
- B. Whose order

XXXVIII. Safety
- A. Dangerous materials
  - 1. Drugs
  - 2. Poisons
  - 3. Radioactive substances
- B. Proper labeling
- C. Control
  - 1. Equipment and appliances
  - 2. Temperatures
  - 3. Infections
- D. Siderails
  - 1. Age range
  - 2. Conditions
  - 3. Type of patient
  - 4. Where obtained
  - 5. By whom
- E. Explosions
- F. Smoking
  - 1. When
  - 2. Where
  - 3. Who
- G. Disposal
  - 1. Broken objects
  - 2. Closed cans
- H. Electric cords

XXXIX. Soliciting and vending
- A. Tips and gifts
  - 1. When accepted
  - 2. By whom
- B. Vending
  - 1. When
  - 2. Who

XL. Suicide
- A. Reporting
  - 1. To whom
  - 2. By whom
- B. Forms necessary

XLI. Suspicious persons
- A. Who to notify
- B. Telephone number

XLII. Telephone
- A. Use
  - 1. Personal
  - 2. Patients
  - 3. Visitors
- B. Handling of incoming and outgoing calls

XLIII. Taxi or ambulance service
- A. Service
- B. How obtained

XLIV. Transfer of patients
- A. Within the hospital
  - 1. Clearing house
  - 2. Reasons
  - 3. Special care units
- B. From hospital
  - 1. Who contacted
  - 2. Responsibility

XLV. Unusual occurrences
- A. Report
  - 1. To whom
    - a. Day
    - b. Evening
    - c. Night
  - 2. Number of copies
    - a. Where sent
    - b. By whom
- B. Emergency action

XLVI. Visitors
- A. Hours
- B. Number
- C. Children
- D. Special requests

XLVII. Wills
- A. Drawing up
- B. Witnessing
  - 1. Who
  - 2. When

continues

Table 9-1 *continued*

Part II. Interdepartmental Policy

Interdepartmental policies are in keeping with overall hospital policies, thus ensuring unity and harmonious relationships among departments. The nursing unit will endeavor to make good use of the professional and technical services which render help to the patient. This requires a clear understanding of how these services can be carried out smoothly to the betterment of all concerned. Coordination of all their activities in obtaining the same final goal may be reached by the use of written policies.

I. Admitting office
  A. Admissions
    1. Type of patients
    2. Time
      a. Elective surgery
      b. Medical care
    3. Reservations
      a. When made
      b. How long
    4. Identification of
       patient
      a. How
      b. When
    5. Signing of consents
    6. Accompanying
       patient to unit
  B. Transfers
    1. Requests
    2. Departments to be
       notified
  C. Discharges
    1. Notification
    2. Request for
       transportation
**II. Barber and beautician
    service**
  A. Arrangements
    1. How contacted
    2. Time
      a. Bed patients
      b. Ambulatory
         patients
  B. Remuneration
    1. Paying patients
    2. Service patients
III. Blood bank
  A. Obtaining
    1. Written requisition

  a. What information
  b. Number of copies
    2. Issuance
      a. By whom
        1) Day
        2) Evening
        3) Night
      b. Rechecking
         information
  B. Reactions
    1. Who notified
    2. Records filed
  C. Replacement
    1. Time
    2. Who
    3. Where
IV. Cafeteria
  A. Hours
  B. Late meals
  C. Who may use
  D. Removal of food
V. Cashier's office
  A. Notification of
     discharge
  B. Check-out time
  C. Information given
  D. Valuables
    1. Safekeeping
    2. Receipt
VI. Dietary
  A. Requisitions
    1. New diets
      a. Therapeutic
      b. House
    2. Extra nourishments
    3. Discharge diets
    4. Change in diet
    5. Late meals

  B. Tray service
  C. Dish room

VII. Electrocardiograms
  A. Requisition
    1. Routine
    2. Emergency
  B. Bed or ambulatory
     patients

VIII. Health service
  A. Hours
  B. Types of service
    1. Routine
    2. Emergency
  C. Who may use

IX. Housekeeping
  A. Assignments
  B. Inspections
  C. Responsibility
  D. Cleaning of patients'
     rooms
    1. How notified
      a. Daily
      b. After discharge
    2. Precautions to be
       taken

X. Laboratory
  A. Requisition
    1. Routine orders
    2. Emergency orders
      a. Who to call
      b. Where
  B. Charting
    1. Hours
    2. By whom
  C. Manual for nurse's
     responsibilities

continues

Table 9-1 *continued*

XI. Laundry
A. Issuance
1. Routine
2. Emergency
B. Disposal of soiled linen
C. Special items
1. Uniforms
2. Patients' clothes
D. Safeguards
XII. Maintenance
A. Requisitions
1. Routine
2. Emergency
B. Inspection of units
C. Movable articles, care of
XIII. Medical library
A. Hours
B. Who may use
C. Overdues
XIV. Medical record library
A. Medical record
1. How compiled
2. Whose property
3. Return of completed record
4. Previous admissions
5. Nurse's responsibility
B. Late reports
C. Release of information
XV. Occupational therapy
A. Hours of service
B. Requisitions
C. Kinds of activities
1. Ambulatory patients
2. Bed patients
XVI. Patient's library
A. Hours
B. Time limits
C. Service
1. Ambulatory
2. Bed patients

D. Overdue books
E. Damage or loss of books
XVII. Personnel department
A. Requisition for personnel
1. Replacement
2. New employee
B. Interviewing
1. Preemployment
2. Postemployment
C. Recordkeeping
D. Assistance given personnel
1. Counseling
2. Grievances
3. Health and welfare program
4. Training
E. Job analysis and specifications
F. Personnel policies
G. General orientation
XVIII. Pharmacy
A. Hours of service
1. Day
2. Evening
3. Night
B. Ordering of drugs
1. Unit supply
2. Prescription orders
C. Narcotic and barbiturate regulations
D. Label changing
E. Inspection of stock drugs and solutions on units
1. How often
2. By whom
F. Safety precautions

XIX. Physical therapy
A. Hours of service
B. Requisitions
C. Types of treatments
XX. Purchasing department
A. Hours of service
B. Requisitions
1. Routine
2. Emergency
3. Types
4. Number of copies
C. Back orders
XXI. Social service
A. Hours of service
B. Referrals
1. By whom
2. Who
C. (Contact) agencies contacted
XXII. X-ray
A. Requisition
1. Information necessary
2. Time
a. Routine
b. Emergency
1) Who contacted
2) Where
B. Preparation of patient
1. Details in procedure manual
a. Prepared by x-ray
b. Kept on nursing units
C. Notification of unit
1. Before and after x-ray
a. Who
b. When
2. Cancellation of x-ray

Source: Sister Jean Marie Braun, S.C.S.C., "A Checklist for Nursing Service Policy Manual," The Catholic Health Association. Reprinted with permission.

Table 9-2 The Nursing Service Procedure Book: A Model for Contents

Sections:

#1	=	Nursing Arts	#7	=	Orthopedic Nursing
#2	=	Medical Nursing	#8	=	Urological Nursing
#3	=	Infectious Disease Nursing	#9	=	Pediatric Nursing
#4	=	Surgical Nursing	#10	=	Obstetrics and Gynecological Nursing
#5	=	Eye-Ear-Nose and Throat	#11	=	Outpatient Nursing
#6	=	Neurosurgical Nursing			

Section	Subject Index
1	Abbreviations, Acceptable
2	Abdominal Paracentesis
1	Admission of Patient to Ward (Routine)
11	Allergy—Skin Testing for (Pediatric Allergy Clinic)
1	A.M. Care (Adult)
9	A.M. Care (Infant)
2	Application of Topical Medications
1	Arterial Blood Samples, Obtaining of
1	Bath, Bed
9	Bath, Infant
10	Bath, Infant Sponge (Demonstration for Mother)
10	Bath, Post Partum Patient
1	Bath, Sitz
1	Bath, Temperature Reducing Sponge
2	Bath, Therapeutic Skin
1	Bath, Tub
7	Bed, Circoelectric
1	Bed Making, Occupied Bed
1	Bed Making, Unoccupied Bed, Assigned
1	Bed Making, Unoccupied Bed, Unassigned
1	Bed Pan, Giving and Removing
8	Bladder, Catheterization of
8	Bladder, Irrigation of Indwelling Catheter
8	Bladder, Insertion of Inflatable Catheter
10	Blanket Technique (Nursery)
1	Blood, Administration of

Section	Subject Index
1	Blood Pressure, Taking of
1	Body, Care after Death (Routine)
3	Body, Care after Death (Infectious Disease)
10	Body, Care of Newborn after Death
10	Bottle Feeding
10	Breast Binder (to Suppress Lactation)
10	Breast Expression, Post Partum
10	Breast, Taking Babies to
7	Buck's Extension with Thomas Splint
3	Care of Patient in Isolation
7	Casts, Plaster (Application of)
7	Casts, Care Immed. Following Applic.
7	Cast, Routine Care of Patient in
8	Catheter, Application of External
8	Catheter, Insertion of Inflatable
8	Catheter, Irrigation of
8	Catheterization of Bladder
4	Central Venous Pressure, Measurement of
4	Chest, Closed Drainage of
7	Circoelectric Bed, Preparation and Use
10	Circumcision of Newborn
4	Circumcision of Adult
1	Cleaning Unit (after Departure of Patient)
1	Cleansing Enema (Adult Patients)
1	Clothing, Care of Patient's
4	Colostomy, Care of Patient with
4	Colostomy Irrigation
1	Death, Care of Body after (Routine)
3	Death, Care of Body after (Infectious)

continues

Table 9-2 *continued*

continues

Table 9-1 *continued*

continues

Table 9-2 *continued*

Section	Subject Index	Section	Subject Index
6	Spinal Puncture (Lumbar Puncture)	1	Transportation of Patient on Stretcher
1	Sputum Specimen, Collection-Preparation)	1	Transportation of Patient in Wheelchair
10	Stillborn Infant, Care of Body	1	Tub Bath, Routine
1	Stretcher, Maxing Standard	2	Tub Bath, Therapeutic Skin
1	Stretcher, Transporting Patient on	7	Turning Patient after Spinal Fusion
4	Surgery, Minor	1	Unit, Cleaning of Patient's
4	Swan Ganz (Pulmonary Artery Cath)	1	Urinal, Giving and Removing
1	Teeth and Mouth, Care of	8	Urine Specimen Collection (Catheterized)
1	Temperature Taking	9	Urine Specimen Collection (Pediatrics)
1	Temperature Taking (Ivac Electronic Thermometer)	1	Urine Specimen Collection, Single Voided
1	Temperature Reducing Sponge Bath	1	Urine Specimen Collection, 24 Hour
2	Therapeutic Tub Bath (Dermatology)	10	Vaginal Douche
7	Thomas Splint, Use with Buck's Extension	10	Vaginal Douche, Solutions for
2	Thoracocentesis	1	Valuables, Care of Patient's
2	Topical Medication, Application of		
5	Tracheostomy, Care of Patient with		

Source: Reprinted with permission of Cook County Hospital, Chicago, IL.

Communication of New Policies*

Distribution

New or revised material should be distributed as soon as possible after it is approved and ready for distribution.

Manuals or individual policies/procedures may be mailed to persons/places listed on a need-to-know distribution sheet. Interoffice mail, hand delivery, or pay envelope issue are methods for dispensing the materials.

A memorandum should be attached to any manual material that is distributed. It should contain: date of distribution; an explanation of the subject; and directions for posting, indexing, adding, deleting, and filing. Even if the material is hand delivered and the instructions are carried

out by the person who delivers the material, the memorandum should be posted on the departmental bulletin board as a reminder that new material is to be implemented.

Implementation of New Policies and Procedures

A new manual or revised individual policies and procedures bring about changes, sometimes suddenly. If personnel are not prepared for these changes, discord, confusion, and resentment may result.

Suggestions for implementation include both the understanding that a mandate exists and that a positive approach to change is important. Some implementation suggestions are:

- Distribute new or revised policies and procedures to the entire staff at the same time. Ask everybody to read and demonstrate that they understand and can perform them. Their signing that they have read and do

Source: Reba Douglass Grubb, *Hospital Manual: A Guide to Development and Maintenance*, Aspen Publishers, Inc., 1981.

understand the information places the responsibility on them.

- Hold a conference or meeting in small departments to discuss and demonstrate new policies and procedures. This can be done as a part of regular meetings that are held weekly or monthly.

- Have a procedure demonstration day. All participants are given a copy of the procedures so they can follow along as demonstrations are made. Return demonstrations from the group also are used to reinforce learning.

  Each participant is given an unsigned posttest, including a few questions from each procedure. At the close of the session, these are analyzed and the questions that were answered incorrectly are emphasized in the next sessions. If too many questions were missed on one procedure, this indicates that further instruction is needed or that the procedure needs to be rewritten.

Personnel who were unable to attend the regular sessions should be scheduled to attend another or work the "buddy system" with one who is experienced in the procedure. Released time for this education program is provided for each employee.

- Place the complete manual on each unit. Discuss one or two revised or new policies and/or procedures at each conference or departmental meeting until the manual has been reviewed by all employees. This would be difficult for a large department or if the manual is large.

- Ask personnel of one nursing unit to demonstrate a procedure to another unit; that unit then demonstrates the procedure to another unit; this continues until all units have participated in a learning session.

- Videotape a procedure and hand out written copies of the process. Let the personnel follow the videotaped action. The tape may be shown as often as necessary.

Chapter 10

Nurses and the Law

PRIMER ON THE LAW*

Nurses have a legal and an ethical duty to practice nursing according to a professional nursing standard of care. Nurses are required to use the same degree of knowledge and skill as reasonably prudent nurses would use under the same or similar circumstances and, if they fail to do so, they can be sued for malpractice by the injured plaintiff.

The Distinction between Negligence and Malpractice

Negligence is the failure to exercise the degree of care that a reasonably prudent person would exercise under the same or similar circumstances. *Malpractice* (professional negligence) refers to negligent acts committed by a person in his or her professional capacity. It is defined as any professional misconduct, unreasonable lack of skill or fidelity in professional or fiduciary duties, evil practice, or illegal or immoral conduct. There are fundamental differences between a lawsuit based on a charge of negligence and a lawsuit claiming malpractice. In a malpractice suit

- the act of negligence must have been committed in the course of carrying out a professional responsibility.
- the statute of limitations is generally shorter than for negligence
- the standard of care will be tested in reference to the behavior of other nurses
- the testimony of an expert witness is usually required to prove the standard of care

When professionals are sued for malpractice they are accorded these added protections; however, they are not available to nurses in jurisdictions where the courts do not recognize that the nurse's actions are those of a professional. The legal concept of professionalism has traditionally considered a profession to require (1) a rigorous and systematic educational program for practitioners, (2) a code of ethics, (3) a strong research program, and (4) a certain authority and prestige associated with the field. The nursing profession has the altruism and the code of ethics and is improving in the area of research; however, in prestige and authority it is still lagging behind other professions.

Source: Unless otherwise noted, Carmelle Pellerin Cournoyer, *The Nurse Manager & the Law*, Aspen Publishers, Inc., © 1989.

Elements Required To Establish Nurse Liability

In order to establish a claim of negligence or malpractice, a plaintiff is required to introduce proof of the four elements of negligence: (1) duty; (2) breach of the duty, which is the failure to meet the required standard of care; (3) causation; and (4) injury.

Duty

The courts have stated that in negligence cases, the duty is always the same, to conform to the legal standard of care or reasonable conduct in the light of apparent risk. The plaintiff must first prove that the person charged with negligence is under a legal duty to exercise due care. There is no legal duty to come to the aid of another unless a legal relationship exists.

A nurse's duty toward a hospital patient is established by providing evidence that the nurse was employed by the hospital in which the plaintiff was a patient. The nurse's duty arises in the context of the hospital-nurse–patient relationship, in which the nurse has a legal and an ethical duty to the patient. Once a duty is acknowledged, the plaintiff must establish the scope of the duty that the nurse was obligated to provide. The plaintiff must prove that the nurse failed to act as a reasonably prudent nurse would have acted under the same or similar circumstances. In order to do this, the plaintiff must introduce evidence of the standard of care that was required; in other words, the plaintiff must demonstrate how the nurse should have acted under the circumstances.

Standard of Care

Although jurisdictions continue to treat nursing malpractice as ordinary negligence, the trend is to hold nurses to a professional standard of care. The plaintiff can prove the standard of care, and the nurse's failure to meet that standard, by the introduction of documentary evidence and the testimony of expert witnesses.

The type of documents that are usually used to prove the standard of care include the following:

- ANA standards of nursing practice, the standards that are published by the specialty professional nursing organizations, and the Joint Commission's standards
- statutes and administrative codes such as the nursing practice act and regulations, the federal hospital regulations, and the hospital licensing standards and regulations
- hospital bylaws and hospital policy and procedure manuals relevant to the standard of nursing practice within the institution

Expert Witness Testimony. The standard of care in a nursing malpractice action must be established by expert witness testimony. The general rule is that witnesses can testify only as to the facts; their opinions and conclusions are not admissible. On the other hand, expert witnesses are presented for the purpose of eliciting their expert opinion as to the matter being litigated. Unlike regular witnesses, expert witnesses seldom have direct, personal knowledge of the actual facts and circumstances of the case. They have generally reviewed the record and formed an opinion as to the nurse's conduct. Both the plaintiff and the defendant may present expert witness testimony. The trial court first determines that the expert witness is competent to testify as an expert on the subject. The court must be satisfied that the testimony to be presented is the kind that requires special knowledge, skill, and experience. The purpose of the expert witness's testimony is to help the jury understand the professional or technical issues that are being litigated. The expert witness is subject to cross-examination by the attorney for the opposing side. The jury decides how much weight and credence to give to the expert witness's testimony.

Traditionally, the standard of care required of health care professionals was that degree of care ordinarily exercised by health care professionals of similar knowledge and skills in the same or similar community. The application of a community standard of care, commonly referred to as the locality rule, is rapidly being replaced with the recognition of a national standard of care so that expert witnesses can be hired from anywhere in the country. The practice of nursing, however, may involve situations in which there are several different, equally safe and efficient ways of performing a procedure. There is no liability if the nurse has followed the approach used by a respected minority of the profession.

Causation

Proximate cause or legal cause requires that the plaintiff prove that a reasonably close connection exists between the defendant's conduct and the plaintiff's injury. Many lawsuits are lost by plaintiffs who are unable to prove the causal relationship. Proximate cause requires a two-pronged inquiry.

1. *Is the defendant's conduct the cause "in fact" of the plaintiff's injury?* Two tests are used to answer this question. First, could the injury have occurred "but for" the defendant's conduct. For example, the nurse's negligent administration of an overdose of medication that results in the patient suffering an adverse reaction. Second, was the defendant's conduct a material and substantial factor in bringing about the injury. This issue is critical when there is more than one defendant.

2. *How far will the law extend the responsibility for the defendant's conduct to the consequences that have occurred?* Foreseeability of the risk of injury is the criterion used to determine the limits of the defendant's liability. If the defendant's failure to foresee the consequences of the action is proven to be a direct cause of the patient's injury, legal causation is established.

Injury

In negligence actions plaintiffs are required to prove that they suffered physical, emotional, or financial injury. The plaintiff is compensated for the injury by an award of money damages that the defendant is ordered to pay. Types of damages include nominal, actual or compensatory, and punitive damages.

Nominal damages are a minimal sum that is sometimes awarded to vindicate a technical right; however, nominal damages cannot be obtained in a negligence action where no actual loss occurred. *Actual* or compensatory damages are the losses sustained by the plaintiff and include medical costs, loss of earnings, impairment of future earnings, and past and future pain and suffering. *Punitive* damages, which are also called exemplary damages, are designed to

punish the defendants and deter others from following their example.

NURSE ACTIONS

Nursing Administrative Actions To Meet Legal Obligations*

The two major legal responsibilities that civil law imposes on nurses and nurse managers are to (1) maintain the standard of nursing care and (2) respect the rights of patients and staff. The following behaviors demonstrate some of the responsibilities that nurse managers must assume in order to fulfill their legal obligations to the patient and to the employer (see also Tables 10-1 and 10-2):

- Hire, supervise, and evaluate the nursing staff.
- Evaluate interaction with the nonnursing staff.
- Develop mechanisms for resolving professional conflicts.
- Participate in the credentialing and evaluation process.
- Implement and maintain the current standard of nursing practice.
- Provide for nursing staff competency through education.
- Evaluate the nursing staff and the level of nursing care being provided to patients.
- Discipline nurses found to be incompetent, reporting to the state board when necessary.
- Participate in the risk management process.
- Respect patients' right to consent or to refuse to consent to treatment.
- Respect nurse's right to fair and equitable treatment under the employment agreement.
- Respect the nurses' and the patients' constitutional rights.

---

*Source: Carmelle Pellerin Cournoyer, *The Nurse Manager & the Law*, Aspen Publishers, Inc., © 1989.

Table 10-1 Nursing Actions Involved in Litigation

Treatment	• Gave enema to seven-month-old infant when contraindicated • Failed to test performance, take safety precautions, and properly connect machine, resulting in air being blown into bloodstream • Failed to cut jaw wires (respiratory distress) • Failed to respond to alarms, used malfunctioning equipment, and failed to supply oxygen when respirator could not promptly be reattached • Failed to implement orders for IV hookup and fetal heart monitoring • Failed to attach fetal monitor • Failed to manage infant's airway (brain damage) • Administered improper oxygen levels, failing to adhere to protocols • Fed infant with baby bottle warmed in microwave oven, resulting in burns • Failed to attend to patient during asthma attack • Allowed mother to walk for hours despite serious vaginal bleeding

Communication	• Failed to notify or advise physician of:
	  —changes in signs and symptoms and patient status
	  —changes in a casted leg resulting from reduced circulation (circulatory compromise)
	  —fetal tachycardia and meconium
	  —pain and vaginal bleeding
	  —increased pulse rate and lack of response to stimuli (intensive care unit)
	  —dehydration, seriousness of condition
	  —late decelerations that occurred during fetal monitoring
	  —jaundice
	  —excessive oxygen levels
	• Failed to chart vital signs for seven and three-quarter hours (labor room)
	• Failed to chart for three hours (labor room)

Medication	• Gave wrong medication upon discharge (gave Alcaine, a topical eye anesthetic; should have given artificial tears) • Failed to discontinue oxytocin (Pitocin) as required by hospital policy when obstetrician was absent • Administered morphine without notifying physician • Failed to give diazepam (Valium) as ordered • Gave excessive dose of disulfiram (Antabuse) • Allowed inappropriate use of intravenous infusion equipment, which resulted in extensive infusing of fluids extravascularly into leg and foot • Gave thioridazine (Mellaril) at night, against physician order; mistakenly gave paraldhyde (intended for patient in next bed) with thioridazine (Mellaril) • Administered meperidine (Demerol) hydrochloride, clinically contraindicated • Administered potassium chloride improperly • Mishandled infusion pump
Monitoring/Observing/ Supervising	• Failed to recognize dehydration and electrolyte imbalance • Failed to observe changes in circulation due to leg cast

continues

Table 10-1 *continued*

- Failed to assess and record vital signs for seven and three-quarter hours
- Discharged maternity patient upon order of physician who later denied giving order (should have notified supervisor)
- Failed to periodically monitor, recognize misuse, and discontinue intravenous therapy
- Improperly participated in obtaining father's signature on a consent form one and one-half hours after infant was born, before he had been apprised of the infant's condition
- Failed to provide one-to-one monitoring in recovery room, which resulted in failing to recognize and respond to cardiac arrest
- Failed to observe adverse reaction to meperidine (Demerol) hydrochloride
- Negligently interpreted recovery room protocol
- Failed to monitor fetal heart rate and contractions every 30 minutes as required by hospital policy
- Was negligent in supervising a psychiatric patient who attempted suicide
- Failed to notice hypoxia
- Improperly assisted patient to bathroom (nursing home)
- Failed to observe mother in labor for three hours
- Failed to observe jaundice
- Failed to recognize signs and symptoms of oxygen deprivation during surgery (nurse anesthetist)
- Was negligent in assigning and supervising a nursing student (student did not take blood pressure for six hours)
- Failed to observe head circumference, intracranial bleeding
- Failed to monitor fetal heart rate

Hospital Management*

- Failure to provide adequate staff to check plaintiff every 30 minutes as physician ordered
- Failure to train emergency room nurses in the same manner as other hospital nurses concerning medication administration
- Failure to establish mechanism for ensuring that patients in labor have given informed consent to the method of delivery
- Failure to establish a mechanism for prompt reporting of any life-threatening situation
- Failure to supervise employees (impaired nurse)
- Failure to enforce internal safety regulations requiring employees to test contents of heated bottles
- Failure to provide immediate treatment of burns
- Entrusting patient's care solely to a nursing student

*Nursing actions for which hospitals were held responsible.

Source: Cynthia E. Northrop, "Nursing Actions in Litigation," *Quality Review Bulletin,* vol. 13, no. 10, October 1987. Copyright 1987 by the Joint Commission on Accreditation of Healthcare Organizations, Chicago. Reprinted with permission.

- Promote an environment of mutual respect and cooperation between health care professionals.
- Promote an environment of mutual respect and cooperation between nursing and hospital management.

Physician Orders and Nurse's Duty*

The major legal consequence of the recognition of nursing as an independent profession has been the establishment of the nurse's duty to review certain physician actions.

Inappropriate Physician Orders

For example, part of a nurse's training includes instruction in the dosages and routes in the administration of commonly used drugs. The nurse has a duty to determine if the physician's drug order is reasonable. This does not mean that the nurse is allowed to decide that one drug would be better than another. It means rather that, if a physician orders an improper dosage, an inappropriate form, or an otherwise unacceptable drug, the nurse should not follow the order. Recognizing the incompatibility of the drug form and the route of administration is within the nurse's area of competence. The nurse's duty extends beyond simply not following the inappropriate order. The nurse must bring the inappropriate order to the attention of the supervisor so that a proper order may be obtained (see Table 10-2).

A nurse who knowingly carries out an incorrect order can be held personally liable for negligence. If a nurse independently initiates care that is harmful to the patient, the nurse is also personally liable. In the first case, the hospital and the physician would also be liable. In the second case, only the hospital would share liability as the nurse's employer. The nursing protocols should clearly delineate which tasks are nursing tasks and which tasks require independent medi-

*Source: Edward P. Richards III and Katharine C. Rathbun, *Medical Risk Management: Preventive Legal Strategies for Health Care Providers*, Aspen Publishers, Inc., © 1983.

Table 10-2 Procedure for Dealing with Inappropriate Physician Orders

- The first step is to double-check the order with the physician who wrote the order.
- If this is done by telephone, the order should be read to the physician to determine if it is understood correctly.
- If the order is correctly understood, the nurse should discuss the specific problem with the physician.
- If the physician does not feel that the order should be changed, the nurse should contact the nursing supervisor.
- The supervisor may decide that the order is proper and instruct the nurse to carry it out, or the supervisor may agree that the order is incorrect.
- If the supervisor agrees that the order is questionable, it will be necessary to seek the opinion of another professional. In questions concerning drugs, a good choice is the hospital pharmacist. In teaching hospitals with 24-hour house staff coverage, it may be possible to ask a resident about the problem.
- If the resident or pharmacist agrees that it might be dangerous to carry out the order, the hospital administration must become involved in the problem.

Note: The criterion for overriding an order must be that the order is medically incorrect and dangerous to the patient.

Source: Edward P. Richards III and Katharine C. Rathbun, *Medical Risk Management: Preventive Legal Strategies for Health Care Providers*, Aspen Publishers, Inc., © 1983.

cal judgment and may not be initiated without specific orders from a physician.

Absence of a Physician Order

A companionate problem is the absence of an order. The nursing staff has a duty to monitor the patient's condition and to report relevant information to the physician through entries in the nurses-notes section of the medical records. If there are acute adverse changes in the patient's condition, there is a duty to report these changes directly to the physician. This does not discharge the nurse's duty to the patient; there is also a duty to see that proper care is provided to the patient. If the attending physician ignores the nurse's complaints or is unavailable and has not assigned the care of the patient to a colleague, another physician must be called in to see the patient. In a teaching hospital, house officers are available to treat the patient. In other hospitals, there must be provisions for providing care when the attending physician is absent or abandons the patient.

INFORMED CONSENT

Overview*

The common law has long recognized the basic societal concept of a person's right to control his or her own body. Each of us is entitled to possess and control our own person free from all restraint and interference by others unless otherwise determined by clear and unquestionable authority of law.

The doctrine of informed consent is one of the primary means developed in the law to protect this personal interest in the integrity of one's body. Under this doctrine, a medical procedure may not be performed without the patient's consent, which is to be obtained only after explanation of the nature of the treatment, substantial risks, and any alternative therapies. This doctrine presupposes that the patient has the information necessary to evaluate the risks and benefits of all the available options and is competent to do so.

There are three basic prerequisites for informed consent: (1) the patient must have the capacity to reason and make judgments; (2) the decision must be made voluntarily and without coercion; and (3) the patient must have a clear understanding of the risks and benefits of the proposed treatment alternatives or nontreatment, along with a full understanding of the nature of the disease and the prognosis. It is the physician's responsibility to provide the necessary

---

The Intent of Informed Consent

- The fact that consent is given does not automatically establish that the consent was informed.

- Express or implied consent must be given after the patient has received sufficient information to make an informed choice.

- It is important to remember that consent is a process, not a document. The document merely codifies and reflects the culmination of the process.

- Written consent alone, without true disclosure and an opportunity for dialogue between the provider and the patient, is generally inadequate.

- Consent forms were developed primarily as a means of establishing that informed consent did in fact occur. However, such forms have been recognized as an important component of the process, as many states mandate that consent forms be used as a part of the decision-making process.

Source: J. Phillip O'Brien, Michael R. Callahan, and Jamie A. Savaiano, "A Practical Approach to the Doctrine of Informed Consent," in *Health Care Ethics*, Gary R. Anderson and Valerie A. Glesnes-Anderson, eds., Aspen Publishers, Inc., 1987.

---

information and facts; it is the patient's responsibility to make the subjective treatment determination based upon his or her understanding of the information and facts provided.

Informed consent applies not only to the patient's right to informed assent, it encompasses a right to informed refusal. A competent adult person generally has the right to decline to have medical treatment initiated or continued.

Nursing and the Informed Consent Process*

In a study of nurses' attitudes toward the informed consent process, it was found that

---

Source: Joan S. Dwyer, "The Decision: To Resuscitate or Not," in Barbara Stewart Heater and Betty AuBuchon, eds., *Controversies in Critical Care Nursing*, Aspen Publishers, Inc., © 1988.

Source: Anne J. Davis, "The Clinical Nurse's Role in Informed Consent," *Journal of Professional Nursing*, vol. 4, no. 2, March-April 1988.

nurses view it as the responsibility of the physician and/or researcher to provide patients with technical information, the range of options available and possible, and the requisite time for reflection. However, the nurse often becomes involved almost immediately after the first interaction focused on obtaining informed consent. If the physician has given the patient the needed information prior to hospital admission, the nurse may first become involved when the intern does an intake interview to gather clinical data. Such interviews often lead to the patient and nurse discussing what treatment the patient will receive.

Consent is considered more informed when the patient has received prior preparation for consent. This prior preparation should include clear communication in understandable language about the procedures that the patients will undergo and an open discussion about the degree of control the patients can exercise and the choices that they can make. Most acutely ill patients do not have much idea of their rights, whereas patients who have a chronic illness and have been previously hospitalized are more likely to have such an awareness.

The consent form itself presents problems that often lead to the patient's discussing the situation with the nurse. In these situations, the patient often initiates the discussion, focuses on the meaning of the words, and wants a more detailed description of the procedures being proposed. A concern voiced by most patients is whether they will feel pain, and if so, how much and for how long. If the pain is more likely to be prolonged, they want some assurance that this will be managed medically.

The major problems that nurses experience with the consent forms themselves are that (1) the words used are sometimes too complex, although not necessarily technical, and (2) sometimes not enough description is given, especially of painful procedures.

Another problem is the timing in seeking consent signatures. Nurses should take into account the stress level of the patient, the urgency of treatment, and the sequence of concurrent events. Nurses should also encourage others seeking consent to do likewise and even suggest, when appropriate, that seeking consent be postponed based on their assessment of the patient.

One way nurses deal with consent problems is to include the patient's significant others (at least one) in the informed consent process. The others may be family members, friends, or a hospital staff person, provided that a relationship defined by the patient as meaningful to him or her exists. Another activity, and one which goes a long way in dealing with the spirit of informed consent as a process grounded in the ethical principle of autonomy, is to have several discussions with the patient and, if possible, the significant others. These ongoing discussions are not always possible because of the urgency and timing of the treatment.

Another major problem in consent is lack of assessment regarding the patient's comprehension of the information given. Many people obtaining consent evidence little knowledge of communication as a process and the importance of establishing and maintaining feedback channels. Therefore, assessment of patient comprehension can be superficial and perfunctory. Some nurses believe that a witness needs to be present to ascertain what actually went on in the consent interaction.

The final concern is that an opportunity be specifically provided for the patient to reevaluate the decision that had been made earlier. Practical considerations are a realistic factor here, but also the idea that consent, once given, does not need to be further discussed comes into play as well. Ongoing discussions, assessment of comprehension, and reevaluation of the initial agreement take time and some interpersonal skill. Time is viewed as being in short supply by those seeking consent, and the extent to which the interpersonal skills are lacking makes informed consent as a process more difficult and less likely to be successful (i.e., to achieve its intended goal). Even for those health professionals who understand the ethical and legal underpinning of informed consent, such an achievement is difficult and, at times, impossible. This, more than all of the other factors, creates the need for the nurse's active involvement in making consent informed.

The Roles of Nurses in Informed Consent

Nurses identify five roles they can assume as forms of active involvement (see also Table 10-3).

Watchdog. This role serves to monitor informed consent situations. Nurses often accompany the patient to witness the consent. They also confer about and report what they saw as violations of the consent process. In this role, they attempt to establish and maintain clear limits regarding their ethical obligations to patients, physicians, and the institution.

Advocate. Nurses assume this role in order to mediate on behalf of patients. As a part of this role, it is important to bring crucial new or additional information to the physician or researcher from the patient or family. For example, the patient's rationale for certain choices and decisions can function to recast the meaning of events and expose the underlying values at play. As advocates, nurses also support the decision-making process per se and the decision made by the patients.

Resource Person. As resource persons, nurses collect, dispense, and report information about all alternatives available, guide patients regarding their informational needs, and clarify the features of consent that the patients misunderstood or overlooked.

Coordinator. Nurses can explore implications for and observe direct and indirect effects on the patient and family. They can integrate treatment and care with the workings of the system so as to try to ensure necessary time for working through any issues that might arise about informed consent.

Facilitator. Nurses can clarify and validate differences in perspective between parties involved in informed consent. They can discuss with patients and families such topics as long- and short-term consequences of choice, suffering, and pain, as well as psychological and physical benefits. As facilitators they try to build in opportunities for reevaluation at a later stage. And finally, they assume the responsibility of getting the team together to discuss aspects of specific situations, including those of informed consent, that raise issues that need to be discussed.

Consent from Persons Other Than the Patient

Incompetency*

Lack of competence to consent to treatment may result from a patient's unconsciousness, the influence of drugs or intoxicants, mental illness, or other permanent or temporary impairment of reasoning power. The essential determination to be made is whether the patient has sufficient mental ability to understand the situation and make a rational decision as to treatment.

Some cases are clear-cut, as where the patient has been adjudicated an incompetent. Many, however, involve subtle determinations of fact where no court has previously assessed the mental capacity of the particular patient involved. These questions are roughly analogous to the situation of the "mature minor." Whenever possible, a hospital or other provider of health services contemplating treatment of a person arguably incompetent should try to obtain "substituted consent" from the person's next of kin or a court order authorizing the proposed treatment.

Patients Adjudicated Incompetent. When a patient has been declared incompetent by a court, the rules regarding consent to treatment are straightforward. An adjudicated incompetent cannot give a legally valid consent, and the authorization for treatment must be obtained from the legal guardian whom the court has appointed to represent the patient's interests. A consent form signed by the guardian is the hospital's or physician's best and simplest protection against liability for unauthorized treatment. At least one state supreme court, however, has ruled that the state's guardianship statute requires even a court-appointed guardian to

---

*Source: "Consents," *Hospital Law Manual*, Aspen Publishers, Inc., September 1985.

Table 10-3 Sample Policy—Nurses' Responsibilities in Informed Consent Procedures

1. Nursing personnel on the unit will review the patient's chart to make sure that the fully completed informed consent form is present.

   - This will take place during the admission process on the unit for patients being admitted the day prior to surgery.
   - For patients already in-house who are being scheduled for surgery, this process can take place any time up to the evening before surgery.
   - For patients having outpatient surgery who are in-house patients, this audit process will take place some time prior to the patient's being sent to outpatient surgery for the procedure.
   - Whenever possible this audit should take place 24 hours or more prior to the scheduled surgery/procedure.
   - When the informed consent form is absent from the chart during this audit, nursing personnel on the unit will notify the operating/administering physician of this deficiency.

2. In cases where the informed consent form has been sent to the hospital with the preadmission packet or sent with the patient to the hospital and for some reason has not been received in the hospital, the operating/administering physician may sign the affidavit form stating that the consent form has been completed and that the form was signed and a copy will be sent or brought from the physician's office to the hospital within 24 hours for placement in the chart. In these cases, the physician may proceed with the surgery/procedure.

3. Nurses/employees may be involved in an informed consent procedure under the following conditions only:

   - The operating/administering physician wishes the nurse/employee to witness the entire informed consent process and to witness the signature by the patient, or
   - The operating/administering physician has obtained the informed consent and wants the nurse/employee to witness the patient's signature only, or
   - The operating/administering physician has obtained the informed consent and places a specific written order stating that the specific surgery/special procedure has been explained to the patient and requests that the nurse/employee obtain and witness the patient's signature on the informed consent form.

4. The nurse/employee will *NOT* answer *ANY* questions relating to the informed consent. The questions will be referred back to the physician doing the consent/explanation. If the patient refuses to sign the form until these questions are answered, the physician will be notified immediately by the nurse/employee.

5. Nurses/employees who participate in the informed consent process to the extent of responding to the patient's questions about the surgery/special procedure jeopardize their protection under the hospital's liability program.

6. The hospital-provided informed consent form is the minimum requirement of placement in the chart. Physicians or group practices preferring to use a special form that they may be using currently or wishing to develop may do so once the form has been approved by the Risk Management office to make sure that it meets the minimum requirements of the Joint Commission. Once these have been approved, a letter will be sent to nursing service listing the physicians and the forms that have been approved in addition to the form.

7. In case of an emergency procedure, please refer to Policy and Procedure XYZ for guidelines.

8. Either the consent form or the affidavit form must be in the chart prior to the operation/procedure or the operation/procedure will be postponed.

9. Any problems with this procedure or with a particular patient or physician should be referred to the Risk Management office if it cannot be handled directly by the floor and/or nursing personnel.

Source: Glenn T. Troyer and Steven L. Salman, eds., *Handbook of Health Care Risk Management*, Aspen Publishers, Inc., 1986.

obtain specific court authorization before consenting to any extraordinary, irreversible medical procedure that would seriously affect the patient's bodily integrity (such as amputation or psychosurgery). Physicians and hospitals should be aware of their state laws in order to ascertain whether a guardian actually has the authority to consent to a particular treatment or procedure.

All states have statutorily defined procedures for adjudication of incompetency. The determination may be general, affecting all aspects of the individual's activities, or may be limited to a particular aspect, such as the ability to decide on medical or surgical treatment.

Judging Competency. In the President's Commission for the Study of Ethical Problems in Medicine and Biomedical and Behavioral Research report, the Commission refers to competency as decision-making capacity. The Commission spelled out the components of decisional capacity: the possession of a set of values and goals, the ability to communicate and understand information, and the ability to reason and deliberate.

Competency assessment usually focuses on the patient's mental capacities: specifically the mental capacities to make a particular medical decision. Does this patient understand what is being disclosed? Can this patient come to a decision about treatment based on that information? How much understanding and rational decision-making capacity is sufficient for this patient to be considered competent? Or how deficient must this patient's decision-making capacity be before he or she is declared incompetent? A properly performed competency assessment should eliminate two types of error: preventing competent persons from deciding their own treatments, and failing to protect incompetent persons from the harmful effects of a bad decision.[1]

*Consent to Treatment of Minors**

The need for consent to a minor's treatment underlies two separate legal questions. The first

relates to the practitioner's liability for battery if valid consent is not obtained. The second concerns the practitioner's right to compensation for services that have not been authorized by someone with legal capacity to make a binding contract.

As a general proposition, the consent of a minor to treatment is ineffective. Thus, the health care provider must secure the consent of the minor's parent or other person standing *in loco parentis* or risk liability to the minor and/or the parent. The general proposition is rarely applied in a rigid manner, however. There are numerous judicial decisions that respond to a variety of special factual situations by declining to impose liability despite the lack of parental consent. Emergencies requiring immediate treatment to preserve the life of or prevent serious impairment to the health of a minor are the most common such situations. If the parents cannot be located within the time available, the courts usually have held that the existence of an emergency obviates the need for consent.

Most states have statutes specifically addressing consent to emergency medical and surgical treatment of minors.

PROFESSIONAL LIABILITY INSURANCE*

An increasing number of lawsuits are being filed against nurses. For many nurses, the unsettled question is whether to purchase professional liability insurance.

Reasons given for seeking coverage beyond that provided by a hospital employer include the following:

- In the event of litigation, the hospital, not the nurse, makes any decisions about settlement or defense, so the nurse's best interests may not be represented.
- If the court determines that the nurse acted outside the scope of employment, he or she is unprotected.

---

[1]James F. Drane, "The Many Faces of Competency," *Hastings Center Report,* vol. 15, no. 2, April 1985.

**Source*: Arnold J. Rosoft, *Informed Consent: A Guide for Health Care Providers,* Aspen Publishers, Inc., 1981.

**Source*: Sister Rosann Geiser and Karen Fraley, "Perinatal Outreach: Liability Issues," *Journal of Perinatal and Neonatal Nursing,* vol. 2, no. 3, © 1989 Aspen Publishers, Inc.

- If the nurse does, in fact, practice outside the hospital's job description (professional committees, outside speaking, educational work), the hospital coverage does not apply.
- Hospitals have the right to seek reimbursement from the nurse for claims paid as a result of negligence.
- Personal assets may in some cases be attached to satisfy a judgment or wages may be garnisheed.
- Hospital insurance is frequently a claims-made policy. This type of policy will cover the nurse only while he or she is employed by the hospital, not years later when the claim is in court.
- The cost of insurance is relatively small in relation to the peace of mind the insurance provides.

Because nurses are in a high-risk field, they should maintain job descriptions that accurately reflect scope of responsibilities. Each nurse should determine the dollar limits of any hospital liability coverage and whether the coverage is of a claims-made or occurrence type. Knowledge of the institution's recent history in litigation involving nurses will provide a background for supplementary insurance decisions (see Table 10-4).

Conditions of a Professional Liability Insurance Policy*

Each insurance policy contains a number of important conditions. Failure to comply with these conditions may cause forfeiture of the policy and nonpayment of claims against it. Generally, insurance policies contain the following conditions.

Notice of Occurrence—When the insured becomes aware that an injury has occurred as a result of acts covered under the contract, the insured must promptly notify the insurance company. The form of notice may be either oral or written, as specified in the policy.

Source: George D. Pozgar, *Legal Aspects of Health Care Administration*, ed 3, Aspen Publishers, Inc., © 1987.

Table 10-4 Deciding on Professional Liability Insurance

Reasons To Obtain Insurance	*Reasons Not To Obtain Insurance*
Nurse is responsible for every action undertaken or omitted.	Nurse is practicing within scope of duties, hospital covers.
Hospitals could seek countersuit if nurse is negligent.	Fear of countersuit is unrealistic. Dollars gained in countersuit by hospital may cause negative effect on RN recruitment and retention.
No coverage is provided for actions outside of job description.	Potential for damage recovery increases risk of lawsuit.
With claims-made policy, no coverage is provided after leaving facility.	Potential conflict exists over percentages of compensation to be paid by nurse and hospital as separate policyholders.
Nurse lacks control if RN representation includes hospital and physicians and has no part in decision to settle or defend.	Potential conflict exists between nurse and hospital attorneys.
Nurse is self-employed, serves on professional committees, or does volunteer work.	
Cost is relatively minimal for protection provided.	

Source: Sister Rosann Geiser and Karen Fraley, "Perinatal Outreach: Liability Issues," *Journal of Perinatal and Neonatal Nursing*, vol. 2, no. 3, © 1989 Aspen Publishers, Inc.

Notice of Claim—Whenever the insured receives notice that a claim or suit is being instituted, notice must be sent by the insured to the insurance company. The policy will specify what papers are to be forwarded to the company. Note that failure to provide timely notification in accordance with the terms of a policy may void the insurer's obligation under the policy. It may not matter that the insurer has in no way been prejudiced by the late notification. The mere fact that the insured has failed to carry out its obligations under the policy may be sufficient to permit the insurer to avoid its obligations. Where the insurer has refused to honor a claim because of late notice and the insured wishes to challenge such refusal, a *declaratory judgment* action can be brought asking a court to determine the reasonableness of the insurer's position. During the period that such action is pending, it is imperative that arrangements be made by the insured to protect him- or herself from the action against him or her that precipitated the claim to the insurer.

Assistance of the Insured—The insured must cooperate with the insurance company and render any assistance necessary to reach a settlement.

Other Insurance—If the insured has pertinent insurance policies with other insurance companies, the insured must notify the insurance company in order that each company may pay the appropriate amount of the claim.

Assignment—The protections contracted by the insured may not be transferred unless permission is granted by the insurance company. Because the insurance company was aware of the risks the insured would encounter before the policy was issued, the company will endeavor to avoid protecting persons other than the policyholder.

Subrogation—Subrogation is the right of a person who pays another's debt to be substituted for all rights in relation to the debt. When an insurance company makes a payment for the insured under the terms of the policy, the company becomes the beneficiary of all the rights of recovery the insured has against any other persons who may also have been negligent.

Changes—The insured cannot make changes in the policy without the written consent of the insurance company. Thus an agent of the insurance company ordinarily cannot modify or remove any condition of the liability contract. Only the insurance company, by written authorization, may permit a condition to be altered or removed.

Cancellation—A cancellation clause spells out the conditions and procedures necessary for the insured or the insurer to cancel the liability policy. Written notice is usually required. The insured person's *failure to comply with any of the conditions can result in nonpayment of a claim by* the insurance company. An insurance policy is a contract, and failure to meet the terms and conditions of the contract may result in the penalties associated with breach of contract, such as nonpayment of claims.

Chapter 11

Ethics

INTRODUCTION

Involvement with patient care often determines the quality and magnitude of ethical considerations facing a supervisor and her or his staff. Nursing departments are by nature intimately involved in patient care and are confronted with numerous serious ethical concerns, including

- the confidentiality of records
- the patient's right to privacy
- the patient's right to information regarding medical procedures and their implications
- the patient's competent consent to treatment
- the patient's right to refuse treatment
- the quality of service provided to severely disabled elderly or terminal patients
- termination of treatment

In addition to recognizing issues, the nursing manager must make decisions that involve ethical concerns. These decisions can be made and ethical issues can be resolved to some extent through collaboration with institutional resources, such as ethics committees, and the use of a decision-making process that carefully iden-

tifies an ethical component in analyzing and arriving at a decision.*

Ethical Considerations in Patient Care**

The Massachusetts Nursing Association has formulated guidelines for nursing staff and managerial actions to promote ethical behavior in the provision of nursing services.

Responsibilities

All nurses are expected to recognize their responsibilities toward their patients. Nurses have a responsibility to recognize when the care and safety of a patient is in jeopardy. This recognition is grounded in the application of sound concepts of patient care, taking into account differing but valid practice techniques. Nurses have a duty, as moral agents, to intervene to

---

*Source: Gary R. Anderson and Valerie A. Glesnes-Anderson, "Ethical Thinking and Decision Making for Health Care Supervisors," *Health Care Supervisor*, vol. 5, no. 4, © 1987 Aspen Publishers, Inc.

**Source: "Ethics for Patient Protection: Guidelines for Nurses," © Massachusetts Nurses Association, 1986. All Rights Reserved.

prevent harm to patients. Nurses should seek the least harmful and least disruptive methods of ensuring patient protection. Nurses who are employed in institutions or groups have a responsibility to make every effort to utilize and exhaust the internal reporting mechanisms before notifying public agencies or the general public; such notification is generally referred to as "whistleblowing." Nurses should seek to minimize harm to colleagues and the institution as well as patients. In crisis or emergencies, a nurse's first and overriding responsibility is to patients.

Nursing Administrator/Manager Actions

- Promote a climate in which employees are encouraged to report those situations which may adversely affect the delivery of quality care.
- Identify those persons or those practices which may cause actual or potential harm to the patient.
- Establish mechanisms for reporting and handling instances of incompetent, unethical, or illegal practice.
- Maintain confidentiality in appropriate circumstances.
- Respond to those situations which involve unacceptable practices by determining through investigation that a problem exists, including verification and documentation of facts.
- Respond further to unacceptable practices by taking actions to halt the harmful practice, such as the following:
  —reporting facts in accordance with established institutional processes
  —ensuring that practitioner(s) receive appropriate notification and referral if a pattern of unsafe practice occurs
  —ensuring appropriate notification and counseling to the injured party if there has been actual or potential injury to the patient
  —adhering to institutional disciplinary policies and procedures when just and appropriate

Staff Nurse Actions

- Identify and confront those individuals on the health care team whose clinical practice clearly presents a danger to the health or safety of the client under their direct or indirect care.
- Report to the appropriate authority the individual whose unethical or unsafe practice has been confronted without an acceptable solution.
- Recognize the necessity of further reporting if the problem is not resolved at the initial reporting level.
- Participate in the development of specific procedures for identifying and reporting incompetent, illegal, or unethical practice.

Determining Whether an Act is Right or Wrong*

A nursing manager needs to recognize when he or she is faced with a situation that involves a moral issue. A balance has to be maintained between classifying all decisions as moral judgments and totally neglecting the ethical implications of any action.

How can a manager be certain of the rightness or wrongness of an action or decision? Three schools of thought provide guidance for determining whether an act is right or wrong:

The first holds that *people should do what is right*. This view assumes knowledge of basic human rights and right conduct (i.e., right to self-determination and well-being, right to know, right to privacy). A right decision is one made in accordance with the person's rules, codes, and rights. This presents a conflict when (a) there is little agreement concerning these rules of conduct; (b) there is a conflict between personal values and the decision's perceived benefit or the survival of a department or institution; or (c) there is a contradiction between two

---

Source: Gary R. Anderson and Valerie A. Glesnes-Anderson, "Ethical Thinking and Decision Making for Health Care Supervisors," *Health Care Supervisor*, vol. 5, no. 4, © 1987 Aspen Publishers, Inc.

rules, for example, the dilemma posed in respecting someone's confidential communication when that person intends to harm someone else.

The second view holds that *a moral course of action is that which provides the greatest benefit to those people affected by the action.* In simple terms, this view states that rightness or wrongness is relative to outcome (whereas the first school emphasizes that one should do what is right regardless of the circumstances). This view assumes knowledge of a decision's benefit and also requires the difficult task of weighing and balancing the consequences for one person against those for others.

A third (less prominent) view suggests that *what is right is what is in the best interest of the person choosing the course of action.* This view advances an individualistic stance and suggests that the "end justifies the means."

To maintain a higher degree of objectivity in decision making, a supervisor might need to examine his or her values and exercise caution in applying these values.

In addition to recognizing issues that involve values, the nursing manager must make decisions that involve ethical concerns. These decisions can be made and ethical issues can be resolved to some extent through collaboration with institutional resources, such as ethics committees, and the use of a decision-making process that carefully identifies an ethical component in analyzing and arriving at a decision.

Types of Ethical Conflicts*

Ethical dilemmas occur when a solution to a conflict encroaches on the interests and welfare of another. For example, society's inclination toward prolonging life may conflict with the patient's autonomy to make decisions about his or her care. Among critically-ill patients, such dilemmas most frequently center around four ethical conflicts: autonomy versus paternalism,

---

Source: Ginger Schafer Wlody, "Technology, Ethics, and Critical Care," in *Advanced Technology in Critical Care Nursing*, John M. Clochesy, ed., Aspen Publishers, Inc., © 1989.

duty (deontological approach) versus outcome (teleological approach), justice versus utilitarianism, and veracity versus fidelity.

Autonomy vs. Paternalism

Autonomy refers to the right of the patient to self-determination and freedom of choice. Autonomy asserts that humans have incalculable worth, deserve respect, and have the right to self-determination. If a competent patient makes a clear statement about his or her wishes, then these wishes should be respected. Freedom of choice requires that full information be given to the patient; thus, informed consent is defined as the right of competent adults to accept or refuse medical treatment on the basis of full information.

Paternalism, on the other hand, claims that beneficence (doing good for others, being helpful) should take precedence over autonomy. Beneficence also involves balancing the benefit of some therapy with the burden of it. For example, in the paternalistic approach a health care worker makes a decision for the patient, saying "It's in his best interest." This type of conflict (autonomy versus paternalism) occurs frequently in the area of technology related to treatment decisions. If a patient needs a technological therapy that the physicians view as lifesaving but the patient views as unnatural and unbearable, he or she may make an informed decision that the benefit does not outweigh the psychological and physical costs. The patient may then refuse the therapy.

Justice vs. Utilitarianism

Justice demands that people have an opportunity to obtain the health care they need on an equitable basis. Utilitarianism states that the morally right thing to do is that act that produces the greatest good (for the greatest number of people, or society).

The current situation, in which there are expensive or limited resources, has forced health care leaders to review outcomes of care. Critically ill patients consume vast resources such as personnel, time, space, highly sophisticated equipment, and pharmacological products.

Provision of intensive care to critically ill patients ultimately has effects on other patients (the moderately ill) from whom resources may have been diverted. Therefore, clear benefit should be gained by the critically ill patient in order to justify the vast expenditures of resources.

Conflicts in this area arise because some physicians and nurses want to provide every available therapy for their patients, even though the cost (psychological and financial) may outweigh the benefits or eventual outcome.

Veracity vs. Fidelity

The concept of veracity refers to truth telling, honesty, or integrity. The nurse, as a professional, has an obligation to tell the truth. Fidelity is related to trust, or to the promises we make. Professional nurses promise to care for a patient to the best of their ability. The American Nurses' Association Code of Ethics puts forth the ethical standards for professional nurses and sets the standards for a trust relationship between the nurse and the patient.

As the nurse carries out this trust relationship and strives to deliver safe, quality care to the patient, conflicts may arise with other responsibilities the nurse has (e.g., to perform a painful or potentially dangerous procedure). Veracity conflicts with fidelity in these situations. Telling the patient truthful information that could cause the patient distress may conflict with protection of that patient.

Professional Integrity vs. Remaining True to One's Own Ethical and Moral Beliefs

Conflicts between professional integrity and remaining true to one's own ethical and moral beliefs occur in various situations. Such conflicts might result in objecting to delivering certain types of treatment or to caring for certain types of patients.

The best-known examples include nurses' participation in abortion when this procedure conflicts with their own religious and/or philosophical beliefs and nurses' caring for AIDS patients. Nurses, however, have traditionally removed themselves from the specific job situation in order to spare themselves the daily con-

flict. This becomes necessary because management cannot function in a situation in which individual nurses are saying such things as, "I don't think homosexuality is right; therefore, I cannot take care of this patient with AIDS."

Factors Affecting Ethical Issues and Ethical Decision Making*

The factors which influence ethical decision making are delineated below.

Patient Needs. Are the patient's physiological needs being met even though the patient has a terminal disease? Does the ICU "dump" (i.e., transfer) the patient out of the unit as soon as he or she is listed as a "no code" or "do not resuscitate"? The family may view the situation this way: One minute the physician in the ICU is doing "everything" he or she can to preserve the patient's life and the next minute fewer and fewer resources are used. Families sometimes value care in relation to the cost and intensity of resources used rather than what the patient needs.

Disease Processes. Which disease processes are affecting the patient? Is a given disease process reversible? Is it terminal? Is it superimposed on a chronic, irreversible process? For example, does the patient have multiple sclerosis and pneumonia?

Patient Rights. Is the nurse familiar with the American Hospital Association's *Patient Bill of Rights*? Does the hospital have a policy? The patient should be consulted and, if possible, participate in decisions that affect his or her care. If the patient is not competent, does the next of kin or guardian have the opportunity to participate in the decision-making process? The patient has the right to privacy and to competent care and the right to informed consent regarding special procedures.

Patient Feelings and Wishes. It is not only the patient's right to have informed consent but to

---

Source: Ginger Schafer Wlody, "Technology, Ethics, and Critical Care," in *Advanced Technology in Critical Care Nursing*, John M. Clochesy, ed., Aspen Publishers, Inc., © 1989.

have his or her wishes followed. If the patient wishes to have a living will or to be considered "do not resuscitate" and is hopelessly ill, these wishes should be honored and carried out according to hospital policy.

Family Wishes. A major focus in recent years has been the promotion of greater patient and family participation in decision making. Frequently, although the patient is alert and competent, the family, or a specific member, will disagree with the patient, usually "putting the patient's feelings down" or disregarding them. This occurs especially if the patient is anoxic, losing consciousness, or handicapped. Family members, because they may have been the patient's caretakers, lose sight of the patient's right to self-determination. Health care workers frequently assume this caretaker type of attitude.

Treatment Team. The treatment team is usually composed of the nurse, physician, respiratory therapist, social worker, and nutritionist. More and more often in large medical centers an ethicist, or a person who acts as an ethicist, is involved in addressing ethical dilemmas with the treatment team and family.

A nurse might consult an ethicist when there are conflicting ideas about what to do in a situation because of different values or principles (a nurse may not be sure whether to support the patient's freedom of choice or the patient's health needs).

Society. Societal changes in attitudes toward access to care, death, the handicapped, and the concept of informed consent are all important factors that influence ethical decision making.

Resource Allocation. Shortages of staff, equipment, and other resources affect the decision-making process.

Legal Issues and Hospital Policies. The nurse must be aware not only of hospital policies related to all these issues but also the legal requirements of the state in which he or she is working. For example, nurses should be familiar with hospital policies on resuscitation, withdrawal of life support, care of the brain-dead organ donor, and levels of care for the terminally ill patient.

A NURSING BIOETHICS COMMITTEE*

The primary function of a nursing ethics committee is to assist nursing personnel in assuming ethical responsibilities. This is accomplished through (1) education, (2) support, (3) decision making, and (4) consultation.

Ethics education for the nursing staff should be ongoing.

The support of knowledgeable peers is crucial for staff nurses to make effective ethical decisions. The mere presence of the committee serves to encourage positive, conscious efforts to solve ethical problems or to prevent them from occurring in the future. Staff nurses and managers are encouraged to bring concurrent and retrospective cases to the committee, which serves as a forum for airing concerns and decision-making.

Decision-making in this context refers to the identification of the ethical issues in the case, the

---

*Source: Barbra J. Edwards and Amy M. Haddad, "Establishing a Nursing Bioethics Committee," *Journal of Nursing Administration*, vol. 18, no. 3, March 1988.

Objectives for a Nursing Bioethics Committee

- To provide a structural format for professional nurses to increase their knowledge of applied ethics.

- To assist nurses in assuming ethical responsibilities and making judgments as professionals affecting change.

- To influence the development of policies on health care standards within the profession and institution.

- To serve as a resource to individual clinicians and managers whose responsibility for high-quality nursing care spans patients, families, and the community.

- To develop support within the system for nurses' active participation in ethical decision making.

- To serve as the group from which nursing representation will be selected to serve on the hospital's multidisciplinary ethics committee.

roles and responsibilities of the parties involved, alternative courses of action, and the consequences of each of the alternatives.

SPECIFIC ETHICAL ISSUES

Many ethical issues confront the nurse in the performance of his or her professional role as a health care provider. Prominent issues include the allocation of scarce resources, the withholding of medical treatment, euthanasia, and "do not resuscitate" orders.

Allocation of Scarce Health Care Resources*

Health care delivery probably has reached a point at which some form of rationing or restriction must be invoked even though society lacks moral agreement about how, or to whom, to deny medical services. Medical triage is being used in a covert fashion. Patients are "allowed" to die, doctors are deciding who shall receive high-tech medical treatments, and cost and delay inevitably kill many who cannot get access to quality health care. The ethical issues can no longer be avoided. Perhaps the most urgent ethical problem is that most health care providers sidestep such questions.

Many ethical issues involve clinical hospital support decisions where there are competing claims for scarce resources. Nurse executives should create forums for dialogue with each other and with appropriate representatives from other disciplines to begin to address these issues. In relation to their role in "distributive justice," there are three basic questions nursing administrators can ask:

1. Do they have a moral responsibility to identify and resolve ethical issues related to the distribution of scarce nursing resources?

2. If so, what kind of knowledge base do they need to enhance their moral reasoning about how to allocate these scarce nursing resources?

3. How, then, can they apply this knowledge base to distributive justice problems arising out of their nursing and administrative practice?

These are meant to be used as a springboard from which many other questions and issues will be raised.

Nursing professionals essentially have a moral obligation to guard the allocation of resources so that the care and safety of patients is not compromised. There is a large body of ethical knowledge and principles on which nurses can base and apply moral reasoning about these issues.

Withholding or Withdrawing Nutritional Support*

The increasing use of life-sustaining technologies in the care of patients has created unprecedented moral and legal questions in health care during the past decade. More recently, the question of whether technology-supported nutrition and hydration can be legally and morally withdrawn or withheld from patients has produced professional and public concern.

On March 15, 1986, the Council of Ethical and Judicial Affairs of the American Medical Association issued a *Statement on Withholding or Withdrawing Life Prolonging Medical Treatment*, declaring that life-prolonging medical treatment and artificially or technologically supplied respiration, including nutrition and hydration, may be withheld from a patient in an irreversible coma even when death is not imminent. In January 1988, the Committee on Ethics of the American Nurses' Association issued its *Guidelines on Withdrawing or Withholding Food and Fluid*, stating, in essence, that there

Source: Mychelle M. Mowry and Ralph A. Korpman, *Managing Health Care Costs, Quality, and Technology: Product Line Strategies for Nursing*, Aspen Publishers, Inc., © 1986.

Source: Sara T. Fry, "New ANA Guidelines on Withdrawing or Withholding Food and Fluid from Patients," *Nursing Outlook*, vol. 36, no. 3, May-June 1988.

are few instances under which it is morally permissible for nurses to withhold or withdraw food and/or fluid from persons in their care.

These statements from the two professions will undoubtedly provide direction to physicians and nurses in patient care decisions. However, neither document is without problems, especially when families are involved in decisions about withdrawing or withholding treatment. This is especially true in decisions involving patients who either did not or cannot make their wishes known.

Euthanasia*

Since an estimated 80 percent of Americans now die in hospitals and nursing homes, rather than at home as in the past, the topic of euthanasia is now openly and often vigorously discussed. The misconceptions and confusion regarding the topic have led to wide disparity among jurisdictions, both in legislation and in judicial decisions. As a result, the American Medical Association, the American Bar Association, legislators, and judges are actively attempting to formulate and legislate clear guidelines.

In order to properly address the topic of euthanasia, it is necessary to understand the precise meaning of the recognized forms. Rhetorical phrases such as "right to die," "right to life," and "death with dignity" have obfuscated rather than clarified the public's understanding of euthanasia.

The division of euthanasia into active and passive categories is, for many, the most controversial distinction. Active euthanasia is commonly understood to be the commission of an act that results in death. The act, if committed by the patient, is thought of as suicide. Moreover, if the patient cannot take his or her own life, any person who assists in the causing of the death could be subject to criminal sanction for aiding and abetting suicide.

Passive euthanasia occurs when lifesaving treatment (such as a respirator) is withdrawn or

withheld, allowing the patient diagnosed as terminal to die a natural death. Passive euthanasia is generally allowed by legislative acts and judicial decisions. These decisions, however, are generally limited to the facts of the particular case.

The distinctions are important when considering the duty and liability of a doctor who must decide whether or not to continue or initiate treatment of a comatose or terminally ill patient. Physicians and nurses are bound to use reasonable care to preserve health and to save lives; so unless fully protected by the law, they will be reluctant to abide by a patient's or family's wishes to terminate life support devices.

Both active and passive euthanasia may be either voluntary or involuntary. Voluntary euthanasia occurs when the suffering incurable makes the decision to die. To be considered voluntary, the request or consent must be made by a legally competent adult and based upon material information concerning the possible ramifications and alternatives available.

Death Defined and Determined

Most cases dealing with euthanasia speak of the necessity that a physician diagnose a patient as being in a persistent vegetative state or terminally ill. This diagnostic role of the physician acts as a limitation on the decision-making role of the family or guardian. Where death is actually present, of course, the termination of mechanical or other similar devices would be a consistent and permissible act.

Relying on the 1968 Harvard criteria set forth by the Ad Hoc Committee of the Harvard Medical School to Examine the Definition of Brain Death, many states now accept that death occurs when there is "irreversible cessation of all brain functions including the brain stem." At least 38 states now recognize brain death by statute or judicial decision.

Nearly half of our states also have enacted laws setting forth statutory guidelines for terminating life support. California, in 1976, was the first state to enact what has been called a natural death or living will act. Such legislation allows the creation of documents which provide a legally recognized way for competent adults to express in advance their desires regarding life-

Source: H. Robert Halper, Esq., and Hope S. Foster, Esq., *Laboratory Regulation Manual*, Aspen Publishers, Inc., © 1987.

crucial medical decisions in the event they become terminally ill and death is imminent.

Oral declarations may be accepted only after the patient has been declared terminally ill. Moreover, the declarant bears the responsibility of informing the doctor to ensure that the document becomes a part of the medical record.

The majority of states allow the document to be effective until revoked by the individual. To revoke, the patient must sign and date a new writing, destroy the first document him- or herself, direct another to do it in his or her presence, or orally state to the physician an intent to revoke. The effect of the directive varies. However, there is unanimity in the promulgation of regulations that specifically authorize health care personnel to honor the directives without fear of incurring liability.

Do Not Resuscitate*

Because the primary goal of medicine is the enhancement of life, it is only when this goal is unattainable that medically life-sustaining intervention creates opposition.

Cardiopulmonary resuscitation is one of the most common medical life-sustaining procedures performed today. The current standard of care as applied to resuscitation efforts requires resuscitation to be implemented by a responsible person or agency when two conditions are met: (1) when there is the possibility that the brain is viable and (2) when there is no legally or medically legitimate reason to withhold it. Although this standard appears to be simple, its application is quite complex.

Application of DNR Orders

A do not resuscitate (DNR) order generally means that cardiopulmonary resuscitation measures will be withheld in the event of an acute cardiac or respiratory arrest. A DNR order does not prohibit other forms of life-sustaining interventions. In critical care units, where the use of

*Source: Joan S. Dwyer, "The Decision: To Resuscitate or Not," in Controversies in Critical Care Nursing, Barbra Stewart Heater and Betty AuBuchon, eds., Aspen Publishers, Inc., © 1988.

sophisticated lifesaving technology is commonplace, many patients continue to receive vasopressors, antiarrhythmics, antibiotics, pulmonary artery catheters, and ventilators despite an order to withhold resuscitation. A DNR order does not and should not imply that the patient's care will be less aggressive or substandard. Nor does it mean that the amount of nursing care required will be reduced.

The legal issue presented here is whether or not the law prohibits a course of medical treatment that excludes resuscitation attempts in the event of cardiac or respiratory arrest and, if not, whether prior judicial approval for the validity of a DNR order is required. In analyzing this issue, it is important to distinguish between the withholding and the withdrawal of medically life-sustaining treatment. While the result is the same in both cases, namely death, the rationale for the final determination will be affected by specific facts concerning the individual in question.

While the courts have acknowledged the right of an individual to have medical treatment withheld, including resuscitation, the decision-making responsibility has not been vested unilaterally in the physician. When the patient is unable to speak for him- or herself, the patient or the patient's family must be afforded the opportunity and the responsibility to share in the decision.

Each case in which there is a decision to withhold resuscitation is unique. It is the facts of the case that influence the application of the individual's rights and principles of law. In determining whether resuscitative treatment can be withheld, it is necessary to identify the nature and application of an individual's rights and the legal implications of upholding or overriding these rights.

An individual can be placed into one or two categories: competent or incompetent. In the hospital setting, the categorization of the adult patient may shift from competent to incompetent due to narcotics, tranquilizers, or general anesthesia; pain may also contribute to an altered state of mental capacity and thus render a patient incompetent. A minor, unemancipated child is always deemed incompetent. The determination of the category dictates which individual rights apply.

Documentation of Nonintervention

Whether the patient is deemed competent or incompetent, the decision-making process must reflect the patient's or family's understanding of resuscitative nonintervention. The medical and legal importance for documenting their reflection cannot be overstated. While the Joint Commission on Accreditation of Healthcare Organizations requires a hospital policy pertaining to informed consent and the medical record to contain evidence of appropriate informed consent, there is no "per se" requirement for a policy on or evidence of the converse of informed consent, namely, informed refusal.

While documentation need not be drafted as a formal agreement or a permit for "informed refusal," there is a logical, legal recommendation for a memorandum of understanding that would provide a minimum standard for the medical record.

Assent by one family member may not mean unanimous assent. If nonintervention is applied, legal recourse by the nonconsenting family members for negligent liability will remain. A written declaration and authorization, preferably signed by the spouse and all adult children, would be of substantial evidentiary proof in the defense of a legal unit.

Slow Codes

A frequently used alternative to DNR orders is the implementation of slow codes. A slow code is generally defined as a slowed response and/or performance time and/or the limited administration of medications in a cardiopulmonary arrest situation. Although the family may be comforted, initially, by the appearance of lifesaving measures, the potential for malpractice litigation remains. The legal liability involved with slow codes arises from the duty of care that is owed the patient and the extent of damages, physical and financial, the patient may suffer.

Although slow codes may sometimes appear to be the appropriate moral response, legally they are not! Resuscitation must be considered an all-or-nothing proposition. If the patient is to acknowledge death as a natural act and if the right to die with dignity is to be effected, then the mutual consent of the patient, either by personal or substituted decision making, and the physician should be expressly recorded as a DNR order. Without a DNR order, resuscitation should be carried out to the fullest.

Judgment of Competency*

Although nurses support and guide patients daily in fulfilling diagnostic treatment requirements, this is not done with ease when patients begin refusing to comply with protocols of health care. Many nurses would welcome a model to follow when there is a need to assess patient competence in order to know whether a paternalistic posture would be justified or whether the patient's sovereign state should be respected. From a legal view, persons are considered competent until it is determined otherwise by a judicial hearing; however, clinical situations that require a nurse to make a competency assessment are a reality and are often of a pressing nature. The autonomy of individuals is seriously respected by nurses, but a paradigm is needed for offering this protection when a patient's competency is being challenged.

As the disease process may affect the patient's mental capacity, so also can interpersonal factors or the real or imagined features of a health care facility. A high level of awareness is needed by the nurse to distinguish a competency assessment issue from these other effects. Available charted models of competency determination can provide some conceptual understanding of how to act in a knowledgeable way, lifting moral choice out of an intuitive base. Judgments of patient competence can be based on understood concepts and are not to be confused with bias held by the health care provider. Although many patients are competent to make decisions about their nursing care and health care, it is important to address those borderline areas of competency that provoke uncertainty and need formulation by nursing.

*Source: Virginia Kilpack, "Ethical Issues and Procedural Dilemmas in Measuring Patient Competence," in *Ethical Issues in Nursing*, ed. Peggy L. Chinn, Aspen Publishers, Inc., 1986.

Patient Self-Determination*

Although the nurse is obligated to act in the best interests of the patient, it is the patient and not the nurse who decides what those "best interests" are. The role of the nurse, however, goes beyond that of merely protecting patients against institutional encroachments on their freedom of choice. It involves actively assisting patients in the exercise of self-determination—helping them to clarify values and beliefs, to develop their understanding of self and of the situation, and to make decisions based on their own goals and wishes.

Three models of practice that may have some relevance for how nurses structure their relationships with patients have been described. The first is the "engineering model," which consists of giving the patient only the facts, usually emphasizing "scientific facts," and allowing the patient to decide. The provider in this model believes that it is improper to get involved in values concerning patient situations and often is unaware of how his or her own values influence the nature of transaction.

The "priestly model" of practice is paternalistic in orientation. The provider expects the patient to follow directions given and operates on the basis of "I know best." A variant of this model is the maternal form, which often assumes

an ultraprotective stance toward the patient while at the same time setting absolute standards for the patient's performance. The "contractual model" of practice provides for shared decision making by the provider and the patient and assumes that both parties have obligations and obtain benefits from their shared endeavors.

The contractual model appears to be most suitable for the nurse-patient relationship given nursing's primary goals. Establishing contractual arrangements by mutual consent and the ongoing process of evaluating progress and making decisions about new courses of action depends on both parties being willing to exchange information and to validate their observations, so that the next step can be taken toward the agreed-upon goals. The process of helping the patient to make decisions that incorporate the patient's own values and concepts of self and health demands far more of nurses, both intellectually and interpersonally, than simply making decisions on behalf of the patient.

The education of nurses who are responsive to the moral as well as the technical components of professional work requires an interpersonal environment that does more than distribute knowledge and promote conformity to established professional norms. It should promote the exercise of self-determination and personal growth of students in a holistic sense through a milieu that encourages independence of observation, originality of thought, dissent from established opinion, tolerance for differences in viewpoint, and respect for the rights and contributions of others.

Source: Jeanne Quint Benoliel, "Ethics in Nursing Practice and Education," *Nursing Outlook*, July-August 1983. Reprinted with permission of the American Journal of Nursing Company.

Part III

Administration

Chapter 12

Financial Managing and Budgeting

FINANCIAL RESPONSIBILITIES AND SKILLS OF NURSE MANAGERS*

Changes in third-party reimbursement, the economics of the nursing and medical professions, organizational diversification, and rising competition make it imperative that managers be well versed in and allocate sufficient time to financial management. Unless nurse managers develop a functional competency in financial management, they may be unable to contribute to financial issues involving their nursing program or organization.

If nurse managers expect to adopt a financial perspective commensurate with their managerial and clinical skills, it follows that they must first learn basic financial concepts and techniques. Such knowledge is a prerequisite to nurse leadership. A solid grounding in financial basics allows nurse managers to acquire power and to participate jointly (with other nonnursing managers) in key decision processes.

Decisions about budgets and financial plans, for example, are constrained by many factors outside nursing services.

First, the philosophy of the chief executive officer (CEO) and the governing board relative to expenditure increases, capital outlays, equipment acquisition, or cost control affects financial decisions for the nursing program.

Second and third, nursing's profile as a revenue generator (or revenue consumer) influences the extent to which funds are allocated for program growth. Nursing is often viewed as a consumer of resources rather than a revenue generator. Nurse managers need to demonstrate how nursing expenditures enhance other service units (e.g., laboratory, radiology, and surgical services) that are revenue earners. In this manner, nursing establishes rights to its fair allocation of resources.

A fourth factor constraining financial plans is the extent to which the proposed plans are cost-effective. This cost-effectiveness is related to nursing's reputation as a credible financial manager. The credibility of proposed budgets is linked to the credibility of nurse managers as financial planners. It is also supported by past efforts at attaining budgets.

Fifth, decisions about nursing expenditures and annual budgets by key decision makers are affected by the perceived thresholds of safe clinical practice.

Other factors affecting financial plans—quality of care and state-of-the-art practice—are related to safe clinical practice. Nursing programs are expected to produce high-quality care and to maintain safe clinical practices. Hence

*Source: Judith F. Garner, Howard L. Smith, and Neill F. Piland, *Strategic Nursing Management: Power and Responsibility in a New Era*, Aspen Publishers, Inc., © 1990.

financial planning hinges on documentation (of quality or low risk) to justify resource expenditures.

Further, resources used in the budgeting process influence financial planning by nurse managers. Reports, information, data files, historical schedules, and similar resources ultimately determine the accuracy of proposals. Consequently, they represent another factor constraining financial plans. This information is usually provided by financial personnel who may not understand the considerations and trade-offs surrounding clinical practice. Nurse managers work with financial officers in guiding their understanding of how nursing functions as an individual financial entity. The final step suggests that expected outcomes from nursing activities influence decisions about allocations to nursing services.

In sum, nurse managers should attempt to control various factors in presenting a solid financial plan to health care decision makers. Financial management is predicated on basics. Without basic knowledge of financial skill areas, it will be difficult if not impossible for nurse managers to contribute an enlightened perspective on nursing services to the rest of the organization.

THE BUDGET PROCESS

Overview*

The budgeting process is a tool for planning, monitoring, and controlling cost. It enables the director of nursing to demonstrate the cost of the nursing care required in each hospital unit. A nursing unit's budgeting process should

- plan for required patient hours
- plan for paid time off, vacation, holidays, etc.
- take into account weekends off
- plan for nondirect patient-care activities
- correlate budgeted positions to actual day-of-the-week staffing patterns by shift

- include measures of performance, both of finances and productivity (in this case productivity equals the ratio of the required patient-care hours based on the patient census and acuity to the actual hours worked)

Budget Coordination*

To ensure an orderly and timely development of the departmental budget program, the coordinating team must be well defined. Usually, the department manager or his or her assistants will assume the role of departmental budget coordinator. This individual will work directly with the total health care facility's budget director, who is frequently the chief financial officer, the controller, or a special budget director, in the preparation of the technical aspects of the budget preparation, execution, and monitoring.

Budget Committee*

Depending upon the size of the department, it may be advisable to form a departmental budget committee of top management and supervising personnel to assist the department's budget coordinator. The departmental budget committee can assist the department manager in the monitoring of the budget and in the budget preparation. Although the budget coordinator does most of the work in the budget preparation, the critical part of the budgeting is performed by the line supervisors and department heads. Unless the parties to be controlled by the budget have a voice in developing the budget and agree with the reasonableness of the final departmental budget, control will be relatively ineffective. To assist in the budget coordination process, a budget planning schedule should be devised.

Cost Centers**

Four cost centers must be considered in preparing a unit budget.

---

*Source: J.N. Althaus et al., *Nursing Decentralization: The El Camino Experience*, Aspen Publishers, Inc., © 1981, based on ''Planning and Budgets: Magic or Math'' by John Fleming in Elsie Schmied, ed., *Maintaining Cost Effectiveness*, Aspen Publishers, Inc, © 1978.

*Source: Allen G. Herkimer, Jr., *Understanding Hospital Financial Management*, Aspen Publishers, Inc., © 1978.

**Source: J.N. Althaus et al., *Nursing Decentralization: The El Camino Experience*, Aspen Publishers, Inc., © 1981, based on ''Planning and Budgets: Magic or Math'' by John Fleming in Elsie Schmied, ed., *Maintaining Cost Effectiveness*, Aspen Publishers, Inc, © 1978.

Administration. Coded to this cost center is the time spent by the head nurse and unit personnel in managing the nursing unit. Some examples of how the time is used include coaching staff, completing performance appraisals, attending meetings, updating and revising unit policies and procedures, unit planning, and nursing research. The head nurse shares the administrative hours with assistant head nurses and staff nurses, depending on management responsibilities delegated to them.

New Training. Orientation of new personnel and orientation of current nursing staff to a new area of responsibility are coded to new training. Also allocated to the NT cost center are the hours spent by nurses who are serving as preceptors to new employees.

Education. Nursing unit educational conferences, in-house educational programs, and independent learning time spent by nurses in the hospital's learning center are coded to the education cost center.

Patient Care. All nursing time spent in patient care is coded to this cost center. Also coded here is the time worked by the unit secretaries.

Hours are estimated for each of these cost centers. The hours for new training, education, administration, and patient care cost centers differ according to the kind of unit and will be negotiated between the head nurse and the director of nursing during actual budget sessions. The nursing unit's overall goal is a summary of the hours and negotiated goals of the four cost centers.

Budget Planning

Factors in Budget Planning*

Nursing service needs are determined by many factors, which the staff should be aware of as budget planning proceeds:

1. The type of patient (medical, surgical, maternity, pediatric, communicable disease, chronically ill), the length of stay, and the acuteness of the illness).
2. The size of the hospital and its bed occupancy. It takes more total personnel in the *large* hospital than it does in the smaller hospital to care for the same number of patients.
3. The physical layout of the hospital, the size and plan of the ward—open ward, small units, private ward.
4. Personnel policies:
   a. Salaries paid to various types of nursing personnel, including pay for overtime.
   b. The length of the workweek and work period as well as flexibility of hours.
   c. The extent of vacation, statutory holidays, and sick leave.
   d. Provision for in-service education programs, including instructional staff as well as relief staff.
   e. Provision for development of staff through university preparation, refresher courses, etc.
5. The grouping of patients: for example, specialized units, such as neurological services and intensive care units, will have differing needs.
6. Standards of nursing care: The kind and amount of care to be given as it affects the number of hours of bedside care, for example, assisting the patient with a fracture to adjust to the degree of independence of which he or she is capable; health teaching, including methods of adjusting to normal living in the community.
7. The method of performing nursing procedures, simple or complex; the method of recordkeeping and charting, for example, whether or not all routine procedures such as baths and back rubs must be charted, all medications must be recorded in the nurses' notes, a work sheet and checking system are in use.
8. The proportion of nursing care provided by professional nurses as compared to that provided by auxiliary personnel.
9. The availability of graduate and allied personnel and the utilization of both

---

*Source: *Nursing Service Budget*, National League for Nursing, Pub. No. 22, 1957. Reprinted with permission.

groups according to competencies and preparation.

10. The amount and quality of supervision available and provided; the efficiency of job descriptions and job classifications.
11. Method of patient assignment, for example, team nursing.
12. The amount and kinds of labor-saving equipment and devices: intercommunication systems; carrier and pneumatic tube systems; electronic monitor for determining vital signs, etc.
13. The amount of centralized service provided: sterile supply; central oxygen service; postoperative recovery room; messenger and porter service; linen service, including distribution of linen.
14. Whether or not nonnursing functions such as clerical, dietary, housekeeping, messenger, and porter services are the responsibility of the nursing department.
15. The nursing service requirements of ancillary departments: clinics, admitting office, health service, emergency department, etc. These activities may be included in the responsibilities of the nursing department but should not be charged to nursing.
16. Reports required by administration, whether simple or complex.
17. Method of appointment of medical staff: size of staff; activities of medical staff; kind and frequency of treatments and orders.
18. Affiliation with a medical school. Inexperienced medical students need more equipment and supplies.
19. The presence, or not, of a school of nursing.

*A Budget Planning Flow Diagram**

Preparation of the budget package can be divided into eight activities. A flow diagram depicting the steps in the budget-planning process is shown in Figure 12-1.

Source: Joan Althaus et al., *Nursing Decentralization: The El Camino Experience*, Aspen Publishers, Inc., © 1981.

1. *Productivity goal determination*. Here the director of nursing services and the head nurse determine the unit's productivity goal for the coming fiscal year.
2. *Forecast workload*. The number of patient days expected on each nursing unit for the coming fiscal year are forecasted.
3. *Budgeted patient care hours*. The number of hours expected to be used in patient care for the patient days are forecasted.
4. *Budgeted patient care hours and staffing schedules*. Here the budgeted patient care hours are reflected in recommended staffing schedules by shift and by day of the week.
5. *Planned nonproductive hours*. The vacation, holiday, education leave, sick leave, etc., hours are budgeted for the coming year.
6. *Productive and nonproductive time*. To aid in the planning process, a graph is used to show head and assistant head nurses how the level of forecasted patient days and therefore the staffing requirements are expected to move up and down during the year. Productive time is the time spent on the job in patient care, administration of the unit, conferences, educational activities, and orientation.

Only steps 7 and 8, "supplies and services" and "capital budget," are concerned with nonlabor expenses.

These eight steps result in a total budget package which goes to the director of nursing services for review. Upon his or her preliminary acceptance of this budget, it is sent to the accounting department, where the forecasted patient days are turned into expected revenue. The budgeted productive and nonproductive time is extended into dollars, as are the costs for supplies and services and other operating expenses that will be allocated to a given nursing unit for the coming year. A pro forma operating statement is then returned to the director of nursing for review, by the director and the head nurse. When the director and head nurse accept the budget, it is returned to the accounting department and forwarded with the rest of the hospital budgets to administration and the board of directors.

Figure 12-1 The Decentralized Budgeting Process

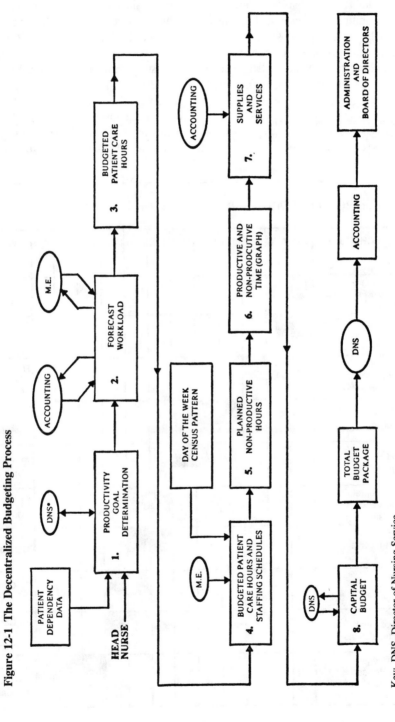

Key: DNS–Director of Nursing Service
      ME–Management Engineer

Preparation and Presentation*

The director must be aware of any special instructions available from hospital administration about preparation of data and the annual procedure for budgeting—and so inform the committee and unit personnel responsible for budget preparation. He or she must also obtain a copy of the hospital calendar budget which will

*Source: Marie DiVincenti, *Administering Nursing Service*, Little, Brown and Company, 1978. Copyright © 1978 by Little, Brown and Company. Reprinted with permission.

provide sufficient information for internal budget planning and a timetable of proposed activities. The nursing budget committee initiates a calendar based on the hospital calendar, which will also serve as a schedule to outline activities leading to the preparation and completion of the nursing budget. (See Figure 12-2.)

Past operations records need to be analyzed, and the overall master staffing plan must be reviewed. Each supervisor should work with his or her head nurses to determine the staff requirements for each unit. They should consider such factors as: (1) assurance of standards according

Figure 12-2 Annual Budget Plan (ABP) for Department of Nursing

SCHEDULE / ACTIVITIES	JUL	AUG	SEP	OCT	NOV	DEC	JAN	FEB	MAR	APR	MAY	JUN	WHO WILL DO/HELP
1. Establish Objectives for the Fiscal Year 1986-1987	■												Dir. of Nursing Assoc. Director
2. Identify Key Issues	■												Dir. of Nursing Assoc. Director Pt. Care Coords.
3. Analyze Performance and Resources		■											Dir. of Nursing Controller Pt. Care Coords.
4. State Basic Assumptions			■										Pt. Care Coords. Dir. of Nursing
5. Set Unit Objectives				■									Pt. Care Coords. Unit Staff
6. Develop Program Strategies and Action Plans						■							Pt. Care Coords. Unit Staff
7. Forecast Income						■							Controller
8. Develop Operational Plans							■						Pt. Care Coords. Unit Staff
9. Prepare Budget Recommendations								■					Pt. Care Coords. Dir. of Nursing Assoc. Director
10. Submit Budget; Review, Revise, and Secure Approval										■			Dir. of Nursing Assoc. Director Pt. Care Coords.

Source: Adapted from J. Ganong and W. Ganong, "APB for Nursing Administration," *Journal of Nursing Administration*, May-June 1973. Reprinted with permission.

to the philosophy and objectives of the hospital and the department of nursing, (2) past experiences of the unit, (3) anticipated needs for the unit, and (4) percentage of unit occupancy.

The estimation of staff for each unit should also include, for example, provision for vacation, sick leave, holidays, average amount of illness per staff member, and on-call pay. The number of hours of nursing care and nursing service hours per patient should be estimated from the total.

As these figures are identified for each unit within the nursing department, there emerges a visible method of interpreting nursing care needs to the nursing budget committee and later to hospital administration.

Consideration should next be given to any new activities that will occur within a unit or have some bearing on the overall department, such as new services for patient care, changes in in-service educational programs, or changes in other hospital departments that affect the nursing services required.

A review of the number of nursing hours per patient per day should be done to determine whether the amount of care provided was comparable to what is considered minimal for safe nursing care. The hours may be maintained by the nursing office or data processing office and available to nursing administration. Each supervisor and head nurse should receive a monthly report of nursing hours and should have a cumulative record from the previous fiscal year to review. These figures must be scrutinized, moreover, to find out whether the quality of nursing care met the predetermined standards of care and whether it could be maintained by using other levels of personnel, with fewer professional personnel, by a prearrangement of duties and responsibilities—for example, the addition of unit clerks to the evening tour of duty.

The next step in the preparation of the budget is to ascertain the amount and kind of supplies needed for the operation of each nursing unit, or those which are for total departmental use. A review of the last fiscal year's expenses provides data for planning. For budgetary purposes, the year's expected expenses can be divided by 12 or, where possible, calculated month by month. Generally, a 5 to 10 percent increase in cost of supplies is figured because of rising prices. Each unit should identify its needs in writing. Each nursing unit also submits a list of its own capital expenditure needs, and they are compiled into the total departmental requests.

As each supervisor or head nurse completes the preparation of the proposed budget, he or she meets with the nursing budget committee to make a formal presentation of the unit's financial request. The purpose of the session is to review the operating and capital expenditures and allow for an explanation and justification of unit requests. To be discussed are: (1) personnel staffing requirements, with a justification if additional persons are needed; (2) general impact of supplies needed for use; (3) capital equipment to be replaced or requested, with documented justification, and other items requiring financial assistance; and (4) in some situations, specific recommendations for equipment and supplies prepared by the nursing unit staff with the chief of staff.

The unit budgets are approved as recommended, or revisions may be requested by the committee. Once the unit budgets are reviewed, classified, and summarized, the next step is to examine the departmental nursing budget appropriation and the actual expenditures for the current year, using information furnished by the accounting department in conjunction with the statistical data, such as average daily census per unit per service for the past year and anticipated census for the fiscal budget year; percentage of bed occupancy by months; average length of patient stay for the past year; total patient days and outpatient visits; nursing service hours per patient per day; number of employees divided into their various classifications; and expenses for supplies.

Budget Presentation

After the nurse director compiles and completes the final draft of the nursing service budget, he or she should carefully reflect on how to present the budget to the controller, budget officer, or hospital administrator. Presentation of the proposed budget affords the nurse director an opportunity to outline future nursing service plans for the department and the hospital, to define goals, and to set forth ideas for achieving the desired results. It also allows him or her to review the department's past achievements and appraise them with some degree of perspective. A carefully planned budget presentation will reflect favorably upon the administration; a haphazard presentation may place the director in a less than favorable position.[1]

Guidelines to Presenting the Budget*

Preparation of a sound budget by nurse administrators is the most important step for ensuring favorable action by the budget committee. Defense of the nursing budget must be clearly stated, the costs must be accurate, and the revenues must be defensible. Much of the selling is done by preparing for it. There are five guidelines, however, that help.

Be prepared to defend the budget. Every program must be carefully thought through. Although each budget committee member will have figures at hand, the nurse administrator must have a detailed overall plan for every program. This will include support for need, objectives, cost of additional resources (personnel, supplies, equipment, space) and source of funding.

Initiate a marketing strategy. This can include selling programs to budget committee members beforehand. An example is joint appointments of nursing professors/instructors as nursing staff in a university medical center. The plan should be carefully made, supported by nursing service and nursing college administrators, and sold to the vice president for academic affairs. Get support of interested parties beforehand, and decide how to use the support successfully.

Anticipate challenges. Who will be against the program? Why will they be against it? Prepare a sound defense for each anticipated challenge. When the nursing shortage is less acute, finance personnel are prone to want to cut salaries and fringe benefits. Be prepared to defend call pay, shift differentials, and clinical ladders.

Be persuasive without being emotional. If the clinical ladder is under attack, present the differences between the performance requirements for each level and relate them to productivity.

Work for win-win situations. Plan fallback positions in the management plan. These could range from optimum to minimally acceptable. Begin with the optimum, and if the committee and chief executive officer want cuts, negotiate. They win concessions, and the nurse administrator wins a program.

BUDGET APPROACHES

1. Zero Base Budget*

Zero base budgeting assumes that no existing program is entitled to automatic approval. Many individuals have identified this process with existing budgetary systems that are based on prior year expenditure levels. Zero base budgeting looks at the entire budget and determines the efficacy of the entire expenditure.

A cost-benefit analysis and the "arithmetic" used in zero base budgeting reviews are concerned with two questions:

- Are the services presently provided being delivered in an efficient manner?
- Are the services presently provided being delivered in an effective manner in terms of the organization's goals and objectives?

A procedure for quantitatively answering these two questions is important; there are seven sequential steps that must be conducted.

- Define the outputs or services provided by the program/departmental area.
- Determine the costs of these services or outputs.
- Identify options for reducing the cost through changes in outputs or services.
- Identify options for producing the services and outputs more efficiently.
- Determine the cost savings associated with options identified in steps 3 and 4.

---

[1]DiVincenti, *op cit.*

*Source: Russell C. Swansburg, Philip W. Swansburg, and Richard J. Swansburg, *The Nurse Manager's Guide to Financial Management*, Aspen Publishers, Inc., © 1988.

---

*Source: William O. Cleverly, *Essentials of Health Care Finance,* ed 2, Aspen Publishers, Inc., © 1986.

- Assess the risks, both qualitative and quantitative, associated with the identified options of steps 3 and 4.
- Select and implement those options with an acceptable cost-risk relationship.

Modifications Based on Review

The concept of cost that is most relevant is *avoidable cost*. An attempt is made to discover what the costs of these services are now and what costs would be incurred if these services were discontinued. In this context, the direct cost of the department is most useful. Indirect cost in most situations should be ignored because it is unavoidable.

Among the options for modifying outputs are the following: elimination of the service, reduction in the frequency of the service, reduction in the quality of the service, or reduction in the amount of the service.

Options for providing services more efficiently should also be seriously examined. The identification of improved ways to provide services is an important activity in efforts to minimize costs.

Risk is a function of two factors: the probability of an adverse consequence and the potential severity of that consequence. In most situations, both these factors are highly subjective. However, some idea of risk, even subjectively determined, is necessary in the overall assessment of the option's desirability.

After the conclusion of this analysis, someone needs to make a decision concerning which specific options should be selected. This designation falls to those involved in the zero base review or the management structure.

2. Forecast Budget*

A critical element in forecast budgeting is the grasp of the upside/downside concept. The upside concept reflects factors that would demonstrate growth or increased demands on services and the cost of providing them. The downside concept would indicate adverse trends

or a decline in the demand for services. Forecasting requires a firm grasp of future events and conditions, and the upside/downside impacts determine the measure of budgetary adjustments to be made over previous budgets.

There are basically two types of forecasting methods to consider. These are mechanical and analytical forecasting.

> *Mechanical forecasting,* also known as historic forecasting, usually involves a straight percentage increase multiplied across the board. It can be used for yearly projections on demands and services. However, it is best to go back three years as the base from which to project.
> *Analytical forecasting* employs the upside/downside concepts and seeks to project realistic figures based on the impact of demands for services. Critical factors to be considered in forecasting are future events or conditions that will affect situation, people, time, and causative controls.

Examples of critical factors that affect situations in health care might be a change in patient days or in patient mix or in patient services.

Examples of critical factors impacting people might be personnel turnover rate or availability of various levels of personnel.

Examples of critical factors influencing time or showing trends toward change might be trends toward more outpatient services, in-service education, or unionization.

Examples of critical factors influencing place might be a move to another location or sharing space or facilities with another department.

Examples of critical factors that affect controls or constraints might be new legislation, Joint Commission demands, or PSRO requirements.

Management Activities

A listing of management activities performed during the forecasting phase of budget preparation would probably include the following:

- Identify the budgetary and forecasting period. This might be 12 months, 18 months, or whatever period is selected.

Source: Kathleen A. Waters and Gretchen F. Murphy, *Medical Records in Health Information*, Aspen Publishers, Inc., © 1979.

- Identify and gather information on future events and conditions affecting people, place, trends, controls, and situations.
- Sort out information into upside/downside influences and trace these to departmental activities and services.
- Translate or convert these impacts into measurable units: hours, people, equipment needed, dollars and cents.
- Communicate to and obtain understanding and acceptance of the forecast by all affected components of your department. (If, for example, you are planning to go into a heavy-scale nursing-audit activity, you can project the .5 full-time equivalent employee increase needed to do ten audits per year.)
- Write out indirect costs debited against department budgets and check into increases in cost and activity for the future.

3. Fixed or Static Budget*

Currently, the fixed or static budget is the most common budgetary approach. This budget is based upon a fixed annual level of volume activity (i.e., number of patient days, tests performed) to arrive at an annual budget total. Usually, these totals are then divided into 12 equal parts for each month of the year. The primary weakness in this approach is that it does not allow for seasonal or monthly variations. To illustrate, assume a nursing station has 36 beds and the nursing supervisor and head nurse anticipate a 75 percent patient occupancy and a staffing requirement of 4.2 nursing hours per patient day. The nursing salary budget would be developed as follows:

- total capacity: 36
- projected percent of occupancy: 75 percent
- projected average daily census: 27
- projected calendar days: 365

---

*Source: Budget approaches 3 to 7 and associated tables are from Allen G. Herkimer, Jr., *Understanding Hospital Financial Management*, Aspen Publishers, Inc., © 1978.

- projected annual patient days: 9,855
- average nursing hours per patient day: 4.2
- annual nursing hours requirement: 41,391
- average hourly rate: $7.50
- annual nursing costs: $310,433
- average monthly patient day census: 822
- average monthly nursing hours requirement: 3,449
- average monthly nursing costs: $25,869

However, this approach is frequently used to prepare a department's initial budget. This is especially true when there is relatively little historical data upon which to project seasonal volume variations. Obviously, this is the simplest budget to prepare, but most managers feel it is too difficult to compare, evaluate, and relate to the department's actual performance, since the fixed budget does not allow for volume variations in the initial plan.

4. Flexible Budget

The flexible budgeting approach establishes relevant ranges of volume activity. A relevant range of activity represents the range of volume or production units from a low point to a higher point. Expanding upon the above illustration, assume the nursing supervisor and the head nurse establish the variations for patient census or occupancy level options indicated in Table 12-1.

Revenue and expense budgets are then prepared to reflect the average revenue and expenses (i.e., staffing requirements) for each of the three volume options. The monthly flexible

---

Table 12-1 Patient Volume and Range of Activity

Volume Options	Total Patient Pay Capacity	Volume Percent	Range of Activity Patient Days
1	36	60–75%	22–27
2	36	76–89%	28–32
3	36	90% & over	33–36

Table 12-2 Computation of Monthly Flexible Nursing Salary Budget

Volume Option	Percent Occupancy	Average Annual Patient Days	Nursing Hours per Patient Day	Avg. Annual Nursing Hrs. Requirement	Avg. Hourly Rate	Average Annual Nursing Salary Budget	Average Flexible Nursing Budget		
							Patient Days	Nursing Hours	Nursing Costs
1	60–75%	8,943	4.2	37,560	$7.50	$281,700	745	3,130	$23,475
2	76–89%	10,950	4.2	45,990	$7.50	$344,925	913	3,833	$28,744
3	90% & over	12,593	4.2	52,890	$7.50	$396,675	1,049	4,408	$33,056

nursing salary budget would be computed as shown in Table 12-2.

In reality, three individual budgets are prepared to reflect the hourly and salary requirements for the various volume levels or relevant ranges of activity. These ranges of activity will facilitate the fitting of budget-level requirements to actual performance of the nursing station.

The two primary disadvantages of this budgeting approach are that it requires more preparation and maintenance time and that it establishes range of activity rather than pinpointing the actual volume activity.

5. Variable Expense Budget

The variable expense budget approach allows the department manager and his or her supervisors to pinpoint the budget plan to the actual performance volume. In practice, the variable expense budget approach establishes a formula to enable the generation of a control budget which is directly related to volume activity. It is computed by using predetermined standards or budgeted rates and multiplying these rates by the actual volume. This eliminates variances that might occur due to volume differences.

To develop a variable expense budget, each cost item must be classified into one of three categories:

1. *Fixed costs*—those that remain essentially constant in the short run, irrespective of changes in output volume.
2. *Variable costs*—those that vary directly (in proportion) with changes in output volume.

3. *Semi- or step-variable costs*—those that are neither fixed nor variable.

This variable expense budget approach is frequently referred to as dynamic cost control. It is effective in departments where it is difficult to budget workload volume, such as nursing, but it requires a considerable amount of preparation, maintenance time, and cost. (See Table 12-3.)

6. Rolling or Moving Budget

The rolling or moving budget concept is basically an expansion upon any of the above-mentioned budgeting approaches. Under this method, the most recent month or quarter is deleted and a new projection is added for a corresponding month or quarter, so that the budget continually projects a fixed period of time, usually a minimum of a year.

The rolling or moving budget approach is especially effective in a department or facility which is exceptionally dynamic as far as costs and volume changes are concerned. Also, this concept ties very nicely into the belief that the budget is a management tool and must be continually monitored and updated.

7. Program Budget

The program budget approach can be very effective when a department manager is interested in projecting estimated revenue and expense of a specific new program.

The program budget is usually developed separately from the conventional budgetary process

Table 12-3 Preparing a Variable Expense Budget

To illustrate the preparation of a variable expense budget, let us assume that the 4.2 nursing hours are divided into the following classifications:

Position	Hourly Standard	Hourly Rate
Head Nurse	0.2	$12.00
Registered Nurse	1.0	9.00
Licensed Practical Nurse	2.0	6.50
Nurse Aide	.5	6.50
Ward Clerk	.5	6.70
Total Average	4.2	$ 7.50

Assume that the head nurse, one registered nurse, one licensed practical nurse, and the ward clerk have been classified as fixed costs and the remaining personnel are considered as variable costs as follows:

	Salary Costs	
Position	Fixed	Variable per Patient Day
Head Nurse	$2,080	
Registered Nurse	1,560	
Licensed Practical Nurse	1,127	
Ward Clerk	1,161	
Total Monthly Fixed Costs	$5,928	
Variable Costs Licensed Practical Nurse 1 hour @ $6.50 =		$6.50
Nurse Aide ½ hour @ 6.50 =		3.25
Total Variable Cost per Patient Day		$9.75

Table 12-3 *continued*

Assume the actual patient days (P/D) for the month were 950. Applying the above standard variable costs, the month's variable expense control budget would be compared to the actual performance as follows:

Description	Control Budget	Actual	Variance
Patient Days	950	950	0
Fixed Costs			
Head Nurse	$2,080	$2,080	0
Registered Nurse	1,560	1,560	0
Licensed Practical Nurse	1,127	1,369	[242]
Ward Clerk	1,161	919	242
Total Fixed Costs	$5,928	$5,928	$0

Description	Control Budget	Actual	Variance
Variable Costs			
Licensed Practical Nurse ($6.50 × 950 P/D) =	$6,175	$6,276	$[101]
Nurse Aide (3.25 × 950 P/D) =	3,088	2,969	119
Total Variable Costs	$9,263	$9,245	$18
Total Nursing Salary Costs	$15,191	$15,173	$18

specific project or program, but the concept should never be considered as the replacement for a budgetary control system.

8. Variance Analysis

Monthly analysis of significant budget variances has a twofold purpose. First, it acts as a control by requiring managers to identify any potential problem areas. Potential problem areas, once identified, are further analyzed. Second, the reports represent a historical account of

and simply serves to supplement the overall department budget. Frequently the time period for a program budget is over the anticipated life of a program or piece of equipment. The program budget concept is a very effective management tool to determine the cost or benefit of a

whatever creates a significant unfavorable variance. The manager as well as the administration become very knowledgeable about the major spending patterns within the institution.*

Action To Be Taken**

Interpretation of the reported results involves not only the identification and justification of specific variances but also the interpretation of the impact that these contributing causes will have on the various levels of cost behavior.

Each of the variances will have some impact on the overall cost behavior. Management's key role is to identify the type of variance, the probable duration of the contributing cause, and the corrective action that must be taken. The following information provides a course of action to be taken based upon specific variances.

Price Variance (Labor)

Management Action

- Determine reasons causing increase in wages and determine if wage increase is permanent or temporary.
- Determine if substitute for labor is acceptable *and* available.
- Determine if wage and salary framework is structured and competitive with your facilities.
- Determine impact (if any) on profitability.

Unit Action

- Assist personnel in identifying alternatives to current personnel disciplines.
- Align available staffing to actual staff needs more closely.

Source: Donald F. Beck, *Basic Hospital Financial Management*, ed 2, Aspen Publishers, Inc., © 1989.

**Source*: Robert B. Taylor, Jr., "Budget Reporting and Control," *Topics in Health Care Financing*, vol. 5, no. 4, Aspen Publishers, Inc., © 1979.

Price Variance (Supplies)

Management Action

- Determine reasons causing price increase and if price increase is permanent or temporary.
- Determine availability of substitute supplies.
- Determine feasibility of reducing price through bidding process or other purchasing techniques.

Unit Action

- Reexamine supply usage by specific volume indicator and reevaluate cost behavior trends.

Efficiency Variance (Productivity)

Management Action

- Determine reasons causing increase/decrease in labor component and assess impact of patient mix, service mix, and the like.
- Determine if labor variance is permanent and, if so, reassess impact of change as cost behavior.
- Examine fringe benefit program and other contributing reasons if variance is due to substantial incurrence of nonproductive labor.

Unit Action

- Change in required labor component will necessitate reexamination of cost behavior.
- Determine impact, if any, on profitability.

Capacity Variance

Management Action

- Determine reasons for increase/decrease in level of use and identify degree of permanence.

- If permanent increase/decrease, assess need for reallocation of resources and reexamine cost behavior.

Unit Action

- Identify specific course of action that can be used to correct (if adverse capacity variance) or sustain (if favorable variance) change in capacity.

TYPES OF BUDGETS*

Though the nursing service budget is referred to in the singular, it reflects several different budget sheet calculations. Projections of personnel needs are an essential element of the operating budget, but the determination of this figure calls for several procedures collectively considered in the labor budget. The various factors of nonlabor expenses are also evaluated separately in, for example, the supplies/services budget sheet and the capital expenditure budget sheet before being fed into the final format of the operating budget.

1. Operating Budget Overview**

The operating budget estimates and determines how much money it will cost to keep a specific nursing unit open next year. The budget estimates future requirements and expenses for personnel, supplies, and other items necessary to the functioning of the unit, which is identified as a cost center. It may also include estimated revenues from patients and other sources.

Formulation of the operating budget should begin months before the beginning of the new fiscal year to provide sufficient time for planning and forecasting. Before beginning to plan an expense budget, the year-to-date report of

---

*Source: Except where noted, excerpts on budget types are from J.N. Althaus, et al., *Nursing Decentralization: The El Camino Experience*, Aspen Publishers, Inc., © 1981, based on "Planning and Budgets: Magic or Math" by John Fleming, in Elsie Schmied, ed., *Maintaining Cost Effectiveness*, Aspen Publishers, Inc., © 1978.

**Source: Arlene N. Hayne and Zeila W. Bailey, *Administration of Critical Care*, Aspen Publishers, Inc., © 1982.

expenditures during the current fiscal year must be reviewed. This report often provides only six or eight months of information; therefore, it must be annualized to project expenditures for the entire year. Then judgments must be made about future directions for the unit. Will any major changes be made in programs or services that might have an impact on the expense budget?

2. Labor Budget

To better understand how the labor budget system works, let's follow a typical budget process at El Camino Hospital. The following account will explore the creation of a labor budget by Shirley, the head nurse of 2-East, a 34-bed surgical unit.

To start, Shirley and her staff have agreed to a 95 percent productivity goal. They have reviewed the census forecast and have found a typical yearly pattern has been predicted. There is no forecast for any changes in the patient mix or the major/minor surgery mix.

To determine the total number of full-time equivalents (FTEs) that are needed based on the productivity goal and anticipated census, Shirley uses a budget worksheet. She takes into account the hours of patient care needed, the vacation and holidays that this staff will accumulate during the coming year, the average amount of sick time used, and other significant factors that will require additional coverage. (An illustration of the procedure is presented in the box "Calculations for Labor Budget Worksheet" and Figure 12-3.)

Upon completion of the budget worksheet, the number of FTEs has been determined: 13 FTEs for the day shift; 9.8 FTEs for the evening; and 5.6 FTEs for the night. A department total of 28.4 FTEs will be required for patient care. Shirley now compares the number with her current number of employees and determines the number of people she needs to hire for each shift, if any. Two questions have been answered: *(1) How much staff should be hired to care for these patients? (2) How much staff should be scheduled on day shift, evening shift, and night shift?*

Now Shirley must ascertain how much staff should be assigned to each shift each day of the

Figure 12-3 Labor Budget Worksheet

NURSING UNIT: ___2 EAST___   BUDGET PERIOD: _____

ANNUAL PATIENT DAYS: 9795

AVERAGE DAILY PATIENT DAYS: 26.9 @ 5.09 H.P.D. 4.84 @ 95% GOAL

AVERAGE DAILY PRODUCTIVE HOURS 136.9 ÷ 8 = 17.12 STAFF x 1.4 = 23% FTE's

AVERAGE DAILY PRODUCTIVE HOURS BY SHIFT

	HOURS		STAFF		FTEs
DAY	44 : 60.24	÷ 8	7.83	x 1.4	10.54
EVE	30 : 49.29	÷ 8	6.16	x 1.4	8.63
NITE	20 : 29.38	÷ 8	3.42	x 1.4	4.79

NON-PRODUCTIVE TIME COVERAGE

SHIFT	HOLIDAYS		E.L.	VACATION	FTES
	HR/ PROD FTE FTE HRS	HR/ PROD FTE FTE HRS	HR/ PROD FTE FTE HRS	HR/ WK WK HRS	HR/ HRS FTE FTE
DAY	56 x 10.54 = 590.2	16 x 10.54 = 168.6	24 x 7.4 = 177.6	32.8 x 40 = 1312	2245.4/2000 = 1.12
EVE	56 x 8.62 = 482.7	16 x 8.62 = 137.9	24 x 6.2 = 148.8	18.2 x 40 = 728	1497.4/2000 = .75
NITE	56 x 4.79 = 268.2	16 x 4.79 = 76.6	24 x 3.2 = 76.8	16.4 x 40 = 656	1077.6/2000 = .54

FTES

	DAY	EVENING	NITE
1. PRODUCTIVE	10.54	8.62	4.79
2. VACATION/ HOLIDAY/EL	1.12	.75	.54
3. AVE. SICK TIME	.475	.237	.147
4. ADMINISTRATIVE	.87	.2	.1
5.			
6. TOTAL FTES HIRED *(1 thru 5)*	13.0	9.8	5.6
7. EDUCATION	.11	.05	.05
8. ORIENTATION	.145	.2	.1
9.			
TOTAL BUDGETED FTES *(1 thru 4 -7 and 8)*	13.26	10.06	5.73
DEPARTMENT TOTAL BUDGETED FTES		29.05	

week. The management engineer will review with Shirley last year's historical census pattern. The census by day of the week has been kept and graphed by the management engineer and will help to determine the most frequent census level for each day of the week for the coming year. The recommended weekly staffing schedule worksheet (Figure 12-4) is used to translate the

Calculations for Labor Budget Worksheet
(Refer to Figure 12-3)

Parameters
Patient day forecast = 9,795 days
Labor standard = 4.84 nursing hours per patient day (HPPD)
Productivity goals = 95 percent
Holidays = 56 hours
Personal/sick day leave = 16 hours
Education leave = 24 hours
Vacation = total number of weeks × 40 hours

On the budget worksheet for 2-East (Figure 12-3), the 9,795 patient days are turned into average daily patient days. The nursing hours per patient day (HPPD) equal 5.09, which is equivalent to the labor standard of 4.84 HPPD at a 95 percent productivity goal. The average daily patient days are multiplied by 5.09 HPPD, resulting in an average daily productive hour requirement for patient care of 136.92 hours. These average daily productive hours are converted into the number of staff, and the number of FTEs required is 23.97 (or 24).

The average daily productive hours by shift are then determined. Here the average daily productive hours of 136.92 are spread across or allocated to the three various shifts. They are allocated on the percentage basis with the day shift receiving 44 percent of the total hours, evening shift 36 percent, and night shift 20 percent. These percentages are based upon management-engineering work done at the hospital; they reflect typical industry standards for hospitals.

The average hours per day for each shift are then turned into the staff required for each day and the number of full-time equivalents required for each shift; days required 10.54, evening 8.62, and nights 4.79 FTEs. These are the full-time equivalents required to take care of the average daily census for 9,795 patient days per year at 4.84 HPPD and with a goal of 95 percent productivity.

Holidays, education leave, and vacation needs are considered under nonproductive time coverage. Using the day shift as an example, the 590.2 hours of holidays, the 168.6 hours of sick leave, the 180 hours of educational leave, and 1,312 hours of vacation amount to 2,248.4 hours of nonproductive time. Dividing this by 2,000 hours, estimating some two weeks off during the year for holidays and sick leave, results in 1.12 FTEs needed to provide nonproductive time coverage for the 10.54 FTEs involved in patient care. These various elements for each shift are summed up in the lower portion of the budget worksheet (Figure 12-3).

The total number of FTEs hired to 2-East for the next fiscal year is reflected in line 6.

expected census level each day into the required staff for each shift each day. This information is then transferred to a recommended weekly time schedule (Figure 12-5), which represents a midpoint or core staffing guide per shift per day for the coming year.

Another question—*How much will the staffing needs vary by day of the week?*—has also been answered.

There is one remaining question: *How much and when can vacation time be scheduled?* In order to answer this question, Shirley and her staff review the forecasted workload (converted to productive patient care hours). The workload is distributed across the year by accounting period and reflects the amount of staff necessary for patient care. The difference between the FTEs required for patient care (28.4) and the total FTEs (29.05) reflects when and how much vacation time may be scheduled; thus the forecasted census is translated into the required number of nursing care hours by pay period.

Figure 12-4 Recommended Weekly Staffing Schedule Worksheet

UNIT ___2-EAST___   CENSUS DATA PERIOD _____

	AVE. CENSUS	H.P.P.D. x CENSUS	HOURS/ DAY	STAFF (÷ by 3)	DAY x 44%	PM x 36%	NITE x 20%
SUNDAY	23.88	5.09	121.55	15.19	6.68	5.47	3.04
MONDAY	27.79	5.09	141.45	17.68	7.78	6.36	3.54
TUESDAY	29.89	5.09	152.14	19.62	8.37	6.85	3.80
WEDNESDAY	30.03	5.09	152.85	19.11	8.41	6.88	3.82
THURSDAY	29.42	5.09	149.75	18.72	8.24	6.74	3.74
FRIDAY	26.16	5.09	133.15	16.64	7.32	5.99	3.33
SATURDAY	22.06	5.09	112.29	14.04	6.18	5.05	2.81
TOTAL FTE'S: (SUM ÷ 5 SHIFTS/FTE)					10.6	3.7	4.8

Figure 12-5 Recommended Weekly Staffing by Shift and Day

UNIT ___2-EAST___   BUDGET YEAR _____

Recommended Time Schedule

	SUN	MON	TUE	WED	THU	FRI	SAT			FT	PT
AVE. CENSUS	24	28	30	30	29	26	22		Full-Time/Part-Time Mix		
DAYS	6	7	7/8	8	8	8	6/7	DAYS	RN	5	4
									LVN		2
									NA	2	
									CUS	1	
PMS	5	6	7	7	4/7	6	5	PMS	RN	4	5
									LVN		
									NA		2
									CUS		1
NITES	2/3	3/4	4	4	4	3/4	2/3	NITES	RN	2	2
									LVN	1	
									NA	1	
									CUS		

The result is the expected number of patient care hours required by shift each pay period across the year to take care of the expected patient census. Shirley adds this information on a staff planning graph, which shows how the workload varies by pay period across the year. The graph (Figure 12-6) also shows from the budget worksheet the number of FTEs that are available for patient care as well as for providing coverage for administrative, education, orientation, vacation, holiday, and average sick time. The difference between the staff available and the expected patient-care requirements is the time available to give the staff their vacations and holidays as well as coverage for these other functions. Thus the last question—*How much and when can vacation time be scheduled?*—has been answered.

Finally, when the vacation and holiday time is scheduled on a personnel budget-by-position form, the labor portion of 2-East's budget is completed.

3. Capital Expenditure Budget

The capital expenditure budget outlines the need for major equipment or physical changes in the plant requiring large sums of money. If an item exceeds some arbitrary amount—say, $100—it is classified as a capital expenditure. The ceiling is established by hospital administration.

These expenses are figured on a capital expenditure worksheet (Figure 12-7). After conferring with the assistant head nurses and the director of nursing, the head nurse will plan for the purchase of new equipment and/or the replacement of existing equipment. The capital expenditure worksheet includes a description of the item, the importance and urgency of its acquisition, and other requested information. Head nurses are required to indicate in which quarter the equipment should be purchased and to specify annual equipment needs for the following two years. The capital expenditure worksheets are used by the purchasing agent and hospital administration in developing a capital expenditure budget for the next three years.

Figure 12-6 Staff Planning Graph

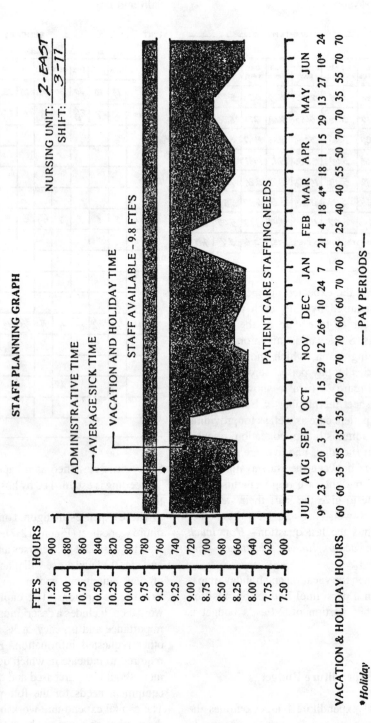

STAFF PLANNING GRAPH

NURSING UNIT: 2-EAST
SHIFT: 3-11

Figure 12-7 Capital Expenditure Worksheet

COLUMN #	1	2	3	4	5	6	7	8		9				10	11
								ESTD COST		*ACQUISITION PERIOD* (5)				*DEPARTMENTAL COMMENTS (JUSTIFICATION)*	*ADMINISTRATIVE COMMENTS/ APPROVAL*
ITEM	(1) DESCRIPTION OF ITEM	(2) PRIORITY	ADDITION	REPLACEMENT	(3) DISPOSAL	(4) RENOVATE	QUANTITY	EACH $	TOTAL $	1st Qtr.	2nd Qtr.	3rd Qtr.	4th Qtr.		
1.															
2.															
3.															
8.															
9.															
10.															

(1) List in order within year, priority, disposals last.
(2) Priority:
  a. Required for accreditation and licensure.
  b. Cost reduction.
  c. Required for objective.
  d. Desired for other reasons (specify).

(3) Disposal:
  T. Trade-in
  S. Sale
  R. Retire & store
  D. Transfer for other use
  J. Scrap

(4) Renovate: Repair & extend useful life.
(5) Acquisition: Indicate *month* desired in column.

REMARKS:—

4. Supplies and Services Budget

The use of medical and nonmedical supplies is based upon the forecasted patient days for the coming year. The average cost of medical and nonmedical supplies is determined from the preceding year's expense plus the expected inflationary increases.

Purchased services are based on historical information and reflect any service contracts particular to that unit. The input for this budget is primarily from accounting data that the head nurse reviews. He or she may make changes based on anticipated changes in the type and amount of supplies required for the coming year. The major tool in figuring the supplies and services budget is the nonlabor expense worksheet, shown in Figure 12-8.

MONTHLY REPORTS*

A variety of reports produced periodically in every facility can give a manager valuable departmental information. The information on these reports enables a manager to evaluate performance on the unit and determine expenses compared to budget.

Three monthly reports that provide the manager with needed information are (1) the labor hours report, (2) the operating statement, and (3) the expense report.

*Source: Elizabeth N. Lewis and Patricia V. Carini, *Nurse Staffing and Patient Classification: Strategies for Success.* Aspen Publishers, Inc., © 1983.

While facilities may vary in what they choose to title these reports, nursing managers should have access and responsibility for interpreting and monitoring their departments' budget activity reports.

1. Labor Hours Report

The labor hours report for a nursing unit should show productive nursing hours as well as nonproductive hours. Productive nursing hours are defined as hours spent hands-on, actually delivering patient care. The categories of productive nursing hours are:

- regular nursing hours (scheduled hours)
- overtime hours
- call-back hours
- contract hours (registry)

Nonproductive nursing hours are defined as the hours spent in areas other than those directly related to patient care.

The category of nonproductive nursing hours includes in-service, orientation, holidays, vacation, sick time, continuing education time, funeral leave, jury duty, and standby.

To determine the nursing hours per patient day, the nurse manager totals the number of productive nursing hours worked and divides this figure by the number of patient days recorded in that accounting period of time. For example, in Table 12-4 there is a total of 1,999 productive nursing hours. If this accounting period showed 349 patient days, the nursing

---

Table 12-4 Labor Hours Report

Town and Country Hospital
Department: 1 South—Medical-Surgical
(2-week period)

Productive Hours				Nonproductive Hours				
Regular Hours	Over-time	Contract Labor	Hours Worked	In-service	Other (vacation, holidays, sick benefits)	Total Hours Paid	FTE Worked	FTE Paid
1,924.5	34.5	40.0	1,999.0	99.0	324.5	2,422.5	24.78	30.28

Figure 12-8 Nonlabor Expense Worksheet

Accounting Period	*1*	*2*	*3*	*4*	*5*	*6*	*7*	*8*	*9*	*10*	*11*	*12*	*13*	*TOTAL*
1. UNITS OF SERVICE:														
Supply Expense														
2. Average Effective Rate—Drugs, Food														
3. DRUGS—FOOD—LINEN EXPENSE (Line 1 x Line 2)														
4. Floor Nourishments (Estimate)														
5. Average Effective Rate – Medical Supplies														
6. MEDICAL SUPPLY EXPENSE (Line 1 x Line 5)														
7. Average Effective Rate—Nonmedical Supplies														
8. NONMEDICAL SUPPLY EXPENSE (Line 1 x Line 7)														
9. Maintenance—Repair Supplies														
10. TOTAL SUPPLY EXPENSE														
FEES & PURCHASED SERVICES														
11. Professional Fees—Physicians														
12. Professional Fees—Administrative														
13. Purchased Services (Estimate)														
14. Equipment Repair & Maintenance Services (Est.)														
15. TOTAL FEES & SERVICES														
GENERAL & ADMINISTRATIVE														
16. Depreciation—Equipment (Assets)														
17. Leases and Rentals														
18. Utilities														
19. Education · Tuition—Travel														
20. Other General & Administrative														
21. TOTAL GENERAL & ADMINISTRATIVE														
22. GRAND TOTAL NONLABOR EXPENSES														

hours per patient day would be 5.72. This is determined in the following manner:

1,999 hours ÷ 349 patient days =
5.72 nursing hours per patient day

The total number of hours paid equals the number of hours worked (productive hours) plus all other hours paid, such as in-service, orientation, vacation, holidays, sick time, jury duty, funeral leave, and educational leave (nonproductive hours).

Also reflected in a labor hours analysis report should be the actual worked and paid FTEs. The total number of full-time equivalents worked is determined by dividing the total number of hours worked by 80, the number of hours in an accounting period. (Usually an accounting period is two weeks in length; a full-time employee would work 80 hours during two weeks [40 hours a week].) The paid FTEs indicate all the full-time equivalents, both productive and nonproductive, that were charged to the department during the particular accounting period (Table 12-4).

2. Operating Statement

The monthly operating statement summarizes a given department's financial performance, which will reflect actual unit operations. The key indicator on this report is:

gross profit = revenue − expenses

In the following discussion of the items that appear on monthly operating statement, refer to Table 12-5.

Unit of Measure: Patient Days. This figure represents the total number of patient days recorded for the month in review. This figure represents the combined total of all medical-surgical (med-surg) units. Table 12-5 shows 2,269 med-surg patient days during this month.

Total Revenue. Total revenue refers to the total number of dollars generated through patient room charges of those 2,269 patients. The total

revenue in the example in Table 12-5 is $646,665 (2,269 × $285 = $646,665).

Regular Salaries and Wages (with Overtime). This figure refers to the total amount of dollars spent on salaries and wages, including the overtime hours (paid at a regular rate), for all nursing staff who worked on the medical-surgical units during this month. In Table 12-5 regular salaries and wages with overtime total $135,309.

Contract. This represents the amount of dollars spent for contract labor from registry services during the month. In Table 12-5 this amounts to $1,760. The reader can further break this figure down as to the actual number of hours this represents if the reader knows that the rate is $22 an hour for an RN. Therefore, if $1,760 were spent on contract labor at $22 an hour, dividing $1,760 by $22 shows that 80 hours of contract services were utilized during this specific month ($1,760 ÷ $22 = 80 hours).

Total Productive Salaries and Wages. This figure, $137,069, shows the combined amount of dollars paid for salaries, overtime, and contract labor during this month.

Overtime Premium. This shows the amount of dollars paid to personnel who worked overtime during this month. In most facilities overtime premium usually signifies funds paid to employees who worked a 12-hour shift. They receive 4 hours of overtime pay. The base rate of that 4 hours is included along with the regular salaries and wages, but this $4,675 figure represents the overtime rate for those 4 hours.

In-service/Orientation. This value refers to the amount of dollars paid to employees for either in-service or orientation time. In this example, totals for in-service and orientation equal $7,529.

Vacation, Holidays, Sick Leave. This figure, $24,258, is the amount of dollars paid to the employees on the med-surg units for vacation time, holiday time, and sick time. Vacation and holiday time can be controlled only in that vacation time should be distributed evenly among

Table 12-5 Monthly Operating Statement

Town and Country Hospital
Department: Medical-Surgical Units Combined*

	Actual	Per Unit	Budget	Per Unit
Unit of measure: pt. days	2,269		2,335	
Total revenue	$646,665	$285.00	$665,475	$285.00
Regular salaries and wages (with OT)	$135,309	$ 59.64	$137,830	$ 59.03
Contract	$ 1,760	$ 0.78	$ 10,000	$ 4.29
Total productive S & W	$137,069	$ 60.41	$147,830	$ 63.31
Overtime premium	$ 4,675	$ 2.06	$ 2,027	$ 0.87
In-service/orientation	$ 7,529	$ 3.32	$ 9,648	$ 4.14
Vacation, holidays, sick leave	$ 24,258	$ 10.70	$ 24,258	$ 10.39
Total nonproductive S & W	$ 36,462	$ 16.07	$ 35,933	$ 15.39
Taxes and other benefits	$ 31,393	$ 13.84	$ 31,357	$ 13.43
Total S, W, & B	$204,924	$ 90.32	$215,120	$ 92.13
Medical supplies	$ 3,558	$ 1.57	$ 4,501	$ 1.93
Office supplies	$ 1,560	$ 0.69	$ 1,548	$ 0.67
Equipment lease/rental	$ 255	$ 0.12	$ 242	$ 0.11
Repair and maintenance	$ 50	$ 0.03	$ 72	$ 0.03
Travel/business meetings	$ 180	$ 0.08	$ 200	$ 0.09
Total other expense	$ 5,603	$ 2.47	$ 6,726	$ 2.88
Gross profit (loss)	$436,138	$192.22	$443,629	$190.00
Gross profit margin percentage	68%		67%	

*Unit cost = actual cost ÷ patient days

employees and calendar months so that not all nursing personnel are absent from the unit at one time. Since holiday time is paid during the pay period in which it occurs, it is ideal to take time off for the holidays during the same period. However, vacation and holiday time are benefits paid and earned by the individual employee. Because they must be paid, one can monitor only how evenly vacation and holiday time are distributed. Sick time can be monitored and controlled to some degree. Nursing managers should document and monitor sick day patterns and follow up on individuals who show an excessive use of sick time. In this example, vacation, holiday, and sick time amounted to $24,258. Nursing managers can further break down this amount of dollars by auditing the unit staffing records and time cards of their employees during this month to determine what portion of this amount was spent for vacation, for holidays, and for sick time.

Total Nonproductive Salaries and Wages. This figure indicates the combined amount of dollars spent on the overtime premium, in-service and orientation, vacation, holidays, and sick leave, that is, all nonproductive time. While the employee is on the premises and may be working during in-service or orientation, this time is actually considered nonproductive time because it may be only indirectly related to patient care. In Table 12-5 this figure equals $36,462.

Taxes and Other Benefits. This value of $31,393 refers to the amount of dollars paid to the employees on the medical-surgical units for taxes and other benefits such as medical insurance, dental insurance, life insurance, and pension plans.

Total Salaries, Wages, and Benefits. This is the grand total of salaries, wages, and benefits paid to the employees; it includes both productive and nonproductive salaries. Total salaries, wages, and benefits (SWB) in Table 12-5 amount to $204,924.

Medical Supplies. This refers to medical care materials and miscellaneous supplies purchased for the unit. This does not include the budgeted capital equipment but rather low-cost, necessary medical supplies such as a new IVAC thermometer, a portable patient scale, bedside bags, medicine cups, and other various nonpatient charge items. The medical supplies charged to the unit in Table 12-5 cost $3,558.

Office Supplies. Office supplies refers to the amount of dollars spent on paper items. This may include chart and requisition forms, depending on the facility. Office supplies could include a new pencil sharpener, staplers, paper clips, rubber bands, etc. Table 12-5 shows $1,560 for office supplies.

Equipment Lease/Rental. This indicates any items that may have been rented or leased for the med-surg unit during this month. Examples include the rental of a Clinitron bed and the lease of an electric typewriter. Table 12-5 shows $255 allocated for the lease or rental of special equipment.

Repair and Maintenance. This refers to the amount of dollars spent on repair or maintenance and charged to the unit. Depending on the facility, this may be either internally charged from the engineering department or externally charged from an outside contracted repair and maintenance service. Examples of this are repair of an electric bed and preventative maintenance or repair of a telemetry unit. In Table 12-5 such repairs and maintenances amounted to $50.

Travel/Business Meetings. This refers to the amount of dollars spent to send the unit managers or any members of the staff to lectures, seminars, or workshops held off of the hospital premises. In Table 12-5 this amounted to $180.

Total Other Expense. This is the combined total sum of the previous five categories (i.e., medical supplies, office supplies, equipment lease/rental, repair and maintenance, and travel/business meetings). In Table 12-5 this amount equals $5,603.

Gross Profit. The gross profit is determined by the amount of revenue ($646,665) less the expenses ($210,527). Another way to express gross profit as illustrated in Table 12-5 is as follows:

Revenue	$646,665
Expenses	− 210,527
Gross profit	$436,138

Gross Profit Margin Percentage. Gross profit margin percentage equals gross profit divided by total revenue. Another way to express this in Table 12-5 is as follows:

gross profit margin percentage (68%) = gross profit ($436,138) ÷ total revenue ($646,665)

3. Monthly Expense Report

The purpose of the monthly expense report is to provide each nursing unit manager with a clear picture of the amount of charges that it has actually incurred in comparison to the current budget. The nursing manager should be able to utilize this data as illustrated in Table 12-6 in order to account for each item and service charged to the department. If total dollar amounts do not agree, this discrepancy needs to be investigated by the manager. Vendor charges on the monthly expense report (Table 12-6) should in turn match the charges in the monthly operating statement (Table 12-5). For example, Table 12-6 states that $1,760 was paid to Kramer's Personnel Pool. The manager should first be able to verify that contract labor in this amount was utilized on the specific nursing unit by checking past staffing records. The nursing manager should multiply the recorded number of hours of contract labor times the hourly rate paid to the contracting agency. In this case if the contracting agency charged $22 an hour for a registered nurse, the nursing manager would expect to find 80 hours of contract service utilized during this month in question and documented in the staffing records ($1,760 ÷ 22 = 80). Second, the manager should be able to find and verify that expense on the monthly operating statement under the subtitle of contract labor.

Table 12-6 Monthly Expense Report

Town and Country Hospital			Month: *April*
Department: Medical-Surgical Units Combined			

Vendor Number	Vendor Name	Invoice Date	Invoice Amount
1. Contract Labor			
K050642	Kramer's Personnel Pool	4-83	$1,760
2. Medical Supplies			
P121550	Daly Hospital Supply	3-83	390
E082345	Marin Health Supplies	12-82	600
J072272	J E H Supplies	3-83	207
V110521	Medical Equipment by Kirby	11-82	2,200
G120449	Gingers Health Supplies	3-83	161
3. Office Supplies			
H070641	M.E.H. Store Equipment	12-82	1,200
M060751	Westlake Office Equipment	1-82	360
4. Equipment Lease/Rental			
R090432	Land-O-Nod Rentals	4-83	165
I062909	Typewriters-R-Us	2-83	90
5. Repair and Maintenance			
C011581	C. Nicholas Repair & Maintenance	3-83	50
6. Travel/Business Meetings			
W061420	Mayfair Travel Agency	1-83	80
B082646	DCRD and SFPD Airlines	3-83	100

COSTS

Definitions*

Variable and Fixed Costs

Variable costs change as output or volume changes in a constant, proportional manner. That is, if output increases by 10 percent, costs should also increase by 10 percent—there is some constant cost increment per unit of output.

Fixed costs do not change in response to changes in volume. They are a function of the passage of time, not output. For example, each month, irrespective of output levels, depreciation cost will be the same.

Direct and Indirect Costs

Costs can be categorized as direct or indirect. A direct cost is specifically traceable to a given

*Source: Allen G. Herkimer, Jr., *Understanding Hospital Financial Management*, Aspen Publishers, Inc., © 1978.

cost objective; for example, salaries and supplies are classified as direct costs. Indirect costs cannot be traced to a given cost objective without resorting to some arbitrary method of assignment. For example, depreciation and employee benefits are indirect costs.

Not all costs classified as indirect may actually be indirect. There are some situations where they could be redefined as direct costs. For example, it might be possible to calculate employee benefits for specific employees; these costs could then be charged to the departments where the employees worked and thus become direct costs.

Controllable and Noncontrollable Costs

What proportion of the total costs charged to a department is the manager responsible for? The answer to this question implies a need to categorize costs into two categories: controllable costs and noncontrollable costs.

Controllable costs can be influenced by a designated responsibility or departmental manager within a defined control period. It is often said that all costs are controllable by someone at some time. For example, the chief executive officer of a health care facility, through the authority granted to him or her by the governing board, is ultimately responsible for all costs.

There is a tendency in developing management control programs, especially in the health care industry, to use one of three approaches in designating controllable costs. First, controllable costs may be defined to be the total costs charged to the department. In most normal situations, this grossly overstates the amount of cost actually controllable by a given departmental manager.

Second, another concept of controllable costs would limit controllable cost to those costs classified as direct. This system is also not without fault: Specifically, there may be fixed costs attributed directly to the department that should not be considered controllable. Rents on pieces of equipment, for example, may not be under the departmental manager's control. There may also be indirect costs, especially costs which are variable, that the department manager can control. For example, employee benefits may legitimately be among the department manager's responsibility.

Third, in some situations, controllable costs are defined as only those costs which are direct/variable. This limits costs which are controllable by the department manager to their lowest level. However, it excludes what could be a relatively large amount of cost influenced by the department manager. Failure to include these costs in the manager's control sphere may weaken management control.

Cost-Benefit/Cost-Effectiveness Analyses

Distinctions*

Cost-benefit and cost-effectiveness analyses are primarily analytical techniques which are used by the manager in making decisions. By their use it is possible to select what is considered

to be an optimal approach from a group of feasible alternatives.

In cost-benefit analysis generally one seeks to value all inputs (i.e., costs) and all outcomes (i.e., benefits) in dollars. Cost-benefit analysis can assist in setting priorities across programs with substantially different outcomes and in the process yield an estimate of the net dollar value associated with each course of action. Cost-effectiveness analysis, on the other hand, can help in choosing among alternative means of achieving a given, presumably desired, outcome possessing a single measure of effectiveness. The price paid to accomplish the more powerful cost-benefit analysis, however, is high, for in valuing all benefits the questionableness of problems of subjectivity arise, such as valuing human life or quality of life in dollars. Despite the conscientious efforts of analysts to attack these issues, many decision makers may not find such valuations palatable.

Finally, a still simpler form of economic analysis is the comparative cost analysis. In this case, the benefits from two projects are presumed or known to be indistinguishable; the choice may be made on costs alone.

Guidelines for Use of CEA/CBA*

Following are 10 principles of analysis that could be used to guide the conduct, evaluation, or use of CEA/CBA studies:

1. *Define the problem.* The problem should be clearly and explicitly defined and the relationship to health outcome or status should be stated.
2. *State objectives.* The objectives of the new approach being assessed should be explicitly stated, and the analysis should address the degree to which the objectives are (expected to be) met.
3. *Identify alternatives.* Alternative means to accomplish the objectives should be identified and subjected to analysis. When slightly different outcomes are

---

*Source: *Analysis of New Health Techniques.* Health Planning Information Series, DHHS, Pub. No. (HRA) 80-14014, 1980.

*Source: *Cost Effectiveness Analysis of Medical Technology,* Office of Technology Assessment, Pub. No. (OTA)H-125, August 1980.

involved, the effect this difference will have on the analysis should be examined.

4. *Analyze benefits/effects.* All foreseeable benefits/effects (positive and negative outcomes) should be identified and, when possible, measured. When possible, and if agreement on the terms can be reached, it may be helpful to value all benefits in common terms in order to make comparisons easier.
5. *Analyze costs.* All expected costs should be identified and, when possible, measured and valued in dollars.
6. *Differentiate perspective of analysis.* When private or program benefits and costs differ from social benefits and costs (and if a private or program perspective is appropriate for the analysis), the differences should be identified.
7. *Perform discounting.* All future costs and benefits should be discounted to their present value.
8. *Analyze uncertainties.* Sensitivity analysis should be conducted. Key variables should be analyzed to determine the importance of their uncertainty to the results of the analysis. A range of possible values for each variable should be examined for effects on results.
9. *Address ethical issues.* Ethical issues should be identified, discussed, and placed in appropriate perspective relative to the rest of the analysis and the objectives of the technology.
10. *Discuss results.* The results of the analysis should be discussed in terms of validity, sensitivity to changes in assumptions, and implications for policy or decision making.

Cost-Effectiveness Analyses*

In cost-effectiveness analysis, the following concepts are most important:

Source: Royal A. Crystal and Agnes W. Brewsterm, "Cost Benefit and Cost Effectiveness Analyses in the Health Field: An Introduction." Reprinted, with permission of the Blue Cross Association, from *Inquiry*, Vol. 3, December 1967, pp. 3–13. Copyright © 1966 by the Blue Cross Association. All rights reserved.

1. There are alternative ways to accomplish an objective and we must select the optimal alternative, which may not be the least costly one.
2. There must be at least two alternative ways to accomplish a task in order to undertake cost-effectiveness analysis.
3. Cost-effectiveness analysis is not cost reduction; it is optimization of an approach to a specific goal or set of goals.

From a managerial standpoint cost-effectiveness analysis is directed by two basic economic considerations: (1) a minimum expectation that in either social or economic terms, for the program being undertaken, there will be a dollar of return for each dollar of investment, and (2) an optimal expectation that one dollar plus some additional increment of economic or social return will accrue for each dollar of investment.

A cost-effectiveness analysis is ultimately reduced to a series of models. These models, which are frequently but not always complex, set out alternatives and indicate the anticipated return of each alternative relative to a given level of investment.

A disciplined look is taken in order to fully analyze information, alternatives, and problems and, where possible, take advantage of various new technological developments which are available.

The initial step is to delineate clear and specific objectives by asking why it is necessary to do a given task and what is expected in return for the undertaking. We do not merely say we want to reduce condition X by 20 percent or add 50 new hospital beds. Rather, we ask why we should be doing this and what our real short- and long-range objectives are. After the objectives have been determined, the cost-effectiveness approach evaluates the alternatives, asking the questions, "To attain this objective, how many alternatives and what types of alternatives are available? Do we only have one way to do the job? Are there two or more alternatives open to us?" It is necessary next to specify what resources are required for each alternative— resources in terms of people, money, equipment, and facilities.

The analyst then prepares cost-effectiveness models for each alternative and also determines the criteria to be used for the selection of the preferred alternative or alternatives.

As the cost-effectiveness models are built, we are concerned with several pertinent measurements which will be used in making a decision and which form parts of the model. These include:

- Measures of effectiveness—the criteria which indicate how well the alternative satisfies the objectives.
- Measures of operational use—the criteria for consideration of alternatives in light of the other responsibilities which must be undertaken.
- Measures of personnel and equipment needed—the determination for each alternative of the number and kinds of people and equipment required.
- Cost factors.
- Measures of cost—the determination of cost for each alternative way of doing the job and the manner in which cost will be measured.

Cost-Benefit Analysis*

Cost-benefit analysis consists of five sequential steps:

1. Articulation of a clear, unambiguous statement of the decision faced and objectives sought by the health planner.
2. Identification of alternative actions or programs that satisfy stated objectives.
3. Identification separately of the costs and benefits associated with the proposed undertaking and each alternative action.
4. Quantitative evaluation of all costs incurred and benefits returned for each action.
5. Comparison of alternatives against explicit decision criteria to yield the preferred program.

Advantages

- Provides a systematic and consistent approach to the evaluation of alternative actions.
- Requires explicit (numerical) statements regarding the values of all recognized effects attributed to the various interventions, thereby avoiding purely subjective judgments.
- Takes a total view of the allocation decision, as opposed to that of a dollar cost alone.
- Yields an explicit appraisement of the net value of undertaking the preferred alternative.

The Cost-Benefit Study*

As part of the evaluation of new ventures or new systems, a well-executed cost-benefit study supports administrative efforts to gain a competitive edge. First, the study provides the basis for sound decision making: It identifies both the actual costs of the present system and the estimated costs of the proposed system or venture. By comparing the two sets of costs, administration can determine the extent of tangible and intangible benefits, as well as the range of risks and opportunities, associated with an impending decision.

A second way the cost-benefit study supports a return on investment is through the association of specific benefits with required system features. Those features with high benefits are the ones that cannot be negotiated away either with the vendor or with programming staffs that might be looking for ways to expedite the installation process. System features with high benefits become the mandatory requirements for the proposed system.

The third way the study helps a hospital gain a competitive edge is in the development of an action plan for realizing the benefits and for controlling costs. The cost-benefit study, then,

---

*Source: *Analysis of New Health Technologies,* Health Planning Information Series, DHHS, Pub. No. (HRA) 80-14014, 1980.

---

*Source: Mike Sullivan, ''The Cost/Benefit Study: A Competitive Edge,'' *U.S. Healthcare* (formerly called *HealthCare Computing and Communications*), May 1987, © 1987 Health Data Analysis, Inc.

provides both the raw data that helps drive the decision-making process and the basic plan for ensuring a favorable return on investment from that decision.

Reasons for a Cost-Benefit Study. Although the underlying reason for initiating any cost-benefit study is to gain a competitive edge, the basic study has been most frequently applied to the evaluation and justification of proposals for new systems or new ventures. The principal reasons administrators choose the cost-benefit study are to

- identify the costs of the present system
- document the constraints in the present system (these became the opportunities with the new system)
- document the favorable features in the present system (these become the risks with the new system)
- identify the costs of the proposed system
- identify the benefits of the proposed system
- identify the mandatory requirements for the proposed system
- develop an action plan for benefits realization
- validate the benefits and the action plan

Proposals for new ventures might include proposals for the opening of an emergency care center, an interface between the hospital computer and ones in physician offices, or the merging of two nursing stations.

Types of Benefits. Identified benefits fall into two broad categories: tangible and intangible.

Tangible benefits, in turn, can be further subdivided into economic and noneconomic. A tangible *economic* benefit is one that can be quantified in terms of dollars and has a direct relationship to the proposed system or venture. A tangible *noneconomic* benefit is one that is directly related to the proposed system or venture but is not readily converted to dollars, such as an improvement in the quality of patient care.

Intangible benefits, on the other hand, are not easily converted to dollars and, at best, have an indirect relationship to the proposed system or venture (see Table 12-7).

FTE Reduction versus Cost Avoidance. Of the five basic types of tangible economic benefits, the identification of FTE reduction versus FTE cost avoidance is, perhaps, the most controversial.

The labor costs associated with the major nursing tasks in the present or manual system must be compared to the estimated costs to perform these same tasks in the proposed system. The difference between the two sets of costs is the identified savings or benefits . . . the FTE reduction or cost avoidance.

In Figure 12-9 the actual time it takes a nurse to perform major tasks in the present system is compared to the estimated time it would take the nurse to perform the same tasks in the proposed system. Timings and volumes are based upon an eight-hour shift, a staffing ratio of one-to-five, an average daily census of 30 patients, and an average acuity of three (on a scale of one to five).

Reading from left to right, the first column shows time in increments of 40 minutes. Reading from bottom to top, note that the first five

---

Table 12-7 Tangible Economic Benefits

Personnel	Material	Equipment	Purchased Services	Revenue Enhancements
• FTE Reduction	• Forms and Supplies	• Typewriters and Copiers	• Agency Personnel	• Bad-Debt Reduction
• FTE Cost-Avoidance	• Inventory Reductions	• Terminals and Printers	• Maintenance Services	• Capture of Late/ Lost Charges
		• Computers		• Reduction of Days in Accounts Receivable

Figure 12-9 Daily Nursing Activities, by Elapsed Time

MINUTES	PRESENT SYSTEM		PROPOSED SYSTEM	
480		100%		100%
440	6. Other Tasks (118 min)		7. Savings/Benefit (90 min)	
400				81%
		75%	6. Other Tasks (118 min)	
360	5. Report (33 min)			
		69%		
320				57%
4. Assessments (70 min)			5. Report (12 min)	
280				
		54%		54%
240	3. Charting (75 min)		4. Assessments (70 min)	
200				
		38%		40%
160	2. Medications (84 min)		3. Charting (50 min)	
120			2. Medications (40 min)	29%
		21%		21%
80	1. Treatments (100 min)		1. Treatments (100 min)	
40				
0				

Source: Mike Sullivan, "The Cost/Benefit Study: A Competitive Edge," *U.S. Health Care*, (formerly called *Healthcare Computing and Communications*), May 1987, © 1987 Health Data Analysis, Inc.

elements constitute the major, time-consuming tasks, while element six represents a group of minor tasks. To significantly impact nursing, the proposed system must impart tasks in the first five areas.

In comparing the graph in the proposed system column with that in the present system column, tasks two, three, and five are the ones impacted for a combined labor savings of 90 minutes per nurse. As previously noted, with a staffing ratio of one-to-five and an average daily census of 30 patients, the individual savings is multiplied by six nurses for a total saving of 540 minutes per shift (days).

Of the identified 540 minutes on the day shift, 480 minutes is FTE reduction while 60 minutes is FTE cost avoidance.

To realize the benefits from the FTE reduction and the cost avoidance, administration must have an action plan in place ready to be imple-

mented shortly after the installation of the new system.

ESTABLISHING THE COST OF NURSING SERVICES

The Importance of Accurate Cost Measurement*

Careful identification of nursing costs is essential for several reasons. First, nursing salary costs represent a large percentage of overall hospital operating costs. Nursing salaries in a typical community hospital usually represent

Source: Paul L. Shafer, Betsy J. Frauenthal, and Catherine Tower, "Measuring Nursing Costs with Patient Acuity Data," *Topics in Health Care Financing*, vol. 13, no. 4, © 1987 Aspen Publishers, Inc.

about 20 percent of the hospital's total inpatient operating cost. Furthermore, for particular types of patients, the cost of nursing care can easily represent more than 30 percent of the total cost of care.

Second, knowledge of nursing salary costs is essential for the preparation of accurate budgets and financial forecasts. How many nursing hours will be required in the next fiscal year, and what will be the associated costs? These two questions can be answered systematically if good nursing cost data by patient type are available. If the hospital plans to start a new service, such as a free-standing urgent care center, nursing cost accounting data can be extremely useful in developing a projection of needed nursing hours and salary dollars.

Third, the identification of nursing costs by patient type is essential for case mix management. Are nursing costs increasing because more cardiovascular surgery and fewer ear, nose, and throat patients are being treated? If the obstetrics product line is expanded by 10 percent, how much will nursing salary costs increase? If nursing salary cost information is developed at the diagnosis-related group (DRG) or International Classification of Diseases, 9th edition, Clinical Modification (ICD-9-CM) level, then the answers to these questions will be readily available.

Approaches*

The first step in cost allocation is to determine the unit of analysis for classifying patients within relevant cost categories. The most commonly used units of analysis have been day of service, diagnosis (medical or nursing), timed functions, or nursing workload units as measured by patient classification system (PCS). The most frequently used cost categories have been cost per patient or length of stay (LOS), cost per patient care unit, and cost per DRG.

Source: Loucine M.D. Huckabay, "Allocation of Resources and Identification of Issues in Determining the Cost of Nursing Services," *Nursing Administration Quarterly*, vol. 13, no. 1, © 1988 Aspen Publishers, Inc.

The significant variation in the amount of daily nursing care needed by different types of patients has important implications regarding the accuracy of alternative methods for costing nursing.

There appear to be four major approaches for allocating hospital nursing service costs: (1) per diem or costs per day; (2) costs per diagnosis; (3) costs per relative intensity measure (RIM); and (4) costs per nursing workload unit based on PCS.

Per Diem Method of Cost Accounting

Per diem or cost per day is the oldest method of allocating resources. It has been used for rate setting and internal managerial control. This cost is calculated by dividing the total nursing costs by the number of patient days for a selected time period. Nursing costs consist of the salaries and fringe benefits for clinical and administrative nursing personnel. This method has been criticized as being inadequate, because it does not accurately represent types of patients and because patient days vary widely in terms of resource consumption.

Cost per Diagnosis

Diagnosis-based methods of accounting for nursing costs attempt to reduce the variability in nursing care requirements by using information above the case mix. The DRG system and several other case mix methods have used medical diagnoses to group patients. Some have also used the nursing diagnosis to group patients and calculate cost per diagnosis. Still others have used the American Nurses' Association's nursing care standards for classifying patients according to nursing care requirements. In one study, nursing diagnosis was a better predictor of nursing care requirements than DRGs based on medical diagnosis. Nursing diagnosis explained two times as much variance as medical diagnosis (DRG) in predicting nursing time.

A system for the development of 23 nursing care categories (NCCs), one for each of the 23 major diagnostic categories from which DRGs are derived, is advocated by Leah Curtin, editor of *Nursing Management*. To stress the nursing aspect of the care and treatment process for DRGs, Curtin also proposes that a detailed nursing care plan, called a nursing care strategy (NCS), be developed for each of the 467 DRGs. Within each NCS, patient care requirement levels may be assessed using a PCS.

Others have advocated that costs for delivering nursing practice be calculated not on the basis of actual practice, as measured by PCSs for staffing, but on the basis of time required to achieve an institution's standard of care.

Cost per Relative Intensity Measure (RIM)

Another method of cost allocation using case mix information is the RIM. A RIM is an arithmetic abstract that serves as a proxy for charges in detailing nursing resource use. A RIM is actually one minute of nursing resource use. The method through which RIMs are costed and ultimately allocated to DRG case mix categories involves a three-step process. First, the cost of a RIM is calculated. A RIM is obtained by dividing the total nursing costs for the hospital by the total minutes of care estimated or nursing resources used to provide care to all patients. Second, the number of minutes used by the total hospital population is determined, including the usual corrections for downtime, such as sick leave, vacation, fatigue, less than maximum efficiency of new employees, and so on. Third, the cost of care for each patient is calculated by multiplying the RIM by the minutes of care required by the patient as estimated by the appropriate equation. Unlike the PCS that looks at staffing needs per shift, the RIM method measures the time spent by nursing personnel in performing nursing and nonnursing tasks during the entire hospitalization.

Cost per Nursing Workload Unit Based on Patient Classification System (Patient Acuity)

Nursing workload–based methods are primarily used to forecast staffing needs. Acuity-level staffing allows nursing managers to staff nursing units shift by shift based on the individual needs of the patients. This method of staffing replaces the more conventional method of determining nurse staffing requirements of the unit based on the daily census.

An increasing number of hospitals have used patient data for allocating nursing costs to DRGs by using the following procedure to calculate the nursing cost:

1. The PCS is used as usual.
2. Patient classification statistics are converted in required hours of care for the course of hospitalization.
3. Patient care hours are then translated to dollar cost.
4. Patients are classified into DRGs.
5. Nursing care costs for patients in selected DRGs are compiled and analyzed in many different ways.

Another method of obtaining workload data recommends assigning nursing functions for patients in each DRG into three categories: daily essential functions common to all patients, physician-dependent functions, and nursing-independent functions. Cost analysis can then be calculated for each of these functions, for patient care units, and for each DRG. This type of workload analysis will provide a useful pricing approach but entails additional data collection.

The following material demonstrates costing of nursing services based on a patient classification system.

Comparison of DRG and Acuity Approaches*

Variability of Nursing Costs by Diagnosis

Only in recent years has the technology been in place to evaluate nursing's contention that patients in different illness categories require different amounts of daily nursing care. It is often true that patients within the same illness category also require different levels of daily

*Source: Paul L. Shafer, Betsy J. Frauenthal, and Catherine Tower, "Measuring Nursing Costs with Patient Acuity Data," Topics in Health Care Financing, vol. 13, no. 4, © 1987 Aspen Publishers, Inc.

nursing care. The development and widespread use of DRGs have provided hospitals with the nomenclature needed to consistently designate these illness categories.

As shown in Table 12-8, there is a significant difference in the actual amount of daily nursing care for patients in selected DRGs. Figure 12-10 presents the calculation of average daily nursing cost used for the patient acuity approach.

At one hospital, estimates of the cost of daily nursing care based on the patient day approach were compared to estimates of daily nursing costs for the six selected DRGs. The results of the analysis are presented in Table 12-9.

The analysis indicates that the patient day approach is fairly accurate if the patients within a DRG have an average acuity level. If, on the other hand, patients in a particular DRG have extremely high or extremely low acuity levels, then the estimates of daily nursing salary costs based on the patient day approach can be significantly inaccurate.

Patient Acuity Systems*

Patient acuity, or classification, systems are management tools designed to measure or forecast the nursing time required to care for individual patients.

Acuity-level staffing results in a more accurate matching of nursing resources to patient needs. By clearly defining the resource requirements of each patient on a nursing unit, an acuity system can assist the nursing department in most efficiently allocating the staff to the various nursing units.

Barriers to Implementation*

If the patient acuity approach for identifying nursing costs is significantly more accurate than the patient day approach, why then is it not used more frequently? Some reasons why the method is not used are as follows:

- The patient acuity system lacks credibility in the eyes of fiscal service personnel. Frequently, fiscal service personnel either have minimal knowledge of the nursing department's patient acuity system or have doubts about the quality of information derived from the system.
- Patient acuity data are not being collected regularly or are not summarized in a manner useful for cost accounting. Frequently, the nursing department will collect patient acuity data on an ad hoc basis. For cost accounting purposes, however, comprehensive patient acuity data must be collected for each patient. Similarly, difficulties arise if patient acuity data are not summarized correctly. For staffing purposes, the nursing department will aggregate patient acuity data by nursing unit. For cost accounting, however, patient acuity information must be summarized by individual patient.
- Acuity information is voluminous and frequently never leaves the nursing department. It is also difficult to enter data into the cost accounting system. A system must be in place to integrate the clinical information with the hospital's financial system to ensure that nursing information for every hospital inpatient is regularly entered into the cost accounting system.

Recommendations for Smooth Implementation*

The following actions will facilitate the implementation of patient acuity–based costing in the nursing department:

1. Fiscal services and nursing must work closely together to develop needed patient acuity data.
2. New billing statistics must be developed and used for patient acuity information.
3. Patient acuity information must be collected each day for each hospital inpatient.

Source: Ibid.

Source: Ibid.

Table 12-8 Comparison of Average Nursing Care Requirements for Patients in Six Selected DRGs

Selected DRG No.	Description	Average Length of Stay	Estimated Nursing Personnel Hours per Day	Overview of Required Nursing Care
138	Cardiac arrhythmia > 69 and/or comorbidity and complication and/or CC	20.1	2.5	Initially this type of patient is in an ICU where high concentration of time is required. Once the arrhythmia is controlled the patient is moved to a medical/surgical unit, where the nursing activity is primarily observational and patient education and discharge instructions are carried out.
36	Retinal procedures	3.3	8.5	These patients require nursing assistance with certain physical activities because of their impaired eyesight. Nursing time is also used for frequent monitoring of vital signs as well as prevention of potential complications and education of the patient prior to discharge.
296	Nutritional and miscellaneous metabolic >69 and/or CC	6.6	11.7	The nursing activities related to the treatments received in this DRG include education, assessment of the gastric system, elimination, monitoring of laboratory work, care of the intravenous catheter, and close observation of daily weights and fluid balance.
197	Total cholecystectomy >69 and/or CC	13.2	12.2	Initially the patient is uncomfortable and requires pain medication and positioning. Nursing activities include frequent initial vital signs, dressing checks, gastric assessment, fluid monitoring, and prevention of post-operative complications.
87	Pulmonary edema and respiratory failure	7.3	27.0	The patients in this DRG are in an acute life-threatening situation requiring immediate and intense medical and nursing intervention.
210	Hip and femur procedures >69	14.9	20.3	The patients in this DRG require significant nursing care due to their age, lack of initial mobility, and inability to perform activities of daily living. These factors make the patient totally dependent on nursing personnel.

Nursing personnel hours include nurse manager, clinical coordinator, head nurse, registered nurse, licensed practical nurse, nursing aide, and unit clerk time.

Source: Paul L. Shafer, Betsy Frauenthal, and Catherine Tower, "Measuring Nursing Costs with Patient Acuity Data," *Topics in Health Care Financing*, vol. 13, no. 3, © 1987 Aspen Publishers, Inc.

First, for cost accounting, the fiscal service department will want to ensure that patient acuity information obtained from the nursing department is well documented, timely, and accurate. Fiscal services must clearly articulate these goals to the nursing department and pro- vide the nurses with the resources they will need to achieve these goals. For example, to enhance the documentation, timeliness, and accuracy of the patient acuity system, the nursing department may need to implement some or all of the following:

Table 12-9 Evaluation of Patient Days as a Basis for Costing Nursing Services

			Direct Nursing Salary Costs				
Selected DRG		Medical (M) or Surgical (S)	Estimate Using Patient Days as Costing Basis ($)	Estimate of Actual Cost ($)	Difference ($)	Full Cost per Day ($)	Difference as a Percent of Full Cost per Day (%)
No.	Description						
138	Cardiac arrhythmia >69 and/or comorbidity and complication (CC)	M	74.91	23.03	51.88	166.78	31.1
36	Retinal procedures >69 and/or CC	S	172.80	75.46	97.34	472.62	20.6
296	Nutritional and miscellaneous metabolic >69 and/or CC	M	74.91	104.26	(29.35)	378.30	(7.8)
197	Total cholecystectomy >69 and/or CC	S	83.34	113.07	(29.73)	486.66	(6.1)
87	Pulmonary edema and respiratory failure	M	136.03	285.48	(149.45)	924.05	(16.2)
210	Hip and femur procedures >69 and/or CC	S	102.31	197.14	(94.83)	673.24	(14.1)

Figure 12-10 Calculation of Average Daily Nursing Cost with Patient Acuity Approach

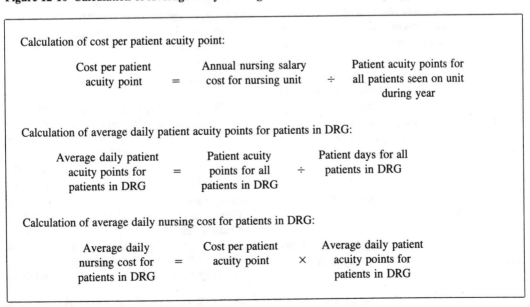

- hire a patient acuity coordinator
- develop new patient acuity forms
- implement an in-service education program related to the patient acuity system
- implement a rigorous data audit process for the acuity system

The second factor needed for smooth implementation of patient acuity–based costing for nursing is the capture of patient acuity data in the hospital's patient billing system. In most hospitals, the charge for nursing services is included as part of the routine room and board charge automatically generated based on the midnight census. Consequently, hospital billing systems have not needed to capture patient acuity data. It is recommended that fiscal service personnel develop new billing statistics that will facilitate the daily entry of patient acuity data into the billing system.

It is advantageous to establish a separate billing statistic for acuity data for each nursing unit or service. In addition, it is necessary to have separate charge codes for each nursing unit or service; this accounts for the different nursing care factors that are either directly or indirectly associated with each unit or service.

Third, it is also recommended that acuity information for all hospital inpatients be collected and entered into the billing system each day. Nursing, data processing, and fiscal service personnel will want to work together to develop an appropriate operational process for entering acuity information into the billing system on a daily basis. Once this is achieved, hospital management will be able to compute the average patient acuity measure per patient per day, per patient per length-of-stay, by nursing service, and by DRG or major diagnostic category.

Variable Billing for Nursing by Patient Classification*

With the added complexity introduced into health care by the prospective payment system

---

Source: Mehmet Kocakulah, Norma Hagenow, and Francine Cope, "The True Costs of Nursing Care," *Health Progress*, December 1990.

and diagnosis-related groups, some health care providers have reevaluated the idea that the daily room rate should include nursing care costs. Nursing managers assert that "hotel services"—the costs of housekeeping and dietary services (room and board)—are fixed costs that should be the same for all patients. Nursing care, on the other hand, is a variable cost: Some patients require much more care than others. Thus some administrators have separated nursing costs from fixed room and board and instituted variable billing for nursing care.

Existing System

Option A in Table 12-10 is a simplified version of a patient's actual bill, used as an example

---

Table 12-10 Comparison of Billing Options

OPTION A: STANDARD PATIENT BILL

Service	Cost	Percent of Total Bill
Medical/surgical/ gynecological semiprivate bed ($178 per day)	$1,068.00	34%
Pharmaceuticals	564.85	18
Supplies	493.72	15
Diagnostic tests	197.90	6.3
Operating and recovery room services	813.50	25
Total charges	$3,137.97	

OPTION B: VARIABLE BILLING WITH NURSING COST BREAKDOWN

	Unit Cost	Unit	Total
Semiprivate bed	$106.80 ×	6	= $640.80
Nursing care			
Class I days	57.71 ×	2	= 115.42
Class II days	73.38 ×	3	= 220.14
Class III days	88.34 ×	1	= 88.34
Class IV days	338.69 ×	0	=
Nursing care total			$423.90

Source: Mehmet Kocakulah, Norma Hagenow, and Francine Cope, "The True Costs of Nursing Care," *Health Progress*, December 1990.

throughout this discussion. The first item on this bill is a semiprivate room at $178 per day for six days. This daily rate is based on overhead costs (room and board) and nursing care, but in setting the rate, providers also consider competitive rates and what insurance companies define as "reasonable and customary" rates.

In a proposed new system, the cost of nursing care is separated from the overhead, using the Hospital Corporation of America's (HCA's) patient classification system. Placement in a nursing classification—Class I, II, III, or IV—is based on assessment of the indicators for nursing intervention and the patient's need for assisted daily living. As patients improve and progress to the next class, they require less nursing care. Thus one day at a Class IV level will cost much more than one day at a Class III level.

In addition to allocating labor, these four classifications help managers monitor nursing productivity. A major efficiency indicator in nursing throughout the United States is *hours per patient day* (HPPD). A recent HCA regional hospital audit indicated the following average number of hours per class per patient day for *direct nursing care* on a general surgery unit:

Class I—2.54 hours
Class II—3.42 hours
Class III—3.89 hours
Class IV—14.90 hours

Direct care reflects activities at the patient's bedside; the audit included two other components—indirect care and constant time—which encompass nursing activities performed away from the bedside.

Indirect care includes all paperwork, documentation, medication preparation, patient transportation, and so forth. *Constant time*, or unit management time, includes on-site education, committee work, administrative duties, and personal time. The total constant time is assigned equally to each patient independent of classification.

For each nursing area, researchers have determined standard hours for direct, indirect, and constant care. The result is *productive hours per patient day*. The figure varies according to nursing area. For example, in the general surgery

unit the internal audit revealed the following figures for a Class II patient:

$$\underset{\text{care (DC)}}{\text{direct}} + \underset{\text{care (IC)}}{\text{indirect}} + \underset{\text{time (CT)}}{\text{constant}} = \underset{\text{HPPD}}{\overset{\text{total}}{\text{productive}}}$$

$$3.42 \quad + \quad 1.48 \quad + \quad 0.3 \quad = \quad 5.2$$

From this foundation, already in place and fully computerized, one can derive the cost of nursing care simply.

Determining a Variable Cost

By building on the existing system, providers can determine a variable labor cost for each patient class. They can obtain the additional unit-specific data easily from routine payroll or operations reports. They can add nonproductive time (benefit hours, based on historical data for the unit) to the previous example to determine *total nursing hours* paid for one Class II surgical patient:

$$\underset{\text{(DC + IC + CT)}}{\text{total HPPD}} + \underset{\text{productive time)}}{\overset{\text{benefit}}{\underset{\text{hours (12\% of}}{}}} = \underset{\text{paid hours}}{\text{total}}$$

$$5.2 \quad + \quad 0.624 \quad = \quad 5.824$$

Total hours paid multiplied by the average hourly rate on the surgical unit gives the *variable nursing care cost* for a Class II patient for one day:

$$\underset{\text{hours}}{\text{total paid}} \times \underset{\text{rate}}{\text{average hourly}} = \underset{\text{cost}}{\text{variable}}$$

$$5.824 \quad \times \quad \$10.50 \quad = \quad \$61.15$$

Using this method, managers can determine labor cost for each department. The *range* on the surgical unit according to patient classification is as follows:

Class I—$48.09
Class II—$61.15
Class III—$73.62
Class IV—$282.24 (1:1 patient to nurse ratio)

To complete the transition to variable billing, one adds an arbitrary *profit margin* (in this case 20 percent) to the labor cost:

	labor cost	+	20% profit	=	total daily rate
Class I	$48.09	+	$9.62	=	$57.71
Class II	$61.15	+	$12.23	=	$73.38
Class III	$73.62	+	$14.72	=	$88.34
Class IV	$282.24	+	$56.45	=	$338.69

Adding this proposed variable billing for nursing care hours to the patient bill in Option A (Table 12-10), one can determine the totals shown in Option B (room and board rate was reduced by 40 percent because it no longer contained the nursing care costs). Total charges for nursing care added to the other charges shown in Option A now total $3,134.67—almost exactly the same as the actual bill. The only difference is that in the actual bill, hotel and nursing costs were 34 percent, whereas the proposed bill shows the costs of the bed were $640.80 (or 20 percent) and nursing was $423.90 (or only 13.5 percent).

As Option A shows, with 20 percent profit, nursing is still only 13.5 percent of the total bill (consistent with research indicating nursing care ranges from 11 percent to 21 percent of total charges billed). This percentage is characteristic of all medical-surgical nursing care costs. In addition to showing that nursing care is cost-effective, billing by classification provides clearly documented evidence, supported by nursing notes, of the costs a hospital incurs in providing care.

Nursing Benefits

Viewing nursing as a profit center, one can evaluate a nursing manager's performance on the basis of business goals. When nursing staffs are recognized as income producers who have increased influence in decision making, they will cease to be the major target in cost-containment programs and will no longer be perceived as an economic drain.

Also, nursing revenues could directly fund programs for nursing in need of subsidy: continuing education for nurses, career opportunities to reward professional development, incentive programs to encourage efficiency in patient care, and nursing research, which has already saved organizations much money.

Cost accounting increases the accountability, professionalism, and control of nurse managers.

Identified costs are more manageable, and the department's and the facility's efficiency increases. Administrators can evaluate departmental performance based on analysis of costs and budget variances. Because nursing costs are derived from valid classification systems, third-party payers may be further persuaded to correlate prospective reimbursement with nursing costs.

FISCAL CONTROL

Manager Education for Monitoring and Controlling Resources*

Data for budgeted positions is usually conveyed by department managers who, in turn, depend on their supervisors for information. Education of the department manager in fiscal operations and enforcement of responsibility and accountability for performance will maximize the nurse administrator's fiscal control (see Table 12-11).

The most fundamental aspects of salary budget development, monitoring, and control must be clearly and accurately relayed. The department's standard, in hours or dollars per patient day, must be understood, including the relationship to volume or units of service. This standard, typically based on average acuity for the department, should be broken down into an allocation for each shift. Based on departmental acuity and volume, a clear guideline is given for staffing, even in the absence of the department manager. Using this guideline, decisions can be easily calculated and traced to the individual decision maker. A cumulative shift report encompassing the 14-day pay period documents fiscal compliance with the departmental standard and in most cases is readily accepted and understood by staff.

The issues of budgeted skill mix, overtime, per diem pay, and registry usage should be thoroughly discussed so that there is an understood priority for making decisions. Standards for staff utilization, overtime, registry, and so forth,

Source: Thomas R. Soule, "Attaining Financial Control in Nursing: Three Basic Factors," *Aspen's Advisor for Nurse Executives*, vol. 6, no. 8, © 1991 Aspen Publishers, Inc.

Table 12-11 Outline of Manager Education Regarding the Control of Resources

Salary Education
1. Human Resource Monitoring/Control
2. Written Human Resource Utilization Standards
3. Monthly Salary Expense Analysis
4. FTE Analysis/Projection

Nonsalary Education
1. Nonsalary Subaccounts
2. Monthly Analysis—Variance Reporting
3. Review of Charging Practices
4. Nonsalary Standards Development
5. Noncapital Purchase Planning

Responsibility
1. Clarify Responsibilities
2. Document Expectations
3. Incorporate into CBPE

Accountability
1. Clarify Accountability
2. Provide Consistent Feedback
3. Provide Positive Support
4. Enforce Accountability

should be clearly defined in writing in order to provide guidance and consistency. Manager feedback based on review of staff utilization and compliance with the department staffing standards are essential. In some cases—depending on how acuity is validated and how frequently acuity and volume are measured, by shift or 24-hour period—solid and objective rationales for variances can be obtained. Control will be expedited with the implementation of written control standards.

As managers' expertise in controlling and monitoring staffing hours develops, efforts can be redirected to the broader picture of salary expenses. Specifically, the relationship of the monthly costs in salary accounts to hours utilized can be evaluated and analyzed. Full participation in projecting yearly units of service and departmental FTEs and positions should be a common expectation for department managers.

Nonsalary Expenses

The second key area for manager education should focus on departmental nonsalary operat-

ing expenses. As with salary expenses, managers should participate in their budgeted yearly allocations in all subaccounts. Managers must be educated in each specific subaccount—what is costed to it and who will be charging against those accounts. All managers should gain expertise in correctly reading the monthly departmental expense reports and identifying unfavorable variances.

Monthly variance reports, based on investigation and identified rationales for unfavorable variances, should be routine and documented. Some of the most meaningful learning will take place when departmental charges from the multitude of internal and external sources are confirmed.

True savings and cost reductions will surface when charging practices are scrutinized by investigating managers. Noncapital supplies and equipment maintenance contracts deserve attention. Frequently allocations by support or ancillary services (e.g., pharmacy or central service) are incorrect, inconsistent, or simply cannot be supported by a sound fiscal rationale. Incorrect practices in ordering and charging out to the cost centers can be put back on track so that nursing operations can be fairly and objectively evaluated. Managers cannot buy-in on their responsibilities unless charging practices truly reflect reality.

Standards for the subaccounts reflecting volume-affected consumable supplies should be considered. By simply involving the managers in evaluating prior monthly costs (dividing actual expense by units of service) for the period, numerical standards can be developed. From these standards for nonsalary expenses, future targets can be adapted according to control or reduction plans. If nurses review in order to utilize better, more cost-effective product brands or to develop a less wasteful system, a lasting financial impact will occur.

Other categories that can be reviewed are noncapital minor medical and nonmedical equipment. A fundamental planning of purchases can be achieved by encouraging a listing of planned purchases consistent with departmental goals. This is not to say that only planned events will occur. But with a sound process, the consistent and equal allocation of monies for emergencies can be accomplished based on the equipment intensivity of the service.

Responsibility

The education of department managers in salary and nonsalary monitoring and control practices will be effective only if accountability and responsibility are clarified up front. If department managers do not accept responsibility for what is expected of them in controlling their departments' expenses, no amount of financial education will help. Furthermore, even if the monitoring and control responsibilities are readily assumed, they will be of little value unless each manager is held accountable for fiscal decisions he or she makes.

One of the most acceptable methods for clarifying the monitoring and control responsibilities is identification of expectations, in writing, with the management group. It is an opportunity to spell out, discuss, and negotiate exactly what responsibilities must be performed by the manager—until consensus is reached.

Timing of reports, acceptable rationales for variances, and implementation of solutions are just a few standards that should be covered. With minor rewording, these standards become a criterion-based performance evaluation.

Accountability

Accountability follows the acceptance of the responsibility. In some cases, it enforces responsibility. The message must be clear that managers *will* be held accountable for decisions that they and their staff make. Staffing decisions, supply purchases, and implementation of cost-effective programs and projects require consistent feedback, which enforces the accountability expected. A positive, supportive, mentoring approach is necessary during the learning phase. Over time, feedback becomes more direct, and accountability for meeting budgetary standards is heightened. Manager buy-in may be encouraged with a pay-for-performance system, monetarily recognizing those managers who have become masters at the art of fiscal control.

Chapter 13

Management of Patient Care

BASIC NURSING CARE DELIVERY SYSTEMS

Overview*

Within the context of nursing practice, the framework for providing nursing services is an important consideration. The system used to deliver nursing care gives the objective observer some idea of the context of care delivery and the philosophy of the organization. Whether it be functional, team, primary, or some modification of one of these, each system reflects a particular philosophy and the way that professional practice of nursing unfolds. The organization must commit itself to a delivery system that will articulate in practice the philosophy, beliefs, and standards that are applied to nursing care and that are acceptable to the institution. While it is argued that some nursing care delivery systems reflect a higher level of professional nursing practice than others, the decision about which system is most effective and most representative of the resources, skills, and abilities of a particular institution's nursing professionals must be made realistically. Appropriate structural and practice strategies can be undertaken within any nursing care system that preserves and promotes high standards of practice. With an understanding of all constraints and pursuing all possibilities available to the nursing organization, the highest level of practice effectiveness must be demanded by the practitioners themselves. It is in that context that any choice of an appropriate nursing care system should be addressed (see Figure 13-1).

Delivery Systems Defined*

A nursing delivery system is a set of concepts defining four basic organizational elements. The definitions of these elements are based on principles that are in turn based on fundamental values. These fundamental values will ultimately determine the quality of the product. If the workers are not valued as independent decision makers by the definers of the principles of work organization, independent decision making will not be characteristic of their practice. If the definers do not believe the average staff nurse has the ability to manage a patient's care (to be distinguished from clinical ability), the system

---

*Source: Timothy Porter-O'Grady and Sharon Finnegan, *Shared Governance for Nursing: A Creative Approach to Professional Accountability*, Aspen Publishers, Inc., © 1984.

---

*Source: Marie Manthey, "Definitions and Basic Elements of a Patient Care Delivery System with an Emphasis on Primary Nursing," in *Patient Care Delivery Models*, Gloria Gilbert Mayer, Mary Jane Madden, and Eunice Lawrenz, eds., Aspen Publishers, Inc., © 1990.

Figure 13-1 Nursing Practice

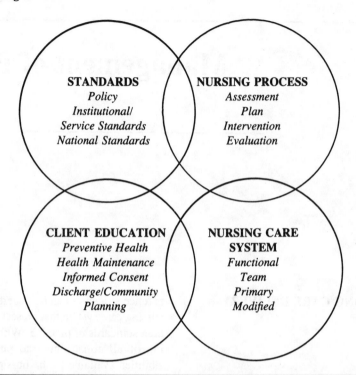

will not give decision-making authority to staff nurses.

The four fundamental elements are

1. clinical decision making
2. work allocation
3. communication
4. management

These four elements—decision making, work allocation, communication, and management—are the cornerstones upon which a delivery system is built. The more clearly they are articulated, the better they will be.

Roles are developed to function within the framework of the delivery system, and that framework impacts the functions in such a way as to support or prohibit various behaviors. For example, imagine a well-qualified, competent nurse functioning one day as a primary nurse, the next as a team leader, and the third day as the medication nurse. The knowledge contained in his or her brain and the skill reflected in his or her hands-on practice and verbal interactions will

differ dramatically depending on the *role* created to fulfill the functions assigned in the context of the expectations inherent in the delivery system.

There is another major way the delivery system impacts work performed and the worker's experience of it. When work is allocated according to tasks rather than patients, a body of knowledge about the patients is simply not accumulated by the staff. This absence of knowledge has a negative impact on the clinical decisions that need to be made. In addition, the absence of patient information severely impacts the quality of data communicated. Data communication is one of the major sources of evidence available after the fact to judge the quality of performance. Delivery system design is the framework within which roles are developed and clinical knowledge is required and formulated.

The Mechanics of Delivering Nursing Care

The continuous search for improvement in the delivery of nursing care has provided administrators with four basic model systems: case, functional, team, and primary care. The construction and mechanics of each system reflect a shifting emphasis in the services provided by health care personnel and in the roles of the patient.

The oldest method of delivering nursing care is the *case system*, where one nurse is involved in nursing observation and care of a single patient. Considered a one-to-one relationship, this method is used today primarily for assignments in intensive care units and for educational demonstrations with student nurses.

The most frequently adopted method is the *functional system*, which focuses on the number of tasks that must be provided to the overall patient population and assigns qualified personnel to the appropriate task. This division of labor into interlinking but separate components is based upon the assembly line production concept found in industry, where the worker's repetition of a single activity leads to increased expertise and efficiency. In the nursing unit the breakdown of activities is translated into patient-care assignments which are specific for each staff member: to provide hygienic care, to distribute medication, to administer treatment or therapy, to instruct the patient, to keep records, and so on. The central authority resides in the charge nurse, who processes all major communications. Though this system has been favored as an economic measure, as in industry, there has been a revision of attitude toward its overall effectiveness in maximum productivity. Comparisons of cost-effectiveness indicate other combinations of nursing care delivery systems are equal to and sometimes superior to the functional method. More important, nurses frequently chafe under this partial involvement, limited to only one aspect of the patient's total health care. Patient-clients are often confused by the endless flow of different caregivers.

The *team system* modifies the depersonalized, skilled-worker approach in a format which focuses on individualized patient health care. Adopted in the 1950s, this system employs a cluster of health care personnel whose varied skills are directed by a team leader to provide total services for a specific patient case. The formation of a team is a cooperative and collaborative venture which involves a professional nurse capable of leadership and health personnel who are technically proficient in their respective roles and capable of participation in a group effort. The care of the patient is conceived of as a group task, with observations, interpretations, and evaluations mutually investigated and shared. The team leader's responsibility is to coordinate, supervise, and engage the full participation of her coworkers in the construction and implementation of nursing care plans for the well-being of the patient-client. (Patient assignments for teams are made by the charge nurse, who also acts as a resource person.)

The most recently developed care delivery method is the *primary care system*, which recalls some of the features of the case system but assumes added dimensions in the nurse's increased responsibility in areas such as coordination and range of patient coverage. The primary nurse has full, 24-hour-a-day, continuous accountability for planning, evaluating, and directing the nursing care of a patient case. The primary nurse establishes a direct relationship with the patient, collecting and assessing data, forming plans, making decisions, and representing the patient's total needs in the coordination of activities with other health personnel and disciplines. When the primary nurse is off duty, his or her relief nurse continues to act in accordance with the care plan he or she has developed. More than one patient case is usually assigned, though this number varies with the nature and treatment of nursing services required and the number of support personnel and systems available in the hospital. The assignment of patient cases is usually the responsibility of the nurse leader, who attempts to match professional expertise or special interests with cases. Occasionally the primary nurse is allowed to pick and choose his or her own patients.

In practice these basic models of nursing care delivery systems have been adapted and altered in new combinations to suit different department needs. Since the team and the primary care systems are the more current and more variable modes of delivering nursing care, further details and information will be provided below. (*Note*: For a comparison of nursing care delivery systems see Table 13-1.)

Table 13-1 Comparison of Three Methods of Delivering Nursing Care

Factor	Method of Nursing Care		
	Functional	Team	Primary
Assignments	Head nurse or nursing coordinator assigns to staff members tasks that fall within their job descriptions.	Team leader assigns to team members tasks that fall within their job descriptions.	Head nurse or nursing coordinator assigns individual patients to professional nurses, matching the patients' needs to the nurses' skills.
Assessment, planning, and evaluation	Related to a specific need of each patient; done by any member of the nursing staff; no continuity.	Related to specific needs of each patient; done by the team leader; a limited continuity depending on how long a person remains team leader.	Related to specific needs of each patient; done by the primary nurse; maximum continuity, since primary nurse remains throughout patient's stay on hospital unit.
Implementation	Different members of the nursing staff do tasks for a given patient.	Each team member does tasks for all patients, according to job description; the team leader often does medications and charting for the team.	Each primary nurse delivers total care to all assigned patients ("For the first time I feel that somebody knows who I am").
Documentation	Staff members make notations on only those actions or aspects of care done by them. *or* A staff member is assigned to "chart" for a given number of patients; usually no nursing care plan is in evidence.	Team leader usually documents care for patients cared for by most, or all, team members; sometimes a team member makes certain entries on patient charts; the team leader documents the nursing care plan.	Each primary or associate nurse documents care given to each assigned patient during shift; the primary nurse documents the nursing care plan.
Reporting at end of shift	A "charge" nurse gives report on patients to another charge nurse; most of the information shared is based on reports of other workers.	The team leader gives report on the group of patients to the oncoming team; most of the information shared is based on reports of other workers.	The primary nurse gives report on each assigned patient to oncoming nurse who will care for the patient; the nurse who reports has interacted directly with all the patients about whom reports are given.

continues

Table 13-1 *continued*

Factor	Method of Nursing Care		
	Functional	*Team*	*Primary*
Responsibility for planning care	No one person is responsible for planning unless this is assigned as a functional task to a specific R N for a given period.	The team leader is responsibile for planning the nursing care for the assigned group of patients.	The primary nurse is responsible for planning the nursing care of all primary patients, from the time they are admitted to a nursing unit until they are discharged from that unit.
Responsibility for providing care	Nursing care is delivered in a fragmented manner, with many staff members interacting with the patient as the various tasks are done.	As in functional nursing, delivery of nursing care is a "mixed bag."	The primary nurse directly delivers all nursing care to the primary patients when on duty.
Decentralization of authority, for continuous decision making and followup of nursing care	Total decentralization— decisions are made on basis of separate tasks done by individual staff members for each patient on the unit.	The team leader makes final decisions about nursing care for the patients in the group on basis of feedback (some of which is lost) from team members.	Each primary nurse makes final decisions about nursing care for the assigned patients.
Accountability to patients, families, peers, physicians, interdepartmental staff, administration, and community:			
For professional actions	Professional nurses are each answerable for their own professional actions.	Professional nurses are each answerable for their own professional actions.	Professional nurses are each answerable for their own profesional actions.
For coordination and outcomes of nursing care	No one nursing staff member is answerable for the coordination and outcomes of nursing care; the head nurse often answers to everyone for the entire staff.	The team leader, who plans care but often does not give it, is answerable for the care of each patient in the assigned group and for the coordination and outcomes of nursing care.	The primary nurse who plans and delivers the care to each assigned patient is answerable for the coordination and outcomes of nursing care.

continues

Table 13-1 *continued*

Factor	Method of Nursing Care		
	Functional	Team	Primary
For follow-up on patient problems	Physicians, administrators, and other interdepartmental personnel can rarely pinpoint responsibility for follow-up on problems.	The team leader is responsible for follow-up on patient problems, which are often generated by other staff.	The primary nurse is responsible for follow-up on problems of assigned patients.
"Passing the buck"	"Passing the buck" prevalent.	Moderate amount of "buck passing" due to change in staff assignments from day to day.	Minimal, if any, "passing the buck" because of constancy of staff assignments to same patients.
Comprehensiveness of care, in terms of:			
Patients' needs	Not possible; focus of care is on tasks, not on the patient as a unique individual with a broad spectrum of needs and resources.	Theoretically, and sometimes actually, possible, since team members are expected to communicate ideas related to patient needs and nursing action to meet those needs; a united approach is the goal; however, plans are often designed with minimal patient/family input, and focus is on nursing action rather than on patient goals.	Inherent in the system, because continuity in same nurse/same patient relationships is maximized; focus of nursing care is on patient goals rather than on nursing action.
Documentation	Nursing care regimens are rarely documented, so individual approaches are inconsistent.	Documented nursing care plans are encouraged but can rarely be demanded, because nursing caseload is too large.	Documented nursing care plans are mandated and are facilitated by smaller caseload of each nurse and by constancy of assignment.
Communication:			
Between nurses and patients or clients	Patient, family, and significant others find it difficult to	Patient, family, and significant others may be confused as	Patient, family, and significant others can clearly identify

continues

Table 13-1 *continued*

Factor	Method of Nursing Care		
	Functional	*Team*	*Primary*
	identify a nursing staff member with whom to relate on a continuing basis.	to identity of the nursing staff member to whom questions and problems may be directed.	the nurse and can share ideas, feelings, and problems freely with this person.
Between nurses and staff of other departments	Physicians, administrators, and interdepartmental staff address questions and problems to nurses or to head nurse on unit, but often satisfactory answers are delayed or are not available.	Same as in functional nursing, except team leader rather than head nurse may be consulted.	All communications are directed to the primary nurse for each patient. Satisfactory answers are more likely to be forthcoming. Persons may find difficulty in locating specific nurses.
Between nurses and supervisors	Instructions often have to be repeated because of changes in staff assignments and lack of consistent documentation of nursing care plans.	Same as in functional nursing.	Dramatic decrease in repetition of instructions for particular patients due to constancy of assignments and mandatory care plans.

Source: Donna R. Sheridan, Jean E. Bronstein, and Duane D. Walker, *The New Nurse Manager*, Aspen Publishers, Inc., © 1984.

Team Nursing*

Objectives

The objectives usually stated for team nursing are to provide

1. adequate staff for good care
2. good experiences for staff members
3. good personnel policies to maintain morale

---

*Source: Russell C. Swansburg, *Management of Patient Care Services*, The C.V. Mosby Co., © 1976. Reprinted with permission.

Assignments

Charge nurses make assignments of team leaders. They assign both team members and workloads to individual teams. Team leaders further break down the workload assignments within the teams. A team member should be able to do the following: (1) when reporting for duty, obtain a written assignment; (2) receive a verbal or taped report on the team's patients; (3) take orders from nursing care plans and doctor's order sheets; (4) verbally review assignment with team leader and organize his or her assignment on a written assignment sheet.

Use of the Nursing Daily Assignment Sheet

1. The Nursing Daily Assignment Sheet is to be used by the team leader to make individual assignments for all team members. It can be used to review activities and progress. The team leader should assign patients to team members matching skills to needs.
2. The first column is to be used for patient identification; the second is to be used for routine or programmed care and level of activity. The other columns provide space in individual time blocks for specialized care or treatment to be performed. There is also space for noting when treatments are completed and pertinent remarks concerning progress or status of patients.
3. One side provides space for additional duties and special activities. For example, unit details, nursing care conferences, classes, and appointments of the team member should be entered in this space (by the member).
4. The location for the form should be decided by the team. It may be a central point so all team members have access to this information, or team members may prefer to retain it in their possession.
5. A team conference should be held during each shift. It should be brief (10 to 15 minutes) and should center around a patient, identification of problems, planned nursing approaches, or updating of a nursing care plan.

Considerations

The following items should be considered in making team nursing assignments:

1. quantitative workload: total direct and indirect patient care activities
2. qualitative workload: specialized needs of patients
3. available staff, including experience level of staff
4. personal factors or qualifications and abilities of staff
5. division of work, including limiting the physical work of registered nurses
6. geography of unit
7. continuity of care
8. type of assignment: team, case, primary nursing, or functional method
9. availability of clerical and housekeeping personnel

Primary Nursing Concepts and Structure*

Philosophy

Primary nursing provides comprehensive and continuous patient care from admission to discharge by using the same RN (primary nurse) to coordinate, evaluate, and provide direct patient care (the RN uses the nursing process in planning this care). The patient's and family's involvement in care encourages a trusting nurse-patient relationship, thereby promoting continuity and effective discharge planning.

Peer accountability, review, and support are integral parts of the primary nursing system and they result in a continuous evaluation of patient care. In primary nursing, the responsibility (and authority) to make decisions about patient care devolves to the individual nurse. This responsibility allows the nurse to act as a change agent and patient advocate.

Structure

The *primary nursing coordinator* is a registered professional nurse who assumes 24-hour-a-day, seven-day-a-week responsibility and accountability for activities of an assigned nursing unit, with the main focus on patient and nursing staff needs. The *primary nurse* is a registered professional nurse responsible and accountable for (1) the nursing process for a specified number of patients, including but not limited to assessing patient needs and planning, implementing, and evaluating all aspects of patient care; (2) the delivery of care 24 hours a day from admission to discharge; and (3) participation in a communication triad between patient and physician. The *associate nurse* is a

---

*Source: Linda Burnes-Bolton et al., ''A Cost Containment Model of Primary Nurses at Cedars-Sinai Medical Center,'' in *Patient Care Delivery Models*, Gloria Gilbert Mayer, Mary Jane Madden, and Eunice Lawrenz, eds., Aspen Publishers, Inc., © 1990.

Major Areas of Primary Nurse Responsibility

There are three major areas of responsibility. First, the primary nurse is responsible for making available the necessary clinical information others need for the intelligent care of the patient in the nurse's absence. This means the nurse not only must be knowledgeable but also must be able to recognize what information is essential for the others to have.

Second, the primary nurse is responsible for deciding how nursing care shall be administered and for making available to other nurses the instructions for care. Instructions left by the primary nurse are to be followed by others caring for the nurse's patients in his or her absence unless an alteration is dictated by a change in a patient's condition. When that happens, the nurse's instructions may be modified to deal with the new situation. Otherwise, they are to be followed by the staff members who care for the patient on the other shifts.

The third major area of responsibility is discharge planning. The primary nurse is responsible for seeing to it that the patient and family (if the family will be caring for the patient after the hospitalization) have been prepared to provide safe and effective care. If the patient is being transferred to an agency that employs nurses, the primary nurse is responsible for communicating any information needed for a smooth transition.

Source: Marie Manthey, "Definitions and Basic Elements of a Patient Care Delivery System with an Emphasis on Primary Nursing," in *Patient Care Delivery Models*, Gloria Gilbert Mayer, Mary Jane Madden, and Eunice Lawrenz, eds., Aspen Publishers, Inc., © 1990.

registered professional nurse who, in the absence of the primary nurse, assumes responsibility and accountability for maintaining individualized quality nursing care for a designated number of patients for an 8-hour period. Keystones of primary nursing are

- continuity of patient care
- centrality of the patient
- responsibility to the patient

- patient advocacy
- centrality of the patient's life style and family
- emphasis on health (in the sense of wellness)
- patient education
- accountability to peers, the patient, and the physician
- goal directedness
- job fulfillment and retainment
- nurse practitioner autonomy
- patient inclusion in planning care

Certain advantages of primary nursing are clear. Nurses who are aware of their patients' diagnoses and the ramifications become more involved with their patients. Continuity of care is fostered by uninterrupted care planning—shift to shift, nurse to nurse, and hospital to home.

Patients realize that someone knows them as individuals from certain cultural and social backgrounds. Primary patients have opportunities to express their needs and concerns, and they will usually feel confident that their nurses will integrate these needs into their care.

Staffing*

"It will cost more to have primary nursing." "You need a higher number of nurse hours per patient." "You need an all RN staff." These are comments often heard from administrators and directors of nursing who associate the increased professionalism expected from primary nursing with increased cost. Some nurse administrators, therefore, dismiss primary nursing as unrealistic for their hospital, "ivory towerish," and costly. If the following principles about staffing are understood, then answers to the above statements come forth:

- Assess present staffing to bring it to an acceptable standard of patient care hours.
- Upgrade positions as vacancies occur.
- Utilize all levels of staff more effectively.

*Source: Karen Ciske, "Misconceptions about Staffing and Patient Assignment in Primary Nursing," *Nursing Administration Quarterly*, vol. 1, no. 2, © 1977 Aspen Publishers, Inc.

- Plan toward future staffing goals.
- Demonstrate what RNs can do as professionals.

The People Doing the Job. Yes, you may need more nursing hours per patient if your present ratio is inadequate for the acute patient needs and shorter stay in today's complex hospital system. If requests must be made for more and higher quality staff to ensure quality care, then the request is valid, no matter what organization is chosen on the unit. The assessment of staff ratio preceding primary nursing just brings to light a problem that might have been existent for years. But because attempts to increase staffing then follow, it looks like the move to primary nursing required higher staffing.

No, it need not cost any more money if you utilize the present staff more effectively.

Head nurse positions in primary nursing become ones of quality control, management of people, and staff development. The head nurse must be freed from the management of things, desk work that can be delegated elsewhere, and routine MD rounds. Decentralizing decision making to the bedside requires a unit leader who has assessed the staff's capabilities, provided for their learning, and allowed and trusted them to function as independently as possible. This is no easy process! If the head nurse is available to *share* the clinical expertise that advanced him or her into the position originally, the staff will develop clinical leadership traits. But if the head nurse previously gained much satisfaction from knowing and being in control of communication about patients or from "running a tight ship," then the adjustment to primary nursing will be difficult and will require defining new satisfactions. Support and education from peers and supervisors will help.

Staff nurses will have intense involvement with a consistent group of primary patients instead of a superficial knowledge of (and consequent superficial involvement with) a whole team. In converting to primary nursing from the team system, two more caregivers are gained—the team leaders. This brings a potential for growth of clinical skills, collaboration with other health team members, and satisfaction from direct patient care.

"The part-time RN cannot be a primary nurse" is another misconception regarding staffing. If the RN's work schedule is so sporadic that two or more consecutive days are never worked, then perhaps this person cannot be a primary nurse. However, if the scheduling can be improved, there are short-term patients, in for only one to three days, for whom a part-time nurse can be primary nurse. The responsibility would entail admission and care each following day. Continuity, concern, planning, and teaching could occur on a limited basis—if goals were realistic. Another option for the part-timer is being a consistent secondary nurse for short-term patients.

The Job Content. It is appropriate to look at what is done by nurses to see what could be allocated to other departments. Transportation of patients is just one of the many examples that we know well.

Routines need to be evaluated, such as bed and bath each day, vital signs at certain frequencies, and the charting of something, no matter how trivial, each shift.

Patient Assignment*

The Method. Some nurses think that there is one *right* way to assign patients. Three patterns have been described in health care literature: geographic, individual, and promotional. Principles to consider in any method are:

1. equal caseload depending on staff ability and hours
2. optimal match between patient need and staff competence made at admission or within 24 hours and maintained through patient's stay unless:
   —a patient-nurse personality conflict exists that cannot be resolved
   —the nurse is going onto a block of nights or on vacation
   —the patient condition changes beyond the capability of the primary nurse
   —the patient requests a change
   —the patient transfers to a room that is inconvenient for the primary nurse

---

Source: Ibid.

3. a variety of patient conditions for staff growth, identified and visible to patient, family, nurses, physician, and other staff
4. the geographic location of rooms

There are advantages and disadvantages to each of the three systems, as shown in Table 13-2. There is no perfect system. Considering all your unique variables, one or a combination of methods can be chosen, keeping the main principles in mind.

Who Are the Primary Patients? Feedback from satisfaction in the nurse-patient relationship, seeing results in goal accomplishment, and working with other disciplines are easier to experience when the patient's length of admission is more than a week. That is why implementation of primary nursing on medical wards is generally more effective than on surgery, where the average length of stay is shorter. These external rewards are important, and there is just not enough time to accomplish them for the one- to two-day admission.

It is also frustrating to try to establish goals for the healthy, knowledgeable person having minor surgery. Certainly extensive planning and teaching cannot be done for the short-term patient, but if conditions related to planning and teaching are identified as needs, they can be referred to other nurses in the community.

Duration of Assignment. Some nurses misunderstand the primary nursing assignment to be absolute, never changing. If difficulties occur between the nurse and patient, there is reluctance to discuss a possible change, because the nurse might feel exposure of the situation would reflect inadequacy.

A solution to this is the head nurse's surveillance of all assignments. The head nurse is ultimately responsible for quality of care. Supervision and education can be provided through patient rounds, chart and care plan audits, conferences, and so on. When nurses want to change patients, problem solving can help staff see their situations more objectively, learn from them, and possibly stay with the patients rather than requesting reassignment.

When patients are readmitted, the choice to remain primary nurse with a patient should be

Table 13-2 Methods of Patient Assignment

Advantages	Disadvantages
Geographic Method	
1. Stable, patients easy to keep track of	1. No guarantee of fair caseload
2. Easier to have consistent secondary coverage	2. Loses patient when transfer to another district
3. Well-organized	3. Unclear who is accountable when off duty for long stretch
4. Easier for health team to learn who has what patient	
Individual Method	
1. Caseload fair	1. Much time spent in making original and daily assignment
2. Variety of cases	
3. Can be maintained when readmitted	2. Wasted steps if patients for any nurse are spread through unit
4. Control by head nurse	
Promotional Method	
1. Screening process, only for best professionals	1. Large caseload
	2. Much delegation of direct patient care
2. Viewed as more status	3. Cost of positions
3. Stimulates staff to show competence	4. Holds back advancement if more nurses are ready to be promoted than positions available
4. Increased role clarity	
5. Reward of increased pay	

left to the nurse. Many times the patient's condition will have deteriorated, as with a cancer patient. It could be stressful for the primary nurse to resume care for such a patient, depending on caseload, emotional reaction to the declining condition, hours, or skills required. When given the option, most choose to remain primary and receive satisfaction in continuing the relationship, even if the patient is dying. However, most nurses appreciate having an "out" in case they need it.

Temporary relief periods might be necessary for the primary nurse whose patient requires heavy care, physically and/or emotionally. This is possible, if it is limited to a few shifts and the patient is informed. Discussing why relief is needed can help the nurse see the problem more clearly, learn, and be more effective.

OTHER OPTIONS FOR DELIVERING NURSING CARE

Newer structures of organization and newer systems of applied practice have been evolving which, while they may not call on the executive to deny the value of traditional approaches, will call on leadership to understand how those approaches are undertaken, the framework within which they were applied, the systems out of which they operate, and the outcomes they achieve. Without building those processes into the deliberations regarding the most appropriate and effective ways of delivering health care services, the nurse executive and other leadership are disadvantaged by their own traditional approaches and belief systems about health care, the role of the nurse, and other professions' roles in making decisions regarding direction, values, and service structures for the future.*

Managed Care and Nursing Case Management**

Nursing case management, with its foundation of *managed care*, is a clinical system for the strategic management of cost and quality outcomes (see Table 13-3). Managed care and case management provide patients and their families with a collaborative plan based on standards of care, yet individualized by groups of clinicians who have expertise in their "case types." Continuity of care is accomplished by managed care.

---

*Source: Tim Porter-O'Grady, *Reorganization of Nursing Practice: Creating the Corporate Venture*, Aspen Publishers, Inc., © 1990.

**Source: Karen Zander, "Managed Care and Nursing Case Management," in *Patient Care Delivery Models*, Gloria Gilbert Mayer, Mary Jane Madden, and Eunice Lawrenz, eds., Aspen Publishers, Inc., © 1990.

Continuity of providers across an entire hospital is achieved through group practices that provide case management.

The six components of managed care, as manifested in the New England Medical Center, a major trendsetter for this system, are

1. *standard critical paths*, which are used as adjuncts to care plans
2. *critical paths*, which are used as bases for change-of-shift reports
3. *analysis of positive and negative variances* from the critical path
4. *timely case consultation* for the caregiver "inheriting" a complex patient care situation
5. *health care team meetings* initiated, conducted, and followed up by nursing
6. *variances aggregated, analyzed, and addressed* by the unit's nurse manager

Structure for Case Management

Nursing case management relies on the unit-based systems of managed care but goes one step further to identify the specific nurses and physicians who will be accountable for the financial and clinical outcomes of designated patients. The four components are as follows:

1. accountability for the clinical and financial outcomes of patients' entire episodes of care
2. the use of caregiver (staff primary nurse) as case manager
3. formal RN-MD group practices
4. increased patient and family participation in and control of health care

The first component, accountability for outcomes, is achieved at the staff nurse level through a combination of primary nursing, managed care, and formal group practice.

Paramount to the nursing case management model is the use of caregiver as case manager (except for training or volume-overload situations). This component differentiates the model of New England Medical Center hospitals from others in which the case manager may be a nurse but is not involved in the direct care of the

Table 13-3 Ground Rules for Case Management

1. Every designated patient will be admitted to a formally prepared group practice composed of an attending physician and staff nurses from each of the units and clinics likely to receive the patient.
2. Each nurse in the group practice will give direct care as the patient's primary or associate nurse while the patient is on his or her geographic unit.
3. Every group practice will assign one of its nursing members to be the case manager who works with the attending physician in evaluating an individualized case management plan (CMP) and critical path for each patient.
4. A critical path for the whole episode of care will be used to manage the care of every designated patient, both at change-of-shift report and during group practice meetings.
5. The nurses in the group practice will meet on a weekly basis at a consistent time and place and maintain a patient roster.
6. Each nurse member of the group practice will communicate immediate patient care issues with the attending physician while the patient is on his or her own unit. The assigned case manager will work through the group and the attending physician for nonemergent issues.
7. Negative variances from critical paths and/or CMPs require discussion with the attending physician and possibly a case management consultation.
8. The group practice will meet to discuss care patterns, policies, specific patients and variances, research questions, and updated knowledge at their own predetermined intervals (e.g., monthly, bimonthly). Minutes will be taken for reference by members who cannot attend.
9. Nurse members of the group practice will negotiate a flexible schedule that accommodates the needs of their case-managed patients and collaborative practices *as well as* the needs of their units.
10. Responsibility of the case manager begins at notification of patient's entry into the system and ends with a formal transfer of accountability to the patient, family, another health care provider, or another institution.

Source: Copyright © Karen Zander, Department of Nursing, New England Medical Center Hospitals, 1988.

patients being managed. *Nursing case management results in ultimate decentralization inasmuch as it delegates accountability for clinical and financial outcomes to specific staff nurses.* To accomplish this, the staff nurse, as case manager, is placed in a case-based matrix at the patient care level (see Figure 13-2). The staff nurse works with certain physicians individually or as a member of a multiunit group of primary nurses. The case manager is both a member of a unit-based staff and a member of the group practice.

The fourth component encompasses new methods for actively involving patients and their families in every phase of care. This includes pre- and posthospitalization phone calls, giving patients copies of their critical paths, using patient portfolios, including patients (when indicated) in team meetings, negotiating meaningful outcomes and discharge plans, and involving them in audits of their responses to interventions.

Role of the Case Manager

The case manager is expected to perform the following unifying functions:

1. Establish a mechanism for notification when a new patient enters the caseload (this includes determining which patients he or she will case manage).
2. Introduce self to the patient or family and explain the role of case manager and group practice.
3. Give patient and family the group practice card.
4. Contact physician(s) to begin sharing assessments, goals, and plans for the patient's episode of illness.

Figure 13-2 Patient Care Level Matrix for Case Management

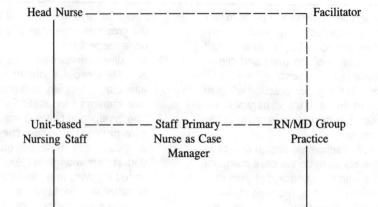

5. Know the anticipated diagnosis-related group (DRG), length of stay, and transfer or discharge dates.

6. Discuss ongoing and future care with the other nursing staff on units (inpatient and ambulatory) to which the patient will most likely be transferred.

7. Negotiate work schedule with the nurse manager to attend weekly group practice meetings.

8. Compare the standard case management plan against the patient's individual needs in such areas as social and economic data, family resources, functional abilities, knowledge needs, potential risk factors and complications, and special issues.

9. Identify a critical path for the patient and place it in the nursing Kardex.

10. Review and revise the individual critical path with the physician(s) within 24 hours of admission.

11. Contact other key members of the patient's team (e.g., the social worker, dietitian, physical therapist, community resources personnel, and others) as needed.

12. Give and monitor the delivery of care and the patient's responses to care every day that the patient is on the case manager's unit.

13. Arrange for continuity of plan and provide coverage during short, long, and unexpected absences.

14. Give the patient and family a time schedule and tell them whom to contact during the case manager's absence.

15. Document the achievement of intermediate goals and clinical outcomes as they occur.

16. Integrate case management information and revised interventions (processes) into intershift report and group practice meetings.

17. Request consultation and feedback before a crisis occurs.

18. Plan, participate in, and follow through with health care team meetings, as needed.

19. Manage the patient's transitions through the system and transfer accountability to the appropriate person or agency upon discharge.

20. Complete a follow-up evaluation.

Variant on the Existing Structures

Differentiated Practice

Differentiated practice as developed by the National Commission on Nursing Implementation Project is a care delivery system that combines the model of primary nursing for all clients with a case management model for the chronically ill or for those with no support system in the home. Its goal is to place nursing in a strategic position to influence hospital operations and medical practice. Some of the potential benefits of differentiated nursing practice include effective deployment of nursing staff into emerging new roles, shared governance that facilitates staff nurse involvement in the clinical decision-making process, and increased clinical management skills, resulting in integration and continuity of care and substantial cost savings.*

Aspects of Differentiated Practice**

The *differentiated practice model* is a system designed to provide distinct levels of nursing practice based on defined competencies that are incorporated into job descriptions. General guidelines for the concept are as follows:

- Current RN practice will be the minimum level at which differentiation of RN competencies will be established.
- Competencies will be consistent with the minimum expectations for the associate degree (ADN) and baccalaureate degree (BSN) levels in the education sector.
- Nurse satisfaction will improve, and thus so will retention, due to placing the authority, responsibility, and accountability for the planning and provision of high-quality, cost-effective nursing care at the staff nurse level.

- Differentiated competencies will be time- and setting-free and will be applicable to nursing practice in any setting.
- Differentiated levels of practice will, in the future, be supported by separate licensure laws and regulatory requirements.

The differentiated competencies for the RN (ADN and BSN) can be developed based on the principles of differentiated educational preparation. The competencies of the currently practicing LPN can be defined and presented in the same format as the ADN and BSN competencies.

The differentiated practice model displayed in Figure 13-3 shows the three major and three minor role components of nursing practice. The three major components—provision of direct care, communication, and management of care—make up the model, and their intersections form the three subcomponents. Direct client care intersects with communication to form patient teaching. Communication intersects with management of care to form coordination with other disciplines. Management of care intersects with direct care to form delegation of care. As shown by the placement of the ADN and BSN circles, the complexity of decision making in the nursing process is the basis for the differentiated levels of practice.

Once the scope of competencies are delineated, the levels of practice, as differentiated by complexity of client, time lines, and structure of the setting in reference to the nursing actions described in the competencies, can then be quantified and documented in the form of competency-based job descriptions specific to each institution or agency.

Cooperative Care*

Cooperative care is a method of delivering nursing care to patients who require hospitaliza-

---

Source: Virginia Del Togno-Armanasco, Susan Harter, and Nannette L. Goddard, "Cost and Quality: Are They Compatible?" in *The Encyclopedia of Nursing Care Quality Volume I: Issues and Strategies for Nursing Care Quality*, Patricia Schroeder, ed., Aspen Publishers, Inc., © 1991.

**Source*: Judy Blauwet and Patty Bolger, "Differentiated Practice in an Acute Care Setting," in *Patient Care Delivery Models*, Gloria Gilbert Mayer, Mary Jane Madden, and Eunice Lawrenz, eds., Aspen Publishers, Inc., © 1990.

Source: Sandra W. Murabito, "Cooperative Care: A Common-Sense Approach for Patient Care Delivery Systems," in *Patient Care Delivery Models*, Gloria Gilbert Mayer, Mary Jane Madden, and Eunice Lawrenz, eds., Aspen Publishers, Inc., © 1990.

Figure 13-3 Model for Differentiated Practice Roles

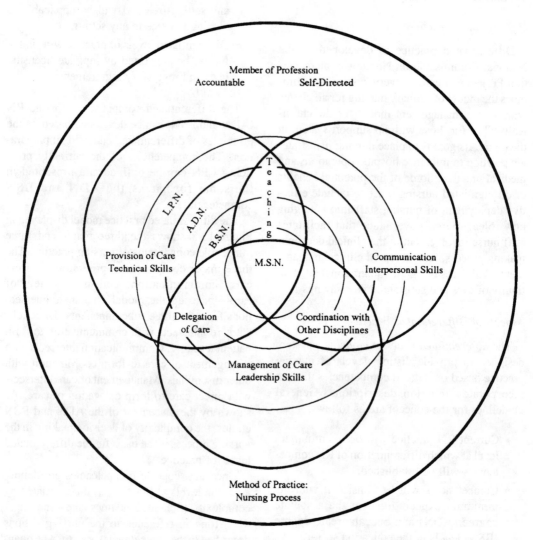

Source: *Associate Degree Nursing: Facilitating Competency Development*. Copyright by Midwest Alliance in Nursing and W.K. Kellogg Foundation. Reprinted with permission.

tion but not necessarily intensive, 24-hour-a-day nursing observation. A self-care philosophy, intensive patient education, and a wellness-oriented atmosphere are crucial to a cooperative care center's operation. Cooperative care centers require involvement of the patient and family as active participants in the care during the hospitalization. Nursing interventions are provided, but the patient maintains a more proactive role in seeking the assistance and guidance of health care professionals.

The cooperative care concept is grounded in self-care principles in the belief that hospitalized patients wish to be active participants in their care. This assumption may or may not reflect reality. The patient's initial response may be one of "culture shock," since expectations regarding traditional hospital services are contradicted.

Second, the model assumes that individuals have the capacity to learn. Patient education is a primary therapeutic tool in the cooperative care system. Theoretically, those persons with mental disabilities, sensory deficits, and age limitations should be excluded from the center. Any patient who is alert, oriented, and clinically stable and has a care partner could conceivably be a candidate for this unit.

Third, the model suggests that a homelike environment is therapeutic to a patient's convalescence. Through simulation of a more familiar atmosphere, the negative connotations of hospitalization are expected to decrease. This is achieved through room decor, provision of privacy, and reduction of restricted patient areas on the unit.

Staffing and Management

Nursing professionals are essential in the cooperative care model. Staff nurses must possess a registered nurse license, a wide knowledge of various medical and surgical specialties, excellent communication skills, and the ability to instruct people in individual and group settings. In addition, staff nurses must be comfortable in relinquishing control to the patient in such a fashion that the patient does not feel abandoned.

The nurse:patient ratio is 1:8 for all shifts, 24 hours a day, 7 days a week. This staffing pattern allows for a more cost-effective unit operation. A nurse coordinator has four support persons to assist and support him or her in administrative activities. They include an associate director of nursing, medical director, assistant nurse coordinator, and unit manager. Each has specific tasks that facilitate the functioning of the center. The associate director of nursing is the nurse coordinator's direct link to the executive director of nursing services and other hospital administrators.

The medical director's primary responsibilities are marketing the cooperative care unit to other physicians and consulting on administrative and policy-related decisions.

The assistant nurse coordinator is philosophically a management position, yet 75 to 95 percent of the work time is involved in direct patient care. This position helps the nurse coordinator maintain communication ties with the day-to-day unit operations. It is also designed to groom nurses with leadership potential for future management opportunities.

The unit manager assists the nurse coordinator in routine plant operation maintenance and ordering of equipment and supplies. Minor clerical accounting duties constitute an additional responsibility.

Evaluation

Drawbacks depend on the setting, implementation, and emphasis of each individual center. Perhaps the major drawback is the need for total project support from the unit level to the top ranks of hospital administration. Lack of understanding or commitment at any level can sabotage efforts. Staff nurses must be able to communicate and practice within the model's assumptions and concepts. Nursing administrators are essential in providing support to the staff and marketing the unit concept to the institution and throughout the community.

Generally, implementation of the cooperative care concept involves a calculated risk. Few centers have been in operation long enough to produce financial analyses that indicate the implications for manpower or cost-benefit reports that suggest that commitment to such an endeavor would be profitable or even feasible. Lack of adequate measuring tools, interaction of multiple intervening variables, and the difficulty of selecting appropriate outcome indicators to demonstrate patient response obstruct quantification of the effects of cooperative care.

NURSING CARE PROCESS

Components*

Following is a brief outline of the components of the nursing process: assessment, planning, implementation and evaluation. (See Figure 13-4.)

Assessment

The assessment component begins with the nursing history and health assessment and ends

---

*Source: Helen Yura, ''Climate To Foster Utilization of the Nursing Process,'' *Providing a Climate for Utilization of Nursing Personnel*, National League for Nursing, Pub. No. 20-1566, 1975. Reprinted with permission.

Figure 13-4 The Nursing Process

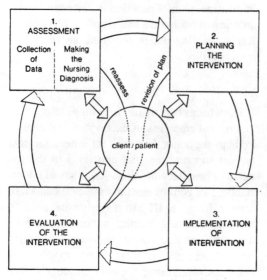

Source: Phyllis E. Jones, ''A Terminology for Nursing Diagnoses'' *Advances in Nursing Science*, vol. 2, no. 1, © 1979 Aspen Publishers, Inc.

with a nursing diagnosis. The purpose of assessment is to identify and obtain data about the client that will enable the nurse and/or client or family to designate problems relating to the client's wellness and illness. If problems exist, then the first step toward solving them is to identify them. The nurse becomes involved with basic human needs that affect the total person rather than one aspect of that person, one problem, or a limited segment of need fulfillment. The nurse validates, organizes, categorizes, compares, analyzes, and synthesizes the data obtained about the client and makes one or more judgments based on these data. Either no problem exists which demands the intervention of the nurse or another member of the health team, or the precise identification is made of all problems (nursing diagnoses) that need to be resolved so that the client can experience optimum wellness. Problems are stated in terms of client problems and result when basic human needs are either not met or are met inadequately. Making a nursing diagnosis requires a high level of intellectual skill. It is a most strategic aspect of the nursing process and concludes the assessment component. Without a nursing diagnosis there is no

reason to continue on into other components of the process. There will be no basis for planning or intervention nor any basis for evaluative judgments about the client's problems.

Planning

The planning component begins with the nursing diagnosis. It is during this component that plans are made with the client to deal with his or her problems as diagnosed. The four purposes of this component are (1) to assign priority to the problems diagnosed; (2) to differentiate problems that could be handled by the client and/or members of the family and those that need to be referred to other members of the health team or handled in conjunction with health team members; (3) to designate specific actions and the immediate, intermediate, and long-term goals of these actions, as well as expected behavioral outcomes for the client; and (4) to write the problems, actions, and expected outcomes on the nursing care plan or the problem-oriented client record. The planning phase terminates with the development of the nursing care plan, which is the blueprint for action, providing direction for implementing the plan and providing the framework for evaluation. This phase draws heavily on the intellectual and interpersonal skills of the nurse.

Implementation

Once the nursing care plan has been developed, the implementation component begins. Depending upon the nature of the problem and the condition, ability and resources of the client, as well as the nature of the action planned, the client or family, the nurse and client, the nurse alone, or nursing team members who are to act or function under the nurse's supervision may be designated to implement the nursing plan. Implementation may be accomplished by the nurse, assisted by nursing team members or in cooperation with health team members. Any one or a combination of or all of these situations may prevail; in any one situation, some planned actions may be accomplished by the client, some by the nurse and others by nursing team members. The implementation component of the nursing process draws heavily on the intellectual, interpersonal, and technical skills of the nurse. Decision making, observation, and communication are significant skills to enhance the success of action. While the focus is action, action is intellectual, interpersonal, and technical in nature.

During the implementation phase the viability of the nursing care plan is tested. The phase concludes when the nurse's actions are completed and the results of these actions and the client's reaction to them are recorded. The quality of the recording about the client and what the nurse chooses to document give direct evidence of the status of goal achievement and individual client reactions. The recording designates the status of and the direction for continued problem solving. The appropriateness and direction of the nurse's actions are determined by the client's behavioral change in the direction of expected behavioral outcome.

Evaluation

Evaluation, the fourth component of the nursing process, follows the implementation of designated actions. Evaluation is always expressed in terms of achieving expected behavioral manifestations within the client. Since specific nurse actions are planned to solve client problems, any judgment about how these problems are being resolved should originate with the client. Evaluation is the natural intellectual activity completing the process components because it indicates the degree to which the nursing diagnosis and nursing actions have been correct. The entire focus of the nursing process is goal-directed. The process is systematically geared to solve diagnosed client problems: specific nurse actions are prescribed which will most successfully induce a specific behavioral effect that will denote that the client's problems have been resolved. Evaluation helps the nurse and the client to determine which problems have been resolved and which need to be reprocessed (including reassessment, replanning, and implementation), and evaluation helps them to diagnose any new problems. The need for nursing research is inherent in the nursing process to test

strategies and their effectiveness in bringing about the expected behavioral changes in the client, accounting for the influencing variables related to the client's individuality.

NURSING DIAGNOSIS

Overview*

A nursing diagnosis focuses on a patient's physical or behavioral response to a problem. In contrast, a medical diagnosis centers on the disease process. Over the last decade, the nursing profession has worked toward standardizing nursing diagnoses. There is now a list of 37 accepted nursing diagnoses (Table 13-4). Developed in a series of national conferences, these are intended to be conditions that nurses diagnose and treat. The goal is to develop a standard nomenclature for nursing diagnoses so that all nurses will be using the same terminology in describing patient problems. The list is amended and revised every few years. You may find it helpful in checking the nursing diagnoses that your staff presently use.

You can also test nursing diagnoses by asking these questions:

- Has enough data been collected? Are the facts accurate and are they related to nursing?
- In analyzing the data, do you see a pattern?
- Is the nursing diagnosis based on scientific nursing knowledge and clinical expertise?
- Can the nursing diagnoses be treated with independent nursing actions?
- Would other qualified practitioners formulate the same nursing diagnosis from the same data?

If the answers are satisfactory, then the nursing diagnoses are ready to use in planning care by identifying goals or expected outcomes for the patient.

_____

Source: Linda Groah and Elizabeth A. Reed, "Your Responsibility in Documenting Care," *AORN Journal*, May 1983. Reprinted with permission.

Table 13-4 Approved Nursing Diagnostic Categories (1990)

Activity Intolerance	Fluid Volume Deficit
Activity Intolerance, Potential	Fluid Volume Deficit, Potential
Adjustment, Impaired	Fluid Volume Excess
Airway Clearance, Ineffective	Gas Exchange, Impaired
Anxiety	Grieving, Anticipatory
Aspiration, Potential for	Grieving, Dysfunctional
Body Image Disturbance	Growth and Development, Altered
Body Temperature, Potential Altered	Health Maintenance, Altered
Breastfeeding, Effective	Health Seeking Behaviors (Specify)
Breastfeeding, Ineffective	Home Maintenance Management, Impaired
Breathing Pattern, Ineffective	Hopelessness
Communication, Impaired Verbal	Hyperthermia
Constipation	Hypothermia
Constipation, Colonic	Incontinence, Bowel
Constipation, Perceived	Incontinence, Functional
Decisional Conflict (Specify)	Incontinence, Reflex
Decreased Cardiac Output	Incontinence, Stress
Defensive Coping	Incontinence, Total
Denial, Ineffective	Incontinence, Urge
Diarrhea	Individual Coping, Ineffective
Disuse Syndrome, Potential for	Infection, Potential for
Diversional Activity Deficit	Injury, Potential for
Dysreflexia	Knowledge Deficit (Specify)
Family Coping: Compromised, Ineffective	Noncompliance (Specify)
Family Coping: Disabling, Ineffective	Nutrition: Less than Body Requirements, Altered
Family Coping: Potential for Growth	Nutrition: More than Body Requirements, Altered
Family Processes, Altered	Nutrition: Potential for More than Body
Fatigue	Requirements, Altered
Fear	Oral Mucous Membrane, Altered

continues

Advantages of Nursing Diagnosis*

Nursing diagnosis is advocated because it:

- assists in organizing, defining, and developing nursing knowledge
- aids in identifying and describing the domain and scope of nursing practice
- focuses nursing care on the patient's responses to problems
- prescribes diagnosis-specific nursing interventions that should increase the effectiveness of nursing care

- facilitates the evaluation of nursing practice
- provides a framework for testing the validity of nursing interventions
- provides a standardized vocabulary to enhance intra- and interprofessional communication
- prescribes the content of nursing curricula
- provides a framework for developing a system to direct third-party reimbursements for nursing services
- indicates specific rationales for patient care based on nursing assessment
- leads to more comprehensive and individualized patient care

*Source: Charold L. Baer, "Nursing Diagnosis: A Futuristic Process for Nursing Practice," Topics in Clinical Nursing, vol. 5, no. 4, © 1984 Aspen Publishers, Inc.

Although some of these assertions may tend to be extravagant in the extreme, there is little

Table 13-4 *continued*

Pain
Pain, Chronic
Parental Role Conflict
Parenting, Altered
Parenting, Potential Altered
Personal Identity Disturbance
Physical Mobility, Impaired
Poisoning, Potential for
Post-Trauma Response
Powerlessness
Protection, Altered
Rape-Trauma Syndrome
Rape-Trauma Syndrome: Compound Reaction
Rape-Trauma Syndrome: Silent Reaction
Role Performance, Altered
Self Care Deficit
    Bathing/Hygiene
    Feeding
    Dressing/Grooming
    Toileting
Self Esteem, Chronic Low
Self Esteem, Situational Low
Self Esteem Disturbance
Sensory/Perceptual Alterations (Specify)

(visual, auditory, kinesthetic, gustatory, tactile, olfactory)
Sexual Dysfunction
Sexuality Patterns, Altered
Skin Integrity, Impaired
Skin Integrity, Potential Impaired
Sleep Pattern Disturbance
Social Interaction, Impaired
Social Isolation
Spiritual Distress
Suffocation, Potential for
Swallowing, Impaired
Thermoregulation, Ineffective
Thought Processes, Altered
Tissue Integrity, Impaired
Tissue Perfusion, Altered (Specify Type) (renal, cerebral, cardiopulmonary, gastrointestinal, peripheral)
Trauma, Potential for
Unilateral Neglect
Urinary Elimination, Altered
Urinary Retention
Violence, Potential for: Self-directed or Directed at Others

Source: Nursing diagnoses approved by the North American Nursing Diagnosis Association (NANDA), 1990.

---

doubt that they either are or have the potential of being ultimately true. However, there are always at least two perspectives for every issue.

NURSING CARE PLANS: THE ROLE OF THE DIRECTOR OF NURSING

Although the director of the department necessarily delegates the direct management of patient care to others on his or her staff—supervisors, head nurses, and team leaders—he or she is responsible for giving them the tools, the support, and the overall direction they need to do their jobs successfully. The nursing care plan is one tool in the management of nursing care of the patient. It is a proposed method of action, indicating the results to be achieved, the steps to be taken in achieving them, and the means to be used. The director of nursing has the responsibility to ensure that the plan is made and the groundwork laid for its effective use.

The following groundwork elements are considered by AHA to be essential to effective utilization of nursing care plans.[1]

1. Clearly Defined Nursing Care Objectives

Objectives consistent with the purpose and goals of the hospital need to be defined for the nursing service. These will be common objectives for the nursing care given all patients, reflecting what the department of nursing believes good care to be. These objectives should be redefined, in turn, for the several clinical departments and the various patient care units in the hospital. With such overall objectives as guides, the nurse has a basis for determining specific objectives for the individual

---

[1] "Practical Approaches to Nursing Service Administration," American Hospital Association, vol. 6, no. 1, Winter 1967.

patient—objectives unique to the patient and his or her individualized nursing care needs.

2. Supportive Policies

Seeing and talking with the patient on admission is the first step in the development of a nursing care plan. Does the nurse who will be responsible for the patient's care have the opportunity and responsibility to see the patient as soon as possible after he or she arrives on the unit? Is the nurse at liberty to talk with the patient, or is the nurse so preoccupied with record forms to be filled out that his or her initial contact with the patient is perfunctory or hurried? Admission policies and procedures need to be established to give the nurse the necessary time and opportunity for this important early contact.

There should also be policies delineating the responsibilities and functions of the various categories of nursing personnel. Since nursing care plans include nursing actions to be taken, the responsible nurse must know who can safely carry out the actions and to whom they can be assigned. It should also be understood that the plans cover the full 24 hours of the day.

Because the successful development and carrying out of a nursing care plan for a patient depend upon knowledge of the patient's illness as well as an understanding of his or her background and personality, the nurse must know the physician's plan for care. Therefore the nurse's relationship with the patient's physician and ability to communicate with the physician are very important. What are the policies and procedures to facilitate communication between nurse and physician? Do nurses make rounds with physicians? What are the reporting mechanisms? How does the nurse work with other departments involved in the patient's care, such as physical therapy, radiology, dietary, etc.?

3. Administrative Support

If nursing care plans are to be a successful tool in the management of nursing care, the support of hospital administration and of the medical staff is essential. Obtaining this support for the nursing department is primarily the task of the director of nursing, who, as a member of top management and a representative of nursing on patient care and intradepartmental committees, is in a good position to interpret to the administrator and the physicians the aims of the nursing service and the means selected to achieve them.

The director of nursing is also in a position to be influential in bringing about the development of hospital policy and administrative procedures that will facilitate the carrying out of nursing care plans—for example, the procedure for delivery of drugs to the nursing unit; the method of handling patient appointments with radiology; and the policy on control of the progress and sequence of events pertaining to the physician's plan for care.

4. Departmental Policies and Procedures

To facilitate the implementation of nursing care plans, appropriate procedures and policies need to be established within the department of nursing itself.

These should be concerned with such matters as, for example:

- Who has the responsibility for initiating a nursing care plan? (Usually it is the head nurse or team leader, depending on how the service is organized.)
- How are new staff members to be oriented?
- What forms are to be used, and where shall they be kept?
- What disposition is to be made of the nursing care plan after discharge of the patient? Are such plans used for a type of nursing audit?
- What provision is made for periodic evaluation and review of the methods for preparation and use of nursing care plans? What are the supervisor's responsibilities for reviewing and evaluating the plans and for helping nurses to improve their skill in planning?

PATIENT EDUCATION

Traditionally, the larger share of the United States' health care dollar was spent on treatment rather than on prevention. However, this pattern is changing, and the rate of change seems to be escalating. Many hospitals have committed significant resources to prevention and others are ready to follow that lead. The concept of preventive medicine is becoming widely accepted.

Hospital-based preventive medicine is beginning to rely more heavily on the educational process. Professionals have long been aware that most of the chronic illnesses being treated involve life-style and personal choice factors. Health education has been addressing such personal risk factors with varying degrees of success. For example, patients with coronary heart disease or cerebrovascular disease have shown decreasing mortality rates, in part due to the decreased consumption of saturated fats, the decreased incidence of cigarette smoking among men, and the dramatic increase in jogging. Some of the credit for these advances can be attributed to health education programs.

Another major concern of health care professionals is patient behavior after discharge. One compliance study revealed that between 15 and 95 percent of orders by physicians were ignored, with resultant relapse and readmission. Again, one of the major causative factors was a lack of understanding of what was to be done and why it was important. To help remedy this situation, educational programs were implemented and were found to increase compliance and reduce readmission.*

Setting Up a Patient Education Program**

Is There a Need for the Program?

Generally, the following categories represent patients who should be considered appropriate candidates for teaching programs: (a) patients

with chronic illnesses/conditions who know little or nothing about their condition or how to care for themselves (e.g., diabetic, COPD, cardiac, and ostomy patients), and (b) patients facing certain treatments, medical equipment, or procedures who don't know what is going to occur (e.g., preoperative patients, patients in labor, patients scheduled for diagnostic tests, new mothers, pediatric patients going for X-rays, and patients having physical therapy or radiation treatments).

More specifically, how should you go about deciding which patient programs to develop first?

1. Utilize the results of the nursing audit that is in effect in the institution. If the guidelines of the Joint Commission on Accreditation of Healthcare Organizations are followed, most of the large specific diagnosis populations are being audited. If in the outcome criteria a criterion relating to knowledge is included, the need for a patient education program may have already been identified.

2. Patients can be surveyed, either by a questionnaire, skills inventory, interview, or a combination of these three. Example: When a diabetic patient is admitted to the hospital, he or she could be given a skills inventory to complete. When completed, the nurse would have the necessary data to set up an individualized program for the patient. Also, if inventories were collected over a period of time, they could be correlated into the foundations of a patient education program.

3. Another area to examine is the rate of readmissions to the hospital, particularly of the patients with chronic conditions. If there is a high frequency of readmission, you may not be doing your job teaching that specific group of patients how to care for themselves at home.

4. Interviewing key medical and nursing staff is perhaps the most subjective way to determine the need for specific patient education but it is one way to assist in determining patient education needs (see Figure 13-5).

*Source: Donald J. Breckon, *Hospital Health Education*, Aspen Publishers, Inc., © 1982.

**Source: Adapted from Lilah Harper, "Developing and Evaluating A Patient Education Program," *Patient Education*, National League for Nursing, Pub. No. 20-1633, 1976. Reprinted with permission.

Figure 13-5 Sample Staff Survey to Assess Health Education Status

The Education Department, with the approval and support of central administration, would like to determine (1) what health education activities have been or are being conducted in this hospital, (2) if the staff members feel that there is a need for an expanded hospital health education program, and (3) the amount of interest in such a program. Department heads and other key people in the hospital are accordingly being asked to complete this brief questionnaire.

Name _____ Position _____ Unit _____

_____ Yes _____No   Has your unit routinely conducted or does your unit routinely conduct any formally planned health education activities for patients, their families, unit staff, or the community at large? If yes, please specify.

Target Group   Educational Activity   Contact Person
1.
2.
3.

_____ Yes _____ No   Do you or your staff spend a significant amount of time conducting informal health education, such as answering questions and explaining procedures? Please estimate the percentage of staff time spent.

_____0 to 10%   _____25 to 50%
_____10 to 25%   _____50 to 75%

_____ Yes _____ No   Do you feel that patients leaving your unit adequately understand their condition and have adequate knowledge for self-care after discharge? Please estimate the percentage of patients who have such knowledge.

_____0 to 10%   _____50 to 75%
_____10 to 25%   _____75 to 100%
_____25 to 50%

_____ Yes _____ No   Do you feel that family members responsible for patient care adequately understand the patient's condition and needed care?

_____ Yes _____ No   Do you feel that patients and families desire more health education than they are currently receiving in your unit?

_____ Yes _____ No   Do you feel that you and the majority of your staff are adequately trained to provide health education for the patients, their families, and the community at large?

_____ Yes _____ No   Do you feel that you and your staff possess adequate time to meet the health education service needs of your unit?

_____ Yes _____ No   Would you like to see the Education Department conduct in-service sessions to assist you and your staff in improving your health education skills?

_____ Yes _____ No   Would you like to see the Education Department expand its services and offer health education activities to _____ your patients, _____ their families, _____ your staff, _____ the community at large?

Source: Donald J. Breckon, *Hospital Health Education: A Guide to Program Development*, Aspen Publishers, Inc., © 1982.

What Will the Program Cost?

The second step in identifying specific program needs is to determine what the cost will be. At this stage of the program development, the determination will have to be a somewhat tentative figure, but it must be examined at this point in order to realistically venture into the project. If it will be unfeasible for the institution to implement the program because of cost, some other decisions will need to be made (i.e., forget the program, modify it to reduce cost, or possibly charge the patient for that particular program). One can't make the above decisions without knowing what cost is involved.

Some factors to consider in determining the cost of an educational program include these:

1. Audiovisuals needed, e.g., movies, filmstrips, charts.
2. Duplicating costs, e.g., patient information booklets, pamphlets.
3. System to be used, e.g., closed circuit television, small groups, one-to-one basis.
4. Staff time involved to design the program, for any training needed by staff, and for the implementation on a day-by-day basis. Will the patient education program increase the budgeted nursing care hours? If so, by what amount? Will the patient education program mean a change in the number or mix of nursing personnel on any specific unit?
5. Possible involvement of other departments. If other departments become involved, how would it affect cost?

Who Will the Teachers Be?

Most nurses in an institution should be involved in patient teaching, some more directly than others. The specific organization implemented will vary from institution to institution, but there are definite responsibilities to be considered.

- Someone in the institution needs to be assigned specific responsibility for determining what programs are needed and for coordinating the development and implementation of the programs. This step will provide accountability and avoid unnecessary duplication (this person may logically be someone in in-service, staff development, or education).
- Someone needs to design the programs. This should be a group activity, involving persons who will probably be doing some, if not all, of the teaching. Also, someone with background in methods of teaching, change theory, and evaluation will be extremely helpful, perhaps again someone from staff development or education.

So, how does one determine which staff nurses to involve?

- Nurses who already include patient teaching as part of their professional practice.
- Nurses who have indicated an interest in teaching, such as teaching in-service classes, participating in nursing grand rounds, teaching in the community, assisting with the orientation of new personnel on the unit, or working actively with students.

The first programs to be developed will run more smoothly if the planning group is interested, involved, and committed.

What Will the Teachers Need to Know?

Assuming that only a portion of the teachers will be on the patient education committee, once the program is developed there will need to be in-service sessions with all of the teaching staff. Also, other nursing department staff will need information sessions so that they can actively support those staff members who are teaching.

Included in the in-service sessions for the teaching staff should be:

1. Purpose of the patient education program.
2. Objectives.
3. Content.
4. Methods of conveying the content. The methods of teaching will be determined by the Patient Education Committee, but the staff nurses will need in-service on the methods. Probable class topics will include:

—How to conduct small group discussions.

—How to speak to large groups.

—Teaching on a one-to-one basis.

5. How to measure if the patient is learning.

6. How to document the teaching-learning process.

7. How to use audiovisual equipment if it is to be used in the presentation.

Funding Patient Education Programs*

There are three basic ways of financing patient education programs. Each has potential and is being used satisfactorily. Similarly, each has its drawbacks. First, costs may be billed to third-party payers in some states. Second, costs may be indirectly carried as part of the daily room rates. The third method is to directly bill patients for educational services rendered. Most often in acute care hospitals, third-party reimbursement comes from private insurance companies and the government's Medicaid and Medicare programs.

Third-party reimbursement for patient education is considered important because most hospital bills are paid by someone other than the patient. Theoretically, if third-party payers are willing to cover health education, ample funds would become available to fund such services. This has already occurred in about a third of the states.

Some services currently are routinely covered by third-party payers. If the education is directly related to the intake diagnosis and is essential to home care, then reimbursement can occur. If, however, the education deals with other health problems or with prevention in general, reimbursement does not occur under most plans. When such coverage does occur, it is usually simply included in the room and board rates.

It is, therefore, incumbent upon those agencies and institutions wishing reimbursement to bill appropriately. For example, if the visit were for "diabetic follow-up to evaluate injection

technique and adherence to diet," it would be more likely to be reimbursed than if it were for diabetic education.

Daily Room Rate

The "indirect costs" mechanism for financing patient education is that by which the health care providers conduct educational programs for patients, but do not separately identify this expenditure on the patient's bill. Such costs are integrated into the patient's "daily room rate" and consequently are indirectly reimbursed by the third-party payers.

The daily room rate is not just a flat rate for rental of a room. Actually, the daily room rate includes charges covering many services, such as (1) three meals a day, (2) 24-hour-a-day nursing care, (3) clean sheets and towels, (4) clean and sanitary facilities, and (5) recordkeeping. Including patient education under this heading is an appropriate way for hospitals to receive reimbursement for a service patients would not receive if identified separately. It is especially appropriate in that patient education has been identified as an integral part of high-quality health care.

Direct Billing

Direct billing is a payment mechanism whereby funds are generated either by directly collecting from the patient receiving the services or from a separate funding agency or a private source. In most hospitals a fee for each service is usually charged. It may also be appropriate for a fee to be charged for health education. Just because health education has been "free" in the past does not mean it must continue to be in the future.

Patient education can be billed at the same rates as other clinical services, or even at lower rates, because physicians often are not involved. Where groups are involved, even smaller fees can be charged. The rates should be set to recover actual costs. If staff time is covered in the fixed rates for comprehensive service, it may be appropriate for only an additional charge to be made for educational materials used.

If the patient is to be billed, the patient should have previously agreed to both receive and pay

---

*Source: Donald J. Breckon, *Hospital Health Education: A Guide to Program Development*, Aspen Publishers, Inc., © 1982.

for the educational service. This is usually facilitated by having physicians issue an educational prescription which the patients voluntarily fill, as they would a prescription for medicine. Under this system, it would be the duty of hospital personnel, whether it be the physician, nurse, social worker, patient education coordinator, or whoever, to convince patients it would be for their own well-being to participate in such programs. Patients should not be coerced into a program with direct billing.

CONTINUING CARE AND THE DISCHARGE PROCESS

Owing to more rigorous monitoring of health care by regulatory agencies and third-party payers, there has been a tremendous increase in the attention given to discharge planning and continuity of care. Shorter hospital stays mean patients have less recuperative time in the hospital, and thus greater demands are placed on patients, families, hospital staff, and community resources.

The terms *discharge planning, continuing care*, and *continuity of care*, although frequently used interchangeably, are defined somewhat differently and should be clearly delineated.

Continuing care has been defined as a hospital-based program which coordinates assessment, planning, and follow-up procedures by providing a multidisciplinary team approach to patients with posthospital needs. *Discharge planning* is frequently used synonymously and has been defined as a centralized, coordinated program developed by a hospital to ensure that each patient has a planned program for needed continuing or follow-up care.

The American Nurses' Association, however, has provided a broader definition, defining discharge planning as that part of the continuity of care process which is designed to prepare the patient or client for the next phase of care and to assist in making any necessary arrangements for that phase of care, whether it be self-care, care by family members, or care by an organized health care provider.

Continuity of care is the term applied to the coordinated delivery of health services on a con-

tinuum. The continuum includes the delivery of health care services in the home through self-care or with the assistance of families or home health agencies. It includes ambulatory settings, such as neighborhood clinics, private practices, and emergency departments, and extends to inpatient hospital care, rehabilitation, or chronic care facilities as well as hospices. The patients' needs and desires for health services will vary considerably, depending on where they are on the continuum at any given time.

In order to achieve the goal of continuity of care, the patient and health care professionals from various disciplines and health care settings work together in a coordinated effort to achieve mutually agreed-upon goals. This involves a multidisciplinary approach to individualized assessment of the patient's health care needs as well as patient involvement in the decision-making process. It is the responsibility of each health care professional involved in the provision of the patient's care to participate in the discharge planning process.*

Discharge Planning

Discharge planning is dependent upon the following six variables:

1. degree of illness (or health)
2. expected outcome of care
3. duration or length of care needed
4. types of services required
5. addition of complications
6. resources available

Continuity of patient care must be planned for. Every patient should have the opportunity to reach his or her maximum potential for recovery. Planning for continuity of care includes planning for the transfer of patients between units within a hospital or nursing home; planning for discharge of a patient from the hospital to the home or to another care facility; and planning for use of

---

*Source: Sally Anne McCarthy, "The Process of Discharge Planning," in Patricia A. O'Hare and Margaret A. Terry, *Discharge Planning: Strategies for Assuring Continuity of Care*, Aspen Publishers, Inc., © 1988.

resources within the community that supplement and reinforce the discharge planning activities of the hospital, nursing home, and other post-hospital care facilities (See Figure 13-6.)*

Preadmission Planning**

Preadmission planning can assist in the continuing care planning process and in the use of outpatient preadmission testing programs. Preadmission planning is intended to be a resource for the physician, the physician's office personnel, the primary nurse, and the social worker as they help to plan for the patient's hospital stay and discharge. A program such as this can assist the patient—and the family—in making an easier transition from home and community into the hospital. The medical staff should view this program, however, as a resource they can use to get the patient through the system in the most cost-effective way, not as an intrusion on their right to practice medicine.

The advantages of a preadmission planning program are as follows:

- To identify before admission the expected posthospital care needs of patients using admission and preadmission screening programs.
- To identify early those patients whose posthospital needs are expected to be complex so that the necessary posthospital resources can be secured in a timely fashion.
- To familiarize patients and their families with the available community resources.
- To coordinate all bookings with physicians and to screen them for appropriateness of admissions, using preestablished admission review criteria.

Source: Unless noted otherwise, excerpts on patient discharge are from Opal Bristow, Carol Stickey, and Shirley Thompson, *Discharge Planning for Continuity of Care*, National League for Nursing, Pub. No. 21-1604, 1976. Reprinted with permission.

**Source*: Nancy C. Zarle, *Continuing Care: The Process and Practice of Discharge Planning*, Aspen Publishers, Inc., © 1987.

- To increase efficiency in the scheduling of diagnostic procedures on an outpatient basis.
- To support quality assurance, utilization review, and risk management efforts by involving patients and families in long-term planning.
- To initiate patient education and preop teaching before admission for elective surgical patients with a selected diagnosis.
- To help the continuing care primary team to begin the discharge planning process sooner and to alert them to those patients with complex discharge needs.
- To help decrease the length of stay and to prevent unnecessary admissions.

Nursing Administrator's Role

The nursing service director should promote an understanding of the needs of such a program:

- Must budget time and money for implementation of a discharge planning program.
- Must provide nursing leadership and involvement in order to ensure continuity of patient care. Problems and procedures should be standard items on the staff conference agenda.
- Must require that discharge planning procedures be written and included in a procedure or policy book.

A manual should be on every unit. Specifically, information on the mechanics of making a referral, an outline of suggested nursing information to complete a referral, and a list of available nursing agencies with their services, addresses, and telephone numbers should be in this manual. A list of potential candidates for referral should also be included. The nursing policies must remain flexible enough to provide for the special needs of a patient. They should also reflect the attitude of the general program objectives.

Discharge planning, an important component of total patient care, should be part of every nurse's patient care plan. It must begin at the

Figure 13-6 Discharge Planning Process

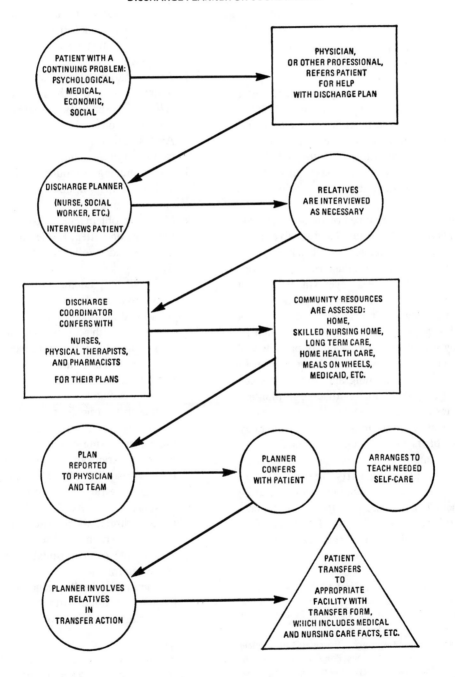

DISCHARGE PLANNING PROCESS
FOR THE
DISCHARGE PLANNER OR COORDINATOR

PATIENT WITH A CONTINUING PROBLEM: PSYCHOLOGICAL, MEDICAL, ECONOMIC, SOCIAL

PHYSICIAN, OR OTHER PROFESSIONAL, REFERS PATIENT FOR HELP WITH DISCHARGE PLAN

DISCHARGE PLANNER (NURSE, SOCIAL WORKER, ETC.) INTERVIEWS PATIENT

RELATIVES ARE INTERVIEWED AS NECESSARY

DISCHARGE COORDINATOR CONFERS WITH NURSES, PHYSICAL THERAPISTS, AND PHARMACISTS FOR THEIR PLANS

COMMUNITY RESOURCES ARE ASSESSED: HOME, SKILLED NURSING HOME, LONG TERM CARE, HOME HEALTH CARE, MEALS ON WHEELS, MEDICAID, ETC.

PLAN REPORTED TO PHYSICIAN AND TEAM

PLANNER CONFERS WITH PATIENT

ARRANGES TO TEACH NEEDED SELF-CARE

PLANNER INVOLVES RELATIVES IN TRANSFER ACTION

PATIENT TRANSFERS TO APPROPRIATE FACILITY WITH TRANSFER FORM, WHICH INCLUDES MEDICAL AND NURSING CARE FACTS, ETC.

Source: Opal Bristow, Carol Stickey, and Shirley Thompson, *Discharge Planning for Continuity of Care*, National League for Nursing, Pub. No. 21-1604, 1976. Reprinted with permission.

time of admission and follow the patient through the progression of his or her illness. Nurses must evaluate each patient's total situation. Merely considering a patient's diagnosis and the related discharge needs as a basis for referral is insufficient.*

Types of Organizational Structures for Discharge Planning**

Discharge planning programs in hospitals come in many shapes and forms. Some hospitals choose to assign the functioning role to the primary nurse at the bedside, others choose to make this the sole responsibility of the social work department, while others have an elaborate structure of team participation with shared responsibilities.

There are several types of models. The first model is the most structured and involves a designated discharge planner (usually a nurse), who has clear responsibility to determine what services the patient may need beyond the hospitalization period. This person is an independent agent, selecting and assessing patient needs. A second model is a variation on the first, in which the nursing and medical staff identify patients with needs and then consult the discharge planner for assistance in determining appropriate services. A third model designates discharge planning activities to specific people. Nurses and social workers assigned to units collaborate on a day-to-day basis and screen patients for post-hospitalization needs (see Table 13-5). Then discharge planning activities are divided between nursing and social services, according to whether home care or nursing home placement referral is needed. In the fourth model the social service department receives requests for patient assistance from medicine and nursing and coordinates all discharge planning activities.

Functions of the Discharge Planning Staff*

1. Screen and study preadmission records
2. Interview, on admission, Medicare-Medicaid patients and patients without insurance
3. Assess patient's needs, stimulate and redirect his or her thinking; encourage self-expression, self-evaluation, and self-determination
4. Assess patient's home situation relative to discharge planning
5. Assist nursing personnel in identifying and assessing patient's needs for discharge planning
6. Identify problems and make appropriate notations on patient Kardex or chart
7. Counsel and involve patient and/or family in:
   a. discharge planning
   b. acceptance of illness, disability, and needed treatment
   c. coping with illness complicated by social and emotional problems
   d. management of finances
   e. self-care and nursing measures in the home situation
   f. reason for transfer to another facility
8. Recommend and assist in placement of patient in nursing home:
   a. arrange transportation if necessary
   b. inform and interpret Medicare, Medicaid, welfare, and community resources
   c. use community resources to supplement and reinforce discharge planning activities of the hospital
9. Make referrals to:
   a. community health agencies
   b. public health departments
   c. psychiatric social workers

---

*Source: Opal Bristow, Carol Stickey, and Shirley Thompson, *Discharge Planning for Continuity of Care*, National League for Nursing, Pub. No. 21-1604, 1976. Reprinted with permission.

**Source: Margaret A. Terry, "Essential Considerations in Setting up a Discharge Planning Program," in Patricia A. O'Hare and Margaret A. Terry, *Discharge Planning: Strategies for Continuity of Care*, Aspen Publishers, Inc., © 1988.

---

*Source: Opal Bristow, Carol Stickey and Shirley Thompson, *Discharge Planning for Continuity of Care*, National League for Nursing, Pub. No. 21-1604, 1976. Reprinted with permission.

Table 13-5 A Discharge Planning Screening Tool

High Risk Factors for Identifying Patients Who May Need Discharge Planning
(Patients are often Type III or IV on PCS)

- ADL dependent (those who cannot manage self-care safely on their own)
- Comatose, semi-comatose
- Disoriented, confused, forgetful
- Dressings and wound care (patients with complicated dressings; patients who cannot do the dressing themselves; patients who will probably not do the dressing unless supervised)
- Equipment and transportation (this function is shared with social services)
- Medications schedules (patients with complex schedules, injections; patients who are noncompliant)
- Ostomies (colostomy, ileostomy)
- Social problems (patients who live alone and could manage with some assistance; those who do not live alone but live with someone who cannot provide adequate care; those who have no home to go to or whose present home is no longer adequate)

- Special teaching needs (e.g., new diabetic, complex diet, injections)
- Terminal, preterminal
- Therapies (O.T., P.T., S.T.)
- Tubes (foley, gastrostomy, supra-pubic, nasogastric, tracheostomy)
- Transfers (transferred here from another hospital or nursing home; patients who will be transferred to another hospital, nursing home, Veterans Hospital, etc.)

Note: Following are the most commonly seen diagnoses of patients who need discharge planning on an acute medical unit:

Arthritis	Diabetes mellitus
Cancer	Emphysema
Cerebral vascular accident	Hypertension
Chronic renal failure	Myocardial infarction
Congestive heart failure	Respirator patients

Source: Linda A. Rasmusen, "A Screening Tool Promotes Early Discharge Planning," *Nursing Management*, May 1984. Reprinted with permission.

---

10. Liaison to maintain continuity of care to:
    a. social service departments
    b. community agencies for posthospital care
    c. various agencies for welfare assistance and placement
11. Liaison between:
    a. hospital and community
    b. social service department and other community agencies
    c. welfare agencies and voluntary charities
    d. departments in the hospital
    e. doctors, patients, and families
    f. hospital and outpatient facilities
12. Resource for:
    a. patient education incorporating available facilities such as the public health nurse

    b. available community facilities
    c. discharge planning for physician and hospital staff
13. Provide inpatient service on a one-to-one basis:
    a. interdepartmental
    b. nursing, ancillary services, chaplaincy, and medical services
14. Establish a system of discharge planning
15. Conduct or participate in continuing education sessions relative to discharge planning
    a. hospital personnel
    b. medical social services
16. Work cooperatively with the physician and social service department for comprehensive discharge planning
17. Obtain necessary physician orders for referrals

Table 13-6 Sample Indicators for Evaluation of Discharge Program

Indicators	Criteria for Determining Degree of Success	Indicators	Criteria for Determining Degree of Success
Hospital Related		**Follow-up of Patients**	
__% decrease in inappropriate admission due to stage of illness in a 6-month period	Appropriateness of admission (use medical criteria)	__% increase in use of community services and resources	Utilization of services postdischarge
__% reduction of overstays in a year or 6-month period	Appropriateness of length of stay Transfer rates to: home care	__% increase in compliance	Satisfaction Compliance with discharge orders Degree of disability 3
Increase from __% to __% patients going to home care, etc.	home nursing home other hospital Planning needs	__% increase in use of planner __% inpatients with discharge plans	months postdischarge, related to planning goals
__% decrease in unmet needs	identified but not met	__% decrease in patient problems	Staff acceptance of program
__% decrease in waiting for admission over 6-month period	Decrease in admission waiting list	due to poor discharge planning information	Feedback from other facilities

18. Assist the health team in understanding the significance of social, economic, and emotional factors in relation to patient illness, treatment, and recovery
19. Provide guidance and aid for patient education
20. Evaluate potential obstetrical clinic patients
21. Assist the patient in the emergency room
22. Encourage development of new resources to meet social service needs
23. Review daily census, coordinate needs of patients, and advise physician of available services
24. Intake for all referrals from physicians on admissions
25. Participate in studies which will contribute toward improving patient care and health programs in the community
26. Make daily rounds to all nursing units to review discharge plans; participate in team conferences on units

27. Attend monthly meetings of audit utilization committee
28. Meet regularly with the utilization review committee
29. Formulate and maintain current departmental policies and procedures
30. Meet with public health and social service personnel
31. Attend orientation for new personnel to explain job functions and to offer assistance when needed
32. Decrease average length of stay of patients in hospital and readmission of patients
33. Keep statistical records of activities and referrals
34. Report monthly to director of nursing and administration on hospital stay and discharge plans for those patients for whom he or she provides help

Chapter 14

Computers and Information Management

INTRODUCTION*

Nursing, like many other professions today, must grapple with information. It must find efficient, effective ways to turn raw data into useful, organized knowledge. Without sophisticated means to process that data, neither the profession nor the industry and public it serves are likely to achieve all the benefits of contemporary health care, nor are hospitals likely to fulfill all their potential as health care businesses.

Advanced computer technology, properly introduced, can yield impressive information-processing results in the nursing profession, in hospitals, and in the health care industry. Nursing information systems can improve both the quality and cost-effectiveness of patient care and the morale of those rendering the care. Although not yet fully proven, these systems hold much promise of making an impact on nursing shortage trends.

To address these driving issues and the projections of skilled personnel shortages, health care managers are demanding information rather than

data. Data represent mere facts, but information assembles those facts that allow managers to make intelligent conclusions and recommendations for decision making. Thus, having accurate, timely, and complete information is essential to address issues effectively.

Nurse management decisions can be enhanced by tracking acuity, cost, and quality data. This information can help nurse management effectively organize patient care delivery, more appropriately measure nurse productivity, identify nursing care costs to assist in making strategic cost-containment decisions, provide a basis for implementing incentive-based compensation programs for measuring and rewarding the provision of quality and cost-effective patient care, and provide objective nursing data to hospital executives.

The evidence clearly shows that the nursing professional can, in fact, be a driving force for the integration of information systems technology in health care (see Table 14-1). Providing a nursing staff with state-of-the-art information tools can be a very effective way of increasing not only the productivity of nurses but also the morale of nurses. In addition, a happier and satisfied nursing staff will promote retention of nurses and present a positive image for the hospital in the eyes of the patient and community.

*Source: Mark S. Gross, "The Potential of Professional Nursing Information Systems," *Secretary's Commission on Nursing: Support Studies and Background Information, Vol. II,* Department of Health and Human Services, December 1988.

Table 14-1 Health Care Information Systems Applications in Nursing

Health care information systems can be applied for the benefit of the nursing profession in a number of ways, including the following:

- A patient assessment application can assist the nurse in quickly and completely assessing a patient's condition at any given time by ensuring that key questions are asked and analyzed.
- A patient classification system can help the nurse determine staffing requirements based on patient care needs by classifying patients according to severity of illness and levels of dependence.
- A care planning system can assist the nurse in specifying and monitoring a treatment plan.
- A charting and documenting system can greatly reduce the amount of paperwork a nurse must complete.
- A QA system can monitor the quality of care being administered by comparing actual care to quality standards.

- Discharge planning systems can assist in effectively planning for the patient's discharge and follow-up care while the patient is still in the hospital.
- Staffing and scheduling systems can assist in appropriately allocating scarce nursing resources to ensure a quality level of care while maintaining complete flexibility of schedules.
- Nurse decisions can be greatly facilitated by having up-to-date and readily accessible patient information.
- Professional nursing systems can incorporate a point of care capability that can include a terminal located at a patient's bedside, in the examination room, or in a patient's home. Information can be collected immediately at the source (the patient), thus easing data entry and increasing accuracy while eliminating duplicate recording of the information.

Source: Mark S. Gross, "The Potential of Professional Nursing Information Systems," *Secretary's Commission on Nursing: Support Studies and Background Information, Vol. II,* Department of Health and Human Services, December 1988.

DETERMINING THE NEED FOR COMPUTERS

Assessment of Existing Information System*

Before deciding whether installing a computerized system will be worth the time and effort, staff should take time to assess the current system and determine if computerization is needed (see Figure 14-1 and Table 14-2).

Staff should begin by assembling all reports received or created. Among these are staffing rosters, personnel and unit schedules, personnel

---

*Source: Patricia M. Haynor and Robin W. Wells, "Taking the Plunge: Selecting a Computerized Staffing and Scheduling System," *Aspen's Advisor for Nurse Executives,* vol. 4, no. 4, © 1989 Aspen Publishers, Inc.

lists by category, wage reports, periodic productivity reports, float pool usage reports, agency personnel usage reports, turnover analyses, acuity data summaries, full-time equivalent (FTE) control, budget statements, and continuing educational in-service activity reports. These form the current information base. The following questions should then be asked:

- How easy was it to assemble the reports?
- What reports do you actually have?
- What information do you receive, and in what format?
- In what time frame do you receive reports—immediately, weekly, monthly, quarterly, annually?
- Who creates reports—you, the nursing department, finance, personnel?

Figure 14-1 Steps in Analysis and Evaluation of Information Needs and Existing Management Information System (MIS)

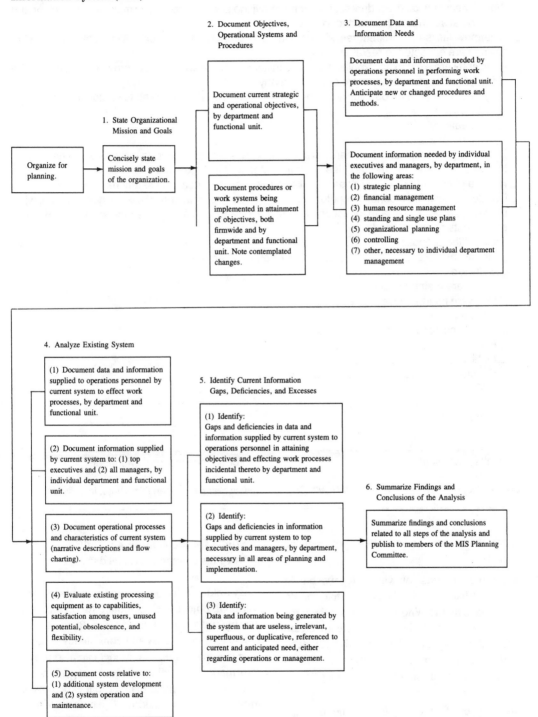

Source: Owen B. Hardy and Clayton McWhorter, *Management Dimensions: New Challenges of the Mind,* Aspen Publishers, Inc., © 1988.

Table 14-2 Checklist for Personal Computer Acquisition

____What present tasks, procedures, or equipment will the personal computer make more efficient and *why*? What savings are expected to result and *why*?

____What new tasks and procedures will the personal computer make more efficient and *why*? What savings are expected to result and *why*?

____Does software exist to accomplish the tasks in items 1 and 2 above? If so, provide the name of the software package and the name of the company.

____Do you plan to take responsibility for the personal computer's use? Who is responsible for:
  _Installation?
  _Maintenance?
  _Ongoing operations?

____Does this proposal include all hardware and/or software required for your foreseeable needs?

____Have space, furniture, and facilities been allocated and included in this proposal?

____Has the plant and properties department approved the electrical and safety requirements?

____Do you expect this personal computer to become a terminal to the hospitalwide system? If so, what provisions have been made for accomplishing that task (e.g., cabling, interface software)? Have all of the costs been included?

____Costs of the proposal:
  _Hardware _____(itemize on another sheet)
  _Software _____
  _Hardware maintenance _____
  _Software maintenance _____
  _Site preparation _____
  _Utilities preparation _____
  _Furniture _____
  _Installation _____
  _Education _____
    TOTAL _____

Approved:

_____   _____

Administrative Staff   Information Resource Manager

Source: Homer H. Schmitz, *Managing Health Care Information Sources*, Aspen Publishers, Inc., © 1987.

- Do the reports actually help you manage better?

- Are there reports you want to receive but do not? What are they? Why is it that you do not have them? Who should create them for you? Is the data base available to create them? Do others understand why you need the information, and are they helpful in getting it to you in a timely manner?

If the answers to these questions include *not enough, not relevant, not timely, from outside the department,* and *they really do not help manage better,* it is time to act.

A Model for Determining a Unit's Nursing Information Needs*

By linking information requirements to organizational objectives, a model for determining nursing information needs can facilitate congruence of objectives and consistency of action by nurse managers. The model can also provide information tailored to a nurse manager's need in a concise, systematic manner that expedites and improves decision making. The process of deter-

*Source: Alice M. Thomas, "Determining Nurse Manager Requirements," *Nursing Management*, vol. 17, no. 7, July 1986. Reprinted with permission.

mining information needs places nurse managers in a position to analyze their jobs, which provides structure, a change of focus, and a better understanding of the job.

The model will guide the interview between the computer analyst and the nurse manager, thereby ensuring uniform results and good utilization of time; no time is wasted deciding how or what to do. Finally, the model is good for all levels of nurse managers, which is ideal, since the information requirements will be uniform and gaps in information assimilation and responsibilities may be identified in the interview process.

An Eight-Step Process

This model comprises eight steps.

1. Understand department objectives. The nurse manager must have a good understanding of the organization's goals and objectives and the objectives of the manager's unit. An example of a unit objective is "to maintain a level of staffing to meet patients' needs."

2. Identify critical success factors (CSFs). The nurse manager determines the CSFs for each objective. These are the few key areas where things must go right for the organization to flourish, tasks that must be accomplished successfully for the unit to achieve its objectives. Each CSF should be written as a short expression (e.g., "scheduling"). The number of CSFs varies for each objective and for each nurse manager but will generally number three to five. Examples of CSFs include a regular staff complement, a relief staff complement, qualified staff, scheduling, and performance appraisals.

3. Identify specific performance measures. The nurse manager must identify the specific performance measures for each CSF. The performance measures should be expressed in quantitative terms if possible. The dimensions of quantity, quality, cost, and time may prove useful as a starting point for generating performance measures.

4. Identify information required to measure performance. The information required must relate to the performance measure. If the performance measure is "actual-to-budgeted staffing patterns," the information required would be summaries of actual versus budgeted staffing for each unit and for the entire area of responsibility.

5. Identify major decision responsibilities. This step involves determining the major decision responsibilities of the nurse manager in order for the manager to achieve the unit's objectives. It is important here to eliminate any decisions of a minor nature in order to ensure that the manager does not become inundated with information.

6. Determine the specific steps required to complete each major decision. The nurse manager articulates the various decision steps for each decision. A decision flow chart may be developed at this time to represent the decision process. This step may be difficult for decision situations that are poorly understood. However, this exercise may result in an improved understanding of the decision process and the information requirements.

7. Determine the information requirements for each decision. Keeping in mind the unit objectives, the nurse manager indicates to the analyst the information that is most supportive of each activity involved.

8. Verify the information requirements. This is done jointly by the analyst and the nurse manager. Any revisions that are deemed necessary are made at this time. The nurse manager must be confident that the identified information requirements are complete and accurate.

PLANNING AND IMPLEMENTATION

See Figure 14-2 and Table 14-3 for guidance in planning and implementing a management information system.

Overcoming Resistance to Computers*

Reasons for Resistance

Many nurses are hesitant to begin using a computer and, indeed, computer resistance is the

---

*Source: Sandra E. Gibson and Mary Ann Rose, "Managing Computer Resistance," *Computers in Nursing*, vol. 4, no. 5, September-October 1986.

Figure 14-2 Planning Steps in Designing and Implementing a Management Information System (MIS)

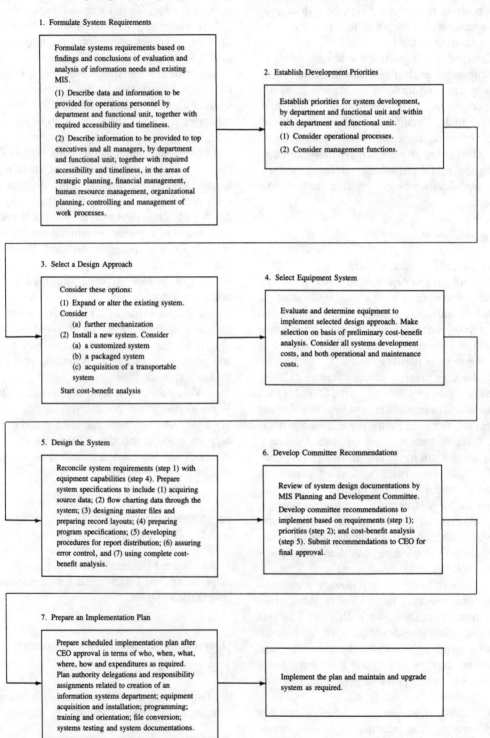

1. Formulate System Requirements

> Formulate systems requirements based on findings and conclusions of evaluation and analysis of information needs and existing MIS.
>
> (1) Describe data and information to be provided for operations personnel by department and functional unit, together with required accessibility and timeliness.
>
> (2) Describe information to be provided to top executives and all managers, by department and functional unit, together with required accessibility and timeliness, in the areas of strategic planning, financial management, human resource management, organizational planning, controlling and management of work processes.

2. Establish Development Priorities

> Establish priorities for system development, by department and functional unit and within each department and functional unit.
>
> (1) Consider operational processes.
> (2) Consider management functions.

3. Select a Design Approach

> Consider these options:
>
> (1) Expand or alter the existing system. Consider
>   (a) further mechanization
> (2) Install a new system. Consider
>   (a) a customized system
>   (b) a packaged system
>   (c) acquisition of a transportable system
>
> Start cost-benefit analysis

4. Select Equipment System

> Evaluate and determine equipment to implement selected design approach. Make selection on basis of preliminary cost-benefit analysis. Consider all systems development costs, and both operational and maintenance costs.

5. Design the System

> Reconcile system requirements (step 1) with equipment capabilities (step 4). Prepare system specifications to include (1) acquiring source data; (2) flow charting data through the system; (3) designing master files and preparing record layouts; (4) preparing program specifications; (5) developing procedures for report distribution; (6) assuring error control, and (7) using complete cost-benefit analysis.

6. Develop Committee Recommendations

> Review of system design documentations by MIS Planning and Development Committee.
>
> Develop committee recommendations to implement based on requirements (step 1); priorities (step 2); and cost-benefit analysis (step 5). Submit recommendations to CEO for final approval.

7. Prepare an Implementation Plan

> Prepare scheduled implementation plan after CEO approval in terms of who, when, what, where, how and expenditures as required. Plan authority delegations and responsibility assignments related to creation of an information systems department; equipment acquisition and installation; programming; training and orientation; file conversion; systems testing and system documentations.

> Implement the plan and maintain and upgrade system as required.

Source: Owen B. Hardy and Clayton McWhorter, *Management Dimensions: New Challenges of the Mind*, Aspen Publishers, Inc., © 1988.

Table 14-3 Guidelines for Setting up a Nursing Information System

The following are suggestions that will help make the move to computer operation a smoother transition.

- Involve nursing service from the beginning.
- Assign a nurse committee to evaluate the following:
  —patient care information needed
  —nursing service management information (staffing, schedules, etc.) needed
  —administrative information (statistical data for budgeting, meeting standards, etc.) needed
- Study the options for going with a full system or selected functions that are most needed and cost-effective.
- Review available systems using both manufacturer's information and on-site observation.
- Select a system based on the following:
  —suitability to needs
  —ease of operations
  —training time needed for staff
  —capacity for updating

- Develop customized information requirements to program into the system (limited access, care plans per diagnosis, pharmacology data, etc.).
- Determine location of terminals as message centers for nursing stations and nursing service.
- Work closely with provider of systems and programs for on-site installation and training.
- Plan orientation and training of personnel. Organize training according to the priority of their roles.
- Provide support staff at time of implementation.
- Provide ongoing training to compensate for turnover.
- Evaluate the system in operation.
- Keep up with state of the art by adding new functions, updated features, or program refinements that are desirable for the facility.

Source: Esther Kinnaman, "Computers in Nursing: How to Orchestrate a (Relatively) Painless Changeover." Published in *RN*. Copyright © 1982 Medical Economics Company Inc., Oradell, N.J. Reprinted by permission.

most prevalent negative phenomenon associated with computer use. Computers can be threatening. Many nurses who have spent years developing and expanding their nursing skills are proud of their complex, demanding practice. Faced with the introduction of computers, they must return to the role of learner to master a new skill, although a fairly simple one compared with the complexities of caring for patients. It is common knowledge that every 14-year-old is a "computer whiz," and this makes the situation worse. Nurses, particularly older nurses, may be hesitant to attempt to learn a skill unrelated to those they have already developed. Additionally, some nurses may have a fear of failure related to a previous bad experience with a computerization effort.

Computers may also be resisted for social reasons. Some nurses derive a major portion of their job satisfaction from the opportunity the job provides for interaction and communication with coworkers and patients. Removing these social benefits could prompt strong dissatisfaction. This is enhanced if there is a socially acceptable attitude of animosity toward machines (e.g., telephone-answering machines).

There may also be more abstract reasons. Professional nurses usually have high human values and may have ideologic barriers to accepting anything that could deprive the patient of professional contact. This may be of particular concern on primary nursing units where nurses feel a high degree of commitment to individualized care.

Strategies for Dealing with Resistance

Assess the Presystem Environment. An appraisal of the presystem environment may alert management to impending problems. Before the system is brought into the unit, the manager should consider the following factors:

- *Identify whether the new system will solve the problem of the current system.* Usually a manager who attempts to change a system that already works evokes cynicism from the staff; the chances of success are low.
- *Determine the support that can be expected from upper-level administration.* Implementation may go more smoothly if the influencing powers in the organization support the introduction of a computerization effort.
- *Determine what hardware and software should be available for immediate use.* Insufficient software and hardware verification before installation may cripple the operational capacity of the unit and weaken enthusiasm. Nurses willing to try computer use will be discouraged if they attempt to use a computer, have difficulty, and then find that the difficulty is the result of inoperable or incompatible equipment.
- *Assess the staff's attitude and level of exposure to computerization.* The amount of exposure may have an impact on how health professionals respond to computerization. Research demonstrates that extensive and daily experience with computers produces positive attitudes toward computerization. A nurse whose family uses a computer at home may have less resistance than one who has only seen the movie *War Games*.
- *Determine the effect implementation may have on the current reward structure.* A reward structure often acts as an incentive to carry out the project. The chances of success may be improved when familiar rewards are retained with the new implementation. For example, the computer's ability to store material compactly in a central location may be a positive reward to a nurse who has a very cramped office.

Focus on the Causes of Resistance. Identifying the reasons for resistance should help the manager develop strategies that address the problem directly. For example, in-service education begun well ahead of implementation can alleviate inaccurate perceptions and help nurses realize how computerization can help accomplish nursing and patient goals.

Market the Computerization Effort. The specific benefits of using computers should be identified and explained to potential users. Throughout the computer in-service sessions, the manager should present examples of favorable computerization efforts in similar nursing organizations and emphasize the support of top management. Potential users should also be assisted to identify how automation helps personal goals for advancement within organizational goals.

Involve the User. User acceptance of the computerization effort is crucial to success. Encouraging the user to participate in the design, implementation, and evaluation can help develop feelings of ownership and commitment to the new system. Managers should provide opportunities for employees to voice their fears and misconceptions from the beginning of the computerization effort.

COMPUTER APPLICATIONS IN NURSING

Applications for Nursing Administration*

At present, computers generate many quantitative and qualitative statistical reports, such as room use and turnover studies, that once required long, tedious hours of compilation and analysis. Nursing administrators are able to program the computer to reproduce administrative forms, evaluations, proficiencies, and disciplinary actions. Yearly evaluations, promotion dates, and other valuable information can be generated months in advance to facilitate counseling. Information regarding risk management (i.e., incident reports and their follow-up) can be stored and used to track trends. Standards of care, procedures, and protocols can be stored

*Source: Barbara J. Robertson and Tonya E. Grinde, "Future Innovations in Computer Technology for Operating Room Services," *Perioperative Nursing Quarterly*, vol. 2, no. 4, © 1986 Aspen Publishers, Inc.

and easily produced for the staff's quick perusal. Messages to staff and other departments can be entered into the electronic mail, and the manager can later track who has read and received these messages.

Images specifically designed for creating newsletters, flyers, and bulletins can be produced by software packages. The computer can be programmed to design simple or complex data forms. Annual reviews and certifications along with annual physicals and tuberculosis clearances for staff can also be entered, stored, and retrieved so that follow-up can be simplified. Protocols or documents with expiration dates can be programmed to appear automatically and can be revised easily and updated. Data forms designed for one unit can be adapted for use in other units of the medical center.

Data for nursing audits are no longer a tedious process of compilation and review. Managers can track statistical data, trends, and improvements easily. Enforcement and adherence to policies and protocols may be less of a burden as the information needed by nurse administrators can be easily retrieved with computer programs.

Scheduling

One hospital has developed a nurse scheduling program that will provide outputs for biweekly nurse time schedules for up to six weeks, individual nurse time schedules, and a daily time schedule that can be used as a confirmation sheet for timekeeping. Tracking on-call rotation is a valuable part of this scheduling package. Scheduling can be accomplished based on trends. On-call and vacation schedules can be easily programmed, as well as off-tour and extended-tour assignments. The percentage of rotation can be monitored as well as deviations related to sick leave and emergency leave.

Communication

The traditional view of computers as data base management tools neglects their role as a medium for communication. The medical center environment, with its broad-based distribution of terminals, presents an opportune vehicle for improved communication. Users may send messages to an individual or a group. Once the message is sent, the user can query the system for the dates and time sent. Electronic mail is the communication medium of the future.

Education

Educational modules as well as minutes and attendance at meetings can be entered on the computer. Special bulletins and notices for workshops, seminars, and meetings can be entered. Job announcements or vacancies can be displayed or sent via the mailing system. Also, annual classes for cardiopulmonary resuscitation, safety, blood transfusion, and other institutional requirements can be stored and retrieved. An orientation file can be compiled and maintained.

Computer-assisted instruction (CAI) is a possible resolution to practical teaching–learning problems because faculty can reduce repetitive, tedious tasks. CAI can stimulate actual nursing practice and provide invaluable realistic learning exercises for nurses. A networking system may be instituted for learning needs. Community hospitals offering in-services may propose to share this information. Staff biographical data can be compiled to obtain statistical data and be used for networking.

The Future

Nurses' dreams for the future include the integration and facilitation of their administrative, clinical, and educational roles through the computer. Programs to anticipate include (1) intelligent scheduling systems for staff and patient operative procedures; (2) totally automated supply services based on physician preference that include accounting programs for billing and supply replenishment; (3) electronic communication within a service and between services (preoperative checklist, reports) or agencies; (4) automated statistical reporting capabilities (room utilization, infection rates, turnover, nursing audits); (5) automated policy and procedure manuals; (6) CAI for operating room nursing staff and patients; (7) totally automated postoperative monitoring equipment; and (8) an electronic patient chart.

Computerizing the Nursing Process*

The key feature of successful future medical information systems will be the broadly based integration of all clinical, administrative, and financial data. Since the bedside is the focus for patient care delivery, it is at the bedside that all such integrated data must come together to enhance both the process and the documentation of patient care. This process will be driven largely by a comprehensive order set detailing all activities concerning each patient. This order set will use both diagnostic and treatment orders (generally physician generated) and patient care orders (generally nursing generated).

The first step of the nursing process involves examining and interviewing a patient in order to delineate problems and progress toward a resolution, as well as to create a baseline profile, and is known as the nursing assessment. This step is typically followed by problem identification, and a care plan specific for the patient is created.

Once a plan of care is instituted, it should be reevaluated periodically and modified as necessary. Through both the medical and the nursing care processes, the status of the problems and the current treatments to resolve them are reassessed regularly, the current progress is documented, and the cycle repeats until the problem is solved or the patient is discharged.

Each of these components of the nursing care cycle lends itself well to bedside-based automation. It is worthwhile to examine each of these areas in turn to understand how automation can affect the nursing care process, especially in the context of optimizing nursing operations performed primarily at the bedside. Under diagnosis-related groups (DRGs), this pursuit of operations enhancement should be a key focus of the nursing department, allowing it to continue the delivery of high-quality care in a cost-constrained environment.

*Source: Mychelle M. Mowry and Ralph A. Korpman, *Managing Health Care Costs, Quality, and Technology: Product Line Strategies for Nursing,* Aspen Publishers, Inc., © 1986.

Nursing Assessment

Computerized bedside-based nursing assessment records the specific data relevant for a particular patient. Using a branched logic approach, in which nonproblem areas are addressed in outline and problem areas in detail, the nurse can be assured that no important topics are missed. For example, if the nurse ascertains that the patient recently experienced significant weight loss, the system will prompt the nurse to ask a series of questions related to diet, exercise, life-style changes, etc. (hospital-defined criteria). If this change did not occur with the patient, the system will prompt the nurse through the next series of general questions. The nurse then is assured that topics of concern involving the patient are covered in appropriate detail. With simple menu entry techniques, the assessment can be done in about the same time it takes to interview the patient. However, at the completion of the computerized assessment, all data gathered are available immediately to all levels of health care providers. This means that other providers seeking allergy, diet, or other information already gathered by the nurse will be able to do so without having to disturb the patient to make yet another entry of the same data. These other providers, especially nurses on following shifts, can easily review significant findings selectively for each patient. This kind of data capture has a substantial beneficial effect on the productivity and quality of care of all providers.

In addition, and very important, the system now can be used to assist in the development of the patient's problem list. As the assessment process continues, problems usually associated with certain responses can be identified and filed. In terms of patient care cost issues, the detection of a greater number of problems early in a patient's hospital course could contribute to an earlier discharge.

It must be emphasized that the primary use of the computer is as a clerical assist/memory jog. The intent of such assessments is not the creation of a computerized nurse; rather, it is the replacement of handwritten recording tasks to make them more complete and error free. This process also makes the data derived from the assessment available immediately to a more extensive user community by eliminating the review of the handwritten documents by both the creator and other professionals.

This kind of information recording gives physicians the opportunity to refer to nursing assessment forms for additional clinical and psychosocial information regarding their patients. The data also are more consistent between and among nurses. Finally, the system assists in pinpointing patient problems. In each of these areas; significant time can be saved in the assessment process.

Care Planning

Upon completion of the automated assessment process, the computer system assists the nurse in the selection of an appropriate problem list for each patient. This list is created in part from computer analysis of information derived during the assessment and from any other specific problems the nurse may wish to establish. For each problem established, a number of typical etiologies are available for selection. After identification of the problem/etiology pair, the system immediately presents to the nurse a list of possible goals and procedures for this problem set. Again using menu selection, the nurse chooses which goals and modalities are desired for this patient. The process is much more efficient and much less error prone than the manual method since it involves no copying; no retention of facts in human memory; and no references to books, cards, or other paper aids.

Once the nursing interventions are selected, both processess identified as problems in the manual system are handled automatically.

The data regarding the treatments are integrated immediately back into the patient's care schedule and are available at once to all other providers for the individual. All future care and assessments for the patient are tracked against the care plan and therefore allow updates in reaction to individual responses; a record is also kept of all these changes.

When the entire nursing process is on-line, it becomes a rapid and simple process to gather data on the most effective treatments for all clinical problems. It is also possible to ascertain the most cost-effective personnel (by skill level, education, or experience) for solving the problems. For example:

- Is it more effective and efficient to ambulate a postoperative patient or to encourage turning, deep breathing, and coughing?
- Is it better to ambulate three times a day or five times?
- Should ambulation be combined with intermittent positive pressure breathing (IPPB) therapy?
- Is it effective to teach the postmyocardial infarction patient in the hospital or in the clinic environment after discharge?
- How much of the teaching information is retained?
- Who is the most effective teacher—the registered nurse, the clinical nurse specialist, the physician, the licensed practical or vocational nurse, the therapist, the discharge planning nurse, or any combination?

Kardex and Patient Schedule Maintenance

The strengths of a computer system lend themselves well to the creation of an automated Kardex and patient care schedule management scheme. As each physician order is entered into the system and as each nursing intervention is created as part of the assessment and care-planning process, the required observations and treatments can be entered automatically and immediately into an automated patient Kardex and care schedule.

Because these documents are referred to via a cathode ray terminal (CRT) and because the CRT is located at the patient's bedside, the nurse can assess immediately what services are due simply by calling up the care schedule at the bedside (Table 14-4). This record will reflect the most recent actions of all providers. As changes are made in physician, ancillary, or nursing order sets, the Kardex and patient care schedule automatically and immediately show the new information. Overdue orders are easy to identify and may be addressed expeditiously.

Table 14-4 Sample Patient Care Schedule

					Fri 28 Mar 91 10:22	
Location	Name	Number	Sex	Birthdate	Age	Physician
5807	Smith, Suzanne	1541342	F	4Dec1933	51Y	Ingold, J.

Schedule for: Fri, 29 Mar 91

(1)	0715 ACT:Position Pt	(11)	prn	MED:Dmrl/Vistrl	(21)	MSC:Pants/Gown
(2)	0731 ACT:UpAdLib	(12)		MED:Actmnph/Cod	(22)	ASM:Trnsport Asm
(3)	0744 NTR:Diet as Tol	(13)		MED:Acetaminoph	(23) lun	NTR:Diet as Tol
(4)	0845 HYG:PeriCare	(14)	cons	RAD:Con Ultsnd	(24) 1301	ACT:Position Pt
(5)		(15)	misc	IV:D5/45Saline	(25) 1501	ACT:Position Pt
(6)	0905 ACT:Position Pt	(16)		NTR:I&O	(26) pm	ACT:Up Ad Lib
(7)	MED:Valium	(17)	1101	ACT:Position Pt	(27)	HYG:Peri Care
(8)	MED:Ampicillin	(18)	day	PSY:Reduce Anx	(28)	CMF:Protect Skin
(9)	0936 LAB:CBC	(19)		LAB:SMAC	(29) 1701	ACT:Position Pt
(10)	1019 ORD:Bauer,D	(20)		RAD:Abdomen	(30) sup	NTR:Diet as Tol

Patient Care Options

(A) Assessment	(N) Nurse Change Orders	(R) Provider Register
(B) Chart Review	(O) Order Entry	(T) Shift Summary
(C) Face Sheet	(P) Care Planning	(U) Unscheduled Procs
(K) Kardex	(Q) Review Queue	

Source: Mychelle M. Mowry and Ralph A. Korpman, *Managing Health Care Costs, Quality, and Technology: Product Line Strategies for Nursing*, Aspen Publishers, Inc., © 1986.

Charting and Continuing Asessment

With the availability of a bedside-based computer tool, it becomes clear that most charting need not be regarded as charting per se; rather, it is a continuing nursing reassessment of the patient's status. This continuing assessment generally can be keyed to the problem list and care plan. Even an unusual event unrelated to any current patient problem needs to be assessed in the context of the possible emergence of a new problem, rather than in just the mere notation of an isolated fact.

Because the system is apprised continuously of the patient's problems, previous assessments, and care, the transformation of charting into a continuing reassessment lends itself well to automation. In this milieu, when nurses come on shift and visit each patient under their care, they can reassess the problems, therapies, and the changes to both immediately. These then can become changes in care plans, responses to existing plans, new problems to be listed, or potential problems evaluated but excluded from the list.

A computer system does not make a good physician or nurse. Their roles involve high-level, integrative, intuitive tasks to which a computer does not lend itself. However, the clerical component of nursing patient care can be well addressed by a bedside-based computer system. With such an operation, notations regarding a patient can be made as they are observed and therapies recorded as they are performed; each of these then can be keyed back to the patient assessment and care planning cycle, allowing both extensive concurrent and retrospective data analysis and evaluation as well as continual updating of the supporting documents: the Kardex, the care schedule, and the care plan. Finally, because the computer can perform clerical tasks instantly, the amount of professional time invested in such work can be decreased substantially.

Patient Care Factors That Could Be Flagged by Computers

- Clinicians at the bedside may choose to review only the abnormal blood pressures on their postoperative patients and may prefer to be made aware of others if they are not performed as scheduled.
- Clinicians may choose specific (and different) exception criteria for data to be displayed at shift end for oncoming nurses so that time is not wasted reviewing the 80 percent of the previous shift's activities that were nonexceptional.
- Nurse managers at the unit level may choose to review patient care plans in which outcome criteria were not met and the length of stay exceeded the DRG limit.
- Managers might review all patients who fell out of bed and also received narcotics prior to the incident.
- Nurse managers over several units may want to review medication errors only on the day shift or specific shifts/units in which actual nursing care hours exceeded budgeted hours and compare this with acuity levels.

Source: Mychelle M. Mowry and Ralph A. Korpman, *Managing Health Care Costs, Quality, and Technology: Product Line Strategies for Nursing*, Aspen Publishers, Inc., © 1986.

Automated Patient Classification Systems

As discussed, the future of nursing service automation will include bedside-based terminals that facilitate documentation as part of the care-giving process. Terminals will be available wherever patients are located or care processes are executed. In this situation, the terminal becomes a valuable tool to assist nurses and other direct caregivers in performing their duties more efficiently with a much higher quality of information processing. This type of terminal networking and availability sets the stage for an accurate, objective, and dynamic patient classification process.

Characteristics. The following characteristics are essential for an effective automated patient classification system:

- valid and reliable, measuring accurately and consistently what it claims to measure
- objective, so that user subjectivity does not influence results
- quick to compute for the user; it should not add to the workload
- simple, so that users can acquire expertise quickly
- capable of being updated easily to keep pace with changing technology and nursing and medical practice patterns
- capable of extensive statistical analysis of the data
- capable of categorizing and timing direct and indirect patient care activities
- flexible, so that activity categorization is defined by individual hospital preference
- capable of producing management reports for budgetary planning and control, productivity tracking, educational needs, workload balancing, nursing care modality comparisons, and quality assurance
- adaptable to all patient care areas, including emergency department, clinics, critical care units, and medical-surgical units

Uses.* A computerized patient classification system can be used to perform the following tasks:

- determining changes in patient mix on a given unit
- determining staff mix ratios based on intensity
- identifying peak workload times as they relate to admissions, transfers, or discharges
- automating the procedure for determining nursing care hours

---

Source: Carol Birdsall and Patricia Valoon, "Management Information System," in *Handbook for First-Line Nurse Managers*, Joyce L. Schweiger, ed., © 1986 John Wiley & Sons (Fleschner Publishing Co.).

The use of a patient classification system to identify changes in patient mix is most helpful. A system that assists with the identification of changes in the total hours of care required and the trends toward consistent change in patient mix on any unit provides valuable information for the first-line manager. For example, if a patient in halo traction were to be admitted to an orthopedic unit for the first time, staff would be unfamiliar with organizing the care for that patient and hence probably spend more time than is really needed in caring for the patient. If this type of patient became the norm for that unit, a system that would identify the change in mix and the intended hours of care needed for this type of patient would be helpful when justifying the need for additional staff.

Peak load times for unit activities, including the number, time, and type of admissions, transfers, and discharges, can be accumulated with a patient classification system. It is possible to develop a management tool for time management that can be useful for planning in-service classes, staff meetings, staff conferences, and break times.

Nursing care hours are another function that can be maintained quite easily with either a patient classification system or a nurse staffing program. Most departments of nursing are required to keep records of the nursing care hours provided by staff for each unit. This information is readily adaptable to a computerized staffing or patient classification system.

Clinical Applications of a Computerized Information System*

Clinical applications can be divided into three major categories:

1. charting functions related to the patient's medical record

*Source: Carol Birdsall and Patricia Valoon, "Management Information System," in Handbook for First-Line Nurse Managers, Joyce L. Schweiger, ed., © 1986 John Wiley & Sons (Fleschner Publishing Co.).

2. selected nursing and medical requirements for the evaluation of the quality and appropriateness of patient care
3. clinical information screens

Charting Functions Related to the Medical Record

To identify those charting functions that readily lend themselves to charting in the system, a complete analysis of the various components of nurse charting will provide the information needed to make appropriate decisions. Many departments of nursing have charting standards and policies that can be used as a starting point: standards or policies related to vital signs; medications; unit tests; intake and output or fluid balance; IVs; criteria or standards for admission or transfer to or discharge from the operating room, recovery room, etc.; height/weight; treatments/procedures; and patient care notes or nursing progress notes.

The first-line manager should examine each item and how and where it is currently charted and who utilizes the information. The items most frequently used by other health professionals should be considered (e.g., vital signs):

- Are they presently graphed?
- Does that work well?
- Will the computer system be able to graph?
- Will it be necessary to buy additional hardware to do this?
- Are vital signs charted with medications for selected drugs?
- Is that option available with the new system?
- If the system of charting related to graphing temperatures and other vital information has to be changed, who will be most affected by the change and how can the change be made to best serve the users?

The first-line manager should develop a scoring system for each of the functions.

- Would compliance or availability of the information be improved if data were put on-line?

- Do the institution's standards include the need for ongoing cumulative fluid balances on patients?
- Are fluid balance sheets kept at the bedside, and if so, who records intake and output?
- If this information is to be placed into the system, who will do it and when will this occur?
- Will it mean double charting for the nurse, and, if so, will the staff comply?

Medication administration and charting often occur together, particularly with a unit dose system that provides a method of charting at the bedside. Conversion to a computerized system requires charting at a computer terminal. The first-line manager should plan to discuss this aspect at length with nursing staff in order to develop policies for charting that will facilitate compliance.

Narrative notes offer another set of problems related to the computer. Staff who do not type may have a difficult time entering notes into the system if it is the expectation that all narrative notes by typed. The other major factors that limit lengthy narratives are, of course, computer capacity and paper volume. Printouts are usually automatic following each entry. Most systems are not programmed to accumulate charting entries equal to a full page. How voluminous will the chart become with the added volume of paper? Who will manage the paper flow? How will staff and physicians locate information in the chart if all the entries are on the same-color paper? Mandating complete charting into the system may not benefit the institution.

Chapter 15

Nursing Reports and Record Systems

MANAGEMENT REPORTS

Function of Reports*

Nurses often fail to recognize the importance of transferring their documentation skills to the reporting of significant events related to managerial tasks and responsibilities. A monthly managerial summary provides a historical data base for reference purposes, a format for objectively examining time spent on various projects and results achieved, and a record of issues and problems that either recur in a cyclic pattern or are resolved after one occurrence. The monthly summary also provides a quick reference from which the nurse manager can prepare a quarterly or annual summary of unit or departmental activities.

Additionally, a monthly summary provides a communication tool by which the nurse manager can let the supervisor know what he or she has achieved. Many nurse managers, novices in particular, seem to believe that everyone knows what nurse managers do and that appropriate credit will be given. This is not always the case. However, a good monthly summary allows the

*Source: Frankie C. Nail and Enrica K. Singleton, "An Approach to Nurse Managerial Reporting: An Essential Task," *The Health Care Supervisor*, vol. 8, no. 2, © 1990 Aspen Publishers, Inc.

nurse manager to assess his or her contribution toward the accomplishment of the overall goals of the organization. A review of 6 to 12 consecutive monthly summaries will allow the nurse manager to discern whether his or her goals are synchronous with those of the next-level administrator and the organization as a whole. These reports can also be useful to the manager in preparing for annual self-evaluations and performance evaluation conferences with the supervisor.

Pointers on Managerial Reporting

Managerial reporting should focus on achievements (outcomes) rather than on activities (processes). The monthly managerial summary should never be used as a log for recording the manager's use of time in various activities. The organization's primary interest is in whether goals are being achieved. The nurse manager may include issues encountered that are related to the goals of the organization, to the need for (or implementation of) major policy changes, and to new programs or methods initiated at the unit or departmental level that will contribute to the accomplishment of organizational goals.

Quantifiable data should be used whenever possible. Most administrators are concerned about the bottom line and are therefore accustomed to dealing with numbers. Therefore, nurse managers must quantify whenever possible.

Reports should be concise. Limit the report to one page, if possible. A two-page report should be necessary only when a month has been truly exceptional. A one-page report is twice as likely to be read as a two-page report and three times as likely to be read as a three-page report. If details are essential for clarification of segments of the report, the information should be included in an addendum.

Managerial reports should highlight accomplishments of the manager as achieved through his or her staff. Positions rather than individuals should be the frame of reference, unless an individual commendation is in order. However, a report should not be used to list names of persons who have experienced circumstances that could be conceived as negative.

Reports should include any follow-up information that was promised in a previous report. For example, suppose the nurse manager initiated a new medication administration record in response to physician complaints and indicated that a six-month evaluation would be conducted. Six months later the results of that evaluation should be reported.

The report should be submitted at about the same time each month, even in unusual circumstances. For example, if a nurse supervisor elects to report on the tenth of each month for the previous month and plans to be on vacation on the tenth of next month, he or she should prepare the report early.

A consistent report format should be selected and used. This will facilitate review in a short period of time.

Deciding To Write Occasional Reports*

The first task in preparing a report is to be clear about its purpose. For example, is it supposed to point up inadequacies in nursing service or good or poor utilization of personnel skills or to provide baseline information for experimenting with new patterns of personnel assignments?

To whom, primarily, is the report being made? Is it directed to nursing service, hospital administration, or the board of trustees? City commissioners or a department of hospitals? Some other audience? The substance of the report is determined by the findings and the audience.

How is the report to be used? Is it for internal use or publication; for use in improving nursing service through staff education; to get approval, from a higher level than nursing service, for change or expansion; to justify additional budget; to spark action or change; to inform participants and others about findings?

How significant are the findings? Are they pertinent to all nursing units in the hospital or limited to the unit or units studied? Do they confirm beliefs for which factual support was needed? Have they revealed new information important to better patient care or more efficient management? Do they support action desired by the nursing service?

If some kind of action seems advisable, recommendations suggesting change should be stated. Recommendations might include specific actions needed; restudy to determine, after a reasonable interval, whether changes recommended have been effective; or studies of phenomena important in patient care.

NURSING FORMS[1]

Among the significant forms in the medical record of each patient are the nursing records. These records are maintained for each patient and cover pertinent information of patient care. Forms are usually provided for data on admission, initial professional assessment, daily notations, and information on discharge of the patient. Many nursing services are now entering various data into designated sections of a master

----

*Source: How To Study Nursing Activities, DHHS, PHS No. 370.

[1]*Note*: For a full discussion of forms design, forms committees, and forms management and reproductions of almost a thousand varied forms covering every aspect of nursing administration and management, see *The Nursing Forms Manual*, edited by Howard S. Rowland (Aspen Publishers, Inc., © 1985).

record, whenever possible, rather than using separate forms.

Designing Forms*

The following questions summarize the targets used in creating effective documents through forms design.

- Where does the form originate; that is, what department originally enters data onto the form or enters the form into the system to be used by others?
- What individual enters data on the form?
- What information should be on the form?
- What information is currently being entered on the form?
- Who ascertains the completeness of the data entries?
- Where will the form finally be filed?
- Who will use the information on the form?
- Who will receive copies of the form?
- How long should the form be retained?

Guidelines for Designing Forms

The following guidelines should prove helpful in knowing where to begin and what steps to take in designing a form.

1. Assess each form individually to
   a. ensure its necessity
   b. avoid duplicate recording
   c. ensure it integrates with the existing records system
2. Determine the purpose of the form, which will determine information to be included.
3. Identify benefits that will be derived from introduction of the form into the record.
4. Design forms as simply as possible; do not clutter them with headings, captions, or instructions.
5. Consider use of unstructured, multipurpose flow sheets. They will eliminate the

need for several special forms to monitor special care factors and reduce chart bulk.
6. Plan all forms in the record to be a uniform size.
7. Place form titles and patient identification consistently on every form.
8. Include space for at least
   a. full patient name
   b. medical, health, or client record file number
9. Consider printing headings and captions in bold print.
10. Line up headings to provide an uncluttered appearance and to promote ease in locating desired information.
11. Consider logical sequence of subject headings.
12. Use white paper with color-coded borders for quick identification of different forms; colored paper may be difficult to read or photocopy.
13. Select captions that clearly state what information is to be entered.
14. Use a box arrangement to save time in checklists.
15. Plan spacing according to the specific method of documentation.
    a. Typewritten entries: set lines according to number of lines per inch on a typewriter and to accommodate vertical spacing.
    b. Handwritten entries: set lines far enough apart to ensure readability.
    c. CRT or computer printout format: set margin, spacing, and punctuation clearly.
    d. Consider the period of time each side of the form covers.
16. Identify certain portions that are restricted for use by designated staff or groups (e.g., medical records service, infection control committee, utilization review committee); those areas should be surrounded with bold lines.
17. Consider printing on both sides of the sheet to maximize paper use and reduce chart bulk.
18. Consider printing on reverse side to facilitate reference when form is in chart

Source: Kathleen A. Waters and Gretchen F. Murphy, *Medical Records in Health Information*, Aspen Publishers, Inc., © 1979.

holder and/or fastened at top as a closed record.

19. When possible, eliminate the need for a special form by utilizing a rubber stamp on an existing form.

20. Allow sufficient space for signatures of those making entries.

21. Because newly designed forms often need revisions, mimeograph or photocopy a small supply for trial use.

22. Use good quality paper stock in final printing to avoid dog-earing and tearing and to ensure permanence; 20-pound weight paper stock is recommended for long-term use.

23. Card stock should be avoided since it creates bulk, is difficult to handle, and may complicate photocopy technique.

24. Stock only a six-month supply of the form to prevent waste in the event of a revision or change in documentation procedures.

25. Always introduce a proposed new form before implementation and preferably during initial design phases; this promotes input by those making entries and using the data.

26. Complete final review and approval of the draft form prior to implementation; this is accomplished by a multidisciplinary forms committee that includes the medical record administrator.

27. Simple printed instructions will ensure uniformity if a form is to be used by various departments.

28. If instructions are detailed, prepare separate directions regarding
    a. purpose
    b. use
    c. instructions for completion
    d. staff responsibilities
    e. references, if any

29. Include the name, address, and city of the facility on forms that are likely to be sent elsewhere.

30. Identify all forms by
    a. a descriptive and simple title
    b. a stock control number
    c. the month and year of first, revised, or last printing

Forms Appraisal Checklist*

1. Is the form necessary, or is there some existing form that could be adapted to fill the need?

2. Has the entire procedure for use of the form been checked? Would a written procedure help?

3. Can the form be combined with some other form, or some other form be eliminated by it?

4. Could the time period covered by the form be lengthened?

5. Are all copies necessary? Could one copy be routed to more than one location?

6. Have users been consulted?

7. Have those responsible for it approved it?

8. If a revision, can it be distinguished from the previous form?

9. Does the form clearly indicate its use?

10. Is the size standard and no larger than necessary?

11. Does the design complement the writing method?

12. Is routing indicated on each copy?

13. Are margins sufficient?

14. If for outside use, will it fit a window envelope? Could it be designed as a self-mailer?

15. Should copies be numbered or have a place for a number?

16. Is spacing correct?

17. Is all fixed information printed, so that only variable items need to be filled in?

18. Are important items properly placed? Are reference items properly located?

19. Are like items grouped?

20. Are signature spaces large enough?

21. Has the number of digits or the typical fill-in been indicated?

22. Is the number of copies ideal for all purposes?

23. Are detailed printing specifications complete?

24. Do paper colors facilitate use?

25. Have requirements been correctly estimated?

*Source: Courtesy of University of South Alabama Medical Center, Mobile, Alabama.

26. Has a low order point been established?
27. Has disposition of old forms been determined?

DOCUMENTATION

The Uses of Documentation

Documentation is a communication tool. It is quality assurance; it is validation that the patient has been served and that outcomes have been achieved. Furthermore, if pertinent information is documented, documentation becomes a timesaver.

Documentation may also serve as a management tool. By identifying issues and documenting them, nurses can make decisions. Moreover, documentation serves a legal purpose: if services are not provided, a legal suit could be drawn. Note, too, that if a service was provided and not documented, a court of law views it as *not* provided. Documentation is essential because the regulatory agencies are monitoring bodies. Documentation is also helpful for statistical and planning purposes. Ask, ''How many referrals have been made in the last six months?'' If the referrals are not documented and recorded in some fashion, the assumption is that no referrals have been made.

Documentation has a purpose—especially in a time of early discharging activity. It is critical that all areas of concern (i.e., teaching, health needs, equipment needs, and orders) be documented and communicated in a timely continuing care process. See Figure 15-1 for an illustration of the documentation process.*

Documentation Systems**

The types of documentation systems fall into two main categories, with variations within each category: traditional and focused.

Source: Nancy C. Zarle, *Continuing Care: The Process and Practice of Discharge Planning*, Aspen Publishers, Inc., © 1987.

**Source*: Christina L.S. Evans and Sharon K. Lewis, *Nursing Administration of Psychiatric-Mental Health Care*, Aspen Publishers, Inc., © 1985.

Traditional, or Source-Oriented, Documentation Systems

In the traditional, or source-oriented, system, each discipline generally charts separately on one patient in separate areas of the medical record. Although this system may facilitate each discipline's review of the patient's progress in relation to the discipline, there is no documented blending of patient information to create an overall picture of the patient's progress and current status. Verbal exchange of information must serve to consolidate treatment approaches. Within this system, formats may vary among disciplines, depending on the collaborative nature of the organization.

Focused Documentation Systems

The focused documentation system requires that charting be done according to certain pre-identified issues. In each system, documentation focuses on these specific identified issues (e.g., problems, topics, goals, exceptions) through the course of the patient's treatment. All disciplines chart in the same section of the medical record. This practice provides a continuous picture of the patient's progress in general, as well as in relation to specific identified areas.

There are four components to all focused documentation systems: defined data base; complete problem list, with numbered and titled problems (topics/goals/etc.); treatment plans, with correspondingly numbered and titled entries; and progress notes, numbered and titled according to problem (topic/goal/etc.).

The *data base* should be composed of all patient information necessary to identify focus areas, determine appropriate treatment plans, and delineate goals or outcomes. Information is gathered not only on admission but also throughout the course of treatment and serves as a foundation on which to base treatment.

In order to develop a *problem list,* the organization must identify its specific focus. If a focus is major, ongoing, or apt to have an impact on treatment or its course, it should be included on the identified list.

Treatment plans, both initial and revised, must address all items on the list of previously identified items. These plans must be tailored to

Figure 15-1 Nursing Documentation Process

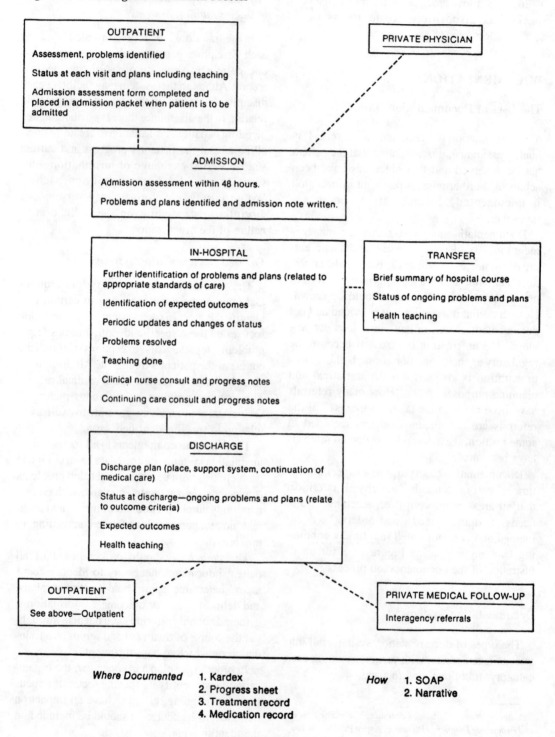

```
┌─────────────────────────────────────────────────┐
│                   OUTPATIENT                     │
│                                                  │
│  Assessment, problems identified                 │
│                                                  │      ┌──────────────────────┐
│  Status at each visit and plans including        │      │  PRIVATE PHYSICIAN   │
│  teaching                                        │      └──────────────────────┘
│                                                  │
│  Admission assessment form completed and         │
│  placed in admission packet when patient is to   │
│  be admitted                                     │
└─────────────────────────────────────────────────┘
```

OUTPATIENT

Assessment, problems identified

Status at each visit and plans including teaching

Admission assessment form completed and placed in admission packet when patient is to be admitted

PRIVATE PHYSICIAN

ADMISSION

Admission assessment within 48 hours.

Problems and plans identified and admission note written.

IN-HOSPITAL

Further identification of problems and plans (related to appropriate standards of care)

Identification of expected outcomes

Periodic updates and changes of status

Problems resolved

Teaching done

Clinical nurse consult and progress notes

Continuing care consult and progress notes

TRANSFER

Brief summary of hospital course

Status of ongoing problems and plans

Health teaching

DISCHARGE

Discharge plan (place, support system, continuation of medical care)

Status at discharge—ongoing problems and plans (relate to outcome criteria)

Expected outcomes

Health teaching

OUTPATIENT

See above—Outpatient

PRIVATE MEDICAL FOLLOW-UP

Interagency referrals

Where Documented
1. Kardex
2. Progress sheet
3. Treatment record
4. Medication record

How
1. SOAP
2. Narrative

Source: Barbiasz, Hunt, and Lowenstein, ''Nursing Documentation,'' *Journal of Nursing Administration,* June 1981. Reprinted with permission.

the individual patient to reflect the patient's strengths and weaknesses. Generally, these plans should also include assignment of treatment responsibilities, patient involvement, discharge planning, and specific areas of needed patient education. If an organization chooses to follow the original problem-oriented documentation system, the plans would also be grouped according to diagnosis, therapeutic measures, parameters to monitor the progress of therapy, and patient education.

Under this type of documentation system, *progress notes* can be divided into three types: narrative notes, flow sheets, and discharge notes. The types of notes used are based on previously defined organizational and departmental needs. All disciplines chart on the same forms in the patient's record and indicate, through a preestablished mechanism, the focus of each individual note. The format for the actual charting varies.

Open Treatment Record

An additional variant on any documentation system is the use of an open treatment record. By definition, this process allows and encourages patients to read and review their personal treatment records. Practiced in an inpatient psychiatric-mental health setting, for example, this would seem a logical option, inasmuch as sharing responsibility with the patient is a fundamental concept of a therapeutic community.

Computers and Documentation*

Computer systems that provide for documentation based on nursing diagnoses in the patient record afford greater chances for ensuring the communication of care and coordination of information among various health care providers. The documented diagnostic label pro-

vides a focus for intervention and evaluation of patient responses.

In an automated, integrated patient record where nursing assessment data are linked to a plan of care, and the plan of care forms the basis of the documentation system, there exists a higher probability that completion of the nursing process cycle will be evidenced in the patient's chart. Complete documentation reduces risk and promotes nursing research.

Computer systems afford *access* to nursing diagnosis information. In a typical scenario, the computer transforms the clinical data entered by the staff nurse into a useful clinical report. The nurse manager could also obtain a record of all patients with a particular diagnosis. Thus, the computer system provides access to stored information in a variety of retrieval formats.

Although access to patient information is possible without a computer, the computer system provides the advantage of rapid, efficient retrieval within seconds. In contrast, manual access is not only cumbersome and costly, but also difficult to justify in terms of the resources needed.

Improving Charting*

Since chart documentation is the proof that nursing care was given, much of the attention to reducing legal liability has been directed to that activity. Managers face the problem that, with increased workloads and decreased use of overtime, nurses often give care that is uncharted. When malpractice cases go to court, the hospital's and nurses' defense is being based increasingly on the nurses' notes.

However, many staff nurses, frustrated with the choice of giving care or completing voluminous records, elect to forgo their charting responsibilities. When confronted, they blame short staffing. Sometimes, inadequate staffing is the problem, but more often it is one of needing to improve productivity.

Source: Carol Ramano and Patricia Flatley Brennan, "Computerizing the Documentation of Patient Care," in *Implementing Nursing Diagnosis-Based Practice: Managing the Change*, Constance D'Argenio, ed., Aspen Publishers, Inc., © 1991.

Source: Barbara Rutkowski, *Managing for Productivity in Nursing*, Aspen Publishers, Inc., © 1987.

Table 15-1 Administrative Actions to Improve Charting Practices

The following activities are recommended for nurse managers who wish to obtain a higher or superior level of chart documentation.

- Place charts in proximity to patients at the bedside or on medication carts so that nurses can chart care as it is given.

- Establish a pattern for assigning major care plan reviews to nurses.

- Develop checklists, flow sheets, and pre-printed patient instructions that minimize nurses' writing, while guaranteeing a uniform quality of care.

- Work with individual staff members to help them in managing their time more effectively.

- Assist staff members in learning to write brief, comprehensive notes that tie the care plan into interventions and results.

- Work with staff members to develop standards of care that guide them in providing effective care at the required productivity level.

- Ensure that standard care plans are available for the most common problems in the unit or center.

- Ensure that treatment protocols are written to aid nurses in performing their jobs more productively.

- Establish a method to use in ensuring that staff members comply with current policies and procedures.

- Analyze how this effort feeds into the performance appraisal process.

Source: Barbara Rutkowski, *Managing for Productivity in Nursing,* Aspen Publishers, Inc., © 1987.

To assist staff members in being more aware of their charting practices, it is helpful to audit a patient chart collectively as an exercise in determining its defensibility, as if it were the only representation of care that could be used in court. When the nurses see how much explanation is needed to make sense out of their notations, they are usually motivated to improve. This motivation should be used to improve the criteria followed in performing concurrent patient care audits and chart audits, as a part of a QA effort. See Table 15-1.

Chapter 16

Staffing

INTRODUCTION

Overview*

Staffing is the process of determining and providing the acceptable number and mix of nursing personnel to produce a desired level of care to meet the patient's demand for care.

A staffing program consists of four phases:

1. A precise statement of the purpose of the institution and the services a patient can expect from it, including the standard and characteristics of the care.
2. The application of a specific method to determine the number and kinds of staff required to provide the care.
3. The development of assignment patterns for staff from the application of personnel guidelines, policy statements, and procedures.
4. An evaluation of the product provided and judgment reflecting the impact of the staff upon quality.

Staffing methods attempt to establish a set of patterns for supplying nurses to patient areas

---

*Source: *A Review and Evaluation of Nursing Productivity,* DHHS, Pub. No. (HRA) 77-15, 1977.

based upon some predicted average workload conditions. Then, when patient demands increase or decrease on a unit during a particular time period, it is necessary to reassign on-duty personnel to balance the staff to patient needs. This dynamic staffing or allocation process makes use of a number of adjustment techniques (see Chapter 18). Whichever method is utilized, it is important to base decisions on some work-load measuring system.

In adopting patient classification and workload systems, the determination of patient need becomes more objective and the allocation process simpler. Reassignment remains a judgmental process based upon supervisory decisions to move personnel between units to balance demand.

It should be noted that even though staffing processes tend to be effective, the system of providing nursing care also relies heavily upon proper scheduling practices. Scheduling is an important factor in providing sufficient staff to meet patient demands. Therefore, any staffing appraisal should include a reassessment of the institution's nurse scheduling policies and practices as well.

Before any attempt is made at restaffing a nursing service area, it is recommended that a proven workload measuring system be adopted and the data be collected over a sufficient time period in order to understand the patient demand. Also, when collecting workload data, it is recommended that all scheduling policies and practices be reviewed and some effort be made to predict future scheduling criteria. Finally, it is recommended that based upon the workload measurement system and the scheduling policies and procedures, the institution attempt to devise an allocation process which balances patient need with available personnel while maintaining personal fairness and consideration without affecting patient care. For an explanation of the elements needed to establish a staffing system, see Tables 16-1 and 16-2.

Factors Affecting Selection of a Staffing System*

Particular institutions have unique policies, structures, and people that must be served by a staffing system. However, certain key factors should be considered when evaluating most staffing systems.

Range of Acuity

Considering patient acuity as a determinant of nursing activity and associated staff needs is important in the selection of a staffing system. Indicators such as activities of daily living, frequency of medications and vital sign monitoring, and number of diagnostic procedures scheduled all relate to the frequency of nursing intervention and, therefore, to resource consumption.

Patient acuity classification systems, if developed appropriately, can serve as an indicator of nursing workload and as an aid in predicting staffing needs. Patient acuity as documented by an objective and reproducible classification scheme can be the supporting logic of a staffing system.

Patient Mix

The mix of patients will usually affect two key factors related to nursing care. First, the patient mix will affect the general expectations of the nursing staff relative to care and treatment. This expectation could affect staffing requirements to support associated activities. Second, should the level of health of the patient population be substandard, staffing will be affected due to increased intensity of care.

The following questions on patient mix should be considered. Are there both low- and high-acuity patients on the same nursing unit, or are all the patients of similar acuity? Are there several types of medical or surgical subspecialties represented, or do all of the patients have similar medical diagnoses? Are the patients demographically homogeneous? Issues such as patient case type, diagnosis, length of stay, intensity of care, and physician routines must also be considered and reflected in nursing staffing decisions.

Nursing Skill Mix

There is no doubt that capabilities differ among RN, LVN, and nursing assistant skill levels. This difference must be considered within the context of a specific nursing unit. Each hospital's expectations for each skill level are unique. If a recommendation is made that a high-skill employee be required to perform a task that requires no special training or skills, this recommendation must be challenged in the interest of cost-effectiveness. It is also likely that the capabilities of individuals within a nursing skill classification will vary.

Resource Consumption Patterns

Each of the above points will have an effect on nursing resource consumption. It is the challenge to the nursing manager to optimally utilize nursing resources to meet the true needs of the physician and patient while being prudent in the allocation of resources. It is a difficult challenge, but one that will have to be addressed through the patient classification systems and staffing models of the future.

---

*Source: Charles C. Gabbert, "Nursing Staffing, Scheduling, and Productivity," in Nursing Administration and the Law, Karen Hawley Henry, ed., Aspen Publishers, Inc., © 1986.

Factors Influencing Staffing*

A number of factors affect staffing—among them are the number of patients, the acuity of the individual patients (patient classification), the need for time standards for some of the more repetitive tasks, provision for type of nursing practiced, and the need to provide allowances for other professional aspects of nursing.

Specifically, here is a list of factors influencing staffing:

- *Characteristics of staff.* What is the mix of skill levels? Are many on the staff young and inexperienced or is the group more settled, not out to "remake nursing"? What are the levels of educational and experiential preparation? How many are there in total numbers and by position? What are the head nurses' orientations to nursing care? To what extent are registry nurses used for unit staffing (and how are the decisions made as to the number of registry nurses needed)? What is their general social and ethnic background? Are many of them graduates of foreign schools?

- *Domain and boundaries of nursing services.* What services is the nursing department responsible for? Do these include, for example, the operating room, errand and escort service, outpatient department, emergency services, special research or treatment units? Is the nursing department "extensible" according to the time of day and weekend, for example, are dietary and pharmacy services on evenings and nights the responsibility of nursing? Are ward clerks or unit managers responsible to nursing administration?

- *Place in formal and informal authority structure.* Is the informal authority of the nursing department congruent with its place in the formal structure? What actual power does it have?

- *Latitude for flexibility.* Is the prevailing consensus one of "doing things alike," or is there flexibility for delivery of care by different methods? Can, for example, primary care be used on one unit and team nursing on another?

- *Administration.* What is the degree of centralization and general organization? Are many persons in middle-management or supervisory positions? What is the prevailing management style? Is it, for example, organization- or person-oriented?

- *Teaching programs.* Is the hospital associated with a school of nursing? If so, are there joint appointments? How extensive is staff involvement with student teaching?

- *Turnover.* Are nursing staff attracted to the area for limited times such as for recreational or education purposes? Do new graduates of area schools tend to stay short periods and then move on? What is the turnover rate for differing skill levels?

- *Group cohesiveness.* How closely knit are the unit staff? Are they "small work groups" or a collective of persons?

- *Resources available within the department.* Are there persons skilled in staff development or in-service education? Are there certain individuals with particular clinical skills, research skills, language facility?

- *Standards of care.* Are the standards clearly spelled out and available to all staff? How many standards are informal, unwritten ones? Do the nursing units set their own objectives and, if so, are they reviewed and revised on a routine basis? Are standards of care fairly uniform across the nursing areas?

- *Priorities in non–patient care activities.* How much emphasis is placed on formal educational development, participation in research activities, in-service, and staff development?

- *Professional activity.* How much active involvement is there with professional organizations?

---

*Source: *Methods for Studying Nurse Staffing in a Patient Unit*, DHHS, Pub. No. (HRA) 78-3, May 1978.

Table 16-1 The Staffing System

Process	Focus	Description	Used for/Purpose	Decision Based on	Method Used
Staffing	On long range unit needs	Supplies the average numerical assessment of staff personnel needed to service a unit 1. by skill position level 2. on each shift	Annual budget	Historical data or previous documented experience of patient census and nursing hours required (level of patient demand)	Census forecast; by assessment of previous year's collection of unit census reports
Measurements	On patient needs	Determines level of care and requirements of staff performance to meet that level	Supply of data		
Nurse Activity Study	On actual performance of nursing function	Observes a comprehensive list of nursing tasks performed on the unit; assessed for time standards and skill levels [a one-time study]	Calculation of standard nursing hours for delivery of patient care per day	Analysis of time study	Work sampling Self-reporting
Patient Classification	On patient needs	Identifies degree of nursing care needed by the patient population in a given type unit (from minimal to maximum)	*Short Range* Actual census of patients and need levels for the day to determine staff readjustment *Long Range* Provides, at end of month and year, data on level of patient occupancy	Assessment of the intensity of patient needs for nursing care on any given shift or day	To construct classification system; application of standards for nursing care To use classification system: daily census report and assessment by delegated nurse

Workload Index	On daily patient needs and available scheduled staff	Quantifies the amount of care needed to be given, and identifies the number of personnel required to meet that need	to be used for forecast of future needs on the unit Daily estimations of under- or overstaffing on the unit for short-range allocations	Comparison of the unit's actual census (patient count and degree of need) and the current on-duty staff, with the assessed standard number of personnel needed to give that level of patient care	Workload index: formula or workload tables
Scheduling	On nurse-worker as well as unit needs	Aligns the work-hour conditions of the nurse worker (40-hour week, vacations, etc) into a unit staffing pattern to provide for the requisite 24-hour-a-day patient coverage	Distribution of budgeted nursing personnel to meet unit's anticipated staffing needs on three shifts a day and weekends	1. Unit staffing positions 2. Required unit coverage 3. Hospital policies (unit organization shift hours, on weekends, vacations etc.)	Variety of methods are used, the most innovational being cyclical scheduling or block patterns Can be calculated manually or with computer assistance
Daily Adjustments (or allocations)	On short-range unit needs	Provides for an increased or decreased supply of nursing personnel if the units actual working load on any given day is above or below the average need anticipated	Correction on a daily basis of any imbalance between the regularly scheduled staff and the actual patient workload	Short range: daily census reports of workload and data on scheduled staff Long range: census forecast of seasonal peaks and lags in patient admissions	Imbalances corrected by a variety of methods: floats, nursing pools, transfers between units, temporary help from agencies, part-time employees, controlled admission

Table 16-2 Staffing Policy Checklist

The following list provides a very convenient outline for evaluating the nursing department's staffing policies.

Employee Categories
1. Full-Time
   1.1 Hours Worked per Week
   1.2 Weekends Worked per Schedule
   1.3 Benefits Calculation
2. Part-Time
   2.1 Hours Worked per Week
   2.2 Weekends Worked per Schedule
   2.3 Benefits Calculation
3. Float Pool
   3.1 Hours Worked Status
   3.2 Weekends Worked per Schedule
   3.3 Scheduling Pattern
   3.4 Assignment Method
   3.5 Line of Authority
   3.6 Salary and Benefits Paid
   3.7 Differentials Paid
   3.8 Orientation Provided
4. On-Call Pool
   4.1 Availability Requirements
   4.2 Weekends Worked per Schedule
   4.3 Assignment Method
   4.4 Line of Authority
   4.5 Compensation Calculation
   4.6 Orientation Provided

Scheduling
1. Authority and Responsibility
2. Length of Cycle Rotation
3. Posting Time
4. Reporting Responsibility

Assignments
1. Placement Determination
2. Basic Care Requirements

Days Off
1. Rotation Pattern/Service
2. Weekend Rotation
3. Special Requests
   3.1 School Schedules
   3.2 Change Status

Weekends
1. Definition
2. Family Member Schedules

Scheduling Requests
1. Request/Response Procedure
2. Weekend Requests
3. Educational Days
4. Emergency Leave
5. Failure To Report When Scheduled

Trade Procedure
1. Acceptable Trades
2. Request/Response Procedure

Vacations
1. Request/Response Procedure
   1.1 Time to Submit
   1.2 Place to Submit
2. Approval Guidelines
   2.1 Seniority Preference
   2.2 Who Decides
   2.3 Number Limitations
3. Change Request
4. Extended Vacations

Holidays
1. Paid Holidays
2. Request/Response Procedure
3. Approval Guidelines
   3.1 Granting Criteria
   3.2 Number Limitations
4. Unexcused Absence on a Holiday
5. Vacation During Holiday Period

Illness
1. Notification Procedure
2. Extended Days
3. Illness on Duty

Leave of Absence (LOA)
1. Request/Response Procedure
2. Paid Leave Time Interface

Failure To Report to Work
1. Consequences

Transfers
1. Request/Response Procedure
2. Approval Guidelines

Temporary Reassignment
1. Who Will Float
2. Refusal Consequences
3. Equitability

Absenteeism
1. Percentage Acceptable
2. Days Absent Patterns
3. Disciplinary Action

Tardiness
1. Percentage Acceptable
2. Disciplinary Action

Irregular Hours Worked
1. Report/Return Home
2. Called after Shift Begins
3. On-Call Availability

continues

Table 16-2 *continued*

Low-Census Procedures	*Overtime*
1. Selection Process	1. Payment Guidelines
1.1 Sequence Followed	2. Availability
1.2 Patient Care Safety Levels	*Family Policy*
2. Benefits Accrued	1. Family Member Assignment
3. Paid Hours	2. Time Off Policy

Source: West Coast Medical Management Associates, Inc., Westlake Village, Calif., 1980. Adapted with permission.

- *Presence of unionization.* Are either nonprofessional or professional staff unionized? If so, what do the contracts cover? What is the resultant climate within the nursing department after election or non-election of union representation?
- *Traditions and history.* Although linked with institutional traditions and history, the nursing department may have its own unique blend of traditions and past events that are informally influential in the organization of services and esprit de corps.
- *Trends in nursing care delivery.* To what extent are emerging and/or unclear roles in existence? Decisions, for example, relative to having clinical specialists in an organizational staff versus line relationship will prompt critical examination of traditional supervisory roles.

All the foregoing factors, as noted, may be seen as having variable influences on the total plan of services to be given in the institution. To get at the overall plan of nursing services and a staffing program that results in individual unit staffing plans and organization of care, however, attention must be focused on what goes on at the unit level in determining the actual care given and the evaluation of nursing care and patient outcomes.

The right side of Figure 16-1 makes more specific the various kinds of daily events and crises that may arise to cause discrepancies between the staffing plan and organization of care and the actual care given to and received by the patient. They include changes in census, patient needs, physicians' schedules, and supporting services available, as well as staff fluctuations due to illness, emergencies, days off, vacations, etc., and the variabilities in the capabilities of total staff on duty because of these unplanned fluctuations. Because very little can be done to alter the occurrence of these types of changes and crises, their influence is depicted as operating in one direction. Personnel needs for satisfaction and demands for organizational maintenance (represented by its subelement: "Demands for Input into Informational and Record System" in the diagram), however, are subject to alteration by "what's going on" and may have a definite influence on the outcome. Thus, they are depicted as having a two-way, or interactive, relationship with the system.

The left side of Figure 16-1 depicts the interdependency of all groups within the hospital in the process of evaluation of the actual nursing care given. As indicated, no one measure of "care" is, or probably could be, employed exclusively (e.g., expected patient outcomes by medical standards may or may not be accompanied by patient satisfaction). Similarly, the level of personnel satisfaction is involved in the process, as are the congruences and coordination with the services of medicine and of other departments. Actual care is always evaluated against certain nursing standards, and, finally, cost of providing the nursing care is a critical factor in the evaluative process. As with the other components, the open system features of the framework allow for the evaluation of the nursing care to feed back into planning for future nursing services, the staffing program, the overall plan of nursing services, and the "negotiated agreement." The open system features also make it clear that the system of events recycles and is repeated continuously.

Difficulty in Assessing Staff Requirements*

There is absolutely no doubt that there are resource management problems in nursing at all levels, and nurses need appropriate tools and approaches to assist in their decision making. Every day, head nurses and unit leaders make assessments of patient needs and staff capabilities and, using some model, create assignments in order to ensure that appropriate care services are delivered. This process may be repeated several times during each shift as the situation changes. Also, each day, decisions are being made at an administrative level as to how many nursing personnel at each level of skill should be assigned to each patient care unit. Such allocation of personnel to units and the subsequent assignment each individual receives can vary widely in terms of workload. Thus, a huge process of resource management, occurring at several levels in the nursing hierarchy, happens each day in each institution. Throughout the nation, the vast majority of decision making in this process is based on the experience of those involved and their abilities to mentally juggle many complex factors to predict care workload and determine staffing requirements. This feat becomes monumental when one considers the fact that there are nonpredictable occurrences and variation in patients' needs and nurses' skill levels and competencies.

Nonroutine, Nonpredictable Occurrences

Nursing units, as a rule, experience more than their share of unexpected events, which drain staff time. Unexpected physicians' visits and orders, patients going "sour," interruptions from support departments and other nursing personnel, observation of previously unidentified patient needs, and visits from friends and family members are among the many occurrences that the nursing staff must cope with each day. In addition, some "routine" things can quickly take on an air of uniqueness. Answering call

lights, admitting and transferring patients, and preparing patients for surgery or diagnostic tests all tend to confound traditional resource management techniques.

Variation of Patients' Needs

One necessary component for personnel resource allocation is an adequate description of the total set of objectives which must be accomplished. On a patient unit, patients' needs represent this component and categorization schemes exist today which effectively divide patients into groups according to their self-sufficiency. Although research has documented that nursing personnel spend less time with self-sufficient patients than with total care patients and that patient classification schemes are important to the staffing function, the implementation of these schemes has been widely avoided due to the time-consuming process of obtaining the information required.

Overlapping Skill Levels

There is no longer any doubt that tremendous overlap exists, in terms of capability for meeting certain patient needs, between RNs, LPNs, and aides. Resource allocation models have great difficulty in accepting and dealing with this fact, while practicing nurses know it as reality and must deal with it in decision making. Complicating this is the additional problem of role definition. It is still difficult to point to any single concept of the role of the RN, LPN, and aide which can be translated into concepts describing their capacity to accomplish patient care activities.

Varying Individual Competencies

A great deal of the adequacy of a patient's care depends upon the individual competencies of the nursing staff; and nursing personnel categories are neither equal nor uniform. Differences are due to such factors as educational programs (there are several different types of programs which prepare the RN), experience, motivation, and other individual factors. For those addressing the resource allocation problem, this knowl-

*Source: Louis Freund and Ronald Norby, "A Model for Staffing and Analysis," Nursing Administration Quarterly, vol. 1, no. 4, © 1977 Aspen Publishers, Inc.

Figure 16-1 Relationship of Factors Entering into Provision of Nursing Care at the Unit Level

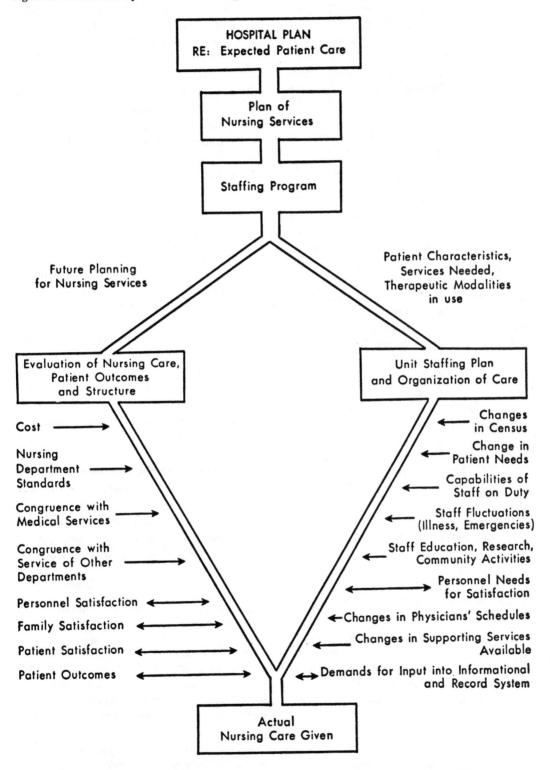

Source: *Methods for Studying Nurse Staffing in a Patient Unit*, DHHS, Pub. No. (HRA) 78-3, May 1978.

edge creates special difficulties. Personnel at each skill level should not be considered equal, yet most models require this assumption and leave sensitivity to differences up to the implementer. In practice, however, these individual differences in competency are extremely important variables, and hence models which cannot accommodate them are largely ignored by nurses.

What is needed are methodologies and techniques particularly responsive to nursing resource management which are acceptable to the nurses involved, actually obtain better solutions to problems than nurses can achieve without assistance, and have a foundation in theory that enables administration to more fully understand how this multifaceted resource is utilized at every level.

Perhaps of equal importance is that such methodologies not function in isolation but become an integral part of a larger analytical model. Too often, nurse staffing is considered as an end in itself. That is, efforts are directed solely at readjusting or otherwise providing individuals to cover workload. While important, this must be accomplished with consideration directed toward many other factors such as desired quality levels; goals related to allocation of responsibility for care delivery; the effect of staffing on morale, turnover, and absenteeism; personnel cost; actual ability to meet workload, recruitment, etc.

Forecasting Manpower Needs*

Manpower forecasting is the prediction of needed health care and the availability of personnel to perform the needed health care functions for some future time period. Each department is expected to forecast future supply and demand, areas of expected operations and manpower needed taking into consideration expected turnover, retirements, vacation benefits, etc., by training and utilizing their personnel. The main steps in the manpower planning process are:

1. *Analyze the present supply situation by making an inventory of your work force:*
   - How many employees do you have by unit, skill, age, sex, education, classification, career interest, and length of service?
   - Analyze present work force trends and problems: absences, turnover, vacancies, recruiting problems, numbers in training, standards, and wage/salary distribution.
   - Analyze organizational structure and manpower policies: duplications, underutilizations, supervision ratio, and policy problems.
2. *Analyze the demand situation—short and long term:*
   - Analyze organization plans and future priorities: activity changes, types of work, needs forecast, and budget forecast.
3. *Analyze productivity trends and review technological changes, productivity experiences of the past, and governmental/ environmental changes.*
4. *Evaluate and update the forecast:*
   - Analyze the flows and trends in the supply of manpower in relation to future needs.
   - Prepare tentative manpower forecast.
5. *Evaluate and update the forecast periodically:*
   - Inaugurate and evaluate related processes of recruitment, selection training, career planning, and organizational development.

Centralization vs. Decentralization in Staffing*

Decentralization is the assignment of decision-making accountability away from the central office and close to the operational level—in nursing, to the patient care unit level. While maintaining responsibility for overall operations

*Source: Joan Holland, "Workshop: Manpower Planning to Meet Needs," *Health Care Management Review,* vol. 1, no. 4, © 1976 Aspen Publishers, Inc.

*Source: Joyce Rhodes, "Staffing and Resource Development," in *Managing for Productivity in Nursing,* Barbara Rutkowski, Aspen Publishers, Inc., © 1987.

of their departments, nursing middle managers acquire the opportunity to focus on more general issues and concerns.

An important element in decentralization is the elimination of multitiered levels of authority, with concurrent increases in the number of middle management positions. The role of the head nurse assumes increased importance as the manager of patient care and related activities. Each unit staff participates actively in the determination of patient care quality and administrative procedures and is held accountable for decisions made. When managed properly, this can improve staff morale and produce feelings of enhanced importance and an increased willingness to contribute.

Table 16-3 compares centralized and decentralized methods of staffing that a nursing department should review before deciding which method best relates to its organization, philosophy, and needs.

When staffing is controlled at the unit level, knowledgeable nurses close to the point of action can meet needs swiftly. Moreover, staff members learn to accept accountability for keeping their unit staffed so that they do not experience unnecessary shortages.

As each unit assumes responsibility for covering its staffing needs, it is more likely to contact sister units to arrange cross-training, building in flexibility for times of census changes. When staff members know before floating which units they may work, they can learn about specialized medicines and treatments in advance. For example, one head nurse printed a list of the 30 most common drugs administered on her unit. This list was given to potential floats so they could become familiar with the drugs before working on the unit.

Decentralized operations still can use on-call personnel, but these persons are assigned to areas in which they have the most competency. Then they can be called as needs arise. However, criteria for minimum work shifts and staff development need to be developed so that these float nurses remain safe to administer care.

Table 16-3 Comparison of Two Methods of Staffing

Decentralization	Centralization
Maximizes unit staffing.	Manages staffing of nursing departments as a whole.
Minimizes or eliminates a centralized float pool.	Maximizes utilization of float pool.
Gives head nurse accountability for the entire staffing budget.	Gives head nurse accountability for staffing budget on the unit.
Gives head nurse responsibility for 24-hour staffing and scheduling.	Gives head nurse responsibility for 24-hour patient care.
Provides for contingency staff backup from companion or sister units, per diem (on-call) staff, increased hours of part-time staff, or overtime when shortages occur.	Permits reassigning float personnel when shortages occur.
Assigns selection of all unit staff members to head nurse.	Assigns core unit staff selection to the head nurse.
Provides that head nurse keeps updated record of current staff skills.	Centralizes updated record of skills required.
Puts decision making at the unit level.	Puts decision making in the central office.
Promotes relationships among sister units.	Does not emphasize relationships between like specialties.
Commits staff to making method successful.	Depends more on central office management for success.

Source: Joyce Rhodes, "Staffing and Resource Development," in *Managing for Productivity in Nursing*, Barbara Rutkowski, ed., Aspen Publishers, Inc., © 1987.

STAFFING SYSTEMS

Guidelines for Establishing a Staffing Program*

In order to initiate a staffing program, which includes as its purpose the projection of the amount of staff needed, and in order to begin the educational program associated with building understanding of the comprehensiveness and complexity of staffing, *a nursing service administrator* is advised to employ the following steps:

1. Organization of a committee of the nursing staff for purposes of becoming informed about staffing—its purpose, philosophy underlying the concepts, objectives, methodology—and to gather information about the populations of patients being served.

2. Appointment of an individual to assume responsibility for the program.

3. Collection of data about personnel needed to predict the requirements:
   - personnel policies
   - personnel statistics: average number of workdays; average number of holidays, vacation, illness, leave of absence for various purposes; turnover rates; supply; etc.
   - current number of personnel, by category, in the department and individual nursing units
   - cost

4. Collection of data about patients:
   - by individual nursing unit—admission and discharge rates or visits to clinics; average length of stay; occupancy or turnover rate; and any other type of data which will be useful
   - consideration of use of a classification scheme and methodology

5. Review of staffing patterns currently used by nursing unit and documentation of rationale employed.

6. Involvement of the committee in the selection of a staffing methodology and the staffing policies and patterns desired and feasible; recognition of constraints that exist in the adoption of the ideal.

7. Introduction of the methodology to collect data regarding patients and statement of why it was selected (the rationale).

8. Writing up of staffing policies which will be generally applied:
   - the placement of holidays (attached to weekends or not)
   - the type of work assignment adopted
   - the maximum and minimum number of consecutive days to be worked before a day off
   - the number of weekends off per month (or unit of time)
   - the number of shifts to be worked by each classification (whether all are straight shifts, or two-shift rotation, or three-shift rotation)
   - the number of weeks per shift, if rotation shifts are used
   - placement of vacation (distributed over the year or not)

9. Calculation of the number of personnel required, by shift, by type of nursing personnel, through use of the methodology adopted.

10. Adjustment of the number to provide leadership and coverage to plan for implementation of staffing policies.

11. Planning for how the evaluation of the staffing and scheduling will be made.

12. Implementation of the staffing program.

13. Evaluation of the program.

Using a Staffing Study Committee*

Once it has been determined that a study will be done, a study committee consisting primarily

*Source: *Nursing Staff Requirements for Inpatient Health Care Services,* American Nurses' Association, Pub. No. NS-20, 1977. Reprinted with permission.

*Source: *Methods for Studying Nurse Staffing in a Patient Unit,* DHHS, Pub. No. (HRA) 78-3, May 1978.

of members of the nursing service administrative group and the hospital administrative staff should be designated. In addition to specifying the number and types of units, the desired schedule, and the nature and scope of the final report, the study committee is responsible for appointing a study coordinator and assigning the necessary supporting people as observers, data clerks, and assistants.

Committee Members

Study Coordinator. The coordinator is the key person in the conduct of the study and should be selected from the nursing service staff.

Since the position of coordinator may require full-time activity, the coordinator's release from regular duties is essential during the time the study is being made and the report written. Some hospitals may want to have the study coordinator continue in a position that will provide continuity for the initiation and supervision of any reorganization decided upon. It is the responsibility of the coordinator to supervise the training of the observers and other members of the study team.

The coordinator carries out the following activities:

1. Instructs and supervises the study team.
2. Assigns and trains observers.
3. Orients other hospital personnel and patients.
4. Prepares study materials and data collection forms.
5. Selects the patient samples.
6. Monitors and edits observers' record taking.
7. Assists with the analysis, interpretation, and evaluation of the data.
8. Prepares the study report.

Other Members. The other members of the study team, including data clerk and typist, are selected by the study committee. The data clerk will be needed to assist in preparing statistical tables and is usually chosen from the business office because of experience with business machines and data computation.

Head Nurses or Charge Nurses. The head nurses or charge nurses of the unit or units selected for study are vital members of the study team. They are directly responsible for categorizing patients according to nursing care requirements. They use their nursing judgment to assess the adequacy or inadequacy of the staffing on their unit, and they also assist the study coordinator. Their importance in providing complete support to the study project cannot be overestimated. These nurse leaders set the tone of the units on which the studies are carried out.

Their activities, in brief, are to:

1. classify patients according to indicators and guidelines for nursing care requirements
2. record their perceptions of the adequacy or inadequacy of staffing on their units for the periods studied
3. assist the study coordinator in checking observer reports
4. orient patients to the study

Observers. If the observers are to be selected from the nursing service staff, the study committee appoints the observers. Nurses selected to be observers should carry out their observations on units other than their own.

Responsibilities of Committee

The function of the staffing study committee is to produce a set of staffing policies and procedures that satisfy the unique needs of the nursing service.

Among the policies and procedures that they would be responsible for creating are:*

- A written statement of the purpose, philosophy, and objectives of the nursing program of care.
- A written statement of the purpose, philosophy, and objectives of staffing.

*Source: *Nursing Staff Requirements for Inpatient Health Care Services,* American Nurses' Association, Pub. No. NS-20, 1977. Reprinted with permission.

- An identification of the data base (i.e., the information regarding patients, staff, and costs).
- A written statement of the rationale for the selection of the staffing methodology employed.
- A coherent set of personnel policies and procedures related to scheduling and plans for implementation.
- A statement of basic staffing patterns for each nursing unit.
- A set of performance standards for the nursing staff.
- A plan for supplementing staff at times of staff illness, emergency leave, and prolonged heavy workloads and for reducing the staff when prolonged light workloads occur.
- A quality assurance program to measure quality of care.
- A written plan for evaluating the staffing program which includes identification of a system for monitoring the success of the program, for examining the staffing patterns at regular intervals in light of changing conditions, and for initiating appropriate changes.

Selecting a Staffing System

While it may be tempting to select a staffing system successfully used in another hospital, you should be forewarned that what is appropriate for one hospital is rarely appropriate—without modification—for another hospital.

The difficulty lies in the range of variable factors: organizational systems, patient-unit arrangements, nurse-support systems, levels of technology, employment policies, hospital architecture, etc.

Essentially the parameters of what is being measured in one hospital are different from those being measured in another. These parameters affect the end figures on which staffing calculations are based—that is, the time standards for nursing activities, the total available nursing

hours, the actual workload, the proportionate distribution of nursing hours and work among staff skill levels, the decision rules for patient classification, and so on.

The process of gathering information to arrive at these figures is called data collection. It is a process which each nursing service unit should employ, using techniques of measurement which are generally applicable and valid in order to produce the unique figures for particular departments and units. Once these base figures have been established, they can then be adjusted to accommodate new conditions or new standards and thus satisfy the changing as well as the continuing needs of the nursing service.

Criteria*

Following are a set of criteria that could be used in selecting the best staffing system for your unit or department:

- It encompasses enough pertinent variables in its application to produce valid results;
- It utilizes measurement devices that produce reliable and valid data about these variables;
- It is simple, in that it is not time consuming and can be applied by the personnel within the institution with a minimum of consultant specialized personnel in its application;
- It provides baseline data that can be used in comparative studies within the institution or within a set of similar institutions in the delivery system;
- The cost-benefit can be predicted and is worthwhile. A more costly methodology may in the long run be less expensive in terms of benefit; and
- It is responsive to changes in the delivery system, such as the introduction of new positions or elimination of old and the creation of new supporting systems to the nursing care delivery system.

---

*Source: Nurse Staffing Methodology, DHEW, Pub. No. (NIH) 73-433, 1973.

Staffing: Model System 1*
(Emphasis on Utilization Control)

The "Staff Utilization Control System" provides a means for predicting nursing requirements so that available personnel can be assigned to the nursing units where they are most needed. In addition, the reporting system provides data which can be used in a variety of ways to manage more effectively.

The control system described here is one that is currently being used in several Texas hospitals. It is intended to provide a typical example, since many variations are possible. The procedures and reports would have to be adapted to your special requirements and conditions.

Nurse Staff Table

The first step in implementation of the control system is to develop the nurse staff table. Figure 16-2 provides an example of a nurse staff table for one hospital. This table is developed directly from study results so that requirements reflect the nursing philosophy and procedures in your hospital. The required hours of care determined for each patient classification and shift are converted to equivalent nursing personnel and arranged in tabular form to simplify estimating personnel requirements.

When the nurse staff table is complete, all of the basic information necessary for implementing a staff utilization control system is available. The patient classification plan used during the study now becomes an integral part of the system for predicting nursing requirements. The only change in this procedure results from the fact that it is necessary to *predict* patient classification rather than record it during the shift, as was done during the study. If patient classification and nursing care plans are incorporated into a single procedure, a simple one-step planning process is provided which results in the patient classification.

Source: SMS Nursing Service Study Guide: Staff Utilization (A Project of The Texas Hospital Education and Research Foundation), Shared Management Systems for the Texas Hospital Association. Reprinted with permission.

Patient Classification Procedure

Eight criteria for measuring the intensity of care to be provided have been established. (See Figure 16-3.)

- These are elements of physical care and comprise a high percentage of the nursing care which requires the greatest amount of time. They are: Diet, Vital Signs, Respiratory Aids, Suction, Cleanliness, Toileting/Output, Turning/Assisted Activity, and Isolation.
- This measurement will be used to assess the classification of each patient and determine if he or she is to be considered total, partial, or minimal.

Total the number of points in all elements of physical care. Compare the total number of points with the conversion table. Place the patient in the appropriate classification.

Staffing Requirements Report

The following is a typical procedure for predicting nursing staffing requirements and preparing a staffing requirements report. (See Figure 16-4.)

The staffing requirements report is prepared by the head nurse each day, covering a 24-hour period beginning at 7 A.M.

1. Determine patient classification for each patient on the unit (check appropriate blanks). Check "Discg." blank for patients expected to be discharged that day and no other classification is required.
2. When a patient is admitted to the unit during the day, initiate a patient classification plan. The patient should be classified as an admit during the first shift he or she is on the unit. Enter the number 1 after "Admission" at the bottom of the staffing requirements report. Check the appropriate blanks to indicate the patient classification for the remaining shifts of the 24-hour period.

The staffing requirements report is revised as necessary at 7:00 A.M. the next day. Significant

Figure 16-2 Nurse Staff Table

	NURSE STAFF TABLE	
	PERSONNEL REQUIRED INCLUDING BOTH DIRECT AND INDIRECT CARE/ADMINISTRATIVE ACTIVITIES	EXAMPLE

NO. PATIENTS	ADMIT		DISCH.		MIN. CARE			PAR. CARE			TOT. CARE		
	D	E	D	E	D	E	N	D	E	N	D	E	N
1	.16	.16	.14	.11	.16	.12	.07	.25	.15	.10	.33	.31	.22
2	.32	.32	.28	.22	.32	.24	.14	.50	.30	.20	.66	.62	.44
3	.48	.48	.42	.33	.48	.36	.21	.75	.45	.30	.99	.93	.66
4	.64	.64	.56	.44	.64	.48	.28	1.00	.60	.40	1.32	1.24	.88
5	.80	.80	.70	.55	.80	.60	.35	1.25	.75	.50	1.65	1.55	1.10
6	.96	.96	.84	.66	.96	.72	.42	1.50	.90	.60	1.98	1.86	1.32
7	1.12	1.12	.98	.77	1.12	.84	.49	1.75	1.05	.70	2.31	2.17	1.54
8	1.28	1.28	1.12	.88	1.28	.96	.56	2.00	1.20	.80	2.64	2.48	1.76
9	1.44	1.44	1.26	.99	1.44	1.08	.63	2.25	1.35	.90	2.97	2.79	1.98
10	1.60	1.60	1.40	1.10	1.60	1.20	.70	2.50	1.50	1.00	3.30	3.10	2.20
11	1.76	1.76	1.54	1.21	1.76	1.32	.77	2.75	1.65	1.10	3.63	3.41	2.42
12	1.92	1.92	1.68	1.32	1.92	1.44	.84	3.00	1.80	1.20	3.96	3.72	2.64
13	2.08	2.08	1.82	1.43	2.08	1.56	.91	3.25	1.95	1.30	4.29	4.03	2.86
14	2.24	2.24	1.96	1.54	2.24	1.68	.98	3.50	2.10	1.40	4.62	4.34	3.08
15	2.40	2.40	2.10	1.65	2.40	1.80	1.05	3.75	2.25	1.50	4.95	4.65	3.30
16					2.56	1.92	1.12	4.00	2.40	1.60			
17					2.72	2.04	1.19	4.25	2.55	1.70			
18					2.88	2.16	1.26	4.50	2.70	1.80			
19					3.04	2.28	1.33	4.75	2.85	1.90			
20					3.20	2.40	1.40	5.00	3.00	2.00			
21					3.36	2.52	1.47	5.25	3.15	2.10			
22					3.52	2.64	1.54	5.50	3.30	2.20			
23					3.68	2.76	1.61	5.75	3.45	2.30			
24					3.84	2.88	1.68	6.00	3.60	2.40			
25					4.00	3.00	1.75	6.25	3.75	2.50			
26					4.16	3.12	1.82	6.50	3.90	2.60			
27					4.32	3.24	1.89	6.75	4.05	2.70			
28					4.48	3.36	1.96	7.00	4.20	2.80			
29					4.64	3.48	2.03	7.25	4.35	2.90			
30					4.80	3.60	2.10	7.50	4.50	3.00			

Figure 16-3 Patient Classification Plan

PATIENT CLASSIFICATION
PLAN

A.   RESPIRATION AIDES AND SUCTION

1 point — Bedside humidifier __
    — stand-by routine suction __
2 point — cough & deep breath q 2 hrs. __
    — oral suction PRN __
    — NASAL - pharnygeal suction PRN __
3 point — continuous O₂ __
    — cough & deep breath q 1 hr __
    — TRACH suction q 1 hr. __
4 point — TRACH suction q 30 min. c̄ pt.
    responsive __
5 point — TRACH suction q 30 min. c̄ pt.
    unresponsive __

B.   CLEANLINESS

1 point — self bath, bed change __
2 point — assist bath, bed change __
    — sitz bath __
3 point — assist bath, occupied bed __
    — partial bath given, bed change __
    — bathed & dressed by personnel (peds),
    bed change __
4 point — bathed & dressed by personnel, special
    skin care, occupied bed __

C.   ACTIVITY

1 point — up in chair c̄ help once in 8 hrs. __
2 point — up in chair c̄ help twice in 8 hrs. __
    — walk c̄ assist. __
3 point — walk c̄ assist. of 2 personnel __
    — turn q 2 hrs., bed fast __
4 point — turn q 1 hr., bed fast __

D.   DIET

1 point — feed self, or family feeds __
2 point — feed self c̄ supervision __
3 point — feed self c̄ constant staff presence __
4 point — feed patient totally by personnel __

E.   TOILET

1 point — toilet s supervision __
    — specimen collection __
2 point — toilet c̄ supervision __
    — uses bed pan __
3 point — toilet c̄ stand-by supervision __
    — daily colostomy irrigation __
4 point — incont. average output __
5 point — incont c̄ diarrhea __

F.   VITAL SIGNS

1 point — TPR routine __
2 point — V.S. q 4 hrs. __
    — night check q 1 hr. __
3 point — V.S. & observation q 4 hrs. __
    — V.S. q 2 hrs. - vital signs monitored __
4 point — V.S. & observation q 1 hr. __
5 point — BP - pulse - respiration & neurological
    evaluation q 30 min. __

G.   INTAKE & OUTPUT

1 point — routine I & O __
    — strain all urine __
2 point — Clinitest and Acetest __
    — I.V push medications __
3 point — gastrostomy feeding q 4 hrs __
    — N/G tube irrig q 2 hrs __
4 point — continuous I V __
    — blood transfusion __
    — hourly output __
5 point — tube feeding more frequently than
    q 4 hrs __
    — drainage c̄ frequent dressing changes __

H.   MISCELLANEOUS

1 point — modified isolation __
2 point — strict isolation __
3 point — pt pre-op (for OR in 24 hrs or less) __
    — pt post op (had surgery in past 24 hrs) __
    — pt. on continuous monitor __
4 point — patient instruction __
    — patient markedly disturbed __

	POINTS
A	___
B	___
C	___
D	___
E	___
F	___
G	___
H	___
TOTAL	___
Classification	

Conversion Table
1 - 9 Minimal
10 - 21 Partial
22 - 30 Total
    31 Transfer to ICU

Figure 16-4 Staffing Requirements Report

SMS

STAFFING REQUIREMENTS REPORT

EXAMPLE

FOR 24 HOUR PERIOD BEGINNING 7 AM –   (DATE) 4/30

ROOM/BED	REV.	DISCG.	MIN. CARE D	MIN. CARE E	MIN. CARE N	PAR. CARE D	PAR. CARE E	PAR. CARE N	TOT. CARE D	TOT. CARE E	TOT. CARE N
101-A						X	X	X			
102-A			X	X	X						
103-A						X	X	X			
104-A						X	X	X			
105-A						X	X	X			
105-B						X	X	X			
105-C											
106-A						X	X	X			
106-B			X	X	X						
106-C									X	X	X
109-A											
109-B											
109-C			X	X	X						
109-D											
110-A	X										
110-B			X	X	X						
111-A			X	X	X						
111-B			X	X	X						
112-A			X	X	X						
112-B			X	X	X						
113-A			X	X	X						
113-B			X	X	X						
114-A			X	X	X						
114-B			X	X	X						
SUBTOTALS			12	12	12	6	6	6	1	1	1
SUBTOTALS			11	11	11	8	8	8			
TOTALS			23	23	23	14	14	14	1	1	1

ROOM/BED	REV.	DISCG.	MIN. CARE D	MIN. CARE E	MIN. CARE N	PAR. CARE D	PAR. CARE E	PAR. CARE N	TOT. CARE D	TOT. CARE E	TOT. CARE N
115-A			X	X	X						
115-B			X	X	X						
116-A											
116-B						X	X	X			
117-A			X	X	X						
117-B											
118-A			X	X	X						
118-B			X	X	X						
119-A						X	X	X			
119-B											
120-A						X	X	X			
120-B						X	X	X			
121-A			X	X	X						
121-B		X									
122-A											
122-B						X	X	X			
123-A			X	X	X						
123-B			X	X	X						
124-A						X	X	X			
124-B						X	X	X			
125-A			X	X	X						
126-A						X	X	X			
127-A			X	X	X						
128-A			X	X	X						
SUBTOTALS			11	11	11	8	8	8			

STAFFING GUIDE HOURS

	DAY	EVE	NIGHT
ADMISSIONS			
DISCHARGES	2) .28		
MINIMUM CARE	23) 3.68	23) 2.76	23) 1.61
PARTIAL CARE	14) 3.50	14) 2.10	14) 1.40
TOTAL CARE	1) .33	1) .31	1) .22
PREDICTED STAFF REQUIRED	40) 7.79	38) 5.17	38) 3.23

changes are recorded and totals entered to indicate the correct number of patients in each classification and for each shift during the preceding 24-hour period.

The information provided on the staffing requirements report serves two general purposes.

1. It predicts nursing requirements for each unit so that immediate action can be taken for optimum use of available staff.
2. It provides historical information for evaluating utilization and planning changes to improve use of personnel in the future.

Although nursing administration can start using this information to allocate personnel as soon as the staffing requirements report has been implemented, substantial improvement in staff utilization should be expected to require long-range projects to develop and test alternative approaches to staff planning and control. The implementation of a simple and effective system of utilization reports will ensure that the information necessary to support these improvement projects is available.

The original copy of the staffing requirements report provides the correct number of patients in each patient classification and the required hours for each nursing unit. Provisions should be made for maintaining a record of the number of patients in each classification since this "patient mix" will become an important factor in any system for planning future nursing staff requirements and budgets. The required hours, or staffing table hours, for each unit are recorded daily on the Weekly Nursing Utilization Report.

Weekly Nursing Utilization Report

The weekly nursing utilization report (Figure 16-5) will become the central document in your staff utilization control system. The information related to actual hours used and census is required from the beginning of the study to provide for evaluation of current staffing patterns.

The weekly nursing utilization report is prepared for each nursing unit. Actual hours worked for each personnel skill are also recorded daily and totaled. The utilization percentage is calcu-

lated for each day and shift by dividing the staffing table hours by total hours used. The midnight census is recorded and the average hours per patient day calculated to provide additional information for analysis.

The staffing table hours and hours used are totaled at the end of the week and weekly utilization calculated for each shift. The average hours per patient day are also calculated on a weekly basis.

"Skills Mix %" reflects the percentage of total hours used by each of the major personnel skills. This relationship of skill hours to total hours can be effectively used to ensure staffing patterns which are compatible with nursing objectives.

One copy of the weekly nursing utilization report should be returned to the appropriate head nurse, with the original filed in nursing administration. Graphs of utilization for each unit can be used to illustrate improvement trends and point out the need for corrective action.

Goals for Skills Mix Ratio

The skills mix ratio provides one simple way to express the relationship of RN hours to LVN hours to AUX hours on a nursing unit. For example, if 120 hours were worked on a nursing unit, including 30 RN hours, 60 LVN hours, and 30 AUX hours, the skills mix ratio would be 25%–50%–25%.

RN	30 Hours	25%
LVN	60 Hours	50%
AUX	30 Hours	25%
	120 Hours	100%

Nursing administration is responsible for determining the proper skills mix for each unit. The skills mix ratio provides a means of expressing your plan so that a goal can be established for each unit which is compatible with both quality and economic objectives for that unit. No guidelines have been developed for this ratio, although the example used (25%–50%–25%) is typical of ratios in existing programs.

An example of how the skills mix ratio is determined is provided in Figure 16-6.

Figure 16-5 Weekly Nursing Utilization Report

<table>
<tr><td colspan="3">☀ SMS
WEEKLY NURSING
UTILIZATION REPORT</td><td colspan="6">UNIT: I</td><td colspan="2">EXAMPLE
WEEK OF: 7-15-80</td></tr>
</table>

DAY	7-15	7-16	7-17	7-18	7-19	7-20	7-21	TOTAL WEEK
				-------DAY-------				
STAFFING TABLE HOURS	46	41	31	44	44	37	53	296
HOURS USED RN	16	16	8	16	16	8	16	96
LVN	9	16	16	8	8	8	20	85
AUX	48	39	32	56	56	32	48	311
TOTAL HOURS USED	73	71	56	80	80	48	84	492
UTILIZATION %	63	58	55	55	55	77	63	60
				-------EVENING-------				
STAFFING TABLE HOURS	33	28	23	30	29	25	49	217
HOURS USED RN	10	8	8	8	8	8	8	58
LVN	16	16	18	16	16	18	16	116
AUX	24	24	16	24	24	24	24	160
TOTAL HOURS USED	50	48	42	48	48	50	48	334
UTILIZATION %	66	58	55	63	60	50	102	65
				-------NIGHT-------				
STAFFING TABLE HOURS	16	14	16	14	14	13	20	107
HOURS USED RN	8	8	8	8	8	8	8	56
LVN	8	8	8	8	8	8	8	56
AUX	32	16	--	16	24	8	24	120
TOTAL HOURS USED	48	32	16	32	40	24	40	232
UTILIZATION %	33	44	100	44	35	54	50	46
				-------TOTAL-------				
STAFFING TABLE HOURS	95	83	70	88	87	75	122	620
HOURS USED RN	34	32	24	32	32	24	32	210
LVN	33	40	42	32	32	34	44	257
AUX	104	79	48	96	104	64	96	591
TOTAL HOURS USED	171	151	114	160	168	122	172	1,058
UTILIZATION %	56	55	61	55	52	61	71	59
MIDNIGHT CENSUS	23	21	18	23	24	19	27	155
HOURS/PATIENT DAY	7.4	7.2	6.3	7.0	7.0	6.4	6.4	6.8

							SKILLS MIX %	20	24	56
ACTIVITY			-------UNMEASURED HOURS---------					RN	LVN	AUX

Figure 16-6 Nursing Care Hours and Utilization Report

UNIT	PT. DAYS	% OCCUP.	CARE HOURS	% UTIL.	% RN	% LVN	% AUX.	HRS.PER PT.DAY	% OCCUP.	% UTIL.	% RN	% LVN	% AUX.	HRS.PER PT.DAY
				CURRENT MONTH							YEAR TO DATE			
1 East	1405	97	5881	97	32	41	27	4.2	87	93	32	42	26	4.4
1 West	1265	89	5207	92	29	42	29	4.1	82	91	30	43	27	4.2
2 East	1031	83	5046	88	33	44	23	4.9	73	84	32	40	28	5.3
2 West	1234	85	5343	98	32	43	25	4.3	77	89	30	46	24	4.6
3rd.	1285	89	5661	92	28	45	27	4.4	82	89	32	45	23	4.4
SUBTOTAL	6220	89	27138	94	31	43	26	4.4	80	89	31	43	25	4.5
CCU	163	--	2132	--	55	45	0	13.1	--	--	56	44	0	14.6
ICU	4	--	88	--	55	45	0	22.0	--	--	55	45	0	22.0
SUBTOTAL	6387		29358		33	43	24	4.6			33	43	24	4.8
Adm. & Supv. Hours Worked	6387		1576					.25						.26
Hours Paid Not Worked	6387		1670					.26						.28
Orientation Inservice, Etc.	6387		293					.05						.04
DEPT. TOTAL	6387		32897					5.15						5.38

NURSING CARE HOURS AND UTILIZATION REPORT

MONTH: FEBRUARY 1980

EXAMPLE

Improvement Projects

After studying the staffing patterns that emerge from these staff utilization reports, you may want to initiate improvement projects appropriate for your department or a particular unit. Among such projects might be the following:

Relative Staff Utilization Percentage. Review current staffing patterns and correct any obvious inequities which result in consistently high or low utilization percentages for a specific unit or shift.

Skills Utilization. A considerable amount of data are available concerning activities of personnel in each skills classification. Consistently low or high utilization of personnel in a specific skills classification suggests an adjustment in staffing patterns to correct inequities in distribution of work.

There are many factors to be considered when evaluating skills utilization in relation to determining the desired or optimum skills mix ratio (RN hours—LVN hours—AUX hours).

1. Services or tasks that actually create workload.
2. Policy that determines who can perform a specific task or service.
3. Skills that will provide best or better patient care in the performance of a specific task.
4. Availability of personnel in any one skills classification in relation to workload.
5. Job enlargement—increasing the responsibilities for personnel in each classification will result in more interesting work for all employees.

6. Economics—use lowest skill acceptable in order to minimize overall cost.

The information necessary for reviewing current staffing patterns and assignment policies and practices is now available. The best time to review skills utilization is when these data are current.

Personnel Interunit Transfer and Nursing Pool. The accomplishment of high average staff utilization is often dependent on development of more effective procedures related to transfer of personnel from one unit to another based on workload. Charts illustrating the variations in daily workloads and actual hours worked for each nursing unit will normally show considerable potential for improvement in matching hours worked to estimated requirements. The implementation of a better system for interunit transfer will often improve this condition.

The determination of optimum staffing for each unit at some point below the peak requirements and the assignment of part-time nursing personnel to units when peak periods are predicted have proven effective in increasing average utilization. The nursing pool is also often used as a means of providing personnel for units when peak workloads occur.

Work Distribution. Projects which result in action to shift nursing workload from one period of the day to another and reduce extreme variations in workload during the day offer opportunities for improving utilization.

Scheduling Innovations. Scheduling changes and use of part-time personnel to provide supplementary staffing during certain days or periods of the day can result in better matching of hours worked to estimated requirements.

Development of Part-Time Nursing Resources. Any use of part-time work schedules normally requires action to develop sources for qualified part-time nursing personnel. A specific project designed to make these schedules desirable and develop sources may yield significant results.

Cyclic Scheduling. Often, development of a cyclic scheduling system which improves the distribution of hours worked in relation to requirements will improve average utilization, as well as eliminate inequities in existing scheduling systems.

Off-Unit Activities. If the study indicates a relatively high occurrence of off-unit activities (errands), it suggests the possibility of an analysis to determine if other alternatives (errand service) should be considered. Improvements might be limited to specific assignments on the nursing unit to ensure the most economical performance of these activities.

Methods Improvement. The completed study has provided detailed information concerning both direct care and indirect care/administrative activities, including identification of the specific services/procedures which require the most time. Opportunities for improving services and reducing the time required are present and the lists of tasks developed provide an important source of projects. Generally speaking, those tasks which require the greatest amount of your time will have the highest potential for improvement.

The assignment of small task-analysis teams of nursing personnel to investigate specific tasks and recommend improvements is an essential part of an on-going improvement program. This activity will help to create and maintain interest in effective nursing care as well as result in tangible savings.

Nurse Staff Planning. The staff utilization control system provides data which can be used for more effective staff planning and budgeting. A project to develop a formal staff planning system for budgetary control based on these data can result in better communications between nursing and hospital administration concerning nursing requirements.

The basic system, which is simple, uses historical data concerning census, patient mix, and the actual staff utilization percentages you have experienced on each unit to forecast the same factors or quantities during the coming weeks or months.

Staffing: Model System 2*
(Emphasis on Budget Control)

Overview

The nurse staffing system is composed of five major components: staffing standards, annual budgeting, schedule planning, daily assignment, and management reporting and control.

The staffing standards portion of the system establishes the critical workload-to-staff relationships that are used in each of the three planning cycles, and consequently is the key feature of the total system. The annual budgeting, schedule planning, and daily assignment sections represent the staff planning activities that take place yearly, every three to seven weeks, and on a daily basis, respectively. The effectiveness of planning efforts is then measured and reported by the management reporting and control section, which provides feedback on a periodic basis.

There are several assumptions inherent in this staffing system:

1. There is a small group of float or PRN nursing personnel who are not permanently assigned to a specific unit.
2. Nurses who are normally assigned to nursing units must expect limited reassignment to similar units.
3. The nurse staffing function is consolidated in a central staffing office with overall responsibility for nurse staffing, including the establishment of time schedules, authorization of overtime, assignment of float personnel, and reassignment of unit staff.

Classifications of patients are not intended to directly relate to the medical conditions of the patients; rather, they are indicative of the time requirements for providing nursing care. The staffing standards utilized in this system are designed for use with established classifications, providing a more accurate determination of staffing needs.

Step 1: Developing Classification Criteria. In developing staffing standards by patient classification, implement the patient classification process first. This involves a number of time-consuming steps, including definition of classification criteria, testing of criteria for validity, and training of nursing personnel to use the classification scheme. Once the patients are routinely classified by degree of care required, it becomes an easier task to develop staffing standards for each classification.

Step 2: Determining the Workload Index. The actual determination of staffing standards is accomplished using a variety of input sources. Available historical data on actual nursing hours per patient day are analyzed for determination of past performance and comparison with data from similar hospitals. The primary data for the staffing standards come from direct time study and random sampling of unit operations. In addition, head nurses can provide a valuable source of information on appropriate staffing levels. The results of the work measurement activities and discussions with nursing personnel are summarized by patient type, employee type, and shift to establish "goal" nurse hours per patient day for each patient type. (See Table 16-4.) A reasonableness test is performed by using each unit's actual distribution of census by patient type to calculate a weighted average of total hours per patient day using the developed standards. These results can then be compared to historical data and similar data from other hospitals.

The Annual Budget and Staffing

The preparation of an annual budget for nursing is the first step in the overall staff planning cycle. The budgeting process uses a forecast of census by unit and data from the staffing standards table to establish unit staffing levels. The census forecast is prepared for each unit on a monthly basis and is based on past trends and

Source: Thomas F. Kelley and W. Andrew McKenna, "An Integrated Nursing Staffing System" (paper presented at the Seventh National Conference, AHE, Hospital and Health Services Division, February 1976). Partners, Touche Ross & Company, Atlanta, Ga. Reprinted with permission.

Table 16-4 Goal Distribution of Nursing Hours by Patient Type for General Medical/Surgical Units

| | Patient Type | | | | Weighted |
	A	B	C	D	Total
7-3 Shift:					
RN	.74	.53	.37	.24	.48
LPN	1.39	.99	.69	.45	.89
T-A	.95	.68	.48	.30	.61
	3.08	2.20	1.54	.99	1.98
3-11 Shift:					
RN	.55	.40	.28	.18	.36
LPN	1.04	.74	.51	.33	.67
T-A	.72	.51	.36	.23	.48
	2.31	1.65	1.15	.74	1.49
11-7 Shift:					
RN	.39	.28	.19	.12	.25
LPN	.72	.52	.37	.23	.46
T-A	.50	.35	.25	.17	.32
	1.61	1.15	.81	.52	1.03
Total	7.00	5.00	3.50	2.25	4.50
Expected Distribution of Patient Type	15%	40%	35%	10%	

A: maximum care; B: complete care; C: partial care; D: self-care.

projections of future changes in patient load. Of course, the census forecast by unit must tie directly to other hospital forecasts used for budgeting. The usual approach to budgeting is to have one source in the hospital for all volume forecasts to ensure consistency in all revenue/expense projections.

After completion of the forecast, unit staffing requirements by month are established using a standard staff budgeting form. The next section provides a detailed procedure for completion of the form. The budgeting form (Figure 16-7) uses the appropriate goal hours per patient day and the projected ADC to compute required FTEs by employee type and shift. Note that there is a provision for five day per week coverage for one head nurse and two unit secretaries that are not part of the census-related staffing. No relief coverage is provided for the head nurse, and relief coverage

for the unit secretaries is provided from the float pool.

Procedure for Completion of Staff Budgeting Form

Following is an outline of the process for completion of the staff budgeting form (Figure 16-7). There will be 12 monthly forms completed for each unit and the float pool.

1. Using the appropriate staff budgeting form for your unit, enter the projected average daily census (ADC) for the unit and period on line 2 of the form. Also complete lines 1, 3, 4, and 5.
2. Multiply the *goal hours* (7) for each position by the ADC to obtain *daily hours* (8).
3. Enter the number of days covered in the period (e.g., 30 for the month of September) in the fourth column (9) and multiply by *daily hours* in the third column (8) to obtain *planned hours* (10). Note that the number of days covered in the period have been preentered for head nurse and unit secretary positions.
4. Enter the planned *cost per hour* for each position for the time period in the sixth column (11). This dollar per hour figure should include the impact of shift differentials, charge pay, and planned merit increases. Multiply the fifth column by the sixth to obtain *total cost* (12).
5. Obtain the required *FTEs* (13) for each position by dividing *planned hours* (10) by the *work hours in the time period* (5).
6. Compute totals for *planned hours, total cost,* and *FTEs* for the entire unit.
7. Calculations can be cross-checked by the following:
   a. Divide the total of the *planned hours* column by line 5. The result should equal the total of the *FTE* column.
   b. Multiply the total goal hours by line (2), then by .175. The result should approximate total FTEs excluding the unit secretary and HN positions.
   c. Obtain the average unit rate by dividing total cost by total FTEs. Compare this number to other units as a reasonableness test.

Figure 16-7 Staff Budgeting Form—General Medical-Surgical/OB-GYN Units

Unit: _____(1) Time Period: _____(4)

Projected Average Daily Census: _____(2) Work Hours
In Time Period: _____(5)

Beds Available: _____(3)

(6) Position Title	(7) Goal Hours	(8) Daily Hours (7) × (2)	(9) Days Covered In Period	(10) Planned Hours (8) × (9)	(11) Cost per Hour	(12) Total Cost (10) × (11)	(13) FTEs (10) ÷ (5)
7–3 Shift							
HN		8.0	21.6				
RN**	.48						
LPN	.89						
Tech./Aide	.61						
Unit Sec.†		8.0	21.6				
Total	1.98						
						7–3	☐
3–11 Shift							
RN							
LPN	.36						
Tech./Aide	.67						
Unit Sec.†	.46	8.0	21.6				
Total	1.49						
						3–11	☐
11–7 Shift							
RN	.25						
LPN	.46						
Tech./Aide	.32						
Unit Sec.							
Total	1.03						
						11–7	☐

		Hours	Cost	FTE
Total	4.50	☐	☐	☐
			(A)	(B)

☐ Unit Avg. Rate
(A) ÷ (B)

Total materials

Total 4.50

Hours ☐

Cost ☐ (A)

FTE ☐ (B)

☐ Unit Avg. Rate (A) ÷ (B)

**Total RNs including charge nurses and staff nurses.
†Day off for unit secretaries will be staffed from the float pool.

The staff scheduling process matches the working hours of budgeted personnel to provide 24-hour-a-day patient coverage. The staff schedule should be developed based upon a repeating pattern for each cycle. For further information, see "Approaches to Scheduling" in Chapter 17.

Daily Staffing Assignments or Adjustments

This procedure is performed daily for each shift and unit by the central staffing office. The purpose and objectives of the daily staffing procedure are

- to alter the scheduled staff complement based on the *actual* census and patient mix by unit
- to react to unplanned absences due to illness, etc.
- to assign "float" or PRN nurses to a unit and to effect transfers of staff nurses between units if needed

The adjustments are based on reported census by patient classification for each unit. Each nursing station prepares a shift report which includes a summary of current census by classification. A copy of this report goes to the staffing office. The staffing coordinator then calculates the required nursing coverage based upon unit census and patient mix using a table of staffing (Table 16-5) prepared from the staffing standards and a shift staffing report (Figure 16-8). The end result of the calculation is the required staffing by employee type and by unit for the upcoming shift.

Once the staffing requirements are established, the staffing coordinator assigns float personnel to units requiring additional staffing and reassigns other unit personnel if required. An important consideration in the quality of patient care is to control the mix of regular, full-time staff in a unit relative to float and part-time staff in that unit, making sure that continuity of care is achieved through the full-time staff.

Table 16-5 Table of Staffing Requirements for 7–3 Shift (All Units Except Intensive Care and Nursery)

| | Type A | | | | Type B | | | | Type C | | | | Type D | | |
Census	RN	LPN	T/A	Census	RN	LPN	T/A	Census	RN	LPN	T/A	Census	RN	LPN	T/A
1	.00	.25	.25	1	.00	.25	.00	1	.00	.25	.00	1	.00	.25	.00
2	.25	.25	.25	2	.25	.25	.25	2	.00	.25	.25	2	.00	.25	.00
3	.25	.50	.50	3	.25	.50	.25	3	.25	.25	.25	3	.00	.25	.00
4	.25	.75	.50	4	.25	.50	.25	4	.25	.25	.25	4	.00	.25	.25
5	.50	.75	.50	5	.25	.50	.50	5	.25	.50	.25	5	.25	.25	.25
6	.50	1.00	.75	6	.50	.75	.50	6	.25	.50	.25	6	.25	.25	.25
7	.75	1.25	.75	7	.50	1.00	.50	7	.25	.50	.50	7	.25	.50	.25
8	.75	1.50	1.00	8	.50	1.00	.75	8	.50	.75	.50	8	.25	.50	.25
9	.75	1.50	1.00	9	.50	1.00	.75	9	.50	.75	.50	9	.25	.50	.25
10	1.00	1.75	1.25	10	.50	1.25	.75	10	.50	.75	.50	10	.25	.50	.50
11	1.00	2.00	1.25	11	.75	1.25	1.00	11	.50	1.00	.75	11	.25	.50	.50
12	1.00	2.00	1.50	12	.75	1.50	1.00	12	.50	1.00	.75	12	.25	.75	.50
13	1.25	2.25	1.50	13	.75	1.50	1.00	13	.50	1.25	.75	13	.50	.75	.50
14	1.25	2.50	1.50	14	1.00	1.75	1.25	14	.50	1.25	.75	14	.50	.75	.50
15	1.50	2.50	1.75	15	1.00	1.75	1.25	15	.75	1.25	1.00	15	.50	.75	.50
16	1.50	2.75	2.00	16	1.00	2.00	1.25	16	.75	1.50	1.00	16	.50	1.00	.50
17	1.50	3.00	2.00	17	1.00	2.00	1.50	17	.75	1.50	1.00	17	.50	1.00	.50
18	1.50	3.25	2.25	18	1.25	2.25	1.50	18	.75	1.50	1.00	18	.50	1.00	.75
19	1.75	3.25	2.25	19	1.25	2.25	1.50	19	1.00	1.50	1.25	19	.50	1.00	.75
20	1.75	3.50	2.50	20	1.25	2.50	1.75	20	1.00	1.75	1.25	20	.50	1.25	.75

Figure 16-8 Shift Staffing Report (Excerpt)

Sample Units

7–3 Shift
Date:

	Census	RN	LPN	T/A		
A	5	.50	.75	.50		
B	15	1.00	1.75	1.25	2 North	
C	12	.50	1.00	.75		
D	3	—	.25	—	U.S.	Total
Req.	2.00	3.75	2.5		1	9.25
Act.	2	3	3		1	9.00
					Variance	(0.25)

	Census	RN	LPN	T/A		
A	2	.25	.25	.25		
B	11	.75	1.25	1.00	3 North	
C	12	.50	1.00	.75		
D	3	—	.25	—	U.S.	Total
Req.	1.50	2.75	2.00		1	7.25
Act.	2	3	3		1	9.00
					Variance	(1.75)

Shift Summary of all Units

	RN	LPN	T/A	U.S.	Total
Req.	13.25	21.00	13.25	8	55.5
Act.	15.00	18.00	14.00	7	54.0
Var.	1.75	(3.00)	.75	(1)	(1.5)

Reporting System

A series of management reports are produced to control the effectiveness of the staffing system. These reports measure the difference between

- planned and actual census by unit for the period
- expected and actual mix of patients by acuity of care classification
- "planned," "required," and "actual" staffing hours and cost

The reports are produced on a daily basis and summarized upwards for different management levels at weekly and monthly intervals.

- Daily reports are used by assistant directors of nursing to identify problem units on a current basis, in terms of:
  —unusual census fluctuations
  —patient classification problems
  —inappropriate staffing levels or mix
- Weekly reports are reviewed by the director of nursing to assess the overall department performance and to analyze trends for discussion in weekly staff meetings, etc.
- Monthly reports are reviewed by hospital administration to ensure adherence to overall hospital financial plans and objectives.

The key to effective management control lies in a detailed analysis of variances. Therefore, the reporting system must isolate the following types of variances in terms of both hours and dollars:

- *Planning variance.* This is the difference between budgeted staffing and required staffing. It measures the effectiveness of the utilization forecast procedure.
- *Efficiency variance.* This is the difference between the required staffing and the actual staffing. It reflects the effectiveness of the staffing office in matching daily patient care needs with the available nursing resources.

The management reporting system must also include reporting on quality of care and monitoring of patient classification. Quality-of-care monitoring through nursing audits and other tools is used to relate quality of nursing care to productivity changes, since productivity increases at the expense of patient care quality are usually unacceptable. In addition, staffing by patient classification requires a method of auditing classifications to discourage misuse of the system.

PATIENT CLASSIFICATION SYSTEMS

Overview*

The primary objective of the first generation of patient classification systems was to predict nurse staffing levels from shift to shift. Today, the objectives have greatly expanded. Information related to productivity monitoring, long-range planning, budgeted staff tracking, trend analysis, costing, and charging and the linking of patient classification information to a wide variety of pertinent data such as quality criteria, length of stay, nursing diagnoses, and medical care data are among the frequent demands. Nursing executives now use workload information for negotiating contracts with HMOs, evaluating trends in patient care demands, and generally minimizing economic risks.

With these and other expanded requirements of patient classification data comes the added pressure to repeatedly demonstrate the accuracy of the information. The methods traditionally employed for maintaining and monitoring the reliability and validity of patient classification systems are increasingly being recognized as inadequate for the complexity and sophistication of the expanded objectives.

With the advent of microcomputers and relational data base software, nursing executives are now able to track reliability and validity on an ongoing basis. Because patient classification data are retained, they can be used to provide more accurate workload predictions and descriptions. Further, the ability to identify the source of problems with unit-specific instruments or nurse classifiers leads to the required corrective mechanism. Increased confidence in the reliability and validity of the workload data provides the staff nurse with direct evidence of the accuracy of the patient classification instrument and provides the nursing executive with a significantly stronger tool in budget planning and tracking, contract negotiations, and financial risk reduction.

*Source: Phyllis Giovannetti and Judith Moore Johnson, "A New Generation Patient Classification System," *Journal of Nursing Quality Assurance*, vol. 20, no. 5, © 1990 Aspen Publishers, Inc.

Components of Patient Classification Systems*

An objective, effective patient classification system contains the following components:

1. flexibility
2. utilization by nursing personnel
3. compatibility with nursing philosophy and productivity goals
4. capability of justifying why nursing hours per patient day do not comply with the budgeted figure
5. ability to be tracked to provide staffing and acuity patterns

Many systems involve three components: a patient classification system, management reports, and monitoring tools. These form an information system enabling the nurse manager to respond to changes in the patient population and quality of care provided and to plan for the future use of nursing resources.

Each institution should develop its own criteria and definitions to fit its objectives and circumstances.

Types of Patient Classification Methods**

Descriptive Method

This is probably the oldest method used. In it, the nurse assigns the patient to a category that best describes the level of care needed. Standards are written to describe the various levels of categories. The narrative descriptions of categories are very general in nature. A predefined nurse-to-patient ratio required to achieve these standards is used to determine the nursing personnel needed.

The problem with this type of system is the subjectivity of the nurse evaluations of the severity of a patient's illness. It has been found that nurses do not consistently interpret the same patient's illness the same way. An example of a

*Source: Barbara Rutkowski, *Managing for Productivity in Nursing*, Aspen Publishers, Inc., © 1987.

**Source: Ibid.

descriptive patient classification system is presented in Table 16-6.

Checklist of Nursing Tasks Method

The checklist of nursing tasks method is based on descriptions of activities that have been identified and sometimes timed using the industrial engineering approach. Each activity pertinent to a particular patient is given a weight to show the degree of time needed to perform the tasks. The weights are summed to give a total for each patient. The total determines the patient type (Table 16-7).

The problem with this method, as with the descriptive method, is the subjectivity of the nurse. In both methods, the staffing is determined by the nurse's assessment of the patient and assignment to a level. One nurse's assessment can differ from another's for the same patient; so, too, can nursing tasks and the method of performing them. There also are differences from unit to unit. With this lack of consistency, the validity and reliability of these types of patient classification systems are questionable.

Patient Needs Method

The last type of patient classification system to be examined is based on patient needs. It identifies nursing resource requirements according to patient's dependence on nursing personnel. A list of patient needs has been identified, with weights assigned to the needs or indicators. These weights have been validated through time and motion studies. Each patient's selected indicators' weights are totaled. The person is assigned to a patient type corresponding to the totaled score. An acuity factor is assigned to each patient type that translates the workload of all the patient types into a relative workload comparable to a central frame of reference, such as the type II patient. The workload thus is expressed in relative terms.

In a system using four patient types, the total workload for patient types I, III, and IV would be expressed in workload terms relative to the most common one—type II (see Table 16-8). Desired hours that the nurse should provide for one unit of workload are identified by nursing

Table 16-6 Sample Descriptive Patient Classification System

Category I: Minimal Care
Patients who are convalescing and no longer require intensive, moderate, or maximum care. These patients still may need supervision by a nurse in the course of a day, even if only at infrequent intervals. This care group also includes patients who require diagnostic studies, minimal therapy, less frequent observations, and daily care for minor conditions; who are awaiting elective surgery or have difficulty arranging transportation between home and hospital; or whose home environment temporarily makes discharge undesirable or impractical.

Category II: Moderate Care
Patients who are moderately ill or are recovering from the immediate effects of a serious illness and/or an operation. These patients require nursing supervision or some assistance ambulating and caring for their own hygiene. They may be ambulatory for short periods.

Category III: Maximum Care
Patients who need close attention throughout the shift; that is, complete care patients who require nursing to initiate, supervise, and perform most of their activities or who require frequent and complex medications or treatments.

Category IV: Intensive Care
Acutely ill patients who have a high level of nurse dependency, including those requiring intensive therapy and/or intensive nursing care and whose unstable condition requires frequent evaluation with adjustment of therapy.

Note: The category best describing the patient reflects the patient type. The nursing division may set the hours of care required by each patient category.

administration. That workload plus the desired target nursing hours per unit of workload provide the total nursing hours required for caring for the patients. The total hours divided by eight hours yields the number of staff persons required to accomplish the required nursing hours for the unit's patient needs.

With this system, the skill mix needed for each patient is identified, as is the shift distribution of the staff, and the data are arranged in two tables. Using these two tables, the appropriate

Table 16-7 Checklist of Nursing Tasks Patient Classification System

	Points	Check If Applicable		Points	Check If Applicable
Nutrition and Elimination			*Mobility*		
1. Eating: Self	1	_____	1. Activities:		
Assist	2	_____	Complete Bedrest	4	_____
Feed	3	_____	Turn	3	_____
2. Fluid Balance:			ROM	3	_____
Intake	2	_____	TCDB	1	_____
Output	2	_____	Dangle	2	_____
Bed Weight	2	_____	Bedside Commode	2	_____
Standing Weight	1	_____	BRP	1	_____
Levine	2	_____	Chair	2	_____
Hemovac	1	_____	Ambulate	2	_____
Encourage Fluids	2	_____	Up Ad Lib	0	_____
Restrict Fluids	2	_____	2. Mode of Transfer:		
3. Bladder: Voiding	1	_____	Stretcher	2	_____
Catheterize	2	_____	Wheelchair	2	_____
Strain Urine	1	_____	Cardiac Chair	2	_____
Foley	2	_____	Bed	3	_____
Clinitest	1	_____	*Bath and Skin Care*		
Acetest	1	_____	1. Bath: Self	0	_____
Testape	1	_____	Assist	2	_____
4. Bowels: Regular	1	_____	Complete	3	_____
Colostomy	3	_____	Bedbath	3	_____
Enema	2	_____	Tub	2	_____
Education			Sitz	1	_____
1. Routine	1	_____	Shower	1	_____
2. Reinforcement	2	_____	2. Mouth Care	2	_____
3. New diagnosis/complete			3. Positioning	3	_____
teaching	3	_____			
Safety					
1. Bedrails: Half	1	_____			
Full at HS	2	_____			
Full Constantly	3	_____			
2. Restraints	3	_____			
Total Points	_____	_____	Total Points	_____	_____

Total Points Column 1 and 2 _____

Type I = 0–18 points; requires 0–3 hours of care   Type III = 37–60 points; requires 7–10 hours of care
Type II = 19–36 points; requires 4–6 hours of care   Type IV = 60 + points; requires 11 + hours of care

Source: Barbara Rutkowski, *Managing for Productivity in Nursing*, Aspen Publishers, Inc., © 1987.

staff mix for each shift is identified. The skill mix and shift distribution tables may vary from institution to institution, depending on the nursing department's philosophy of care delivery.

This system is more valid and reliable because it is based on patient needs that are the same within the institution as well as between institutions. It permits one hospital to compare itself with others. It defines the patient types in hours of required care rather than by terms such as "self-care," etc., which increases the system's objectivity.

Table 16-8 Patient Needs Classification System

I. (65%) A PATIENT WHO REQUIRES ONLY MINIMAL AMOUNT OF NURSING CARE (An average of 2.8 nursing hours per 24 hours)

Examples

- A patient who is mildly ill (generally termed convalescent).
- A patient who requires little treatment and/or observation and/or instruction.
- A patient who is up and about as desired; takes his or her own bath or shower.
- A patient who does not exhibit any unusual behavior patterns.
- A patient without intravenous therapy or many medications.

II. (100%) A PATIENT WHO REQUIRES AN AVERAGE AMOUNT OF NURSING CARE (An average of 4.3 nursing hours per 24 hours)

Examples

- A patient whose extreme symptoms have subsided or not yet appeared.
- A patient who requires periodic treatments and/or observations and/or instructions.
- A patient who is up and about with help for limited periods; partial bed rest required.
- A patient who exhibits some psychological or social problems.
- A patient with intravenous therapy with medications such as IV piggybacks every six hours.
- A newly admitted patient, either surgical or medical, who is a routine admission and not necessarily acutely ill.

III. (135%) A PATIENT WHO REQUIRES ABOVE AVERAGE NURSING CARE (An average of 5.8 nursing hours per 24 hours)

Examples

- A moderately ill patient.
- A patient who requires treatments or observations as frequently as every two to four hours.
- A patient with significant changes in treatment or medication orders more than four times a day.
- An uncomplicated patient with IV medications every four hours and/or hyperalimentation.
- A patient on complete bed rest.

IV. (200%) A PATIENT WHO REQUIRES MAXIMUM NURSING CARE (An average of 8.6 nursing hours per 24 hours)

This classification is most often used in intensive care areas.

Examples

- A patient who exhibits extreme symptoms (usually termed acutely ill).
- A patient whose activity must be rigidly controlled.
- A patient who requires continuous treatment and/or observations and/or instructions.
- A patient with significant changes in doctor's orders more than six times a day.
- A patient with many medications, IV piggybacks, and vital signs every hour and/or hourly output.

The total amount of time required to care for each patient determines his or her classification.

Note: The percentage figure is the relation of care in the category to the daily standard of 4.3 hours. For example, Category I requires only 65% of the standard daily hours, or 2.8 hours. This four class system is patterned after Joint Commission guidelines. To acquire a nursing hours baseline, use was made of historical data. The number of hours per patient day was derived by taking the previous year's number of patient days divided by the number of paid nursing hours; the quotient was 4.2. Since nursing and fiscal affairs both wanted to increase patient care hours, the figure was adjusted to a baseline of 4.3 hours. Other estimates of nursing hours can be calculated from nurse activity studies.

Source: E.A. Schmied, "Nurse Staffing After Hospitals Merge," *Nursing Administration Quarterly*, vol. 2, no. 1, © 1977 Aspen Publishers, Inc.

Developing a Patient Classification System*

The development of an appropriate patient classification system should be based on an objective approach (see Figure 16-9). There are essential characteristics of such a system that are important in establishing a base for the development of a patient data monitoring mechanism. Patient classification should relate not only to the level of staffing but also to the impact of acuity on the processes of delivering nursing care.

All patient classification systems must meet some basic criteria:

- They must identify patients in conjunction with each other so that they can be classified into relatively clear categories of care.
- There must be a systematic and organized approach to the classification and integration of various patient types and components.
- The timing of each classification must be identified so that the numbers of classifications and the time it takes to deliver care can be consistent with the service offered.
- The calculation must make provision for the utilization of human resources and their application to the requirements for patient care.

There are almost as many patient classification systems available as there are institutions using them. The elements listed should be consistent within almost any such system.

The nurse manager must be careful to conduct a balanced and systematic assessment of the variables that go into the design of the classification system. Following are some key questions to be addressed.

Are objective processes being used to determine the relationship between nursing staffing needs and patient acuity levels?

Is the financial framework which provides the resources for nursing care flexible in responding to changes in acuity?

What do acuity and patient classification measures indicate when correlated with financial, standards, and quality indexes that define the nursing care expectations on an individual unit, department, or service?

How deeply is the nursing staff involved in the process of classifying and utilizing the data for determining patient care needs and staffing levels?

Does the patient classification system serve as a component of the data base that assists the manager in making decisions on allocation and utilization of human resources for delivering standard-based nursing care, meeting the predefined levels of quality, and operating within the prescribed financial limits?

MEASURING NURSE ACTIVITY

Criticism of Measuring Techniques*

The criticisms leveled at the various techniques for quantitatively measuring nursing activities are important to note:

- A narrow view of nursing practice results from the use of work measurement techniques. Their use implies that nursing work is distinctly procedural in character: task-oriented with specific beginnings and endings.
- There is a lack of precision in the results of these sampling methods. One can raise questions as to whether the nursing practice observed is the most effective that *can* be provided. Omissions of care are not identified. So too, in many reports using these techniques, evidence is markedly lacking that the data presented are objective, reliable, and accurate. The reliability of raters and the problems of error in recording or reporting data are seriously ignored.

Source: Katherine H. West, *Infection Control in the Emergency Department,* Aspen Publishers, Inc., © 1988.

Source: This section consists of material adapted from *Nurse Staffing Methodology*, DHHS, 1973, Pub. No. (NIH) 73-433, and Chapter IV of *Development of Methods for Determining Use and Effectiveness of Nursing Service Personnel*, San Joaquin Hospital, 1976. [PHS No. 1-NU-34038 Laurel N. Murphy, Project Director.]

Figure 16-9 Flowchart for Patient Classification System Work Plan

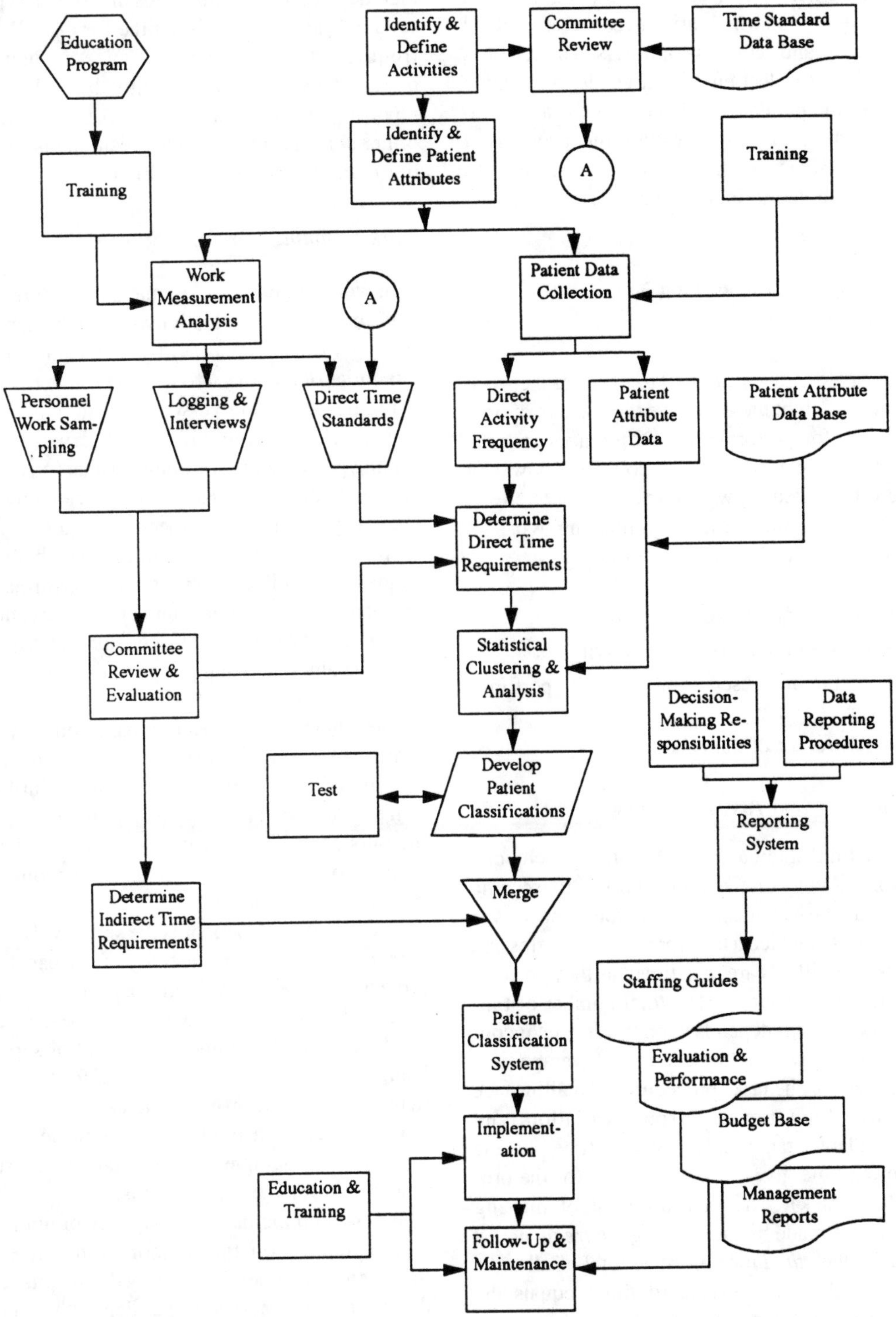

Source: Charles C. Gabbert, "Nursing Staffing, Scheduling, and Productivity," in *Nursing Administration and Law Manual*, Karen Hawley Henry, ed., Aspen Publishers, Inc., © 1986.

- The result is that patient classification schemes reflect specific nursing tasks, a number of which arise because of medical order and acuteness of illness. The schemes do not reflect emotional needs, orientation of the patient, instruction needs, and comfort other than through the process of providing physical care. Few have even attempted to include these items.

Techniques of Measuring Nurse Activity*

Four techniques are used to measure the work of nurses; all of these involve the concept of time required for performance. Differences in techniques reside in how data are collected, how they are categorized, how amounts of time are estimated, and how minutely nursing work is described. The four techniques are

- time study and task frequency
- work sampling of nurse activity
- continuous observation of nurses performing activities
- self-report of nurse activity

Time Study and Task Frequency

The time study and task frequency technique involves analyzing nursing work into specific tasks and task elements. A decision is made as to the points at which a task (procedure) begins and ends. Individuals are then timed as they perform the task (procedures). The total number of timings (sampling) depends upon the degree of confidence one wishes to place in the average time obtained for the task (procedure). An allowance is made for fatigue, personal variation, and unavoidable standby. The average time plus the allowed time gives a *standard time* for the procedure (task). The measurement of nursing activity is made by multiplying the *frequency of task* by the *standard time*. The total of all tasks multiplied by their standard times equals the volume of nursing work. The basic documenta-

tion in staffing approaches using this technique includes a manual of hundreds of "standard procedures" and a "standard time for each." The frequency of task performance is usually obtained by a checklist, with the individual reporting his or her performance of the task, his or her skill level (defined by position classification), and the place of performance.

Work Sampling

In work sampling technique (a procedure also used to measure productivity—see Chapter 20) nursing work is identified by major and minor categories of nursing activities. Through random sampling of nursing personnel as they perform their work, observers obtain observations of nursing personnel performing various activities. The total number of observations divided by the frequency occurring in a specific category yields the percentage of total time (during which observations were collected) spent in the performance of that activity. The total number of observations to be made is determined in advance and is based upon the amount of sampling required for confidence in the data sampled.

The categories that occur most frequently are *direct care* and *indirect care*, indicating that most individuals studying the problem of utilization are interested in the amount of time spent by the nursing personnel with the patient in direct care as opposed to the time away from the patient. (See Table 16-9.)

The observer also records the skill level of the person performing the activity. One can then project the direct care hours per shift as compared with time for other activities. These values can be used to determine the amount of service being provided by the nursing staff for that particular census and mix of patients.

Early studies in the hospitals indicate that a five-day work-sample study generally yields sufficient data for most evaluations.

Work sampling has the advantage of not having to depend on the memory (and time to record) of personnel. Its primary disadvantage is that short observations do not depict the whole complex of an activity sequence. Also, observers need to be trained, supervised, and tested for reliability.

Source: Ibid.

Although work sampling is a relatively non-intrusive procedure, having observations made of one's activities every 10 or 15 minutes can be irksome to staff, though there is a tendency to ignore the observer after the first several rounds of observations. Observing personnel when they are in a patient's room may also be an irritant to the patient. A brief explanation by staff or observers before observational rounds begin that a nursing activity study is taking place will usually be adequate.

In the work sampling form (Table 16-9), *direct care* refers to any nursing activity which is patient-centered; *indirect care* refers to activities which are away from the patient but are in preparation for or in completion of direct nursing care; *unit care* refers to activities necessary for the general coordination of the unit or well-being of the patient population—not for a specific patient. *Personal time* includes meals, breaks, standby, and socializing with other personnel.

A category for "other" activities was also provided on the recording form; observers were instructed to check this space and describe the activity when they were unsure how to code it. It was found that almost all "other" activities could be coded under the 22 categories provided.

Continuous Sampling

Continuous sampling follows the same general pattern of categorization in work sampling except that an observer follows or accompanies only one individual for an extended period of time in the performance of his or her job. The observer may also observe the nursing work performed for one patient or for more if they are in the same room or if they can be observed concurrently (usually called *direct patient care sampling*).

Continuous observation of all personnel on a unit, with recording made in detail of all activities performed, is not justified or feasible. One observer can usually follow only one other person—an exorbitantly expensive and slow way to gather data if many personnel are involved.

Direct Patient Care Sampling. The purpose of direct patient care sampling is to determine the amount and source of direct care to patients by

1. determining the amount of direct nursing care provided to each category of patient (patient categories are discussed in "Patient Classification Systems" above)
2. determining who provides the direct nursing care

The direct care sampling procedure consists of making observations of the services received by patients. A set of patients is selected and at specified intervals of time the direct care activities taking place are recorded. Here, too, the observer also records the level (e.g., RN, LPN, aide, or student) of the person performing the activity. This information can then be used to determine the number of hours of direct patient care provided for the existing patient population and mix from the amount of time spent with individual patients.[1]

Self-Reporting

In self-reporting, the individual checks a predetermined list or logs in diary form the tasks he or she has performed. The entries in the diary or log may be made at time intervals or may be made at the close of a major category of work or a specific task assignment. The self-reports are analyzed by sorting the entries into categories or classes of tasks similar to those for work sampling or by the development of themes or problems describing the activity.

When conscientiously carried out, a large amount of data can be collected. Observers do not have to be hired and/or trained. The method may thus be seen as less costly, but this may not be true. A thorough orientation of all staff members must be done—when all shifts are involved and when one takes into account days off, float persons, and part-time persons, the problem of orientation is considerable. And even with a complete orientation, constant monitoring is necessary. Initial "best of intentions" can wear off rather rapidly and individuals may simply forget to record. Without a strong commitment to the study, resistance can develop. Recording

---

[1]*Methods for Studying Nurse Staffing in a Patient Unit*, DHHS, Pub. No. (HRA) 78-3, May 1978.

Table 16-9 Work Sampling Form

WORK SAMPLING

Hospital _____ Unit _____ Shift _____ Observer _____ Day of Study _____ Date _____

Description of Activity	HN,CN	RN	LPN	NA, Ord.	Stu.	WC	HN,CN	RN	LPN	NA, Ord.	Stu.	WC	HN,CN	RN	LPN	NA, Ord.	Stu.	WC	HN,CN	RN	LPN	NA, Ord.	Stu.	WC
Time:																								
1 Communication with Patient &/or Family																								
2 Medications, I.V. (administering)																								
3 Nutrition & Elimination																								
4 Patient Hygiene																								
5 Patient Movement																								
6 Positioning, Exercising																								
7 Rounds or Assist M.D. or Other with Pt.																								
8 Routine Checks, Patient Rounds, Symptom Observations—Nursing Personnel Only																								
9 Specimen Gathering and Testing																								
10 Treatments and Procedures—Nursing Only																								
11 Vital Signs																								

Direct Care #1-11

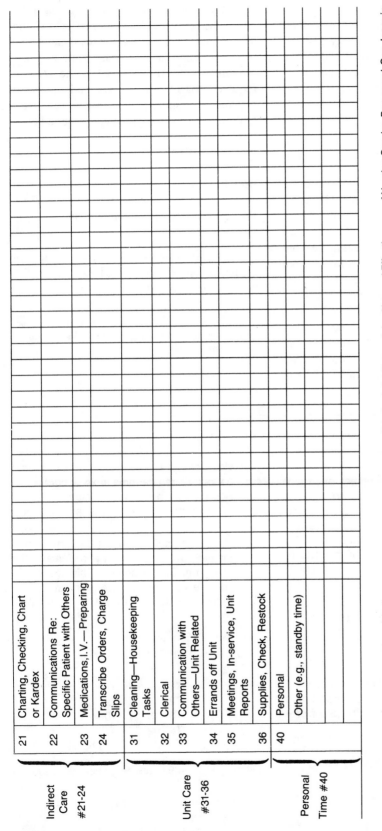

Indirect Care #21-24	21	Charting, Checking, Chart or Kardex
	22	Communications Re: Specific Patient with Others
	23	Medications, I.V.—Preparing
	24	Transcribe Orders, Charge Slips
Unit Care #31-36	31	Cleaning—Housekeeping Tasks
	32	Clerical
	33	Communication with Others—Unit Related
	34	Errands off Unit
	35	Meetings, In-service, Unit Reports
	36	Supplies, Check, Restock
Personal Time #40	40	Personal
		Other (e.g., standby time)

Source: Laurel N. Murphy, Project Director, *Development of Methods for Determining Use and Effectiveness of Nursing Service Personnel*, San Joaquin Hospital, 1976. PHS No 1-Nu 34048.

is tiresome and staff can easily begin to see it as an additional burden in an already busy day. Much depends, too, on the complexity of forms used and the time required to mark them. The method is commonly used, however, and many find that the results are accurate enough for their needs.

THE WORKLOAD INDEX

Patient classification does not measure the amount of care required by patients. However, the category a patient falls within can be correlated with the total amount of nursing care required by that patient. Patients within the more acute categories will have to be allotted more nursing time than patients in the less acute categories. When these correlations are formalized, it is called a workload index.

Briefly, here is how a workload index is created. The results of patient classification and measurements of nursing services provided are combined to obtain the hours or minutes of direct patient care for each class of patient for each shift during the period of observation. The total minutes or hours of care, then, for any population of patients in a unit can be estimated and so give an objective basis for arriving at the services required for the given mix and census of patients. The estimated workload is presented in terms of the total amount of care required of the staff.*

How to . . .

*How To Calculate Required Nursing Hours***

The workload work sheet is used to calculate the mean number of nursing hours required on the unit (see Table 16-10).

_____

Source: R.K. Dieter Haussman, Sue T. Hegyvary, and John F. Newman, *Monitoring Quality of Nursing Care—Part II*, DHHS, Pub. No. (HRA) 76-7, Appendix 6, July 1976.

**Source*: Ibid., Appendix 4.

Table 16-10 Workload Work Sheet

---

1. Unit: _____
2. Find the daily average number of patient types 1–4 on the unit. (To do so, add the number of Type 1 patients each day in the month and divide by the number of days in the month. Do the same calculation for Types 2, 3, and 4.) Enter the number of each type in Column A.

	A	B†	C
Average number Type 1 -		01	
Type 2 -		03	
Type 3 -		07	
Type 4 -		14	

3. Multiply each number of Column A by the number in Column B. Write the product in Column C. (Column B is the mean hours required for each patient type, based on pre-

†Column B lists the mean hours required for each patient type. In this example the ratios are 1:3:7:14. Each hospital unit must establish its own ratio according to need and available resources.

vious study; C is the number of nursing hours required per type in 24 hours.)

4. Add the four numbers in Column C. Enter the number in the blank at the right.

_____

5. Divide the total of Column C by the sum of the daily average number of patients on the unit (from Step 2 above). This figure tells you the number of hours per patient day required. Enter the answer in the blank at right.   _____

Example: Patient unit 3 West
(Steps 2–4) Average patient mix:

	A	B	C
T1 -	08	01	08
T2 -	10	03	30
T3 -	15	07	105
T4 -	02	14	28
	35		171 hours

(Step 5) $\frac{171}{35}$ = 4.9 hours per patient day required

How to Calculate Available Staff Hours
  by Skill Level*

Table 16-11 is the companion of the workload work sheet used to calculate the mean number of nursing hours required on the unit. It is used to calculate the mean number of hours available from each nursing category and should be completed each month for each unit being monitored.

How To Develop Staffing Tables**

Staffing tables can be developed so that when the number of patients per classification is known, the number of staff needed can be obtained directly from the table.

Suppose that each staff member provides three hours of direct patient care, while Category I, II, III, and IV patients require 20, 45, 60, and 180 minutes of direct care respectively. A staffing table such as Table 16-12 will enable a user to estimate staff needs as follows.

Suppose there are 15 Category I patients, 10 Category II patients, 5 Category III patients, and 1 Category IV patient. Under I (the second column of Table 16-12) for 15 patients, 1.7 staff members are needed; under II for 10 patients, 2.5 staff members are needed; under III for 5 patients, 1.7 staff members are needed; and under IV for 1 patient, 1.0 staff member is needed. $1.7 + 2.5 + 1.7 + 1.0 = 6.9$, so seven staff members are needed.

The entries in Table 16-12 were prepared as follows:

> Multiply a selected number of patients (1 through 24, in this case) by the number of minutes of care determined for a given patient category; convert this to hours by dividing by 60. Divide the result by the number of hours of direct care a staff member provides (three in this case). The resulting quotient is the entry in the table for the given number of patients.

For example, 10 patients in Category II require $(10 \times 45) \div 60 = 7.5$ hours of care. Then $7.5 \div 3 = 2.5$ FTE staff members.

It is important to note that corresponding tables should be prepared for each unit for each shift, since the entries depend upon the hours of direct patient care given by each staff member in that unit, as well as the minutes of care required by the different classes of patients in that unit.

Staffing tables developed as a result of studies conducted on specific units will reflect the staffing conditions in existence at the time of the study. If the unit was operating in an understaffed condition during the study, the staffing tables will underestimate staff needs. Conversely, if the staff was observed to have excessive personal time during the study, the staffing tables will overestimate staff needs. The head/charge nurse's perception of adequacy is the key to the development of proper staffing patterns. If the unit was overstaffed during the study, staffing estimates from the table could be "rounded down" or decreased. Additional perception-of-adequacy data could then be taken and comparisons of direct care given per staff member could be made with similar units. Ideally, six months after new staffing patterns had been established, repeat studies could be done to determine the impact of these changes.

GRASP® WORKLOAD SYSTEM*

The GRASP® workload system is founded upon three major assumptions concerning effective hospital and nursing management:

1. No two patients, even given the same diagnosis, will require the same amount of care. Therefore, census figures, without attention to values of intensity of care, can be misleading.

*Source: Ibid.

**Source: *Methods for Studying Nurse Staffing in a Patient Unit*, DHHS, Pub. No. (HRA) 78-3, 1978.

*Source: Diane Meyer, Director, The GRASP System. Reprinted with permission. *Note:* GRASP® is proprietary to MCS, Inc., Morganton, North Carolina (sole agents), and protected by copyright and trademark registrations in the United States and Foreign Countries.

Table 16-11 Available Staff Hours by Skill Level Work Sheet

1. Unit: _____
2. Obtain a list of *all nursing staff* on the unit. Include all full- and part-time employees. Include the head nurse, RNs, LPNs, aides, and any other category you may include in giving nursing care, such as medication technicians. Do not include clerks or unit managers, and do not include nursing supervisory staff who cover more than one unit. Make separate work sheets for each category: (1) RN, (2) LPN, (3) aide and orderly, and (4) other.
3. Starting with the RN category, calculate the *total number of hours worked by each nurse* on the unit this month. Use time cards or staffing roster to ascertain information.
4. Add the hours worked by each person in the category to find the *total number of hours worked by that category* on the unit this month. Enter that number at the right.   _____
5. Divide the total number found in Step 4 by the number of days in the month. (Do not divide by the number of days worked. If for December, divide by 31.) Enter the answer at the right. _____
6. Divide the answer from Step 5 by the number of beds on the unit. Enter the number at the right. This number is the mean number of nursing hours of this category available per patient day on that unit.

7. Repeat Steps 3–6 for LPN staff. Enter the result from Step 6 at the right.   _____
8. Repeat Steps 3–6 for aide staff. Enter the result from Step 6 at the right.   _____
9. Repeat Steps 3–6 for "other" category if applicable. Enter the result from Step 6 at the right.

_____

Example:

	RN Staff	Hours Worked This Month
(Steps 2 & 3)	1. (RN name)	168
	2. (RN name)	164
	3. (RN name)	156
	etc.	etc.
(Step 4)	Total =	1720 hours (for 10 RNs)

(Step 5) $\dfrac{1720 \text{ hours}}{31 \text{ days}} = 55.5$ RN hours per day

(Step 6) $\dfrac{55.5 \text{ hours}}{35 \text{ patients}} = 1.59$ RN hours per patient day

	LPN Staff	Hours Worked This Month
(Steps 2 & 3)	1. (LPN name)	168
	2. (LPN name)	170
	etc.	etc.
(Step 4)	Total =	2016 hours (for 12 LPNs)

(Step 5) $\dfrac{2016}{31} = 65.0$ LPN hours per day

(Step 6) $\dfrac{65.6}{35} = 1.85$ LPN hours per patient day

	Aides and Orderlies	Hours Worked This Month
(Steps 2 & 3)	1. (aide name)	166
	2. (aide name)	156
	etc.	etc.
(Step 4)	Total =	675 (for 4 aides)

(Step 5) $\dfrac{675}{31} = 21.8$ aide hours per day

(Step 6) $\dfrac{21.8}{35} = 0.62$ aide hours per patient day

Total nursing hours available per patient day:

RN	= 1.59
LPN	= 1.85
Aide	= 0.62
Total	= 4.06

Table 16-12 Table for Calculating Number of Staff Personnel Needed Based upon Patient Class and Staffing During Study Period (Excluding Ward Clerk)

Direct Patient Care Sampling

Hospital _____ Unit _____ Date of Study _____
Shift _____ Type of Unit _____

Number of Patients	Number of Staff Members Needed for Category			
	I	II	III	IV
1	.1	.3	.3	1.0
2	.2	.5	.7	2.0
3	.3	.8	1.0	3.0
4	.4	1.0	1.3	4.0
5	.6	1.3	1.7	5.0
6	.7	.5	2.0	6.0
7	.8	1.8	2.3	7.0
8	.9	2.0	2.7	8.0
9	1.0	2.3	3.0	9.0
10	1.1	2.5	3.3	10.0
11	1.2	2.8	3.7	11.0
12	1.3	3.0	4.0	12.0
13	1.4	3.3	4.3	13.0
14	1.6	3.5	4.7	14.0
15	1.7	3.8	5.0	15.0
16	1.8	4.0	5.3	
17	1.9	4.3	5.7	
18	.2	4.5	6.0	
19	2.1	4.8	6.3	
20	2.2	5.0	6.7	
21	2.3	5.3	7.0	
22	2.4	5.5	7.3	
23	2.6	5.8	7.7	
24	2.7	6.0	8.0	

2. Measurement of patient care needs for budgeting and planning staffing must be based on the care the patient should have rather than what care he or she has received. Measurement of the status quo isn't likely to lead to improved quality care.
3. If the nursing workload is balanced on a given unit—that is, if the hours of patient care required are equal to the hours of nursing care available—then there is the opportunity for increased quality of care, decreased cost, and increased personnel satisfaction.

How GRASP® Works

Based on the assumptions stated above, the GRASP® system *quantifies individual patient care needs* as the basis for determining nursing unit workloads. The nucleus of GRASP is the patient care hour (PCH), which is a measurement unit equal to one hour of care required.

In contrast to more subjective classification systems, PCHs provide a workload measurement and administrative decision-making system based on an objective assessment of the unique care requirements of individual patients. Thus the PCH is a more meaningful unit of measurement, which replaces the "patient/day" unit currently used by hospital administration in many reporting activities.

Moreover, PCHs permit continual comparison between patient care requirements and nursing care available. Central to the operation of the GRASP system is a PCH chart (see Figure 16-10) listing significant elements of physical care, indirect care, family and patient teaching, emotional support, and nursing process.

Nurses update the PCH chart each shift, assessing the amount of care their patients will require in each 24-hour period based on medical orders and nursing care plans. The patient care assessment can be represented by this formula, which can be easily adjusted to fit individual hospitals and health care facilities:

$$\text{Total Patient Care} = \text{Nursing Process} + \text{Physical Care} + \text{Indirect Care} + \text{Teaching and Emotional Support} + \text{Delay and Fatigue}$$

By coupling the PCH chart assessment, with parallel retrospective charting, a nurse can determine the total patient care requirements and ensure quality care and complete documentation for each patient each day. (See Figure 16-11 for a schematic view of the process.)

Figure 16-10 Patient Care Hour Chart

UNIT **Forest** DATE **11-15-85** SHIFT **Day**

Pt. Name	S. White	Doc	Sleepy	Sneezy	Grumpy	Bashful	Droopy	Happy		
ASSESSMENT (Select as applicable)										
Initial/Admission Assessment	(5)	5	5	5	5	5	5	5	5	5
Update Assessment	1	(1)	(1)	(1)	(1)	(1)	(1)	(1)	1	1
PLANNING (Select as applicable)										
Initial Care Plan Development	(2)	2	2	2	2	2	2	2	2	2
Update/Revise Care Plan	1	(1)	(1)	(1)	(1)	(1)	(1)	(1)	1	1
IMPLEMENTATION (Select as applicable for each element)										
LEARNING/COPING (Select as applicable)										
Planned teaching	2	2	2	(2)	(2)	2	2	2	2	2
Special/planned emotional reassurance	5	5	5	5	(5)	(5)	5	5	5	5
DIET (Select highest applicable)										
Self/Family feed or NPO (intake assess only)	(1)	1	1	(1)	1	1	1	(1)	1	1
Feeds w/assistance	8	8	(8)	8	8	(8)	(8)	8	8	8
Tube/gastros. feeding w/intermittent ⟋ q4h	12	(12)	12	12	12	12	12	12	12	12
Total feeding by Personnel	14	14	14	14	(14)	14	14	14	14	14
ELIMINATION (Select highest applicable)										
Toilets w/o supervision (output assess only)	(1)	1	1	1	1	(1)	1	(1)	1	1
Foley care (includes bedpan x 1)	4	4	4	(4)	4	4	4	4	4	4
Toilets w/supervision; commode chair, bedpan	6	6	(6)	6	6	6	6	6	6	6
Toilets w/constant supervision	10	10	10	10	(10)	10	(10)	10	10	10
Colostomy care & irrigation	16	16	16	16	16	16	16	16	16	16
Incontinent care	23	(23)	23	23	23	23	23	23	23	23
CLEANLINESS (Select as applicable)										
Bathes self (includes AM & PM Care)	(3)	3	3	3	3	(3)	3	3	3	3
Bathes w/help or superv. (Incl. AM & PM Care)	4	4	(4)	(4)	4	4	4	(4)	4	4
Bathed by personnel (Includes AM & PM Care)	7	(7)	7	7	(7)	7	(7)	7	7	7
VITAL SIGNS/MEASUREMENT (Select Highest applicable)										
Routine vital signs (TPR, BP) BID-TID	(2)	2	2	2	2	(2)	2	(2)	2	2
Vital signs QID or close observation qih	3	3	3	(3)	3	3	(3)	3	3	3
Vital signs q4h	5	5	5	5	(5)	5	5	5	5	5
Post-op vital signs or vital signs q2h	9	(9)	9	9	9	9	9	9	9	9
TURNING/ASSISTED ACTIVITIES (Select highest applicable)										
Walk w/assistance or up in chair w/asst.-OD	(2)	2	2	2	(2)	2	2	2	2	2
Walk w/asst. or up in chair w/asst.-BID or TID	4	4	4	(4)	4	4	(4)	4	4	4
Bedrest-turn q2h (including skin care)	16	16	16	16	16	16	16	16	16	16
MEDICATIONS/FLUIDS ADMIN. (Select all applicable)										
Oral meds., drops, suppos. or ointments	2	2	2	(2)	(2)	(2)	(2)	2	2	2
Injection (estimate prn's)	3	3	3	(3)	3	(3)	3	(3)	3	3
I.V. medications	4	(4)	4	(4)	4	4	4	4	4	4
Initiate/monitor blood transfusions	8	6	6	6	6	6	6	6	6	6
Hyperal. or secondary IV's or Chemotherapy	12	(12)	12	12	12	12	12	12	12	12
Continuous I.V. Care	14	(14)	14	(14)	(14)	14	14	14	14	14
SUCTIONING/RESPIRATORY AIDS (Select all applicable)										
Trach. suction QID; or gastric/oral suction	5	5	5	5	5	5	5	5	5	5
Trach. suction q-3-4h	8	8	8	8	8	8	8	8	8	8
Cough & deep breathe/leg exercises	9	9	9	9	(9)	9	(9)	9	9	9
OTHER DIRECT NURSING CARE (Select as applicable)										
Simple dressings or special skin/decub care	3	3	3	3	(3)	(3)	3	3	3	3
Specimen collection	(3)	3	3	(3)	3	3	3	3	3	3
Isolation Technique	(5)	5	5	5	5	5	5	5	5	5
Complex dressing change (q6-8h)	10	(10)	10	10	10	10	10	10	10	10
Restraint Care	12	12	12	12	12	12	12	12	12	12
INDIRECT CARE	(6)	(6)	(6)	(5)	(6)	(6)	(6)	(6)	6	6
EVALUATION (Select as applicable)										
REVIEW/EVALUATE/DOCUMENTED CARE GIVEN	1	(1)	(1)	(1)	(1)	(1)	(1)	(1)	1	1
TOTAL (Tenths Hrs.)	30	100	27	53	82	36	52	20		
Patient Care Hours (PCH)	3.0	10.0	2.7	5.3	8.2	3.6	5.2	2.0		

UNIT TOTAL PCH

40.0

Note: Chart values (expressed in tenths of hours) have been increased to reflect 100% of direct physical care interventions (as typically only 85% are planned and predictable). Chart values will vary depending on facility layout and unit procedures. Instructions on developing PCH charts, documentation forms, and various applications of PCH data to hospital administration such as admitting, staffing, billing, budgeting, etc., are available from MCS Inc., Box 1774 Morganton, North Carolina 28655.

Figure 16-11 The GRASP® System Workload Model System

ASSESSING CARE NEEDS
Charge nurse assesses 24-hour
patient care requirements based
on medical orders and nursing
care plans.

ADMITTING   ADMINISTRATION

ANALYSIS OF WORKLOAD◄————COMPUTING————►MONITORING WORKLOAD
Admitting compares PCHs and   Clerk (or computer) computes   Daily, weekly, and monthly
NCHs (hours of patient care   PCHs (hours of care required) on   productivity and utilization data
required and hours of nursing care   each unit, relays totals to   are reviewed by nursing
available) on all units.   admitting, and records for   management.
                                     reporting purposes.

PLANNING FOR ADMISSIONS   AUDITING CARE   PLANNING STAFF BUDGETS
Admitting clerk estimates PCHs   Supervisors spot check patient   Director of nursing analyzes
on incoming admissions with   care assessment and delivery on   average hours of patient care
guidelines by diagnosis and   an ongoing basis.   required, by unit, to determine
condition.   staff needs.

DISTRIBUTING WORKLOAD   ASSIGNING NURSES   LONG-RANGE PLANNING
New admissions are assigned by   Nurses are assigned to 8 hours of   Director of nursing and
distributing patients, balancing   patient workload, balancing staff   administrator study cumulative
the PCH workload among units.   loads on the units.   data and plan future budgets and
                                                                          long-range expansion.

ADJUSTING STAFFING————►ONGOING QUALITY PATIENT◄————OTHER APPLICATIONS
Before each shift, current PCH   CARE   Potential applications are many,
data are sent to the staffing office.   e.g., refined cost accounting for
Floats are assigned properly and   DRGs for even charge systems by
PRN s called if needed.   care received, rather than simply
                                                                         by beds, becomes possible.

Chapter 17

Scheduling

OVERVIEW

The basic problem of scheduling is to provide patient care every day around the clock using nurses who generally work five days a week, one shift per day, and prefer to have weekends off. Scheduling is usually done by nursing supervisors for the units or floors for which they are responsible. They estimate patient care requirements and allocate the available nursing staff to the days of the week so that these requirements are approximately satisfied and hospital personnel regulations observed. They try to schedule the nursing staff so that each nurse gets his or her share of weekends off and none of the nurses is rotated to evenings or night shifts for an unduly long time, and they also try to accommodate individual nurses' requests for specific days off. Often a schedule is prepared every other week, specifying work days and days off for each member of the nursing staff over the ensuing two weeks.

Preparation of the schedule is a time-consuming task for the nursing supervisor and there is usually dissatisfaction with the results:

1. Coverage tends to fluctuate widely, particularly in the case of RNs; the number of RNs assigned to a given unit on a given shift may vary from day to day by a factor of two or more.

2. In their position of total authority over schedules, supervising nurses are apt to be suspected of favoritism, particularly when they try—as is often necessary and desirable—to take into account the desires and constraints of individual nurses.

3. The attempt to resolve scheduling and allocation problems can result in excessive use of overtime.

4. Schedules frequently have to be changed on short notice because of changes in patient care requirements, illness of a nurse, etc.

The vast majority of hospitals schedule and allocate nurses on an informal basis. The rejection of more systematic methods appears to reflect in part the belief that nursing, as a profession, is not amenable to formal scheduling and allocation procedures, that too many variables must be taken into account, and that most nurses are not quantitatively oriented and would therefore resist any system involving computers and possibly in part the failure of previous efforts to take into account some variables that were important to nurses.*

---

*Source: Reprinted with permission from Socio-Economic Planning Sciences, Vol. 7, Christopher Maier-Rothe and Harry B. Wolfe, "Cyclical Scheduling and Allocation of Nursing Staff." Copyright 1973, Pergamon Press, Ltd.

Objectives*

The objectives of a scheduling and allocation procedure are to assign working days and days off to individual members of the nursing staff so that

1. adequate patient care is ensured while overstaffing is avoided
2. a desirable distribution of days off is achieved
3. individual members of the nursing staff are treated fairly
4. individuals know well in advance what their schedules are

Factors in Scheduling Decisions**

Among the factors that should play a part in scheduling decisions are the following:

1. The different levels of nursing staff—registered nurses, licensed practical nurses, and nurse's aides—have different capabilities. LPNs and aides are legally allowed to perform only certain functions. Even within these categories, individuals can be classified by degree of experience and by the amount of responsibility they are able to assume.
2. Nursing coverage must, of course, be provided 24 hours a day, 7 days a week. Nursing requirements are typically lower during the evening and night shifts than during the day shift. Saturday and Sunday requirements tend to be 20–30 percent lower than weekday requirements, depending on the medical service, due to a lower patient census, fewer new physician orders, or both.

3. Vacations and time off for holidays must be staggered to ensure continued patient coverage and equitable treatment for nurses.
4. Weekend days off are highly prized by the nursing staff, preferably both days in a row. Next in preference is two or more days off in a row in the middle of the week.
5. Long stretches of consecutive working days (usually defined as more than five in a row) are undesirable.
6. Despite a salary differential, the evening and night shifts are more difficult to staff than the day shift. As a result, schedules must provide for "rotation"; daytime staff must work on the other two shifts from time to time. Also, staff on evening and night shifts may sometimes have to work on the day shift in order to attend special programs, training courses, etc.
7. Most nurses prefer to remain on one nursing unit rather than being "floated" or shifted from one unit to another, partly because of the competence and expertise they are able to develop in a particular unit and partly because of the camaraderie of continued association with the same group. However, there are some nurses who do not mind, and in fact prefer, floating because of the variety of experience it gives them.

Criteria for Evaluation*

A scheduling system can be assessed by observing how well it functions in terms of the following:

Coverage: The number of nurses (by skill class) assigned to be on duty is in relation to some minimum number of nurses required.

---

*Source: Reprinted with permission from *Socio-Economic Planning Sciences*, Vol. 7, Christopher Maier-Rothe and Harry B. Wolfe, "Cyclical Scheduling and Allocation of Nursing Staff." Copyright 1973, Pergamon Press, Ltd.

**Source: Ibid.

---

*Source: D. Michael Warner, "Computer-aided System for Nurse Scheduling," *Cost Controls in Hospitals*, edited by J.R. Griffith, W.M. Hancock, and F.C. Munson, Health Administration Press. Reprinted with permission.

Quality: A measure of a schedule's desirability as judged by the nurse who will have to work it. This measure includes weekends off, work stretches, single days on, split days off, and certain rotation patterns in addition to how a schedule conforms to the nurse's requests for days off for a particular scheduling period.

Stability: A measure of the extent to which nurses know their future days off and on duty and the extent to which they feel that their schedules are generated consistent with a set of stable policies (e.g., weekend policy, rotation policy).

Flexibility: The ability of a scheduling system to handle changes, such as from full-time to part-time, from rotation to working only one shift, and special requirements—class schedules of nurses, requests for days off, vacations, leaves of absence, etc.

Fairness: A measure of the extent to which each nurse perceives that he or she exerts the same amount of influence upon the scheduling system as other nurses.

Cost: The resources consumed in making the scheduling decision.

Guidelines

1. Schedules should represent a balance between the needs of the employee and the employer (patient care). When conflicts arise, patient care should have priority.
2. Schedules should distribute fairly the "good" and "bad" days off among all employees.
3. All employees should adhere to the established rotation. Exceptions should be rare and granted only if the employee is requesting two weekdays off (working every weekend). All requests and exceptions should be in writing and should specify the period of time off requested.
4. Advance posting of time schedules allows employees to plan their personal lives. Therefore, absenteeism and requests for changes are reduced.

5. Time schedules should not be a mystery nor a tool of control or discipline.
6. There should be a mechanism for emergency changes to accommodate both employee and employer.
7. Schedules must conform with all labor laws and hospital and departmental policies.
8. Schedules should be established to provide correct numbers and mix of personnel, allowing continuity, which is essential for quality care.
9. Schedules should be consistent, enabling work groups to develop teamwork, another contributor to quality care.*

Constraints

The more constraints involved, the more difficult any type of scheduling becomes.

- Number of weekends off—1 in four, 1 in three, every other weekend.
- Maximum length of consecutive days worked—i.e., no more than six, etc.
- Whether the days off should be together or split.
- Payroll and overtime considerations (i.e., five work days per week—ten days per pay period).*

Cautions

- Giving more or less of one variable affects the ability to give more or less of the others.
- There is no one schedule that will work for all hospitals and all departments.
- Select several different schedules that complement each other and develop the best cyclical schedule for your department.

Source: Patricia L. Eusanio, "Effective Scheduling—The Foundation for Quality Care," *Journal of Nursing Administration*, January 1978. Reprinted with permission.

- Experiment with combinations of different schedules.*

CENTRALIZED, DECENTRALIZED, AND SELF-SCHEDULING

Centralized Scheduling**

Under centralized scheduling one person in the nursing administration office plans coverage for all nursing units. A master staffing pattern is developed for these units and staffing is based on a preestablished standard. This staffing coordinator has access to clerical help to type, process, and distribute the master plan to the units. The coordinator knows the number and availability of staff on any given day and therefore is able to make the necessary day-to-day changes when sickness or other emergencies occur. The coordinator is able to do this by rotating nurses from one floor to another to achieve the best coverage throughout the hospital. Such a person is important in keeping nurses involved in nursing rather than nonnursing functions.

The pitfalls of centralized scheduling are many. The staffing coordinator, unaware of the implications of clinical problems, may not understand that nurses need certain clinical expertise if they are rotated to more specialized units. Nurses are often placed into regimented schedules and offered no choices and few options for change. They are not included in the decision-making process, which leads them to frustration and feelings of helplessness and insignificance.

Policies for Centralized Scheduling

Without specific policies for scheduling employees, consistent and equitable treatment of

*Source: Thomas Kliber, *Modes of Scheduling*, Blue Cross of Western Pennsylvania, 1978.

**Source: Gloria Swanberg and Eunice L. Smith, "Centralized Scheduling: Is It Worth the Effort," *Nursing Administration Quarterly*, vol. 1, no. 4, © 1977 Aspen Publishers, Inc.

nursing staff is impossible. Typically, policies relate to approved shifts, number of weekends off, identification of weekend days for the night shift, minimum and maximum consecutive workdays, time lapse between shifts if personnel rotate, and the scheduling of holidays and vacations. Policies for both full-time and part-time employees should be delineated.

Head Nurse Participation. Head nurses should be held accountable for personnel expenditures over which they have control. This requires that they *participate actively* in determining the staffing needs for their individual units and *understand fully* the method of projecting full-time equivalents and calculating nursing hours per patient day (actual hours worked and total paid). Employees in staff departments with expertise in collecting and reporting statistics should furnish regular, timely, brief reports to their head nurses for quick reference in monitoring actual hours compared to budgeted hours.

Head nurses who have participated actively in determining the staffing needs, have projected the personnel budget for their units, and have meaningful, timely information regarding achievement of budgetary goals can and will be accountable for personnel expenditures over which they have control. If they have the authority to prepare and control their budgets, understand and support the scheduling policies, and have an opportunity for effective communication with the scheduler for their units, they will have little hesitancy to relinquish responsibility for scheduling personnel.

When the difference between line and staff functions is not understood, both by head nurses and by employees in the scheduling office, conflict may arise. The head nurses may feel they have lost authority, particularly when a question arises regarding the adequacy of the staff on their units to meet current needs. When employees in the scheduling office are not clear regarding their responsibilities and authority, they may feel totally responsible for controlling the budget, and their reactions may be extreme—either too rigid, alienating line personnel and impeding effective nursing, or too accommodating, attempting to do everything anyone requests.

Line vs. Staff Responsibilities under Centralized Scheduling

Confusion in responsibility and authority may result in staff personnel making decisions in areas where line managers are accountable.

Line positions in the nursing department are supervisory (management positions at the level of head nurse and above); these nurses are accountable for nursing care of patients on specified units or services. When scheduling is centralized, the employees in the scheduling office are in a staff relationship with management personnel in the nursing department.

The *line* functions for which the nurses in management positions should be responsible are the following:

1. Establishing and controlling the personnel budget.
2. Developing a master staffing pattern based on patient needs and the methods of assignment.
3. Developing procedures for adjustment of staff on a daily basis.
4. Establishing requirements for each position on the staff (such as assignment to an intensive care unit or charge responsibility).
5. Developing employees to meet requirements of their positions and evaluating their performance.
6. Hiring, promoting, disciplining, and discharging employees.

The *staff* functions for which the central scheduling office is responsible are the following:

1. Gathering facts and preparing reports for line personnel to facilitate budgeting.
2. Scheduling employees according to policies in staffing patterns established by line personnel.
3. Implementing procedures for reallocation of staff to meet daily needs; consulting

with immediate superior when demand exceeds supply.
4. Implementing procedures for position control.
5. Maintaining records needed by line managers for evaluation (regarding absenteeism, for example).
6. Maintaining effective communications with appropriate departments, such as payroll and personnel.

Decentralized Scheduling

Decentralized scheduling has helped to solve some frustrations. Nurses have more input into staffing patterns because the responsibility for staffing is entrusted to the unit supervisor, who is aware of the clinical needs and personal needs of the staff nurses. However, because the supervisor is not an expert in staffing methods and does not have access to clerical help, long tedious hours are spent in nonnursing functions. The schedule remains confusing and inconsistent in spite of sincere efforts.

Self-Scheduling*

Self-scheduling is the process by which staff nurses on a unit collectively decide and implement the monthly work schedule. Given the criteria for adequate unit staffing for each 24-hour period by the head nurse, each staff nurse chooses which day and shift he or she will work.

To implement a self-scheduling system, the head nurse sets up a series of meetings to

1. identify problems with the existing scheduling system
2. present self-scheduling as an alternative system

Source: Michelle Luckhardt Miller, "Implementing Self-Scheduling," *Journal of Nursing Administration*, March 1984. Reprinted with permission.

3. establish a few practice sessions with self-scheduling

Then, if the staff is in agreement to pursue self-scheduling as an alternative form of scheduling, the head nurse posts large signs containing specific criteria the staff must follow in filling out their monthly schedules. The criteria must indicate the number and mix of RNs, LPNs, and nursing assistants (NAs) needed to give quality nursing care to the patients for all shifts each day of the week.

After the criteria are posted, the staff nurses are obligated to fill in their schedules and to check the schedule periodically for conflicts that result from over- or understaffing. When these situations occur, and they will, the staff nurses must negotiate with one another to meet their scheduling needs and the needs of the unit.

Generally, it is helpful if the night and evening nursing staff fill in their schedules first, so that day staff can determine when they must rotate. The head nurse must emphasize to the night and evening staff, however, that they must cover their shifts as evenly as possible to be fair to the rotating day staff. Also, the rotating staff should be given criteria as to the expected frequency of rotations per month (Table 17-1).

Additional signs should remind the nursing staff of their own professional scheduling obligations. For example, preceptors should plan their schedules to coincide with their preceptees. Primary nurses and associate nurses should coordinate their schedules to provide for maximum continuity in their patients' care. Nurses also must remember to plan their schedules to include committee meetings, classes, and seminars they must attend.

Usually, vacations and holidays are handled through a sign-up sheet at the beginning of the calendar year and are supervised by the head nurse according to nursing department policy. For example, if there is a nursing department policy that no more than two nurses from the same unit can be on vacation simultaneously, then the group must adhere to this policy in negotiating their vacations. Holidays may be handled in various ways. There might be a sign-up sheet for the year's holidays to be negotiated

Table 17-1 Monthly Rotation Schedule

Rotation	Frequency (per month)
RNs to nights	3 nights
RNs to evenings	3 evenings
LPNs to nights	2 nights
LPNs to evenings	3 evenings
NAs to evenings	4 evenings

at the beginning of the year or every staff nurse might agree to work every other holiday. This also might be decided either by the group or nursing administration. Special requests for days off are simply designated by writing an "R" in the appropriate space.

Most important, the nursing staff must understand that it is their obligation to switch with a nurse of the same professional level (e.g., an RN switches with an RN, etc.) unless otherwise approved by the head nurse. It is not the responsibility of the head nurse to switch individual nurses to obtain adequate staffing. That is the responsibility of the nursing staff, RNs, LPNs, and NAs.

The head nurse will need to monitor the process occasionally for irregularities (e.g., paying overtime to an overzealous staff nurse), ensure fairness for the less assertive staff members, and nudge the process along if enthusiasm wanes.

Eliminating Obstacles to Self-Scheduling

Any dramatic change, such as self-scheduling, will meet with some degree of resistance. Staff nurses must either have or acquire appropriate interpersonal skills with which to negotiate their schedules with one another and develop the maturity to accept responsibility for adequately staffing the unit. These interpersonal skills do not develop overnight.

Specifically, the greatest resistance to this change will stem from the disruption of the staff's routine. Success with self-scheduling depends on the staff's ability and motivation to check and revise the monthly schedule periodically to ensure that the guidelines for adequate staffing for their unit are followed.

Flextime and Job Sharing*

Total Flextime. Under a total flextime arrangement, employees may come and go as they please; they need only to put in whatever total hours are required of them for the workweek (usually 35 to 40). They are of course required to accomplish the work expected of them.

Total flextime is impractical for all employees except for those rare individuals whose work is so totally independent of the work of others as to be appropriately accomplished at any time at all. Also, even when total flextime may appear appropriate within a work group, it can present problems or at least perceptions of problems in that it is vulnerable enough to potential abuses to appear to be uncontrollable.

Limited Flextime. Limited flextime allows workers the option of establishing their own starting and quitting times on the condition that they be present for a specified block of time that may be relatively broad or narrow.

Team Flextime. Under the team flextime concept all employees of a department or clearly designated team agree on their starting and quitting times as a group. This arrangement has been particularly popular with tightly unified work groups, such as operating room teams who may choose to arrange their schedule around surgeons' operating practices.

Job Sharing. Job sharing consists of two or more people working part-time and mutually arranging their schedules so as to fill one single position. The most common job-sharing situations involve two part-time employees filling one full-time position. One pertinent example would be the position of department secretary in the department of surgery in a particular hospital; this position is filled by two half-time employees who each work alternating weeks of three days and two days.

---

*Source: Charles R. McConnell, *The Health Care Supervisor's Guide to Cost Control and Productivity Improvement*, Aspen Publishers, Inc., © 1986.

APPROACHES TO SCHEDULING*

The Traditional Approach. Starting "from scratch" each month, the head nurse (or supervisor) makes the decision "by hand," taking into consideration quality and coverage. The major advantage of the traditional approach is its flexibility: Since the process is begun from scratch, any changes in the environment can be worked into the new schedule. Its disadvantages include coverage and quality that is uneven, nonstability (unless policies leave little flexibility), and high cost.

Cyclical Scheduling. First a four-week, six-week, etc., schedule which provides even coverage and high quality is determined for each unit, then this schedule is repeated period after period. Advantages include high quality (if the quality of the initial schedule is high), even coverage, high stability, and low cost. The overwhelming disadvantage is inflexibility to survive the changes which characterize the majority of nursing units.

The environments where cyclical scheduling seems to have the best prognosis are those that are the most stable, where nurses do not rotate between shifts, and where new nurses can be hired into an open cyclical "slot."

Computer-aided Traditional Scheduling. A third approach uses a computer to aid in keeping track of policies and past working patterns of nurses and to aid in the fast and more complete search through possible schedules for "good" ones. This approach offers the flexibility of the traditional approach but reduces operating costs considerably, and it can produce high-quality schedules consistently. It also facilitates incorporation of policies which add stability. The approach's advantages are most dramatic in situations where nurses rotate among shifts or where the nursing unit environment is subject to chronic change.

---

*Source: D. Michael Warner, "Nurse Staffing, Scheduling and Reallocation in the Hospital." Reprinted with permission from the quarterly journal of the American College of Hospital Administrators, *Hospital & Health Services Administration* (formerly *Hospital Administration*), Summer 1976.

Table 17-2 A Five-Week Cyclical Schedule

Nurse	S	M	T	W	T	F	S	S	M	T	W	T	F	S	S	M	T	W	T	F	S
#1	D				D					D	D					D					D
#2			D				D	D				D					D	D			
#3	D					D				D				D	D				D		
#4		D					D	D					D				D				D
#5			D	D					D					D	D					D	

Nurse	S	M	T	W	T	F	S	S	M	T	W	T	F	S	S	M	T	W	T	F	S
#1	D					D				D				D	D				D		
#2		D					D	D					D				D				D
#3			D	D					D					D	D					D	
#4	D				D					D	D					D					D
#5			D				D	D				D					D	D			

It has been estimated that approximately 97 percent of all hospitals use the traditional approach, 2–3 percent use some version of cyclical scheduling, with only a few using a computer-aided approach.

Cyclical Schedules

*Overview**

The cyclical schedule is a schedule that covers a designated number of weeks (cycle length) and then repeats itself. The cyclical schedule assigns the required registered nurses, licensed nurses, and total staff to each unit in a manner consistent with average patient care requirements, hospital personnel policies, and the nursing staff's preferences for the distribution of days off.

Cyclical Schedule Structure. Table 17–2 shows a simple cyclical schedule. There are five nurses and the cycle length of the schedule is five weeks. Days off are denoted by *D*. The first row indicates working days and days off for the first nurse, the second row for the second nurse, and so forth. The first nurse has the first Sunday off,

then a Thursday, then Tuesday and Wednesday off, and so on, until the five weeks are up, at which point the entire pattern of working days and days off begins again. The overall pattern of working days and days off is exactly the same for all of the nurses; the only difference is that it begins in a different week for each nurse. Thus, the schedule followed by the first nurse in the first week is followed by the second nurse the following week, the third the week after, and so on. The weeks start with Sunday and end with Saturday. Each nurse works five days a week, works at most four days in a row, and has two out of five weekends off. Four of the five nurses are always present except on Tuesdays and on weekends, when only three are present.

Problems. A schedule must meet staffing requirements and must be consistent with the hospital's personnel policies. Patient care requirements fluctuate from day to day and even from hour to hour; minimum staffing requirements consist of the minimum number and mix of nursing staff required to accommodate average patient care requirements.

It is not always easy to obtain agreement on minimum staffing requirements. Estimates from nursing supervisors tend to be somewhat biased in favor of more people, while estimates from hospital administration may be biased in the opposite direction. It is thus advisable to consult

Source: Except where noted, excerpts on cyclical scheduling are reprinted with permission from *Socio-Economic Planning Sciences*, vol. 7, Christopher Maier-Rothe and Harry B. Wolfe, "Cyclical Scheduling and Allocation of Nursing Staff." Copyright 1973, Pergamon Press, Ltd.

both sources. If patient care requirements fluctuate widely from day to day, it may also be worthwhile to analyze actual staff coverage over an extended period of time and to conduct interviews to find out what happened on days with a particularly large or small number of nurses on duty.

Hospital personnel policies usually reflect agreements reached between the administration and the nursing staff regarding the distribution of days off for nurses. These agreements specify, among other things, the precise beginning of the workweek, the number of days per week that must be given off, the maximum number of working days in a row, how many holidays are to be given off, the duration of vacations, and how many weekends are to be given off. They limit the types of cyclical patterns that are feasible. For instance, if four days off every two weeks are specified instead of two days off each week, the possible range of cyclical patterns is considerably increased.

Cyclical Pattern Alternatives*

Before a cyclical schedule can actually be assembled, patterns of working days and days

---

Source: Ibid.

off must be found which are consistent with requirements outlined.

Feasible patterns of working days and days off could be found through some algorithmic approach such as integer programming or a heuristic approach.

In one examination of scheduling for unit coverage by 12 staff members (5 RNs, 2 LPNs, and 5 aides), governed by various weekend, vacation, and other policy constraints, there were constructed 14 feasible alternatives, as shown in Table 17-3. The first four describe a 10-week cycle with a total of four weekends off, the next four a 12-week cycle with a total of five weekends off, and the last six a 12-week cycle with four weekends off. For easier comparison of the individual alternatives, the relative frequencies of occurrence of four-day weekends off, three-day weekends off, and so forth, are shown in Table 17-4, which indicates the pattern of days off for four of the alternatives. (A three-week schedule is shown in Table 17-5.)

The nurses preferred the cycles with more weekends off and therefore rejected the 12-week schedule with four weekends off. They were initially quite excited about the possibility of long weekends, a feature offered only rarely under the old scheduling procedures, but their enthusiasm was quickly dampened when they

---

Table 17-3 Fourteen Alternative Cyclical Patterns

Length of Cycle (weeks)	10				12				12					
No. of Alternative Patterns	1	2	3	4	5	6	7	8	9	10	11	12	13	14
No. of 4-day weekends off	1	0	0	0	1	0	0	0	1	0	0	0	0	0
Relative frequency (%)	10	0	0	0	8	0	0	0	8	0	0	0	0	0
No. of 3-day weekends off	0	2	1	0	0	2	1	0	1	2	2	1	1	0
Relative frequency (%)	0	20	10	0	0	17	8	0	8	17	17	8	8	0
Total No. of weekends off	4	4	4	4	5	5	5	5	4	4	4	4	4	4
Relative frequency (%)	40	40	40	40	42	42	42	42	33	33	33	33	33	33
No. of 2-day periods off	2	2	2	2	2	2	2	2	3	4	3	4	3	4
Relative frequency (%)	20	20	20	20	17	17	17	17	25	33	25	33	25	33
No. of single days off	6	6	7	8	8	8	9	10	7	6	8	7	9	8
Relative frequency (%)	60	60	10	80	67	67	75	83	58	50	67	58	75	67
No. of 6-workday stretches	2	2	1	0	2	2	1	0	4	2	0	1	0	0
Relative frequency (%)	20	20	10	0	17	17	8	0	33	17	0	8	0	0
No. of 5-workday stretches	2	2	1	0	2	2	1	0	3	4	3	2	2	2
Relative frequency (%)	20	20	10	0	17	17	8	0	25	33	25	17	17	17

Table 17-4 Days Off in Patterns 1, 4, 6, and 11

	Week in Cycle											
	1	2	3	4	5	6	7	8	9	10	11	12
Sunday	1 4		1 4		1	4		1 4				
	6 11		6	11	11	6	11	6		11	6	
Monday		4	1	1		4						
					11	6	6					11
Tuesday					4	1	1 4			1 4		
			11	6	6				11	6	11	
Wednesday	4				4	1	1		1 4			
		6 11			6				11	6	11	
Thursday						4		1	1 4			
		11	6					6 11	6	11		
Friday	1	1	4					4				
	6 11					11	11				6	6
Saturday		1 4			1	4	1 4			1 4		
		6	11			6 11	11	6		11	6	6 11

Table 17-5 Three-Week Schedule for Nursing Unit Staff

Nurse	S	M	T	W	T	F	S	S	M	T	W	T	F	S	S	M	T	W	T	F	S
A	x	o	x	x	x	x	o	o	x	x	x	o	o	x	x	x	o	o	x	x	x
B	o	x	x	x	o	o	x	x	x	o	o	x	x	x	x	o	x	x	x	x	o
C	x	x	o	o	x	x	x	x	o	x	x	x	x	o	o	x	x	x	o	o	x

Note: This three-week schedule of nursing service averages 37⅓ hours per week per person. Longest work span is four days. Schedule provides for seven days off, including one weekend, and an extra day.

Source: *Practical Approaches to Effective Functioning of the Department of Nursing Service,* 1972. Reprinted by permission of the American Hospital Association. This publication is no longer available.

realized, however, that these could usually only be achieved by allowing longer stretches of working days in a row.

The advantage of presenting to the nurses alternative cyclical patterns is that the trade-offs between desirable distributions of days off on the one hand and undesirable stretches of working days on the other are made quite explicit, and the choice is made by the nurses rather than imposed upon them.

Six- and Seven-Week Schedules. For six- and seven-week schedules see Tables 17-6 and 17-7.

Two-Week Schedule. In a repeated two-week pattern, each staff member receives every other weekend off, plus one weekday off during the beginning or end of the week. The net effect is that no one works more than four consecutive days. Each member is assigned an individual two-week pattern to repeat continuously.

Table 17-6 Six-Week Cyclical Scheduling

	M	T	W	T	F	S	S	M	T	W	T	F	S	S	M	T	W	T	F	S	S	M	T	W	T	F	S	S	M	T	W	T	F	S	S	M	T	W	T	F	S	S
1		X	X						X	X						X	X						X	X						X	X						X	X				
2				X							X	X						X						X	X						X							X	X			
3	X	X				X	X	X	X				X	X					X	X						X	X						X	X						X	X	X
	2	2	2	2	2	3	3	2	2	2	3	3	3	3	2	2	2	3	3	2	2	2	2	3	3	2	2	2	3	3	2	2	2	3	3	2	2	3	2	2	2	2

2		M	T	W	T	F	S	S	M	T	W	T	F	S	S	M	T	W	T	F	S	S	M	T	W	T	F	S	S	M	T	W	T	F	S	S	M	T	W	T	F	S	S
1		X	X						X	X						X							X	X						X	X						X	X				
2				X	X	X					X	X	X					X						X	X						X							X	X			
3	X	X	X				X	X	X				X	X			X	X				X	X					X	X			X	X							X	X	X	
4				X			X	X			X			X	X				X						X				X	X			X					X				
	3	3	3	3	3	3	2	2	3	3	3	3	3	3	2	3	3	3	3	2	3	3	3	2	3	3	3	3	3	3	3	3	4	3	3	3	3	2	3	3	2	2

ALTERNATE 2		M	T	W	T	F	S	S	M	T	W	T	F	S	S	M	T	W	T	F	S	S	M	T	W	T	F	S	S	M	T	W	T	F	S	S	M	T	W	T	F	S	S
1		X	X						X	X						X							X	X						X	X						X	X				
2				X							X	X							X						X	X					X							X	X			
3	X	X	X				X	X	X				X	X			X	X				X	X					X	X			X	X							X	X	X	
4			X	X			X	X			X			X	X				X						X				X	X			X					X				
5	X	X				X	X	X	X				X	X			X	X				X	X					X	X			X	X							X	X	X	
	4	4	3	3	4	4	4	4	4	4	4	4	4	4	4	4	4	3	4	4	3	4	4	4	3	4	4	3	4	4	4	4	4	3	4	4	4	4	3	4	3	3

continues

Table 17-6 *continued*

TWO WEEKENDS IN SIX CONSECUTIVE SINGLE DAYS OFF
SEVEN CONSECUTIVE DAYS WORKED
TEN WORKED PER PAY PERIOD

Source: Thomas Kliber, *Modes of Scheduling,* Blue Cross of Western Pennsylvania, 1978. Reprinted with permission.

Table 17-7 Seven-Week Schedule

NURSE	WEEK	1							2							3							4							5							6							7						
		S	M	T	W	T	F	S	S	M	T	W	T	F	S	S	M	T	W	T	F	S	S	M	T	W	T	F	S	S	M	T	W	T	F	S	S	M	T	W	T	F	S	S	M	T	W	T	F	S
Straight 1 days		d	d	d	d	o	d	d	d	d	o	o	d	d	d	d	o	d	d	d	d	o	o	d	d	d	d	o	o	d	d	o	o	d	d	d	d	o	d	d	d	d	o	d	d	d	d	o	d	d
Straight 2 evenings		o	e	e	o	o	e	e	e	e	o	o	e	e	e	e	o	e	e	e	e	o	o	e	e	e	e	o	o	e	e	o	o	e	e	e	e	o	e	e	e	e	o	e	e	e	e	o	e	e
Straight 3 nights		n	o	n	n	n	n	o	n	n	o	o	n	n	n	n	o	n	n	n	n	o	n	n	o	o	n	n	n	n	o	n	n	n	n	o	n	n	o	o	n	n	n	n	o	n	n	n	n	o
Rotating 4 d-e-n		o	d	d	e	o	d	d	d	d	o	o	e	e	d	d	o	n	n	o	d	d	d	o	d	d	e	e	o	d	d	o	d	d	e	o	e	e	o	n	n	o	d	d	o	e	e	o	n	n
Rotating 5 d-e-n		d	d	d	o	d	d	d	d	o	o	d	d	o	d	d	o	d	d	o	d	d	d	d	o	d	d	o	o	d	d	o	d	e	e	o	o	d	d	o	o	d	d	o	d	d	d	o	d	e
Rotating 6 d-e		e	o	o	d	d	o	o	d	o	o	d	d	d	o	o	d	d	d	o	o	d	o	d	d	o	d	e	e	d	d	d	o	o	d	d	d	d	o	d	d	d	d	d	d	d	o	d	d	d
Rotating 7 d-n		d	n	o	o	d	d	d	o	d	d	d	d	d	o	d	o	d	d	d	d	o	d	n	o	o	d	d	d	d	n	o	o	d	d	n	d	d	o	o	d	d	d	d	d	d	d	d	o	d

Note: Staffing standard for this unit calls for three nurses on day tour, one on evening tour, and one on night tour. On basis of 40-hour week, seven nurses are required. Nurse man-hours per week total 280; days, 3 × 56 hours (8 hours × 7 days) = 168; evenings, 1 × 56 hours = 56; nights, 1 × 56 hours = 56. Key: d = day, e = evening, n = night, o = off.

Source: *Practical Approaches to Effective Functioning of the Department of Nursing Service*, 1972. Reprinted by permission of the American Hospital Association. This publication is no longer available.

*Advantages**

Cyclical scheduling, once established, provides all of the following advantages:

1. The amount of highly skilled professional time spent on scheduling functions is reduced. Once a master rotation plan has been developed, trained clerical personnel can prepare and maintain schedules—freeing nursing time for more direct patient care functions.
2. The "good" and "bad" days off are spread equitably among all employees. The premises of cyclical scheduling require standard rotation of days off—distributing "good" days, such as weekends, fairly among all.
3. Schedules can be known in advance (almost ad infinitum) by each employee. This contributes to personnel satisfaction by making it easier for employees to plan their personal lives. It also reduces the number of absences that occur because of social events. By knowing their time schedule far in advance, nurses can plan many of their social events to occur on their scheduled days off.
4. The scheduling of correct numbers and mixes of personnel on duty each day is simplified. Once a master schedule has been developed which provides the correct number and mix of personnel, it can be virtually recopied each time period. The need to continuously count and adjust while developing a schedule is abolished.
5. Continuity of care is provided by minimizing "floating." With the correct number and mix scheduled each day for each unit, the "plug-the-holes" process is virtually eliminated.
6. Work groups develop team synergy by stabilizing scheduled days off and lessening floating. A master schedule provides coverage for days off by the same part-time or full-time personnel—allowing the advan-

tages of stabilized work groups to evolve. This aspect of scheduling is frequently overlooked, resulting in a helter-skelter selection of nurses who must work with great disadvantages.

Computer Scheduling

*Overview**

In concept, the scheduling task is simple; it involves a matching of each nurse's scheduled days off and days on duty to the particular staffing requirements of a given nursing station for a given day for a given shift. In practice, it is far from simple. No matter how carefully the scheduler works things out, it seems that a day inevitably comes when half the staff is scheduled for a day off, and the scheduler must do some heavy bargaining and fast rearranging in order to come up with a minimum complement. Or, conversely, a day comes when everybody is scheduled to show up and does. In such a situation, one can only wish that all this skilled experienced nursing talent had turned up when it was really needed, not just when it was scheduled to appear.

Under these circumstances, it is not surprising that those who are concerned with the problems of the hospital as a functioning system have turned to the computer for some help in solving the nurse scheduling problem. In response, the computer and its programmers have come up with some very ingenious schemes, some of which even work moderately well. The most sophisticated of these are the fully computerized on-line systems which produce a nurse-by-nurse printout of who goes where and when.

Schedules under this system take a variety of individual and system constraints into account and the computer prints out what, in its opinion, is the optimal solution—given that somebody has to take the duty.

The kind of work the computer does best: sifting through large masses of data at nano-

Source: Patricia L. Eusanio, "Effective Scheduling— The Foundation for Quality Care," *Journal of Nursing Administration*, January 1978. Reprinted with permission.

Source: John Jameson, "A Computer Assisted Solution to Optimal Nurse Staffing" (AIIE Conference Paper, February 1976), Blue Cross of Western Pennsylvania, 1976. Reprinted with permission.

second speed, rejecting data which do not fit the constraints, and printing out an optimal solution. However, the nurse scheduling problem must first be translated into computer language by setting constraints to be applied to the scheduling algorithm. For example:

> *Constraint 1*—No nurse will be scheduled to work more than ten shifts in any two week pay period.
> *Constraint 2*—Each nurse will be given three weekends off in six, etc.

One system takes into account such factors as the existence of a "float" nurse and part-time staff and calculates a daily workload index for each nursing unit in order to determine not only when a nurse should be scheduled to work but where exactly he or she should go. The system also takes into account such factors as requested days off and vacations and schedules accordingly. The only apparent flaw in this system is that it requires a fairly extensive operations research job on each nursing unit it covers before the computer has enough data to make its decisions.

Making the Transition*

When introducing automation in the scheduling office, the importance of addressing staff satisfaction with a well-designed software system is imperative. Prior to beginning automation of scheduling, current scheduling practices within the organization must be evaluated. Automation of a poor scheduling and staffing system will produce similar poor results . . . only quicker.

The following concerns should be addressed:

- What is the current scheduling practice?
  —Who currently generates the schedules?
  —How much time does schedule generation and modification require?
  —How are schedules communicated to a central staffing office?
  —How are schedule changes communicated?

- Do current policies and procedures exist regarding
  —weekend rotations?
  —shift rotations?
  —granting requests?
  —overtime?
  —variable shift lengths?
- If these policies and procedures are in existence, are they consistently applied within the organization?
- What is the outcome of the current scheduling practice and systems?
  —Does scheduling of staff match the requirements of patients in the units?
  —What do quality of care measures reveal with current scheduling practice?
  —What is the level of staff satisfaction regarding their schedules?
  —What is the cost of current scheduling practice in staff turnover, overtime, and outside agency utilization?

This survey of present practices will become the first step in an assessment of computerization needs for scheduling.

SHIFTS

Overview*

There has been much discussion of the benefits of altering the traditional patterns in scheduling, the standard eight-hour shifts, to new and different configurations.

Labor Laws and Unusual Shifts

The Fair Labor Standards Act supplies the basic provisions governing hour and wage regulations and determines the conditions under which overtime pay is allocated. Two conditions are set for employees working in the hospital services industry:

Source: William P. Sheridan and Clare Mitchell, "Automated Scheduling: The First Step or Last," *Healthcare Computing and Communications*, September 1987.

Source: "Review and Analysis of Changed Work Schedules in Hospitals," William Clint Johnson, Manpower Administration, Department of Labor, May 1975. (Unpublished Contract Grant DL 91-48-72-37.)

1. In a one-week period, overtime is paid for time in excess of 40 hours in the weekly period.
2. In a 14-day period, overtime is paid for time in excess of 8 hours in any day or 80 hours for the 14-day period.

These conditions permit a freedom in scheduling arrangements without incurring high additional costs for overtime wages. Depending on which base is chosen and the designated start of the workweek, little or no extra expense is incurred with a 10-hour shift for four days a week, a 12-hour shift for three days one week and four days the next, or a 9-hour shift for seven consecutive days on and seven off. Two daily meal periods, 30 minutes each, are disallowed from the hour count on the longer shifts.

Various configurations can be worked out to meet special demands of the nursing units and hospital departments. However, employees must agree in advance to the work-hour arrangements. Statements of the work arrangements should be added as an item of the hospital's preemployment policy.

Shift Options*

It is important for staff nurses and nursing administrators to be aware of the various options in work schedules, as well as the advantages and disadvantages of each. The staff nurse will then be able to select the scheduling pattern best suited to meet his or her need. The nurse administrators will be able to select the scheduling pattern best suited to meet the staffing needs of their floor or unit.

Eight-Hour Shifts

Planning staffing for employees on the eight-hour shift includes arranging for staffing for three shifts—days, evenings, and nights. The day shift begins at 7 AM and ends at 3:30 PM, the evening shift begins at 3 PM and ends at 11:30

PM, and the night shift begins at 11 PM and ends at 7:30 AM. Full-time employees on the 8-hour shifts work five days a week for a total of 40 hours per week. Staff may work permanent days, evenings, or nights, or they may rotate to different shifts.

Advantages of the 8-hour shift may include these:

- The traditional work day is 8 hours. Therefore the body does not have to adjust to an extended workday.
- Staff may have the option of selecting from three shifts the shift they prefer to work.

Disadvantages of the 8-hour shift may include these:

- The 8-hour shift schedule does not allow staff to have every other weekend off.
- It does not permit the employee to have several consecutive days off.
- The 8-hour shift results in unsafe traveling times. Individuals on the evening shift leave work at 11:30 PM and individuals on the night shift come to work at 11 PM.
- Nurse administrators must plan staffing for three different shifts.

Ten-Hour Shifts

The most popular configuration for the 10-hour shift is the 10-hour day, four days a week (the 4/40 workweek). (See Table 17-8.) Various other configurations include: two days of 12-hour shifts followed by two days of 8-hour shifts, or seven days of 12-hour shifts followed by seven days off. Other institutions have utilized 10-hour days on either one or two shifts. Some have used a 10-hour shift, 5-hour shift, 10-hour shift for days, evenings, and nights respectively in order to recruit more part-time nurses for the evening shift.*

Advantages of the ten-hour shift may include these:

- It allows for several consecutive days off.
- Employees can have more weekends off.

---

*Source: Except where noted, material on shift options is from Sherri R. Rasmussen, "Staffing and Scheduling Options," Critical Care Quarterly, vol. 5, no. 1, © 1982 Aspen Publishers, Inc.

---

*Source: DHHS, Pub. No. (HRA) 77-15, 1977.

Table 17-8 Personnel Staffing Schedule: Ten-Hour Shift

No.	NAME	1ST WEEK							2ND WEEK							3RD WEEK							4TH WEEK						
		S	M	T	W	T	F	S	S	M	T	W	T	F	S	S	M	T	W	T	F	S	S	M	T	W	T	F	S
A-1		X		X	X			X	X			X	X		X	X		X	X			X	X		X	X			X
B-1			X		X	X		X		X			X	X	X		X			X	X	X		X			X	X	X
		1	2	1	1	1	1	1	1	2	1	1	1	1	1	1	2	1	1	1	1	1	1	2	1	1	1	1	1

LONG WEEKENDS

No.	NAME	S	M	T	W	T	F	S	S	M	T	W	T	F	S	S	M	T	W	T	F	S	S	M	T	W	T	F	S
A-2		X		X	X			X	X		X	X			X	X	X		X	X		X	X		X		X	X	X
B-2			X				X	X		X				X	X		X				X	X			X			X	X
		1	1	2	1	1	1	1	1	1	2	1	1	1	1	1	1	2	1	1	1	1	1	1	2	1	1	1	1
		2	3	3	2	2	2	2	2	3	3	2	2	2	2	2	3	3	2	2	2	2	2	3	2	2	2	2	2

Source: Thomas Kliber, *Modes of Scheduling*, Blue Cross of Western Pennsylvania, 1978. Reprinted with permission.

- Individuals on different shifts have an opportunity to work together, improving staff interpersonal relationships.
- The overlap of shifts allows for more personnel at busy times and for lunch and dinner coverage.
- Staff members are able to take advantage of unit classes, hospital in-services, patient care conferences, staff meetings, and interdisciplinary conferences occurring during the overlap of shifts.
- During overlap of shifts, staff may have the opportunity to work on unit and hospital projects and committees.

Disadvantages of the ten-hour shift may include these:

- The longer work hours may lead to fatigue of staff.
- With the prolonged workday, the workdays seem to be all work, with little time for relaxation.
- The 10-hour shift also results in unsafe traveling times for the evening and night shift staff.
- It requires more employees than the 8- and 12-hour shift schedules.
- Nurse administrators must plan staffing for three different shifts.

To implement such a shift, changes, such as the following, would be necessary:*

- Establishment of a new system of priorities (e.g., baths no longer given in the morning).
- Holidays and vacations scheduled in terms of hours rather than days. For example:

5-day week: 10 holidays × 8 hours = 80 hours
4-day week: 8 holidays × 10 hours = 80 hours

*Seven on—Seven off.*** When the longer shift of 10 hours is combined with a pattern of

*Source: Thomas Kliber, *Modes of Scheduling*, Blue Cross of Western Pennsylvania, 1978.

**Source: DHHS, Pub. No. (HRA) 77-15, 1977.

seven days of work followed by seven consecutive days off, you have a 7/70 schedule, a radical departure from traditional schedules.

At Mercy Medical Center in Dubuque, Louisiana, the same number and mixture of personnel is on duty 7 days a week, with each employee given every other weekend off. The staff is split into two groups, each nurse working 70 hours in a two-week period (there are two 10-hour shifts and one 5-hour shift each day). Other changes include standard extra pay for working holidays and the scheduling of in-service and educational programs during the employees' time off. Among the administrative benefits of the new schedule have been a reduction (by 26 percent) in employee turnover, nursing care hours, and overtime hours. Results of a survey conducted by an independent research group showed that RN satisfaction was 6 percent above industry norms and 8 percent above the hospital employee norm, but less for part-time employees.

Following are the principal benefits of the seven on—seven off shift:

- increased utilization of space and equipment
- improved service to patients
- increased morale and efficiency
- greatly reduced absenteeism
- reduced personnel costs

Twelve-Hour Shifts

Planning staffing for employees on the 12-hour shift includes arranging for staffing for only two shifts—day and night. The day shift begins at 7 AM and ends at 7:30 PM; the night shift begins at 7 PM and ends at 7:30 AM. Full-time employees on the 12-hour shift may work three days for two weeks and four days a third week; in other words, 36 hours per week for two weeks and 48 hours per week for one week. This averages 40 hours per week. Staff may work permanent days or nights or they may rotate from one shift to the other.

Instead of head nurse and assistant head nurse being assigned to evening shifts and no night shifts, it is possible to have the busy part of evening shift covered by supervisory personnel and the slow part relegated to limited coverage—

a savings for the hospital of at least half of supervisory salaries used formerly for the evening shift. Other advantages of the 12-hour shift may include these:

- Twelve-hour shifts provide for several consecutive days off.
- Employees can have more weekends off (e.g., every other weekend).
- Employees have more time to pursue recreation and leisure interests.
- Twelve-hour shifts allow safe traveling hours.
- Employees have fewer days on duty, therefore decreasing traveling time to and from work.
- Twelve-hour shifts decrease the time spent in change-of-shift reports—two per 24 hours compared with three for the 8- and 10-hour shifts. This provides more time for patient care, patient teaching, or staff education.
- The same nurse is caring for a patient when physicians make morning and afternoon rounds. Thus the nurse is able to describe to physicians the patient changes and treatment effectiveness.
- Fewer staff positions are needed.
- Twelve-hour shifts seem to be a drawing card for recruitment.

Disadvantages of the 12-hour shift may include these:

- The longer working hours may lead to fatigue of staff.
- The half-hour allotted for change-of-shift report may not be sufficient time.
- Attendance at in-service education programs, staff meetings, and nursing care conferences may be reduced because nurses work fewer days.

How does one bring about an organized schedule change? As with all changes, it requires in-depth planning, supervised implementation, and evaluation.

Planning Phase. To begin, the literature on 12-hour shifts is reviewed. Other institutions, floors or units, and personnel already on 12-hour shifts or who have experience with 12-hour shifts are contacted. This will point out further advantages, disadvantages, and suggestions for implementation.

Important in the planning phase is involvement of the nursing staff in this change. Nurses should be involved in the development of a written proposal to change to 12-hour shifts. The entire nursing staff should understand the use of 12-hour shifts in other institutions, the foreseeable use of 12-hour shifts on their floor or unit, and the advantages and disadvantages mentioned in the literature. Possible strategies to minimize the disadvantages can be discussed with the staff.

A proposal for implementation of the shift should include the following:

- Which floors or units will be involved in the schedule pattern change.
- When the schedule change will be implemented and how long the trial period will be (usually three to six months).
- Specification of shift hours. Usually the first or day shift is from 7 AM to 7:30 PM, and the second or night shift is from 7 PM to 7:30 AM.
- A discussion of meals and coffee breaks during a 12-hour shift. Breaks include one 30-minute meal period and two or three 15-minute coffee breaks or rest periods.
- The schedule pattern for full-time and part-time staff. Full-time employees work three days for two weeks and four days a third week.
- Discussion of holiday, vacation, and sick time. These benefits are usually unchanged and are the same as for full-time staff on an 8-hour shift.
- Payroll considerations. Shift differential and overtime pay must be addressed; overtime pay is usually paid for any hours in excess of 40 hours per week.
- Time for staff development classes. Most classes are only 8 hours long; therefore, the

other 4 hours of the shift are either spent working or taken as vacation or leave of absence.

- Advantages and disadvantages plus strategies to minimize the disadvantages.
- Plans for evaluation.
- A breakdown of the duties for the day shift and night shift for each floor or unit.

Implementation. The proposal for 12-hour shifts is carried out in the implementation phase. During implementation it is crucial for head nurses, supervisors, and staff nurses to assess how the new shifts are working out. Nursing administrators should be available to answer questions staff may have regarding the shifts and to identify problems, develop strategies to solve the problems, and communicate these strategies to the involved staff.

Evaluation. The evaluation process should include several phases. The first phase takes place immediately on completion of the trial phase; the second, one year after implementation; and the third is ongoing. Areas to be evaluated include quality of patient care, job satisfaction among nurses, cost-effectiveness, the work environment, the health status of the nurses, and nurse fatigue and alertness.

Chapter 18

Adjustment Techniques for Staffing

In the 1990s meaner and leaner hospital environment, staff adjustments have taken on more complex and serious overtones. The last-minute daily scramble to cope with an unexpected surge in the patient population or an intensification of patient care needs has always been considered part of the job. Harried and overwrought, the nurse manager, over the years, has developed a number of techniques to control the daily crisis situation. These are discussed below, with special emphasis given to the handling of understaffing, the most common of problems.

The real difficulty today lies in the cost-containment need to terminate staff—which can result in an insufficient number of employees. To soften the harsh reality of the staff reduction trend, several terms have been adopted to indicate different levels of termination and the motivation behind them. *Layoff* traditionally refers to letting go of employees until conditions get better. This may be optimistic thinking, although staff members may get rehired on a part-time basis if the cuts were too drastic. *Reductions in force* is more definitive, referring to a permanent termination of employees due to required staffing changes. The term *downsizing* may be used as a euphemism, as it suggests streamlining operations and readjusting positions. Frequently, however, staff cannot be relocated and

are let go. As a result, some procedures are made more efficient, others more narrow in scope or discarded.

Whichever term is used, the nurse manager must plan ahead, exercise tact, and be aware of the constraints and ramifications of the manner in which staff reduction is performed.

DAILY STAFF ADJUSTMENTS

Staffing adjustments should not be confused with regular scheduling. Scheduling is concerned with planning for personnel usage throughout the year—taking into account the changing needs due to shifts, seasons, holidays, vacations, and the full range of predictable factors.

Staff adjustments, on the other hand, are concerned with unexpected conditions, the day-to-day variations in need or situation that result in overstaffing or understaffing.

Unfortunately, such variations cannot be accurately forecast. Adjustments must be made not only if supply is to be matched with demand but also if the amount of absenteeism on any given day is to be reckoned with.

Staff adjustment can be called reallocation, and it is done centrally (or decentrally, among divisions of the hospital) each shift, with the assignment of the float nurses and/or the "pull-ing" of nurses from the units to which they were originally scheduled.[1]

The process is in two phases. First, the demand for nursing care services must be measured on each unit, taking into account the current number, type, and condition of patients.

The second stage is to adjust such demand to the supply, which includes the "core" staff (permanent staff scheduled to a particular unit), the float and/or "pull" staff, and outside resources.

There are a wide range of techniques available for making adjustments for both understaffing and overstaffing.

Methods for Handling Understaffing

If a specific station is understaffed while another is overstaffed, a nurse may be floated (i.e., reassigned to another station). Pool personnel can also be used to cover shortages on specific stations. If it becomes apparent that the nursing stations in total will be understaffed for a given shift, several steps can be taken. Part-time employees assigned to nursing units and assigned to the nursing pool can be contacted and requested to work an extra shift. In addition, an "on-call" pool has been developed to cover in such situations; these people can also be contacted. Another mechanism to add needed personnel is to utilize temporary professional nurse agencies. Basically, the system has been constructed so as to be able to expand on short-term notice; however, anticipation of and planning for these situations are of key importance.[2]

One considerable concern when using any short-term adjustment technique is the adequacy of preparation of nurse replacements in a practice arena which is becoming more and more clinically specialized. To combat this problem, some nurse managers are utilizing a preparatory system called *cross-training*.

Cross-training is the preparation of individuals to function effectively in more than one area of professional responsibility. Within nursing, cross-training involves the preparation of registered nurses for delivery of patient care in more than one clinical specialty at an institution.

Nurses cannot be expected to maintain competency in specialties that are not similar. Therefore, nursing departments should establish companion or "sister" units—cross-training groups that are comparable and related. Examples of cross-training groups include

- labor, delivery, and postpartum care nurses, newborn nursery, pediatrics
- neonatal intensive care unit and pediatric intensive care unit
- intensive care unit, coronary care unit, emergency care nurses
- medical-surgical preoperative and postoperative units, medical units
- mental health units, substance abuse units, eating disorder units
- day surgery and recovery nurses

The cross-training program should provide for the same orientation to the unit as is provided all new employees. In-service education and staff development activities are shared between nursing and education departments. Skill checklists for all specialty orientations should be completed, kept available for reference, and filed according to the hospital procedure.[1]

Advantages of cross-training for the manager include increased ability to deal with changes in census and acuity and greater availability of qualified nursing personnel. Apparently, for the staff member, the process heightens professional satisfaction, providing increased stimulation as a result of exposure to more than one unit.

---

[1]D. Michael Warner, "Nurse Staffing, Scheduling and Reallocation in the Hospital," *Hospital & Health Services Administration*, Summer 1976.

[2]Merrill Lehman and Q.J. Friesen, *A Centralized Position and Staffing Control Administered by Non-Nursing Personnel*, Methodist Hospital, St. Louis Park, Minnesota, 1975.

[1]Joyce Rhodes, "Staffing and Resource Development," in *Managing for Productivity in Nursing*, Barbara Rutkowski, ed., Aspen Publishers, Inc., © 1987.

Note: A more recent development which extends the cross-training concept is *clustering*. Clustering refers to using multi-unit-trained staff interchangably in two or more related units on any given day. This system maximizes the resource pool for each of the clustered units.

1. Floating Nurses

Few nursing administrators like the idea of using floating nurses, yet running a nursing department would often prove unmanageable without them. A national survey of *Nursing '75* discovered that 54 percent of all nurses have to float; 42 percent said they are often pulled from one unit to another. Many of them are unhappy doing it; most of those who were against floating felt that nurses couldn't provide quality of care in a variety of hospital units. Others clearly indicated that they liked familiar surroundings and wanted to feel that they were part of a group. Obviously, the use of floating nurses should be minimized. But when they are used, here are some suggestions for making them more comfortable and effective.

1. Conduct an in-service program where head nurses of different units explain the special demands and procedures of their units. Have nurses take notes or distribute summaries which can be used as a reference guide during the float assignment.
2. Allocate assignments that a float can perform with confidence. Ask nurses to list unit preferences and keep a file of potential float nurses for each unit. This also builds up a corps of float nurses who become familiar with particular units.
3. Delegate a "float-orientation nurse" in each unit who will give the floater a 15-minute introduction to unit needs and arrangements as well as answer questions.
4. Inquire of the float nurse, after the shift is over, what aspects on the unit were most difficult. Include explanations of these matters in the next orientation.
5. Remember courtesies; thank both the float nurse and the head nurse from whose unit he or she was released.

2. Nursing Pools—Permanent*

A nursing pool can be of key importance to the staffing system, as it provides needed flexibility.

Source: Excerpts on Methods 2, 3, and 4 are from Merrill Lehman and Q.J. Friesen, *A Centralized Position and Staffing Control Administered by Non-Nursing Personnel*, Methodist Hospital, St. Louis Park, Minnesota, 1975.

The size of the pool can be varied by the staffing coordinator to meet projected patient care needs. For example, in the Methodist Hospital in St. Louis Park, Minnesota, there are three separate area pools—a medical-surgical pool, a pediatrics-OB/GYN pool, and an intensive care pool. Nurses who are recruited for each of the pools receive orientation to all stations within their respective areas and to each nursing station in the hospital. While they may float to any station in the hospital, the nurses in the pools normally float only within their area of training. Each nurse reports to the assistant staffing coordinator before each scheduled shift to receive his or her station assignment.

Pool nurses are scheduled on a monthly basis, as are all employees in the hospital. As permanent vacancies occur on nurses' stations, pool employees transfer to a nurses' station, thus providing the hospital with a reservoir of trained employees who can fill permanent station assignments.

3. Flying Squad

An added "wrinkle" to the system normally not seen in many hospitals is the use of a "flying squad." The flying squad, normally consisting of two nurses, is not assigned to any specific station, but moves from station to station throughout the shift based on varying needs of the stations during the shift. The flying squad members carry pocket pagers so that head nurses in need of additional help can easily reach them. The flying squad will actually work on several different stations during each shift, thus often overcoming the necessity of providing extra staff on several stations just for the purpose of meeting peak activity times. Again, flexibility is added to the system.

4. Controlled Admissions

The first day of patient stay, particularly for nonelective admissions, imposes more than twice the demand on nurse staff than do subsequent days. Given some choice in placing a new admission, plus knowledge of the number of intensive and first-day patients on each unit, there is a potential for stabilizing workloads by selective admission to units.

5. Part-time Employees*

Part-time employees may work either the 8-, 10-, or 12-hour shifts, but work only part-time. Hospitals throughout the country offer part-time work.

Advantages of part-time work may include these:

- Part-time employment may broaden an individual's horizons beyond home or school, increase income, give ego satisfaction, and help maintain nursing skills.
- Hospitals frequently give part-time employees hospital benefits prorated according to the percentage of time they work.
- Since part-time nurses receive hospital orientation, they are aware of the various resources, policies, procedures, and standards of care.
- Part-time nurses work at the same hospital consistently and are therefore usually better informed about hospital policies and procedures.
- When part-time nurses' outside responsibilities decrease, they are likely candidates for full-time work.
- Part-time nurses tend to work more than their share of unpopular hours.

Disadvantages of part-time work may include these:

- The educational and administrative expenses are higher for part-time than for full-time employees, because it is likely to cost as much to orient a part-time nurse as a full-time nurse.
- Part-time employees decrease continuity of patient care because they only work part-time.
- Since they only work part-time, part-time nurses may not develop the commitment that full-time employees do.

---

*Source: Sherri R. Rasmussen, "Staffing and Scheduling Options," *Critical Care Quarterly*, vol. 5, no. 1, © 1982 Aspen Publishers, Inc.

6. Per Diem Employees*

Per diem (or prn) nurses are hired by the hospital to work as needed. Per diem nurses plan their schedules with the hospital. Then if the hospital finds that on a given day it does not need the per diem nurse's help, the per diem nurse is canceled for that day. Per diem employees may work whatever schedules the hospital offers. Advantages of per diem employment include these:

- Per diem nurses usually are allowed to make their own work schedules, except that a set number of weekends and nights must be scheduled.
- Per diem nurses receive more money per hour than do career or part-time nurses.
- Out of desire to keep the job, prn nurses are more apt to fill in when staff are needed to work.
- Per diem nurses are frequently required to work a set percentage of weekends and nights, which may decrease the friction between career and per diem employees.
- Per diem nurses are interviewed and hired by nursing service. Therefore nursing service is aware of the educational and experiential level of each per diem nurse. With this information, their assignments can be made so that they work on the floors or units where they have experience.
- Per diem nurses work at the same hospital consistently. Therefore, they are better informed about the unit and floor environments and about the hospital's policies and procedures.

Disadvantages of per diem work may include these:

- Per diem nurses do not receive hospital benefits such as sick pay, vacation and holiday pay, and insurance.
- Per diem nurses are employed by hospitals only when career positions are open and temporary staffing is needed. Per diem nurses therefore do not have job security.

---

*Source: Ibid.

7. Shared Services Pool*

One shared services organization, composed of seven member hospitals, implemented a program to provide nursing personnel on an on-call or as needed basis to its member hospitals. The organization itself employs nursing personnel who are sent into the member hospitals upon request to compensate for census peaks, vacations, and employee absenteeism. Three individuals manage the nursing personnel department: a director, a scheduling coordinator, and an RN consultant.

With few exceptions, utilization on a day-to-day basis does not vary significantly. Requests for personnel usually decrease beginning Friday before any three-day weekend or holiday and are usually higher on days hospital employees are paid. Requests by shifts also remain fairly constant in distribution. Fifty-nine percent of the total requests are for the 7–3 shift, 29 percent for the 3–11 shift, and 12 percent for the 11–7 shift.

Requests for nurses are received by telephone and logged on scheduling sheets by the department coordinator. Requests are received from as little as one hour to up to several weeks before the shift to be filled begins. Although nursing personnel call in for scheduled work at weekly intervals, they are called by the coordinator for last-minute requests.

Nursing personnel are oriented in each hospital in which they decide to work. The length and type of orientation depend upon the institution's needs.

A cost formula has been developed to compute the actual cost of personnel on the basis of current and projected salary levels, shift differentials, and taxes.

Hospitals are charged a flat hourly rate for each classification of personnel regardless of the individual's salary level or the shift worked. However, a shift differential is paid. The rates are calculated to cover personnel costs and program overhead and include a 4 percent contingency factor.

A break-even point was reached after the program had been operative for about 12 months and a sufficient volume had been attained. The current rates for the shared services personnel are about 12 percent lower than those of area commercial pools.

Temporary Help Agencies*

No matter how methodically planned, there will be peaks and valleys and unanticipated discontinuities in either patient census or staffing needs or both. It is just this circumstance, the need to have vacancies filled economically on a per diem basis, that makes privately run temporary help agencies so useful.

These agencies are the legal employers of nurses (and other health service workers) whom they recruit, interview, and place in institutions with which they have agreements. In addition to placement they offer the worker such services as withholding tax accounting, bonding, and malpractice insurance. The hospital pays a fixed amount per shift. Aside from saving on recordkeeping and payroll expenses, the hospital is relieved of the duty to contribute to social security, unemployment insurance, and workers' compensation and provide holidays, sick leave, vacations, bonuses, health plans, and inservice training for agency people.

Advantages

The first and most obvious advantage of using supplemental agencies is cost. Besides a saving per shift in payroll, clerical work, and fringe benefits, there is a reduction in hidden administrative expenses. Only a minimal full-time staff need be supported, and the need for maintenance of a part-time pool is eliminated. The overall efficiency of matching available part-time personnel in a community with the flexible needs of its institutions' fluctuations in demand or need for staff is a very attractive concept.

Another advantage to hospital management is the fact that agency-employed part-timers can be used as a lever or disciplinary force. They are a

Source: Douglas K. Woollard, "Shared Services Organizes Its Own Nursing Pool," *Hospitals*, vol. 50, no. 10, May 16, 1976.

Source: Madalon M. Amenta, "Staffing through Temporary Help Agencies," *Supervisor Nurse*, December 1977. Reprinted with permission.

constant reminder to possible balky permanent staff that they can be replaced easily and cheaply. They might help in cutting down absenteeism, turnover, and overtime pay.

There is considerable saving of middle management effort. Supervisors sometimes spend 60–75 percent of their time securing shift coverage. It takes only a few minutes to call the agency and say, "We need ten nurses for the 11–7 shift Wednesday night." Agencies provide an immediate backup in emergencies, such as "flu" decimating a staff, holiday absenteeism, or local disasters that strain the health care system.

Disadvantages

There are, however, many disadvantages in this whole arrangement. Sometimes a nurse's credentials have not been thoroughly checked before he or she is sent to a job. Even when a nurse has been responsibly certified, before being sent to a facility, there is no guarantee he or she will be properly oriented after arrival. Hospitals think agencies should handle it and vice versa. While some agencies do keep the orientation literature and the procedure manuals of their client institutions on file, their use is optional.

Other abuses affect patient safety and quality of care. Some hospitals will not hire associate degree graduates as regular staff until they have had experience, yet they take whomever the agency sends.

In general, any temporary people present problems for the head nurse, since they are not familiar with the hospital, the unit, its procedures and policies or routines of care.

A head nurse can spend a minimum of one hour, possibly up to two hours, with each new temporary orientee before the "helper" even comes up with the inevitable questions that all beginners ask; all orientations need reinforcement throughout the day. At best, the charting of new people has to be checked; at worst, actually done. Extra time slips must be filled out. There may be any number of other added paperwork chores, depending on the particular circumstances.

When an institution comes to rely on temporary agency help for a fixed proportion of its staff, not just in the extraordinary situation, there is a documented downward spiral in quality of care and staff morale. In the beginning, regulars welcome temporaries as help in a crisis and relief from imposed overtime. Then, as a temporary-regular mix becomes a stable condition, and the hospital stops hiring new regulars to fill vacancies, more regulars leave and the hospital hires even more temporaries. For the regulars who remain, there are incrementally heavier patient loads and unattractive schedules. Soon they start leaving. To fill the gap, still more temporaries are hired. As soon as a certain ratio (around 33⅓% temporaries) becomes fixed, the difficulties faced by the regulars become so great and the knowledge of it so widespread in the community that fewer and fewer good nurses are willing to sign on as regular staff. The best people in town stay away; the least able take the jobs. Ineluctably, overall quality of care deteriorates.

This brings us to the most fundamental disadvantage of overreliance on temporary help, the deleterious effects on patient care. The modern health care system is fragmented enough without patients having to see a different nurse, not just every shift, but for every procedure. Vital energies that otherwise might go into recuperation are used up in the repeated adjustments to relays of people. When a professional nurse doesn't see a patient many times a day or even daily, he or she can't pick up the significant changes in status that mark improvement or decline. The nurse has no baseline on which to make judgments about the effects of care and treatment. Temporaries barely manage the procedural work; they can't begin to approach teaching and counseling.

Guidelines for Using Temporary Help Agencies

Temporary help agencies do have a place, but that place must be well defined. Criteria should be devised and responsible surveillance imposed. (See Table 18-1 for the elements of a model agreement.)

The ideal arrangement fits the right person to the right temporary job in a bona fide emergency. The agency itself should keep records indicating the specialties, the hospitals, and the units nurses not only prefer but seem most suited

Table 18-1 Supplemental Staff Agency and Hospital Interactions

AGREEMENT[1]

Agency Agrees to

-screen nurse to verify qualification (license) and competence (previous experience) (records available to hospital on demand)

-pay nurses—including responsibility for taxes, FICA, etc.

-assume responsibility for workers' compensation and general liability

-require employees to work within hospital policies and procedures

-pay for one-day orientation for each nurse

-release agency nurse for permanent hospital employment after 14 days' written notification from the nurse, upon mutual agreement between the nurse and the hospital

-maintain shift rates for one year, amended only by mutual agreement.

Hospital Agrees to

-use contracted agencies exclusively, *if they can meet our needs*

-notify the agency of cancellations more than one hour before the shift or pay for four hours (hospital reserves the right to then employ the nurse for four hours)

-authorize the director of nursing designee to ask any agency nurse deemed incompetent, negligent, or engaged in misconduct to leave with payment only for hours worked

-provide a one-day orientation for each nurse

-maintain the shift rates for one year, amended only by mutual agreement.

DOCUMENTATION FOLLOW-UP[2]

External

To familiarize the agency with the nursing department, the hospital should:

-provide position descriptions and applicable policies to the agencies.

-provide written evaluations on each agency employee assigned to the hospital

-provide copies of applicable nursing policies and procedures on each nursing unit

-provide all positive and negative observations regarding agency employees functioning at the hospital as well as all incidents involving the agency nurses.

Internal

The hospital should maintain a file of agency employees who are preferable, to include:

-Verification of license and renewals.

-Evidence of pre-employment physical examination.

-Evaluation, following ten shifts, and annually thereafter.

-Documentation of inservices, annual CPR certification, and safety and infection control reviews.

-Skills checklist.

[1]*Source*: Donna R. Sheridan, Jean E. Bronstein, and Duane Walker, "Using Registry Nurses: Coping with Cost and Quality Issues," *Journal of Nursing Administration*, October 1982. Reprinted with permission.

[2]*Source*: Adapted from "Agency Nurse Guidelines," *Help News*, Vol. 4:6, June 1981, Alexander & Alexander.

for according to documented feedback from the facilities at which they have already worked.

The hospital nursing department should be especially aware of the hiring practices of the agencies it uses. Crucial is the knowledge of the quality of a nurse's work experience and depend-

ability. These should be rigorously investigated and monitored. As a rudimentary precaution, identification should be checked when the nurse first comes to work and a record of his or her past experience and performance in the hospital should be maintained. If the nurse refuses to work with certain kinds of patients (those with infections, those on respirators, etc.), both the agency and the hospital should know.

When determining which units to staff with temporaries, nursing administration must deliberate long and carefully. Generally it should use regular staff in high-pressure units where the pace is swift and new situations arise quickly, because these are the areas where orientation is difficult and mistakes with grave consequences are most likely to occur. It is here that the temporary nurse can be most easily traumatized.

As a general rule, it is more sound to restrict the use of temporaries to less pressured areas where vacancies can be anticipated well in advance and a thorough orientation given. Vacations and holidays can be planned far ahead of time in an orderly, reasonable way.

Another safety and quality measure for nursing administration would be for it arbitrarily to limit the total percentage of overall use of temporaries on any given unit. All staffing patterns should be reevaluated at six-month to one-year intervals and reformulated on the basis of current staffing standards, statistical records, changing needs, values, and practices.

Finally, since nursing administration is liable for the temporary nurse who is not performing adequately, it should provide charge nurses easy access so that problem temps will be identified and will not be reassigned until their defects are dealt with. An agency should know it will be dropped if it persists in not meeting the standards of the hospital or honoring its requests.

Short-Term Overstaffing*

In the Methodist Hospital (St. Louis Park, MN), they have been able to contract their staffing to meet short-term decreased patient care requirements. This is done by means of a requested absence (RA). If it is found that the nursing stations in general will be overstaffed on a given shift or during a given period, the

assistant staffing coordinator will contact scheduled nursing employees and ask if they would prefer not to work. Often nursing employees are willing to comply with the request. Since this method is mutually agreeable to both the nursing service and the employee, an efficient means of dealing with temporary overstaffing is created. During the employment interview and the staffing orientation session, employees are notified of this option. The option has proved to be quite popular.

Policies for Implementation

- The staffing office may request that an employee take an RA day or the staff member may initiate the request for an RA day by notifying the staffing office. The RA must be mutually agreeable to both the employee and the staffing office.
- Employees contacted to take an RA day are responsible for notifying the staffing persons if they are to work charge, etc., on the proposed RA day.
- The total RAs taken by one employee may not exceed 20 days (160 hours) for one year.
- There will be no loss of time in calculating benefits during a requested absence.
- RA days may not be used in lieu of leave of absence days.

HANDLING STAFF REDUCTIONS

Developing a Staff Reduction Plan*

It is imperative that a staff reduction plan for nursing be developed in advance of the need for it, so that a thorough and objective system can be designed. Last-minute plans for a layoff are invariably ill conceived and implemented and result in more organizational chaos than is necessary. The time to plan for a staff reduction is before a crisis occurs, when there is time to think

---

*Source: Merrill Lehman and Q.J. Friesen, *A Centralized Position and Staffing Control Administered by Non-Nursing Personnel*, Methodist Hospital, St. Louis Park, Minnesota, 1975. Reprinted with permission.

*Source: Katherine W. Vestal, "Staff Reduction: The Nursing Administrator's Role," *Nursing Administration Quarterly*, vol. 8, no. 2, © 1984 Aspen Publishers, Inc.

clearly and objectively about the staff reduction process.

This plan must be designed to include issues related to not only the employees being laid off, but also the employees who remain. The remaining employees represent a far larger group and require careful reassurance about the organization and their own job security.

Basic areas that should be addressed are the following.

- *Indicators for decisions regarding staff reduction.* At what point, financially or otherwise, will the decision be made to reduce staff? What criteria will be used to determine the number of positions to be abolished? Which positions will be eliminated? What will the target staff mix and numbers be?

- *Options and alternative plans.* What options, long- or short-term, will be considered? What are the criteria to determine if long- or short-term problems exist? What are the advantages and disadvantages of each option?

- *Criteria for determining employees to be reduced.* What policies on staff reduction exist? Are the criteria clearly spelled out (e.g., seniority, job performance, etc.)? Are there union contracts prescribing layoff procedures? Are data available on each employee to assist in ranking (e.g., length of employment, special qualifications, age, race, education, sex, job performance evaluations)?

- *Implementation plan.* Has a timetable been developed that allows time for the reduction process to be conducted smoothly? Who and what will the reduction affect, and where and when will the effects occur? Have all managers been thoroughly educated in the process? Have employees been informed of the deteriorating financial state of the institution? Is the plan workable and reasonable?

- *Evaluation plan.* Is there a plan to evaluate the staff reduction process? Are mechanisms for communicating with staff in place? Could the process have been handled better in any manner?

The value of a cohesive, well-designed, and well-written plan cannot be underestimated. In fact, such a plan actually allows the nursing administrator to be more sensitive to the staff during difficult times, rather than be sequestered in a room, initiating a crisis plan. A nursing plan, coordinated with the entire hospital personnel arena, allows nursing to be at the forefront in policymaking and to protect essential positions as difficult decisions are made.

General Approach to Limiting or Reducing Staff*

Staff reduction is never popular no matter where it takes place, be it in industry or the health care field. However, there are times when circumstances make it necessary.

There are some general points which should be kept in mind by nurse administrators when considering action leading to staff cuts.

- Staff adjustments should take into account activities and the corresponding skill level required. Wholesale and indiscriminate reductions could purge the nursing service of valuable people having important talents. This should be avoided.

- The total staffing in an area should initially be adequate. A 5 or 10 percent across the board cut in all nursing unit rosters, while of minor consequence to overstaffed areas, can seriously hinder operations where units are already undermanned.

- The means of effecting the staffing reduction should be carefully weighed. Some causes of action have greater impact than others. If the same ends can be achieved through expected normal attrition or encouragement of early retirement, this is certainly a better approach than causing wholesale layoffs on an indiscriminate basis. While the latter is certainly quick and sure, the former, taking some amount of planning and work, would produce the more positive results from a personnel relations standpoint.

---

*Source: "Selected Procedures and Methods of Staff Reduction," Haricomp Guide Series Publication, Pub. No. 79a, 1975. Reprinted with permission.

Long-Term Techniques for Downsizing*

In the following discussion of how to reduce staff, an attempt has been made to present the less extreme methods first and the more drastic measures last. The exact rank is open to individual preference. (Table 18-2 contains a different sequence of staff reduction measures.)

Attrition. If time permits, staffing can be adjusted on a long-term basis through attrition. Such action can be difficult if

- the rate of attrition, departmentwide, is low
- the rate of attrition in a given unit (because of size or type of work) is low
- the time to achieve reduction is short

While attrition is not necessarily the way to end up with optimum staffing in a department (it's possible that the most productive persons will leave), it is one of the most "painless" means of reducing staff.

Overtime. Work should be planned in order to be accomplished in a normal workweek. In cases where the workload varies because of sudden heavy inputs that cannot be normally handled or deferred, overtime can be authorized. The same argument holds for emergency work.

A review of overtime hours might point out the need for a revamping of personnel scheduling. Too often inflexibility in scheduling can induce overtime where it could otherwise be avoided.

Transfers and Promotions. Where there are apparent cases of under- as well as overstaffing, efforts should be made to transfer employees within the hospital and between nursing service units, keeping requirements in mind.

This can be encouraged by posting job openings for which any qualified employee can apply. Worker morale and loyalty can be significantly improved with this type of well-administered program. In other circumstances the personnel department may have to act as the agency to match personnel from over- to under-staffed departments.

Source: Ibid.

Table 18-2 Sample Sequence for Downsizing

Step 1: Attrition—over the course of three months only essential vacancies are filled.

Step 2: Temporary early retirement—a temporary early retirement program is offered to all eligible employees.

Step 3: Elimination of management positions—the management structure is streamlined and positions are eliminated.

Step 4: Conversion of a number of full-time to part-time positions—to increase the percentage of variable staff, designated full-time staff become part-time.

Step 5: Terminations—implemented as a last step to minimize actual numbers affected (depends on effectiveness of previous steps).

Source: April J. Rozboril, "Systematic Downsizing: An Experience," *Journal of Nursing Administration*, vol. 17, no. 9, September 1987.

Promotion from within is based on similar arguments and further encourages employee performance in the hope that when appropriate openings occur, they will be filled from within.

Leave of Absence (LOA). The department should encourage the taking of extended leaves of absence such as educational LOAs. The impact on the budget would not be major inasmuch as usually only the barest of benefits are carried in cases of authorized LOA.

Reemployment could be contingent on there being positions open at the time a person on leave would seek to return. The exception to such a policy would be with respect to military leaves, for which the returning employee is guaranteed a position.

Retirement Phase-outs. Hospitals have long kept employees on the payroll even though they have passed the widely recognized retirement age of 65. Following such a practice unfortunately penalizes the hospital in many ways. The elderly employee may present a picture of marginal productivity (in labor-intensive, non-professional positions) and increased injury/illness days; yet often, because of seniority, they enjoy the largest salaries and the most vacation days in their job classification.

Replacement might be possible or a shift to a lower paid position as part of an evaluation of duties and/or a departmental organization.

Minimize Part-time Staffing. An attempt should be made to minimize the use of part-time staff.

This might be done through rescheduling existing full-time personnel or combining the workload of many part-timers to create a lesser number of positions.

Elimination or restriction of hiring of temporary or supplemental staff should be considered. Where the reason for using such personnel is uneven scheduling of workload, attempts should be made to balance the ''peaks and valleys'' with the resulting loss of need for temporary help. Another common situation which causes a ''need'' for staff is the failure to preplan vacation schedules. A disciplined policy for taking earned vacation time should cause few if any staff shortages during these times.

Interhospital Transfers. Where severe overstaffing exists, the personnel department might attempt to arrange employee transfers to other hospitals in the area where appropriate positions are open. These workers would be considered as ''new employees'' in their new employment, but would also enjoy relative job continuity.

Management Engineering. Management engineering can be of use to the department in indicating performance levels and improvement areas.

A review can be made to determine if, in fact, a valid need exists for the hiring of new or replacing vacant positions in the department.

A check could also be made to determine if positions could be reclassified to a lower level based on existing departmental requirements.

Usually savings can be effected with the creation of a vacancy, since the new employee could be paid at the reclassified, lower rate.

Disciplinary Enforcement. In tight labor markets or when there is a high demand for personnel, enforcment of disciplinary policies tends to become relaxed. A problem worker will be toler-

ated because replacing him or her could be difficult. The reverse corollary is also true.

Incompetency and Probation Dismissals. In somewhat of a similar vein, supervisors and head nurses may have identified some of their staff as being incompetent in the work required of them. When faced with a staff cut, various means should be taken to encourage these employees to resign.

Also, as a prelude to a general layoff, consideration should be given to the dismissal of employees currently on a probationary status.

Layoff. A layoff of staff should be a last resort after all other attempts at trimming personnel have been exhausted.

People affected by the layoff should be given a thorough explanation of the circumstances and be informed of what efforts were made to find positions for them by the personnel department.

They should further be advised that as circumstances change, they will again be considered for employment, but this period of layoff could last for an extended number of months.

Finally, they should be fully informed of their unemployment status and told of their unemployment entitlements.

Preventing Labor Problems Stemming from a Reduction-in-Force Action*

Responsible managers who want to avoid major labor-management problems will give careful consideration to the legal precepts and practical factors that should guide decisions about a reduction in force (RIF).

The RIF policy should be developed by the executive management team with the advice of the hospital's labor relations consultant or labor attorney. All levels of management should be trained in the interpretation and application of the policy.

Fairness can be achieved by a RIF policy that is designed to treat similar cases alike, avoiding

*Source: Richard Ashton and JoAnne Ashton, ''RIF: The Legal and Practical Considerations,'' *Aspen's Advisor for Nurse Executives*, vol. 1, no. 2, © 1985, Aspen Publishers, Inc.

partiality, discrimination, or arbitrariness in selecting employees to be laid off. Ideally, the RIF policy should provide for psychological and vocational counseling, placement services, and severance pay.

In a unionized hospital, the procedure for a RIF will be established by the contract. Deviation from the terms of the contract by either party will result in a labor dispute that will have to be resolved by arbitration or litigation. In those hospitals where union contracts do not exist, a RIF policy should be established to guide all levels of management in planning for and implementing employee reductions. A properly developed policy will reduce the risk of acting illegally and will greatly assist in the maintenance of constructive employee-management relationships during and following the RIF.

A RIF policy should be designed to provide the hospital and nursing management with the greatest staffing flexibility possible while still being fair to the employees affected by its application.

*Minimizing the Risk of Discrimination.** The possibility that, in a layoff, the varying discrimination acts may come into play must also be examined. Strict seniority-based layoff procedures are the safest to use and easiest to implement. This, however, presupposes that the initial determinations as to which units will be subject to layoffs are based on objective criteria. An employer's decision to make reductions in a particular department or classification, although facially neutral, could have an adverse impact on protected groups if the chosen department or classification has a disproportionate number of protected employees. Thus, employers are well advised to review how the policy will work when applied during an actual layoff *before* a layoff is announced. If the "test run" results in a disproportionate impact on a particular protected group, the policy should be reexamined for hidden bias.

_____

Source: Martin E. Skoler, *Health Care Labor Manual*, Aspen Publishers, Inc., © 1981.

Part IV

Operations

Chapter 19

Operational Reviews

THE COST- AND QUALITY-EFFECTIVE NURSING DEPARTMENT*

In 1988, the National Commission on Nursing Implementation Project identified four major characteristics of effective, high-quality, cost-effective nursing departments: delivery-related features, evaluation-related features, market-related features, and policy-related features.

Included among the *delivery-related features* are (1) working relationships among nurses, physicians, and other members of the health care team; (2) roles that incorporate authority, autonomy, and responsibility and offer appropriate compensation; (3) involvement of nurse managers in preparing the budget, managing resource utilization, and preserving a safe practice climate with acceptable outcomes; and (4) market knowledge concerning the ability to efficiently produce a service that will sell or draw consumers.

Evaluation-related features include (1) mechanisms for determining consumer satisfaction and providing feedback to the unit and to the practitioner, along with the monitoring of

retention rates; (2) a consumer feedback mechanism; (3) supervisor and peer evaluation; and (4) a nursing QA program. Additional components include an evaluation mechanism for assessing cost-effectiveness, quality standards, and productivity standards; a reliable and valid classification system; information systems with outcome measures; staff participation in designing cost accounting and reporting systems; and staff education about the systems.

Market-related features include features that affect the demand for nursing services, such as (1) the involvement of practicing nurses in the selection and evaluation of technology and programming used in the provision of client care, (2) information systems that track utilization patterns, (3) consumer input and regular program evaluation, and (4) involvement of nurses in public relation activities of the organization.

The *policy-related features* identified affect nursing's ability to influence overall policies in the organization. These include (1) the formal placement of nursing so as to allow it to influence policy formation and implementation relevant to the organization as a whole, (2) membership of middle-management and clinical nurses in institutional committees that set policies and procedures for patient care at the operational and patient unit levels, and (3) the possession by nursing of accountability and authority over the fiscal resources for nursing practice.

Source: Virginia Del Togno-Armanasco, Susan Harter, Nannette L. Goddard, "Cost and Quality: Are They Compatible?" in *The Encyclopedia of Nursing Care Quality Volume I: Issues and Strategies for Nursing Care Quality*, Patricia Schroeder, ed., Aspen Publishers, Inc., © 1991.

Quality and Cost Indicators

To evaluate quality, each health care facility must first define and accept for itself a concept of quality. Secondly, it must identify all cost factors affecting the achievement of this quality. Once these concepts are defined and identified, they must be integrated into the facility's daily operational components. These actions result in the identification of patient care service as an essential indicator of the organization's overall performance.

Examples of *quality indicators* that can be utilized are the achievement level of nursing care standards, length of stay variances attributable to nursing actions, infection rates, and patient incidents attributable to nursing actions. *Cost indicators* affecting the achievement of quality that need to be evaluated are compliance with staffing standards, professional to nonprofessional personnel ratios, budgeted to filled position ratios, patient acuity, and compliance with salary and nonsalary budgets.

Source: Virginia Del Togno-Armanasco, Susan Harter, Nannette L. Goddard, "Cost and Quality: Are They Compatible?" in *The Encyclopedia of Nursing Care Quality Volume I: Issues and Strategies for Nursing Care Quality*, Patricia Schroeder, ed., Aspen Publishers, Inc., © 1991.

ORGANIZATIONAL AND MANAGEMENT EFFECTIVENESS

Essential Principles*

The Joint Commission recently distributed for review 12 key principles that are intended to characterize a health care organization's commitment to improve continuously its quality of care. These principles represent the first major step in the Joint Commission's plans to refocus

*Source: "Proposed Principles of Organizational and Management Effectiveness for Healthcare Organizations," *Agenda for Change Update*, vol. 3, no. 1, February 1989. Copyright 1989 by the Joint Commission on Accreditation of Healthcare Organizations, Chicago. Reprinted with permission.

and streamline its standards and to monitor organizational performance more effectively.

One of the prerequisites for improving an organization's clinical performance is organizational and management effectiveness. Therefore, the Joint Commission set out to identify those principles of organizational and management effectiveness that could serve as a basis for measurable indicators of effectiveness and for standards on which to base accreditation decisions.

1. Organizational Mission. The organizational mission statement clearly expresses the commitment to improve continuously the quality of patient care. The commitment is translated into measurable objectives and action plans through the organization's strategic, program, and resource planning processes. The mission statement and plans are mutually developed and regularly evaluated by the governing board and managerial and clinical leadership.

2. Organizational Culture. The organization fosters a culture that promotes a high degree of commitment to quality patient care. In promoting this culture, the organization seeks the involvement of all those who use or provide its services. The organization encourages self-assessment, open communication, appropriate participatory decision making, and fair conflict resolution among all levels of clinical and managerial personnel.

3. Organizational Strategic, Program, and Resource Plans. Strategic, program, and resource plans are based on a broad range of assessments pertaining to the external environment, access to care, adequacy of patient volume to support clinical competence, and quality of care judgments rendered by patients, their families, health care practitioners, other employees, payers, the community, and other organizational care providers. The planning process addresses the financial support needed to meet short- and long-term goals to improve the quality of patient care.

4. Organizational Change. The governing board and managerial and clinical leadership continuously assess the need and recognize opportunities for change prompted both internally and externally in order to plan and implement change in support of quality patient care.

5. Role of Governing Board and Managerial and Clinical Leadership. The organization's commitment to improve continuously the quality of patient care is reflected in the roles and performance of the organization's leaders. These expectations are translated into definitions of authority and responsibility and specific work objectives contained in written role/position descriptions. These leaders articulate the organization's values involving the continuous improvement of quality patient care, and they systematically seek, measure, and use the judgments and evaluations of patients, their families, health care practitioners, other employees, payers, the community, and other organizational care providers as an ongoing method of evaluating and improving the quality of patient care.

6. Leadership Qualification, Evaluation, and Development. The governing board and managerial and clinical leadership consist of well-qualified people who possess the knowledge, skills, attitudes, and vision for achieving the objective of measuring and continuously improving the quality of patient care. The leadership is regularly evaluated for its effectiveness in acquiring, utilizing, and coordinating resources and using information to promote the quality of patient care as delineated in their role expectations (e.g., job descriptions). In support of this effort, there is a well-conceived plan that addresses both internal and external opportunities for the growth and development of leaders to improve continuously the quality of patient care.

7. Clinical Competence of Independent Practitioners. Initial assessment and continued monitoring and evaluation of practitioners' clinical skills are intended to ensure that high-quality patient care is provided by each independent practitioner.

8. Human Resources. Recruitment, development, evaluation, and retention policies and practices are instituted to ensure that the health care practitioners and others who support patient care are competent and have appropriate skills, attitudes, and knowledge. Adequate staffing levels are maintained to meet the individual's role expectations as well as the organization's goals of continuously improving the quality of patient care.

9. Support Resources. Facilities, equipment, and technology will be acquired and maintained in accord with the mission statement and strategic, program, and resource plans. The decision-making process regarding facilities, equipment, and technology is characterized by broad-based participation among relevant parties.

10. Evaluation and Improvement of Patient Care. The monitoring, evaluation, and continuous improvement of patient care are overseen by the governing board and involve appropriate individuals and organizational units. This organizationwide assessment process integrates data from quality assurance, risk management, and utilization review and seeks ongoing feedback on the quality of care from patients, their families, health care practitioners, other employees, payers, the community, and other organizational care providers. The analysis of this information is used for short- and long-range planning decisions and is reflected in departmental objectives and job performance measures.

11. Organizational Integration and Coordination. To achieve continuous improvement of quality patient care, organizational leaders will ensure that there is appropriate communication, coordination, conflict management, and integration among relevant parties. Each department develops policies and procedures that recognize its responsibilities to other departments' efforts to improve the quality of patient care and explicitly delineate its responsibility for communicating and coordinating its patient care efforts with these departments.

12. Continuity and Comprehensiveness of Care. There are effective linkages developed and maintained with external care providers to ensure access, continuity, and comprehensiveness of care received by patients, including care before admission and after discharge.

Leverage Points for Increasing Organizational Effectiveness*

Leverage points are those few places where changes, often made with little intervention, within an underlying structure have pervasive results.

A key concern is how to find leverage points. How does one determine which structures to adopt? How does one know the operating forces and their strengths? Changes in seven primary leverage points can make a significant impact on patient care and nursing.

1. Leadership. Nursing leaders who make a difference stand for something, articulate a vision, and are committed, even under pressure. They empower themselves and others and create organizational structures that get results; they go beyond what seems ordinary to take risks. To redesign the work of nursing is to be vulnerable, because, in letting go of sacred cows, redefining quality, restructuring decision making, and offering incentive pay, leaders risk standing alone.

2. Governance. Governance defines power, reporting relationships, decision making, and access to information, and it is often the basis for managing conflict. Nurses, who make life and death decisions at the bedside, cannot be governed by a structure that renders them powerless in the organization. Shared governance offers one way to shift control and the power base. For organizations contemplating shared governance models, key considerations are the readiness of nurses and the potential for using the model organizationwide. Well-executed work redesign incorporates all departments, since shared governance by nursing alone risks "backlash."

3. Staffing and Scheduling. Clearly defining and coordinating centralized and decentralized functions and holding appropriate persons accountable can make significant differences in work and nurse-nurse relationships. Although this sounds simple, it is not. The key is balance.

Authority and accountability for staffing must be held by the nurse manager, with some scheduling responsibilities delegated to a centralized staffing office. This office functions in a staff or consultant relationship to the manager and not as a replacement.

Essential for well-managed scheduling are competent budgetary management and reporting systems that provide appropriate information when needed and in an understandable form consistent with reports used by the fiscal department. All players need to know what it costs to provide patient care and what revenues they generate to really share in the organization's work.

4. Rewards and Incentives. Organizations that have flexible plans (offering childcare as well as tuition support), that pay on the basis of performance, that use a pay scale not capped prematurely for nurses, and that recognize and promote nurses can exploit the complex needs of employees for rewards and incentives.

5. Career Development. Career development, along with training, compensation, and supervisory practices, is part of supporting and managing work.

Typically, career development practices have been fragmented and have not been compatible with creating challenging work and motivating individuals to approach their potential. Mentorships and partnerships with other practitioners are steps in the right direction, but they need to be complemented by practices such as providing regular sabbatical leaves and giving rewards for doing things differently and by structures such as those supporting "think tanks" comprising those at the bedside as well as their leaders.

6. Connections between Nursing and Other Departments. Work sampling provides objective information about apparently subjective problems. Issues such as reducing the amount of time between an order for medication and its administration are examined, solved, and monitored by steering committee members from involved departments. The departments directly involved have the benefit of ideas from those who are not.

Keeping the connections in place after a work redesign project and spreading connections

*Source: Gloria Gilbert Mayer, Mary Jane Madden, and Eunice Lawrenz, eds., *Patient Care Delivery Models*, Aspen Publishers, Inc., © 1990.

beyond the steering committee can be achieved in several ways. Organizationwide shared governance, multidisciplinary ad hoc groups for problem solving, and having people deal directly with those with whom they have a problem are examples of methods that have made a difference. Alignment of all disciplines toward organizational goals requires that changes made in the redesign process become part of the culture of the organization.

7. Physician-Nurse Collaboration. Work redesign offers a systemic way of resolving systemic problems. A multidisciplinary project requires the full participation of physicians who have organizational power or who provide informal leadership. As physicians and nurses share issues and "walk in each other's shoes," a foundation for mutual respect and trust is laid. Not surprisingly, nurses and physicians discover a strong, shared commitment to patient care. As the depth of the commitment to patients is uncovered and trust grows, nurses and physicians move from being adversaries to becoming *real* allies.

Collaboration between physicians and nurses requires negotiating roles. This can be done only by the physicians and nurses involved, and it necessitates a time commitment from each person. Once begun, the process becomes part of the cultural norm and is expected and rewarded. Organizations with a reputation for collaborative relationships between nurses and physicians hold a unique market position with respect to nurse recruitment and retention.

ASSESSMENT OF ORGANIZATIONAL PERFORMANCE

Overview*

When an examination of the organization's performance is undertaken, all of the indicators of productivity, costs, and quality are reviewed. In order to identify important trends, data are

Source: Vi Kunkle, *Marketing Strategies for Nurse Managers: A Guide for Developing and Implementing a Nursing Marketing Plan*, Aspen Publishers, Inc., © 1990.

collected retrospectively, preferably five years back. Budgeted data are compared to the actual by service or by unit. Some of the questions to be explored here are these:

- How cost-efficient is the nursing department?
- How productive is the nursing department?
- What were the self-defined quality ratings by unit and service?
- Is there an inverse relation between quality and productivity?
- Are some services more efficient than others?
- Is overtime justifiable?
- Do salary cost increases exceed the consumer price indexes?
- Are there appropriate levels of professional care?
- Are negative trends sporadic or subtle indications of major problems?

In order to provide the highest quality for the best price (the best value), the nursing department monitors the cost, productivity, and quality indicators monthly and annually, plotting five-year trends. Financial, productivity, and quality problems are identified by service and unit. Other questions for analysis are as follows:

- If productivity is increasing and hours per patient day (HPPD) decreasing, is quality affected? In other words, has short staffing affected quality?
- If overtime is increasing, are the actual staff positions less than budgeted (acuity data included in budgeted staff)? What justifies the overtime?
- If productivity is low and productive HPPD high, is low census the problem? If not, are vacations being given properly, or are there orientees on the unit?

Most administrators make use of a reporting format that can be used on a monthly basis to monitor unit financial management, productivity, human resource management, quality of care, and organizational development.

An Operational Audit*

An *operational audit* is an independent appraisal of the adequacy, effectiveness, and efficiency of an operational process. It entails determining the following general objectives:

1. What is the purpose of this operation? How effectively is the purpose being accomplished?
2. Is the purpose of the operation in congruence with the overall philosophy and purpose of the organization of which it is a part?
3. How effectively and how efficiently are the assets and resources (including personnel) utilized, accounted for, and safeguarded?
4. How reliable and useful is the information system supporting the operation? How well controlled is it?
5. What is the extent of compliance with outside contractual obligations, industry standards, and governmental laws and regulations?

Types of Questions in an Operational Audit

- What specific relationships exist with physicians, other departments, and external agencies, organizations, vendors, etc.?
- What credentials are necessary for the staff? How are they documented?
- What resource constraints exist in terms of staffing, equipment, space, supplies, and storage?
- What possibilities exist for marketing?
- Are departmental policies and procedures current?
- Is staff turnover a problem?
- Is recruitment difficult?
- Are any major projects planned or being implemented?
- Is the organizational chart in the department job description current and accurate?

Source: William L. Scheyer, ed., *Handbook of Health Care Materiel Management*, Aspen Publishers, Inc., © 1985.

- Does pricing adequately cover costs?
- What are the major problems the department faces?
- What sorts of routine analysis are performed?

Before concluding the interview, ask for a tour of the department and permission to interview the staff. Be observant of work conditions, employee attitudes, and diligence to the job during these periods.

1. Review the organization's long-range plan for applicable goals. Determine the current status of goal implementation.
2. Review applicable corporate policies and procedures and check for compliance.
3. Review departmental goals and objectives. Are they consistent with the long-range plan? Are they measured?
4. Review the departmental policy and procedure manual. Verify that required policies are in place and followed. Comment on discrepancies between policy and practice.
5. Review the quality assurance plan. Check for compliance. Review any written quality assurance reports prepared.
6. Review pertinent compliance and regulatory requirements. Acquire evidence that each requirement is complied with. Comment on any deviation.
7. Review the department description. Verify its accuracy through interviews and personal observation.
8. Determine consistency of goals, objectives, and policies and procedures at the corporate and departmental levels.
9. Review the job descriptions for all department personnel. Determine their accuracy through interviews with department management and staff and personal observations. Note any discrepancies.
10. Review the staff personnel files for
    - proof of licensure
    - discipline not in accordance with organizational policy
    - excessive staff turnover

11. Review patient or other opinion poll responses and incident reports. Note any repetition of complaints or incidents that indicate areas of potential liability.

12. Prepare flow chart of operations where applicable, based on your understanding of department operations gained through the above work. Submit the preliminary flow chart draft to the department director for review. Incorporate any revisions into the final copy. Analyze the flow chart for control strengths and weaknesses and consistency with external, corporate, and departmental dicta.

13. Review computer programming or systems requests and their current status. Evaluate the logic for acceptance or rejection of these.

14. Review the financial and utilization reports prepared by the accounting department. Analysis of these should give the auditor an understanding of department utilization of financial and personnel resources. Growth rates, seasonal variations in expenses and revenue, control of overtime, and so on, should become evident.

15. Review any formulas that compute departmental productivity standards. Determine whether or not these formulas are reasonable as a basis for standards.

16. Review past capital budget requests. Determine the reasonableness of the rationales for acceptance or rejection of these requests. Identify capital requests that may require construction work for installation. Is the construction costed and included in the cost of the capital request? If not, why?

17. Obtain a blueprint of the department floor plan. Evaluate how well the floor plan design accommodates the department's needs.

18. Review procedure manuals. Are they informative? Adequate? Understandable? Understood? Complied with? Consistent with corporate policies and procedures?

19. Conclude by referring to the audit objectives at the beginning of the program.

Evaluate to what extent the questions raised in the objective statements can be satisfactorily answered. Be specific.

20. Draft a report. Include all noteworthy comments and recommendations.

21. Plan future review and follow-up.

ORGANIZATIONAL CULTURE AND CLIMATE

Understanding the Organizational Culture*

Once the department's mission has been defined and a strategy formulated, the supporting structures, processes, and management of the organization—its *culture*—must be brought into alignment with the mission and the strategy. This often demands significant realignment to achieve effective implementation of the new mission and strategy.

Every health care organization has its own culture—one that can be measured, compared with the cultures of similar organizations, and managed to complement mission and strategy.

Culture is a body of learned practices that employees of an organization share and that they transmit to new employees. Simply stated, culture is "the way things get gone in the organization." The two principal approaches for measuring culture are the anecdotal approach and the quantitative approach.

Managing the culture for competitive advantage is the key to successful implementation of strategy, and executive management must take the lead.

Learning about the Culture

The Anecdotal Approach. Anyone who has worked in a health care or another organization develops a sense of the culture. Talk to people in that organization, and the stories will begin to provide a picture of the culture. This is what is meant by the anecdotal approach. Although

---

*Source: Michael R. Cooper and James B. Williams, "Managing Cultural Change to Achieve Competitive Advantage," in *Handbook of Health Care Human Resources Management*, ed 2, Norman Metzger, ed, Aspen Publishers, Inc., © 1990.

these stories and company myths provide a picture of the culture, they are not measurable, and their "fit" with a particular strategy can be difficult for the health care executive or manager to evaluate.

The Quantitative Approach. The quantitative approach to culture measurement relies on objective data about the organization and its culture. These data are gathered through face-to-face interviews; observation; analysis of organizational levels, staff size, and reporting ratios; and systematic collection of perceptions about the culture through questionnaires. Information is collected about *management practices*—what managers do and how they do it. With this approach, culture can be measured in a way that enables comparison with other organizations and provides a basis for making changes in the organization's culture and monitoring their effects.

A framework has been developed to organize and condense information about culture in a meaningful and useful way. The core dimensions to be examined in each culture assessment are as follows:

- *Clarity of direction*: the extent to which the organization relies on formal and complete planning systems and has established clear courses of action. (Have plans and goals been well formulated? Have the strategy and the plans and goals been communicated to appropriate management down the line?)
- *Decision making*: the degree to which decisions are systematically formulated, implemented, and reviewed. (Are information systems providing the information needed for decision making? How centralized is the decision-making process? Are the organizational structure and staffing levels appropriate in light of the strategy?)
- *Organization integration*: the degree of coordination, cooperation, and communication among units in the organization.
- *Management style*: the pattern of encouragement and support for initiative taking and openness. (How much freedom to act do managers have? Are managers encouraged to take risks, or does top management

send out a "play it safe" message? How are conflicts aired and resolved?)
- *Performance orientation*: the degree of emphasis placed on individual accountability for clearly defined end results. (Are the managers held accountable for achieving these results?)
- *Organizational vitality*: the dynamic nature of an organization as reflected by its responsiveness to change in its business environment, the development of pace-setting programs, and the creation of venturesome goals. (Is this a fast-paced, market-responsive organization, or is it conservative and slow paced?)
- *Management compensation*: the extent to which the compensation system is seen as internally equitable, externally competitive, and tied to performance. (Is the compensation program consistent with the business strategy and designed to elicit appropriate behavior?)
- *Management development*: the degree to which the organization provides opportunities for advancement and developmental experiences to prepare people for higher-level jobs.
- *Identity*: the organization as a place to work and the image projected to employees and outside constituencies.
- *Quality of care*: the perceived extent to which the organization delivers high-quality health care, encourages employees to focus on providing quality care, and provides them with the necessary resources, direction, and support to accomplish this goal; also, the degree to which employees judge their work to be of high quality.

Understanding the Hospital Climate*

A hospital culture impacts decision making, performance, activity, relationships, and com-

*Source: Mark B. Silver, "Success Strategies: Victor or Victim?" in *The Health Care Executive Search: A Guide to Recruiting and Job Seeking*, Earl A. Simendinger and Terence F. Moore, eds., Aspen Publishers, Inc., © 1989.

mitments. Before implementing plan, a health care leader must first know what are the perceptions within the corporate climate. Achieving needed changes requires that there must be accurate identification of the positive as well as the negative perceptions which operate within the hospital. Meaningful data are needed; diagnosis must precede the planning.

Identification. Identify what the staff is proud of and what makes the hospital special. What are the positive, energizing sets of beliefs or emotional forces within your hospital. List the positive attitudes and perceptions that knit the staff together.

Correction. What does not need fixing? What is working well here and should not be changed? Internally, what is being done right and effectively? Where is cohesiveness and cooperation in meeting the external challenges evident?

Structure. How clear and effective are assignments, tasks, and the organizational charts? To what extent does the hospital's structure facilitate or hinder the achievement of goals? How does its structure facilitate or hinder coordination in getting jobs done?

Systems. Where do the arteries of information flow or get clogged? Are you getting adequate and sufficient information downward or between departments? Identify where you need more reliable, faster, and more current communications.

Symbolism. A culture rewards and reinforces acceptable behaviors; management pays attention and gives emphasis to what it considers important by rewarding different results. What symbolic behaviors tell you what is acceptable and what is not acceptable? What symbolic behaviors are rewarded or punished here? To what does management pay great and ongoing attention or pay little or inconsistent attention?

Shared Values. Cohesive and consistent beliefs provide pride and direction through visions. List positive values and visions of this hospital. List negative values, which hide in the "little corners" among the employees.

Strategy. Key result areas and identified ways to achieve successful and sustainable

effects are critical in competitive times. Identify where you are getting mixed signals (confusion) regarding strategy. What strategy targets of this hospital do you want to know or have clarified?

Barriers. "We versus they" barriers can paralyze action. Where is the administration enslaved and encumbered by bureaucratic habits, out-of-date systems, unnecessary rituals, and comfort? Identify ways you can de-layer, de-value, and de-manualize. What rules, which interfere with relations, can you change?

Trust. Describe the level of team interaction and trust in your hospital. List adjectives you hear which reflect trust and openness between people. Identify situations or areas where there is organizational gridlock, lack of decision making because of artificial walls, broken trust, and poor communication.

MANAGEMENT OR OPERATIONAL CONTROL

The Distinction between Operational and Management Control Systems*

The purpose of operational control systems is to ensure that specific tasks are carried out in accordance with well-defined expectations. The performance of a task is monitored continuously, and whenever it is found not to be within the standard, prespecified corrective mechanisms are triggered so that the task is ultimately carried out satisfactorily.

Management control systems are typically based on retrospective assessments of trends and are more likely to require subjective judgments. In contrast to operational controls, the corrective action in a management control system can seldom be defined a priori and is designed to affect all instances of the future performance of a given task rather than merely correct, as operational controls do, each individual deviation as it is detected. For instance, in some institutions the

---

Source: Leon Wyszewianski, J. William Thomas, and Bruce Friedman, "Case-based Payment and the Control of Quality and Efficiency in Hospitals," *Inquiry* 24, Spring 1987, © 1987 Blue Cross and Blue Shield Association.

management control system for the surgical operating room suite is based on regular reports that provide the percentage utilization of operating room capacity, number and type of procedures performed, length of waiting queue, and similar measures. If these measures show decreasing utilization of the operating room suite's capacity in the face of a lengthening queue for elective procedures, the control system triggers an investigation into the possibility of inefficient scheduling of the operating rooms and other operational problems, resulting in corrective actions to eliminate future underutilization of operating room capacity.

The differences between operational and management controls make them complements. Operational control systems are best for rectifying the occasional deviation from a specified standard—for example, a drug reaction—but they are not well suited for repeated, systematic deviations from the standard, such as a pattern of inappropiate prescribing of drugs by one or more physicians. Detecting and correcting such a problem are much more the province of management controls. Accordingly, some management control systems monitor how frequently an operational control triggers corrective actions, and when an undesirably repetitive pattern of such corrections occurs, the management control system initiates changes in the appropriate administrative and organizational areas to eliminate the pattern.

Example: Controls in the Operating Room

Operational Controls. Characterized by routine application and well-defined, immediate corrective measures, operational controls are well suited to ensure compliance with many common requirements of operating room management. Such requirements include laboratory tests routinely ordered preoperatively to anticipate possible surgical complications or uncover contraindications for certain types of surgery: white blood cell count, hemoglobin concentration, chest film, and basic liver and kidney function tests.

Harm to the patient will be minimized and quality of care thereby safeguarded if operational controls ensure that no surgery is performed unless all applicable prerequisites have been satisfied. In addition, unnecessary preoperative stays as well as last-minute cancellations of the surgical procedure can be avoided—thereby also saving the consequent costs of idle operating rooms—if for elective cases a set of operational controls prevents scheduling of a time slot for the operating room unless all necessary tests have been ordered and the requested date allows sufficient time for the results to be received and evaluated before the operation. Additionally, other controls can monitor test results to make certain that all test results have been received and to flag any findings so outside the norm as to require cancellation of the procedure.

All such controls require linkages between the operating room scheduling system and the system for ordering tests and reporting their results. If the linkages are not already in place, establishing them is within the reach of the many organizations in which these separate functions are already computerized.

The process of developing operational controls may itself lead to an increase in efficiency. Once it becomes clear that surgical procedures will be canceled if certain test results are not available on time, the medical staff may review the need for all preoperative tests and conclude that some are altogether unnecessary whereas others ought to be required more selectively. The net result would be a gain in clinical efficiency from the reduction of preoperative testing costs and higher quality of care through elimination of the risks associated with unnecessary tests.

Management Controls. Management controls can similarly have a positive effect on quality and efficiency in the operating room. In the operating room suite, a management control system might monitor how often requests for scheduling operating room time are turned down by operational controls because the necessary prerequisites have not been satisfied and how often surgery is automatically canceled by the operational control system because test results are not available or the results are outside acceptable norms. These are costly and disruptive events that may indicate inadequate handling of cases. When such events occur too often, management controls can prompt the formulation of appropriate educational or administrative interventions to reduce their incidence.

Management control systems can also be used to monitor the quality and efficiency of the surgical care provided. For instance, length of operating room time can be monitored as an indicator of both the quality and efficiency of the surgeon's technique. If standard times are established for the most frequently performed procedures, a pattern of excessive departure from those times, in either direction, is cause for further investigation and possible remedial action. Although such a pattern sometimes reflects nothing more than differences among surgeons in the pace of work, it can also be an indication of hurried and poor surgical technique or a repetitive history of intraoperative complications. Similarly, unsatisfactory performance can be identified not only by monitoring reports of normal tissue removed but also by monitoring the amount of blood and blood components transfused intraoperatively and during the immediate postoperative recovery period for specific procedure groups.

Chapter 20

Productivity

OVERVIEW

It has been said that people produce more when they know the following things about their work:

1. what they are supposed to do
2. what authority they have
3. what their relationships are to other people in the organization
4. what constitutes a job well done in terms of specific results
5. what they are doing exceptionally well
6. where they are falling short
7. what they can do to improve unsatisfactory results
8. that there are appropriate rewards for work done exceptionally well
9. that what they are doing and thinking is of value
10. that the supervisor has a deep interest in and concern for them
11. that the supervisor truly wishes them to succeed and progress.[1]

In more formal studies[2] researchers have identified ten primary factors that need to be taken

into account if an organization is to achieve the systemwide changes that are essential to raising its productivity and improving its performance. Paraphrased, these are:

1. employee compensation tied to performance and to sharing in productivity gains
2. participation of workers in decisions affecting their own and related jobs
3. job enlargement, including challenge, variety, wholeness, and self-regulation
4. employees' sense of involvement in the total organization
5. adequate safety conditions, pay, fringe benefits, and working conditions
6. simplification of channels of communication and authority
7. resources at workers' disposal to facilitate work effectiveness and reduce frustration associated with getting the job done
8. improved work methods that have involved workers in their planning and work
9. opportunities for greater employee "stewardship," that is, direct care of and attention to coworker needs
10. allowance for flexibility in relation to type of incentive and authority patterns

Using the foregoing list of ten critical factors, the nursing administrator should attempt to diagnose his or her department's strengths and weaknesses in order to set priorities and assess the

---

[1]Max B. Skousen, "Increasing Individual Productivity through Motivation Controls," *Meeting the Productivity Challenge*, American Management Association, 1960.

[2]Reprinted, by permission of the publisher, from *Productivity: The Measure and the Myth* by Mildred E. Katzel, pp. 34–36, © 1975 by AMACOM, a division of American Management Associations. All rights reserved.

potential for improvement in each area, so that decisions can be made as to which areas are most promising of favorable results. Needless to say, workers should be involved in the diagnostic work, in determining priorities, and in planning the course of action.

The nursing administrator should realize that there are many approaches to dealing with organizational problems, and that each organization should choose the approaches best suited to its own situation. Large organizations will be able to use the skills of qualified staff to deal with these matters. Smaller organizations have the advantage of being able to move somewhat more directly. Whatever methods are selected, the overall direction of the effort should be placed at a high level in the organization, because of the scope of the changes that are likely to be made, the functions that will probably be affected, and the policy decisions that almost inevitably will result.

Characteristics of Productivity-Excellent Hospitals*

In a recent study of highly productive hospitals, the following data was drawn:

- Almost all productivity-excellent hospitals appear to have a CEO who relates high productivity to high employee morale.
- Some productivity-excellent hospitals had been in financial difficulty and made noteworthy comebacks.
- The main cause given for favorable morale at these hospitals is job security. Equitable compensation and benefits and effective employee-management communication were listed next in frequency. Other factors referred to were (1) confirmation that the organization is successful and (2) confidence of employees that their jobs are important.
- A large majority of hospitals are using or are preparing to use productivity perform-

ance monitoring, a nursing acuity system, a nonlayoff strategy, cost accounting, strategic planning, and performance appraisal to determine a bonus or salary increase for management personnel.

- Employee employment security was ranked higher as a management value by the productivity-excellent hospitals than either community relationship enhancement or employee compensation and benefits.
- Turnover rates for productivity-excellent hospitals are substantially under the national health care average.
- Most productivity-excellent hospitals involve nonmanagement employees in management decision making.
- High staff morale is usually directly associated with high productivity. Four categories of how highly productive employees feel about their organization emerge from this study as causal factors of morale. The employees feel that their jobs are important to the organization and that the organization has concern for its employees (they have *tangible* evidence of this). They have a feeling that the organization is oriented to success—a winning team. Last, there is a feeling that people in the organization interact effectively.
- Effective communication occurs both up and down the organization and at all levels.

NURSING PRODUCTIVITY

Factors Affecting Staff Productivity*

Productivity can be defined as the ratio of output, in terms of products and services, to input, in terms of resources consumed. The productivity of the nursing staff is measured by the number of nursing hours (resource inputs) provided to meet the demands of the mix of patients (services output) on a nursing unit.

---

*Source: Fred F. Fifield, "What Is a Productivity-Excellent Hospital," *Nursing Management*, vol. 19, no. 4, April 1988. Reprinted with permission.

*Source: Charles C. Gabbert, "Nursing Staffing, Scheduling, and Productivity," in *Nursing Administration and Law Manual*, Karen Hawley Henry, ed., Aspen Publishers, Inc., © 1986.

The primary inputs affecting nursing staff productivity are the characteristics of the staff, the patients, and the nursing unit itself. Staff characteristics include the level, mix, qualifications, experience, and stability of staff members. Obviously, well-educated, experienced, highly motivated nurses will be more productive than those with less education, experience, and motivation. Patient characteristics include the number of patients to be cared for and their ages, diagnoses, and treatments. Many acutely ill patients with complicated diagnoses that require multiple treatments will make greater demands on the nursing staff than a few patients with less severe problems. Unit characteristics refer to the unit's size, layout, and location as well as the equipment and services available on the unit. A well-designed working area that is in close proximity to equipment and services used by the staff will greatly boost staff productivity compared to close, cramped quarters that are inconvenient to the services and equipment used.

The primary outputs of the staff are acuity-adjusted patient days, improved patient health, patient satisfaction with service, medical records, and patient education. Methods of assessing staff output and productivity include the patient classification system, cost accounting, budget and general ledger reports, position control, and quality monitoring.

The challenge to managers of nursing resources is to maximize the productivity of those resources to optimize costs and to preserve an appropriate quality level. Peter Drucker has said that productivity is *the* job of a manager, and the management of productivity is the true test of a competent manager.

There are many factors that bear upon nursing staff productivity. They do not affect all organizations equally, or in the same way, but must be considered when managing nursing staff productivity. Among these factors are

- a patient classification system that reflects resource consumption
- a nursing utilization system that prospectively allocates staff and retrospectively monitors productivity
- a scheduling system that allows for planning of nursing resource assignments, yet is sufficiently flexible to respond to changes in demand
- nursing staffing and personnel policies that support productive resource use (e.g., every third weekend off rather than every other weekend off, permitting ''doubling back'' with only eight hours off between shifts)
- an optimal mix of skills that allows individuals to do the jobs they are trained to do in response to demand
- an efficient interface between nursing and ancillary departments regarding patient access, with a master scheduling system in place for each patient
- a physical plant layout that minimizes unnecessary travel and activity on the part of nursing personnel
- flexible medication, meal serving, and shift reporting procedures that prevent peaking of workload
- an ability to forecast census and patient mix in order to plan resource allocation
- nursing managers who are constantly looking for better ways to do things with less resources

These are generalized factors that affect many hospitals in different ways. The important point to consider is that, if each element of this short list of factors were to be addressed, productivity in any nursing department would be positively affected to a substantial degree.

Approaches*

The study of nursing productivity is the study of how to deliver the best nursing care in the most appropriate manner at the lowest cost. In this sense, nursing productivity is a concept which ties together all the factors involved in the provision of quality nursing care.

Criteria frequently used in evaluating nursing productivity include nursing hours per patient

---

*Source: A Review and Evaluation of Nursing Productivity, DHHS, Pub. No. (HRA 77-15), 1977.

day, ratios of staff to patients, cost per patient day, numbers of encounters, and many more. Depending upon the health care setting and the persons performing the evaluation, each of these items may represent a meaningful, if simplistic, measure. But even with these simple, often accepted performance indicators, there tend to be inconsistencies in the manner in which hours, dollars, numbers, and ratios are determined.

Following are some suggestions on specific approaches.

Measure of Nursing Productivity. Develop a measure of nursing productivity based upon nursing outcomes, through the following steps:

- Define nursing outcomes and determine how these should be measured. Include the following:
  —health status
  —patient knowledge
  —patient satisfaction (measured indirectly and directly)
- Define patient-oriented goals based on these nursing outcomes.
- Measure the extent to which these goals are achieved (this is a measure of nursing quality).
- Utilize this nursing quality measure as a part of a nursing productivity measure (the other part being efficiency—use of resources to deliver the quality).

Role Definition. Improve the role definition of the nurse at all levels from director of nursing service to staff nurse, and do it both in leadership and clinical areas.

- Utilize personnel at levels consistent with their competence and preparation.
- Provide management training for nurses at the master's level and through in-service education.
- Involve the nurse in the development of his or her own role.
- Study the disparity between nursing education and nursing practice and determine how to reduce or eliminate it.

Participative Management. Encourage experimentation with and research into participative nursing management.

Incentives. Develop and use quality, financial, and other incentives for both individuals and the institution. Determine through research the extent to which incentives can affect productivity.

Technological Factors. Investigate the interrelationship of various factors which affect nursing productivity, for example, the relationship between nursing care organization (team, functional, primary) and facility design.

Mechanization and Automation. Develop a model for nursing productivity which will:

- utilize quantified outputs and inputs
- fit into a model of health services evaluation
- utilize as inputs nursing personnel, facilities, equipment, supplies, etc.
- provide output measures of patient health status, knowledge, and satisfaction

Productivity System Issues*

When implementing a productivity system, the following issues must be considered.

Acceptable Range of Productivity. Because most employees in a nursing department work either 8- or 12-hour shifts, it is often difficult to arrive at 100 percent productivity. Because much of the care on a nursing unit is time sensitive (meaning it must be performed at specific moments), it is not always possible to have exactly the right staffing available at a given time. It is, therefore, essential that a reasonable range of productivity be established as a standard for comparison. This range is often between 85 percent and 115 percent.

---

*Source: Letty R. Piper, "Patient Acuity Systems and Productivity," *Topics in Health Care Financing*, vol. 15, no. 3, © 1989 Aspen Publishers, Inc.

Direct and Indirect Care. The care on a nursing unit can be described as direct, indirect, fixed, and variable. Direct care is the actual care provided to patients. Indirect care is the documentation, direction, and planning of the direct care. Fixed care is the minimal required staffing for a unit; this does not vary with the acuity. Variable care is the component of care that is directly driven by the acuity.

Most acuity systems are quite good at measuring direct care and often have additive factors that also account for the indirect time directly related to the direct care. However, in units such as the emergency department, delivery suites, and intensive care units, there is a larger component of indirect care due to the uneven flow of patients. For example, although a nurse may have the time to care for additional patients, there may not be any additional patients available.

Fixed and Variable Components. When establishing a productivity system, it is important to determine the variable portion of staffing. This component should be compared with the acuity standard, and the fixed portion should be compared with a per-diem or per-shift standard. On a nursing unit, the head nurse and clerk are often fixed and the staff registered nurses and nurses aides are variable.

Updating and Validation. Systems are designed to be used for periods of years. Because the policies and procedures of the department are frequently altered by technology, physical layout changes, and practice pattern modifications, it is essential that the user understand how the time values assigned to indicators or descriptions were established so that the values can be modified or validated over time. Patient acuity systems must not remain stagnant but must have the flexibility to change with the practices that they measure.

In conjunction with validation, it is necessary to note that there are always differences in the amount of time various individuals need to perform a task. However, it is also important to note that, frequently, two tasks can be performed simultaneously or in an abbreviated fashion, thereby altering the productivity equation.

Productivy and the Supervisor*

All nurses must have a concern about that elusive element—productivity—which relates not only to quantity of output by employees but to the quality of their performance.

In a factory, the measurement of productivity presents no difficulty. The operator produces so many widgets per hour; they are inspected and a record is made of spoilage; and management knows how many useable items have been produced, how much wastage has occurred. In a hospital unit, such appraisals of an employee are not easy. Much more reliance has to be placed on general impressions of the employee's abilities, cooperativeness, and availability when needed; the speed with which assignments are performed; and the quality of outcome. The usual definition of productivity is "man-hour output," but that is applicable on the hospital floor only in the lowest-level activities.

This does not mean that the supervisor cannot evaluate personnel, spot deficiencies, and point out ways of improvement. What it does mean is that the supervisor, even more than the industrial foreman, must be close to the staff, observing them more keenly. The foreman can tell what's happening by looking at the end result; the hospital supervisor, especially the professional, has to keep a sharper eye on the work in process.

The reason for this vigilant supervision is not only to deflect the dangers of error. Also important is the supervisor's responsibility for providing affirmative leadership. In the industrial setting, discipline after the event may be enough to cope with bad performance; in the hospital, mishaps must not only be forestalled but the employee must constantly be motivated to provide the highest possible quality of personal service.

Leadership Styles

The nurse manager or administrator stands at the head of the work team. How effectively he or

---

Source: Aaron Levenstein, "The Issue of Productivity," *Supervisor Nurse*, December 1975. Reprinted with permission.

she coordinates and maneuvers depends on his or her ability to lead the members of the team to obtain their maximum level of performance. An inappropriate leadership style can reduce staff morale, motivation, and productivity. Overabundant tight supervision or the opposite, extremely lax supervision, can end in unfortunate results, with personnel who are underutilized, resentful, and frequently absent.

The leadership qualities of the nurse manager function both in long-range and short-range situations. In terms of the long-range relationship of the manager to subordinates, the underlying philosophy of the leader plays a crucial part. One authority cites two categories of leaders who have an effect on productivity levels.

The work-centered leader focuses on the technicalities of the task and views workers as quantitative factors in the mechanism. When the mechanism falters, the nurse manager will investigate the dimensions of the task, the workings of the system, or the number of personnel. The discontent or inappropriate placement of staff, the human element, are not considered as factors in attaining maximum performance.

The person-centered leader identifies the individual worker as the major resource in a complex system, the hub of the "wheel of productivity." This manager will attempt to introduce the right people into the various systems and then give due recognition for accomplishment to the workers, not the system.

Productivity has been shown to be substantially higher among employee groups whose supervisors have been person-centered.

A style of leadership, however, cannot be too rigidly adopted. Whether bureaucratic, autocratic, or democratic (see Chapter 1 for a discussion of "Leadership Styles"), the nurse manager must bend at times to the exigencies of particular situations. The manager must be able to perceive the nature of the immediate problem and shift approaches accordingly. This does not imply that the manager should become an unpredictable weather vane; rather the manager should superimpose over his or her basic leadership philosophy a flexible manner adaptable to individual situations. In this way he or she will set the scene for improved staff morale and productivity.

The Productive Supervisor: Self-Evaluation

As a supervisor your first task in seeking to make others more productive is to make yourself more productive. By increasing your display of leadership you can help to motivate your people towards better performance.

Questions a supervisor should ask him- or herself:

1. Confronted with a problem, do you take positive action—making a decision, issuing orders, setting things in motion?
2. Do you provide fluent and readily understood responses to questions that are addressed to you by colleagues, subordinates, and superiors?
3. In assigning and scheduling work, are you specific about the time or the date when you will expect completion?
4. Do you establish priorities so that people know what is "rush" and what can wait a reasonable period of time?
5. Can you see the interrelationship between various problems so that by linking them you can work more efficiently?
6. Do you make "terminal decisions" so that you can "close the books" on a particular problem instead of leaving things "up in the air"?
7. Do you issue orders, when necessary, that are specific and leave nothing to the employee's imagination—and do you issue open-ended orders when you want to encourage employee initiative?
8. Do you make it a practice to obtain facts, information, and advice from all of your subordinates?
9. Do you make similar requests for information and counsel from your superiors without a feeling of embarrassment?
10. Do you call for an exchange of ideas with others, outsiders included, before acting on an issue?
11. Do you seek face-to-face personal contact with others?
12. Do you patiently explain your reasons to your subordinates?
13. Do you inform your staff of actions that you plan to take?

14. Do you show courtesy in dealing with people even if they are your subordinates, sincerely using phrases like "Please," "Thank you," and "I suggest"?

15. Are you sometimes informal with your subordinates so that they see you as genuinely friendly?

WORK SIMPLIFICATION

The ideal design of any work operation should aim to make the procedure productive, smooth-flowing, and simple.

Principles*

Work simplification is the organized application of common sense to find easier and better ways of doing work. This organized and systematic approach to improvement and problem solving is a step-by-step procedure. It provides a guide to thinking that makes improvement easier and is also a desirable and continuous way of performing everyday work. Making use of the pattern helps one organize and "sell" one's ideas for improvement.

The following questions concerning work simplification should be addressed.

Can We Eliminate? In far too many instances we devote much time to studying various activities for possibilities of improvement without asking the most important question, "Why do we perform this activity?" If we succeed in eliminating the operation or even part of it, the ultimate in work simplification is achieved.

Can We Combine? This opportunity for improvement is one that should not be overlooked. Whenever two activities can be combined, they are often performed for a little more than the cost of one activity, and the make-ready and put-away details of one of the operations are eliminated.

Can We Change the Sequence? The flow diagram or template layout of the area often helps here. By changing the sequence of an activity, we may be able to eliminate the backtracking. Although much of the order in which the details are performed is necessary as a part of the process, in many instances a change of sequence can be made with consequent saving.

Can We Improve or Simplify? Unfortunately, many attempts to make improvements in the past have started without the benefits of an organized approach to this question. Failure to find improvements has resulted in stifling creativity, accepting things as they are, and taking no steps to improve them. We should question everything.

Can We Change the Place? Naturally, the question "where?" challenges the place where the operation is performed. Why is it done there? Too many times work is done in one place or department mainly because it has always been done there. Can we change the person? Challenging the detail with the question "who?" often results in the discovery that it could be done better by some other person. The questions "how?" and "why?" challenge the method of doing a particular activity. A part of the philosophy of work simplification is, "It is not *what* we do, but the *way* we do it." Often we can more than double productivity by improving the method. Improvement generally means a study of the motions used in the performance of the job. Simplification of these motions is accomplished by utilizing the principles of motion economy.

A Six-Step Job Improvement Plan*

The proper method of work simplification is a logical, orderly approach to the solution of a problem, frequently referred to as the job improvement plan, which includes the following six steps:

1. Select a job to improve.
   –Ask what needs improvement most.

Source: Robert M. Sloane and Beverly LeBov Sloane, *A Guide to Health Facilities*, 2nd edition, The C.V. Mosby Co., 1977. Reprinted with permission of the author.

Source: Ibid.

–Make the best use of your time by selecting the right job.

2. Get the facts.
   –Select the appropriate analytical technique.
   –Look at each detail of the job.
3. Challenge the job.
   –Challenge each detail of the job.
   –List the improvement possibilities.
4. Develop the improvement.
   –Evaluate all possible solutions.
   –Chart the new method.
5. Install the improvement.
   –Sell your idea to all concerned.
   –Get approval, and then get your idea installed.
6. Follow up.
   –Follow through to be certain that the improved process is fully operating so that the full gains are being realized.

Several of these techniques and the forms used are demonstrated in the following material. (*Note*: The technique of work sampling is discussed later in "Measuring Productivity.")

Work Distribution Chart*

There are many analytical techniques for implementing a work simplification program. Six of them are briefly outlined in Table 20-1. (Two are illustrated in Figures 20-1 and 20-2.)

The work distribution chart (Figure 20-2) is designed for analyzing the functions performed in a department or unit. When properly prepared, it enables us to see clearly in one place

- the work activities performed and the time it takes to perform them
- the individuals who are working on these activities
- the amount of time spent by each person on each activity

---

*Source: Addison C. Bennet, *Methods Improvements in Hospitals*, J.B. Lippincott Company, © 1964.

Here are some ways in which the work distribution charting technique can help in developing improvements in the way things are being done:

It indicates what activities take the most time.

It points out the unnecessary work that is being performed.

It indicates whether or not skills are used properly.

It indicates whether or not any employees are doing too many unrelated tasks.

It points out tasks that may be spread too thinly throughout the department or unit.

It shows whether or not work in the unit is distributed evenly.

To begin with, the preparation of a work distribution chart is made possible through the use of a *task list* and an *activity list*. The information that is entered on these records is assembled subsequently onto a work distribution chart.

The task list is used to develop a listing of the duties actually being performed by each employee in the department or the unit, indicating the estimated number of hours spent per week on each duty. This listing of tasks should be made out for each position presently occupied in the organizational unit, including the department head and supervisory positions. If difficulty is encountered in estimating time spent on each task, it may be necessary for the employee to maintain a record of hours spent on each activity over a period of one or two weeks so as to establish a proper allocation of time.

The activity list is used to record the major activities that are performed or that should be performed to fulfill the objectives of the department or the unit. The list should be prepared by the supervisor of the organizational unit.

The next step is to assemble these data in such a way as to be able to analyze them conveniently. This is accomplished by transferring the information found on the activity list and the task lists onto a work distribution chart. First, rank each activity, assigning a number. Starting at the extreme left of the sheet, rule a column for activities, followed by a column for each em-

Table 20-1 Analytical Techniques for Work Simplification

The Analytical Technique	*When It Should Be Used*
1. The flow process chart	A work study situation in which it appears desirable to follow the actions pertaining to a *single* person, a *single* material, or a *single* form. This would include (a) the activities of a *person* who is involved in a straight sequence of events, with some movement from place to place; (b) the handling of any single *material* that flows through a connected series of events; (c) the flow of a single-copy or single-part *form*. (See Figure 20-1.) (Although this vertical type chart may be ideal for gathering and recording facts relating to a single item involving process, the procedure flow chart (a horizontal-type chart) is more adaptable to work procedures of a more complex nature.)
2. The flow diagram	A work study situation in which it appears desirable to examine the *paths* of movement of people, paperwork, or materials. This form of analysis is particularly useful in work where (a) the distance traveled is excessive; (b) the flow is complicated; (c) the work area is congested; (d) backtracking is evidenced. The flow diagram in its simplest form is used to supplement the flow process chart.
3. The organization chart	A work study situation in which it appears desirable to analyze and evaluate the present organizational structure of a department or unit. This chart can be helpful in providing a broad overall view of the department or unit as it now exists.
4. The work distribution chart	A work study situation in which it appears desirable to examine in greater detail the work being done in a department or unit. This chart will present clearly in one place (a) the work activities performed by the department, and the total time it takes to perform them; (b) the individuals who are working on each of these activities; (c) the amount of time spent by each person on each activity. (See Figure 20-2.)
5. The procedure flow chart	A work study situation involving the performance of many different work routines by individuals in different capacities and, perhaps, in different departments. It is also recommended for charting the details of procedures which involve the flow of multicopy or multipart forms.
6. Work sampling	Work study situations in which the functions being investigated are nonrepetitive in nature. This technique makes it possible to gather detailed information that would be difficult to obtain by means of continuous observation.

ployee in the unit. On the right side of each of these columns, allow space for the entry of hours per week. Review all task lists for the purpose of identifying each entry with an activity number appearing on the activity list. Enter in each appropriate employee column all the tasks that have been classified as number 1. At the same time, record the number of hours spent on activity 1 by each employee. When all information has been entered on the chart, total the time entries for all employees as well as for all activities. Both of these totals should be the same. See Table 20-2 for a summary of the process involved in analyzing work distribution.

Figure 20-1 Flow Process Chart

PRESENT METHOD ☑ PROPOSED METHOD ☐

FLOW PROCESS CHART

PAGE 1 OF 1

SUMMARY: 1 TRIP	PRESENT	PROPOSED	DIFFERENCE
○ OPERATIONS	7		
⇨ TRANSPORTATIONS	8		
□ INSPECTIONS	1		
D DELAYS	3		
▽ STORAGES	2		
DISTANCE TRAVELLED	740 FT	FT	FT
TIME MIN.	45		

JOB HANDLING VALUABLES OF PRIVATE AND SEMI-PRIVATE PATIENTS

Subject Charted NURSE

CHART BEGINS AT NURSES' STATION

CHART ENDS AT NURSES' STATION

CHARTED BY L. WEEKS DATE 10/25/61.

	DESCRIPTION OF EVENT	OPERATION / TRANSPORT / INSPECTION / DELAY / STORAGE	QUANTITY	DISTANCE IN FEET	MIN TIME	NOTES
1	AT NURSES' STATION	○⇨□D▽				3rd FLOOR
2	GETS ENVELOPE AND FORM	○⇨□D▽			1	
3	FILLS IN NECESSARY DATA	○⇨□D▽			2	
4	WALKS TO PATIENT'S ROOM	○⇨□D▽		30	1/2	
5	CHECKS VALUABLES WITH PATIENT	○⇨□D▽			5	
6	RECORDS AMOUNT + KIND OF VALUABLES ON ENVELOPE + FORM	○⇨□D▽			2	
7	SIGNS TEMPORARY RECEIPT	○⇨□D▽			1/2	
8	DETACHES TEMPORARY RECEIPT AND GIVES TO PATIENT	○⇨□D▽			1/2	
9	WALKS TO ELEVATOR	○⇨□D▽		180	3	
10	WAITS FOR ELEVATOR	○⇨□D▽			5	AVERAGE OF 6 TRIPS PER DAY
11	RIDES TO MAIN FLOOR	○⇨□D▽		35	1	
12	WALKS TO CASHIER	○⇨□D▽		125	2	
13	GIVES VALUABLES TO CASHIER	○⇨□D▽				
14	WAITS WHILE VALUABLES ARE CHECKED + PERMANENT RECEIPT OBTAINED	○⇨□D▽			10	
15	WALKS TO ELEVATOR	○⇨□D▽		125	2	
16	WAITS FOR ELEVATOR	○⇨□D▽			5	
17	RIDES TO NURSING FLOOR	○⇨□D▽		35	1	3rd FLOOR
18	WALKS TO PATIENT'S ROOM	○⇨□D▽		180	3	
19	GIVES PERMANENT RECEIPT TO PATIENT	○⇨□D▽			1	
20	RETURNS TO NURSES' STATION	○⇨□D▽		30	1/2	
21	AT NURSES STATION	○⇨□D▽				
22		○⇨□D▽				
23		○⇨□D▽				
24		○⇨□D▽				

Figure 20-2 Work Distribution Chart

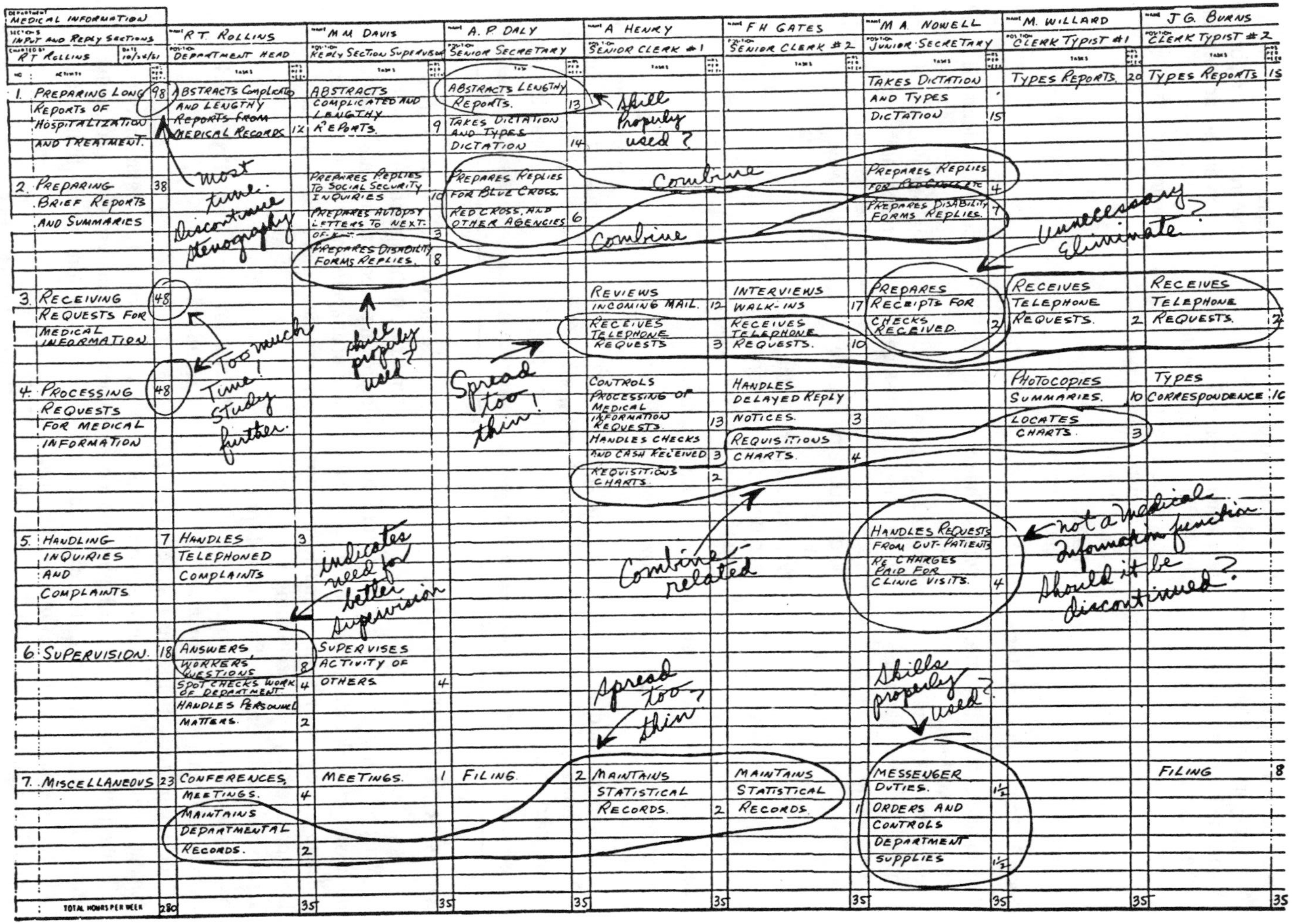

Department: MEDICAL INFORMATION
Sections: INPUT AND REPLY SECTIONS
Charted by: R T ROLLINS Date: 10/24/61

No.	Activity	Hrs. per week	R.T. ROLLINS, DEPARTMENT HEAD — Tasks	Hrs.	M.M. DAVIS, REPLY SECTION SUPERVISOR — Tasks	Hrs.	A. P. DALY, SENIOR SECRETARY — Tasks	Hrs.	A. HENRY, SENIOR CLERK #1 — Tasks	Hrs.	F.H. GATES, SENIOR CLERK #2 — Tasks	Hrs.	M.A. NOWELL, JUNIOR SECRETARY — Tasks	Hrs.	M. WILLARD, CLERK TYPIST #1 — Tasks	Hrs.	J.G. BURNS, CLERK TYPIST #2 — Tasks	Hrs.
1.	PREPARING LONG REPORTS OF HOSPITALIZATION AND TREATMENT.	98	ABSTRACTS COMPLICATED AND LENGTHY REPORTS FROM MEDICAL RECORDS	12	ABSTRACTS COMPLICATED AND LENGTHY REPORTS.	9	ABSTRACTS LENGTHY REPORTS.	13					TAKES DICTATION AND TYPES DICTATION	15	TYPES REPORTS.	20	TYPES REPORTS	15
							TAKES DICTATION AND TYPES DICTATION	14										
2.	PREPARING BRIEF REPORTS AND SUMMARIES	38			PREPARES REPLIES TO SOCIAL SECURITY INQUIRIES	10	PREPARES REPLIES FOR BLUE CROSS, RED CROSS, AND OTHER AGENCIES	6					PREPARES REPLIES FOR [illegible]	4				
					PREPARES AUTOPSY LETTERS TO NEXT OF KIN	3							PREPARES DISABILITY FORMS REPLIES.	7				
					PREPARES DISABILITY FORMS REPLIES.	8												
3.	RECEIVING REQUESTS FOR MEDICAL INFORMATION	48							REVIEWS INCOMING MAIL.	12	INTERVIEWS WALK-INS	17	PREPARES RECEIPTS FOR CHECKS RECEIVED.	2	RECEIVES TELEPHONE REQUESTS.	2	RECEIVES TELEPHONE REQUESTS.	2
									RECEIVES TELEPHONE REQUESTS	3	RECEIVES TELEPHONE REQUESTS.	10						
4.	PROCESSING REQUESTS FOR MEDICAL INFORMATION	48							CONTROLS PROCESSING OF MEDICAL INFORMATION REQUESTS.	13	HANDLES DELAYED REPLY NOTICES.	3			PHOTOCOPIES SUMMARIES.	10	TYPES CORRESPONDENCE	10
									HANDLES CHECKS AND CASH RECEIVED	3	REQUISITIONS CHARTS.	4			LOCATES CHARTS.	3		
									REQUISITIONS CHARTS.	2								
5.	HANDLING INQUIRIES AND COMPLAINTS	7	HANDLES TELEPHONED COMPLAINTS	3									HANDLES REQUESTS FROM OUT-PATIENTS RE CHARGES PAID FOR CLINIC VISITS.	4				
6.	SUPERVISION.	18	ANSWERS WORKERS' QUESTIONS	8	SUPERVISES ACTIVITY OF OTHERS	4												
			SPOT CHECKS WORK OF DEPARTMENT	4														
			HANDLES PERSONNEL MATTERS.	2														
7.	MISCELLANEOUS	23	CONFERENCES, MEETINGS.	4	MEETINGS.	1	FILING.	2	MAINTAINS STATISTICAL RECORDS.	2	MAINTAINS STATISTICAL RECORDS.	1	MESSENGER DUTIES.	1½			FILING	8
			MAINTAINS DEPARTMENTAL RECORDS.	2									ORDERS AND CONTROLS DEPARTMENT SUPPLIES	1½				
	TOTAL HOURS PER WEEK	280		35		35		35		35		35		35		35		35

Table 20-2 Analyzing Work Using a Work Distribution Chart

Step 1. Analyzing All Activities

| Taking each activity listed vertically in the column at the extreme left of the chart, ask these questions. | *What* is the purpose of the activity? *Why* is it necessary? *Why* is this activity a function of this department? *What* activities take the most time? *Why?* *What* is a reasonable time for each activity? etc. | These questions will help to determine the importance of each activity and whether any activity can be eliminated. |

Step 2. Analyzing Each Task of Each Activity

| Taking one activity at a time, read horizontally across the chart and ask these questions about each task assigned to it. | *What* is the purpose of the task? *Why* is it necessary? *Where* should the task be done? *When* should the task be done? *Who* should perform the task? *Who* duplicates or overlaps in performing the task? etc. | These questions will help to determine whether each task is being done in the right place, at the right time, by the right person, and in the right way. |

Step 3. Analyzing Each Person's Tasks and Activities

| Taking one person at a time, ask these questions concerning each duty or task listed vertically in the assigned column. | *How* closely related are the duties? *How* are skills utilized? *How* heavy is the workload? *How* repetitive are the tasks? etc. | These questions will help to uncover unrelated tasks, misuse of skills, uneven distribution of work, and tasks spread too thin. |

MEASURING PRODUCTIVITY

(*Note*: See Chapter 16, "Staffing," for a full discussion of work measurement techniques.) In order to achieve staff savings and to monitor labor productivity on a continuing basis, labor standards are essential. Their development requires not only technical expertise, but also the exercise of managerial judgment.

The techniques available for developing standards are varied, ranging from the simple utilization of historical data to highly refined, predetermined time systems. Three are adaptable for hospital use: (1) estimating the time required to perform a given task; (2) the classical time and monitor study approach; and (3) the historical data evaluation approach.

Regardless of the method used to develop standards, if the standards are to be effective in improving productivity and reducing cost, hospital managers must be held accountable for performance against these standards.

Process for Developing Productivity Standards*

A supervisor (or management engineer or other work analyst) will ordinarily begin the process of setting productivity standards for a

---

Source: Charles R. McConnell, *The Health Care Supervisor's Guide to Cost Control and Productivity Improvement*, Aspen Publishers, Inc., © 1986.

department by assessing the department's work and identifying all tasks that are done. Standards are most frequently established in order of the proportion of the department's time that various tasks require; that is, the first tasks for which standards are set are usually those that consume the largest part of the employees' time.

Assuming that a particular task has been identified and that a productivity standard is to be set, the process may proceed as follows.

1. *Identification of Steps.* The content of the task is analyzed for the purpose of identifying all steps involved, all inputs required, and all supporting activities that may have to take place for completion of the task. Special attention is given to identifying clearly recognizable starting and ending points for the task.

2. *Evaluation of Each Step.* The content of every step is evaluated in detail, and every effort is made to alter the steps in the interest of improving productivity while not adversely affecting quality. Such evaluation will usually include attempts to reduce delays, reduce travel or handling, improve materials and equipment, and improve workplace layout.

3. *Determination of Time.* Using one of the methods previously outlined—stopwatch time study, predetermined motion times, or work sampling—*normal time* for the task is determined. Normal time is the bare clock time, unaltered by allowances for performing the task.

4. *Calculation of PFD Factor.* An appropriate factor is applied to compensate for personal, fatigue, and minor delay time that may be experienced. Commonly referred to as a PFD (personal, fatigue, and delay) factor, this may be established for the institution as a whole or for a specific department by extensive work-sampling study. Many hospitals use institutionwide PFD factors, most of which fall in the range of 15 to 20 percent. If the organization's PFD factor is 17 percent, for example, the normal time referred to in the preceding step is multiplied by 1.17 to arrive at the *standard time*, the time required by a qualified and properly trained person working at a normal pace to complete the task.

5. *Identification of Work Units.* If not already accomplished, the department's *work units* should be clearly identified. These work units are the common units of service that constitute the department's output, such as admissions (the admitting department), discharges (the medical record department), square feet of building space service (the housekeeping department), bills rendered (the patient billing function), tests (laboratory), procedures (radiology), meals served or patient days (food service).

6. *Final Calculations.* Determine the *work unit time per occurrence* for each task. When such times for all tasks having a bearing on producing a unit of service are added together, the result will be the *standard time per unit of service*.

7. *Establishing the Relationship of Indirect Tasks.* It is next necessary to account for *indirect tasks* that are not accounted for in the standard thus far but nevertheless necessary to the production of the department's output. These can be handled in two ways.

1. If there is a reasonable relationship between the indirect tasks and the units of service produced, that is, if the indirect work varies up or down as the units of service vary up or down, the indirect tasks (at least some of them) can be added to the standard as an additional per-unit allowance. For example, obtaining supplies, cleaning up after working, and preparing certain reports might be includable in the standard.

2. If there is no direct relationship between indirect tasks and amount of output, indirect time may be expressed as an amount of constant time per day. Certain supporting activities, foremost among them supervision, secretarial support, and attending meetings, are departmental activities that occur roughly to the same extent regardless of variations in levels of output. For example, a given department may function at all times using one supervisor and one secretary over a broad range of output levels. Thus the resulting standard

for an entire department is often a two-part expression—hours of constant time per day and time per unit of service.

8. *Applying the Productivity Standard.* The resulting *productivity standard* is applied in measuring and monitoring the department's productivity. Common forms of hospital productivity standards include

- admitting: hours/calendar day, plus hours/admission
- food service: hours/calendar day, plus hours/patient day
- housekeeping: hours/calendar day (with staffing based on square feet of area)
- laboratory: hours/calendar day, plus hours/test; or hours/calendar day, plus CAP units
- medical records: hours/calendar day, plus hours/discharge
- nursing (for specific nursing unit): hours/patient day
- physical therapy: hours/calendar day, plus hours/modality

9. *Setting Up a Target Utilization Factor.* It may at times be necessary to alter a department's productivity standard further to account for interference factors referred to earlier. Interference factors result from forces beyond the control of the supervisor, such as sporadic workload arrival, the need for standby coverage, and problems with physical layout. A *target utilization factor* may be established for this purpose. Usually based on a combination of measurement, observation, and judgment, a target utilization factor recognizes that practical productivity is often less than theoretical productivity. If a department's target utilization factor is 90 percent (an official recognition that 90 percent utilization is the maximum practical utilization for this department), the variable portion of the standard (the hours per unit of service) will be divided by 0.90 (inflated by ten percent) to reflect this. (The constant portion of the standard, the hours per calendar day, remains unadjusted.)

10. *Conclusion.* With or without the necessary adjustment of a target utilization factor, the

productivity standard for a department will be of the form—usually two-part, but occasionally a single expression—described above. This productivity standard makes it possible to value the department's output in terms of work time so output may be compared with work time applied as input.

*Additional Factors to Consider in Setting a Productivity Standard**

In addition to the essential work content of a job, a number of additional factors will have a bearing on the manner in which a productivity standard is set. The more significant factors include these:

- *The degree of repetitiveness of the task.* A task that is performed only occasionally does not allow opportunity for the worker to get fully up to speed, unlike a task that is done over and over again. For many tasks, repetition builds familiarity, which in turn builds output efficiency.
- *The fatigue potential of the job.* Some tasks, through either physical or mental demands, induce fatigue to an extent that can markedly affect performance time. Virtually all tasks induce fatigue to some degree: A person who enters a job fresh and rested is capable of greater performance than one who is tired from hours of work. This must be recognized in the time standards.
- *Dependence on other employees.* Many tasks are such that they cannot be completed alone; they require the accompanying efforts of other persons or they require related tasks to be accomplished first or perhaps between steps. This dependence, which is manifested in what may appear to be idle time, must be reflected in the time standard as long as it is valid.
- *Interference.* Natural disruptions sometimes prevent a worker from seeing a task through to completion, or work does not arrive in a time sequence that matches the worker's capacity. An interrupted task, one

---

Source: Ibid.

that must be stopped and restarted several times (such as the typing of a report by a secretary who doubles as a receptionist and thus must stop frequently to answer inquiries), will take longer because of the stops and starts than would otherwise be required. As to the timing of work arrival, a worker may be available to work but have nothing to do at times because no work has arrived. Some emergency room staffs experience interference factors in this respect; because of the essentially random arrival of patients they cannot always be gainfully occupied, but minimum staffing requirements dictate that a staff must always be there.

Chapter 21

Quality Care and Improvement

OVERVIEW

Evolution of the Quality Concept*

Historically, the quality of health care has been measured through analysis of mortality and morbidity records, improvements in professional education, and establishment of professional standards of care, credentialing, and reimbursement. In the last few decades the thrust toward controlling quality and working towards quality health care has intensified. In response to public concern about escalating health care costs, the government has also enacted several legislative efforts to ensure cost effective care. The Joint Commission continues to measure compliance to its standards but has changed its focus several times.

Quality control, a concept of the 1970s, examined the operational and structural requirements needed to keep a unit operational. It had little to do with the clinical processes related to patient care, but it supported clinical practice. [For information on quality control which is once again considered significant as a part of total quality management, see Chapter 19, Operational Reviews.]

The 1980s ushered in the concept of quality assurance at the departmental level (e.g., the nursing department) which was then brought to the unit level (e.g., the operating room). The 1970s short-term focus on a specific medical diagnosis or procedure has been replaced with a Ten-Step Joint Commission monitoring and evaluation of high-risk, high-volume, and problem-prone aspects of care over a period of time.

Under this approach, care that is given is measured against predetermined standards. Problems and areas of noncompliance with standards are identified and resolved through appropriate action. Evaluation of the effectiveness of corrective actions is accomplished by ongoing monitoring. Quality assurance in the 1980s focused on the identification and correction of problems.

In the 1990s the concept of quality is still evolving. The focus is now on continuous quality improvement (CQI). CQI is not another model for conducting quality assurance activities; it is a management style that supports and enhances the efforts of quality assurance. The focus is on improving care and service. CQI requires examination of the processes of care and service in order to improve outcomes.

Quality assurance and continuous quality improvement are complementary. Quality assurance activities enable identification and resolution of problems. Continuous quality improvement goes beyond the problem-oriented

---

*Source: Joanna Eisenberg, "Quality Assurance—Continuous Quality Improvement," in *The Manual of Operating Room Management: An Administrative Patient Care Resource*, Cynthia Spry, ed., Aspen Publishers, Inc., © 1990.

approach; the data derived from monitoring is used to continuously improve—*even in the absence of problems*.

For the CQI concept to succeed, quality must be a priority at all levels within the organization. Staff must be encouraged to improve care. There must be multidisciplinary and interdisciplinary review of systems and service with efforts focused on improvement of processes and systems.

Quality assurance/improvement programs must continue to ensure compliance with federal, state, regulatory, and professional requirements. The Joint Commission Ten Steps, with its focus on patient outcomes, remains the solid foundation for a quality assurance program; however, programs must now incorporate the CQI concepts that affect processes outcomes and must be continually improved. See Figure 21-1 for an illustration of quality measurement.

Figure 21-1 Measurements of Quality

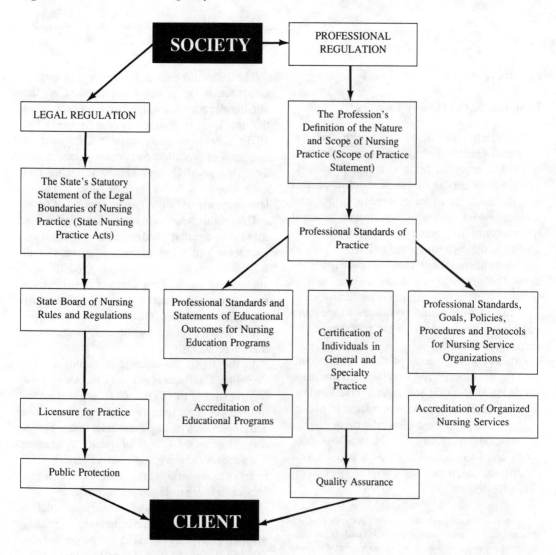

Source: Reprinted from *California Nurse*, p. 10, with permission of California Nurses' Association, © July/August 1987.

Assessing Quality of Nursing Care*

To assure quality, nursing care must be assessed in terms of outcome, content, processes, resources, and efficiency—in that order of priority.

1. Assessment of Outcome

Quality of nursing care received should principally be measured by the outcome of that care. The assessment of outcome focuses on the alteration in the health status of the consumer. Positive indices that can be used in assessing the alteration in the consumer's health status include the following:

- an increase in the consumer's health knowledge
- the degree of application of that knowledge
- the degree of the consumer's participation in his or her health decision making
- the degree of responsibility that the consumer assumes for his or her health behavior
- the consumer's ability to maintain positive health behavior
- the degree to which the consumer's right to choices that affect his or her health are ensured
- the consumer's ability to utilize health services, both personal and community, with efficiency and economy
- the consumer's ability to function in work and personal roles
- longevity

Assessment of the outcome of nursing care also seeks to account for negative outcomes for the consumer of health services which may be attributed wholly or in part to nursing intervention or the lack thereof. Negative indices include the following:

---

*Source: Wisconsin Regional Medical Board, "Assessing Quality of Nursing Care," *Nursing Administration Quarterly*, vol. 1, no. 3, © 1977 Aspen Publishers, Inc.

- failure to maintain or improve his or her health status
- lack of continuity of care
- failure to identify and respond according to factors actually or potentially detrimental to his or her health
- disability
- discomfort
- dissatisfaction
- complications
- prolongation of illness
- unwarranted death

2. Assessment of Content

Secondly, the quality of nursing care should be assessed in terms of content. Content is the nursing care that is actually given in a specific instance. Content is assessed by the application of standards of nursing practice developed for specific nurse-consumer situations. For example, assessment of content involving a burn patient in an emergency room would differ from an assessment of content involving a coronary patient in the same setting. Similarly, assessment of content to improve the health status of a two-year-old would differ from that for a fifteen-year-old.

3. Assessment of Process

Assessment of process in nursing care focuses on the nature and sequence of events in the delivery of that care. This assessment takes into consideration such aspects as the nature of the interactions among the consumer, nurse, other health care workers, and significant others; the extent to which nursing care objectives have been reached; the specific techniques or procedures used; the degree to which the consumer and significant others have been involved in the entire process; the degree of skill with which nurses have carried out the nursing care as compared with that established by clinical nurse specialists; the coordination among different components of the system and among members of the team; appropriate utilization of each of the available components of the system; and the continuity of care.

4. Assessment of Resources

Assessment of resources in nursing care focuses on the properties of the resources used to provide that care and the manner in which they are organized. Nursing care resources include staff, consultants, collaborating disciplines and services, physical structures, facilities, equipment, supplies, administrative structure, operating procedures and policies, and maintenance. A climate conducive to providing quality nursing care is a prime resource. Resources should be evaluated in terms of their accessibility, availability, appropriateness, and acceptability.

5. Assessment of Efficiency

Efficiency is the attainment of quality nursing care reviewed in relationship to the manpower, supply, equipment, space, and other resources of the provider and the appropriateness, acceptability, and cost to the consumer. Efficiency is frequently referred to as the cost-benefit ratio. It is concerned with determining whether there is a less costly way to achieve the same quality nursing care.

Consumers must be assured an equivalent standard of quality nursing practice in any care setting. Standards of practice are established by clinical specialists in the field who have at least master's degree preparation in clinical nursing and demonstrated expertness and by appropriate external bodies. It is the responsibility of practitioners to develop concordant standards of practice within the specific practice setting.

The perspective of the consumer needs to be included in this evaluation process. In the identification of criteria for use in evaluation, the patient and family unit that receive care and the populace in general should be participants, since the outcomes or end results of care will be stated in terms of benefit to the recipients of service. For the function of allocation of resources, the populace must be informed about the health status of the community, region, or state and the results of resource allocation. Again, the users need to assist in identification of criteria so the results of evaluation are stated in terms which are meaningful to them.

The Current Focus of Quality Assurance Activities

The pursuit of quality in health care is being revolutionized. Quality assurance (QA) activities have routinely evolved in their focus, but they have never enjoyed such attention, recognition, and support.

Quality-related programs and activities in health care have evolved over time. Precipitated by changing expectations on the part of the Joint Commission on Accreditation of Healthcare Organizations (Joint Commission), QA standards of the 70s focused on chart audits. In the 80s a formal, organizationwide QA program that oversaw the monitoring and evaluation of care was prescribed. Increasing emphasis was placed on participation of all disciplines and departments in the QA program. The movement of QA into the 90s has expanded and gained speed. Emphasis is being placed on quality improvement philosophy, including a personal and organizational commitment to quality; ultimate focus on the needs of consumers; and efforts toward continuous improvement.*

Three New Directions*

Three distinct issues appear to be changing the focus of health care quality programs.

First, the *definition of quality* and its essential components has broadened. Twenty years ago, it seemed that the quality of health care could be described by the documentation found in patients' medical records. The skills and behaviors of health care providers, as evidenced by such documentation, were considered the ultimate parameters of quality. It has become increasingly clear that quality health care involves much more. It is unquestionable, for example, that quality care must begin with educated, skilled, and committed caregivers who are oriented to the expectations for their role within a given organization. Additionally,

*Source: Patricia Schroeder, "Improving Health Care Quality in the Nineties," in *The Encyclopedia of Nursing Care Quality Volume I: Issues and Strategies for Nursing Care Quality,* Patricia Schroeder, ed., Aspen Publishers, Inc., © 1991.

research-based practice must guide the care of these knowledgeable practitioners.

Ensuring quality also involves meeting the needs and expectations of patients, physicians, and payers—three different and essential customer groups. Organizational culture, leadership, costs, productivity, and efficiency are additional components. Because of this multi-faceted vision, the description, measurement, and ultimate improvement of quality are increasingly complex.

The second issue changing health care quality programs is the *measurement of quality*. First, scientific methods of measurement are increasingly necessary. QA evaluation requires sound methods in order for the resulting data to be sound. Furthermore, data from QA evaluation are being used to create significant change within organizations, so faulty data based on inaccurate measurement methods carry a great risk. Precise methods are in the process of being developed. In 1989 the federal government established an organization—the Agency for Health Care Policy and Research (AHCPR)—that is investigating and defining outcome measures of quality health care. In addition, both large-scale and small-scale research on patient outcomes is being carried out. Clinical practice guidelines are being developed by expert multidisciplinary teams.

In addition, the measurement of quality has decidedly shifted from addressing the process of care to addressing the outcomes of care. This is a backward swing of the pendulum: Outcome-based evaluation criteria were the foundation of many chart audits in the seventies.

The return to outcome measures has been fostered by many outside of the care delivery setting. Consumers and third-party payers of health care are increasingly asking what outcomes they can expect from care received and money paid. Further, the Joint Commission has moved boldly into the outcome arena, requiring that patient outcome indicators be used for monitoring and evaluating activities. They have begun development of outcome indicator sets for which mandatory data collection will eventually be necessary. The resulting data are to be used internally within the health care setting, by the

Joint Commission on its periodic surveys, and for the development of a national data base.

The third issue changing quality programs is the shift from a QA philosophy to a quality improvement (QI) philosophy. Taking the lead from industries outside of health care that have achieved dramatic success in improving the quality of their products and services, some have begun to apply QI principles to health care settings.

The premise of QI is that quality can always be made better. Rather than comparing oneself to a national norm of mediocrity, improvement can only be demonstrated through comparing oneself to oneself over time. QI embodies the message that quality will not be improved simply as a result of inspection. It must be built into the people and the processes carrying out the work of the organization. QI uses workers at the point of service to define quality, measure its achievement, and create innovations to constantly improve. A QI program requires active involvement of all within the organization, from the mailroom to the boardroom. Visible, supportive leadership is essential.

Monitoring Quality*

The systematic review and evaluation of standards of care and practice will take place in an environment of multidisciplinary collaboration and with an emphasis on clinical research that will link nursing practice to patient outcomes.

Determination of the focal point for quality-related activities will be the caregiver–care receiver encounter and a results-oriented evaluation of patient outcomes. The shift is from the review of organizational characteristics to an analysis of the long-term impact of the care delivered on a patient's state of functioning or wellness. The purpose set forth by the Joint Commission is to foster an internalization of commitment to quality within the organization through an ongoing monitoring and feedback

Source: Mary Ellen Connington and Pamela Dupuis, *Unit-Based Nursing Quality Assurance: A Patient-Centered Approach*, Aspen Publishers, Inc., © 1990.

Types of Review

Since retrospective and concurrent review have different advantages, both should be implemented in an institution's quality assurance program. The same tool can and should be applied in both reviews.

Retrospective Review. *Retrospective review* is a critical examination of past or completed work with a view to improvement. Documentation in the patients' (medical) records is the source of data for the review. Retrospective review is a required dimension of quality assurance.

Retrospective review has the advantages of use of data for the full continuum of care and evaluation of the results of care for a large series of comparable cases. Impressions gained by practitioners from single cases in which they are personally involved and without systematic study of quantifiable aspects are not always borne out by systematic review of a large number of cases.

Concurrent Review. *Concurrent review* is a critical examination of the patient's progress toward the desired alterations in health/wellness status (outcomes) and patient care management (activities) while patient care and treatment are in progress. Documentation of care in the patient's record, and interview, observation, and inspection of the patient, are the sources for data. In some programs, concurrent review is also a required dimension of quality assurance programs. Reviews required by the Social Security Amendments ask for certain pre-admission, admission, and length of stay monitoring while the patient is receiving care. Concurrent review has the advantage of providing the opportunity to make changes in ongoing care. It can also guide the work of the professionals.

---

system. The institution will oversee the integration of quality control into every aspect of organizational life and will measure the quality of the practitioner by the quality of patient outcomes.

Standards of care and practice will be measured by generic, predetermined clinical indicators shared among all similar health care organizations. The indicators will not be the only determinants of quality, but they will serve as triggers for review and corrective action. The focus for institution-specific efforts to determine quality will continue to be on the development of indicators that address high-risk, high-volume, and problematic issues.

Interinstitutional sharing will increase, making use of aggregate data bases and standardized collection modes. Thresholds of evaluation established in the past on the basis of uni-organizational experience will be enhanced or altered through the availability of the multi-organizational indicator data base of peer group institutions. The data base will be updated through the frequent and ongoing submission of institution-specific results of QA monitoring. Therefore, evaluation will be continuous and, although based on individual patient review, will address aggregate clusters of patients to more effectively focus on patterns and trends and to facilitate relevant conclusions regarding appropriateness of care, timeliness of services, efficient utilization of resources, and quality of patient outcomes.

Patient outcome standards will be the primary measure of quality and will determine the appropriateness of clinical practice. The expectation will be that the results of the ongoing monitoring of outcomes will have to be practitioner-specific in order to provide a data base for the credentialing of the future. Evaluation methodology that links nursing and professional practice standards directly to patient outcome will anticipate the future in the continuing evolution of quality assurance.

COMPONENTS OF A QA PROGRAM

The Flow of Responsibility*

There are many individuals, groups, and committees that have responsibility for the development and implementation of the quality assurance program. The focus of flow of responsibility in the nursing department changes as the steps of the quality assurance process change. The many roles for staff in the quality assurance program are identified in Table 21-1.

---

*Source: Anita W. Finkelman, *Quality Assurance for Psychiatric Nursing*, Aspen Publishers, Inc., © 1990.

Table 21-1 Quality Assurance Role Responsibilities

Nurse Administrator

1. Participates in the development of the overall nursing department quality assurance plan.
2. Approves the nursing department quality assurance plan.
3. Ensures that the nursing department quality assurance plan is coordinated with the hospitalwide plan.
4. Reviews implementation quarterly.
5. Reviews and participates in decisions regarding changes required.
6. Monitors the overall program to ensure that it meets accreditation and professional standards.
7. Acts as a role model for all nursing staff communicating the importance of a quality assurance program focused on excellence.

Nursing Supervisory Staff

1. Develop unit quality assurance plan with unit staff.
2. Participate in the development of the overall nursing department quality assurance plan and ensure that the unit plan is coordinated with the overall plan.
3. Ensure that the plan is implemented and that the results are utilized to assist in decision making related to patient care.

4. Assist in teaching staff and sharing results about quality assurance.

Quality Assurance Coordinators

1. Coordinate the unit quality assurance activities with the assistance and guidance of the head nurse.
2. Implement the data collection as identified on the plan.
3. Maintain the records of the data collection activities and, in conjunction with the head nurse, prepare the required reports.
4. Assist the head nurse in staff development related to quality assurance.
5. Act as a role model for staff in communicating the importance of quality assurance to the entire staff.
6. Attend quality assurance meetings as scheduled.

Staff Nurses

1. Participate in developing the unit quality assurance plan.
2. Collect data as assigned and report data.
3. Participate in staff meetings to discuss the results of the quality assurance program.
4. Implement required changes in daily practice to provide excellence in care.

Source: Adapted from *Nursing Economics*, No. 6, p. 286, with permission of Anthony Jannetti, Inc., © 1986.

The flow of responsibility is not downward or upward but rather circular. Emphasis on a particular group changes with the process. Each step in the process requires a variety of skills and participants. At specific points, some skills and participants are more important than others. When one group does not participate actively at the appropriate time, this affects the entire process and each person's responsibility. Some people will take on too much responsibility, and others will abdicate theirs.

Nurse Administrator and QA Objectives

The nursing profession and the Joint Commission's quality assurance standards clearly recognize that the nurse administrator has the ultimate responsibility for the quality of the nursing care provided in the nursing department. The fulfillment of this responsibility can occur in a wide variety of ways, although certain fundamentals apply universally.

First, there must be an excellent communication system in place to allow critical data to reach the nurse administrator. The nurse administrator needs to be involved in the development of this communication system so as to ensure that it provides the required data for decision making.

Second, the authority to make decisions intended to resolve problems is an essential component of responsibility. Without the power to initiate change, the nurse administrator cannot fulfill his or her responsibility.

Third, although the level of direct participation by the nurse administrator in the quality assurance program will vary, any program that does not have a nurse administrator who is enthusiastic, supportive, and a participant in the quality assurance process will probably not be successful. Even when quality assurance is decentralized and unit based, the nurse administrator still retains ultimate responsibility and must provide overall guidance.

Finally, with responsibility comes the need to emphasize excellence in the nursing care provided. It is easy to make the quality assurance process into a negative process. However, the result will be a program that fails to fulfill its purpose.

Writing A Quality Assurance Program Plan*

Step 1: Statement of Purpose or Goal. In stating the purpose, the following question should be answered: What is the intention of the quality assurance program? An example of what could be stated is this: "The purpose of the quality assurance program or the goal of the quality assurance program for nursing service is to establish a planned and systematic process for the monitoring and evaluation of the quality and appropriateness of patient care and for resolving identified problems."

Step 2: Listing of Objectives. Objectives should define what is to be accomplished by carrying out a QA plan. Some plans include both long-term and short-term objectives. Long-term objectives act as a guide to the overall program. Examples include these:

- evaluating compliance with the established standards of patient care

- identifying problems and developing strategies to resolve identified problems
- recognizing and improving the quality of nursing care provided to patients
- identifying nurses with performance problems

Short-term objectives reflect the emphasis for the next one or two years. Examples include these:

- revising QA reporting tools
- researching and selecting a software package for sorting QA information and writing reports

Step 3: Description of Role Responsibilities. Although accountability for QA programs is the ultimate responsibility of a nurse administrator, in most organizations many nurses are involved in quality assurance. At this point in the plan, describe the roles and responsibilities of every member of the QA team.

Step 4: Description of Structure. The structure should indicate the manner in which the work of quality assurance will be completed. State the particular model that has been chosen. If a unique model has been created at the facility, describe it and include a diagram of the structure. Be sure to explain how this nursing department structure relates to the organizationwide QA program and how reports get to the governing board.

Step 5: Description of QA Committee Functions. The QA committee will oversee the process of monitoring nursing practice. Although some committee functions may be determined by the QA model selected, responsibilities that might be considered include scheduling regular meetings, conducting an annual evaluation of the QA program, receiving and responding to QA reports, and providing ongoing QA education and training.

Step 6: Description of How Monitoring and Evaluation Will Be Conducted. For QA monitoring results to be useful, the information needs to be summarized. A convenient way to organize the QA reporting schedule is to collect

---

*Source: Anne-Marie Ducquette, "Approaches to Monitoring Practice: Getting Started," in *The Encyclopedia of Nursing Care Quality Volume III: Monitoring and Evaluation in Nursing*, Patricia Schroeder, ed., Aspen Publishers, Inc., © 1991.

data for three months (or one quarter) and then report the findings. While there may be "formal" time frames for reporting, any evidence of significant clinical problems must be followed up immediately.

The Monitoring and Evaluation Process (Joint Commission Viewpoint)

The monitoring and evaluation process is designed to help health care organizations effectively use their resources to manage the quality of the care or services they provide. Monitoring and evaluation activities involve the ongoing examination of care provided, the identification of deficiencies in that care, and improvement, as necessary, of the quality of care. Appropriate monitoring and evaluation activities are ongoing and integrated with other monitoring and evaluation activities throughout the organization.

The monitoring and evaluation process assists both in identifying patterns of care that may not be evident when only case-by-case review is performed and in identifying situations in which case review is likely to be most useful in identifying correctable deficiencies in care and opportunities to improve care. Although it will not identify every case of substandard care, the monitoring and evaluation process will help the organization identify situations on which its attention could be the most productively focused.*

The Ten-Step Monitoring and Evaluation Process**

The following ten steps are necessary for effective monitoring and evaluation in an organization, department, or service.

*Source: Copyright 1988 by the Joint Commission on Accreditation of Healthcare Organizations, Chicago. Reprinted with permission.

**Source: This most current version of the Joint Commission's model is applicable to all departments and was obtained from *Monitoring and Evaluation: Physical Rehabilitation Services*. Copyright 1988 by the Joint Commission on Accreditation of Healthcare Organizations, Chicago. Reprinted with permission.

1. Assign responsibility.
2. Delineate scope of care.
3. Identify important aspects of care.
4. Identify indicators related to these aspects of care.
5. Establish thresholds for evaluation related to the indicators.
6. Collect and organize data.
7. Evaluate care when thresholds are reached.
8. Take action to improve care.
9. Assess the effectiveness of the action and document improvement.
10. Communicate relevant information to the organizationwide QA program.

The Sequence. Visual representation of the monitoring and evaluation process is shown in Figure 21-2 as it functions from step 2 to step 10. Appropriate staff members delineate scope of care, identify important aspects of care, identify indicators, and establish thresholds for evaluation to facilitate monitoring and evaluation of care provided in a particular department or service. Data pertaining to the indicators are collected, and the aggregate level of performance is compared with the threshold for evaluation. If the threshold is not reached, further evaluation is not necessary. Those findings are included in the regular report to the organizationwide QA program. When the threshold is reached, the important aspect of care is evaluated to determine whether a problem or opportunity for improvement is present. If a problem or opportunity for improvement is identified, the cause is determined and corrective action is taken. After a sufficient period of time, the effectiveness of the actions is assessed, and the findings are reported to the organizationwide QA program. Monitoring and evaluation is continued to identify any future deficiencies in care.

What To Monitor. To delineate the scope of care for a given department, its personnel should simply ask themselves the following question: "What is done in this department?" The answer to this question will be an inventory including the types of patients served, the conditions and diagnoses treated, the treatments or activities performed, the types of practitioners providing

Figure 21-2 The Monitoring and Evaluation Process

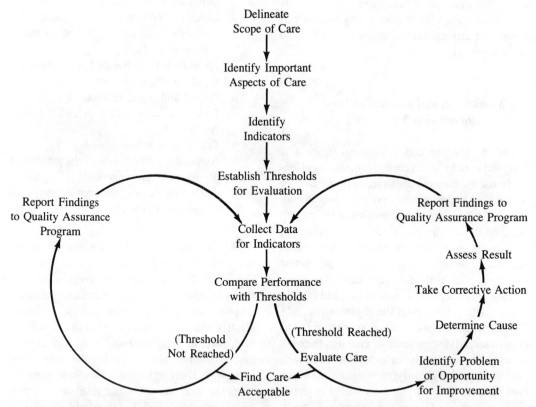

Source: *Monitoring and Evaluation: Physical Rehabilitation Services*. Copyright 1988 by the Joint Commission on Accreditation of Healthcare Organizations, Chicago. Reprinted with permission.

care, and even the sites where care is provided and the times it is provided. This inventory provides a basis for subsequent steps in the monitoring and evaluation process.

After the scope of care is delineated, department personnel should ask themselves a more specific question: "Which of the things we do are the most important?" The answer to this question should lead to identifying important aspects of care—the aspects on which monitoring and evaluation will be focused (see Table 21-2). To use the organization's resources effectively (including professionals' time) in quality assurance, the activities chosen should be those with the greatest impact on patient care. Therefore, priority should be given to those aspects of care for which one or more of the following is true:

- the aspect of care occurs frequently or affects large numbers of patients
- patients will be at risk for serious consequences or will be deprived of substantial benefit if the care is not provided correctly (including providing care that is not indicated and failing to provide care that is indicated)
- the aspect of care has tended in the past to produce problems for staff or patients

High-volume, high-risk, or problem-prone aspects of care should be the highest priority for monitoring and evaluation.

In order to monitor the important things being done in the department efficiently, indicators should be identified for each important aspect of care.

Table 21-2 Sample Schedule for QA Monitoring Program

FREQUENCY

MONITORS/EVALUATIONS	January	February	March	April	May	June	July	August	September	October	November	December
I. Quality Indicators												
• Medication errors	X	X	X	X	X	X	X	X	X	X	X	X
• Patient falls	X	X	X	X	X	X	X	X	X	X	X	X
• Patient satisfaction	X	X	X	X	X	X	X	X	X	X	X	X
• Patient correspondence	X	X	X	X	X	X	X	X	X	X	X	X
• Narcotic discrepancies	X	X	X	X	X	X	X	X	X	X	X	X
• Infection control												
—Isolation problems	X	X	X	X	X	X	X	X	X	X	X	X
II. Standards												
• Patient identification	X	X	X	X	X	X	X	X	X	X	X	X
• Sponge/needle counts	X	X	X	X	X	X	X	X	X	X	X	X
• Product evaluation	X	X	X	X	X	X	X	X	X	X	X	X
• Nursing process (proposed for quarterly evaluation)	X			X			X			X		
—Assessment												
—Planning												
—Intervention												
—Evaluation												
—Documentation												
• Committee minutes										X		
• Nursing practice manuals												
• Licensure	X											
• Education program documents												
• Administrative documents (proposed annually)												
III. Problems												
• Problems/omissions in care	X	X	X	X	X	X	X	X	X	X	X	X

Source: Courtesy of the Hospital of the University of Pennsylvania, Philadelphia, Pennsylvania.

DEVELOPMENT OF INDICATORS AND THRESHOLDS FOR EVALUATION

Definitions*

The use of "indicators" and "thresholds for evaluation" is an important component of any monitoring and evaluation program. Their use will focus attention on high-priority areas of practice and facilitate an objective identification of problems needing further analysis and peer review.

An *indicator* is a well-defined, objective variable used to monitor the quality and/or appropriateness of an important aspect of patient care. An indicator can be a resource, process, clinical event, complication, or outcome about which data should be collected through monitoring activities. Examples of indicators include death, hospital-acquired infection, a severe adverse drug reaction, pressure sores, and unanticipated transfer to the acute care unit, and full participation in planned therapy sessions.

Each *threshold* for evaluation is a pre-established aggregate level of performance applied to a series of cases performed by a practitioner, service, department, or organization related to a specific indicator of the quality and/or appropriateness of an important aspect of care. When the threshold is reached, evaluation of the quality and appropriateness of the important aspect of care is initiated. For example, one possible threshold for a hospital-acquired infection indicator is 5 percent. When the measured aggregate level of performance pertaining to the indicator reaches the threshold, further evaluation is necessary.

Both indicators and thresholds for evaluation should be determined by the department or service staff and should be derived from communication with knowledgeable individuals and a review of pertinent health care and QA literature.

The Clinical Indicator*

Defining, understanding, and quantifying appropriate clinical indicators in nursing are critical to the comprehensive effectiveness of both unit-based and departmental quality assurance programs. With the Joint Commission on Accreditation of Healthcare Organizations' new Agenda for Change and the public's heightened sensitivity to health care delivery systems, it is imperative to identify and consistently use appropriate, measurable indicators.

Clinical indicators are defined by the Joint Commission as a quantitative measure that can be used as a guide to monitor and evaluate the quality of important patient care and support service activities. Indicators should not be thought of as direct measures of quality, but rather as markers or barometers that can identify areas and issues that warrant closer evaluation.

Indicators should reflect and measure the structure, processes, and outcomes of nursing care. Structure indicators address the potential to deliver high-quality patient care. They evaluate structural aspects required for care, such as staffing requirements, necessary credentials, and equipment preparation or readiness. Process indicators focus on the actual manner in which care is delivered. Effectiveness, timeliness, and appropriateness of care rendered are examples of process issues. Outcome indicators assess exactly what the name implies: the end result (desirable or undesirable) of care delivered. It represents the composite of all other variables. While it is important to examine all three aspects of care delivery, emphasis should be directed toward evaluating the outcomes of nursing care.

Basis for Measurements

Indicators can be further refined and applied to nursing practice. According to the Joint Commission, there are two general types of indicators: sentinel event and rate based. A *sentinel-event indicator* identifies a grave, untoward

*Source: Monitoring and Evaluation: Physical Rehabilitation Services. Copyright 1988 by the Joint Commission on Accreditation of Healthcare Organizations, Chicago. Reprinted with permission.

*Source: Anne Dearth Williams, "Development and Application of Clinical Indicators for Nursing," Journal of Nursing Care Quality, vol. 6, no. 1, © 1991 Aspen Publishers, Inc.

process or outcome of care. Usually, and ideally, the incidence of this type of indicator will remain low (e.g., hospital-acquired decubitus ulcer). A *rate-based indicator* identifies patient care outcomes or processes of care that may require further assessment based on significant trending or variances from thresholds over time (e.g., percentage of patients prepared for discharge). Indicators may be expressed as either desirable or undesirable measures based on the aspect of care you wish to monitor.

It is helpful to approach rate-based indicators as two more distinct types: occurrence indicators and compliance/performance indicators. *Occurrence indicators* are usually dedicated to identifying outcomes of care, while *compliance/performance indicators* are used to assess processes of care delivery. Occurrence indicators also can frequently measure the occurrence of patient complications. This is significant because a large majority of nursing activity focuses on the prevention of a wide variety of patient complications, thereby lending itself to measurement of the outcomes of the preventive nursing interventions.

Several important issues need to be remembered when designing and implementing nursing indicators. First and foremost, quality assurance activities, while similar to research, should not be confused with this more exact science. Due to the numerous, uncontrollable variables in patient care settings, generalized assumptions are difficult to make appropriately across patient populations. In addition, when measuring patient outcomes it is important to realize that individual outcomes cannot be guaranteed through routine quality assurance activities; rather, outcome indicators assess the overall past outcomes for similar patient populations.

Designing Indicators

Clinical indicators can be tailored to express almost any specialized patient process or outcome. Process and outcome indicators can be used simultaneously to more effectively evaluate any aspect of care. In fact, it is vital that indicators be as specific to the aspect of care as possible so that a thorough evaluation of nursing care can be implemented.

Quantifying indicators can be simplified when the aspect of care that is being measured is expressed in the form of a rate or ratio of events for a defined population and time frame. In other words, an indicator is measurable when a rate is used as follows:

$$\text{Outcome indicators} = \frac{\text{Number of patient care events}}{\substack{\text{Total number of patients or} \\ \text{total number of times at risk} \\ \text{for above event (for a given} \\ \text{period of time)}}}$$

$$\text{Process indicators} = \frac{\substack{\text{Number of times ``procedure} \\ \text{X'' or ``standard Y'' is} \\ \text{successfully completed/} \\ \text{implemented by a nurse}}}{\substack{\text{Total number of times} \\ \text{procedure or standard is used} \\ \text{(for a given period of time)}}}$$

Indicators should also be flexible enough so that they can be revised periodically to reflect the most accurate and specific measure of the aspect of care being evaluated. Examples of specific clinical indicators can be reviewed in Table 21-3.

To help ensure more valid indicator rates, several reliable data sources must be used. Consistent numerator and denominator definitions applied appropriately to credible data sources can strengthen the value of an evaluation. Specific, defined criteria must be utilized to assist in the measurement process of the indicator.

Data can be obtained from a combination of incident reports, direct observation and tracking on individual units, medical record reviews, unit event logs, and occurrence screening during utilization review activities.

Determining a Threshold of Evaluation*

The threshold of compliance or threshold of evaluation is a numeric figure or percentage that indicates the frequency with which compliance with a standard is expected. Thresholds of eval-

Source: Mary Ellen Connington and Pamela Dupuis, *Unit-based Nursing Quality Assurance: A Patient-centered Approach*, Aspen Publishers, Inc., © 1990.

Table 21-3 Examples of Clinical Indicators

Aspect of Care	Indicator	Indicator Type	Quantifiable Measure
Management of patients on ventilators R/T self-extubations	Occurrence of self-extubations	Outcome	No. of patients who self-extubate No. of patients intubated
	Compliance with standard of practice (R/T ventilator management)	Process	No. of times standard of practice (on ventilator management) is successfully followed/implemented No. of times standard of practice is utilized
Discharge education	Occurrence of well-prepared patients at discharge	Outcome	No. of patients who successfully completed discharge program No. of patients discharged
Discharge planning R/T continuity of care/support	Occurrence of discharged patients well prepared for community reintegration	Outcome	No. of patients referred to community support groups or resources No. of patients discharged
Medication administration R/T prevention of administration errors	Occurrence of medication errors	Outcome	No. of medication errors No. of doses dispensed
	Compliance with medication administration procedure	Process	No. of times procedure on medication administration is followed successfully No. of doses dispensed (no. of times procedure is utilized)
Patient safety R/T prevention of patient falls	Occurrence of patient falls	Outcome	No. of patient falls No. of patients at risk or no. of patient days
Management of premature infant with thermoregulatory problems R/T prevention of hypothermia	Occurrence of hypothermia events	Outcome	No. of hypothermia events No. of patients at risk or of patient days
	Appropriate implementation of management of thermoregulation protocol	Process	No. of times management of thermoregulation protocol is successfully followed or implemented No. of times protocol is utilized

uation delineate precisely the allowable deviation from the standard. The threshold is set prior to the collection of data and serves as an internal trigger or "red flag" for the nurse manager. Compliance levels below the predetermined threshold warrant review and usually corrective action. Compliance levels equal to or above the threshold warrant positive reinforcement for the staff and signify satisfactory or acceptable patterns of care.

Thresholds of evaluation are often expressed as percentages, although they can also be expressed as integers and decimals. Thresholds can be defined in absolute terms as "all or none." In this mode, the threshold of compliance is expressed as a percentage and is set at either the 0 percent limit or the 100 percent limit. For example:

100 percent compliance. All patients will receive their correct medications in the correct dosage at the correct time via the correct route without exception.

0 percent compliance. There will be no medication error occurrences.

Both of the statements mean the same. One is stated in the positive, and one in the negative; however, both are absolutes. There is no allowance for deviation from the standard. Generally, the department or organization should adopt one consistent approach to stating outcomes (either in the negative or the positive). It is simply a matter of wording. Either way, a 100 percent or a 0 percent compliance threshold would automatically mandate review of each error.

Absolute evaluation thresholds have their greatest application in the area of risk management and for critical practice issues that may result in fatal outcomes. Absolute thresholds should be set judiciously and reserved for issues of critical importance because they require significant effort to attain and maintain. Basically, thresholds modify standards by allowing ranges for recognition of both competent clinical care and the need for corrective action for outcomes and clinical practice patterns that are not optimum.

IMPLEMENTING AND USING A QUALITY ASSURANCE PROGRAM

Developing a Quality Assurance Manual*

Operationally, each nursing unit or professional service should create a unit QA manual

Source: Carolyn G. Smith Marker, "The Marker QA Model for Quality Assurance, Monitoring and Evaluation in Professional Practice," *Journal of Nursing Quality Assurance*, vol. 1, no. 3, © 1987 Aspen Publishers, Inc.

with all activities labeled. All methods, mechanisms, and tools that capture the data of the activities are then housed in the appropriate sections of the manual. The area QA plan is at the front of the manual, and the quarterly reports and annual summation are placed at the end. After the reporting mechanism has summarized the data being reviewed for the quarter, along with accomplishments, the manual can be thinned of obsolete data. This thinning process keeps the QA manual orderly and current.

Sections

Standards Development. Although the area's standards are contained in a standards manual, the QA manual should contain a separate tab labeled "Standards Committee," behind which can be placed the standards committee's validation of their continued work at standards development, their efforts to update standards to respond to changing patient care conditions, and QA findings. Also located here are the specific review activities conducted by the standards committee, namely, documentation reviews carried out periodically validating the implementation of standards and patient response in the nursing progress records.

Continuing Education. The continuing education section of the QA manual should house the area's staff development records for easy staff and manager access and demonstrate that continuing education is a component of QA. It is suggested that three continuing education records be used: (1) a continuing education events list that tracks educational topics addressed throughout the year and the reason for each (e.g., to maintain competency, to create new competency, or to respond to a QA corrective action); (2) a mandatory events list that tracks required review sessions such as cardiopulmonary resuscitation classes, electrical safety updates, and fire and disaster drill attendance; and (3) an individual record for each staff member in which he or she tracks personal continuing education data.

The credentialing section of the QA manual should contain all the information pertaining to staff competency so that it is readily available for staff evaluation programs and regulatory agency visits. It is suggested that three tools be used for this component of QA: (1) a licensure update to annually record the current licensure status of staff members; (2) a credentialing list to annually certify staff in cognitive and skill reviews; and (3) procedure approval lists to grant permission to staff, based on proven competency, to function in high-risk, controversial areas of nursing.

Performance Appraisal. This section of the QA manual should contain a brief narrative explanation of the area's performance appraisal mechanisms, stressing the relationship between QA events and employee evaluation. Staff performance appraisal tools may be added.

Audit Process. The audit section of the QA manual contains all information reviewed by the audit process. It is suggested that six compliance audits be conducted per unit per year: two structure, two process, and two outcome audits. Noncompliance audits should be done as necessary to investigate known areas of low adherence to standards. Miscellaneous audits should include two documentation reviews, one staff and one consumer survey, and one generic review per unit per year.

Monitors. All completed monitors are placed in the concurrent monitoring section of the unit QA manual and summarized in the quarterly QA report.

Risk Management. The risk management section of the QA manual contains the data sources for tracking safety, infection control, and incidents.

Utilization Review. The utilization review section of the QA manual contains all information relative to resource use. It is suggested that three utilization review tools be developed: a unit log, a utilization of the unit record, and a budgetary tracking form.

The unit log records vital statistics on all patients admitted or seen in the area and also contains a section for recording adverse events experienced by each patient, incorporating the concept of generic screens.

The use of the unit record tracks information on staff workload and bed utilization as well as selected volume indicators that are pertinent to the area.

Finally, the budgetary record tracks unit expenditures and compares the current budget status with predetermined budget goals.

Problem Identification. The problem identification section of the QA manual contains all data sources for problem identification and improvement monitoring. It is suggested that four data sources be developed: (1) a problem identification sheet and a problem log, (2) a care conference report sheet, (3) a supervisory report form, and (4) a shift unit report sheet.

The problem identification sheet is used by all employees to report complaints and perceived problems in writing. Because these reports can get wordy and accumulate in volume, they should be summarized by the manager in a written unit problem log.

The care conference report sheet records that care review sessions have been held by the staff. The tool provides an additional source of problem identification, a vehicle for group care planning, and a valuable monitoring tool to track results of corrective actions.

The supervisory report sheet records observations and perceptions of the manager as weekly rounds are made. Areas of compliance and noncompliance with standards are recorded. This tool allows subsequent rounds to become more effective in following up issues of concern by the manager.

Finally, the shift report sheet, completed by each shift leader, provides a summation of the shift's activities and communicates promptly to the manager for follow up any problems with staffing, other departments, bed census, or working relationships.

Evaluation of a Quality Assurance Program*

Review Program Objectives

The first step in a QA program evaluation is to critically review program objectives for utility in directing the evaluation. In this sense, program objectives must be made operational. Since this

*Source: Cathleen Krueger Wilson, "Designing a Quality Assurance Program Evaluation: A Process Model," *Journal of Nursing Quality Assurance*, vol. 2, no. 4, © 1988 Aspen Publishers, Inc.

situation is not always the case, it is useful for the evaluator to pull together key staff and manager program participants in order to accomplish this work. Once objectives are operationalized, criteria that will clearly provide evidence of objective achievement must also be established.

Initially, the group can be instructed to order objectives from most abstract to least abstract and then work to reduce the abstractness. The content of each objective needs to be made very clear. Objectives also must be examined in terms of their short-term versus long-term effects. How long are the effects presumed to last? Finally, multiple or overlapping objectives need to be identified and eliminated.

Once this review has been completed, criteria for objective achievement can be more easily developed by the work group. For example, a QA program objective might be to provide mechanisms for the integration of nursing QA with hospital and medical QA programs. This objective clearly describes organizational structures that are the arena for the integration of all QA activities occurring within the hospital. It is hoped that such integration will bring about systemwide problem identification and resolution. Sample criteria for this objective achievement would include the presence of joint hospital, medical, and nursing QA activities, including meetings, educational opportunities, and multidisciplinary monitors, at a defined level of frequency.

Identify Target Groups

The next step in designing program evaluation is to identify program participants as well as those individuals impacted by the program. Target groups include staff nurses, managers, unit-based committees, nursing division committees, hospital QA committees, and patients. The overall structure of the QA program will determine the target groups available for study.

Two major concerns need to be addressed in relationship to target groups: (1) participation and (2) identification of the presence of new behaviors. For example, several questions can be raised regarding nurses' participation. To what extent does each nurse actually participate in both the monitoring and the implementation of a unit-based system? What are the organizational

arrangements that allow the RN to participate, and are staff nurses given the time to participate? How often do staff nurses participate and in what component of the program? Are these arrangements effective?

Another question to be addressed concerns whether or not the QA program has been modified to require some change in nurses' behavior. For example, moving from a centralized program to a decentralized unit-based program certainly requires new behavior on everyone's part. Also, the introduction of a new manager or new QA coordinator can result in significant changes in expected QA activities. In considering additional target groups for evaluation, potential participants (such as new employees) or program dropouts might reveal useful information regarding the difficulties in acquiring such new behavior.

Compile a List of Program Characteristics

Program activities, procedures, materials, and administrative processes must be clearly identified. This list of key characteristics will guide the selection of evaluation strategies. A work group can be assembled and instructed to create a very detailed list of key QA program characteristics. These features would include (1) activities for which the most resources are allocated; (2) areas of the program needing revision; (3) descriptions of all program activities; (4) frequency and duration of program activities; (5) identification of responsible people; (6) forms of program coordination; and (7) systems in place for identifying, implementing, and following up on program monitors.

Choose an Evaluation Strategy

The next step in designing a QA program evaluation includes issues of both time and evaluation methodology. The evaluator must decide whether to evaluate data over a specified period of time in either a prospective or retrospective manner. Since the Joint Commission on Accreditation of Healthcare Organizations' requirements specify the need for an annual review of QA programs, a year is a common time frame. There are essentially three process model strategies that are applicable to QA program evaluation:

1. analysis of existing documentation
2. observation
3. self-reports from program participants

1. Analysis of Existing Documents. The documentation of QA activities in a hospital can yield a data system that presents a very clear overall picture of the program or an extremely limited view. In order to apply this strategy, the evaluator must carefully examine all existing data sources in existence that are related to QA activities in the hospital organization. Sample sources include the following:

- attendance and in-service logs—QA education
- minutes of all QA-related committees
- incident review committee minutes
- safety committee minutes
- in-house memos related to QA work
- reports summarizing QA monitors and follow-up actions
- staff meeting minutes
- circulation of files on QA in library
- patient satisfaction questionnaires
- QA projects produced by staff
- administrative reports
- organizational charts

Existing records must be carefully examined for their usefulness for achieving the program evaluation goals. Are the data accurate, reliable, and complete? Careful thinking through of data requirements for evaluation is essential at this point.

With a complex QA program, evaluators must be cautioned to discretely sample key data sources and, when absolutely necessary, create a new record to address a particular evaluation need. By avoiding data saturation, the evaluator ensures that time is not wasted sorting through abstract or irrelevant information in order to search for program features.

Once the sources of data to be collected have been identified, a data collection tool can be developed. This tool is simply a list of docu-

ments that indicates how they are named, where they can be found, what activities are to be noted within, their frequency of occurrence, and responsible parties. Once this information is recorded, the data provided are used to match program goals and outcomes and to identify relationships among program components.

2. Observation Strategies. Observation strategies may be used alone or in combination with analyses of documents.

Evaluators interested in employing this strategy must answer several questions. Where are the best arenas for observation? Who should be observed and in what time frame should observation occur? The decision about where to look may be influenced by a need to add to existing documentation or to explore suspected critical differences in program implementation.

The target population for the evaluation will determine who shall be observed. It is imperative that the sequencing of observations be planned carefully, in order to accurately track practice changes attributable to monitoring. Availability of observers and time for training will partially determine instrument choice. If a key program decision, such as whether or not to continue the current QA program, is resting on observational data analysis, then a highly structured approach is recommended. The degree of structure and detail inherent in both the scenarios and the data collection tool is directly related to the degree of accuracy attributable to the data collected. While streamlining the data collection tools will minimize data quality problems, time requirements remain a serious issue with this evaluation strategy.

3. Self-Report Strategies. Self-reports may be used to support other data collected as part of the evaluation. This method relies on interviewing past, present, and future QA program participants. However, in relationship to QA program evaluation, self-reporting methods must be carefully examined before they are implemented.

The formality of the self-report process may vary, similar to the observation methods described previously. Once again, time requirements for training, instrument development, and data collection need to be carefully planned.

The steps involved in implementation of self-report strategies parallel those required for observation. However, noted differences are the communication and psychosocial skills required of interviewers. Careful choice of interviewers through a screening process will address this issue.

The self-report strategy may be extremely useful in determining staff nurses' view of their role in QA activities. Evaluators could structure an interview guide from the program characteristics list and ask staff nurses specific questions about involvement in key program activities.

Organizational Review of Unit-based Quality Assurance*

The term *unit-based QA* can be a real misnomer. Just saying it is so does not really get the job done. Use this eight-point checklist to determine whether your own unit passes.

First, does the unit have a written QA plan? Is the plan developed by the head nurse with staff input? Does it define the objectives, scope, and mechanisms of unit-based QA activities and diagram how the plan integrates with that of the department and hospital? Does the plan explain the ways in which QA events are planned, are systematic, and are ongoing? Is the plan evaluated annually and revised as necessary?

Second, is there a QA calendar hanging on the conference room wall for the year that translates the plan into action each month? Does the calendar reflect clinical topics for monitoring, display compliance factors, and list the staff involved? Do the topics being monitored reflect all the major clinical activities in the area?

Third, is there a unit QA manual organized to house QA work? Is this accessible to the staff at all times, while simultaneously protecting the confidentiality of patients? Are the staff actively using it to enter data as well as regularly review QA findings?

Fourth, is there an organized reporting mechanism to summarize what has been done—data reviewed, problems identified, actions taken, and results achieved? Does this report serve to integrate unit activities with those of other units and tie all the department QA events together?

Fifth, is a "practice model" being used to shape QA activities? Does the chosen model direct QA measures in a comprehensive manner and ensure that issues of standards development, continuing education, staff credentialing, performance appraisal, risk management, utilization review, clinical monitoring (via planned audits and spontaneous, concurrent monitoring "spot checks"), and active problem identification (via unit-specific data sources) are incorporated at the unit level?

Sixth, to what extent is QA incorporated into the daily activity of unit operations? Is there daily tracking and trending of certain volume indicators and weekly clinical monitoring of select clinical topics? Is this integrated into the daily work and assignments of the nursing staff?

Seventh, are all staff involved in some QA events on the unit, not just a few nurses? Do all staff participate in standards development, criteria development, data collection and analysis, as well as formulation of corrective action plans and follow-up monitoring? Is the concept of peer review understood and accepted by most of the staff and put into practice so that they are comfortable monitoring the practice and care of colleagues? Do unit-based performance standards specify that staff actively participate in QA, and are the QA findings reflected in annual staff performance appraisals?

Eighth, finally and most importantly, what visible and measurable improvements in unit operations, staff performance, and patient care are occurring? Do staff members feel positive about their contributions and accomplishments? Are problems actively identified and permanently solved? Is the overall compliance with established standards (procedures, protocols, guidelines, and standards of care) adequate and consistently achieved? Is consumer, nursing, and physician satisfaction high? Are negative incidents below the established thresholds?

Source: Carolyn G. Smith Marker, "QA Forum," *Journal of Nursing Quality Assurance*, vol. 3, no. 3, © 1989 Aspen Publishers, Inc.

Using Results*

The conclusions of QA reviews can often provide directions for constructive activities. For example, some of the potential improvements that can be undertaken include

- modifying nursing care plans and the nursing care process, including discharge planning, for selected patient populations
- implementing a program for improving documentation of nursing care through improved charting policies, methodologies, and forms
- focusing of nursing rounds and team conferences
- focusing supervisory attention upon areas of weakness identified, such as one particular nursing unit or specific employees
- designing responsive orientation and in-service education programs
- gaining administrative support for making changes in resources, including personnel
- using the evaluations based on nursing audit criteria to focus staff attention on individual patient outcomes

The findings can also be utilized by each level of nursing management.

For Nursing Administrators

The measurements

- provide evaluations of particular programs, such as orientation of personnel or establishment of a patient teaching program
- support requests for accreditation or for financing for a particular program
- serve as bases for planning new programs or program changes
- serve to identify areas of strength and weakness in the total nursing program, in specific areas of the program, and in various settings in which a program exists

- determine the influence of varied staffing patterns
- may be used as data in cost-effectiveness studies—for example, studies comparing the quality of care received by patients in varied situations in which costs of staffing vary

For Supervisors and Head Nurses

The measurements

- identify areas of needed patient care improvement
- provide bases for planning in-service education programs
- identify teaching/supervision needs of staff members who give direct care to patients

For Head Nurses and Staff Nurses

The measurements

- provide a "self-examination" of care in their specific nursing unit or setting
- identify particular types of care in which practice may be improved merely by increased attention and conscientiousness
- identify types of care in which improvement will depend on the staff's acquiring additional knowledge and skill

REPRESENTATIVE MODELS

ANA Model for Implementing a Nursing Quality Assurance Program*

Many models describe the flow of activities in a quality assurance review process. The ANA Congress for Nursing Practice Model is a problem-solving process which utilizes process, structure, and outcome criteria as the tools of inquiry. Following are eight steps for implementing the model for quality assurance.

*Source: Helen Benedikter, From Nursing Audit to Multidisciplinary Audit, National League for Nursing, Pub. No. 20-1673, 1977. Reprinted with permission.

*Source: American Nurses' Association, Guidelines for Review of Nursing Care at the Local Level, Bureau of Quality Assurance, DHHS, Pub. No. (HRA) 76-3004, 1976.

1. Identify Values

The first step in implementing this model for quality assurance is to look at social, institutional, and individual values. Any definition of quality implies a consideration of values: what people think of as "good" and as "bad." The values of the culture, the institution, the profession, and the nursing service department will interact to influence the development of the criteria used in the review process. The involvement of nurses at the local level in the establishment of criteria is, therefore, an important aspect of the evaluation system.

For example, identifying values might require consideration of societal values, professional nursing values, and scientific knowledge. One societal value may be the level of health care the consumers are willing to accept and for which they are willing to pay. Professional values are established standards of the profession, as reflected by such statements as the American Nurses' Association's *Standards of Practice* or the *Code for Nurses with Interpretive Statements*.

Specific institutional values will be reflected in concrete ways in the development of criteria and standards. If a specific nursing service department values prevention as an aspect of patient care, a list of criteria for nursing performance in the gynecology unit might include teaching breast self-examination to each patient.

2. Identify Structure, Process, and Outcome Standards and Criteria

Identify the Focus of the Review. Today health is viewed as the ability of the individual to function actively in work, in recreation, and in society. Standards need to be set that define levels of health and establish guidelines to identify how individual patients are progressing toward predetermined goals. These guidelines are developed in the quality assurance review.

The primary purpose of a review system is to assure the patient, the health financers, as well as the profession itself that patients are receiving health care that conforms to criteria established by nursing peers—care that is effective and efficient. The evaluation can focus on the patients, the providers, or the institution, or all three simultaneously. The focus will, in part, be dictated by the values of the institution and of the individuals within the institution.

If the review looks at the care of patients, the review may be limited to groups of similar patients or to a specific number of patients. Such variables as age, nursing problems, degree of illness, ecologic factors, or religious orientation may all be used to identify groups of patients.

If the review looks at the nurse, nursing service departments using team nursing may use groups of nurses or patient care units as the focus. Nursing service departments organized using primary nursing or independent nursing practice may use individual nurses as the focus.

If the review focuses on the institution, it may look at the type of services delivered, the administrative structure, the organization, or the flow of activities. In each case, the focus of the review is different. Review of each group will ask different questions and find different answers.

Review committees should be formed within the committee structure of the institution and should carry administrative sanction. The membership of a committee will depend on the focus and activity of the review program. The purpose of the review will dictate whether the committee will be composed of nurses from one specialty (e.g., pediatrics) or nurses from several specialties. A committee limited to practitioners in one specialty would review health care for patients within that specialty. A committee with membership from several specialties might review total care within an institution. Practitioners in similar agencies can form a quality assurance committee within a geographical district.

When institutional review committees are functioning, the results of several institutional groups can be shared.

Multidisciplinary committees composed of representatives from several health professions may pool the results of individual peer review committees and study patient care in-depth in one specific area. When the focus of the review is on the patient and criteria are being prepared for health care evaluation studies, multidisciplinary committees would be particularly appropriate. The committees could share in the development of the outcome criteria or coordinate the inclusion of criteria developed by several disciplines into the review process.

Identify the Criteria and Standards. After deciding the focus of the review—the patient, the nurse, or the institution—the next step in this review model is to specify the criteria and standards appropriate for evaluating care.

Criteria are predetermined elements against which aspects of the quality of a health service may be compared. Criteria are developed by professionals relying on professional expertise and on the professional literature. In a general sense, criteria may be thought of as specific statements of health care that reflect nursing values.

Criteria are statements of structure, process, or outcome that can be measured. For example: (1) Each nurse will have a minimum of 15 continuing education contact hours per year (structure). (2) A nursing care plan will be written on each patient within 24 hours of admission (process). (3) By discharge, patient names medications (outcome).

If there are existing sets of structure, process, or outcome criteria, the quality assurance review committee will need to decide whether or not modifications are necessary. Whether the review committee writes its own criteria or uses criteria that have already been developed and published, the criteria need to be validated before use in an audit. A common form of validation is by consensus among peers. The rationale for including this step in the identification of criteria is to ensure that the criteria are appropriate, relevant, and useful to the nurses working with the subject under review. The nurse who works daily with the content included in the criteria is in the best position to know if the criteria are appropriate and relevant to the group of patients, the nurse's activities, or the structural setting.

When criteria have been defined, the review committee needs to agree on the level of performance that will indicate when each criterion has been satisfactorily met. This will establish the *standard* for the review, which is a professionally developed expression of the range of acceptable variations from norms or criteria.

If a nursing service department decides that each nurse will have a minimum of 15 continuing education contact hours per year, this becomes a structure criterion which defines a level of expected performance. One must then identify an acceptable standard, which indicates the range of acceptable variation from a criterion for a group of patients, providers, or units. If it is decided that this variation will be satisfactory if at least 75 percent of the nurses have 15 continuing education contact hours, this becomes the acceptable standard for the criterion.

3. Secure Measurements Needed to Determine the Degree of Attainment of Standards and Criteria (Gather Information)

The degree to which actual practice conforms to established criteria provides the information used for making judgments about the strengths and weaknesses of nursing practice. Many methods can be used to measure the level of nursing practice according to the established criteria.

The methods include utilization review, self-assessment, supervisor evaluation, performance observation, and review of records.

Regardless of the method, data should be easily accessible and retrievable. The review may either look at what has happened in the past or what is happening in the present. A chart review that looks at what has happened in the past is a "retrospective" review. A "concurrent" review looks at what is happening in the present, that is, while the patient is receiving care.

Specific questions relevant to the topic of study that the review committee needs to answer include these:

- What is the source of the data?
- How can the data be collected?
- Who collects the data?
- When can the data be collected?

The answers to these questions should reflect consideration of accuracy and efficiency in data collection.

Each criterion should be stated so that it is possible to recognize immediately whether or not it has been met. The results should be tabulated and a decision made as to whether the percentage of yes or no answers corresponds to the standard set for each criterion. When the level of performance does not measure up to the standard established, the criterion for the group has not been met.

4. *Make Interpretations about the Strengths and Weaknesses of the Program*

The degree to which the identified standards have been met serves as a base for pinpointing the strengths and weaknesses of current nursing programs or practice. Attention must then be given to ensuring that this information is properly used to effect appropriate changes in practice.

Part of this step involves identifying the factors related to successful or unsuccessful nursing interventions. For example, if one group of nurses meets the criteria for a given group of patients and another does not, a comparison of procedures or practices might provide insight into methods for improving both.

Sometimes the cause may lie outside the area of nursing control—the information may indicate that the problem lies within the administration of the institution (e.g., insufficient nurses) rather than a deficiency in nursing practice (e.g., lack of appropriate knowledge).

5. *Identify Possible Courses of Action*

When strengths and weaknesses of the nursing practice have been identified, action can be taken to reinforce strengths and to reduce weaknesses. Information from the review should provide a motivation as well as a plan for change. Those who will be affected by this review will see many possible courses of action and should be involved in this process.

The attainment of the standard and available resources serve as the basis for decisions about changes in nursing practice. Alternative actions are numerous. The actions can include continuing education, in-service education, peer pressure, administrative changes, environmental changes, research, reward systems, or self-initiated change. The course of action chosen will be dictated by identified causes of the problem.

Each alternative action will have advantages and disadvantages. Sometimes the mere development of a criteria set by a peer group is enough to change or reinforce the practice of individuals within the group. Likewise, writing of criteria by a multiprofessional group may change the practices of the involved individuals.

6. *Choose a Course of Action*

After several alternative actions have been proposed and examined in light of existing resources and organizations, the best action is selected for implementation. Decisions need to be made with a realistic consideration of the institution's resources. There may be several contributing causes in any one specific case. Where possible, each of these causes should be identified and action taken to alter each one. In some situations, it will not be possible to clearly identify a single cause for the problem. In that case, many possible solutions will need to be explored and a decision made based on the best possible information.

The individual(s) making these decisions will depend upon the organizational structure of the health setting. The nursing or multidisciplinary review committee may propose several alternatives to the director of nursing or other administrative personnel for final decision. The authority for action taken may, however, be delegated to the review committee. In such a situation, the results of review and action taken would be provided to the director of nursing and other administrative personnel as points of information. In PSRO review, the results of the nursing review will be incorporated into facilitywide data.

7. *Take Action*

Improving the quality of care implies a change in behavior. This in turn implies a choice of actions by the decision maker.

Sometimes activities required for change are not controlled by nurses or the nursing service departments. Problems within the organizational structure, such as ineffective policies, inadequate or inappropriate administrators, or environmental conditions should be referred to the appropriate administrators.

Where information is inadequate or skills are lacking, continuing education, in-service educa-

Structure, Process, and Outcome Criteria

1. *Structure criteria* are statements that describe the purpose of the institution, agency, or program. Included are statements about legal authority, organizational characteristics, fiscal resources and management, the qualifications of health professionals and other workers, physical facilities and equipment, and accreditation and certification status. Structure criteria may be written for the patient, for the nurse, or for the institution (e.g., the patient will be situated in a room not less than 10 by 15 feet; the nurse working in a coronary care unit will have successfully completed an ANA approved coronary care course; the institution's staff will have one registered nurse for every ten patient beds). Examples of structure criteria can be found in accreditation manuals, in policy and procedure books, and in statements of philosophy and objectives from institutions and nursing service departments.

2. *Process criteria* focus on the nature, sequence of events, and the activities of health care. Process criteria describe what happens within the institution during the care and treatment activities or to the patient (e.g., the patient newly diagnosed as having diabetes mellitus will receive ten hours of instruction; the nurse will collaborate with the patient about his or her nursing care plan; the institution will record data in a problem-oriented system).

3. *Outcome criteria* pertain to the end results of the health care process and what is focused on the patient. For the patient, an outcome criterion would be a measurable change in the state of his or her health. Outcomes may be positive or negative and are the ultimate indicators of the quality of patient care (e.g., patient has been afebrile for 48 hours before discharge).

tion, or staff development will be the appropriate choices. Nurses on the unit may choose to initiate study of a variety of approaches. In-depth studies of the processes of nursing care and the structure in which this care occurs will be frequently appropriate.

8. Reevaluate

At this point, the cycle begins to be repeated. Each time actions are taken, the progress of nursing practice needs to be reassessed and remeasured. Continual reevaluation of practice in light of established criteria and standards can indicate how well a change is progressing and whether the activities taken to implement change are having an effect.

It is particularly important to monitor and document new programs and nursing practice when several actions have been undertaken simultaneously. Decision makers must use caution in defining a direct cause and effect relationship between a change of policy and a change in behavior of those affected. Careful analysis of the variables in the actions and the results of reevaluation can ensure continued improvement of the quality of nursing care.

Quality Improvement Program*

Quality improvement is an integrated, coordinated approach to objectively and systematically review and evaluate quality indicators for the scope of services and activities within an institution. Quality is a part of all components of work found within a nursing organization: clinical practice, professional staff development, and administrative support. A quality improvement program analyzes all work components to ensure the continuous improvement of services to consumers, nursing staff, and the nursing system as a whole.

The quality improvement program established for the nursing service at Barnes Hospital, St. Louis, Missouri is designed to systemat-

---

Source: Patricia Potter, "An Assessment Tool for Developing Quality Indicators," *Journal of Nursing Care Quality*, vol. 6, no. 1, © 1991 Aspen Publishers, Inc.

ically measure outcomes of the key organizational components for the department (Figure 21-3). In support of professional nursing practice, the nursing department has three operational components: clinical practice (incorporating standards of care and standards of practice), professional development, and administrative support. The quality improvement program incorporates the analysis and evaluation of outcomes and associated processes for each of the operational components.

Each patient care unit within the nursing service develops an annual quality improvement plan. The process begins during the fourth quarter of each year. Nurse managers involve staff in conducting a systematic analysis of the scope and key aspects of service delivered on their particular unit. Nursing staff and members of all other health care disciplines within the hospital have attended workshops on total quality management concepts and strategies.

The analysis is simplified through the use of a quality improvement assessment tool. The tool is divided into three major sections assessing each of the department's operational components. Use of the tool provides a comprehensive survey of unit activities and reveals opportunities for improving the quality of services. The format for each major section of the tool is the same: assessment of scope of services, assessment of key aspects of service, and selection of quality indicators. Each section allows staff to thoroughly explore the uniqueness and characteristics of services offered on their unit. Staff from other health care disciplines—such as medicine, social work, and infection control—can give input to a unit plan. Once completed, the assessment tool allows staff to identify relevant quality indicators.

Clinical Practice

The tool begins with an assessment of clinical practice with the focus on the patient. To conduct an assessment of clinical practice, managers are encouraged to review information from

Figure 21-3 Model for Nursing Service Quality Improvement (*Barnes Hospital, St Louis, Missouri*)

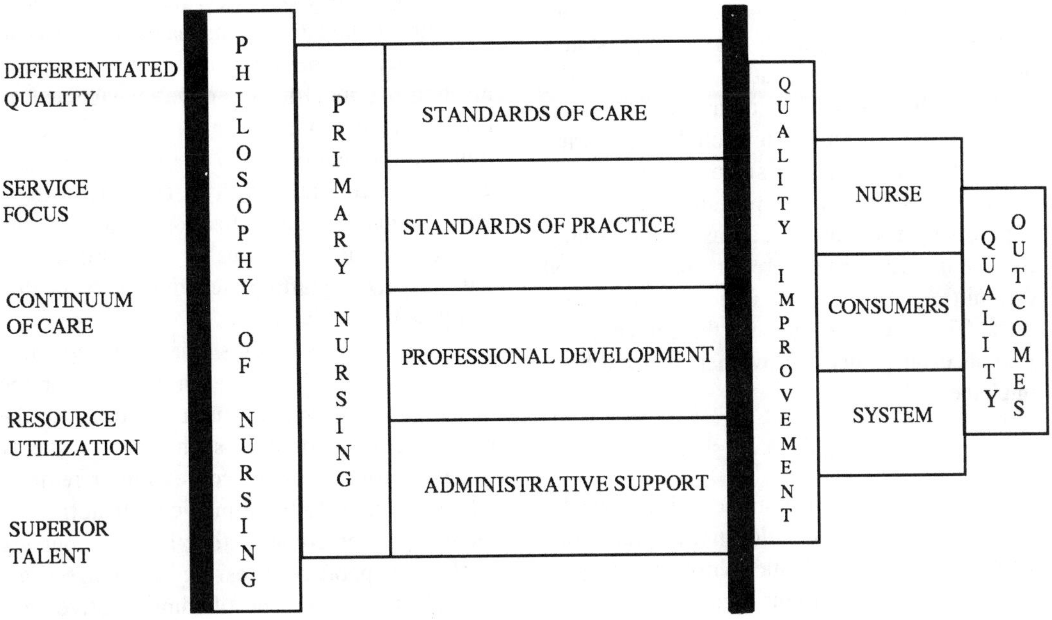

Source: Patricia Potter, "An Assessment Tool for Developing Quality Indicators," *Journal of Nursing Care Quality*, vol. 6, no. 1, © 1991 Aspen Publishers, Inc.

previous quality assurance studies, patient satisfaction surveys, incident reports, infection control studies, nursing protocols and care plans, committee minutes, and even staff performance appraisals. The systematic review of available clinical practice data can reveal trending information that ultimately directs the assessment to relevant practice issues that yield quality indicators.

Following the preliminary review of data, the assessment tool next requires an analysis of the scope of services for the unit.

Next, an analysis of diagnostic and treatment modalities helps staff to systematically review the types of care activities that may warrant evaluation.

Finally, the assessment tool requires staff to review the processes of care delivered by nursing staff. This includes independent and interdependent nursing care activities, such as outcomes of primary nursing, the use of teaching protocols, or the coordination of discharge planning activities. Many units,

The next step in analyzing clinical practice for a unit requires staff to identify key aspects of service. The tool incorporates an analysis of high volume, high risk, and problem areas. The final portion of the clinical practice assessment requires staff to list the clinical indicators suitable for review and evaluation.

The quality improvement plans made by staff are not required initially to include monitoring criteria. Through the support of quality assurance nurses, nurse specialists, and other appropriate disciplines (such as infection control), monitoring criteria are set when unit-based committees plan for each indicator's measurement. This occurs throughout the course of the year once the quality improvement plan has been implemented.

Professional Development

The assessment tool continues with an analysis of professional development issues and activities. Preliminary data involve a survey of information valuable to managers and staff that reflect the educational, research, and other professional activities engaged in by staff over the

previous year. Course attendance records and staff performance appraisals are common sources of data. The scope of services analysis begins with questions regarding the nursing staff's professional attributes, such as education and length of service.

The tool next focuses on the aspects of professional development that are high volume, high risk, or problem areas. An example of a high-risk issue is the outcome of cardiopulmonary resuscitation certification for nursing staff. Do staff acquire and then demonstrate the skills needed for safe and successful cardiopulmonary resuscitation?

Administrative Support

The final section of the assessment tool analyzes administrative support activities. The focus is on the systems designed to support staff in the delivery of care. Again, a preliminary review is conducted, this time to look at information dealing with system operations, professional affairs, and resource management. A staff satisfaction survey, turnover report, staffing proposal, or patient classification report may prove useful in determining what elements to assess. The scope of service review includes questions regarding administrative mechanisms in place to communicate issues on a nursing unit. Communication is critical for effective management to occur. The tool offers insight into existing communication channels and their efficacy. The assessment continues with an analysis of manpower allocation and utilization. Managers and staff explore the problems or deficits that exist with respect to staffing, scheduling, or facility equipment and planning.

Finally, the tool raises questions regarding interdepartmental services necessary for the operation of the nursing unit. Frequently, the role of other departments, such as central supply or respiratory therapy, comes under review. Ultimately, quality improvement activities require greater collaboration between nursing staff and support services. Once managers and staff identify key aspects of administrative services with respect to high-volume, high-risk, or problem areas, indicators of quality are identified. The actual monitoring of indicators under administrative support might become a multi-disciplinary effort.

Initially, the administrative support section of the assessment tool has been the most difficult for staff and managers to complete. Total quality management principles often come into play when analyzing systems of operation that affect more than one group of staff.

Annual Plan

Following completion of the quality improvement assessment tool, head nurses and staff select the quality indicators to be measured for the upcoming year. At least one indicator is selected for each of the organizational compo-nents. Activities of a given unit influence the most appropriate time for select indicators to be measured. For example, at our institution more staff are sent to educational programs during the spring and fall. Measuring the outcomes of such activities are best planned after programs are completed. The yearly plan denotes which indicators are to be measured for specific months of the year and allows staff to repeat measurement of indicators when deficits are identified. Completed plans are reviewed by head nurses and directors and then are submitted to the nursing quality assurance department. Quality assurance staff track the common indicators measured by multiple nursing units to ensure that trends are shared and joint recommendations can be made. Meetings are planned as needed between divisions monitoring similar indicators.

Chapter 22

Risk Management and Safety

NURSING'S ROLE IN RISK MANAGEMENT

The nurse manager should keep abreast of liability issues for nurses, be aware of state and federal legislation impacting nursing practice, monitor the quality of nursing care through regular reports, and keep informed of hospital risk management issues. (See Table 22-1.) In an era of limited resources, risk management data can be extremely valuable in helping nurse administrators determine priorities and make decisions relative to resource utilization in their institutions.

Table 22-1 Functions of Risk Management

1. Protect financial assets of the hospital.
2. Protect human and intangible resources.
3. Prevent injury to patients, visitors, employees, and property.
4. Loss reduction focusing on *individual* loss or on single incidents.
5. Loss prevention to prevent incidents by improving the quality of care through continuing and ongoing monitoring.
6. Review of each incident and the patterns of incidents through the application of the steps in the risk management process: risk identification, risk analysis, risk evaluation, and risk treatment.

Source: Reprinted with permission from *Hospitals*, published by American Hospital Publishing, Inc., © June 1, 1981, vol. 55, no. 11.

The most important area of responsibility and potential liability for nurse managers is that of staff selection, orientation, and continuing education. Nurse managers are responsible for overseeing the quality of care provided by the nursing service and ensuring the competency of the nursing staff. The nursing service should have an established ongoing system for monitoring nursing licensure, nursing skills, and continuing education.

A participative approach to risk management should be fostered. This can be done by encouraging and involving nursing staff in risk management activities. Since the nursing staff are closest to the level of operations, they are most familiar with risks in the patient care delivery system. They serve as a valuable information source and can often suggest ways to prevent these risks. In addition, the chief nurse administrator should hold the administrative staff accountable for being familiar with risks in the environment through the use of risk management and QA data collected by the hospital. These data should be fed back to the staff nurses so that they also maintain an awareness of risks.

Programs to reduce patient risks should be developed in conjunction with the hospital's risk management department. Generally, the highest risks are from slips and falls and medication errors.*

Source: Denise Pelle, "Risk Management," in *Current Strategies for Nurse Administrators*, Mary K. Stull and Sue Ellen Pinkerton, eds., Aspen Publishers, Inc., © 1988.

Components of a Nursing Risk Management Program*

Providing Proper Documentation

Adequate documentation can prevent malpractice claims from being initiated and is invaluable in a successful defense against them. The rules for appropriate documentation emphasize factual information presented as completely and as honestly as possible. A fraudulent record is difficult to defend in a malpractice case. Therefore, all health care providers are encouraged to alter records only if absolutely necessary for patient care purposes and only with the greatest of care to prevent even the appearance of misrepresentation. Accurately timing and dating nurses' notes and progress notes is especially important.

Using Reasonable Standards of Practice

A nurse's failure to document may lead to an erroneous judgment by a jury that the nurse failed to practice in a reasonable manner. Practicing in a reasonable professional manner and documenting that factor are the two best defenses against malpractice claims.

Risk management cannot prevent all malpractice claims. Those that cannot be prevented can be defended successfully by nurses' using reasonable standards of practice. Nurses frequently ask what the standard of care is. This is a significant question, since the nurse's behavior in a specific malpractice case will be measured against reasonable standards of care.

These standards are formulated by the nursing profession. In fact, one of the characteristics of a profession is the ability to set its own standards. Nurses formulate their standards as they practice nursing on a day-to-day basis. Some standards are part of the custom of nursing practice and therefore are not necessarily in written form. Other standards are written, including job descriptions, policies, procedures, association guidelines, textbook material, and nurse practice acts. All of these may be admissible in a mal-

practice case to establish deviations from customary practice. An expert witness testifies in a malpractice case to assist the court in understanding the standard against which the nurse's actions should be measured.

Channelling Information Appropriately

To assist the hospital board and administration in meeting their corporate responsibility, nurses frequently become the eyes and ears of the risk management program. Patient care information at the staff level must be channelled into the system appropriately so that action can be taken if necessary.

For example, if the nursing staff became aware of a physician who was impaired by alcohol (or drug) abuse and whose impairment was interfering with his or her ability to care for patients, such information must be communicated through appropriate departmental channels as well as to the risk management committee. This not only helps the institution meet its corpo-

---

Table 22-2 Checklist of Risk Identifiers

Report If These Occur	
____Wrong dosage	____Infections
____Wrong medication	____Fall from bed
____Medicine to wrong patient	____Fall while ambulatory
____IV infiltration	____Other falls
____Wrong IV rate	____Untimely orders
____Wrong IV solution/dosage	____Wrong treatment/ test
____Other IV errors	____Treatment/test to wrong patient
____Patient complaints	____Delay in results
____Left against medical advice	____Lost orders/results
____Suicide attempt	____Delayed response/ treatment
____Self-inflicted injury	____Orders unclear/ contradictory
____Other patient injury	____Improper criticism/ jousting
____Poor outcome/ complications	____Failure to follow policies/rules
____Death/cardiac arrest	____Miscellaneous

Source: Tools for Quality Assurance Process, Colorado Hospital Association Trust, 1984.

Source: Janine Fiesta, "Nursing and Risk Management," in *Handbook of Health Care Risk Management* by Glenn T. Troyer and Steven L. Salman, eds., Aspen Publishers, Inc., © 1986.

rate responsibility, it also allows nurses to meet their own professional, legal, ethical, and personal accountability responsibilities for patient care. Once a staff nurse communicates the information, the situation then becomes a management or institutional issue to be resolved. If management or the administration fails to pursue appropriate action, the issue becomes one of institutional liability. The same principle applies when the nurse notifies the supervisor that equipment is deficient or unsafe for patient care or that staffing is inadequate. (See Table 22-2.)

Although it is well recognized that such events will occur on an isolated basis in even the best of institutions, the repetitiveness of such problems with no attempted intervention may signal the failure of reasonable standards of care for the institution.

Application of Standards of Care as a Preventive Strategy*

The best prevention/defense strategy against malpractice suits is thorough knowledge of the standard of care applicable in every clinical encounter. (Tables 22-3 and 22-4) The legal standard of nursing care is to act as any other reasonable nurse would act under the circumstances. The client-nurse relationship, environmental factors (e.g., staff-client ratio), client acuity, and clinical needs are factors to consider as part of the circumstances in determining what is reasonable. Reasonableness may be altered by the circumstances.

- "Reasonable" can be defined by reviewing several sources, including nursing experience, education, state nursing practice acts and regulations, other legislation and regulations relevant to the practice area (e.g., home health agency, conditions for participation in Medicare/Medicaid, federal regulations), and previous case law (state or federal, depending on the practice setting and legal issues involved).
- Evidence of the standard of care is usually developed by reviewing the facts of the case

and applying the appropriate standard of care. Standards of nursing care can be found in agency policy and procedure manuals, job descriptions, employment contracts and handbooks, accreditation criteria, AMA certification requirements, statements of professional associations (e.g., ANA, AAOHN, APHA, NAACOG, etc.), and nursing journals and texts.

- If there is inadequate documentation of what the nurse did and how the client responded, then the issue becomes whether the standard of care was met. If the record is inadequate, the nurse may still convince the decision makers through testimony that the standard of care was met. One approach is to establish that the nurse knew the standard of care by using other evidence to show that the nurse regularly and routinely has met the appropriate standard of care. Adequate documentation, however, is part of a reasonable standard of care, and failure to

---

Table 22-3 Guidelines for Reducing Nurse Liability

While following these guidelines may not prevent nurses from being involved in litigation, it should reduce their chances of being involved in a malpractice lawsuit and improve their ability to successfully defend in any lawsuit that is brought against them.

1. Be knowledgeable in your clinical specialty.
2. Demonstrate concern for patients in day-to-day care for them.
3. Collaborate and communicate with other members of the health care team.
4. Be familiar with and follow the hospital's written policies and procedures.
5. Understand the equipment used at the hospital.
6. Document appropriately and accurately.
7. Question any physician order which is not understood or agreed with.
8. Learn how to correct medical record entry errors.

Source: Denise Pelle, "Risk Management," in *Current Strategies for Nurse Administrators*, Mary K. Stull and Sue Ellen Pinkerton, eds., Aspen Publishers, Inc., © 1988.

Source: Cynthia Northrop, "Malpractice and Standards of Care," *Nursing Outlook*, vol. 34, no. 3, May-June 1986.

Table 22-4 Guidelines for Nursing Activities in Risk Prevention

TREATMENT

To minimize the possibility of patient injury as a result of treatment, it is useful to

- adequately orient all personnel to a unit
- test equipment regularly, provide routine maintenance for equipment, and keep records of equipment use
- provide in-service education on treatment methods
- organize a "buddy system" in which peers observe and evaluate each other's techniques and performance
- provide close clinical supervision by peers and supervisors
- conduct clinical audits of nursing practice
- conduct periodic performance evaluations by supervisors and self-evaluations
- develop and support employee assistance programs
- urge prompt notification of the nursing administration of any problems with a physician or other health care team member

COMMUNICATION

Insist on prompt, complete, and accurate recording of data in patients' charts. Such a record makes it possible to recall the condition of the patient, the treatment given, the results of that treatment, and the follow-up. Failing to record data or altering a patient's chart implies a degree of negligence to a jury and certainly does not lessen risk.

Implement staff development programs that will sharpen the assessment skills of staff nurses, improve their ability to judge when a situation needs a physician's attention, and clarify the level of knowledge required by the standard of care for nursing practice.

MEDICATION

In the medication area, vigilance, accuracy, careful attention, and meticulous knowledge of medications and their administration are also needed. In addition, nurses should conduct clinical research that examines modes of delivering medication to patients in order to answer the following:

- Do error rates differ when one nurse per unit is responsible for administering medications, as opposed to several nurses administering medication to their assigned patients in one unit?
- Are there safer ways of giving medications?
- Another strategy for minimizing risk of injury by medication error is to
  —evaluate labeling, packaging, coding, and other aspects of medicine identification
  —encourage all members of the nursing staff to notify the nursing supervisor, the hospital, and the manufacturer, in writing, of any problems, questions, or concerns about the delivery of medications

MONITORING/OBSERVING/SUPERVISING

The nursing staff should have a thorough knowledge and understanding of the hospital's protocols, rules, and policies and procedures. This could be encouraged by periodic review and/or testing.

- Nurses should be expected to follow the current literature in their primary area of practice.
- Workshops to enhance assessment skills and clinical judgment should be made available to all the nursing staff on a regular basis.

Source: Cynthia E. Northrop, "Nursing Actions in Litigation," *Quality Review Bulletin*, vol. 13, no. 10, October 1987. Copyright 1987 by the Joint Commission on Accreditation of Healthcare Organizations, Chicago. Reprinted with permission.

---

meet a standard of care can be reflected simply by failure to record events properly.

- An expert nurse witness is the most appropriate person to provide an opinion about whether a standard of care was met. In some situations in which a nurse's action is ques-

tioned, expert testimony may not be required. Figuring out when expert testimony is required usually rests on determining whether the decision maker needs information beyond what he or she possesses in order to make a decision.

INCIDENT REPORTS*

Most hospitals require the nursing staff to fill out incident reports when a problem in medical care delivery has occurred. (See Table 22-5) These reports are meant to be nonjudgmental,

Source: Edward P. Richards III and Katharine C. Rathbun, *Medical Risk Management: Preventive Legal Strategies for Health Care Providers*, Aspen Publishers, Inc., © 1983.

factual reports of the problem and its consequences. Nurses should understand that filing an incident report is not tantamount to blaming a fellow employee for the problem. More important, it should be made clear that filing an incident report is not an admission of negligence. Incident reports are simply records of all events that are not part of routine medical care. The hospital administration should promulgate lists of events whose occurrence requires the filing of

---

Table 22-5 Sample Policy and Procedure for Incident Reporting

Policy

☐ Safety Committee Responsibilities:

To assess how the internal reporting mechanism is working.
To code incidents according to their potential risk.
To review each incident report for completeness and quality.
To analyze the data obtained and prepare a bimonthly summary report to be sent to the assistant administrator for nursing, directors of division, clinical nurse specialists, the director of staff development and research, the nursing quality assurance/risk management director, and the nursing quality assurance/risk management committee.

☐ Supervisory staff utilize information supplied by the safety committee to teach staff and correct problems.

Procedure

1. Complete an incident report for any unusual occurrence. If in doubt, it is always better to complete a report than not to file one.
2. Complete the report as soon after the incident as possible.
3. Have the staff person involved complete the report, and if more than one staff person is involved, all should participate and sign the report.
4. Make sure the report is accurate and complete.
5. Never put the report into the patient's record or make a comment in the patient's record regarding the completion of a report.
6. Identify only facts in the report.
7. Have the patient's M.D. sign the report.
8. Route the complete report as follows:
   –Initiator sends all copies to the clinical nurse specialist, who routes the report to the designated persons or committees.
   –Copy A is sent to the safety committee.
   –Copy B is sent to the director of the division and then to the assistant administrator for nursing.
   –Copy C is sent to the hospital administrator, who will send copies to the hospital's insurance carrier and attorney.

CAUTION: Never put a copy of the incident report into the patient's medical record or make a comment in the patient's record about completing an incident report.

Source: Anita W. Finkelman, *Policies and Procedures for Psychiatric Nursing*, Aspen Publishers, Inc., © 1986.

an incident report. The staff must also be free to file a report even if the event does not appear on the list of mandatory reports. This allows the incident report to be used as a way of formally asking a question about a questionable procedure. Nurses must feel that they can question the orders of a physician through the filing of an incident report without feeling that they are thereby claiming that the physician is wrong.

The nonjudgmental nature of an incident report is very important because in most cases the incident report will be discoverable in litigation. An accusatory remark in an incident report may gain unintended weight in a legal proceeding.

Reporting Forms

A single-sheet, multiple-copy form is the best approach to incident reporting. The form should contain basic patient identification data, a checklist of different incidents, and a space for written comments. (See Table 22-6.)

The nursing supervisor should review all reports after they are filed but should not prevent a report from being reviewed by the quality control manager. This review enables the supervisor to supply additional information, if needed, and to identify reports that require immediate action.

There should also be a mechanism for directly alerting the administrator if the nurse or other person filling out the form feels that the incident demands immediate attention. The mechanism for direct reporting can be very valuable when the appropriate supervisor is unavailable.

Responsibility for Completing Incident Reports*

Hospitals should develop a clear policy with respect to who is responsible for completing the initial incident report and the more important incident investigation report. Generally, both the incident report and the incident investigation report forms should be completed by

- the hospital staff member involved in the occurrence (where more than one staff member is involved, it is preferable that the person with the most supervisory responsibility complete the report)
- the hospital staff member who discovered the incident (where there is more than one

*Source: Clemon W. Williams, "Guide to Hospital Incident Reports," *Health Care Management Review*, vol. 10, no. 1, © 1985 Aspen Publishers, Inc.

Table 22-6 Guidelines for Incident Report Writing

- Correct report writing means putting on paper total objective findings of an incident or a crime that has come to your attention.
- The written report frequently is the only complete communication with other persons seeking information on an earlier incident or crime.
  - Write the report assuming that the reader has no prior knowledge of the event.
  - Start the report at the point when first informed of the incident, always keeping in mind WHO, WHEN, AND WHERE.
  - Report all dates and times as accurately as possible.
  - Record names, addresses, and phone numbers of participants and witnesses so that they may be located if needed at a future time.

- Document any incident that involves the hospital or has the slightest possibility of later resulting in a lawsuit or litigation. Often, a lawsuit will surface several years after the fact; therefore, be prepared with proper reports that have been accurately documented on file.
- State in the report who (by name) was notified at the time (security director, vice president, management services, president, etc.).
- Duty, incident, and crime reports will be kept permanently boxed and labeled each year and stored in an approved area of the hospital.
- Accurate and complete reports are essential for self-protection and protection of the hospital from the increasing burden of legal suits.

Courtesy of Deaconess Hospital, Cleveland, Ohio.

employee involved, the person with the most seniority should complete the form)
- the hospital staff member to whom the incident was reported

However, in those situations where the person who discovers the incident is involved in the incident or the person to whom the incident was reported is a registry nurse, temporary employee, or volunteer, that person's immediate supervisor should complete the form.

Incident reports should be completed as soon after the occurrence as possible, but in any event should be completed before the person responsible for completing the report form leaves the hospital grounds.

MEDICATION ERRORS

Overview*

If a medication error is detected, the patient's physician must be informed immediately. A written report should be prepared describing any medication errors of clinical import observed in the prescribing, dispensing, or administration of a medication. This report, in accordance with hospital policy, should be prepared and sent to the appropriate hospital officials (including the pharmacy) within 24 hours. These reports should be analyzed, and any necessary action taken, to minimize the possibility of recurrence of such errors. Properly utilized, these incident reports will help to ensure optimum drug use control. Medication error reports should be reviewed periodically by the pharmacy and therapeutics committee. (It should be kept in mind that, in the absence of an organized, independent error detection system, most medication errors will go unnoticed.)

A *medication error* is broadly defined as a dose of medication that deviates from the physician's order as written in the patient's chart or from standard hospital policy and procedures. Except for errors of omission, the medication dose must actually reach the patient; that is, a wrong dose that is detected and corrected before administration to the patient is not a medication error. Prescribing errors (e.g., therapeutically inappropriate drugs or doses) are excluded from this definition.

Medication Error Policy*

Appraisal

The merits of a medication error policy or indeed of any policy can only be measured in terms of results.

1. Are medication errors being reported promptly?
2. Is the perpetrator reacting properly and procedurally?
3. Is there a marked decrease in repeat offenders?
4. Are the educational and corrective measures reviewed constructively?
5. Have union grievances as a result of corrective measures decreased?
6. What seems to be the overall feeling of the staff towards the medication error policy?

Disciplinary Action

Disciplinary action as a result of a medication error will be handled by, and at the discretion of, the nursing administrator or his or her designee. The judgment resulting in disciplinary action will be based on

1. the severity of the medication error
2. the action and reaction of the nurse involved in the medication error
3. the number of medication errors in an annual period

Source: "ASHP Technical Assistance Bulletin on Hospital Drug Distribution and Control," *American Journal of Hospital Pharmacy*, August 1980. Reprinted with permission.

Source: Adapted from Barbara Wilson, "Medication Error Policy," *Supervisor Nurse*, May 1978. Reprinted with permission.

Nine Categories of Medication Error

1. *Omission error*: the failure to administer an ordered dose. However, if the patient refuses to take the medication, no error has occurred. Likewise, if the dose is not administered because of recognized contraindications, no error has occurred.

2. *Unauthorized-drug error*: administration to the patient of a medication dose not authorized for the patient. This category includes a dose given to the wrong patient, duplicate doses, administration of an unordered drug, and a dose given outside a stated set of clinical parameters (e.g., medication order to administer only if the patient's blood pressure falls below a predetermined level).

3. *Wrong-dose error*: any dose that is the wrong number of preformed units (e.g., tablets) or any dose above or below the ordered dose by a predetermined amount (e.g., 20 percent). In the case of ointments, topical solutions, and sprays, an error occurs only if the medication order expresses the dosage quantitatively (e.g., 1 inch of ointment or two 1-second sprays).

4. *Wrong-route error*: administration of a drug by a route other than that ordered by the physician. Also included are doses given via the correct route but at the wrong site (e.g., left eye instead of right).

5. *Wrong-rate error*: administration of a drug at the wrong rate, the correct rate being that given in the physician's order or as established by hospital policy.

6. *Wrong-dosage form error*: administration of a drug by the correct route but in a different dosage form than that specified or implied by the physician. Examples of this error type include use of an ophthalmic ointment when a solution was ordered. Purposeful alteration (e.g., crushing of a tablet) or substitution (e.g., substituting liquid for a tablet) of an oral dosage form to facilitate administration is generally not an error.

7. *Wrong-time error*: administration of a dose of drug greater than $\pm X$ hours from its scheduled administration time, X being as set by hospital policy.

8. *Wrong preparation of a dose*: incorrect preparation of the medication dose. Examples are incorrect dilution or reconstitution, not shaking a suspension, using an expired drug, not keeping a light-sensitive drug protected from light, and mixing drugs that are physically/chemically incompatible.

9. *Incorrect administration technique*: situations when the drug is given via the correct route, site, and so forth, but improper technique is used. Examples are not using the Z-track injection technique when indicated for a drug, incorrect instillation of an ophthalmic ointment, and incorrect use of an administration device.

Source: "ASHP Technical Assistance Bulletin on Hospital Drug Distribution and Control," *American Journal of Hospital Pharmacy*, August 1980. Reprinted with permission.

The nursing administrator reserves the right to institute immediate discipline, including termination, for a medication error which causes irreversible damage to the patient or has the possibility of such damage. The right to institute immediate discipline also applies to any nurse who demonstrates negligence or irresponsibility in his or her reaction to such an error.

In dealing with less serious medication errors, corrective measures will be cumulative according to the number of errors. For the first error,

counseling will be given by the nursing administrator or his or her designee. For the second error, a corrective educational program will be added. For the third, a one-day suspension will be given. The fourth error will be followed by a counseling session, corrective educational programs, and a three-day suspension without pay. If a nurse commits five errors in a year, the nurse is subject to termination. The complete work record of the employee will be considered in cases involving termination.

Chapter 23

Supplies and Equipment

SUPPLIES

Estimating Needs*

To estimate needs, which implies projecting into the future, the following steps are suggested.

1. Analyzing Program Needs

The need for facilities, supplies, and equipment is largely dictated by the kinds of programs and services to be provided. Therefore, an examination of what is required to carry out certain programs or to provide certain services seems a logical starting point in estimating future needs. For instance, if a change in pharmacy functions that affect nursing service is planned, an analysis of operations step by step will indicate what change in the nursing department's facilities, equipment, and supplies will be necessary to carry out its functions effectively within the changed system. The idea is to document as much information and data as possible to substantiate realistic estimates.

---

*Source: American Hospital Association, *Practical Approaches to Nursing Service Administration*, vol. 8, no. 1, Winter 1969.

2. Standardizing Supplies and Equipment

In most hospitals, great strides have been made in standardizing supplies and equipment. The advent of disposables and prepackaged items has accelerated this trend. However, the appearance of new products and new clinical procedures requiring different kinds of supplies and equipment makes it necessary to be alert in order to maintain standardization as far as possible. The purchasing department can be of tremendous help to the department of nursing in this regard. For instance, a system might be established whereby the purchasing department would notify the nursing department when a requisition or request was received for a piece of equipment or an item of supply differing from that primarily used by nurses. The nursing department could then refer the new item to the appropriate committee or group for evaluation and a recommendation as to whether the new item should become standard, be given a trial, replace a standard item, be used only on specific units, be referred to the hospital's standards committee, or be handled otherwise. In other words, to maintain standardization of supplies and equipment, a system should be established to monitor the introduction of new products.

3. Ordering and Maintaining Supplies

Systems for centralized control of supplies are becoming more common in hospitals. In hospitals where the department responsible for purchasing and stores maintains the "floor stock" of supplies, including sterile supplies, according to an inventory standard established by the department of nursing, it is essential that realistic inventories be established and that the flow of items be carefully watched so that inventories can be adjusted to prevent overstocking as well as understocking. In hospitals where each unit requisitions supplies, there should be a written procedure and a system whereby the requisitions are audited by the purchasing or accounting department and reported concurrently to the department of nursing. For instance, if 20 catheterization trays are delivered and used during the month and charge slips for only 15 are recorded, the control system is faulty somewhere.

Although the head nurse is in control, the system of ordering and maintaining supplies should be such that the routine can be delegated to a ward clerk or an aide assigned to the task. Because unexpected situations may arise, the system should also provide for emergency delivery of supplies.

4. Controlling Supplies and Equipment

The systems established for selecting, standardizing, ordering, and maintaining supplies and equipment are all part of the control system. In addition, however, the control system should include an educational component, because all members of the staff are involved in controlling the use of supplies and equipment. To achieve their willing cooperation, they must be instructed in the use of all items, informed about their cost, informed about the program of preventive maintenance for equipment, given assurance that supplies will be available when needed, and—very important—given suitable recognition for ideas that result in better utilization of both supplies and equipment and that reduce costs.

5. Keeping Records of Usage

To estimate future needs, a record of past experience in the use of facilities, equipment, and supplies is helpful. For items such as utilization of a conference room, a record might be kept over a specified period of time as a basis for determining whether more or less conference space and time are needed. If there is a question about the need to increase or decrease the number of pieces of equipment used almost exclusively by nurses—such as roll tables—a record over a specified period of the number of times such a table was needed and was not available will provide a basis for estimates of future needs. If borrowing of certain equipment seems to be excessive, a record of the number of times such borrowing is necessary over a specified period will be similarly useful.

With regard to the use of supplies, reports and information available from other departments (e.g., purchasing, stores, central supply, pharmacy, etc.) are invaluable. If these records are not obtainable or are in a form that is not useful, the director of nursing and the head of the department concerned can usually get together and work out a system that will be useful. For instance, in some hospitals the department responsible for purchasing and stores maintains the "floor stock" of supplies according to an inventory standard established by the nursing department. Records of the numbers of items delivered to the various units are furnished to the department of nursing and are very helpful in estimating future needs. If it is the practice for each unit to requisition supplies, accumulated records kept by the purchasing department can serve the same purpose. Records from the accounting department on patient charges—for example, the number of charges made for disposable catheterization trays on a particular unit—might also be a source of information.

Supply Distribution Systems*

A hospital's distribution system is an intricate network from storage to user points. The goal of any effective distribution system should be to provide the right item to the right place at the right time for the least total cost.

*Source: Jamie C. Kowalski, "Supply Distribution Options—A New Perspective," Hospital Materiel Management Quarterly, vol. 2, no. 2, © 1980 Aspen Publishers, Inc.

Requisition System

The requisition system is basically controlled by each department. Nursing, for example, functions as a materiel manager and keeps track of its own inventories. At a given time or when inventory levels get low, a requisition is prepared and presented to the central storage point. The requisition is then filled, and supplies are delivered to the nursing area, where nursing staff put the items in their appropriate place.

Par-Level System

A par-level system can be defined as one in which the nursing department stores supplies in an assigned location in its own area. Physical stock levels in that area are predetermined, based on a usage rate and the frequency of the replenishment process. At periodic intervals (e.g., every 24 hours, twice a week, or weekly), supply personnel conduct a physical inventory of what is available and order and obtain supplies to return the on-hand levels to the predetermined or par level.

Exchange Cart System

The exchange cart system has been the most popular of all systems implemented by hospitals in recent years. The system is basically the same as a par-level system in that there are predetermined levels and predetermined intervals for replenishing inventory to those levels. In the exchange cart system, however, the cart is used for storage and distribution. A duplicate of each cart in the nursing department is maintained in the storage area so that at the predetermined time the full cart can be taken to the nursing area and exchanged for the depleted cart. The cycle repeats itself at the given intervals.

Evaluating Supply Delivery*

How does one measure the performance of the materiel management department? First and foremost, certain performance criteria should be drawn up by the manager. This is commonly referred to as the statement of services for the department and should be distributed to all of the supply consumers. The following example represents such a statement.

Statement of Services to the Nursing Units

A. A total supply cart exchange program for each nursing unit will furnish 95–99 percent of the supply requirements for each unit for a 24-hour period.
  1. The supply quotas will be individualized according to the needs of each nursing unit.
  2. These supply quotas will be reviewed and updated at least quarterly.
  3. The carts will be exchanged daily at 6:00 A.M.
B. A 24-hour, seven-days-a-week delivery service will be provided for items that are not on the cart.
  1. If you do not have a supply item for any reason, please use the supply "hot-line" and you will receive an immediate response (within 15 minutes) around the clock.
  2. Please do not send unit personnel to central stores to pick up supplies.
C. Equipment rounds to each nursing unit will be made twice daily, seven days a week to check such items as suction machines, K-pads, etc.
D. Monday morning of each week, a check of the miscellaneous equipment (flashlights, stethoscopes, scales, etc.) will be performed. You are to sign that this service was performed.
E. Every attempt will be made to keep your units supplied with the proper items and equipment. In order to assure this, the Central Stores supervisor will make daily supply rounds on each unit, Monday through Friday. If you should have any supply, process, or delivery problems, please bring them to his or her attention.
F. A current supply reference catalog is filed on each nursing unit for your convenience and assistance.

Source: C. Housely, "Let the Consumer Be the Judge," *Dimensions in Health Service*, Journal of the Canadian Hospital Association, September 1977. Reprinted with permission.

Table 23-1 Supply Survey

1. Are your supply and linen carts delivered on time (before 7:00 A.M.)?
   Yes ☐   No ☐

2. Generally, do the supply and linen carts contain all of your needs? Yes ☐   No ☐

3. Cart supply quotas are to be reviewed with you at least quarterly. How long has it been since someone in materiel management reviewed with you your supply needs?

   _____

4. Did you know that only "charge" items have charge tickets and need your attention to process them immediately?
   Yes ☐   No ☐

5. If the supply is not on the cart, can you use the telephone hot-line and receive immediate (within 20 minutes) delivery?
   Yes ☐   No ☐

6. When you have a supply problem, do you feel free to call someone in Central Stores to get immediate action? Yes ☐   No ☐

7. When you call Central Stores, are the attendants courteous?   Yes ☐   No ☐

8. Are they knowledgeable and helpful?
   Yes ☐   No ☐

9. When you phone Central Stores, what is the average delivery response time:
   10–20 Minutes ☐
   20–30 Minutes ☐   30–60 Minutes ☐

10. Do you ever have to send someone to Central Stores to pick up items?
    Yes ☐   No ☐

11. Does the linen cart meet your linen supply needs?   Yes ☐   No ☐

12. If "No," what needs our attention? _____

    _____

13. Equipment rounds to check suction machines, K-pads, etc., are made on your unit 7 days/week at 10:00 A.M. and 2:00 P.M. Did you know this?
    Yes ☐   No ☐

14. In your opinion, are these equipment rounds effective?   Yes ☐   No ☐

15. Also, we check and replace, if needed, items such as flashlights, blood pressure units, stethoscopes, etc., every Monday morning. Did you know this?
    Yes ☐   No ☐

16. Are these items being maintained well on your unit?   Yes ☐   No ☐

17. In your opinion, what area of supply service needs our immediate attention to assist you most? _____

    _____

18. Generally, how would you rate our overall supply service?
    Poor ☐   Fair ☐   Good ☐   Excellent ☐

19. If you indicate "fair" or "poor," simply state why in 25 words or less. Please use the reverse side of this questionnaire.

20. Any other comments are welcomed: _____

    _____

    _____

    _____

After the evaluation criteria have been delineated, persons who use the service should judge the effectiveness. That means that nursing service will be a major contributor to the evaluation process. Periodically the nursing department should complete a questionnaire in reference to supply service. (See Table 23-1.) This information can be used by the materiel manager to improve services to the department and ultimately to the patient.

EQUIPMENT

One key area of supervisory involvement in the management of equipment is gathering and assembling the information required for justifying equipment needs and the potential allocation of capital funds for purchases. Depending on the scope of any undertaking and thus on the depth and extent of the supervisor's involvement, the supervisor may be called on to provide information on why a request is being made.

In most cases, regulation or accreditation requirements are sufficient justification for a purchase. If the equipment is requested to replace existing equipment, the justification for the request will proceed along the lines of demonstrating why and how the existing equipment is no longer adequate. The request for the addition of new equipment to perform a function not previously performed ordinarily involves the provision of a new service. The justification of the equipment purchase is, therefore, a part of the economic and clinical justification for adding the new service.

The manager should be able to explain why the equipment being asked for is the most efficient and effective way of performing the function or address the concern that triggered the request. A justification should attempt to deal with the potential usefulness or applicability of the proposed purchase under present circumstances, within the short run (up to one year in the future) and within the longer run (looking perhaps four or five years into the future).

Assessment of Clinical Implications*

It is often advisable to proceed beyond the general assessment of need to an additional clinically oriented assessment of the likely impact of the new equipment or service on both patients and staff. Any new personnel should be identified at least by skill level and pay grade and work status (full-time or part-time for some specific number of hours per week). This assessment should consider, in addition to the possibility of added personnel in the department, the use of existing personnel at present grade levels or the need to upgrade existing personnel.

Economic Analysis**

Economic analysis should take into account all costs of acquiring and using the equipment, including

- acquisition, which includes purchase price, cost of shipping, and total cost of installation
- estimated cost of all materials and supplies to be consumed in the operation of the equipment
- cost of additional personnel required or cost of essential upgrading of existing personnel
- cost, if any, of training personnel to operate the equipment
- estimated cost of maintenance, service, and repairs
- other applicable costs such as insurance premiums, license costs, various fees, additional power and other utility requirements

Finally, a comparison of alternatives should be undertaken on the basis of equivalent annual costs, that is, the cost of owning and operating each alternative on a per-year basis.

Conducting Equipment Trials*

Equipment trials are an option which should be strongly considered in any major departmental expenditure. Trials prior to selection of new equipment are a valuable means of evaluating both quality and costs in purchase decisions.

Establishing an equipment trial requires planning, staff education and cooperation, and evaluation procedures. The planning phase includes selecting the appropriate test population, establishing time limits, and coordinating sales representatives' activities to meet predetermined trial needs. The "test" population is determined by the use of the equipment; ideally it represents a sample of the nursing care units likely to use the equipment. A trial period should be long enough to be fair to each product, but allowing an evaluation to drag on more than two weeks may decrease enthusiasm and input—especially when more than one company product is involved and the clinical trials will last for months.

Source: Charles R. McConnell, *The Health Care Supervisor's Guide to Cost Control and Productivity Improvement*, Aspen Publishers, Inc., © 1986.

**Source*: Ibid.

Source: Phyllis Barone-Ameduri, "Equipment Trials Make Sense," *Nursing Management*, vol. 17, no. 6, June 1986. Reprinted with permission.

A meeting should be held with each sales representative prior to the trial to review plans and discuss company responsibilities during the period. Based on the predetermined trial length and number of participating units, verify that the company is indeed willing and able to provide the equipment and supplies needed for a successful evaluation.

Clarify the in-service education that will be needed to acquaint staff with the product. Ascertain whether and when the sales representative will be able to meet staff education needs on all shifts. Will he or she be available as a resource person to field questions and solve problems that may arise during the trial?

An evaluation tool should be developed prior to the trial. This tool should measure staff opinion in areas which define gradations of performance from poor to excellent. Evaluation criteria include reliability, ease of learning, simplicity of operation, and/or features which are improvements over currently used equipment. These factors will later be balanced by considerations such as cost, service agreements, and the like.

Part V

Human Resources Management

Chapter 24

Personnel Policies, Salaries, and Benefits

PERSONNEL POLICIES

The Personnel Policy Manual

Personnel policies and procedures are intended to act as a guide for supervisory and staff personnel in day-to-day personnel administration. A personnel policy manual should outline policies toward various aspects of the employer-employee relationship and indicate how those policies are to be administered. Because written policies promote consistency and understanding, manuals can assist a department in achieving uniform interpretations of policy by all personnel. Advantages expected to accrue from use of a manual include understanding, designation of line of authority, and consistency. You can create your own comprehensive personnel policy manual by following the model table of contents in Table 24-1.

Job Descriptions*

A job description is a statement setting forth the duties and responsibilities of a specific job and the characteristics of the individual needed

---

Source: Adapted from ''Practical Approaches to Nursing Service Administration,'' vol. 2, no. 2, 1963, and vol. 8, no. 4, 1969, American Hospital Association.

to perform it successfully. Job descriptions have become increasingly important as a management tool—a tool that management needs to make certain that responsibilities are wisely delegated, work efficiently distributed, talents fully used, and morale maintained.

Usefulness

Selecting Qualified Individuals. A job description that defines the duties and responsibilities involved when special abilities or skills are needed can aid in the recruitment and selection of the right person. Choice of a person who is either underqualified or overqualified can lead to unhappy results for both the worker and the job.

Providing an Evaluation Tool. A job description that spells out responsibilities and duties is an aid to the supervisor in rating the work of an employee. When both the person doing the evaluation and the person being rated know the specifications of the job, the rating can be objective and can be discussed on the basis of how well specific duties are carried out. For example, if making up empty beds is described as one of the responsibilities of a nursing aide, he or she can be rated on how well this is done. In jobs that are less task-oriented, where more is expected in the way of judgment and initiative, the same principle still applies. The employee then is rated on

Table 24-1 Personnel Policy Manual: A Model Table of Contents

continues

Table 24-1 *continued*

8. Grievance Procedures	**11. General Information**	Precautions
		Smoking
Content	Change of Employee Status	Kitchens
	Appearance, Uniforms	Housekeeping
9. Termination	Food Service Department	Oxygen
	Housekeeping and	Exit Ways
Avoiding Mistakes in	Maintenance Department	Regular Fire Checks
Discharging Employees	Ideas and Suggestions	Fire Drills
Verbal Warning	Lost and Found	Other Disasters
Written Warning	Loyalty	General Rules in Case of
Disciplinary Layoff	Parking	Fire
Discharge	Radio Voice Page	
Resignation	Day Care	**Appendices**
Exit Interview	Staff Meetings	
Type of Termination	Telephone Usage	Employee Evaluation Forms
	General Instructions for Safety	Exit Interview Form
10. Patient Care	Fire Prevention	Salary Schedules
	Storage of Combustible	
Admissions	Materials	
Patient Records	Trash Burning	
Discharge or Transfer of	Heating Equipment	
Patient	Electrical Hazards	
Visitors		

Source: Adapted from Thomas O. Harris and Robert E. Scott, *Model Personnel Manual*, American Health Care Association, 1975. Reprinted with permission.

---

the basis of his or her performance in situations that require judgmental decisions.

Making up the Budget. When salaries are equated with the level of responsibility and skill defined by job descriptions, recommendations concerning budgetary salary requirements can easily be justified.

Determining Departmental Functions. The director of nursing using job descriptions can help the hospital administrator to determine where certain functions should be placed and whether some functions performed by the nursing department can be done more efficiently by another department. For example, the nursing department may be performing dietary, housekeeping, or messenger tasks whose transfer to the proper departments would get the job done better.

Classifying Departmental Functions. The director of nursing service can use job descrip-

tions to classify nursing functions according to the levels of skill they require. Better utilization of personnel results when tasks are differentiated on this basis. Comparing job descriptions of the supervisor's and head nurse's duties may result in a realignment of responsibilities that will place controls closer to where the work is done. It may show a divided responsibility that makes controls ineffective.

Preparing Job Descriptions

Collecting Information. In a hospital where no job descriptions exist for nursing service personnel, the AHA suggests the following procedures for preparing them.

1. Prepare a simple form on which each employee may list his or her own duties; he or she may also be asked to fill in other information listed above. This will furnish information on what each person is currently doing.

2. Have the supervisor review each form with the individual worker and add comments about what the supervisor perceives the job to be.
3. Group all forms received from workers whose jobs are comparable, and from them prepare a general summary of the requirements for each job.
4. Compare all summaries to determine whether functions and tasks are assigned to the proper jobs, and make any necessary revisions to minimize duplication and overlapping.
5. Prepare specifications for jobs having comparable overall requirements. Include general requirements and standards that must be met by an applicant which are useful for administrative purposes and for establishing salary ranges.
6. Prepare for each specific job a description setting forth its characteristics, duties, and responsibilities. This should be given to employees and used in training new personnel. Note the date when the description was prepared and the name of the person preparing it.
7. Plan for implementation. Discuss the job descriptions with staff members and help the staff to put them into effect.
8. Plan for periodic review and revision as necessary.

In preparing job descriptions, allow for flexibility to give the worker opportunity to exercise initiative. It is well to include a phrase such as "and other related duties as required" to remind both supervisor and employee that the description is not absolutely all-inclusive and that related duties may be assigned on occasion.

When discussing job descriptions with workers, help them to see how their job contributes to patient care, how much other workers depend on them, and how they help in meeting the objectives of the department and of the hospital.

Because job descriptions are written for an individual hospital and a particular nursing service organization, using descriptions prepared in another hospital is unsatisfactory. Situations differ, and jobs are not alike in all hospitals.

Remember that job descriptions are no substitute for supervision. To maintain a high standard of performance, continuing supervision is essential.

Writing Job Descriptions. Observe the following guidelines in formulating job descriptions:

1. Allocate a title which distinctively implies the nature of the job.
2. Introduce the description with a summary of the essential features of the particular job which distinguishes it from all others.
3. Organize the list of requirements and duties in a logical sequence, concentrating on the major work activities, indicating the proportion of time involved, and summing up less significant functions.
4. Write in a clear, concise manner, avoiding ambiguity, overfussy details, excessive conditional words or clauses, and pale, nondescriptive language. Verbs and adverbs should be selected carefully to define the function accurately.
5. Use a standard format for all job descriptions and label all sections appropriately (e.g., major duties, minor duties, qualifications, etc.).
6. Review each proposed job description to check whether it meshes with current practices on the job, or if a new position is being created, whether the duties can be reasonably accomplished.

SALARY POLICIES*

The salary ranges and levels are key ingredients to a successful salary program. They must be substantial enough to attract and retain the most able employees yet modest enough not to waste the hospital's resources.

Each salary range provides for a minimum, a midpoint, and a maximum. The minimum must be high enough for 80 to 90 percent of the candidates to accept it as a starting salary. It must be competitive. The midpoint must be enough to retain the employee once he or she has become thoroughly skilled and contributing to the job. The maximum must be sufficient to retain the

Source: Martin E. Skoler, *Health Care Labor Manual*, Aspen Publishers, Inc., © 1981.

employee, avoiding loss by piracy or disenchantment.

To achieve these objectives the salary range will usually be narrower at entry-level positions, broadening out either on a dollar or percentage basis at higher grades. A common variance in salary ranges is from 20 percent (minimum to maximum) at entry-level positions to 35 to 40 percent at the senior positions (department head). This reflects a greater need at senior levels for salary flexibility to reward a greater variety of skills and to minimize turnover, the impact of which increases dramatically at high levels. Such differences in the breadth of ranges and salary levels introduce a great emphasis on market requirements as opposed to equity requirements. (See Figure 24-1 for a sample set of salary and wage guidelines.)

Figure 24-1 Sample Salary and Wage Guidelines Form

FROM:	Administrator
TO:	Distribution List
SUBJECT	SALARY AND WAGE GUIDELINES
PURPOSE	To provide for a sound, fair and equitable system of compensating hospital employees by paying the best possible wages based on job evaluation, area wages, effect on hospital costs and employee performance.
PAY PERIOD AND WORKWEEK	*Pay Period*—will begin Sunday morning at one (1) minute after Saturday midnight and end fourteen (14) days later at midnight Saturday. *Workweek*—will begin at one (1) minute after Saturday midnight and end Saturday midnight seven (7) days later.
OVERTIME	Authorized overtime will be paid at 1½ times the employee's regular rate for all hours *worked* in excess of forty (40) hours per workweek. Exemptions to the time and one-half provision will be based on the revised Federal Wage and Hour Laws and hospital policy. All overtime must be approved prior to the hours of actual overtime work by the Department Head and countersigned by Administration.
LEAVE	Leave paid hours are hours not actually worked and *will not* be included in the computation of overtime.
GRADES AND STEPS	All nondepartment head positions have been assigned a grade of 1-20. Each grade has a minimum step and eight other steps. Employees may progress within their grade by receiving step increases.
WAITING PERIOD	A waiting period is the length of time an employee must wait before proceeding to the next step in grade. New waiting periods begin with promotions and/or step increases. Merit increases *do not* change the waiting period. The minimum time (waiting period) required to advance from the minimum step to step 1 is six (6) months; from step 1 to step 2, step 2 to step 3, step 3 to step 4, etc., is one (1) year.
EXCEPTION: MERIT INCREASE	The exception to the above waiting period is the employee who is recommended for and received a merit increase (1 step). A merit increase recommendation, however, must be based on at least six (6) months of observed performance.
PROMOTIONS	Promotions will normally result in an approximate 10% increase in salary.
MAXIMUM ADVANCEMENT	Employees will not normally be advanced more than two (2) steps in any twelve (12) continuous months.
WITHHOLDING INCREASES	Step increases may be withheld with proper justification for a period not to exceed forty-five (45) days. If not granted then, a *new* waiting period will begin.

continues

Figure 24-1 *continued*

HIRING RATES

New employees will normally be hired at the minimum step of the position they are filling. New employees may be hired at step 1 or step 2 of the appropriate grade provided the Department Head and the Personnel Director agree. Hiring at above minimum will be guided by the following:

1. Applicants with from two (2) to five (5) years of directly related recent experience or an additional education degree deemed appropriate without experience may be hired at step 1.
2. Applicants with over five (5) years of directly related recent experience may be hired at step 2.
3. Applicants with from two (2) to five (5) years experience (as in guideline 1), and an additional education degree deemed appropriate may be hired at step 2.
4. The above guidelines apply to applicants who the department head feels will be outstanding employees.

TRAINEES

New employees hired as bona fide trainees will normally be paid at 90% of the minimum step established for the position. The trainee will receive an increase to the minimum step when satisfactorily completing the training period. A new waiting period will begin with that increase.

SHIFT
DIFFERENTIAL

Additional compensation will be paid to the following Nursing Personnel who work in ICU, CCU, PCU, OR, RR, and ER:

	Evening	Night
1. RN, Lab Technologist, Respiratory Therapist (Reg.)	$.25 ph	$.30 ph
2. LPN, X-ray Tech., Lab Technician, Respiratory Therapy Technician	$.15 ph	$.10 ph
3. All Others	$.15 ph	$.10 ph

SPECIALTY
DIFFERENTIAL

Additional Compensation will be paid to the following Nursing Personnel who work in ICU, CCU, PCU, OR, RR, and ER:

Staff Nurse	$.15 ph
LPN	$.10 ph
Nursing Assistant	$.10 ph
Unit Secretary	$.10 ph

CALL PAY

Employees subject to call will be paid at a rate of $1.00 per hour of call. Employees on call who are called in to work will be paid at their normal base rate for no less than one (1) hour for the first hour and any time beyond for actual time worked. Call pay stops when the normal shift begins and/or the employee comes to the hospital in response to being called in.

EFFECTIVE
DATES

Salary changes will be effective *only* at the beginning of a pay period.

RESPONSIBILITY
AND AUTHORITY

The Administrator or his or her designee will approve any salary increases. The Personnel Director will be responsible for staff supervision of the Salary and Wage Program.

Submitted by:

Approved by:

_____
Director of Personnel

_____
Administrator

Distribution List

All Departments

Merit vs. Longevity

What will be the basis for individual salary determinations and salary increments? There are two major alternatives for consideration: the merit system and the longevity system.

The Merit Approach

To many, the merit system has a very logical theoretical base. Should not the hard-working employee be rewarded for superior effort and ability? Should not the resources of the organization be directed primarily to substantial contributors rather than to the indolent and mediocre?

The merit system is characterized by the ranges of salary increase that an employee may receive, based on relative achievement reflected by his or her supervisor's recommendation at predetermined review times.

Also common to this approach are the concepts of salary minimum, midpoint, and maximum. The salary minimum is the starting rate for employees not having exceptional experience. The employee then moves to the midpoint by two to three increases, often occurring at, let us say, six-month intervals. The midpoint of the range is also the competitive rate for similar work being done in the community. The spread between minimum and midpoint reflects the learning period necessary to become job competent. Once an employee arrives at the midpoint of the range, salary review periods are longer (at least 12 months), and the basis for any change is exceptional rather than competent performance. The maximum salary is the highest that can be received by a person in a particular salary grade.

Some administrators have taken exception to the merit system and its salary range concept based on problems they have experienced in its operation. For instance:

- If the midpoint is the competitive salary in the community, and particularly if many employees in the area are on a single-rate (union) system, how can employees be recruited at less than that midpoint rate?

- If the range between minimum and midpoint is the learning period, does not the learning period differ from job to job and person to person? Can there be an arbitrary time between minimum and midpoint?

- Can the hospital remain competitive and deny employees some annual increase after they arrive at midpoint? If not, the notion of exceptional performance is in jeopardy.

- Finally, the most common criticism of the merit system is management's imprecise ability to determine degrees of merit, and the resulting small differences in salary between employees. In practice, can management effectively measure the differences in contribution? Is it possible that the employee who is less of a rival to the supervisor and is more deferential receives the larger increase?

This latter criticism is particularly common at entry-level positions, where degrees of merit are more difficult to determine.

These challenges to the basic merit system have resulted in conversion by some hospitals to other systems, such as longevity.

However, many who retain a belief in the efficacy of rewarding merit have developed modifications to meet the weaknesses in the merit program. These include the following:

- Establishment of step increments rather than a range of possible increase and a "go-no-go" decision by the supervisor as to whether a raise is merited or is to be delayed to another specified review date. This decision often must be approved at the next level of supervision.

- Establishment of quantitative bases for evaluation wherever possible (e.g., attendance, typing production speed, etc.).

- Development of participating approaches to performance evaluation, including self-appraisal, objectives-related appraisal, or appraisal by several supervisors.

- Moving to a longevity approach for entry-level positions, where differences in performance are difficult to assess.

Under this program, employees would receive modest longevity increases to midpoint, then be reviewed on the merit system. Other employees, in positions whose achievements are more measurable, would be eligible for merit increases from the minimum.

The Longevity Approach

Much of the structure described under the merit system also applies to any pay increase program based upon longevity. There is still the minimum, midpoint, maximum concept, with a person eligible for salary reviews at stated intervals. The principal difference is that increases are based upon length of service only, irrespective of achievement. The employee's supervisor has no significant say in determining the amount or appropriateness of the increase.

An interesting factor about longevity is the recent growth in its use and its application by various groups. Historically, there has been an emphasis on longevity for nonprofessional groups. Presently, there is a tendency toward a longevity base also among many professional groups.

The growth in the use of the longevity system suggests some important advantages that should be noted here:

- It eliminates a source of real stress between employer and employee, to the extent that employees have been dissatisfied with their supervisors' salary recommendations.
- It effectively counteracts union-organizing claims of arbitrary management by adopting the salary increase approach espoused by unions.
- Finally, it demands that supervisors concentrate on other ways of motivating employees.

There are also disadvantages attributed to any longevity program, including the following:

- There is no tangible way to reward excellence within a particular job.

- There is no way to encourage the resignation of marginal employees by withholding increases.
- Longevity forgoes any leverage provided by the merit program for a continuous, formalized performance appraisal program. This could also lead to a breakdown in the informal day-to-day performance appraisal process. Without this, employees who have taken their jobs for granted may be terminated without what they feel is adequate warning.
- A supervisor has little opportunity to assume responsibility and authority in a highly judgmental area.
- Finally, longevity creates the tendency to have narrow salary ranges (minimum to maximum) to avoid overpaying the modest performer. The regrettable effect of this decision is that exceptional performers are also limited.

Job Changes

Changes in position also require salary administration policies. These can include promotions, lateral transfers, demotions, and reevaluation of positions.

Promotions, by implication, usually involve a higher salary. Frequently, however, due to salary range overlap, an employee already is within the salary range for the new position. Nevertheless, most programs will provide an increase unless the employee is higher than the midpoint of the new salary range, which is a rare situation.

Lateral transfers demand salary review and thorough communications. Usually the employee will transfer to the new position at the same salary, assuming that the same skills are used in the new position. If, however, he or she is using a new set of skills, the salary should be negotiable. It may even be less than before, in fairness to the coworkers in the new department.

An employee may be *demoted* for cause or because of personal preference; the difference is important. Commonly, health care institutions may employ a senior employee who is no longer able to perform his or her old job, whether due to personal disability or a change in the demands of the position. Under these circumstances, many programs allow the employee to transfer, retaining his or her previous salary level, but exclude the employee from merit review raises until the new salary range catches up to the salary level carried over.

When an employee requests a change to a lower graded position (e.g., the RN who wishes to treat patients rather than supervise), the salary should be adjusted to a level no higher than the maximum of the grade for the new position. This is a negotiated process and may result in a salary level lower than the maximum.

Finally, when a job is *reevaluated*, employees should be treated as though promoted. They should be brought at least to the new minimum. To provide a proper spread, increases should also be allowed within the new range up to midpoint.

EMPLOYEE BENEFITS*

Determining Employee Needs

An employer must consider the needs of different groups of employees in selecting desired benefits and in setting priorities. The hospital work force consists of a mixture of full-time and part-time employees. Long-term workers may change their work schedules from time to time. The staff will include a wide variety of skill levels ranging from highly paid professionals to low-paid unskilled workers. Some of the workers will be planning a career in health care, and

Source: Anna M. Rappaport, "Benefit Plan Design Issues Today and through the 1980s," *Topics in Health Care Financing*, vol. 6, no. 3, © 1980 Aspen Publishers, Inc.

others will be temporary, with high rates of termination.

A benefit program should be able to accommodate workers in different circumstances and at different times in their life cycles.

The traditional approach to benefit design has been to develop a single pattern of benefits, with some completely paid for by the employer, some cost shared, and some paid for solely by the employee. The working husband, dependent wife, and minor children model has served as the family prototype around which this pattern was built. The employee's only choice has been whether to participate in contributory coverages. This benefit pattern was chosen to represent a compromise which would best meet the needs of a majority of the work force.

Flexible Benefits

A new approach to benefit plan design is currently developing in the United States. This approach provides for flexible benefits and permits individual employees to tailor a benefit package that best fits individual needs. This new approach is in the experimental stage. (See Table 24-2.)

Such programs involve a core of benefits provided by the employer for all employees, together with numerical credits which allow employees to select additional benefits beyond the core.

The factors which will determine the pattern of benefits that best fits a particular employee are

- family situation
- availability of other sources of benefits
- willingness to assume risks
- priorities of the individual
- general financial situation

Whether this method will work out well over the long term remains to be seen.

Table 24-2 Checklist for Salary and Benefits Negotiation

Salary Factors	(✔)	Fringe Benefits or Perquisites	(✔)
1. Salary range established ($_____ to $_____)	____	1. Stock options	____
2. Minimum acceptable salary ($_____)	____	2. Profit-sharing	____
3. Relocation expenses		3. Pensions and retirement plans	____
3.1 Packing and moving	____	4. Tax shelters _____	____
3.2 Old mortgage	____	_____	
3.3 New mortgage	____	5. Insurance	
3.4 Temporary housing	____	5.1 Medical (including family)	____
3.5 Utility hookups	____	5.2 Life	____
3.6 Furnishings	____	5.3 Disability	____
3.7 Others _____	____	5.4 Dental (including family)	____
_____	____	6. Vacation	____
_____	____	7. Sick leave	____
		8. Discounts	____
4. Salary review plan (date: _____)	____	9. Credit union	____
5. Commission or bonuses	____	10. Education benefits	____
6. Automobile	____	11. Professional dues	____
7. Reimbursable expenses	____	12. Social dues	____
		13. Others _____	____
		_____	

Source: Russell C. Swansburg and Phillip W. Swansburg, *Strategic Career Planning and Development for Nurses*, Aspen Publishers, Inc., © 1984.

Chapter 25

Interviewing Applicants and Orientation

OVERVIEW

The employment interview is a two-way communication process. The employer is attempting to obtain information about a prospective employee. The applicant, likewise, is attempting to obtain information about the prospective employer. In consideration of today's current shortage and recruitment market, it would be advisable to encourage applicant questions and/or readily provide information about the facility and the department. Orientation, too, should be used to win over the newcomer and to clarify the attributes and uniqueness of the working environment. In this way, the applicant has the necessary information to judge whether the fit is right and so avoid a costly error—for both sides.

INTERVIEWING JOB APPLICANTS

The Interview

Following the initial screening by the personnel department, nursing administration should interview all acceptable nurse applicants.

Interview Form

Sometimes the notes taken during an interview are more important than the application form information in determining a job applicant's qualifications. The written record of the interview could be a simple narrative report or a more defined check-off list or fill-in form. A combination of the two concepts may be preferable, namely, a form with check-off items as well as ample space for comments. Such a form provides consistency among interviews and reminds the interviewer of points to be observed, while the blank spaces allow room for qualifying or explanatory remarks.

Interview Plan

The interview often focuses on the "persona" of the applicant. Application forms supply the factual details but interviews supply the live impression of the applicant in action-thinking, organizing, and explaining. After the initial introductions, the following areas of inquiry should be pursued with the applicant.

1. *Personal past experience.* The applicant should be asked to discuss his or her experiences as a child, as a student, and as an employee in other work situations. Questions can be asked about the nature of the experiences—the benefits, obstacles, disadvantages, and assessments.
2. *General attitudes toward nursing, the position available, and the facility environment.* The applicant should be

asked to discuss his or her philosophy of nursing and special interest in the specific position and the hospital in general. If there are criticisms or reservations, these should be explored.

3. *Sense of self*. The applicant should be questioned on immediate and eventual goals and realistic plans to accomplish these objectives. Ask the applicant to evaluate his or her own strong and weak points in professional work and interpersonal relations. Discuss the applicant's responses to authority, responsibility, innovation, and participation.

4. *Personal current experiences*. The applicant should be asked about his or her current or planned marital and family status and whether any conflict might occur between work and private life. Find out about the range of private interests and professional associations which occupy the applicant's leisure time.

5. *Information interchange*. At this point, the applicant may have questions about the position, and the interviewer should respond with forthright answers. Additional information on areas not covered by the interviewer may also be offered by the applicant at this time.

Interview Flow

Careful reading of the interview plan will reveal a flow and ebb to the procedure, a movement from the general to the particular and back again to the general. The first part of the interview acts as a warm-up, but the open-ended quality of the questions should reveal a great deal about the applicant: his or her approach to problems, professional pride, sincerity, etc. By introducing all major topics with a broad, neuter-type question, a spontaneous response can be elicited. The applicant is allowed to direct the conversation to areas which have relevance for him or her, thus offering the interviewer grounds for more specific questions. If the applicant persistently sticks to generalizations, he or she should be asked to provide illumination by describing a situation from his or her experience. The intent is to discover how the applicant handles situations in the working environment and whether these reflect potential personality conflicts, faulty reasoning, lack of understanding, or inability to cope.

In the last phase, when the applicant is more relaxed and is discussing his or her personal life outside of the hospital setting, the interviewer should note those traits which may be of value in the hospital unit. Is the applicant narrow in scope or curious, interested in learning? Are the applicant's interests diverse or focused? Will any interest contribute to his or her value as a worker? Observe also those questions asked and not asked by the applicant. The type of information actively sought by the applicant is indicative of his or her real concerns and of an attempt to assess the situation in terms of his or her needs.

Interview Pitfalls*

Three classic pitfalls that severely block effective communication are the third degree treatment, the leading question, and the loaded question. These are pitfalls that put the other person down in some way or set him or her up for a fall.

The Third Degree

In an effort to get to the bottom line, some interviewers fall into the trap of creating a "stress interview." They use the old third degree treatment, grilling the suspect—oops, the interviewee—with a series of tough, unexpected, anxiety-producing questions (often leading or loaded questions) to test out how quick, sharp, and consistent he or she is.

Unfortunately, this interviewing technique works against the achievement of your goal in the interview, that is, getting to the bottom line, gathering new information and data. The grilling requires a great deal of energy on your part to sustain. As well, it puts the other person on edge and breaks any trust and rapport that you may have established, causing him or her to give you a "whitewash" or simple "yes-no" responses. In effect, you have closed off communication— you have crossed the point of no return.

Source: Paul Koellner, "Planning and Communication Blocks for Effective Interviewing," *Management Perspectives*, April 1977.

The Leading Question

One of the most common communication pitfalls that finds its way into interview situations is the "leading" question. The way the question is phrased suggests a correct answer—"Don't you think or agree that . . . Aren't you in favor of . . . You like . . . don't you?"

The leading question puts words in the interviewee's mouth, forcing him or her to agree with you whether in fact that is the case or not. A leading question is of little help in discovering how the person really thinks or feels. Indeed, one of its major difficulties is that many people will agree with you so as not to jeopardize themselves, especially if the job or the situation is important to them.

The Loaded Question

The "loaded" question is a close cousin to the leading question—it, too, anticipates agreement. The added feature of most loaded questions is that the person is never really sure if the answer he or she gives will or will not cause an explosion—"I thought he did a good job. What do you think?" "That wasn't a very good reason for not completing the assignment, was it?" "When did you stop coming in late?"

The interviewee may not know the answer (in which case he or she is playing Russian roulette), may resent the question, or may answer the question the way he or she thinks it is supposed to be answered. Whatever the case, though, the result is the same—no new information about the person. One of the most classic loaded questions I heard took away any response from the interviewee altogether—"How long do you expect me to tolerate your performance anyway?" The loaded question closes off communication.

Psychological Barriers at Interviews*

Unequal Power

The emotional state of each party in an interview is likely to be entirely different. The interviewer can afford to be relaxed and comfort-

able—perhaps even blasé. The interviewee cannot enter into this relationship in such a relaxed manner, however; it is far too important. Given this situation, it is perhaps even naive to expect that the typical applicant can be at ease during the interview. On the contrary, we should expect in many cases to see an applicant who is ill at ease, uncomfortable, and nervous. This is certainly a very "natural" way to react to a stressful situation. If we convince ourselves that the seemingly comfortable, self-assured applicant is somehow "better" than the uncomfortable and nervous applicant, we run the risk not only of basing our decision on largely superficial personality traits but also of potentially succumbing to the second psychological barrier: "phoney" behavior.

"Phoney" Behavior

Related to the power imbalance inherent in job interviews is what can best be termed "phoney" behavior. Phoney behavior is familiar to anyone who has done extensive job interviewing—the feeling that the applicant is attempting to project an "image," to convey an impression of being a certain type of person. To get a job, many applicants seem to feel, one must be perceived as sociable, highly intelligent, considerate, and so on. They love to "work with people," never have problems with superiors, and are universally liked; they are seeking a job with challenge, responsibility, and an opportunity to prove themselves. The clichés runneth over.

Questions without Answers

The third psychological barrier to effective employment interviewing is the tendency of some interviewers to ask questions that do not really have answers. Some examples of such questions: "Tell me something about yourself," "How would you describe yourself?" and "Where would you like to be 10 years from now?"

Given the power imbalance inherent in the situation and the emphasis on phoney behavior, there is little reason to believe that answers to these questions are completely honest anyway. This puts the interviewer in the position of providing a probably incorrect analysis of a dishonest answer from a tense and uncomfortable applicant.

Source: Richard G. Nehrbass, "Psychological Barriers to Effective Employment Interviewing," *Personnel Journal,* February 1977. Reprinted with the permission of *Personnel Journal,* Costa Mesa, California; all rights reserved.

Overcoming the Barriers

Awareness of these three barriers can aid an interviewer. Awareness, by itself, won't solve the problem but it can emphasize to the interviewer the need to create (to the extent possible) a psychologically safe and supportive atmosphere for the interview. The interviewer can show by behavior and active attention to the applicant that he or she considers the interview to be as important as the applicant does.

A short introductory statement to the effect that the organization is looking for the best person to fit the position, rather than any particular personality type, can also partially alleviate the applicant's felt need to project a certain image.

Perhaps, most importantly, the interviewer can ensure that the interview stresses facts and not opinions or feelings. Through an emphasis on questions that require the applicant to relate factual events from the past, the interviewer can steer the conversation away from projecting an image and towards reality.

A number of these factually oriented questions exist and have been used by some interviewers for years. It is usually a good idea to pair a "positive" with a "negative" question to further reduce the uneasiness of the applicant. Some examples of such questions: "There are always some things about our jobs we like and some we dislike. Tell me a couple of things about your last job that you particularly liked and a couple of things you particularly disliked." This question can also be asked about the applicant's previous superiors. Another such question is, "What were some of the things about your last job that you felt were particularly difficult to do? What were some of the things you did best?"

Avoiding Discriminatory Questions*

Federal laws prohibit employment decisions based on sex, race, color, age, religion, national origin, and handicap. State laws *do* vary, since each state has independent legislation on dis-

crimination. Generally, interviewers can obtain the pertinent regulations from the state department of labor or the state human rights commission.

The nurse interviewer should be cautioned against asking questions that apply to only one sex, race, or group. For example, questions about marital status and children generally are considered discriminatory because, in most instances, the questions are asked only of female applicants.

Other questions that interviewers generally reserve for female applicants include babysitting or child care arrangements, family or spouse reaction to meals not being served on time, and spouse attitudes toward shift work, employment in general, and job-related travel. Questioning the male applicant about his attitude or reaction to a female supervisor has discriminatory implications.

Discriminatory questioning of the older applicant and the handicapped applicant tends to be more subtle. Older candidates should not be questioned about their ability to keep up with younger employees, nor should the over-40 applicant be questioned regarding his or her attitude toward having a younger supervisor. The Rehabilitation Act requires that the mentally and physically handicapped individual be judged solely on his or her ability to do a specified job and thus makes non-job-related selection criteria illegal.

Because there are racially different statistical arrest rates, questions about arrests are generally considered discriminatory. Questions concerning conviction are never disallowed, since this information is public record.

ORIENTATION

Program Scope*

The number of nursing instructors and clerical staff required depends upon the number and type of training programs needed, which may be as

---

*Source: Gaye W. Poteet, "The Employment Interview: Avoiding Discriminatory Questioning," *The Journal of Nursing Administration,* April 1984. Reprinted with permission.

*Source: Grace Matsunaga, *Concerns in the Acquisition and Allocation of Nursing Personnel,* National League for Nursing, Pub. No. 20-1709, 1978. Reprinted with permission.

various as on-the-job skill training for nursing assistants or in-service education for inexperienced nurses requiring special preparation in clinical specialties.

All newly employed personnel are entitled to be oriented to the hospital as a total institution and specifically to the nursing service. (See Table 25-1.) The orientation program usually includes a tour of the physical setting as well as information on the philosophy, goals, and structure of the overall hospital and the department of nursing. Functions of the various members of the nursing team and nursing care standards are usually emphasized. Under normal circumstances, it takes only a few days to orient new employees to the work situation and setting. However, since many new graduates lack sufficient clinical practice in the generic nursing programs, many hospitals have had to combine orientation and in-service education during the initial period of employment in order to prepare the nurse to function as a beginning-level practitioner.

Table 25-1 Self-Learning Manual for RN Orientation–Outline

Section A—General Information
RN/GN Competencies
Organizational Chart
Department of Nursing–Purpose and
  Objectives
Department of Nursing Statement of
  Philosophy
Hospital Map
Policy and Procedure Review Worksheet
Patients Bill of Rights
Code for Nurses

Section B—Documentation
Charting Guidelines
Guidelines for the Use of Nursing Diagnosis
Flow Sheets
Patient Teaching Records

Section C—Transcription of Orders
Transcription Process
Transcription of Medication Orders
Use of the Medication Sheet
Medication Administration Times

Section D—Pharmacy Information
Medicated Large Volume IV's
Ordering Intermittant IV's
Pharmacy Forms
Pharmacokinetics
Aeseptic Technique
Unit Dose System
Medication Calculations

**Section E—Admitting, Transferring and
  Discharging Patients**
Routine Scheduled Admissions

Transfers
  • in house
  • to another hospital or home health care
    agency
  • to a long term care facility
Discharges
  • routine
  • AMA
  • deceased

Section F—General Communication
Shift-to-Shift Report
Patient Classification
Communication with Nutritional Services
Communication with Family Practice
  Center–Residents
Laboratory Reports
Incident Reports
Central Distribution System

Section G—Emergency Plans/Safety
Fire Fighting Plan
Procedure for Evacuation of Patients, Visitors
  and Staff
Tornado Alert
Bomb Threat Plan
Disaster Plan
Hazard Communication

Section H—Suicide Policy
Identifying Suicidal Patients
Suicide Precautions
Case Study

Evaluations

Individualized Training*

The in-service education program to help the new nurse become proficient in clinical nursing skills must be individualized since nurses differ in their educational background and work experience. The observed and felt learning needs can best be identified through the use of a checklist which involves the active participation of both the trainee and instructor. This type of basic preparation may extend from two weeks to over a month, depending upon the learning needs of the nurse. However, if the new nurse is to be assigned to an intensive care unit, he or she will probably require much more time in the training program. The preparation of the new graduate, however, is not the sole responsibility of the in-service education staff. Supervisors, clinicians, and head nurses on the services on which the nurse is assigned are also responsible for closely working with the nurse to further develop his or her competencies in nursing practice and to reinforce knowledge acquired in the formal teaching situation. The supportive help and guidance given to the new nurse in this early phase of employment is crucial for further development of the potentials of the nurse and for a healthy adaptation to the work situation.

If unskilled workers are employed as nursing assistants who will be involved in direct patient care services, they must be provided with on-the-job skill training. They must be taught the knowledge and skills required to perform their defined functions, with measures taken to safeguard the quality of nursing care. To continue their employment, nursing assistants should successfully pass paper-and-pencil tests and a practical examination on skill performance.

Supervised Practice*

The appropriate allocation or assignment of newly recruited nurses cannot be based solely upon the staffing requirements of the various

clinical services if the goal is to retain qualified and competent nursing personnel. A number of hospitals place new graduates on selected general medical-surgical units to gain basic nursing care experience under close supervision and guidance prior to assignment to other clinical specialties. As well, it is often found essential to rotate new nurses to evenings and nights during the initial phase of employment. Nursing administration is responsible for ensuring that these new graduates receive sufficient orientation, supervision, and support in rendering patient care and in carrying out their other assigned functions. The new graduate is vulnerable and will be greatly influenced by the attitudes, expectations, and behavior of the head nurse. The relationship that is established between the new graduate and the head nurse is a key factor in determining the adaptation, productivity, and satisfaction of the staff nurse. Nursing administrators must give thought to assigning the impressionable new staff nurse to head nurses who can serve as healthy role models and who have the interest and patience to work with newly employed nursing personnel.

Specific Approaches to Orientation*

New-Graduate Program

Typically a new-graduate program begins with general nursing orientation, to which are added classes on pharmacology, team-leading theory, care planning, communications, and the contributions of other departments to patient care. Many new graduates perceive such a program to be merely an extension of school, and if there is one thing they don't want more of, it's school. If they don't feel a need to learn something, it is very unlikely that the information will be retained.

New nurses are often action-oriented, with much of their interest and energy absorbed in the new situation, relationships, and roles. If new graduates are offered classroom activities in-

---

*Source: Grace Matsunaga, *Concerns in the Acquisition and Allocation of Nursing Personnel*, National League for Nursing, Pub. No. 20-1709, 1978. Reprinted with permission.

*Source: Unless otherwise noted, excerpts on specific orientation approaches are from Ann Haggard, *Hospital Orientation Handbook*, Aspen Publishers, Inc., © 1984

stead of the direct nurse-patient relationships they want and need, they often refer to such orientation classes as boring and irrelevant.

How long should a program be? There are no magic numbers. Different programs range from one week to over a year. New-graduate orientation programs generally provide all participants with similar experiences. After the standard nursing orientation, a new graduate spends more time on the units without being counted as staff and is usually given more time in class.

The head nurse and unit teacher should meet with each new graduate to review goals, philosophies, experiences, and values. Discuss unit expectations and discover the new nurse's expectations of the job. Let graduates know that a feeling of stress and overload is normal and that exhaustion is a rational reaction to suddenly increased responsibility. A plan for professional development can be agreed on and the responsibility for it clearly placed on the new graduate. This is an important point. Although instructors and unit personnel can offer help and support, the final responsibility for making the adjustment can only belong to the individual. Orientees are being paid to attend seminars, learn needed information, put it into practice, and become functioning members of the health care team.

Buddy System

Each orientee is paired with an experienced staff nurse. On the first day, the staff nurse receives a patient assignment—if anything, a little lighter than usual—and the orientee works with the buddy to care for these patients. Notice that the orientee is not assigned any patients. The whole purpose of this method of orientation is that the new person works alongside the experienced nurse to learn care routines. If one is in a room giving a bath while the other is down the hall passing medications, all the benefits of the buddy system are lost.

As the new nurse becomes more comfortable on the unit, separate assignments are made, with the buddy still available as a resource. If possible, the pair should be scheduled for the same on-duty time through the end of the orientation period.

Orientation Units

Placing orientees on units designated expressly for orientation is a practice seen in some hospitals. The rationale for this approach is that the entire unit is geared toward teaching and there is more supervision available. On some of these units the staff provide the instruction; on others the orientation instructors from the education department work with orientees.

All new nurses are assigned to the orientation unit(s) for a designated period of time, usually the first two weeks of employment. When a nurse is hired, all clinical experience is provided on the special unit. At the end of the orientation unit assignment, the nurse moves to the permanent work area.

Although the instruction received on such a unit is well planned and well executed, several serious drawbacks exist. First, the orientees are placed in an artificial environment that some may resent as being too protected and too much like a student experience in nursing school. Second, the staff of such a unit may rapidly burn out from a heavy influx of orientees. Third, and perhaps most important, orientees are kept from their home unit and permanent work group, delaying bonding and identification and increasing costs, as they still have to be oriented to their own unit.

Competency-based Orientation

Competency-based programs require orientees to demonstrate their mastery of performance objectives within an agreed-on time frame. The knowledge required may be obtained through self-study modules, reading, discussion, or clinical practice. Hospitals using this type of program find that eliminating unnecessary class time saves money, and tailoring orientation to each person's individual needs reduces total orientation hours and increases job satisfaction.

Developing a Learning Contract. The orientation agreement states all the experiences a nurse should complete before proceeding to permanent assignment. In the first meeting with an orientee, the head nurse or instructor explains the contract and negotiates the plan for meeting it. Such a contract serves two purposes: (1) the new nurse knows exactly what is expected and (2) the instructor can pinpoint the learner's weaknesses for later follow-up and evaluation.

The learning contract also provides needed structure. It is essential to provide some sense of the parameters of the environment (time constraints and learning aids available) and of individual learning needs. Orientees who have difficulty diagnosing their own needs and taking responsibility for meeting them find such structure particularly helpful.

Learning Strategies. The key concepts of competency-based education may be listed as follows:

1. Performance itself is the outcome.
2. Learning is self-directed and has reasonable time limits.
3. Learning is self-paced to accommodate individual learning rates.
4. The teacher becomes a resource rather than merely a conveyor of information.

Following these principles, orientees should select their own patient assignments, and both study time and clinical time should be flexible. This can cause problems on the units if head nurses and staff are not knowledgeable and supportive of the concept. Since some content will be taught at the bedside, clinical practice must be excellent, with all nurses serving as potential role models.

Learning Modules. Aside from planned experiences with patient care, orientees may obtain needed content from prepared learning modules. Each module usually has the following elements: title, purpose statement, entry behaviors, objectives, learning activities, and a method of evaluation. For instance, a learning module could be designed to inform learners about competency-based orientation.

Learning modules can be designed to cover a wide range of content. With the addition of equipment and step-by-step procedures, orientees can even learn and practice nursing skills such as setting up for a lumbar puncture, changing ostomy bags, or instituting heart monitoring.

Testing and evaluation can involve written tests, oral explanations, return demonstrations, and performance of the skill in a clinical setting. Although setting up learning modules is initially very time consuming, once the program is implemented the packages can be used over and over again with little additional revision.

Preceptor Programs in Clinical Orientation

A preceptor is an experienced nurse selected according to specific criteria to serve as a resource person to new nurses. Although formal preceptor programs are a fairly new development in orientation, the concept of an experienced practitioner serving as a mentor to a new person has been around for as long as there have been trades and professions. These programs are

---

Orientation Objectives

Orientation objectives for the clinical nurse educator, as formulated by one hospital, are as follows:

- Support the new employee during the transition period to the assigned area.
- Assist the new employee in identifying individual strengths and weaknesses.
- Provide an ongoing appraisal of the new employee's performance during orientation via regularly scheduled meetings.
- Provide an introduction, review of basic skills, and selected learning experiences based upon individual needs.
- Act as a liaison between the employee and the staff, assisting and encouraging the staff to participate in teaching the new employee.

Source: Elaine J. Serra, "Orienting and Developing Professional Nurses in the Practice Setting," in *Human Resource Management Handbook: Contemporary Strategies for Nursing Managers,* Ellen M. Lewis and Joan Gygax Spicer, eds., Aspen Publishers, Inc., © 1987.

expensive to start, because the preceptors must be prepared for their new role.

Selecting Preceptors. The selection of staff nurses to serve as preceptors is usually done by the head nurses. The people selected should be volunteers, but not all volunteers are appropriate choices. Criteria for selection include

- at least one year's experience in the clinical area
- permanent, full-time employee
- consistent high-quality nursing skills and judgment
- desire to work closely with new employees

- ability to instruct others clearly and in a positive, supportive way

Preceptor Preparation. After the nurses have been selected, preparation for their new role should include a workshop and discussion meetings. The workshop should be a minimum of one day in length if the preceptors are to have a basic grounding in what they will be doing. Also, be sure to provide practical experience as well.

Each preceptor should meet with the head nurse to determine how orientation will be conducted on the unit. Table 25-2 presents guidelines for the different roles involved in orientation: head nurse, preceptor, educator, and new employee.

Table 25-2 Roles in a Preceptor Program

	Head Nurse	Preceptor	Nurse Educator	New Employee
Assessment	1. Interviews and hires new employee with input from AHN 2. Administers Clinical Unit Skills Inventory 3. Pretests for theory and clinical abilities 4. Compares new employee to competencies in CORE Curriculum	1. Reviews results of and explains use of • Clinical Skills Inventory • CORE Curriculum • Objectives • Other tests given to new employee 2. Direct observation of new employee's clinical performance	1. Reviews results of • Clinical Skills Inventory • CORE Curriculum • Other tests given 2. Direct observation of new employee's performance	1. Completes and updates Clinical Skills Inventory self-assessment of current performance level 2. Identifies own learning needs
Planning	1. Selects Preceptor for new employee 2. Informs Nursing Education, Preceptor, and Unit Staff of new employee's hire date and learning needs 3. Assigns new employee to orient day shift and/or off shift	1. Has planning conference with new employee first clinical day 2. Writes mutually agreed upon goals and objectives to increase skill and performance level of new employee	1. Informs Preceptor and Unit of first clinical day 2. Assists Preceptor in writing goals and objectives	1. Writes mutually agreed-upon goals and objectives with Preceptor

continues

Table 25-2 *continued*

	Head Nurse	Preceptor	Nurse Educator	New Employee
Implementation	1. Provides orientation and Preceptor time for new employee	1. Is not "in charge" while precepting 2. Provides Learning Center time for new employee 3. Provides learning activities for new employee 4. Acts as clinical resource for new employee 5. Holds weekly conferences to review progress on technical and process skills 6. Gives ongoing feedback regarding performance 7. Validates skills according to protocol	1. Provides new employee with general hospital orientation 2. Provide Preceptors with Preceptor Training Program 3. Assists Preceptor in locating appropriate learning activities	1. Reads procedure and policy manuals 2. Initiates own learning experiences 3. Follows learning activities outlined in CORE Curriculum and follows "Guidelines for Integrating Nursing Process into Practice"
Evaluation	1. Evaluates orientee's progress by observation and feedback from orientee and Preceptor 2. Conducts 3-month evaluation conference with Preceptor and new employee 3. Determines if orientation needs to be extended 4. Assigns new employee to permanent status	1. Confers with new employee about progress at end of orientation 2. Give feedback to HN regarding new employee performance 3. Provides written evaluation to new employee using • Goals and objectives • Direct observation • Clinical Unit Skills Inventory • Process to practice tool	1. Assists Preceptor and new employee in evaluating new employee's progress 2. Consults on any proposed extension of probation or orientation 3. Evaluates orientation and updates learning programs as needed 4. Reviews orientation evaluations and gives feedback to Preceptors and Head Nurses	1. Conferences with Head Nurse and Preceptor at end of orientation 2. Evaluates Preceptor program and orientation 3. Writes self-evaluation of progress with use of Clinical Unit Skills Inventory and mutually set goals and objectives

Source: Nancy Plasse and Janet Reiss Lederer, "Preceptor: A Resource for New Nurses," *Supervisor Nurse*, June 1981. Reprinted with permission.

Cost-Effectiveness Analysis of Orientation*

Analyzing Program Costs

Each program should be analyzed in terms of what it costs to produce and present as well as evaluate. How many hours did each instructor put in developing the class (research, arranging for rooms and refreshments, composing handouts, etc.)? How many hours were actually spent in class?

To those hours should be added any time spent on follow-up: putting away equipment, reading completed assignments or classwork, grading tests, completing records, etc. Add preparation hours to class hours and hours spent on follow-up and multiply the total by the instructor's hourly salary. Add to that any time spent by anyone else involved in the class: other instructors, the secretary who did the typing, the audio-visual technician who videotaped something, etc.

Now calculate the costs of the materials you used. How much did the film cost, or the transparencies, or the slides? Divide that total cost by the number of times instructors expect to use this item in order to determine the cost of a single showing. What were the costs for photocopying the syllabus, handouts, case studies, and tests? Multiply the number of copies by the cost per copy to get the total cost.

Take the attendance sheet and note the categories of employees who were in the class: RN, pharmacist, unit secretary, physical therapist, etc. Build in a mechanism for discovering who attended on their own time—have a space to

_____
Source: Ann Haggard, *Hospital Orientation Handbook*, Aspen Publishers, Inc., © 1984

check on the roll sheet or a box on the application form. Anyone who was not paid to attend is not added to the cost. But all participants attending on paid time are part of the cost analysis, and orientation is a required class where everyone is paid to attend. Multiply the relevant hourly salaries (personnel department can give an average hourly salary for each category of employee) by the class hours and add them all together to get the cost to the institution of having those people participate.

Put in any other program costs such as consultant fees, workbooks, refreshments, etc., and add all these figures together to find out the total cost of the course.

Analyzing Program Benefits

Learning outcomes range from attendance only (the participants were there and breathing, but that's all you can say for sure) to consistent on-the-job performance without external reinforcement, calculated on a 1 to 5 scale. This data can be obtained only by observation and follow-up during and after class. If most participants can pass a written test, the class achieved a 2; if they successfully complete a simulated problem in class, a 3; if they apply content to actual work situations with reinforcement from another person, a 4; and so on.

When presenting such findings to administration, stress the fact that 70 percent of a hospital's operating budget goes to payroll costs. With such a tremendous investment already committed to employees, it only makes sense to develop them to the greatest extent possible. If new employees leave soon after hire because of inadequate orientation, the hospital suffers a double penalty of recruitment induction costs and an overworked staff more likely themselves to terminate employment.

Chapter 26

Labor Relations

UNIONIZATION IN THE HOSPITAL

Changing Times and Attitudes*

Traditionally, health care employees have not embraced the notion of collective bargaining, but times are changing. Unionization is not exactly a foreign concept to registered nurses. Indeed, some registered nurses have for some time viewed unionization as a potential tool to enhance the role of the professional nurse as a clinical decision maker. On the other hand, the majority of nurses have historically resisted positive identification with unionization.

Today's decrease in resistance is reflected in a variety of attitudes. Many registered nurses, who comprise a large and significant employee group, are turning more to unionization as a means of upgrading their position in hospitals. Some RNs may view unionization as the most promising avenue available to them through which to address professional practice issues and improve their economic and career status. Nurses are experiencing dissatisfaction with their profession, becoming more concerned with

the limited autonomy of the nursing role and practice as a member of the health care team and management's lack of communication and desire to involve registered nurses in decision making concerning patient care and other matters related to health care. Clearly, a growing proportion of professional nurses want to be viewed as movers and shakers within the patient care and hospital management teams.

Coupled with the above, is the interest union organizations are showing in the health care industry. While collective bargaining in hospitals experienced unprecedented growth as a result of the 1974 health care amendments to the Taft-Hartley Act, there has been a decline in the number of union members in the traditional industrial organizations. Thus, as unions move from industry-related into service-related organizations, the health care industry is a major target for increasing union membership roles.

In addition to the stance taken by the nursing professional associations, the National Union of Hospital and Health Care Employees voted to affiliate with the Service Employees International Union, leading to an alliance of the two largest health worker unions. This marriage may thrust health care organizing into the forefront, as the United States has more than six million health workers, 90 percent of whom are not unionized. The breadth and reach of the vis-

---

*Source: C. Nick Wilson, Carol Lee Hamilton, and Ellen Murphy, "Union Dynamics in Nursing," *Journal of Nursing Administration*, vol. 20, no. 2, February, © 1990 J.B. Lippincott.

ibility and power of the "super union" may be a more potent source of professional power for the registered nurses.

Whether or not predictions of union growth in the registered nursing ranks become a reality or not may very well depend upon the hospital and nursing management's response to professional nurses' burgeoning dissatisfaction.

Pressures of inflation, legislated cost-containment activities, an increasingly tight nursing labor market, compensation, and professional issues have created an unsettling situation for the registered nurse. These same conditions imply that collective bargaining with union representation is a possible, if not probable, scenario for registered nursing personnel in hospitals.

Vulnerability to Union Organizing*

No employer is perfectly invulnerable to union organizing. For management ever to believe so is a form of smugness that represents a considerable measure of vulnerability.

Vulnerability is relative to a number of factors. However, experience has shown that organizing drives—most originating inside the organization as employees reach out for representation—usually originate with employee dissatisfaction with some or all of the following.

Quality of Direct Supervision. Quality of supervision is a key factor for all employees whether professional or nonprofessional. The organization is vulnerable if

- insufficient attention is given to placing managers out of consideration for communications skills, leadership, and problem-solving abilities and the like (as opposed to making placement decisions on technical skills alone)
- there is little or no emphasis placed on management development
- top management fails to act on apparent supervisory weaknesses (discrimination, harassment, favoritism, neglect, etc.)

---

*Source: Charles R. McConnell, *Managing the Health Care Professional*, Aspen Publishers, Inc., © 1984.

- no effort is made to stimulate and promote upward communication, and no readily accessible channels are open to employees

Organizational Stability and Job Security. The organization is vulnerable if

- there are frequent surprise shifts in workload and work distribution
- there is a history of instability, leading the employees to anticipate periodic layoffs
- there is no rational, consistent approach to layoff, recall, and bumping
- surprise changes occur in job structure and assignments
- new methods and new equipment are introduced without advance notice
- minimal information is provided about opportunities for advancement or for training and development

Compensation and Benefits. The organization is vulnerable if

- pay rates are not comparable with other health care organizations and other relevant competitors
- there is no reflection of individual performance in the granting of raises
- there are internal inequities in pay
- employees do not understand how their pay is determined
- there is no job evaluation program or other systematic approach to grading jobs and setting rates of pay
- employees are dissatisfied with their benefit plans as compared with the plans of other employers
- arbitrary changes in benefits occur by surprise
- employees lack knowledge of the details of their benefit programs

Input to Organizational Processes. For this area of concern of particular importance to professional employees, the organization is vulnerable if

- employees feel that they have no input into the form and structure of their jobs or no voice in how their work is done
- employees feel that they have no say regarding decisions that affect them
- employees receive no management response to their suggestions, problems, and questions

Problem Resolution Process. The organization is vulnerable if

- discipline is not applied fairly, uniformly, and consistently
- disciplinary actions are taken without extending employees a reasonable opportunity to correct their behavior
- there is no formal, consistent, multistep problem or grievance resolution procedure

Evaluation of Employee Climate*

The most important questions that health care executives should ask in appraising the overall level of employee satisfaction or dissatisfaction are these:

1. Does the employee believe that he or she is regularly treated with courtesy, respect, and dignity?
2. Does the employee believe that he or she is treated as an individual with unique needs, skills, and aspirations?
3. Does the employee believe that management makes personnel decisions fairly, without regard to race, sex, age, religion, nationality, or the like?
4. Does the employee believe that his or her supervisors are careful to avoid favoritism in directing work, imposing discipline, and dispensing rewards?
5. Does the employee believe that his or her efforts and loyalty are known and appreciated by immediate supervisors and by higher management?

6. Does the employee believe that management has and will *voluntarily* grant reasonable, competitive wage increases and improve fringe benefits?
7. Does the employee believe that day-to-day working relations are friendly and relaxed?
8. Does the employee believe that the workplace is attractive, healthy, and safe?
9. Does the employee believe that his or her job is secure from unwarranted discharge or layoff?
10. Does the employee believe that his or her work is genuinely important to the welfare of patients and the community?
11. Does the employee believe that he or she has received adequate training?
12. Does the employee believe that the institution itself is managed in a highly professional manner so that he or she can be proud to identify with it?
13. Does the employee believe that his or her job holds promise for a better future, that he or she will be offered opportunities to upgrade skills, enjoy greater responsibility, and achieve higher earnings?

If these questions can be answered affirmatively, employees will have little interest in union representation. But note that each question is framed in terms of employee perceptions, not objective reality. Health care executives often have an unrealistic sense of their employees' true feelings. Not uncommonly an institution that believes it has been a model employer learns to its dismay that employees have a distinctly negative opinion of it.

The Organizing Campaign*

Union Organizers and Their Strategies

Organizers are specialists in identifying sources of employee dissatisfaction. If they find no legitimate complaints among employees,

---

Source: Martin E. Skoler, *Health Care Labor Manual*, Aspen Publishers, Inc., © 1981.

*Unless otherwise noted, excerpts are from Warren H. Chaney and Thomas R. Beech, *The Union Epidemic*, Aspen Publishers, Inc., © 1976.

they will magnify minor ones. They are usually well informed about personnel problems in the health care field and can quickly identify low morale, uncompetitive wages, high-handed supervision, and other sources of employee dissatisfaction.

Typically, they pose as all things to all employees. To black workers, they denounce "racism" and promise "equality" under a union contract. To kitchen workers, they criticize poor ventilation and unpleasant working conditions and promise that the union contract will make things better. To aides and orderlies, they emphasize wages and job security, making promises about how the union will improve both. To nurses they stress professionalism, while to nonprofessionals they stress "solidarity." Their job is to convince employees that they should be dissatisfied with the status quo—regardless of the objective situation.[1]

Employee Organizing Committees

An organizing committee can play a vital role in the campaign because its members (if they are chosen with care) enjoy a trusted relationship with their fellow employees. The professional organizer, on the other hand, is an outsider whose motives are unknown and credibility is untested.

An organizing committee customarily meets several times a week throughout the campaign. It supports the organizer in these major respects: identifying other employees who might favor the union; supplying information about potential campaign issues and about grievances, problems, and changing sentiments within the institution; evaluating the effectiveness of the union's and management's strategies; and performing the "leg work" of the campaign, such as soliciting union authorization cards and distributing handbills.[1]

Steps in Organizing

Union organizing attempts primarily incorporate one or more of three steps.

---

[1]Martin E. Skoler, *Health Care Labor Manual*, Aspen Publishers, Inc., © 1981.

Step 1: The Hospital Survey. Background information is a necessary part of any campaign. Unless the organizer has a thorough understanding of the hospital, its policies, its key people, its problems, etc., a formalized strategy cannot be developed. Consequently, the first step is to do a "target" survey.

Initially, the organizer spends several hours simply observing the facility, talking to cafeteria employees, workers in housekeeping, nurses, and so on. From such conversations the organizer attempts to determine the number of employees per shift; employee breakdown by sex, age, race, etc.; what eating and drinking facilities are nearby; available transportation facilities for the employees; and special problems the facility might face.

The second part of a survey involves establishing contact with the existing labor movement in the community. Here the organizer determines the labor position of the mass media; the labor history of the organization; names of employees who are active in community work such as churches, civic groups, and politics (these persons often make good initial contacts); names of former employees who belonged to a union; a general idea of wages, conditions, and problems; community relations with the target facility; community reaction to organized labor; and meeting dates and places for local union groups.

Step 2: Selecting the Employee Leaders. Having completed the initial survey of the facility, the organizer is now ready to make contact with the employees of the health care facility. Most union organizers are primarily interested in finding employees who are respected by fellow workers and who have informal influence within the health care facility. These are the workers that an organizer will depend on for "internal leadership" and information about the specific problems and complaints of the employees.

The labor organizer courts potential internal leaders. The benefits of the union are explained, and an attempt is made to build up the trust of the leaders. The organizer tries to get leaders for every faction within the organization—for the women, the men, the minority groups, etc. The organizer creates committees and encourage mass participation.

Step 3: Showing the Union Presence. In Step 3 the union will begin actively to distribute handbills and/or begin seeking authorization card signatures for the purpose of forcing an election. The purpose of this first handout distribution is little more than to show union presence. Such leaflets tend to be general in nature and are usually prepared by the union's international or national office.

Once the "internal leaders" begin bringing the organizer the signed union authorization cards, the organizer dramatically steps up the campaign by seeking the trouble spots, evaluating internal leadership, determining the area in which to build additional support, and determining the best areas for the key supporters within the health care facility.

Demand for Recognition

Early in a campaign the union usually will send a telegram, letter, or even the organizer in person demanding recognition as the official bargaining unit for the health care employees. This demand for recognition usually asserts that

1. the union has been officially designated as the exclusive bargaining agent by the majority of employees in the bargaining unit
2. the union is prepared to begin immediate bargaining with management
3. the union is prepared to present its authorization cards to management or to a third party to validate its claim of majority representation
4. the employer should beware of violating its "employees" statutory rights guaranteed under the National Labor Relations Act

The purpose in sending this demand is to seek voluntary recognition without an election. Failing that, the demand is reflected in the official petition for an election filed to initiate the National Labor Relations Board's election procedures. Usually, the hospital's labor counsel

will send a standard letter to the union stating that the hospital doubts that the union represents an uncoerced majority of employees; the hospital believes that the best method for determining the true wishes of the employees is through the secret ballot; the hospital has no knowledge of the method by which the union solicited authorization cards and, thus, cannot accept their validity; and the hospital recommends that the union file an election petition with the NLRB, which has jurisdiction over such activities.

Union Authorization Card

The typical union authorization card simply authorizes the union to act as an employee's agent for purposes of collective bargaining with the hospital.

In addition, the card serves four other important purposes. The first one is to satisfy the NLRB's 30 percent showing of interest requirement. In other words, the union must obtain a 30 percent show of interest by signed authorization cards or employee signatures on a petition to file with the NLRB to hold a secret ballot election (conducted by the NLRB).

Second, the authorization cards are usually a reliable barometer of the employee sentiment within the hospital.

Third, authorization cards are useful as a check on an overzealous union organizer who might forge or persuade employees to sign cards without regard to the employees' real interest in the union.

Fourth, a hospital can be ordered by the NLRB to bargain with the union even if the union lost the election. This can happen if 50 percent or more of the employees have signed authorization cards *and* the hospital is guilty of serious unfair labor practices, which tend to preclude the possibility of conducting a second election. (See Table 26-1.)

The Election

Having failed to get management to agree voluntarily to collective bargaining, it now becomes necessary to carry the campaign toward an election. The majority of effort is spent on encouraging those that signed the cards to actu-

Table 26-1 Limits on Management's Right to Oppose Unions

Under the Taft-Hartley Act, there are four management unfair labor practices that pertain to the organizing stage.

1. **Interference, restraint, and coercion.** Seven major types of management conduct are proscribed: (1) violence, (2) espionage, (3) surveillance, (4) threats, (5) promises of benefit, (6) coercive interrogation, and (7) interference with the right of employees to communicate with each other.

2. **Assistance to or domination of a labor organization.** This prohibition is intended to protect the integrity of unions. For example, management may not assist a union's organizing efforts by giving it money, free office space, free legal counsel, information about employees, or the like. Moreover, management may not apply its rules in a disparate fashion among unions. It may not, for example, permit professional organizers of one union to enjoy ready access to the institution's premises while barring a second union's organizers.

3. **Discrimination to discourage or encourage union membership.** The classic example of discrimination to discourage union membership is the discharge of a leading union adherent shortly after management becomes aware of his or her role in an organizing campaign. Less obvious but equally illegal types of discrimination to dis-

courage union activity are closing a facility to avoid union activity, blacklisting union adherents, demoting union adherents, reducing wages or fringe benefits, withdrawing traditional overtime opportunities, supervising employees more strictly than has been customary, increasing the severity of penalties for minor employment offenses, and withholding wage increases promised before the organizing campaign began. It is equally illegal to discriminate against employees *to encourage* union membership by taking hostile action against employees who decline to support a union favored by the employer or granting benefits to employees who agree to support the union favored by management.

4. **Discrimination against an employee because he or she filed charges or gave testimony under the NLRA.** This is a rarely used prohibition, intended to protect employees' *access* to the NLRB. An employer may not retaliate against an employee who has either filed unfair labor practice charges or given testimony that the employer does not like by engaging in any form of discrimination in the terms or conditions of employment.

Source: *Health Care Labor Manual*, Aspen Publishers, Inc., November 1988.

ally vote for the union. Inside the health care facility the prounion employees try to persuade the other employees to support the effort. Participation is the key word in a union organizing attempt. The organizers create all types of committees:

1. membership (accumulates potential members, names, groups)
2. publicity (discusses union information within the facility)
3. distribution (does mimeographing, hands out pamphlets, maintains mailing lists, etc.)

4. strategy (works with organizer in developing tactics and strategies for the campaign effort)
5. community (explains the need for the union to the community and tries to get its support)

Another primary purpose for getting as many inside workers as possible on committees is to prevent management from claiming that the union activity is the result of "outside agitation" or to protect the organizing effort from the attack that it is the work of "a minority of disgruntled employees."

*Organizing Campaigns and the Health Care Professional**

An organizing campaign among health care professionals differs in several ways from one involving nonprofessionals. A professional campaign, for example, typically involves the circulation of a huge number of letters and memoranda, far more than in a campaign involving nonprofessionals. Both sides emphasize the potential impact of unionization on patients, whereas in a campaign among nonprofessional hospital employees, the parties emphasize the impact of unionization on employees virtually to the exclusion of patients. And throughout the campaign, issues of professionalism are raised over and over again. Management typically questions whether high professional standards can be maintained in a unionized health care setting, whereas the union (or association) maintains that unionization is consistent with high professional standards.

The typical campaign involving nonprofessionals is fundamentally a contest between management and the union. They alone circulate letters and other written materials. Only they call meetings to explain their views. But, in an organizing campaign involving professional employees, individual professionals—usually on their own initiative—write long, argumentative letters to their colleagues for or against unionization. Committees of employees spring to life to advocate and oppose collective bargaining. In short, a campaign involving professionals is far more lively and unpredictable.

The professional association that undertakes to organize nurses for collective bargaining purposes has a supreme advantage that traditional labor unions do not enjoy: It is not a complete stranger either to the employing organization or to professional employees. The crux of the professionals' campaign, therefore, usually involves the association's claim that it is still the custodian of the traditional values of the nursing or medical profession, contrasted with management's claim that the association should be seen

by professional employees for what it has become and seeks to be (namely, a labor union that, like the Teamsters, calls strikes and disciplines members).

ROLE OF THE NURSE ADMINISTRATOR IN LABOR NEGOTIATIONS

Caught In Between*

Staff nurses ordinarily look to their supervisors and director for the support, problem solving, and decision making needed to keep any organization, large or small, functioning smoothly. They also expect you to serve as an open communication channel to administration, passing on information regarding both their personal needs—such as salary and benefits—and their professional interests—such as education, career development, and relations with the medical staff and other hospital personnel and departments. These expectations are quite realistic. Indeed, the role of intermediary comes with the managerial territory. And, provided you can maintain the confidence of both the staff below you and the hierarchy above, it can be a rewarding role to play.

But the picture changes when a union organizing campaign begins. Supervisory and staff nurses suddenly become adversaries and find themselves on different sides of the fence. This "we" against "them" atmosphere is created because under labor law, supervisory personnel are defined as "management," while those being supervised are considered "labor."

What a Manager Can and Cannot Do**

The individual manager is the member of management whom the employees know best.

Source: *Health Care Labor Manual*, Aspen Publishers, Inc., November 1988.

Source: Anthony Lee, "How To Rise above the Cross-Fire of a Union/Hospital Battle," *RN*. Reprinted with permission of Medical Economics Company, Inc., Oradell, N.J.

**Source*: Charles R. McConnell, *Managing the Health Care Professional*, Aspen Publishers, Inc., © 1984.

The manager may indeed be the only member of this mysterious entity called *management* whom most employees know on a first-name basis or with whom they are on speaking terms. Thus as employees see this manager, so are they likely to see all management and the organization itself. If they see the manager as unconcerned, uncaring, distant, or indifferent, so are they likely to view the organization as a whole.

It follows then that the manager is in a key position when dealing with the threat of unionization. The individual manager is the link that ties the employees to higher management and thus to the organization. The manager's long-term behavior has a great deal to do with whether the department is a fertile ground for union organizing activity, and the manager's conduct and actions during a union organizing campaign exert a significant influence on the employees' reaction to the organizing drive.

Under the law, employees have the right to organize and the institution has the right to work within legal boundaries to remain union free. The contest, however, is somewhat one-sided in that the conduct of the employer—and of the employer's representatives—is subject to far more scrutiny than the conduct of the union.

The manager's introduction to preventive labor relations should begin with thorough orientation in the pitfalls of behavior to be avoided. Although the rules are many, they fall into a simply described mode of behavior; what the manager cannot do during a union organizing campaign is captured in the TIPS rule.

During union organizing activity the manager cannot

- *threaten* employees, perhaps with possible loss of employment or other consequences
- *interrogate* employees about their union activities or sympathies
- *promise* employees favored treatment or other rewards for opposing the union
- *spy* on employees to determine involvement in union activities

A list of more complete, specific prohibitions appears in Table 26-2. Despite the length of the list, however, one can readily see that each specific prohibition relates to one of the four TIPS—threaten, interrogate, promise, and spy.

However, for every *cannot* there is a *can*—and then some. Refer to Table 26-3. All the items in this exhibit avoid the TIPS prohibitions. Note one extremely important consideration—although it is true that the manager cannot ask about union interest and activity, the manager can listen to anything that the employees volunteer. The implications of this are far-reaching indeed, for it is the manager who has cultivated interpersonal skills and has become a sympathetic, nonthreatening listener who is readily made aware of what is going on in the department.

It is to the manager's advantage—at all times, but especially during a union organizing campaign—to know the employees as individuals and know them well. Although people cannot be stereotyped and there are few reliable generalizations concerning employees' receptiveness to a union, it is nevertheless possible to make some reasonable judgments as to how certain employees might react under organizing pressure. Often the employee sympathetic to the union's cause may

- feel unfairly treated by the organization and believe that reasonable work opportunities have been denied
- feel that the organization has been unsympathetic regarding personal problems and pressures
- express a lack of confidence in management and be unwilling to talk openly with members of management
- feel unequally treated in terms of pay and other economic benefits
- take no apparent pride in affiliation with the institution
- exhibit career-path problems, having either changed jobs frequently or having reached the top in pay and classification while still having a significant number of working years remaining
- be a source of complaints or grievances more often than most other employees
- exhibit a poor overall attitude

Table 26-2 What the Manager Cannot Do When a Union Beckons

- Ask employees for information about organizing activities or union matters. Employees may *volunteer* such information; you may listen, but you must not *ask*.

- Attend union meetings or participate in any undercover activities to find out who is or is not participating in union activities.

- Attempt to prevent internal organizers from soliciting memberships during nonworking time.

- Grant pay raises or make special concessions or promises to keep the union out.

- Discriminate against prounion employees in granting pay increases, apportioning overtime, making work assignments, promotions, layoffs, or demotions, or in the application of disciplinary action.

- Intimidate, threaten, or punish employees who engage in union activity.

- Suggest in any way that unionization will force the institution to close up, move, lay off employees, or reduce benefits.

- Deviate from known institution policies for the primary purpose of eliminating a prounion employee.

- Provide financial support or other assistance to employees who oppose the union, or be a party to a petition or such action encouraging employees to organize to reject the union.

- Visit employees at home to urge them to oppose the union.

- Question prospective employees about past union affiliation.

- Make statements to the effect that the institution "will not deal with a union."

- Use a third party to threaten, coerce, or attempt to influence employees in exercising their right to vote concerning union representation.

- Question employees on whether they have or have not signed a union authorization card.

- Use the word *never* in any statements or predictions about dealings with the union.

It is extremely important for the manager to know the employees' attitudes toward the institution; the manager must develop a keen sense for how well he or she is communicating. Ultimately a labor union has little to offer if employees already feel that the organization is responding to their needs.

How To Prepare for Negotiations*

Several months before negotiation time, you should discuss with the hospital administrator the role of the nurse administrator in contract negotiations. The nurse administrator is in a position to do all of the following:

1. predict the impact of the contract on patient care
2. predict the impact on personnel and financial resources
3. be aware of personnel issues that will arise to be dealt with at contract time
4. be familiar with the goals, personalities, and idiosyncracies of the personnel involved in negotiations
5. implement the contract legally and fairly
6. deal with issues that are a focus of conflict during negotiations throughout the upcoming year

After establishing your involvement in the process, prepare for the time of negotiating.

1. Know your own contract thoroughly. List the difficulties it has created, both from an administrator's perspective and from the

Source: Donna K. DeGraw, "Role of the Nurse Administrator in Labor Negotiations," *Nursing Administration Quarterly*, vol. 6, no. 2, © 1982 Aspen Publishers, Inc.

Table 26-3 What the Manager Can Do When a Union Beckons

- Campaign against a union seeking to represent employees, and reply to union attacks on the institution's practices or policies.
- Give employees your opinions about unions, union policies, and union leaders.
- Advise employees of their legal rights during and after the organizing campaign, and supply them with the institution's legal position on matters that may arise.
- Keep outside organizers off institution premises.
- Tell employees of the disadvantages of belonging to a union, such as strikes and picket-line duty; dues, fines, and assessments; rule by a single person or small group; and possible domination of a local by its international union.
- Remind employees of the benefits they enjoy without a union, and tell them how their wages and benefits compare with those at other institutions (both union and nonunion).
- Let employees know that signing a union authorization card is not a commitment to vote for the union if there is an election.

- Tell employees that you would rather deal directly with them than attempt to settle differences through a union or any other outsiders.
- Give employees factual information concerning the union and its officials, even if such information is uncomplimentary.
- Remind employees that no union can obtain more for them than the institution is able to give.
- Correct any untrue or misleading claims or statements made by the union organizers.
- Inform employees that the institution may legally hire a new employee to replace any employee who strikes for economic reasons.
- Declare a fixed position against compulsory union membership contracts.
- Insist that all organizing be conducted outside of working time.
- State that you do not like to deal with unions.

---

staff viewpoint. Define changes that would make staffing the hospital easier, be beneficial to patient care, and not take too large a proportion of resources. Read the minutes and notes taken during past negotiating sessions. This may be very helpful in giving a perspective on previous negotiations and a sense of the probable direction of future negotiations. List the changes that you anticipate the negotiating team will propose. Assess the importance of each area to them. Communicate this information to the management negotiating team.

2. Be familiar with any other contracts that exist within your facility. Obtain copies of contracts from other facilities within the community, especially those that are in competition with yours for personnel and those that were negotiated by the same

labor organization. If your facility is a corporation, be familiar with other contracts within the corporation, especially those negotiated by the same union. Extract from all these contracts their positions on all major issues, especially wages and major problem areas, and prepare a simple data sheet that compares and contrasts these items.

3. Be familiar with labor laws, especially the Taft-Hartley Act and the Fair Labor Standards Act. Contact both state and federal offices and obtain all pamphlets on wage and hour laws, employment, discrimination, employment of minors if this is applicable, and safety.

4. Be knowledgeable about the management team and who will be the primary spokesperson. It is definitely preferable that the spokesperson be experienced

through previous contract negotiations. (You can be certain that the union representative will be an experienced person.) Discuss the plan for negotiating and determine what areas are negotiable. Most administrators seem to have their "pet peeves" on which they are inflexible. Identify these in advance and estimate the impact on the contract, the employees, and the nurse administrator's task.

5. Assess the community's attitude about unions and collective bargaining. Know whether there is a climate for settlement or strike.

6. Identify the staff who will be part of the union collective bargaining team. Find out whether their primary motivation is patient care, working conditions, wages, unresolved feelings of conflict and anger, or peer pressure. Predict what areas are essential to them individually and collectively to settle. Predict which areas are negotiable and which are extras.

7. Identify the needs of nursing administration. What will help to provide good care to patients, to attract and keep well-qualified staff, and to facilitate the goals and objectives of the nursing department of the hospital? Identify areas that are essential and those that are advantageous. Ideally, vital areas of common concern should be discussed months before contract negotiations time. For example, if a contract change is needed to make it possible to implement ten-hour shifts, discuss the advantages, implications, and problems of the ten-hour shift with appropriate groups from the staff long before it is a part of negotiations.

8. Communicate with other departments who will not have direct representatives to determine any needs and problems they have identified that might be different than those identified by nursing.

When you have gathered sufficient data, prepared data sheets, and considered the implications for your facility, define for the management team areas important to nursing administration to negotiate. This will be very general at this point but will give your team a purposeful direction. You can negotiate more effectively regarding nursing administration needs on the basis of accurate facts, statistics, and analysis.

As you meet with the management team, listen carefully to what others are saying and strive to really understand their viewpoint. It is important to negotiate from a common position.

Prior to moving to the negotiating table, know your team's strategy. Which member will assume the position of spokesperson? How will you communicate concerns to the spokesperson? What is the system for having conferences?

During Contract Negotiations*

During negotiations, the first step will be a proposal submitted by the union. While first proposals tend to be gross exaggerations of expectations, they do serve as an indicator of the direction of the group. Management will normally use this first time together to simply seek clarification on all the issues, take good minutes, and then set dates and times for further negotiations. Management will then withdraw to prepare the first counterproposal.

Compare each proposal to the data sheet previously prepared and calculate the cost of all proposals for the immediate and distant future. Realize that some expenses (e.g., a significant increase for employees with longevity or step increases for education and/or experience) may result in a greater cost in several years than in the immediate future.

Determine if there are significant needs that have not been addressed. This is likely to occur because the union committee is rarely representative of all employee groups and can never speak for all employees. Determine if management's strategy is to introduce these areas into the contract. There may be a real advantage to include some of these in the counterproposals or to save these as trade-offs. Areas such as holiday pay, shift differential, or on-call differential may be much more significant to the nurse administrator than to others. Clarify this to the manage-

---

Source: Ibid.

ment team and supply facts to support your position.

Totally avoid negotiating management rights that are essential to the management of the hospital. These issues usually represent a current concern within the facility and are often related to a single incident or several incidents. It is important to hear those concerns and address them away from the table. Contracts rarely, if ever, settle conflicts about staffing, safety, determination of quality of work, or job descriptions. Avoid building these matters into the contract as they may return to haunt you in situations neither side ever anticipated.

As negotiations progress or deteriorate, remember the following guidelines:

1. Deal with issues, not personalities.
2. Keep all notes and minutes under lock and key.
3. Do not talk about negotiations, especially in a negative manner, except with the other members of your team in a closed room.
4. Be completely fair with the members of the union team in other situations. Do not expect more or less from them than you normally would.
5. Recognize your role as a valuable one and do not accept responsibility for the feelings of others.
6. Accept the fact that you are experiencing extra stress during this time, and have a tangible plan for dealing with this.

Always deal with the issues completely and be very certain not to be libelous, derogatory, or careless. Many grievances are lost on both sides because procedure was not followed exactly, or lost by management for publicly saying or writing something critical of the staff member.

Dealing with grievances and conflicts will normally take only a small portion of the administrator's total time if the communication systems are open. Most time will be spent creating a good environment in which to work. The most effective way to obviate the need for a strong labor union organization is to apply good management techniques, stressing that employees are valuable people. This is especially effective in a small hospital or organization where the nurse administrator knows all the staff and is

able to have a direct impact on the staff members' perceptions of their roles, their jobs, and management. Participatory decision making, fairness, opportunities for growth and creativity, support for the employee who is under unusual stress, some flexibility in scheduling, and warm, enjoyable relationships—these are indicators to the employees that management cares about them. See Table 26-4 for an outline of a sample nursing department strike plan.

ADMINISTRATION OF A COLLECTIVE AGREEMENT

In the eyes of the law, a collective agreement is legally enforceable, just like any other commercial contract. In fact, if a collective bargaining agreement contains no grievance arbitration procedure, the contract is enforceable *only* in the courts or through strike action by the union. The vast majority of collective bargaining agreements, however, provide for enforcement through a multistep grievance procedure that terminates in final and binding arbitration.*

Training the Management Team*

Management should act promptly after a contract becomes effective to ensure that its own representatives—especially first- and second-line supervisors—understand its significant aspects. If supervisors are ignorant of the institution's contractual rights and obligations, management's rights may be eroded and the union's rights may be violated, both at high cost to the employer.

A practical way to communicate the terms of a newly negotiated labor agreement to the managerial-supervisory staff is through a formal training and orientation program.

Training should include instructions about how to respond to grievances. Under the typical collective bargaining agreement, all grievances by the union are first filed with the supervisor. Supervisors must be careful to note whether the union has observed the contract's time limits and

---

*Source: Health Care Labor Manual, Aspen Publishers, Inc.

Table 26-4 Outline for a Nursing Department Strike Plan

BASIC ASSUMPTIONS

A. Patient admissions will be based on nursing staff availability and care requirements of the patient. Admission decisions will be made by nursing management and supported by hospital administration and medical staff.

B. Patients admitted have a right to quality care; therefore, the patient with emergent needs will have priority.

C. Nursing management will support operationalizing these basic assumptions through adjusted assignments and schedules.

D. Nursing departments/units will be consolidated as determined by nursing management.

E. Service departments' staffing will be sensitive and responsive to the needs of open nursing units.

F. Supportive working conditions will be developed and maintained.

WORK FORCE/STAFFING

A. Develop a master nursing staffing schedule coordinated with other departments employing RN staff.

B. Develop plan for controlling sympathetic work force reduction.

C. Communicate with service departments and participate in coordinating for anticipated strike impact.

D. Cancel all nursing department programs.

E. Develop plans to ensure supportive working conditions—continuing through reentry and poststrike phase.

PATIENT CARE MANAGEMENT

A. Plan for systematic reduction of census.

B. Determine consolidation of nursing units and plan for moves.

C. Implement maintenance and remodeling plans and programs on vacated nursing units.

D. Establish productivity levels of available work force.

PLAN FOR REESTABLISHMENT OF SERVICES

A. Prepare facilities for full utilization.

B. Recognize strike work force.

C. Implement reentry of staff through poststrike phase.

---

must respond to the union within the contract's time limitations. Training should also prepare supervisors to reply to a grievance with such clarity that there can be no doubt about the institution's position. Any defect in the union's handling of the grievance should be expressly noted because, if the grievance is carried to arbitration, the institution's defenses may be limited to those set forth by the first-level supervisor in the initial response to the grievance.

To ensure that discipline is administered for the right reasons and by the right procedures, supervisors should be trained in the uses of progressive (corrective) discipline under the contract.

Every supervisor should be encouraged to keep a copy of the collective bargaining contract handy. When questions arise, supervisors should consult the contract and not rely on memory. Moreover, supervisors should be encouraged to consult with the institution's labor relations or personnel director when novel or difficult questions arise. Further, first-line supervisors should consult with the institution's labor relations or personnel director whenever possible before imposing discipline, such as discharge, since under collective bargaining, acts of discipline are usually subject to review by outsiders, labor arbitrators, whose sole interest is to decide whether discipline was just or unjust.

Reviewing the Contract*

As the manager in the nursing unit and as the person responsible for contract enforcement and interpretation, you should follow these principles when you review and interpret provisions of the contract:

Source: Virginia K. Baillie, Louise Trygstad, Tatiana Isaeff Cordoni, *Effective Nursing Leadership: A Practical Guide*, Aspen Publishers, Inc., © 1989.

- Read and reread those sections that affect the employees under your supervision.
- Note limitations, restrictions, or qualifying language.
- Never assume that the language as presented is superfluous or unimportant.
- If you are unclear about an interpretation, *ask for help.*
- Verify your understanding of a contract provision with someone in authority (e.g., your supervisor or the personnel/labor relations director).

There are several principles used to guide interpretation of the contract, particularly if a disagreement appears before an arbitrator.

Residual Rights Theory. What management has not given away, it retains. The contract cannot cover all policies, rules, and procedures concerning the day-to-day activities of employers and employees. Because the contract does not cover all issues, the concept of "residual rights" exists to aid in contract interpretation. This concept may not be agreed upon by the union.

Clear Contract Language versus Past Practice. Clear and unequivocal contract language cannot be ignored nor given a new interpretation by the arbitrator. In situations where contract language is unclear, ambiguous, or incomplete, arbitrators can go beyond the literal wording in the contract.

Past Practice. This relates to a consistent and long history of handling similar questions in one particular way. For example, the way in which management and the union have settled similar grievances is investigated as a potential precedent.

Steps in the Grievance Procedure*

The grievance procedure itself is negotiated and clearly described in the labor-management contract. Ideally, it provides for a series of progressive steps and time limits for submission and

resolution of unresolved grievances to higher and more authoritative management levels. The grievance procedure also will define what a grievance is and the manner of its presentation. This is to guard against emotional excesses on the part of either party.

In one institution a grievance is first initiated through an informal discussion. This is just a talking stage during which the employee informally presents his or her complaint to the supervisor, usually as soon as possible after the violation has occurred. The collective bargaining agent has the right to be present. The following sequence of steps is then utilized.

Step 1. If the grievance is not adjusted by informal discussion, written notice of the grievance is given within 5 to 10 workdays to the supervisor. A written response from this level of authority should be received within 3 to 5 workdays. Many institutions have forms upon which formal grievances are submitted. The employee, delegate, and supervisor are present for any discussions at this time.

Step 2. If the response to Step 1 is not satisfactory, a written appeal may be submitted within 10 workdays to the director of nursing or his or her designee. Parties to discussions at this stage are the employee, SNA representative, grievance chairperson and/or delegate, and the director of nursing or designee. Again, written response will be provided in 5 workdays subsequent to these meetings. In many bargaining units, the positions of delegate and grievance chairperson are separated. Generally, the grievance chairperson is an officer in the bargaining unit, and though apprised of the grievance at the early stages, he or she may become more actively involved at the later stages. Whether the person is a delegate or grievance chairperson will depend on how the bargaining unit is structured.

Step 3. The employee, SNA representative, grievance chairperson, and/or delegate, director of nursing, and director of personnel meet for discussions. The 10- and 5-day time limits for appeal and answer are again observed.

Step 4. This final step is arbitration. It is invoked when no solution suggested is acceptable at all. Present at these meetings are an arbitrator who is a neutral third party selected by

Source: Elaine Beletz and Mary T. Meng, "The Grievance Process." *American Journal of Nursing*, February 1977. © American Journal of Nursing Company. Reprinted with permission.

both parties involved, the SNA representatives, employee and hospital representatives, and any others who may be called as witnesses. The submission of a grievance to this step may be required in 15 days of Step 3. In some contracts there is a step between 3 and 4 which provides that the grievance be taken to someone in hospital management before going to arbitration; however, this is not usual.

Often a statement included in each of the steps states that if the time limits are not observed by one party, the grievance may be considered resolved and further action barred. The contract also usually specifies how an arbitrator is selected. One should remember that, in some cases, the employer also has the right to state a grievance and use the procedure to resolve it.

Handling Grievances*

The following points may prove helpful when approaching a grievance:

1. The objective of the grievance procedure is not to achieve conquest. Remember you do have to work with one another after resolution of the grievance, so treat each other with courtesy and respect.
2. Don't threaten or bluff each other. On the other hand, this is not an unheard of tactic. Some people use it all the time, others only when a ticklish situation seems to require a firmer approach. If you have investigated properly, you will be able to spot this part of the strategy.
3. Don't withhold facts or information relating to the grievance. This rule is essential to good faith in bargaining.
4. Both the bargaining unit and the management team must present a solid front when faced with one another; therefore, do not, whatever your position, exhibit internal disagreements or disputes.
5. Expediency is a must; delaying tactics serve only to heighten emotions. However, allow time for consideration of all of the facts.

6. Don't blame the other if he or she takes advantage of your mistakes. Learn from them and don't repeat them the next time.
7. Stay objective. Emotionalism usually leads to further problems.
8. Evaluate and anticipate the other party's position and possible response. The implementation of decisions or the filing of grievances may require planned strategy. As time permitted, you might role-play all grievances, just to make sure you had thoroughly planned for all contingencies.
9. Utilize all the resources available. Seek guidance from those in authority, which for the supervisor will be those in higher administrative positions, and for the delegate, his collective bargaining organization. You will be able to make a much more rational decision and plan a better course of action.
10. The right to representation is one of the advantages of being under the auspices of a collective bargaining unit. The supervisor should neither fear, nor refuse to meet with, the grievant's representatives. "Arbitrators generally recognize the employee's right to union representation at least commencing with the first step of the grievance procedure."
11. The bargaining unit representative, though in a unique position, is not immune from reprimand or discipline. When not involved in bargaining unit activities, the delegate is an employee, responsible to the rules and regulations of the institution, and the employer has the right to a full day's work and an acceptable level of performance. However, while handling grievances, the delegate is not really considered an employee. He or she is considered the representative and advocate of the employee who filed the grievance.
12. On occasion, discussions in settling grievances become quite heated and emotional. Neither party has to tolerate personal abuse. The meeting should be adjourned and rescheduled at a time when the talks can continue on a more objective level. Occasionally, super-

---

Source: E. Beletz, "Some Pointers for Grievance Handlers," *Supervisor Nurse*, August 1977. Reprinted with permission.

visors when dealing with unions have been faced with language that constitutes obscenity. No one has to put up with this. In fact, an arbitration ruling has noted the differences in profanity, vulgarity, and obscenity. The first two categories may be acceptable, even if not liked, but the latter is not acceptable. "Use of foul or abusive language directed at supervision is also regarded as a punishable offense when it exceeds the 'conversation level' of the work group."

13. If you are a supervisor or a delegate, you may deny the grievance based on the feeling that none of the cited violations have occurred. This does not limit the employee from pursuance of the grievance and seeking redress at the next step in the procedure.

14. You should not submit to emotional appeals as to what is fair. The contract is the sole determinant of what is fair; if necessary, a neutral third party will be utilized to interpret the contract. What one person considers fair may not necessarily be seen in the same light by the other.

15. Be prepared to give or take acceptable compromises and alternative solutions within the framework of the contract, no matter which party suggests them.

16. Know the strengths and weaknesses of the issue for either side.

17. Integral to bargaining are solutions which may also accommodate future changes

and needs. Therefore, you must think ahead.

18. Pat formulas do not settle grievances or solve problems. A formula would negate the needed judgment and flexibility which is so necessary to grievance handling.

19. Know where your bottom line is for compromise.

20. Observe the time limits. If you do not, the bargaining unit may lose the right to continue the grievance to the next level, or both the bargaining unit and management may lose in an eventual arbitration.

21. It is wise to remember that once a grievance is filed, it may chain-react and almost any imaginable outcome may end up as the solution. However, a carefully written grievance should obviate this possible outcome.

22. When adjusting a grievance, you have to know yourself very well. As with any interaction between people, your statement is colored by your temperament and is interpreted by the other party in accordance with his or her own temperament.

23. "Gloating" over a "win" is human; just remember, you may "lose" the next one; don't become overconfident.

24. One of the most important points in grievance handling is being a good detective. Get all the facts and information, the witnesses, the documentation. Find out whether any similar situation ever occurred and what the decision was.

Chapter 27

Communication and Interpersonal Relations

COMMUNICATION

Experts say we only hear one-quarter of what people say to us.

One researcher who studied 100 American industries discovered that the president of the average company got only 90 percent of the information the board of directors wanted the president to give company employees. The department heads (listen well, nursing supervisors) got only 50 percent of the information. The foremen (are you listening, head nurses?) got 30 percent. And the nonmanagement employees—for whom the information was intended—got only 20 percent of the information.

Misunderstandings are usually caused by the fact that whenever communication is attempted between two people, there are at least six messages—each somewhat different—involved in the communication:

1. what you mean to communicate
2. what you actually communicate
3. what communication the other person *receives*
4. what communication the other person *thinks* he or she receives
5. what the other person *says*
6. what you *think* the other person says

Improving the Communication Climate*

Communication climate is the degree to which an organization permits—and preferably promotes—a free and open exchange of ideas and information among its members.

There are three key components of communication climate: the amount or *quantity* of information exchanged among people, its *quality*, and the number and nature of *channels* available for relaying the information.

Quantity. Essentially, the communication climate in an organization is favorable when the quantity of information exchanged among people is sufficient to allow them to carry out their assigned jobs knowledgeably and confidently. When too little information is exchanged, whether among superiors and subordinates or

---

Source: Corwin P. King, "Keep Your Communication Climate Healthy," *Personnel Journal*, April 1978. Reprinted with the permission of *Personnel Journal*, Costa Mesa, California; all rights reserved.

among peers in the same or different departments, confusion and uncertainty could well result. People may not know what is expected of them in their jobs and so won't be able to meet expectations, and further, they might not understand how their jobs relate to others' work. Among peers, this may lead to a failure to cooperate in solving common problems.

Though it is usually less of a problem, exchanging too much information can also be harmful, for it can easily create a state of information overload for people. Faced with more information than they can conveniently handle, they may simply ignore most of it, and in the process ignore essential information which is needed for their jobs. Additionally, when it comes from superiors, too much information may have negative motivational effects, implying that people are too dull and irresponsible to do anything on their own. In time, this may cause them to "live down to the label," refusing to take initiative and passively waiting for instructions on even the simplest of tasks.

Quality. Essentially, the quality of information is good when it is clear, relevant, accurate, and consistent from the standpoint of those who receive it. The value of clarity and relevance should be obvious, for information which fails to meet the needs of people's jobs, at least in terms which they can understand, is worthless. The value of accuracy and consistency should also be obvious, since information which is inaccurate and inconsistent cannot be relied upon.

Channels. Information is exchanged through two kinds of channels in an organization, vertical (including downward from superiors to subordinates as well as upward) and horizontal (including internal, among peers in the same department, and external, among peers in different departments). Regardless of classification, however, good channels for information have the following characteristics.

First and foremost is the fact that they exist where they are necessary, and second is the fact that people who need to use them have access to them—preferably easy access. When channels do not exist, or when people are not aware that they do, employees may not know where to turn

for important information about their jobs and so may be denied that information. When channels do exist but people do not have access to them, the situation may be even worse, for it is highly aggravating to know where to find information but not be able to get it. If people must spend too much effort to get information, they may just do without it and trust to their own resources, however good or bad they may be.

Another characteristic of good channels is that they are direct and official. Direct channels are desirable because they are simpler and faster and usually more reliable. When information is conveyed indirectly through third parties, there is little guarantee that those who need the information will receive it accurately and on time.

As a rule, the more channels people have access to in an organization, the more they are likely to communicate. When people are asked to suggest ways of improving an organization's communication climate, they often suggest ways of improving the frequency of communication by developing more and better channels or by better utilizing the channels that exist.

How To Communicate*

How we respond to people in the communication process has a great deal to do with their reactions. There are three ways of responding to people and problems. First is the repressive level, where the response is very unsatisfactory. The second is to minimize what the person feels to be a legitimate problem. In the third way, you try to understand what is being said. Try to identify with the person and his or her view of the situation.

Climate and communication work hand in hand. Be open and interested. Try to deemphasize the hierarchical differences, play down the power differentials. Level more with people in an open way characterized by frankness,

---

*Source: Robert K. Burns, "Techniques for Strengthening Intra and Interdepartmental Operations and Coordination," *Hospital Topics*, March-April 1975. Reprinted with permission.

integrity, and openness. If you lay out the problem and get the people themselves involved in solving it, they are better able to pass judgment on themselves than you are. There isn't anything you need to tell a person about his or her shortcomings and deficiencies that you can't convey indirectly and without demeaning the person. If you demean people, they will only become defensive and fight back.

If you ask two or three pertinent questions, the individual can come up with the problem him- or herself. It is psychologically much easier for the person to find and state the problem and take corrective action on his or her own than for you to tell the person, for that is self-imposed control.

The Art of Asking Questions. When you ask an employee a question, you are indicating that you think it would be valuable to hear the employee's ideas and suggestions, and that should make him or her feel valuable as a person. It is better to ask than to tell.

When asking people questions, use the kind of methods that give you the kind of information you desire. If you need the facts about something, ask a factual question. To get the facts, do two things: First identify and isolate what you need to ask, and then differentiate and separate it in terms of the desired answer. Ask the questions what, when, which, where, why, who, how, and how many until you get all the information you need.

Involving Subordinates. One test of leadership is getting the other person to do the work that needs to be done the way it should be done because that's the way he or she wants to do it. That exemplifies authority based on cooperation instead of authority imposed from above.

Try to clarify the work by taking a look at the job, decide what the mission is, then break down the job into key areas. Talk things over with the people you work with—boss and subordinates. Get agreement and commitment from everyone and work together as a team. Many people say that to do that is giving up one's prerogatives. Hogwash! You're not giving up anything, you're getting something. You're getting ideas, suggestions, and motivated people.

Supervisor-Employee Communication*

The relationship between supervisor and employees should be congenial, show mutual caring without undue familiarity, be personal but not show favoritism, and be relaxed but purposeful. From this relationship the supervisor can be as directive as the situation requires while allowing employees all the freedom and flexibility in the performance of duties as their competence allows. Good communication builds a relationship that strengthens the supervisor's ability to motivate the best efforts of the team because the members are satisfied with the relationship.

Supervisory relationships can be considered in four phases: meeting, knowing, enabling, and directing. These are somewhat sequential but are also intertwined.

The tasks of the *meeting* phase are for the supervisor to learn about the employees' experience, aptitudes, and skills; to help them become oriented to the job; to create expectations for instruction and feedback processes that the manager will use; and to establish expectations about work attitudes and quality of performance. This usually is a short phase occurring at the beginning of the relationship.

Skills include the ability to give information clearly; to model appropriate action; to listen; and to communicate empathy, respect, and warmth. Basic friendship skills are used. Generally a personnel office helps with some of these tasks.

The effect of the meeting phases is that both levels obtain information about each other, size each other up, and lay the basis for the relationship. The employees are introduced to the job and become part of a work group.

The task of the *knowing* phase is to know the person. This means going beyond biographical and vocational facts to such intangibles as attitudes and motivation.

Source: George M. Gazda, William C. Childers, and Richard P. Walters, *Interpersonal Communication: A Handbook for Health Professionals*, Aspen Publishers, Inc., © 1982.

The supervisor learns the employees' capacity for doing assigned work and gains an understanding of how to improve that capacity. The supervisor finds out who the employees are; their attitudes and opinions; preferences for work, for fun, and for people; and their motivators—what makes them tick. It also is important for supervisors to learn to accept characteristics that were disliked at first but that do not hurt the employees' work performance.

In the *enabling* phase, the supervisor uses the skills of giving encouragement and praise, pointing out performance problems or missed goals, giving advice and instruction frequently, and in other ways using the transition dimensions. The primary task here is informal. Later formal performance reviews will show what the employees need to change in order to be more successful on the job. These efforts all are directed toward helping the employees see how personal success comes by helping the organization advance by providing opportunities for staff members to grow professionally through work, which results in their working hard because personal needs are met through the job. This has benefits for productivity and effectiveness, especially over the long term.

In the *directing* phase, the supervisor enforces rules, sets deadlines, gives ultimatums, and takes disciplinary measures as appropriate. Here the action dimensions, especially confrontation, may be used. This includes dealing with inappropriate talk and responding to an angry person.

The use of the directing phase dimensions usually results in some resistance, which is in proportion to how meaningful the relationship has been. This may strain the relationship, either temporarily or longer.

The supervisor's behavior, for the most part, is nondirective in the knowing phase and becomes increasingly directive in moving through the enabling phase to the highly directive behaviors of the directing phase. Nondirective, gentle supervisory behaviors of persuasion, encouragement, asking, listening, and cooperating are quite in contrast to the directive, tough, supervisory behaviors such as forcing, demanding, telling, and coercing. These, however, also are legitimate under certain conditions.

Using only gentle behaviors or only tough behaviors works for a while but good supervision requires the full range of actions. Optimal performance comes when the supervisor can concentrate on enabling employees to do their best but can shift to the gentler approach of the knowing phase or the tougher approach of the directing phase when either of those are indicated.

Confrontation

Probably the most difficult task in supervision is talking with an employee about such things as deficiencies in performance of duties, infractions of rules, or undesirable interpersonal relationships.

The acceptance of any confrontation depends upon (1) a good base relationship and (2) skillful use of the confrontation itself.

The confrontation occasion does not need to be extremely uncomfortable for either supervisor or subordinate. It can, in fact, be a time of constructive advance in skills and understanding for both parties. These suggestions can maximize the benefits of these occasions. The supervisor should do the following:

1. Be careful not to get overly caught up in the crisis of the moment but keep the long-range relationship in mind.
2. Take care not to accuse prematurely, listen to the employee's story, and be alert for new data that are relevant to the situation.
3. Give employees an opportunity to take the initiative in explaining and correcting the situation, follow the principle of allowing them to do as much for themselves as they are capable of doing.
4. Put the criticism and the problem area in perspective by discussing employees' areas of strength. To let employees mistakenly feel that they are doing nothing right is tragic, but it happens frequently. Again, stay alert for the effect of the interaction on the employees.
5. Provide the best protection against remedial supervisory work by prevention of problems through clear task assignment

and other preparation of employees to carry out their duties.

6. Avoid ''hit and run'' confrontation. Things rarely are as simple as they appear on the surface, so allow for explanation of the problem and ample time for interaction.

Nurse Administrator's Guidelines for Communication

Identification of Weaknesses

The effective use of information depends upon effective communication links. Every administrator plays a vital role in this system, both as a transmitter and as a recipient of information. To help you assess and identify communication weakspots, review the questions below.

Do you receive information from *your staff* which is excessive, minimal, inaccurate, or basically routine? Do you hear requests for supplementary information or further explanations? Do you hear complaints about information arriving too late?

Do you receive information from *hospital management* which is untimely, insufficient, overabundant, garbled, or imprecise? Do you hear (or do you recognize) that your communications are late, unnecessarily time consuming, or in need of revision?

Do you receive reports from *other department heads* or send reports to them that are purposeless, inconsistently informative, or inappropriate? Are your conferences overlong, excessive in number, vague in objectives, or indecisively concluded?

Effective Leadership Communication

Behind the exchange of information in the communication process are larger concepts which the nurse administrator hopes to convey to his or her staff: standards of performance, motivation toward effective functioning, and acceptance of innovations. Communication is a force for influencing staff direction. Indirect and direct means can be used. Indirectly, the nurse administrator sends out signals by his or her own behaviour. All the lectures about standards and attitudes will be ineffective if subordinates observe contradictions and lapses in the nurse administrator's own actions. Most people learn to communicate through example.

For direct communication, it is important that messages are not only given but heard too. The first step is to promote a responsive communication climate in the department where staff members feel comfortable in expressing their underlying reactions, attitudes, and problems. The following steps may help you communicate clearly with your subordinates:

1. Consider your objectives in advance, forming a plan for communication: why, when, how.
2. Express yourself with unmistakable clarity. Be concise and tick off main points by emphasizing them.
3. Formulate messages in a manner which is attuned to the subordinate's self-interest, creating greater acceptance.
4. Be sensitive to differences in needs, experiences, and frames of reference among various subordinate levels; adjust messages accordingly.
5. Avoid didactic language. Use conversational language but be aware that words have different shades of meaning, assuming coloration from the type of situation or the background of the listener.
6. Be a listener as well as a talker. Encourage openness and observe accurate criticisms and fresh approaches. Strive for feedback from subordinates to confirm whether the message has been comprehended.
7. Follow-up conversations and meetings with memos or reports to the staff. Let them know that action has resulted from communication or, in the case of individual criticisms, that progress has been noted.
8. Use a variety of communication methods to reinforce an important message or select a single most appropriate method according to the nature of the message: conversations, notes, official memos, meetings, conferences, and reports.

The Skill of Listening

Many nurse administrators are trained to communicate effectively, but few are prepared properly to receive the wealth of information found in the attitudes, opinions, and suggestions of others. By learning to listen well to the words of staff members in conversations and meetings, by learning to read the manner of expression with which these words are conveyed, the administrator is able to keep in contact and to direct activities more successfully.

The groundwork of effective listening is built on the practice of the three A's:

Availability. Be accessible to your staff, willing to listen to statements in meetings, impromptu conversations in the hall, or discussions from drop-in visitors.

Attentiveness. Be receptive in your manner of listening, maintain eye contact and bodily attention. During the conversation, listen non-evaluatively, encouraging the speaker to express him- or herself freely and nondefensively. Avoid the raised eyebrow or other comments of scepticism of the moment. Reserve judgmental assessment until after the speaker has delivered his or her piece in full. Practice courtesy and request clarification if anything is unclear.

Acceptance. Understand the speaker's frame of reference. Sense how background and experience influence a point of view. Perceive and accept the emotional content as well as the verbal message. Suspend any prior prejudice to a particular mode of expression or the delivery of contrary ideas. Lastly, guarantee the right of others to speak out, focusing disagreement or criticism on the message content and not on the speaker's "outspokenness."

Quiz on Listening Habits

Assess your own listening abilities by answering whether you find yourself acting in the following ways.

Do you . . .

1. Act impatient, fidget, or seem poised in mid-flight while others are speaking? Yes No
2. Pretend attentiveness, barely tracking the conversation while your mind is on other thoughts? Yes No
3. Selectively listen, picking out partial facts, ideas, or underlying feelings but ignoring the whole content? Yes No
4. Fail to ask questions when a statement is unclear? Yes No
5. Frequently have to check back and verify details because you misunderstood the information? Yes No
6. Become easily distracted from the conversation by nearby noises and activity? Yes No
7. Judge a message as unworthy because of the speaker's appearance or delivery? Yes No
8. Pride yourself on predicting what the speaker will say before it is said? Yes No
9. Dismiss statements or arguments of others without a hearing because you are certain you're right? Yes No
10. Stifle conversation by making constant corrections or asserting your own viewpoint? Yes No
11. Spend more time in forming your answers than in concentration on what is being said? Yes No
12. Prefer talking, speaking, telling, lecturing, or sounding off to the state of listening? Yes No

Total _____

If your honest response to all the questions is an unqualified no, then you've attained perfection as a listener. Most people cannot make claim to that ideal; they admit to several of these bad habits. However, if you answer yes to half the questions or more, you're losing contact with your subordinates. Start listening to yourself and start changing your listening habits.

Using Feedback Constructively

An incident occurs, an attitude is expressed, and you are sufficiently annoyed with the behavior of a worker to set on a course to change that behavior. How do you communicate that message?

Step 1.   Suggest a private talk at an appropriate time in a place where the discussion will not be interrupted or overheard.

Step 2.   Present the facts, not an evaluation, of the behaviour observed. Shore up the facts with accurate details.

Step 3.   Give the worker time to draw his or her own inferences, such as "I guess I didn't control my temper." If none are forthcoming or there is disagreement with the worker's inference, then express your own.

Step 4.   Double-check the validity of your inference and the communication of your message. Ask the worker to comment on the accuracy and meaning of what you said. Is his or her response in line with what you were trying to convey?

Step 5.   Describe the impact of the worker's behavior on coworkers and let him or her judge whether this is a desirable reaction.

Step 6.   Ask the worker for plans or actions that will be taken to correct the behaviour. Guide the discussion with discreet suggestions of your own. Check if these messages are accurately perceived.

How To Prepare a Speech*

One of the most important elements of successful speaking is the speaker's preparation. Most speech experts agree that preparation for speaking is a simple step-by-step process. The first task that any speaker faces in preparing a speech is to determine and limit the purpose of the speech. The speaker then assembles relevant support materials, plans the organizational pattern, and decides how to begin, develop, and conclude the speech.

*Source: Principles and Techniques of Instruction, U.S. Air Force (AF 50-62), 1974.

Purpose

Every successful speech has a clear and definite purpose designed to achieve a particular audience reaction. This purpose is the goal or objective for the speech. Like other goals, the purpose serves to guide the speaker in all phases of speech preparation and final delivery.

Within such limitations as the occasion, place, time, speaker's ability, and audience background, all speeches have been traditionally classified according to one of three general purposes: to inform, to persuade, or to entertain.

To Inform. The speaker's purpose is to inform when he or she helps an audience to understand an idea, a concept, or a process or broadens the range of the audience's present knowledge. All informative speeches have a clear organization, supporting facts, and illustrative examples and comparisons.

To Persuade. In the speech to persuade, the speaker wishes to change or reinforce existing beliefs, stimulate activity, or increase emotional involvement. A distinguishing feature of the persuasive speech is its appeal to an audience's emotions in addition to its appeal to their intellectual reasoning.

To Entertain. The speech to entertain has as its objective the enjoyment of the audience. This type of speech, then, is characterized by information which is interesting, unusual, or humorous.

Once the general purpose has been selected, the speaker is ready to form the specific purpose by stating the precise response desired from the audience. When writing the specific purpose, the speaker must conform to the needs of the audience, the limitations of time, and any limitations inherent in the situation.

Research

With the purpose of the speech in mind, the speaker now proceeds to the second step—gathering material on the subject. The source of this material is the speaker's own experience or the experience of others gained through conversation, interviews, and written or observed material. The person concerned with giving a good speech will probably draw from all of these sources.

The next step is to evaluate the material gathered. The speaker will probably find that there is enough material for several speeches. The speaker must now combine some ideas, eliminate others, and perhaps bolster some ideas that appear in the research materials. At this time, the speaker will probably see that the ideas are beginning to form into some type of pattern.

Determining the Pattern

- The *time or chronological pattern* is used when the material is arranged according to the order in which a number of events took place.
- The *spatial or geographical pattern* is very effective in describing things. When the spatial pattern is used, the speech material is developed in some directional sequence.
- The *topical pattern* is used when the subject has within itself divisions well known to the speaker and the audience.
- The *cause and effect pattern* is also used in speaking, but does not lend itself to all topics. When using the cause and effect pattern, the speaker may first enumerate specific forces, then point out the results which follow; or the speaker may first describe conditions, then discuss the forces which caused them.
- The *problem-solution pattern* organizes material in terms of problems (needs) and solutions (plans). The problem-solution pattern is particularly effective with a persuasive speech.

The Outline

An effective outline helps to make a good speech. By establishing the structural form of the speech, the outline facilitates evaluation. Is the thinking clear? Is each point treated according to importance? Does the speech need more support material? Are ideas in the proper sequence? Such evaluation questions will ensure that the speech has unity, is coherent, and has a smooth progression from beginning to end.

The first step in the rough draft is listing the main points and arranging them in a systematic sequence. Once this is accomplished, the speaker inserts subpoints and decides which support material will best verify and/or illustrate each point. Then comes the crucial question: Does the draft cover the subject and fit the purpose? If not, the speaker revises the draft.

Delivery

One object of speech delivery is to achieve a sense of direct communication with the audience. Both the speaker and the listeners must feel that they are in touch with each other. The speaker must believe in both the content and the need to communicate the same. This may not be a permanent conviction, but it must be the conviction of the moment.

Variety in voice is one secret to effective delivery. The speaker may vary the loudness, pitch, and rate of utterance, but the variations must be in harmony with the meaning, emotional content, and emphasis. One effect of movement is that the audience tends to follow the speaker's body as he or she moves across the platform. This effect can be used to gain attention or to aid in the transition from one point to the next. Too much movement becomes distracting while too little movement becomes boring for lack of change.

Gestures should appear natural, definite, and well timed. They should never draw attention from the point they are emphasizing. Any gesture should be harmonious with the speaker's attitude, conviction, and topic.

Use of Notes

Through the use of notes in delivery, the speaker can remain flexible and responsive to the needs and attitude of the audience.

The use of notes allows the language and phrasing of the speech to remain flexible. The speaker is not restricted to reading a set speech. He or she can vary the support material collected during the preparation to meet the needs of the audience. Notes used wisely have certain advantages, namely, to stimulate memory, to help with the reporting of complicated information, to help vary the support material to meet the needs of the audience, and to ensure organizational accuracy during delivery.

CONFLICT*

One of the main characteristics of any organization is that it is made up of human beings in interaction with each other. In such circumstances it is well known that conflicts will arise, and will sometimes result in detrimental side effects to the parties involved or to the organization as a whole. A study by the American Management Association revealed these findings:

- Managers spend an average of 20 percent of their time dealing with conflict.
- They feel that their ability to manage conflict has become more important over the last ten years.
- Conflict management is rated as of equal or slightly higher importance than planning, communication, motivation, and decision making.
- Managers emphasize psychological factors as sources of conflict: misunderstanding, communication failure, personality clashes, and value differences.

In fact, conflict in organization is probably inevitable due to the nature and design of the structure itself. The modern progressive organization recognizes the fact, however, that conflict, both internal and external, exists in any healthy organization and attempts to both benefit by desirable types of conflict and resolve or eliminate detrimental conflict. A certain degree of conflict within and between individuals and groups may increase creativity, satisfaction, performance, and effectiveness.

Conflict is a dynamic process, a type of behavior, involving two or more parties in opposition to each other. It can be overt or covert. Of the two, the covert is the more dangerous, because the harbored feelings of individuals can drain an untold amount of energy, both physical and psychological. Once conflict is acknowledged, then energies and resources can be channeled to dealing with and resolving it.

In order to be able to deal effectively and constructively with conflict, the manager must understand and must be able to analyze the various sources of conflict that may be found in people, things, or conditions. It is important to diagnose as correctly as possible the underlying causes of conflicts because they are not always what they appear to be on the surface.

Sources of Conflict

A typical source of conflict is when two people or two units have mutually exclusive goals—goals which cannot be reached simultaneously. An example would be when two or more managers of equivalent ranking are competing to replace their superior who is about to retire. Then there is the case of the person justifying failure by pointing to the errors of a colleague.

Groups or individuals that are committed to reach their goals will want to ensure that they have all the resources required. In any organization, resources are limited and all demands cannot be satisfied to the same degree. This is a frequent area of conflict.

Competition for status often leads to conflict. The concern of people with their position relative to others has much influence on their behavior and performance. An example of frequent conflict is when a young, highly educated person is called upon to supervise the work of older persons who have gained their status through their years of experience with the organization.

In a large organization, people will have different backgrounds and different value systems and will perceive things from different viewpoints—a possible cause of conflict, especially when not understood. Those in different functional departments will have varying beliefs and opinions on what is best and how it should be done. Perceptual differences between people in different areas can be accentuated because they interact with a different public. Difference of position in the hierarchy can also give rise to significant differences in perception of events.

---

*Source: Ross Smyth, "The Sources and Resolution of Conflict in Management," *Personnel Journal*, May 1977. Reprinted with the permission of *Personnel Journal*, Costa Mesa, California; all rights reserved.

Conflict also occurs frequently between first-line supervisors and managers at higher levels. The supervisor will be seeking short-term solutions to immediate problems, whereas the manager will be considering longer term solutions.

Management of Conflict

The way conflict is managed rather than suppressed, ignored, or avoided may contribute significantly to the organization's effectiveness. It can even be exploited as a means of promoting effective changes in the organization. The goal is to achieve a creative, acceptable, and realistic resolution of conflicts. In a conflict situation, the manager can be the initiator, defendant, or conciliator. In any case, knowledge of conflict management can give him or her a considerable advantage.

There are basic styles of conflict resolution, the oldest being through suppression or removal of the adversary. The emphasis is placed on immediate production of results without much concern for the people involved or the longer term ramifications.

An opposite style of conflict resolution is characterized by a strong desire to maintain harmony at all costs and to sacrifice any potentially positive and constructive results in the name of peaceful coexistence. A similar style is to cajole people to retreat from their positions and not attempt to achieve a constructive solution.

A middle-of-the-road type of resolution is by compromise, in which case there are no winners or losers. A workable solution is sought rather than the optimum one. People are often called upon to compromise their convictions, and a minority is called upon to endorse a position that would be supported by a majority.

The most highly recommended method in an organization receptive to change is the problem-solving style which seeks the optimum solution—which may in reality be the maximum satisfaction of all concerned. We start by recognizing that intelligent strong-minded people have legitimate convictions about what is right—at least from their perspective. We must therefore analyze the situation to identify the causes of conflict; ensure that each party reveals

its thoughts and feelings on the issue; and ensure that each is sensitive to the needs of the others.

All parties must have a vested interest in the outcome and feel that they share the common goal of solving the problem rather than accommodating different points of view. The latter point is particularly important in preventing the conflict from being viewed as a win or lose situation.

Constructively managed conflict can focus attention on the goals of the organization rather than on the individual's or group's subgoals; it can lead to innovation and energize people to activity. Conflict is part of the process of change and adjustment of the status quo. Contrary to past belief, conflict can be a controllable element in organizations and hence can be adjusted to minimize its destructive and maximize its constructive aspects.

UNDERSTANDING PEOPLE'S VALUES

Values—Old and New*

Based on 16 years of observation and research, Professor Graves of Union College found that people seem to evolve through consecutive levels of "psychological existence" which are descriptive of personal values and life styles.[1] Relatively independent of intelligence, a person's level of psychological existence can become arrested at a given level or it can move upward or downward depending on that person's cultural conditioning and perception of the opportunities and constraints in the environment. A diagrammatic version of Grave's framework is presented in Figure 27-1.

Level 1. The *reactive* level of existence is most commonly observed in newborn babies or in people psychologically arrested in, or regressed to, infancy. They are unaware of themselves or others as human beings, and sim-

---

*Source: M. Scott Myers and Susan S. Meyers, "Adapting to the New Work Ethic," *Business Quarterly,* Winter 1973. Reprinted with permission.

[1]Clare W. Graves, "Levels of Existence: An Open System Theory of Values," *Journal of Humanistic Psychology,* Fall 1970.

Figure 27-1 Levels of Psychological Existence

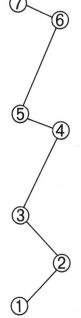

EXISTENTIAL

High tolerance for ambiguity and people with differing values. Likes to do jobs in his or her own way without constraints of authority or bureaucracy. Goal-oriented but toward a broader arena and longer time perspective.

MANIPULATIVE

Ambitious to achieve higher status and recognition. Strives to manipulate people and things. May achieve goals through gamesmanship, persuasion, bribery, or official authority.

EGOCENTRIC

Individualistic, selfish, thoughtless, unscrupulous, dishonest. Has not learned to function within the constraints imposed by society. Responds primarily to power.

REACTIVE

Not aware of self or others as individuals or human beings. Reacts to basic physiological needs. Mostly restricted to infants.

SOCIOCENTRIC

High affiliation needs. Dislikes violence, conformity, materialism, and manipulative management. Concerned with social issues and the dignity of human beings.

CONFORMIST

Low tolerance for ambiguity and for people whose values differ from his or her own. Attracted to rigidly defined roles in accounting, engineering, and the military and tends to perpetuate the status quo. Motivated by a cause, philosophy, or religion.

TRIBALISTIC

Found mostly in primitive societies and ghettos. Lives in a world of magic, witchcraft, and superstition. Strongly influenced by tradition and the power exerted by the boss, tribal chieftain, police officer, schoolteacher, politician, and other authority figures.

---

ply react to hunger, thirst, urination, defecation, sex, and other periodic physiological stimuli. Few people remain at this stage as they move toward adulthood; however, those at the threshold of subsistence in some of the larger cities of the Middle East seem to be little beyond this stage of existence. People at this level are generally not found on payrolls of organizations.

Level 2. Most people, as a matter of course, move out of the reactive existence to a *tribalistic* stage. Tribalism is characterized by concern with feelings of pain, temperature control, and safety and by tacit submission to an authority figure, whether a supervisor, police officer, government official, teacher, priest, parent, big brother, or gang leader. Tribalism is commonly observed in primitive cultures where magic, witchcraft, ritual, and superstition prevail. For example, the Bantu, who work in the coal, gold, and diamond mines of South Africa, are largely

tribalistic. People at this level are locked into the rigid traditions of their tribe and are dominated by the tribal chieftain or his or her substitute.

Level 3. Egocentrism is an overly assertive form of rugged individualism. This person's behavior reflects a philosophy which seems to say, "To hell with the rest of the world. I'm for myself." He or she is typically premoral—thus unscrupulous, selfish, aggressive, restless, impulsive, and, in general, not psychologically inclined to live within the constraints imposed by society's moral precepts. To this person, might is right, and authoritarian management, preferably benevolent, seems necessary to keep him or her in line. Typical group techniques are not usually successful for this type of person, but structured participative management, properly administered, promises to be an effective strategy for getting the person out of this egocentric mode.

Both egocentrism and tribalism are found in U.S. ghettos—not as a function of ethnic determinants, but rather as a result of cultural disadvantage. Now that equal opportunity laws are accelerating the employment of minority people, egocentric and tribalistic behavior is more prevalent in organizations.

Level 4. Persons at the *conformity* level of existence have low tolerance for ambiguity, have difficulty in accepting people whose values differ from their own, and have a need to get others to accept their values. They usually subordinate themselves to a philosophy, cause, or religion and tend to be attracted to vocations circumscribed by dogma or clearly defined rules. Though often perceived as docile, the conformist will assert or sacrifice him- or herself in violence if his or her values are threatened. For example, in 1954, the normally law-abiding Archie Bunkers of Little Rock, Arkansas, erupted in violence against equal opportunity measures which violated the predominant value system of that region. Conformists prefer authoritarianism to autonomy, but will respond to participation if it is prescribed by an acceptable authority and does not violate deep-seated values. They like specific job descriptions and procedures and have little tolerance for supervisory indecision or weakness. People at this level have been the mainstay of the hourly work force since the beginning of the Industrial Revolution.

Level 5. The fifth level of psychological existence is characterized by *manipulative* or materialistic behavior. Persons at this level are typically products of the Horatio Alger, rags-to-riches philosophy—striving to achieve their goals through the manipulation of things and people within their environment. They thrive on gamesmanship, politics, competition, and entrepreneurial effort, measure their success in terms of materialistic gain and power, and are inclined to flaunt self-earned (as against hereditary) status symbols. Typical of level 5 persons are business managers, who define their goals and strategies in terms such as cash flow, return on investment, profits, share of the market, and net sales billed and generally focus on short-term targets such as the quarterly review or annual plan. They tend to perceive people as expense items rather than assets.

Level 6. People at the sixth, or *sociocentric*, level of existence have high affiliation needs. Getting along is more important than getting ahead, and the approval of people they respect is valued over individual fame. At this level people may return to religiousness, not for its ritual or dogma, but rather for its spiritual attitude and concern with social issues. Many members of the original "hippie" cult were sociocentrics—their hirsute and dungareed appearance being a symbolic put-down of the organization-man appearance approved by the establishment. On the job the sociocentric responds well to participative management, but only on the condition that he or she and valued others believe in the product or service. The sociocentric tends to articulate protests openly, but characteristically dislikes violence and would counter authoritarianism with passive resistance. Sociocentrics are frequently perceived as cop-outs by 4s and 5s, and their behavior is not generally rewarded in business organizations. As a result, persons at this level who do not ultimately capitulate by regressing to the organizationally accepted modes of manipulation and conformity or adapt by evolving to the seventh level of psychological existence may become organizational problems because of alcoholism, drug abuse, or other self-punitive behavior.

Level 7. Individuals at the *existential* level of existence have high tolerance for ambiguity and for persons whose values differ from their own. On the job their behavior might say, "O.K., I understand the job to be done—now leave me alone and let me do it my way." In some respects they are a blend of levels 5 and 6 in that they are goal-oriented toward organizational success (level 5) and concerned with the dignity of fellow human beings (level 6). Like the level 5, they are concerned with organizational profits, the quarterly review, and the annual plan, but they are also concerned with the 10-year or 50-year plan and the impact of the organization on its members, the community, and the environment. Like the level 6, they are repelled by the use of violence. However, their outspoken intolerance of inflexible systems, restrictive policy, status symbols, and the arbitrary use of authority is threatening to most level 4 and 5 managers, and they may be expelled from the organization for reasons of nonconformity or insubordination.

RELATIONS WITH YOUR STAFF

Developing a Helpful Attitude with Staff*

- Effective supervisors are characterized by a belief in the nurse's ability to grow.
- The nurse supervisor's expectations of the nurse can facilitate or retard his or her development.
- Nursing supervisors who convey empathy, positive regard, and genuineness contribute to the personal growth of the nurse, constructive change, and the facilitation of learning.
- In order to establish a helping relationship, the nursing supervisor and the nurse must clarify mutual expectations, establish common goals, and initiate cooperative action.

Respect

Respect or positive regard means expressing care and concern for the individual by communicating that the person's ideas, feelings, and opinions are valued. In interactions with the nurse, the nursing supervisor can convey recognition of the nurse's basic drive to grow, to develop, and to realize potentials. The behavior of the nursing supervisor can demonstrate a belief that nursing staff members are responsible for their actions and are capable of using their own resources to solve the problems they encounter in the work situation.

1. Providing Positive Feedback on an Informal Basis. There is a tendency to focus on weaknesses rather than on strengths. Frequently,

positive feedback is not directed to the person involved. The nursing supervisor may speak favorably to others about a nurse, but unfortunately the nurse may never hear the praise.

2. Minimizing Defensiveness in Confrontation Interviews. For example, when confronting a nursing staff member who has been consistently late or absent, compare the statement, "What am I going to do about you?" with the following one: "You've been consistently late for the past three days. This interferes with care to patients and I want to know what you're going to do about it." The former statement is apt to elicit excuses and place the relationship on a parent-child basis. The latter statement, directed toward future action, conveys that the person is responsible for his or her own actions and implies that he or she must do something about this situation.

3. Promoting the Involvement of Nurses in Decision making. By asking, "Do I reward compliance and dependency or initiative and autonomy?" the nursing supervisor can begin to assess the quality of communication he or she has established with the staff.

Empathy

Empathy refers to seeing and understanding the other person from his or her own frame of reference, putting oneself in the other person's shoes. For the nursing supervisor, this means communicating interest in how the nurse is responding to work experiences. With the stress and demands of many work situations, the nursing supervisor's empathic understanding can contribute to the nurse's growth and learning and lead to his or her increased ability to act effectively in the situations encountered. There are several ways in which this can be fostered.

1. Focusing on What Is Not Being Expressed as Well as on What Is Being Expressed. Attempt to understand the nurse's experience and seek to explore what is not being expressed.

2. Refraining from Acting on the Evaluation of Others. This is particularly important in new relationships. Everyone makes initial evalua-

---

*Source: Mary A. Trainor, "A Helping Model for Clinical Supervision," *Supervisor Nurse*, January 1978. Reprinted with permission.

tions and judgments about others. What is suggested is to avoid acting on these judgments until more information is available.

3. Increasing Attention to Listening. The willingness to listen conveys acceptance and an attempt to understand the other person. Furthermore, an ability to listen has been shown to be a characteristic which differentiates successful groups from unsuccessful groups.

Genuineness

Genuineness, a third characteristic of the helper, refers to a willingness to be honest about oneself and to enter a relationship without presenting a front or facade. When the nursing supervisor communicates values, convictions, and ideas to members of the nursing staff, he or she is presenting him- or herself honestly and accurately—and also nondefensively, accepting the fact that being human means having deficiencies, making mistakes, and not having all the answers. Accepting and acknowledging his or her own strengths and limitations will encourage staff members to be more genuine. Verbal interactions which are sincere and spontaneous facilitate attempts by others to relate effectively and naturally. The following techniques may serve as a guide to developing genuineness in helping relationships with nursing staff.

1. Responding Nondefensively. Accepting one's limitations means accepting the consequent deficiencies and mistakes. For example, a nurse may ask a question regarding some aspect of nursing that is unfamiliar to you. A response such as "You should know that" or "I think it would be more useful if you found out about it" sets up a barrier and a facade which prevents authenticity. The reality of the situation is that no one person can know everything. Simply stating "I don't know" and then referring the staff member to an appropriate resource communicates that you are being honest, direct, and real. In addition, it conveys the attitude that admitting a lack of knowledge is acceptable and that resources are available in these situations.

2. Minimizing Playing a Role and Hiding behind a Mask. Frequently, situations occur when the clinical nursing supervisor feels threatened and may experience a need to impress others with his or her knowledge and achievements. This may occur with nurses or with other nursing supervisors. Consider the continual changes occurring in most work situations. These changes may be related to complex technologies used with patients, to computer programming, or to recent graduates with a different view of nursing. Each of these situations can be threatening, and in an attempt to cope with feelings of insecurity there may be a tendency to focus on one's knowledge and achievements. This prevents an honest and open exchange between oneself and other persons. It is recognized that changes are threatening to most people, but if the nursing supervisor expresses his or her response to the situation openly and honestly, it will help others to respond in a similar manner.

3. Creating an Environment in Which Other Persons Feel Free To Disagree and Express Their Own Ideas. In such an atmosphere curiosity is valued, questions are welcomed, and groups are encouraged to pursue their own goals. This is not to say that one must accept all suggestions made by nurses. What is meant is that a genuine response to others fosters their ability to be honest, genuine, creative, and authentic.

4. Expressing Feelings Appropriately. Many people have difficulty expressing feelings, particularly angry feelings. When these feelings are not appropriately expressed, they are overtly acted out. One way of examining this is to look at the feedback system. Problem-centered feedback focuses on negative behavior, but in a manner which seeks to find a solution to the problems caused by such behavior. Consider the example of a nurse who is resisting a change that has been recently introduced. Her repeated complaints and whining are aggravating. A response might be, "You've expressed a number of concerns about this new medication system. I'm getting frustrated because the explanations I've given to you do not seem to help. Could we talk about this? Perhaps this can be further clarified." This kind of response focuses on the feeling and allows one to be genuine. It also provides a feedback system dealing with the problem rather than the personality.

Personnel Cliques*

Satisfying the individual's need for belonging, prestige, recognition, etc., is the primary function of the informal group. The informal group is a natural unit in which work decisions and judgments are reached. It provides an atmosphere for testing new procedures and creates standards of conduct for its members.

Group standards of behavior pervade the informal social organization. Management may either benefit or suffer from the group's standards and group pressure to conform. It depends on how close the goals of the group are to the goals of management.

Members

The group member experiences certain pressures to conform to group standards and norms. The individual point of view becomes aligned with the group's point of view, and since the group satisfies the member's social needs, he or she accepts the group's goals. The member wants to be "well regarded" by the other members. A member who exceeds the group's accepted level of output may find him- or herself ostracized. Any deviation from group standards may cause the member to be isolated and be given the "silent treatment." The member may be left out of group activities. More direct methods of pressuring the individual to conform include letting management know of the deviant's "mistakes," flooding his or her desk with work, or even sabotaging his or her equipment.

Leaders

It is sometimes hard to identify the group leader. The group spokesman is not necessarily the leader. There may be different leaders for different group functions.

The group's leader tends to be the member who most closely conforms to the group's stand-

ards and norms, or the one who has the most information and skill related to the group's activities. The leader must enable the members to achieve their private goals as well as the group's goals.

The informal leader can sometimes mold and change the group's goals and norms. When the leader speaks, the group listens and is influenced. But if the leader tries to change things too fast, he or she can lose the role of leader.

Managing Cliques

Management must recognize that informal groups exist. Once this is acknowledged, management should gather as much information as possible about the existing groups. Who belongs to which informal groups? What are the goals of the different groups? Are they opposed to the organization's goals? What are the operating techniques of the groups? How cohesive are they?

The supervisor can gain cooperation only by respecting the group's standards and norms. Supervisors have been characterized as the "people in the middle." They are formal leaders, but must rely on more than the authority of the formal organization to get successful results. They must build acceptance of themselves by the informal group and, in effect, attain some portion of the role of informal leader.

A good supervisor knows what the group expects and adjusts his or her behavior accordingly. The supervisor must make *fair* demands of the group and emphasize "getting the job done" rather than use authority for its own sake. Rules imposed on the group should be reasonable. Time-honored customs should be respected whenever possible. The supervisor must weigh the implications carefully before taking a position at odds with the accepted practices of the group.

Informal leaders should be given a chance to gain recognition by working with rather than against management. It is important to build good relations with informal leaders—pass information to them, ask them advice, have them train others. However, it is necessary to be aware of the danger of cooperating so far that it becomes favoritism.

Source: Richard S. Muti, "The Informal Group—What It Is and How It Can Be Controlled," *Personnel Journal*, August 1968. Reprinted with the permission of *Personnel Journal*, Costa Mesa, California; all rights reserved.

Should management try to build cohesiveness? There is no clear answer to this question. Cohesive groups display teamwork, higher morale, lower turnover and absenteeism and are easier to supervise. But highly cohesive groups may not readily accept new employees. They may not cooperate well with outsiders. Consequently, competition and hard feelings between rival groups can develop. However, if the group is cooperative, or even neutral, management should obviously try to encourage cohesion. If an informal group is antagonistic, management should try its best to change the group's attitude. But failing in that, it should attempt to weaken or destroy the power of the group.

Note: See Table 27-1 for a questionnaire regarding interpersonal relations.

COLLEGIAL RELATIONS: PHYSICIANS AND ADMINISTRATORS

Collaborative Relations with Physicians*

The physician-nursing relationship is a reciprocal one. The exchange relationship is one in which nursing needs physicians for patient referrals and physicians need nursing to deliver nursing care to their patients. The manner in which care is delivered can be a direct reflection of the physician's judgment. Additionally, nursing can alter the efficiency of physicians by making hospital rounds organized or disorganized. On the other hand, physicians can produce nurse turnover by creating a tense working environment for nurses. In the ideal situation, both nurses and physicians collaborate, taking the time to discover how each type of professional can make the workplace more efficient for the other.

Nursing Representation on Physician Committees

Physicians make decisions in hospitals by committee and majority rule. Although nurses

*Source: Vi Kunkle, *Marketing Strategies for Nurse Managers, A Guide to Developing and Implementing a Nursing Marketing Plan*, Aspen Publishers, Inc., © 1990.

cannot be voting members, nurses can influence the vote. Nursing representation is now required on most physician or hospital committees by the Joint Commission. This positions nursing in the physician decision-making arena. Active involvement, however, occurs by working with the chairperson to become a regular part of the departmental agenda. In so doing, nursing educates, communicates, and influences. Benefits include high visibility for nursing, input into patient care decisions, and better working relationships between the medical staff and nursing.

Nurse-Physician Joint Practice Committee

The joint practice committee is a standing committee of both the medical and nursing staffs, consisting of an equal number of physicians and nurses as voting members. The ideal number is five physicians and five nurses, three of whom are staff nurses. The purpose of the committee is to examine, discuss, collaborate, and come to a consensus on any issue affecting the way in which care is given. This committee is the most effective tool for establishing a good working relationship with physicians. The decisions rendered in the committee are challenged by neither the medical staff nor nursing because of the composition and standing of the committee. Examples of agenda items are

- critical nurse staffing issues
- problems with support services that prevent nursing from carrying out the plan of care, such as delayed laboratory reporting, delayed medication delivery, and lack of adequate supplies
- problems and issues related to house staff affecting nursing's ability to provide care to patients
- inappropriate requests by specific physicians for nursing to perform medical practice procedures
- physician complaints about nursing's care delivery system, chart forms, or method of assignment of nursing staff
- new nursing procedures or systems expected to affect medical practice

Table 27-1 Questionnaire: Supervisor's Interpersonal Relations

1.	Do you have a thorough understanding of the institution's goals and your part in meeting the objectives of the institution?	Yes	No
2.	Do you avoid confusion and have a clear understanding of what is expected and how to do it?	Yes	No
3.	Do you offer suggestions or constructive criticism to your immediate supervisor and ask for additional information when necessary?	Yes	No
4.	Do you build team spirit and group pride by getting everyone into the act of setting goals and pulling together?	Yes	No
5.	Do you schedule time for meetings with your subordinates and with your superiors?	Yes	No
6.	Do you encourage each of your employees to come up with suggestions about ways to improve things?	Yes	No
7.	Do you make it easy for your employees to approach you with job or personal problems?	Yes	No
8.	Do you keep your employees informed on how they are doing?	Yes	No
9.	Are you too busy with operational problems to be concerned with your employees' personal difficulties?	Yes	No
10.	Do you give your employees a feeling of accomplishment by telling them how well they are doing in comparison with yesterday or last week or a month or a year ago?	Yes	No
11.	Do you build individual employee confidence and praise good performance?	Yes	No
12.	Do you use personnel records and close observation to learn exactly which skills each employee has so that his or her best abilities may be used?	Yes	No
13.	Do you let your employees know how jobs are analyzed and evaluated and what the job rates and progressions are?	Yes	No
14.	Do you attempt to rotate employees on different jobs to build up skills for individual flexibility within the group?	Yes	No
15.	Do you train your employees for better jobs?	Yes	No
16.	Are you developing an understudy for your job?	Yes	No
17.	Do you hold a good person down in one position because he or she may be indispensable there?	Yes	No
18.	Are you doing things to discourage your subordinates?	Yes	No
19.	Are you aware of sources of discontentment or discouragement or frustration affecting your employees?	Yes	No
20.	Do you listen to the ideas and reactions of subordinates with courtesy?	Yes	No
21.	If an idea is adopted or not adopted, do you explain why?	Yes	No
22.	Do you usually praise in public, but criticize or reprove in private?	Yes	No
23.	Is your criticism constructive?	Yes	No
24.	Are you aware that a feeling of belonging builds self-confidence and makes people want to work harder than ever?	Yes	No
25.	Do you ever say or do anything that detracts from the sense of personal dignity that each of your employees has?	Yes	No

Source: Norman Metzger, *The Health Care Supervisor's Handbook,* 3rd edition, Aspen Publishers, Inc., © 1988.

Both nursing and the medical staff may place items on the agenda for discussion and recommendations. Recommendations from the committee go to the nursing and medical executive committees for approval. Physicians accept the committee's decisions because of its standing as a bona fide medical staff committee written into the professional staff bylaws and governed by majority rule.

Physician Unit Representative Program

Another effective tool for creating a good working relationship with the medical staff is the physician unit representation program. The chief of staff appoints a physician to each of the nursing units to act as a physician liaison and representative for mediconursing issues needing immediate attention. The purpose of the program is to

• provide crisis intervention between the medical and nursing staffs
• defer appropriate problems and issues to the joint practice committee
• resolve urgent problems in collaboration with unit nurse managers

Consequently, critical problems are resolved before becoming magnified and unmanageable. Esssentially, the physician representative and nurse manager collaborate on critical problems requiring immediate resolution, while the joint practice committee collaborates on issues requiring extensive problem solving and research.

Resident Orientation Program

To initiate positive relations between the nursing and medical staffs from the very beginning, nursing mangement could organize a formal resident orientation program for new house staff. Orientation includes unit protocols; unit-specific orders for laboratory, radiology, and pharmacy; introduction to key nursing staff; explanation of unit layout; and standing orders of attending physicians. Resident orientation could be written and scheduled annually with the arrival of the new house staff.

Executive Management Teams*

A major responsibility of the nurse executive is to function as a member of executive management teams. This is becoming an increasingly critical responsibility as nurse administrators work more closely with all agency departments to provide cost-effective, quality nursing care.

For the most part, nurses are comfortable working with patient care teams and participating as effective team members. Nurse executives, however, usually have less experience and expertise in building and maintaining executive interdisciplinary teams.

Executive interdisciplinary teams differ from patient care teams in several ways. In executive teams, the focus of concern centers around the department or organization; for the patient care team, the focus is the overall welfare of the patient or client. Hospital bureaucracy, power, and politics directly affect the definition of and movement toward executive team goals; patient care teams can use social interactions and peer pressure to accomplish goals. Diplomacy, negotiation skills, and use of power-based strategies or alliances are requisite skills of nurse executives in team building; facilitation skills that allow for sharing of knowledge and communication among peers are necessary for leadership of patient care teams. If the nurse administrator is to be effective in his or her role, these differences must be acknowledged and appropriate techniques employed to maximize team-building efforts.

The Nature of Team Building

Team building is the process of deliberately creating and unifying a group of people into an effective and efficiently functioning work unit so that specified goals are accomplished. The team-building process is designed to assist the work group in becoming more adept at pursuing its objectives and in identifying and resolving its own work-related problems. Team building is a

*Source: Mary J. Farley and Martha H. Stoner, "The Nurse Executive and Interdisciplinary Team Building," Nursing Administration Quarterly, vol. 13, no. 2, © 1989 Aspen Publishers, Inc.

continuous process that goes through several stages and takes time, energy, and effort to accomplish.

Nurse executives who are familiar with individual member tasks as well as group tasks are in a better position to help the team to achieve the ideal outcomes of each stage. Table 27-2 presents a compilation of the stages of team growth, the identifying characteristics of each stage, and the member and group tasks. The ideal outcomes represent the successful accomplishment of member and team tasks during each stage.

Nurse executives need to be aware of the negative forces and actively work to alleviate

Table 27-2 Stages of Team Growth

Stage	Characteristics	Member Tasks	Team Tasks	Ideal Outcomes
1. Orientation	Opinions expressed cautiously	Learning what is expected and relating this to self	Development of trust in others	Acquaintance with colleagues
	Artificial politeness	Making social comparisons (including needs)	Definition of boundaries	Beginning of involvement and identification
	Ambiguous relationships	Asking, "How do I belong to this group?"		Productivity only skin deep
	Efforts unfocused			
2. Adaptation	Social mechanisms developing that serve to differentiate members	Finding appropriate role for self, both personally and professionally	Provision of structure and climate conducive to maximization of freedom	Group roles developing Common language developing
	Team identity beginning		Team identity beginning	Rules and norms developing
3. Emergence	Bargaining Alliances forming Power struggles Dispute, disagreements, and defending of opinions	Finding identity as a team member with ability to communicate, differ, confront, and collaborate	Determination of who is in control Determination of how control is exercised Determination of what happens to delinquents	Increased comfort with differences Emergence of shorthand ways of talking Emergence of "we" identity
4. Working	Achievement of complementarity and gestalt	Making honest disclosure Reaching individual decisions and negotiating solutions	Decision making Planning Productivity	Cohesiveness of team members Feedback readily accepted Enthusiasm high Conflict and dissension dissipate as attitudes are modified

them so that teamwork may be effective and successful. The forces that may tear a team apart include such things as different needs, values, and world views of team members; professional rivalries; contradictory institutional priorities; misunderstandings between team members; and lack of commitment to team goals. Therefore, the nurse executive must be sensitive to individual needs and must use diplomacy in managing conflict.

Suggestions for Building Executive Interdisciplinary Teams

The welfare of the nursing profession may depend on the nurse administrator's ability to work with, build, and maintain effective interdisciplinary teams at the executive level. The following guidelines for building successful executive interdisciplinary teams provide suggestions for nurse administrators. The list include principles that relate especially to executive interdisciplinary teams.

1. Obtain political and organizational support for the proposal, plan, or anticipated goals from the chief executive officer or hospital administrator.
2. Keep conscious diplomacy in mind and contact potential team members to share a vision of positive outcomes that may occur as a result of team participation. It may be necessary to raise individual awareness of the problem or issue, keeping in mind that each potential team member will view participation from a "what's in it for me?" standpoint.
3. Call a team meeting at a convenient time for all team members. An agenda should be sent to each member ahead of the meeting, and the meeting should be conducted in an expeditious manner.
4. Clarify the purpose of the team, sharing all information available. Encourage participation as the group jointly sets clear, challenging, but realistic goals. Without clear, specific goals, the team has no measuring stick for accomplishments. Participation in goal setting contributes to

commitment. Each member of the team ought to understand the goals and how he or she fits in the group efforts toward goal accomplishment.
5. Seek commitment from each team member for accomplishment of team goals.
6. Keep in mind that threats to individual power and/or protection of personal or departmental "turf" may influence behavior. Sensitivity to these needs along with good conflict management techniques will move the team forward.
7. Create an atmosphere of cooperation and satisfying relationships. Praising team members and encouraging members to support each other enhance cooperation.
8. Accept and appreciate the differences of the individual members and departments. Personal needs are part of the human condition.
9. Communicate, communicate, communicate. Members of organizations are often apprehensive of executive team activities.

RELATIONS WITH OTHERS*

With Supportive Departments

Because nonnursing tasks are now undertaken by separate departments, today's first-line manager has much less power than did his or her predecessor. Who are the collateral persons with whom the first-line nurse manager must bargain and coordinate? High on this list are the directors of those departments that provide essential supportive services and supplies. Laundry, pharmacy, materials management, and dietary departments are major examples. Most problems with such departments relate to the logistics of supply, that is, getting enough of the right supplies or services to nursing whenever and wherever they are needed.

Many health institutions hire systems analysts or have a department for operations research. Where such persons or departments exist, the

---

Source: Adapted from Barbara J. Stevens, *First-line Patient Care Management,* Aspen Publishers, Inc., © 1983.

first-line nurse manager should utilize them to solve logistics problems.

Where such assistance is not available, the nurse manager and his or her counterpart in the collateral department may undertake their own analysis of the system. A flow chart may reveal system defects and suggest solutions to the nurse's problem.

With Clinical Specialists

The most difficult relation often occurs within the nursing department itself, between first-line managers and clinical specialists. First-line managers may feel themselves to be competing with clinical specialists for power within nursing. When clinical specialists work in a staff position, a dangerous behavioral cycle may develop between specialist and first-line manager:

1. In order to protect his or her own authority and power, the first-line manager fails to consult the clinical specialist about care problems.
2. The clinical specialist, frustrated over his or her lack of input into the care system, makes a bid for administrative power, trying to supplant the first-line manager.
3. The first-line manager responds to this threat by even greater exclusion of the clinical specialist.

Such a cycle of behavior involves a confusion of two sorts of power: administrative power and professional power.

The first-line manager must perceive his or her job as one of using scarce resources appropriately. Certainly the clinical specialist's knowledge is a scarce resource, one that should be utilized to the fullest degree possible.

With Patients

Patients are persons with whom negotiations are required. When patients are treated as objects, there is no need for collateral relations; objects are to be manipulated and used. To say that such manipulations are carried out "for the patient's own good" is not enough to justify ignoring the personhood of the patient. The growing sensitivity of both patients and nursing staff to this problem is manifested in the popularity of the so-called Patient's Bill of Rights.

Obtaining "informed consent" requires communicating at several levels. At the first level, it simply involves a choice between giving and withholding information from the patient. Sometimes a patient is not told that he or she has options. Many patients are bullied into accepting a given treatment without prior discussion.

At the second level, communication requires that the treatment be described in terms intelligible to the patient. Few patients are familiar with medical terminology, and the first-line manager must forsake terminology for simpler descriptive language. The first-line manager must go beyond clear description and make an effort to be sure that the patient understands what he or she is saying.

The third level of communication involves informing the patient of the full implications of a treatment choice. Knowledge of the implications may evoke an emotional response as well as a cognitive one. It is one thing for a patient to know that part of his or her mandible will be removed; it is another thing to know the impact of that surgery on his or her speech, ability to eat, and appearance. Nurses may shrink back from trying to communicate the full impact of treatment to patients, for conveying this information often requires the nurse to inflict pain. Yet patients and their families may feel deceived if the full impact of a treatment is not known prior to its inception.

Chapter 28

Job Satisfaction and Motivation

JOB SATISFACTION AND JOB PERFORMANCE

Job performance is the result of the interaction of two variables: (1) ability to perform the task and (2) amount of motivation. Ability to perform the task is an obvious variable. To the extent that people are put in jobs which demand skills and abilities that they do not possess, or possess to a degree below that required, lower-than-desired levels of job performance should be expected. Increasingly this requires a complete understanding of job requirements and a thoroughness in screening applicants to ensure that they have the necessary skills and abilities.

Motivational Factors*

The second determinant of job performance is the amount of motivation. This in turn is a function of the following motivational factors:

- need for achievement
- belief that one is being well paid

---

*Source: Burt K. Scanlon, "Determinants of Job Satisfaction and Productivity," *Personnel Journal*, January 1976. Reprinted with the permission of *Personnel Journal*, Costa Mesa, California; all rights reserved.

- job requiring skills and abilities valued and believed possessed
- feedback
- opportunity to participate
- performance instrumental to promotion, wage increases, coworker acceptability, etc.

Several factors deserve special comment. The individual's need for achievement is one. Unfortunately, no way has been determined to precisely pinpoint this. Once employed, the need can change as a result of all kinds of considerations: the kind of training programs; how the job is designed; style of supervision received; changes in motivational patterns.

Also, individuals enter jobs with certain preconceived ideas about "how good they are"—their skills and abilities. Right or wrong, if a person thinks his or her skills and abilities are not being utilized and developed, a motivation problem occurs. It is perhaps worth noting that most people overestimate themselves and therefore, tend to perceive themselves as being underutilized. Truth or falsity is not the issue; an individual's perception of the situation is the important factor.

The importance of feedback and having an opportunity to participate has been widely publicized. Motivation requires more than just physical involvement in a job. It demands mental and emotional involvement also.

Environmental Factors*

Environmental factors also play a key part in motivation. Among these factors are:

- communication
  - —appreciation of one's efforts; praise when it is due
  - —knowledge of the organization's activities and intentions; inclusion in the employer's goals and plans
  - —knowledge of where one stands with the organization at any given time; appraisal
  - —confidentiality in personal dealings with management; tactful disciplining and reasonable privacy
- growth potential
  - —the opportunity for advancement; career ladders and promotional paths
  - —encouragement in growth and advancement; skill training, tuition assistance for formal education, and management training for potential supervisors
- personnel policies
  - —reasonable accommodation of personal needs, as in work scheduling, vacation scheduling, sick time benefits
  - —reasonable feeling of job security
  - —organizational loyalty to employees
  - —respect for an individual's origins, background, and beliefs
  - —fair and consistent treatment relative to other employees
- salary administration
  - —fair salary and benefits relative to others in the organization, in the community, and in one's specific occupation
- working conditions
  - —the physical working conditions relative to what is expected or desired

---

*Source: Charles R. McConnell, *Managing the Health Care Professional*, Aspen Publishers, Inc., © 1984.

The Manager's Role*

The department manager can have an influence on both motivating factors and environmental factors. However, the extent of possible influence depends partly on the job—specifically what the manager has to work with—and partly on the organization—how much latitude the individual manager is allowed.

For all employees the manager has at least some ability to arouse motivation and to prevent dissatisfaction from taking over.

The true motivating factors—the opportunities listed previously—represent that capacity for the fulfillment of needs that are largely, if not entirely, psychological. As compared with the nonprofessional, the professional employee is more likely to be operating on a level of psychological need fulfillment. This should suggest to the manager that the professional employee would be more effectively managed through an open, participative management style that allows the employee the maximum possible opportunity for self-determination.

Let us consider the manager's likely impact on the five environmental factors surrounding the professional's work:

1. Communication. The immediate manager is always the key to communication with employees at all levels. Whether professional or nonprofessional, an employee's overall level of satisfaction often hinges completely or at least in large part on communication that is controlled by the manager. Communication serves many important needs in answering for the employee many questions, such as "How am I doing?" "Am I appreciated?" "Am I trusted and regarded with respect?" "Am I kept advised of what is happening in the organization?" "Am I treated as truly a part of the organization?" These questions and more are answered both directly and indirectly by the manager in the all-important one-to-one relationship with the employee.

2. Growth Potential. The manager has somewhat limited influence in the area of growth potential. Quite simply, the manager cannot

---

*Source: Ibid.

create opportunities that may not be there because there are few openings for promotions or because short, restrictive career ladders are involved. The manager can, however, adopt a positive attitude that encourages employees to fix their sights on the existing opportunities.

3. Personnel Policies. As a member of the larger management group, the individual manager may have input into the formulation of personnel policies. Regardless of the extent of one's involvement in setting policy, however, the manager always has a key role in assuring the consistent application of personnel policies to all employees. Inconsistency of treatment tends to be a major dissatisfier for many employees.

4. Salary Administration. Ordinarily the manager has little or no role in determining the salary structure of the organization. However, in hiring and promoting people and in granting pay raises the manager may well have a key role in the consistent and equitable application of the salary structure. Often the principal determinant of an employee's level of satisfaction with the job's pay is that person's perception of how well he or she is paid relative to others, especially others of comparable skill who do the same kind of work.

5. Working Conditions. The manager has an active role in watching out for the well-being of the employees. Something as seemingly simple as inadequate lighting in the office or insufficient space in the parking lot can lead to dissatisfaction if not acted on. The manager, in many ways the advocate of the employee, partly ensures that the work gets done by ensuring that working conditions are reasonable or tolerable. The manager should serve as a channel through which complaints about working conditions are aired and problems are reported and corrected.

Administrative Actions to Maximize Job Satisfaction*

1. Establishment of Committees To Review Problems. Establish committees with members

Source: Tina Filoromo and Dolores Ziff, *Nurse Recruitment: Strategies for Success*, Aspen Publishers, Inc., © 1980.

representing all levels of the nursing staff. These committees should be directed to address such topics as staffing and scheduling, including the amount of rotation an individual does in a week or a month as well as the number of weekends a nurse must work within a given period.

The committees might also give staff members an opportunity to voice their opinions about such personnel policies as uniform dress guidelines and the method by which employees are evaluated for job performance.

2. Maintenance of an Open-Door Policy. Be sure that the door to nursing and hospital administration is open to staff nurses. Create an atmosphere that encourages nurses to voice complaints and offer suggestions. Prove that you are listening to these suggestions and opinions by always trying to provide answers—if not immediately, then at some specified later date.

3. Maintenance of Adequate Staffing. First, plan a realistic method for delivery of patient care based on the number and kinds of staff currently available. Don't try to do primary nursing when you have personnel only for a team or functional approach. Set guidelines for the system you have chosen, and carry them out as efficiently as possible on a 24-hour basis. A single system is less frustrating to employees than a fragmented system that changes with each shift.

4. Specific Activities. There are many other steps you can take to increase job satisfaction (see also Table 28-1):

- Reinterview new employees at various times after employment. Such interviews may uncover areas of concern or dissatisfaction that you will be able to deal with at once and so prevent the individuals from leaving your hospital frustrated and needlessly upset.
- Staff nurses look for ongoing educational opportunities. Be sure that you offer the chance for the nursing staff on all shifts to participate in in-house programs and in programs outside the institution.
- Be sure your staff members are aware that nursing administration always offers them

Table 28-1 Key Factors in Job Satisfaction

Twelve key factors emerged from two major research projects that examined the attitudes of health care workers and the factors that made them satisfied with their jobs.

1. *Input.* Workers want the opportunity to speak up about their jobs. They want the chance to suggest change and to perceive that they are heard by management and supervision. In the studies this was a particularly strong concern of RNs.

2. *Worker-supervisor relations.* The supervisor is the key to organizational harmony and the success of motivational programs. Supervisors must know how to accomplish their jobs and how to be fair, understanding, mature, and helpful. In the studies this factor was a particularly strong concern of RNs and allied health professionals.

3. *Discipline/grievance.* Workers desire policies and procedures that are fair and unbiased. Policies and procedures can act as powerful motivators.

4. *Work environment.* The environment has to be perceived as clean, comfortable, and safe. These items often emerge as particular concerns of allied health professionals.

5. *Breaks and meals.* Workers feel the need for time off during working hours. Breaking away appears essential to RNs, who often get little or no time to rest because of staffing situations.

6. *Discrimination.* Workers of all job classifications display a general aversion to racial, sexual, and professional discrimination. Fairness in this dimension is highly critical and is more of an issue for female workers than for male workers.

7. *Work satisfaction.* Workers will be motivated if they have jobs that make them feel good about themselves. Individuals need to feel they have a future in the organiza-

tion, and their workload must be perceived as reasonable. This dimension presents a particular challenge for the supervisor in areas where workers have limited upward mobility because of training or educational constraints.

8. *Performance appraisals.* Appraisal and feedback must occur on a regular and timely basis and must be equitable. Supervisors must be thoroughly trained in appraisal methods.

9. *Clarity of policies, procedures, and benefits.* Workers must understand and possess *working* knowledge of policies and procedures and particularly of their benefits. It is the supervisor's responsibility to serve as a teacher and a resource person in this area.

10. *Pay and development opportunities.* Workers want pay that is fair in comparison with the pay of competing health care institutions and with the community in general. Nurses are particularly concerned about development opportunities, including both continuing education and the opportunity to grow within the organization.

11. *Decision making.* Workers want something to say about how the institution or agency is managed; they want to experience a true vested interest.

12. *Style of management.* The attitude projected by top management through the individual supervisors is an important factor. Health care workers want to be associated with an organization that cares about workers and patients alike.

Source: Paul E. Fitzgerald, Jr., "Worker Perceptions: The Key to Motivation," *The Health Care Supervisor,* vol. 3, no. 1, © 1984 Aspen Publishers, Inc.

---

promotional opportunities before looking outside of the hospital to fill positions. Utilize a well-planned procedure for posting job openings, one that is fair to all employees.

- Horizontal mobility is as important to nurses as traditional vertical mobility. Your mobility plan should also include a well-defined and strictly observed transfer policy that is fair to each employee and allows for mobility within the institution for the purpose of professional growth and development.

MOTIVATION

Motivation Theory*

Management's Task: The Conventional View

The conventional conception of management's task in harnessing human energy to organizational requirements can be stated broadly in terms of eight propositions. In order to avoid the complications introduced by a label, let us call this set of propositions "Theory X":

1. Management is responsible for organizing the elements of productive enterprise—money, materials, equipment, people—in the interest of economic ends.
2. With respect to people, this is a process of directing their efforts, motivating them, controlling their actions, modifying their behavior to fit the needs of the organization.
3. Without this active intervention by management, people would be passive—even resistant—to organizational needs. They must therefore be persuaded, rewarded, punished, controlled—their activities must be directed. This is management's task. We often sum it up by saying that management consists of getting things done through other people.
4. The average man is by nature indolent—he works as little as possible.
5. He lacks ambition, dislikes responsibility, prefers to be led.
6. He is inherently self-centered, indifferent to organizational needs.
7. He is by nature resistant to change.
8. He is gullible, not very bright, the ready dupe of the charlatan and the demagogue.

Source: Reprinted, by permission of the publisher, from "The Human Side of Enterprise," by Douglas M. McGregor, *Management Review*, November 1957, © 1957 by American Management Association, Inc. All rights reserved.

The human side of economic enterprise today is fashioned from propositions and beliefs such as these. Conventional organization structures and managerial policies, practices, and programs reflect these assumptions.

In accomplishing its task—with these assumptions as guides—management has conceived of a range of possibilities.

At one extreme, management can be "hard" or "strong." The methods for directing behavior involve coercion and threat (usually disguised), close supervision, tight controls over behavior. At the other extreme, management can be "soft" or "weak." The methods for directing behavior involve being permissive, satisfying people's demands, achieving harmony. Then they will be tractable, accept direction.

This range has been fairly completely explored during the past half century, and management has learned some things from the exploration. There are difficulties in the "hard" approach. Force breeds counterforces: restriction of output, antagonism, militant unionism, subtle but effective sabotage of management objectives. This "hard" approach is especially difficult during times of full employment.

There are also difficulties in the "soft" approach. It leads frequently to the abdication of management—to harmony, perhaps, but to indifferent performance. People take advantage of the soft approach. They continually expect more, but they give less and less.

Currently, the popular theme is "firm but fair." This is an attempt to gain the advantages of both the hard and the soft approaches. It is reminiscent of Teddy Roosevelt's "speak softly and carry a big stick."

Is the Conventional View Correct? The findings which are beginning to emerge from the social sciences challenge this whole set of beliefs about man and human nature and about the task of management.

Perhaps the best way to indicate why the conventional approach of management is inadequate is to consider the subject of motivation.

Physiological Needs. Man is a wanting animal—as soon as one of his needs is satisfied, another appears in its place. This process is unending. It continues from birth to death.

Man's needs are organized in a series of levels—a hierarchy of importance. At the lowest level, but preeminent in importance when they are thwarted, are his *physiological needs*. Man lives for bread alone when there is no bread. Unless the circumstances are unusual, his needs for love, for status, for recognition are inoperative when his stomach has been empty for a while. But when he eats regularly and adequately, hunger ceases to be an important motivation. The same is true of the other physiological needs of man—for rest, exercise, shelter, protection from the elements.

A satisfied need is not a motivator of behavior! This is a fact of profound significance that is regularly ignored in the conventional approach to the management of people. Consider your own need for air: Except as you are deprived of it, it has no appreciable motivating effect upon your behavior.

Safety Needs. When the physiological needs are reasonably satisfied, needs at the next higher level begin to dominate man's behavior—to motivate him. These are called *safety needs*. They are needs for protection against danger, threat, deprivation. Some people mistakenly refer to these as needs for security. However, unless man is in a dependent relationship where he fears arbitrary deprivation, he does not demand security. The need is for the "fairest possible break." When he is confident of this, he is more than willing to take risks. But when he feels threatened or dependent, his greatest need is for guarantees, for protection, for security.

The fact needs little emphasis that, since every employee is in a dependent relationship, safety needs may assume considerable importance. Arbitrary management actions, behavior which arouses uncertainty with respect to continued employment or which reflects favoritism or discrimination, unpredictable administration of policy—these can be powerful motivators of the safety needs in the employment relationship *at every level*.

Social Needs. When man's physiological needs are satisfied and he is no longer fearful about his physical welfare, his *social needs* become important motivators of his behavior—needs for belonging, for association, for acceptance by his fellows, for giving and receiving friendship and love.

Management knows today of the existence of these needs, but it often assumes quite wrongly that they represent a threat to the organization. Many studies have demonstrated that the tightly knit, cohesive work group may, under proper conditions, be far more effective than an equal number of separate individuals in achieving organizational goals.

Yet management, fearing group hostility to its own objectives, often goes to considerable lengths to control and direct human efforts in ways that are inimical to the natural "groupiness" of human beings. When man's social needs—and perhaps his safety needs, too—are thus thwarted, he behaves in ways which tend to defeat organizational objectives. He becomes resistant, antagonistic, uncooperative. But this behavior is a consequence, not a cause.

Ego Needs. Above the social needs—in the sense that they do not become motivators until lower needs are reasonably satisfied—are the needs of greatest significance to management and to man himself. They are the *egoistic needs,* and they are two kinds:

1. Those needs that relate to one's self-esteem—needs for self-confidence, for independence, for achievement, for competence, for knowledge.
2. Those needs that relate to one's reputation—needs for status, for recognition, for appreciation, for the deserved respect of one's fellows.

Unlike the lower needs, these are rarely satisfied; man seeks indefinitely for more satisfaction of these needs once they become important to him. But they do not appear in any significant way until physiological, safety, and social needs are all reasonably satisfied.

The typical organization offers few opportunities for the satisfaction of these egoistic needs to people at lower levels in the hierarchy.

Self-Fulfillment Needs. Finally—a capstone, as it were, on the hierarchy of man's needs—

there are what we may call the *needs for self-fulfillment*. These are the needs for realizing one's own potentialities, for continued self-development, for being creative in the broadest sense of that term.

It is clear that the conditions of modern life give only limited opportunity for these relatively weak needs to obtain expression. The deprivation most people experience with respect to other lower-level needs diverts their energies into the struggle to satisfy *those* needs, and the needs for self-fulfillment remain dormant.

Management and Motivation. The man whose lower-level needs are satisfied is not motivated to satisfy those needs any longer. For practical purposes they exist no longer. Management often asks, "Why aren't people more productive? We pay good wages, provide good working conditions, have excellent fringe benefits and steady employment. Yet people do not seem to be willing to put forth more than minimum effort."

The fact that management has provided for these physiological and safety needs has shifted the motivational emphasis to the social and perhaps to the egoistic needs. Unless there are opportunities at *work* to satisfy these higher-level needs, people will be deprived; and their behavior will reflect this deprivation. Under such conditions, if management continues to focus its attention on physiological needs, its efforts are bound to be ineffective.

People *will* make insistent demands for more money under these conditions. It becomes more important than ever to buy the material goods and services which can provide limited satisfaction of the thwarted needs. Although money has only limited value in satisfying many higher-level needs, it can become the focus of interest if it is the *only* means available.

The Carrot-and-Stick Approach. The carrot-and-stick theory of motivation (like Newtonian physical theory) works reasonably well under certain circumstances. The *means* for satisfying man's physiological and (within limits) his safety needs can be provided or withheld by management. Employment itself is such a means, and so are wages, working conditions, and benefits. By these means the individual can be controlled so long as he is struggling for subsistence.

But the carrot-and-stick theory does not work at all once man has reached an adequate subsistence level and is motivated primarily by higher needs. Management cannot provide a man with self-respect, or with the respect of his fellows, or with the satisfaction of needs for self-fulfillment. It can create such conditions that he is encouraged and enabled to seek such satisfactions for *himself*, or it can thwart him by failing to create those conditions.

But this creation of conditions is not "control." It is not a good device for directing behavior. And so management finds itself in an odd position. The high standard of living created by our modern technological know-how provides quite adequately for the satisfaction of physiological and safety needs. But by making possible the satisfaction of low-level needs, management has deprived itself of the ability to use as motivators the devices on which conventional theory has taught it to rely—rewards, promises, incentives, or threats and other coercive devices.

The philosophy of management by direction and control is essentially useless in motivating people whose important needs are social and egoistic. Both the hard and soft approach fail today because they are simply irrelevant to the situation.

People, deprived of opportunities to satisfy at work the needs which are now important to them, behave exactly as we might predict—with indolence, passivity, resistance to change, lack of responsibility, willingness to follow the demagogue, unreasonable demands for economic benefits. It would seem that we are caught in a web of our own weaving.

A New Theory of Management

For these and many other reasons, we require a different theory of the task of managing people based on more adequate assumptions about human nature and human motivation. Call it "Theory Y," if you will.

1. Management is responsible for organizing the elements of productive enterprise—

money, materials, equipment, people—in the interest of economic ends.

2. People are *not* by nature passive or resistant to organizational needs. They have become so as a result of experience in organizations.

3. The motivation, the potential for development, the capacity for assuming responsibility, the readiness to direct behavior toward organizational goals are all present in people. Management does not put them there. It is a responsibility of management to make it possible for people to recognize and develop these human characteristics for themselves.

4. The essential task of management is to arrange organizational conditions and methods of operation so that people can achieve their own goals *best* by directing *their own* efforts toward organizational objectives.

This is a process primarily of creating opportunities, releasing potential, removing obstacles, encouraging growth, providing guidance. It is what Peter Drucker has called "management by objectives" in contrast to "management by control." It does *not* involve the abdication of management, the absence of leadership, the lowering of standards, or the other characteristics usually associated with the "soft" approach under Theory X.

Difficulties in Applying Theory Y

People today are accustomed to being directed, manipulated, controlled in organizations and to finding satisfaction for their social, egoistic, and self-fulfillment needs away from the job. This is true of much of management as well as of workers.

Another way of saying this is that Theory X places exclusive reliance upon external control of human behavior, while Theory Y relies heavily on self-control and self-direction. It is worth noting that this difference is the difference between treating people as children and treating them as mature adults. After generations of the former, we cannot expect to shift to the latter overnight.

Steps in the Right Direction

Decentralization and Delegation. These are ways of freeing people from the too-close control of conventional organization, giving them a degree of freedom to direct their own activities, to assume responsibility, and, importantly, to satisfy their egoistic needs.

Participation and Consultative Management. Under proper conditions, participation and consultative management provide encouragement to people to direct their creative energies toward organizational objectives, give them some voice in decisions that affect them, provide significant opportunities for the satisfaction of social and egoistic needs.

Performance Appraisal. Even a cursory examination of conventional programs of performance appraisal within the ranks of management will reveal how completely consistent they are with Theory X. In fact, most such programs tend to treat the individual as though he were a product under inspection on the assembly line.

A few hospitals have been experimenting with approaches which involve the individual in setting "targets" or objectives *for himself* and in a *self*-evaluation of performance semiannually or annually. Of course, the superior plays an important leadership role in this process—one, in fact, which demands substantially more competence than the conventional approach. The role is, however, considerably more congenial to many managers than the role of "judge" or "inspector" which is usually forced upon them. Above all, the individual is encouraged to take a greater responsibility for planning and appraising his own contribution to organizational objectives; and the accompanying effects on egoistic and self-fulfillment needs are substantial.

Applying the Ideas

The not infrequent failure of such ideas as these to work as well as expected is often attributable to the fact that a management has "bought the idea" but applied it within the framework of Theory X and its assumptions.

Delegation is not an effective way of exercising management by control. Participation becomes a farce when it is applied as a gimmick or a device for kidding people into thinking they are important. Only the management that has confidence in human capacities and is itself directed toward organizational objectives rather than toward the preservation of personal power can grasp the implications of this emerging theory. Such managment will find and apply successfully other innovative ideas as we move slowly toward the full implementation of a theory like Y.

Herzberg's Theory

The usual personnel practices used to instill motivation are

1. reducing time spent at work
2. spiraling wages
3. fringe benefits
4. human relations training
5. sensitivity training
6. communications
7. two-way communication
8. job participation
9. employee counseling

However, as Frederick Herzberg (*The Motivation to Work,* Wiley) points out, the factors involved in producing job satisfaction (and motivation) may be quite different from the factors that lead to job dissatisfaction.

Herzberg first categorized specific job aspects into major job factors. Reporting on various studies totaling several thousand employees in nonhospital occupations, he found the job factors, in order of importance to the employees, to be

1. security
2. opportunity for advancement
3. company and management
4. wages
5. intrinsic aspects of job
6. supervision
7. social aspects of job
8. communication
9. working conditions
10. benefits

However a different perspective was provided when he then sought to isolate those factors that caused job satisfaction from those that caused job dissatisfaction.

Motivating Managers*

An organizational environment or atmosphere must be created that motivates the manager by optimizing opportunities to be him- or herself, to exercise his or her skills and talents, and to experience success. This calls for administration to make progress toward such ideals as these:

- *Self-determination* as an operating principle that gives strength to the total organization as it gives strength to its individual members. The intent is not to demolish the hierarchies of responsibility and accountability that are essential in any human institution; rather it is to strike a proper balance between higher authority and individual freedom, between hierarchical action and unjustifiable interference, so that the individual manager has sufficient control over his or her own destiny as a contributor to organizational outcomes.

- *Nonconformity* that purposefully avoids the kind of unity that can rapidly replace the elements of conflict and difference that are so essential to any growing institution.

- *Interdependency* that can take us a long way toward curing the ills of the traditional hospital structure—interdepartmental rivalries, inadequate coordination, and the impulse to become consumed with operational problems and concerns at a parochial level.

- *Open communication* that accepts all essential information, makes available frequent and informal communication among organizational members at all levels, and provides the ''sensing devices'' needed to determine and appraise operational problems and progress.

- *Flexibility* evolving out of an enchantment with change based on the desire not only for

---

Source: Reprinted by permission from *Hospitals*, vol. 51, no. 6, March 16, 1977. Copyright 1977, American Hospital Association.

different programs and processes, but, more significantly, for different results. This ideal departs from a perpetuation of stagnant organizational structures and arrangements and leads us to a search for a more stimulating atmosphere for people at work.

- A *humanistic environment* established with a concern about the quality of the manager's work life. Unless the human factors are carefully integrated and harmonized with the more measurable criteria of effectiveness, work itself, as an investment of the manager's own capacity, time, and effort, may yet well lose its meaning and value.

With respect to evaluative strategies and mechanisms, administration must give attention to the development of a framework for advancing and assessing organizational and managerial success, a framework that embraces such elements as these:

- A *goal achievement process* that requires departmental and individual objectives that are compatible with and contributory to overall hospital goals. Objectives should be concerned with what must be accomplished and should provide a good balance of "results expected."
- *Measurable standards and expectations* that give greater meaning to the established objectives and provide an effective way for discerning the degree to which functional purposes and individual objectives are being met.
- *Performance criteria* that are to be found in the documentation of departmental purposes and objectives, policies and procedures, and position descriptions.
- *Management information systems* that ensure the availability of information that is timely and fully presented so that the manager will know how he or she is doing and can make the kinds of decisions and take the kinds of action that will further his or her performance and results.
- A *performance review and appraisal process* that is future-oriented and moves the

manager into assuming more responsibility. Emphasis must be on performance and results and must take into account the developmental needs of the individual manager.

How *Not* To Motivate*

Incompetent workers are often made, not born. With a little effort, you can squelch enthusiastic workers' initiative and cut their efficiency in half.

You can actually demolish their common sense so that they will apply your instructions to obviously inappropriate situations. The quality of their work will decline while their errors increase. Then, when their confidence plummets, you can let them go.

You can even get their replacements to follow the same path. If any of your workers retain their capabilities, you can make sure that they find better jobs elsewhere or are promoted out of your department.

As a result, you will become busier and busier, buried under a burden of work, completing tasks that your subordinates should have completed and reinstructing them in procedures that they should have learned long ago.

How can you accomplish this unfortunate situation? How can you destroy your subordinates' confidence and watch it crumble? The answer lies in your attitude toward them and the way you treat them.

Sure-fire Techniques

1. *Be so vague about what you want your subordinates to do that they cannot pinpoint precisely what you want.* In other words, don't mention any specific cases or show any examples to which they can refer. Give your instructions matter-of-factly, as if you had no doubt that anyone of minimum intelligence would understand them. Give criticism in the same

---

*Source: "Sure-Fire Ways to Wreck Employee Competence," *Hospital Topics,* November-December, 1975. Reprinted with permission.

way so that they won't know what they can do to correct their performance.

2. *Give an audible sigh of resignation if they ask you to clarify something you have explained.* Imply that no one has ever asked you to clarify such simple instructions. Remember to avoid giving them any examples that would clear up the problem.

3. *If they ask the same questions more than once, point out that you have already answered those questions.* Sometimes you can do this even when a subordinate asks the question the first time—especially if his or her confidence has already been shaken. You may be able to convince the subordinate that his or her memory is failing—which should make him or her feel guilty for having unnecessarily taken up so much of your valuable time.

4. *Make an obvious effort to contain your impatience if the subordinate still doesn't understand what you mean.* This time, instruct him or her so slowly—in minute detail, with very simple words—that you underscore your low opinion of his or her intelligence. Continue to give the subordinate this kind of explanation and impression on other occasions—even when the subordinate insists that he or she understands.

5. *Be sure to criticize specific acts—even where the error is minor and would have been corrected in the normal course of events with no harm done.* You can, in fact, make a game out of trying to catch subordinates in "errors" of procedure. Monitor their work closely and point out minor details that they could have accomplished "better" some other way.

6. *Always give them step-by-step instructions, but leave out an explanation of the purpose or expected results.* This makes it impossible for them to claim that another procedure would better serve the purpose. Be specific enough to prevent them from exercising their initiative.

7. *Change your instructions from time to time as subordinates proceed with a proj-*

ect. It may help sometimes to deny having given the earlier instructions—particularly if the results do not seem to be turning out too well.

8. *If unforeseen problems arise from following your instructions, insist that the subordinates always return to you for the solution.* Don't let them solve the problem themselves, even if they claim they know how to do so. If they challenge this restriction, tell them that there are many details you cannot give them because of lack of time.

9. *Give subordinates deadlines that you know they cannot meet.* When they fail to meet them, as expected, you can blame it on their lack of efficiency.

10. *Improve on everything subordinates do.* Tell them that you do this only to make their work acceptable. Then if they start taking two or three times as long to complete tasks in a futile attempt to meet your "rigorous" standards, point again to their lack of efficiency. Or, if they give up and do each task carelessly, point out how slovenly they are.

Following these guidelines will ensure two things: (1) Your subordinates will be totally demoralized, and (2) you need not worry about being promoted to a position that you cannot fill.

Note: For further discussion on ways to keep staff satisfied and morale high, see Chapters 29 and 30.

JOB ENRICHMENT

Job Design: A Strategy for Improving Satisfaction*

After nurse managers have determined that their nursing program or organization climate is less than desirable, they must devise strategies to promote its potential well-being. Numerous

---

Source: Judith F. Garner, Howard L. Smith, and Neill F. Piland, *Strategic Nursing Management: Power and Responsibility in a New Era*, Aspen Publishers, Inc., © 1990.

strategies are available. Many concentrate on motivation and reward strategies. One strategy that has been recommended for improving the nursing program or organization climate is job design. It consists of three ingredients.

Job Enlargement. Nurses are assigned more tasks to improve the challenge of their job and to reduce boredom. For example, instead of just performing triage, a nurse may be delegated the responsibility of defining a treatment plan and schedule for patient follow-up. This instills variety in the task and relieves the boredom of repeating a single task.

Job Enrichment. Nurses are incorporated into decision-making processes of the nursing department and are assigned more meaningful tasks. By sharing decisions about the service delivery process, their work tasks acquire more meaning. They are no longer simply repeating tasks but are active in and appreciative of the complexity surrounding health care services. For example, a licensed practical nurse at a clinic may log in patients and then assign them to examination rooms. Under a job enrichment strategy, he or she might participate in determining which patients will be scheduled for return visits during the following week and which will be scheduled for another week because of an excessively busy schedule. The job includes more tasks that require decision-making discretion.

Job Rotation. Nurses periodically rotate in assignment in completing the various tasks that are included in a service. In this strategy, nurses come to know, appreciate, and complete all the tasks in a specific service. Variety prevents boredom. Additionally, there is greater flexibility because more nurses are capable of filling in at any specific point if illness or absenteeism occurs. Bottlenecks can be prevented. For example, a nurse executive in a consulting firm may be required to write proposals, to present the proposals to clients, to undertake the proposed analysis, to write up the analysis, to present the results to clients, and to undertake the follow-up. After rotating through each of these tasks, spending perhaps four months on each task or a combination of tasks, the nurse executive can fill in at any point in the process as necessary. Furthermore, by purposefully scheduling rotation it is unlikely that the nurse executive will be bored with any assignment.

The premise underlying job enlargement, job enrichment, and job rotation is that job variety and flexibility in assignments leads to fewer bored and more satisfied personnel. (See Figure 28-1.)

Establishing a Job Enrichment Program*

1. Get the support of subordinate supervisory personnel.
2. Train or acquire personnel with knowledge of job design and job enrichment theory to work as consultants.
3. Identify the jobs that need to be enriched by using questionnaires, opinion and attitude surveys, observation, and the reports of supervisors.
4. Define specifically what supervisors are responsible for doing in the job enrichment program and spell out how they should do it.
5. Redesign the jobs selected for enrichment by
   a. performing job and work flow analysis
   b. selecting a group of people who represent instructors and training-support personnel to generate ideas for enriching the job
   c. brainstorming the job
   d. screening and selecting ideas for implementation on a trial basis.
6. Redesign the job and implement the changes on a time-phased basis.
7. Establish a means of interchanging ideas and experiences.
8. Evaluate results based on feedback and analysis and redesign the job as needed.

*Source: K.S. Bagadia and M.M. Baker, "An Update on Job Enrichment," *Industrial Management*, May-June 1977. Reprinted with permission.

Figure 28-1 Variables Contributing to Satisfaction and Affecting Retention. Successful efforts recognize the interaction of numerous variables, such as those portrayed here.

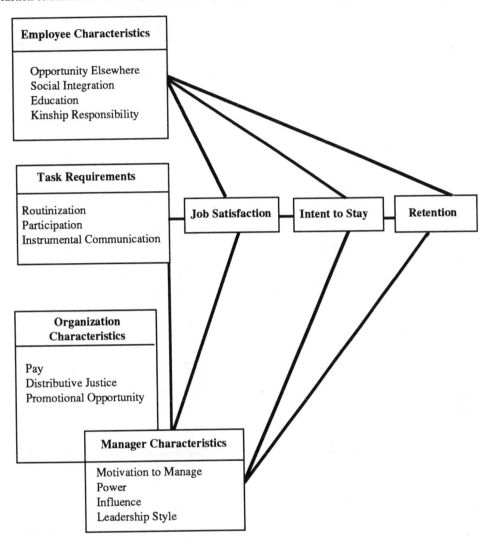

Source: Reprinted from "Manager Impact on Retention of Hospital Staff: Part 1" by R.L. Taunton, S.D. Krampetz, and C.Q. Woods, *Journal of Nursing Administration,* vol. 19, no. 3, p. 15, with permission of J.B. Lippincott Company, © March 1989.

Chapter 29

Absenteeism and Turnover

How do administrators go about the job of combatting the drain on manpower caused by excessive turnover and absenteeism? Those administrators who have been most successful in meeting these problems preplan their work and allow for absences. They keep accurate and complete records of attendance. They provide for exit interviews and analyze separations to find the real reasons for discharges, voluntary quits, and absences from the job. They carefully select new workers; make use of training, safety, and health programs; and cooperate with community agencies to provide child-care, shopping, banking, transportation, and recreational facilities. They make careful analyses and evaluations of the facts and take steps to identify and relieve or eliminate the causes of employee dissatisfaction because they are aware that management cannot afford to ignore either excessive rates of turnover or unrealistic reasons for absenteeism or lateness.

Excessive turnover and absenteeism are expensive to both employers and workers in terms of money, morale, and wasted manpower. Some turnover and absenteeism must be expected, but excessive rates can be reduced by sound personnel policies in which management and labor work closely together.

RELATIONSHIP BETWEEN ABSENTEEISM AND TURNOVER*

Absenteeism and turnover are generally seen as forms of employee alienation or withdrawal from an organization. The nature of the relationship between absenteeism and turnover consists of three parts. In the first case, absenteeism is a form of withdrawal behavior that represents an alternative to turnover. Here the employee does not desire termination nor does he believe his employer will terminate him for his behavior. Some condition related either to the job or to the employee personally seems to justify the absence and restores the individual or the employment relationship to equilibrium. The second position identifies a continuum of withdrawal, with absenteeism preceding turnover. The individual's decision to absent himself from his job is just a miniature version of the more important decision he makes when he quits his job. In the third case, there is no consistent relationship

---

Source: Donald L. Hawk, "Absenteeism and Turnover," *Personnel Journal*, June 1976. Reprinted with the permission of *Personnel Journal*, Costa Mesa, California; all rights reserved.

between absenteeism and turnover. An individual's decision to terminate will depend upon (1) the relative importance of a particular job to other factors in the individual's life, or (2) his perception of alternative employment opportunities which are superior to his current job.

Factors in Absenteeism

- *Demographic factors*. Female workers have a higher absolute absenteeism rate and it is rising faster than that of males. Age is inversely related to absenteeism while the highest rates are in the 18–25 year old age group and the lowest in the 40–65 group. Both unmarried males and females have a lower absenteeism rate than the married group.
- *Personal life*. Traumatic experiences or abnormal pressure levels in one's personal life can result in higher absenteeism rates as the individual takes the time required to restore some semblance of psychological equilibrium.
- *Need state*. If an individual is obtaining most or all of his need satisfaction off the job, he will subordinate both his job and the time spent on it to his outside projects.
- *Organization policy*. Salary continuance or sick pay plans may contribute to absenteeism in two ways. First, if an employee feels his peers are contributing less to the organization than he is, the existence of a liberal sick pay program will help that employee make up his mind to stay home. Although a sick leave policy does not necessarily encourage absenteeism, it does seem to authorize it. Second, in a case where the sick pay program provides no payment for the first two or three days of absence, an employee is enticed to remain off the job until he becomes eligible for sick pay for his total absence.
- *Work planning and scheduling*. The natural work cycle, which creates substantial differences in an employee's workload, may result in absenteeism immediately following the peak level. Employees feel that

this absenteeism is justified because it represents a return to equilibrium, that is, the job requires intensive work during a period of time and thus the employee rests to return to normal prior to the next peak.

Factors in Turnover

- *General economic conditions*. Historically studies have shown that turnover follows directly (with practically no lag time) the peaks and troughs of the general economy.
- *Local labor market conditions*. The concept of a local larbor market refers not only to a limited geographic area but also to the supply-demand ratio for a particular occupation or profession.
- *Personal mobility*. In addition, the individual's own skill or background will greatly influence his mobility and thus be a potential cause of attrition.
- *Job security*. The number of involuntary transfers and terminations in a department directly affect an individual's perception of job security and impact on his feelings about the fairness or equity of policy. If he perceives the work environment to be volatile, that is, unstable or unpredictable, then his tenure may well be affected.
- *Demographic factors*. Females have a much higher turnover rate than males. Married males and middle aged married females have the longest average tenure while unmarried young females have the shortest tenure.

Factors in Absenteeism Leading to Turnover

The level of job dissatisfaction will directly influence both the rate of absenteeism and turnover.

- *Supervisory style*. Supervisory style can affect job satisfaction in several ways. First when work planning and scheduling is perceived as arbitrary and/or inefficient, employees react to the "punishing" supervisory incompetence by withdrawing. Second, role ambiguity created by unclear performance expectations can cause high levels of psychological stress. Third, the lack of feedback on performance and the perceived inequity of performance appraisal can often reduce job satisfaction.

- *Interpersonal relationships.* An organization structure which creates and/or reinforces destructive competition, reduces team spirit, group pride, or group cohesiveness and causes job dissatisfaction.
- *Working conditions.* A working environment which is unsafe or interferes with efficient, productive work contributes to job dissatisfaction.
- *Salary.* There are two elements related to salary that can affect the individual's satisfaction level. The first of these and perhaps the most obvious is wage rate. If an individual's wage rate is substantially below that of the area average he will be dissatisfied. The second case and perhaps the more important is the intraorganization dimension of salaries, that of wage level. If there are substantial differentials in wage levels, employees may perceive the wage structure to be arbitrary and inequitable when compared to the work required.
- *Job expectations.* From interviews, orientation training, and perhaps job descriptions, individuals develop preconceptions of what a job will be like. If an individual's job expectations are a great deal different from what he finds his job is really like, he is apt to be dissatisfied with his decision to join the company.
- *Job fit.* When through selection, placement, and/or promotional practice, an individual's capabilities are systematically underutilized and/or there is no career path available to him, he becomes dissatisfied. The contrary is also true. Should the job require more ability than the individual has, the individual will feel incompetent and be dissatisfied.
- *Job design.* Jobs with low motivating potential (i.e., low skill variety, low task identity, low task significance, little autonomy, and little or no feedback from the job itself) produce employee dissatisfaction.

Developing an Absenteeism/Turnover Reduction Strategy

After discovery of an absenteeism or turnover problem most organizations react one of three ways:

1. They develop an elaborate "control" program.
2. They adopt a current fad.
3. They implement a program that worked well for some other organization.

Since the causes or the circumstances surrounding absenteeism or turnover problems are not necessarily the same, these programs inevitably have less than the desired effect or fail outright.

It is for this reason that careful diagnosis of management's absenteeism/turnover position must precede the formulation of any plans to deal with the problem. The first step in this diagnosis should be a detailed analysis of both absenteeism and turnover data.

Next, the costs of the problem should be identified. If the cost is significant enough to merit an investment in change, the next step is to identify which of the major variables listed are contributing most to the absenteeism/turnover problem.

In determining which are the most significant causal variables, valuable information can be obtained from

1. a review of exit interview data, especially where similar reasons for termination occur frequently
2. an analysis of current performance problems (e.g., substandard work output)
3. the administration and analysis of an appropriate attitude survey

Implementation of the most appropriate and direct solution will then provide the best return (i.e., maximum results for minimum investment).

ABSENTEEISM

Rate and Cause*

The rate of unscheduled absenteeism reported for hospitals in one extensive survey was an average of 2.8 days per year per employee for small hospitals and 3.9 days per year per employee for large hospitals. The average for all hospitals was 3.2. Almost 40 percent of hospitals indicated their rate as less than 1 day per employee. On the other end of the scale, 2 percent of hospitals reported a rate of 12 or more days of unscheduled absences per year per employee. Illness was clearly the most frequent cause of absence listed by all hospitals, regardless of size or geographic region. Other causes, in order of importance, were family health, other problems, and injuries.

Control Methods*

Supervisors must assume the bulk of responsibility for reducing absenteeism. Often supervisors are aware that certain employees are chronic absentees, but the personnel department must make sure that supervisors have adequate training in handling problems of this kind. (See Figure 29-1.) The personnel department should provide the supervisor with statistical information reflecting absenteeism patterns in this department.

The one-day absence, the worker's "inalienable right" to use up allotted sick days one by one, is the scourge of an efficient nursing service. Supervisors who reason with staff members about the department budget problems caused by recurrent absences offer them scant cause for changing their habits.

Conversations with habitual offenders in which the supervisor warns of an inverse relationship between absences and advancement are considered too heavy-handed. Appeals to team loyalty, and some nasty comments from those forced to work harder that day, may have some

___

*Source: NIOSH *Hospital Occupational Health Services Study*, U.S. [Survey of 5,298 Hospitals] Pub. No. (NIOSH 75-154), 1972

impact. But most effective, many supervisors have found, is the careful recording of absences and the documentation of absence patterns. In this way personnel know that supervisors know what's going on.

Many hospital administrators handle these short-term absences in a more systematic fashion, using select rewards, penalties, and surveillance devices. The following control methods are used.

Bonus for Health. Employees receive full pay for any of the allotted sick days they don't take. Another method gives one day's pay for accruing x amount of sick days.

Checkup and Surveillance. This method takes the one-day sickness excuse at face value and sends the returned absentee down to the employee health clinic to explain the causes (symptoms?) to the doctor. A more concerned attitude is seemingly displayed in a variation of this method where a nurse hired for this purpose actually visits the absentee worker's home to find out how the worker feels or if medical help is needed. This solicitude fools no one, nor is it meant to. In one hospital, substantial reductions in sick leave time have been achieved since the method was instituted.

Penalties. Many hospitals deduct the first day of illness but some use a system of make-up work. For example, absences unaccompanied by doctor's notes on scheduled weekends must be made up by work on the employee's next off-weekend.

TURNOVER

A certain degree of attrition is healthy, especially when it leads to refinement of practices. If there were no terminations, there would be no room for new and fresh ideas. However, leaders of nursing service must be aware of the costs of turnover to the hospital, the department, and clinical units. In addition, although non-quantifiable, the resulting effect on patient care should also be taken into consideration.

In metropolitan areas, where job change is easier due to proximity and number of choices,

Figure 29-1 An Absenteeism Control Program for Chronic Abusers

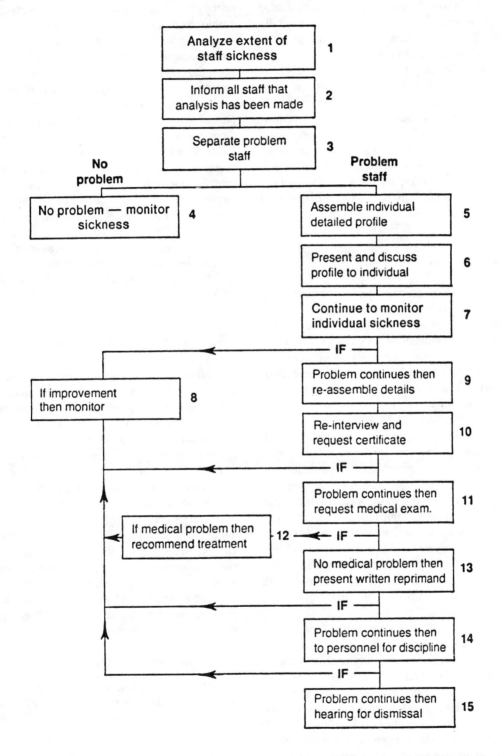

Source: Romeo Circone, "Controlling Sick Leave Abuse," *Dimensions in Health Service,* Journal of the Canadian Hospital Association, April 1978. Reprinted with permission.

the turnover rate sometimes reaches 150 to 200 percent. It would seem that many nurses change jobs, hoping to find a difference, but generally find the new position quite like the previous one—and quite as frustrating.

An HEW study ("The Geographic Distribution of Nurses," 1973) found that the mean number of workdays a new, inexperienced RN spent on the job before assuming full responsibilities was 39.1, or about eight workweeks.

Therefore, if your hospital's turnover rate is, let us say, 70 percent, the average position is filled each 68 weeks, and the new inexperienced employee is not fully productive 12 percent of her average tenure.

Factors in Nurse Turnover

In order to assess the nature and extent of the turnover problem among nurses at Johns Hopkins Hospital, the nursing administration at the hospital initiated a program of voluntary, unstructured "exit interviews" with resigning nurses (excluding dismissals and retirements). Interviews were conducted by the "Employee Relations Nurse."

Data obtained from the interviews provide evidence of the role of organizational factors in determining turnover. Of the reported reasons for resigning, 42 percent had to do with dissatisfaction with working conditions (e.g., scheduling, workload, extent of support staff, method of patient assignment, nurse-physician relations, supervision, and opportunities for advancement), 26 percent had to do with career mobility (especially taking another position with better salary or hours), and 32 percent had to do with personal circumstances (e.g., family relocation, marriage).

Analysis of factors such as the above which have a direct impact on turnover has resulted in a distinction between voluntary and involuntary turnover. Turnover is considered voluntary when the nurse has control over leaving a position, involuntary when departure is for reasons beyond his or her control.

Much explorative research has concentrated on voluntary turnover and various work environment factors which can be associated with reten-

tion of personnel. Generally, economists focus on the salary benefits provided as well as existing employment opportunities. Sociologists and social psychologists enumerate such factors as the authority structure (centralization of power), access to job-related information, level of professionalism, staff integration (friendships), work routinization, justice (where merit receives positive sanctions such as pay, recognition, or other rewards), and an array of factors tucked under the umbrella of job satisfaction.

Among the prime causes of turnover found in recent research were length of service, job satisfaction, level of professionalism, integration, age, pay, distributive justice, routinization, and the amount of hours worked. In an era of nursing shortages, more personal and professional reasons for resignation and turnover are delineated in data on current studies (see Figures 29-2 and 29-3).

Factors in Management Turnover*

Professional employees generally know or believe that they can change employment easier than others, so they are less likely to tolerate what they see as unsatisfactory conditions and less likely to balk at stepping out into the unknown territory represented by a job change.

The manager must come to recognize that the same kinds of needs that first brought the worker into the profession—the need to achieve, to do interesting work, to be challenged, to do something of value, and such—are often the same kinds of needs that stimulate the professional to change organizations. This claim of the impact of professionals' psychological needs on turnover can be supported by a simple examination of the reasons why higher-level employees quit their jobs for new employment.

Why Valued Employees Quit

A brief report appearing in the monthly news publication of the American Society for Personnel Administration (ASPA) discussed turnover

---

Source: Charles R. McConnell, *Managing the Health Care Professional*, Aspen Publishers, Inc., © 1984.

Figure 29-2 Reasons for Nurse Resignations.

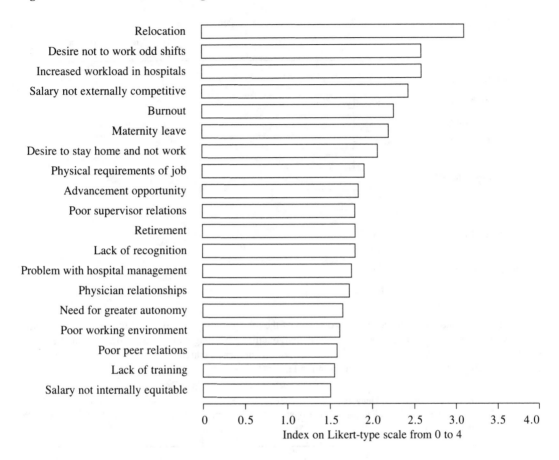

Note: *These reasons were offered in more than 14,000 exit interviews over a 4-year period in 7 southeastern states.* In analyzing the exit interviews with RNs, this study noted how often each reason for resigning was given and scored them all on a scale of 0, ("never") to 4, ("always").

Source: Reprinted from "Hay Study Ties Shortage to Ancillary Cutbacks; Finds Quality of Care 'Directly Threatened'," *American Journal of Nursing*, vol. 88, no. 9, September 1988. Copyright © by the American Journal of Nursing Company. Used with permission. All rights reserved.

under the title of "Eight Reasons Why Good Employees Leave Jobs." According to the report the reasons why top-level people leave jobs are, in order of importance, the following:

1. Lack of Job Satisfaction. This was given as the most common reason for people leaving supposedly good jobs. Indeed it has been established time and again that employees who are unhappy because they do not feel useful or valued, who are generally dissatisfied with what they are doing, are likely to seek employment changes that appear to offer greater job satisfaction.

2. Lack of Challenge. An organization's best potential producers are usually those people who need to have the limits of their knowledge and skill tested regularly. An organization that does not utilize the full talents of its employees, and does not listen to these employees and take their suggestions seriously, tends to lose precisely those employees whom it should be most interested in retaining.

Figure 29-3 Factors Contributing to Nursing Turnover.

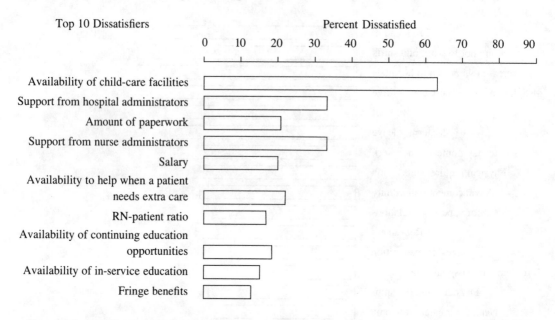

Top 10 Dissatisfiers ... Percent Dissatisfied

Note: Lack of child-care facilities is the worst part of the job agree nurses who will leave and those who will stay. On nearly every item, more leavers are dissatisfied, but high percentages of stayers also are dissatisfied. Are the dissatisfied stayers the nurses who skip from one job to another in search of better conditions? Or are they trapped and disgruntled? Will they one day join the leavers?

Source: Reprinted from Florence L. Huey and Susan Hartley, "What Keeps Nurses in Nursing: 3,500 Nurses Tell Their Stories," *American Journal of Nursing*, February 1988. Copyright © by the American Journal of Nursing Company. Used with permission. All rights reserved.

3. Dissatisfaction with Supervision. Uncommunicative or authoritarian supervision—or bossism—makes employees feel that they are not allowed to think for themselves. A style of management that demands blind obedience and prohibits active participation eventually drives away quality employees, precisely those employees whom the organization should most wish to keep.

4. Dissatisfaction with Organizational Image. An organization that develops an image as a loser, perhaps through shrinkage of its volume of business or its share of the market or the loss of vital or prestigious services, experiences continual difficulty retaining employees who are strongly growth-oriented. The professional who sees him- or herself as going places or making a name eventually seeks an organization that like-

wise appears to be on the rise (if not already there).

5. Incompatibility within the Work Group. This reason for leaving can surface at any time within any organization and at any level. It essentially involves personality clashes between and among persons who must work together on a regular basis. Although no worker is immune to possible incompatibility, the professional, with more interorganizational mobility, is more likely to seek active relief by changing jobs.

6. Inadequate Pay. An organization that does not remain competitive in regard to salaries and benefits stands to lose a number of its valued employees. The notion of equity in compensation is particularly important; what is important is not so much what a person may be paid in absolute amounts but rather what the person is paid relative to others. Money sometimes holds persons longer in the face of other dissatisfactions. However, if the pay is the only satisfactory condition of a person's employment, it never ensures contentment with employment.

7. *Lack of Confidence about Eventual Success in the Job.* Employees who may feel that they are in over their heads often tend to escape that feeling by quitting. The organization that fails to take active steps to develop its employees and demonstrate that it wants them to succeed eventually loses many potential long-term employees.

8. *Location of the Organization.* Some organizations—health care organizations among them—inevitably find it necessary to move the primary business to a new location. Though much more pertinent to nonhealth businesses in general, this can be a factor in employee resignations in any organization. Depending on the distance of the move—whether a few blocks, across town, or across the country—some employees may choose not to move with the organization.

Costs of Turnover*

Turnover is expensive to an institution because the costs of turnover include recruiting and selecting a replacement, socializing the replacement with regard to hospital norms, overpayment of the replacement during the period of learning when he or she cannot produce at full capacity, overtime work performed by others during the period between the turnover and the replacement's achievement of full capacity, and achieving social adjustment between the nursing unit and its new member.

That is why nursing administrators require up-to-date records of the turnover rate in order to estimate more accurately their total budget. It also allows them to identify areas of weakness as well as opportunities for cost reduction.

---

*Source: *Suggestions for Control of Turnover and Absenteeism,* U.S. Department of Labor, 1972.

Three distinct cost components are usually examined: recruitment, on-the-job training, and termination. By estimating the appropriate wage rate for the amount of time spent by hospital personnel in each of these phases of employment, nurse managers can determine hospital costs for nurse turnover.

Recruitment Costs

Interviewing. Time is spent by personnel staff in handling applications, holding preliminary interviews, and processing initial forms.

Physical Examination. Time is spent by medical personnel in conducting routine health examinations.

Clerical Staff. Time is spent completing records and payroll forms.

Orientation. Time is spent off regular job duties (nonoperational) by one or more staff members and the new employee, based proportionately on the wage rate for each person involved.

On-the-Job Training Costs

Time To Reach Proficiency. The complexity of duties and the difference in worker backgrounds vary the amount of time needed to reach proficiency. However, the supervisor should be able to provide an average time estimate.

Excess Wages Paid for Duties Performed. Until the new staff member learns the job requirements, he or she cannot be working at full capacity.

Estimated Costs of Supervision during Training. Wages of supervisors during instruction periods are based upon the amount of time spent in direct contact and the number of trainees involved during the training period.

Termination Costs

Payment of Wages. A departing employee is paid for nonproductive time, that is, salary is received through checkout and exit interview periods.

Exit Interview Expenses. Depending on how elaborate the hospital's system is, costs vary but are essentially based on salary time for the interviewee.

Clerical Staff. Again, time is spent for completion of records and payroll forms.

When all these factors are calculated to arrive at a turnover cost, expenses can be quite high, particularly for personnel in the nursing department.

Based on these cost components, a nursing department may have an average turnover cost of thousands of dollars, which multiplied by the total number of terminated personnel can add up to a substantial sum. Considering the high rates of turnover frequently reported by nursing departments, it would appear necessary for reasons of cost as well as efficiency to investigate methods of reducing staff turnover.

A Formula for Determining Turnover*

Hospitals may use the following formulas for compiling, computing, and recording turnover.

Separation Rate: The number of separations (includes all persons who left for any reason—resignation, dismissal, layoff) during the month is divided by the total number of workers on the payroll in the pay period ending nearest the 15th of the same month; the result is then multiplied by 100.

$$\frac{S \ (separations)}{E \ (employment)} \times 100 = T \ (separation \ rate)$$

Example:

$$\frac{20 \ separations}{100 \ employees} \times 100 = 20\% \ separation \ rate$$

Quit Rate: The number of quits or resignations during the month is divided by the total number of workers on the payroll in the pay period ending nearest the 15th of the same month; the result is then multiplied by 100.

$$\frac{Q \ (number \ of \ quits)}{E \ (employment)} \times 100 = R \ \begin{array}{c} (resignation \\ rate) \end{array}$$

Example:

$$\frac{10 \ resignations}{100 \ employees} \times 100 = 10\% \ \begin{array}{c} resignation \\ rate \end{array}$$

In addition, the American Hospital Association encourages hospitals to consider calculating the stability factor, which reflects the number of positions with no changes in staffing related to total authorized positions for a given month. This figure counteracts distortion caused by the turnover of one position several times. When one position turns over three times, this is reflected in the turnover rate, tending to make the staff appear unstable. (See Table 29-1 for a summary of different methods of calculating turnover rates.)

Vacancies and Turnover*

Vacancies can be related to several causes. Among the most obvious are insufficient supply of nurses for employment in an area; inadequate numbers of nurses qualified for certain types of positions, such as intensive care and coronary care; or institutional attributes that decrease the attractiveness of the hospital to potential nurse employees. When the rate of vacancies is high, strategies for recruitment should be based on an accurate assessment of the causes. See Table 29-2 for examples of causes and strategies.

Table 29-2 shows average vacancy and turnover ratios for RNs in community hospitals classified by bed size, control, and geographic region. Table 29-4 shows the average vacancy ratios for full- and part-time RNs by type of hospital unit among all responding community hospitals. Intensive and/or coronary care units had by far the highest vacancy ratios for both full- and part-time positions.

---

*Source: Suggestions for Control of Turnover and Absenteeism, U.S. Department of Labor, 1972.

---

*Source: Marjorie Beyers, Ross Mullner, Calvin S. Byre, and Suzanne Whitehead, ''Results of the Nursing Personnel Survey, Part 2: RN Vacancies and Turnover,'' *Journal of Nursing Administration,* May 1983. Reprinted with permission.

Table 29-1 Summary of Different Methods of Calculating Turnover Rates

Profile of a Nursing Department: At the beginning of the year, 290 nurses were employed. During the year, 100 nurses left and 120 nurses were hired. By the end of the year, 96 of the new nurses were still employed.

	Definition, by Method	Calculation	Rate
Accession rate	$\dfrac{\text{Number of new employees}}{\text{Average number of employees}}$	$120 \div \dfrac{290 + 310}{2}$	40.0%
Separation rate	$\dfrac{\text{Number of employees leaving}}{\text{Average number of employees}}$	$100 \div \dfrac{290 + 310}{2}$	33.3%
Stability rate	$\dfrac{\text{Number of beginning employees remaining}}{\text{Number of employees at beginning}}$	$\dfrac{190}{290}$	65.5%
Instability rate	$\dfrac{\text{Number of beginning employees leaving}}{\text{Number of employees at beginning}}$	$\dfrac{100}{290}$	34.5%
Survival rate	$\dfrac{\text{Number of new employees remaining}}{\text{Number of new employees}}$	$\dfrac{96}{120}$	80.0%
Wastage rate	$\dfrac{\text{Number of new employees leaving}}{\text{Number of new employees}}$	$\dfrac{24}{120}$	20.0%

Source: Paul B. Hoffman, "Accurate Measurement of Nursing Turnover: The First Step in Its Reduction," *Journal of Nursing Administration,* November-December 1981. Reprinted with permission.

Table 29-2 Vacancy Causes and Recruitment Strategies

Vacancy Cause	*Recruitment Strategy*
Insufficient supply of nurses	Develop liaisons with schools of nursing Develop unique opportunities for clinical experiences that will be attractive to schools of nursing
Insufficient number of nurses qualified for intensive or coronary care	Establish an exchange program for nurses with another hospital that has a quality program for intensive or coronary care Arrange an individualized study and clinical practice experience in a recognized hospital for selected staff nurses
Institution does not attract nurses	Assess the organizational structure, management practices, and public image of the hospital; change the structure, improve management practices, and make the changes visible so that the public knows that the hospital has a new image. Assess the community to locate potential nurse employees; determine how the hospital can become competitive in employment

Table 29-3 RN Vacancy and Turnover Rate by Hospital Type

	Full-time		Part-time	
Hospital Classification	Vacancy Ratio	Turnover Ratio	Vacancy Ratio	Turnover Ratio
Bed size				
6–99 beds	23.7%	3.4%	18.8%	8.8%
100–299 beds	16.5	8.6	16.1	8.3
300 + beds	13.3	9.6	18.0	16.1
Control				
Nongovernment, not-for-profit	14.7	7.4	16.7	11.3
State and local government	20.5	7.8	17.7	8.9
Investor-owned	18.4	11.2	20.7	14.9
Geographic region				
Northeast	9.3	6.9	9.0	14.7
South	20.6	9.6	25.8	13.8
North Central	15.5	5.9	15.2	7.3
West	17.9	9.6	11.9	10.4

Reducing Turnover

Computerized accounting systems can develop turnover data into useful management tools by correlating them with personnel and job characteristics. Detailed data collection can result in recommendations for hiring and allocation of personnel.

A number of techniques have been adapted to reduce turnover. The "exit interview" can provide significant assistance in determining which

Table 29-4 RN Vacancy Rate by Hospital Unit

	Average Vacancy Ratio	
Type of Unit	Full-time	Part-time
Intensive and/or coronary care units	22.1%	24.7%
All other inpatient bed units	15.5	16.4
All other inpatient areas	8.0	7.3
All outpatient areas	07.3	
All outpatient areas	8.4	5.1

approach might be best for the specific department.

1. The Exit Interview*

The exit interview can be a valuable source of information concerning reasons for labor turnover. A few factors contributing to turnover, for example, death or retirement, are not controllable. However, numerous factors which give workers cause for leaving an organization are controllable, and a carefully conducted exit interview will help bring these to light. The exit interview is not intended to absolve the supervisor of the responsibility to maintain conditions that keep turnover low. It is intended to provide additional assistance after the supervisor has done his or her utmost toward retaining a desirable worker.

Exit interviews offer opportunities to

- determine the real reasons employees wish to resign
- retain competent employees by exploring the causes of the dissatisfaction and trying

*Source: Suggestions for Control of Turnover and Absenteeism, U.S. Department of Labor, 1972.

to find a solution for their grievances or problems

- clarify complaints against employees who are separated involuntarily
- promote good relations with employees who separate voluntarily or involuntarily
- obtain reliable data on problem areas which will enable management to set up corrective measures

A person of mature and sympathetic outlook should be selected to conduct the interview. A friendly atmosphere is important. The interviewer's purpose is to get information, not to argue with the employee over his or her reasons for leaving. With understanding and tact, valuable information concerning causes of separation may be obtained. Even though the employee leaves, he or she may leave with friendly feelings and a better understanding of the hospital and with the assurance that the exit interview will not be detrimental to getting a good reference.

In order to offset the reluctance of an employee who has not given frank and candid statements during the exit interview, a questionnaire may be sent to the employee 30 to 60 days after termination. (It should be accompanied by an explanatory letter and a self-addressed, stamped envelope.) The questionnaire should contain questions concerning the employee's feelings about the hospital, and his or her job and supervisor.

If the employee has become established in a new job, he or she may feel freer to give candid, objective answers. These answers can be checked against information given in the exit interview and discrepancies noted. These additional comments can supplement the information gathered in the exit interview. Analysis of information gathered in this manner over a period of time will pinpoint areas in which corrective action may be taken.

Exit interviews should be held in a private office where the employee will feel at ease and may speak without fear of being overheard. Where this situation is impossible, conditions of maximum privacy should be arranged. Interviews with employees, for the most part, follow a general pattern by progressing through the following stages.

Informal Conversation of General Interest. Every effort should be made to establish rapport with the worker. An atmosphere of "quizzing" will elicit little useful information. A chat about something of general interest can be steered around to the principal reason for the interview in a pleasant and informal manner.

The Employee's Own Statement. The employee should be given every opportunity to tell why he or she wishes to resign, if that is the reason for the interview. Interrupting the employee to influence his or her statements should be avoided. Attention to all remarks is important for subsequently directing the interview to an effective conclusion.

Questioning by the Interviewer. When the employee finishes his or her statement, the interviewer should ask appropriate questions in an attempt to determine, in the case of an employee who plans to resign, the true reasons for the dissatisfaction—the employee's attitudes, feelings, and motivations. The interviewer should do the following:

- Ask for specific information about the situation described and evaluate it in view of statements made by the supervisor.
- Ask the employee if he or she has (1) explored the possibility of taking training to obtain greater satisfaction in his or her present position or to prepare him- or herself for promotion or (2) explored the possibility of transfer to another unit in the nursing department.
- Suggest ways in which the present situation might be improved to the worker's satisfaction, or state what arrangements might be made to transfer him or her to another job, paying careful attention to the employee's reaction to all suggestions.
- Attempt to restate in specific terms the problems the employee may encounter in leaving the organization and encourage him or her to try to adjust to the present situation

with whatever changes or improvements are suggested. Sometimes, stimulating interest in the importance of the employee's job to the completed product or services of the company or pointing out the loss in seniority that will result from his or her separation will be effective in retaining the worker.

Final stage of informal conversation. Closing stages of the interview are important to ensure a mutual understanding of any arrangements agreed upon and to plan for any follow-up required. The interview should close on a friendly basis, even if the employee persists in the decision to leave. The employee should be made to feel that he or she will be given every consideration if he or she cares to return.

Since so many eventualities are considered in an outline for an exit interview, the process may appear rather complicated and time consuming. An experienced interviewer can usually conduct a satisfactory interview in from 15 to 30 minutes.

2. Rewards*

In one investigation the influence of specific safety, social, and psychological rewards and incentives on the rate of nursing staff turnover was studied. Results indicated that 59 percent of the RN's who left their staff positions could have been influenced to stay on the job by rewards and incentives—of which 34 percent could have been easily held on the job. The remaining 41 percent could not have been influenced to stay on the job. The categories of rewards were specified as follows.

Safety Rewards, and Incentives. Salary, vacation time, sick leave, weekends off, opportunity for part-time work, hours per day, insurance, and retirement programs.

Social Rewards and Incentives. Maternity leave; child-care facilities; a different supervisor; a different head nurse; social contact with coworkers, nursing superiors, and doctors; and opportunities to share opinions and feelings with other registered nurses and doctors.

Psychological Rewards and Incentives. Educational opportunities, job responsibility, recognition of work, help from peers and superiors, career advancement, and participation in research.

The data revealed that psychological rewards were perceived as more important than safety or social rewards. The unanimous choice of psychological rewards over safety and social rewards strongly indicates that nurses left jobs for lack of internal rewards. More specifically, that while external rewards may draw a person to a job, internal rewards keep the person there.

Higher pay did not retain nurses, nor were they influenced by a specialty area. Most nurses wanted opportunities to attend educational programs, to continue course work for credit, to seek career advancement, and to have their work recognized by peers and supervisors.

3. An Ombudsman*

Before creating this innovative program, the yearly attrition rate at Beth Israel Hospital in New York was 37 percent or more. A few years later it had dropped to 14.5 percent.

A position was created for a nurse recruitment and retention coordinator who really functions as an ombudsman for the professional staff.

The coordinator is expected to emphasize helpfulness and empathy and encourage staff members to seek solutions to problems rather than to seek other employment.

Interviews are scheduled at three months, six months, one year after employment, and yearly thereafter. They provide nurses with an opportunity to express themselves freely and offer

Source: Methods 2, 4 and 5 are excerpted from Joanne McCloskey, "Influence of Rewards and Incentives on Staff Nurse Turnover," *Nursing Research*, May-June 1974, © American Journal of Nursing Company. Reprinted with permission.

Source: Regina Bloch, "The Nurse Ombudsman," *American Journal of Nursing*, October 1976, © American Journal of Nursing Company. Adapted with permission.

them a release from problems which might otherwise be suppressed.

A great deal of counseling takes place during the interview. Personal problems may involve baby sitting, housing, or finances; occupational problems may relate to a change of assignment, interpersonal relations, or simply a clarification of policy.

Reports in writing are sent to the director of nursing. Urgent problems are reported verbally. Frequently, a problem brought to the ombudsman can be resolved then and there merely by bringing it into the open and talking it out. At other times the director of nursing may feel that intervention is necessary and ask an associate director to investigate or to resolve a complaint. But all complaints are studied to identify any pattern of repetitive problems. All complaints are categorized under major headings, such as orientation, administration, policies, staffing, promotions, and the like. Under these major headings, statements by staff are listed anonymously. When a problem has been resolved, the manner of resolution also is entered into the record.

Twice a year the problem list is reviewed, and changes are made in the light of it.

4. A More Intellectual Atmosphere

Nursing service administrators might try to provide a more intellectual atmosphere for nurses to hold staff nurses on the job by providing in-service education programs which allow nurses to actively participate, providing time off and tuition waivers to nurses who wish to continue their education, and hiring a nurse research coordinator to plan and participate with staff nurses for nursing research on their units.

5. Career Advancement

Changes might be made in the traditional career advancement pattern of staff nurse to team leader to head nurse to supervisor to a pattern related more to levels of practice such as staff nurse to clinician to clinical specialist. Nursing administrators might provide a more positive working atmosphere to help maintain the staff nurse's self-esteem by emphasizing team nurs-

ing or instituting primary nursing care; allowing nurses to have more decision-making power, especially in primary care; insisting upon problem-oriented charting for nurses; and training supervisors and head nurses in leadership skills.

6. Using the Nurse Recruiter*

One emerging response to the need to understand and control nursing turnover is the expanding role of the nurse recruiter. Nurse recruiters are in an ideal position to monitor the flow of nursing personnel into and out of the system, to compute turnover and vacancy rates, and to map resignations by location within the hospital. Furthermore, nurse recruiters frequently conduct employment interviews with newly hired nurses and exit interviews or follow-up interviews with resigning nurses. These activities provide important information about nurses' expectations for their jobs and their assessments of their work experiences within the hospital.

Other Recommendations for Reducing Turnover**

7. Allow Voluntary Transfers between Nursing Units

Because of the staffing needs of the hospital when they are hired, nurses with specialized training often are assigned to units where they have little or no opportunity to make use of their special skills and knowledge. Still other nurses develop special interests, expanded by extra education of various types, that are underutilized by the hospitals. Transfers between nursing units would permit better use of these special skills and knowledge, and both nurses and patients should benefit. Some of the complaints about

---

Source: Carol Weisman, "Recruit from Within," *Journal of Nursing Administration*, May 1982. Reprinted with permission.

**Source*: James L. Price and Charles W. Mueller, "How To Reduce the Turnover of Hospital Nurses," *Handbook of Health Care Human Resources Management*, edited by Norman Metzger, Aspen Publishers, Inc., © 1981.

repetitive work seem to be the result of insufficient use of special skills and knowledge.

Such transfers must be voluntary, of course. If the nurses are not willing to transfer, such movement constitutes a punishment and decreases job satisfaction and commitment. It is necessary only to note the hostility to "pulling" among nurses—involuntary transfers for one shift—to appreciate the necessity of keeping the moves voluntary.

A policy of allowing transfers requires that vacancies throughout the nursing department be posted officially in some manner. Information transmitted informally is not always accurate and often is kept among a few close friends. Organizations therefore should depend primarily upon formal means to transmit information about vacancies.

8. Hold Regular and Brief Meetings of the Nursing Units during Working Hours

The frequency of the meetings naturally will vary for the different units, but once a week seems to be sufficient. The scheduling of the meetings should be arranged so that the maximum number of part-time nurses can attend, because these are the individuals for whom the sessions are especially important. Seldom should a session last longer than about 45 minutes.

A supervisor who meets regularly with the members of the unit will be constrained by the pressure of the group to share information and to allow greater participation in its operation. The meetings also provide an opportunity for supervisors to receive information from the staff nurses and for the latter to communicate among themselves. Upward and horizontal communication is as important as downward communication.

9. Promote Primarily from Within the Nursing Department

The present career structure allows for relatively few promotional opportunities for nurses; these limited openings should be reserved primarily for the current staff members. Implementation of such a policy naturally will require an official posting of vacancies for existing staff before outsiders are notified.

Hospitals cannot, of course, promote entirely from within. Situations sometimes arise when the existing staff does not possess the needed qualifications or when an outsider clearly has superior competence.

10. Create an Alternate Career Structure for Staff Nurses

The occupations in a career are ranked in terms of money, prestige, power, rights, and responsibilities. The career commonly available to most hospital nurses consists of the following sequence: staff nurse, unit supervisor, assistant nursing director, and nursing director. Most notable is the fact that this career mostly consists of administrative positions; only the lowest, that of staff nurse, is primarily professional.

For instance, there might be four levels in an alternate career ladder for staff nurses: staff nurse I through staff nurse IV. Each step should result in a significant increase in money, prestige, rights, and responsibilities. Without these increases, a genuine alternate career does not exist. Administrative rights and responsibilities probably will increase somewhat as a nurse progresses through the sequence of levels.

11. Hire More Local Nurses Who Are Married and Who Have Children

Local nurses are likely to have parents and siblings living in the area who constitute a constraint not to leave the hospital. Marriage and children create relatives that further constrain turnover. In addition to this kinship responsibility, local nurses are likely to have close friends working in the hospital. These generally will be the result of long residence in the community and may constrain turnover slightly.

Aggressive recruiting will be necessary to locate local nurses who are married and who have children. Many of these nurses will have left the labor force and will not respond to the typical newspaper advertisement. The existing staff generally will be aware of many of these nurses in the community and can serve as a valuable aid in recruiting.

Since many local nurses will have left the labor force, they usually will require special training before they can start working again. Public schools in the area, such as community colleges, should provide regular nurse refresher courses, since the benefits of such training will accrue to no single work organization.

The hospitals may have to provide extra flexibility in working hours to accommodate these nurses. There is nothing sacred, for example, about three eight-hour shifts. This extra training and flexible scheduling will be costly for the hospital, but will be less than the considerable benefits received by the lower turnover of these nurses.

12. Hire More Nurses Who Are 30 and Over

Previous comments about local nurses who are married and who have children also are applicable to nurses 30 and older. Aggressive recruitment will be needed to locate and hire these nurses, and once they are hired extra training will be necessary, since many of them will have been out of the labor force for some time. The extra costs, however, should be less than the benefits because of reduced turnover among these nurses.

Chapter 30

Recruitment and Retention

OVERVIEW*

Recruitment and retention are parts of a continuous process. Recruitment is supported by a satisfied and stable nursing staff who "sell" their institution to the students and experienced nurses with whom they interact. Retention is fostered by the recruitment of nurses who see themselves "fitting" the culture of the hospital and who find that their career aspirations may be met by the opportunities for professional growth and advancement provided by the organization.

To successfully obtain and maintain its share of the dwindling nursing resource, a hospital must match the incentives provided by its competitors while differentiating itself in one or more areas as a progressive leader that visibly supports its nursing staff. The special niches created by the hospital must be marketed aggressively both to its existing staff and potential recruits. The hospital not only must focus its efforts in the immediate geographical area but also must compete regionally and nationally.

To track its efforts, the hospital must decide in advance what are acceptable attrition rates and maintain records on the costs of RN replacements and programs aimed at retention. While a zero percent turnover is not only unrealistic but also undesirable, the institution should decide what its target rates are for turnover so that allocation of resources for recruitment can be planned. The comparison of costs of recruitment and retention can assist the organization to ensure that a disproportionate amount is not directed toward recruitment. The hospital must focus continually on the fact that retention is the most cost-effective way to maintain an adequate nursing resource.

Hospitals cannot be satisfied with currently successful recruitment and retention activities but must work with other health care organizations and agencies on long-term ways to address the shortage of nurses. One method may be to cooperate with community efforts to introduce high school students to nursing as an attractive profession. Another approach may be to work with businesses and schools of nursing in efforts to retrain a displaced work force from another industry.

The institution must address administrative, organizational, professional practice, and professional development characteristics to compete successfully with others for the limited

*Source: Catherine DeVet, "Nurse Recruitment and Retention in an Urban Hospital," in Managing the Nursing Shortage: A Guide to Recruitment and Retention, Terence F. Moore and Earl A. Simendinger, eds., Aspen Publishers, Inc., © 1989.

nursing resource available. The hospital that involves its own staff in the planning of the retention program will be the one that selects those characteristics that are most meaningful to its particular nursing population and creates a program that meets the widest variety of individual preferences. As the nursing work force becomes more diverse in types of personalities and career stages yet more specialized in practice, the retention factors will need to become more individual. The hospital that is futuristic will not stop at creating a general retention program but will plan refinements of the program to meet the changing expectations of its nurses.

The philosophy of the hospital must be articulated clearly so that a nurse may select an environment that is congruent with his or her own values. Simply recruiting "any warm body" will not build a stable work force. The organization must establish an identifiable "corporate culture" and consistently act in congruence with the norms of the culture. A nurse employed in an institution that shares his or her value system is less vulnerable to the recruitment efforts of another organization since the work environment is part of the nurse's own identity.

To be satisfied, nurses must feel a sense of worth in their jobs. Nurses must also see that their jobs are recognized and valued by nursing and hospital administrators and physicians as well as by their colleagues and patients. Therefore, hospitals must plan and implement recognition and reward programs for their nursing staff as part of a comprehensive approach to retention. Adequate compensation alone will not retain nurses. The environment in which the nurse works must convey a sense of esteem and worth for the nursing care provided to patients.

Early career nurses need an opportunity to perform well on the job through the support of supervisors and peers and to receive adequate feedback on the contributions they are making to the organization. Midcareer nurses need autonomy to make decisions and to work more independently. Advanced career groups need incentives that maintain or rekindle their excitement in their jobs. One creative way to accomplish this is to develop nurses on units into various "expert" roles and title them as consultants in the specific area.

Any program must be based on the needs as expressed by nurses in assessments conducted by the institution and by the needs expressed by individual nurses to their managers. (See Table 30-1.)

RECRUITMENT FROM THE NURSE'S POINT OF VIEW

Nurse Expectations*

The more qualified nurses graduating from baccalaureate and master's programs are seeking positions in institutions that offer salaries and work responsibilities commensurate with their educational preparation, work experiences, and clinical interests. What new graduates are seeking in a position is perhaps best reflected in the advertisements published in the nursing journals. Some cater to the nurse's desire for self-development or to the nurse's wish to function as a nursing practitioner. Some stress the opportunity for advancement.

It is interesting to note that comments regarding the fringe benefits and salaries are usually at the end of the advertisement. While these items may be minimized, experience has shown that they are extremely important in attracting nurses, but not necessarily in retaining them.

Increasingly, nurses are interested in greater specialization in the various clinical fields—intensive care, medicine, pediatrics, psychiatry, and others—and are less willing to function as generalists who rotate to any service in the hospital.

How Nurses Select a Hospital**

In studies conducted at one hospital nurses were asked to assign a weight to the criteria (listed below) used in selecting a hospital for

---

*Source: Grace Matsunaga, "The Nurse Executive and Nursing Manpower," Concerns in the Acquisition and Allocation of Nursing Personnel, National League for Nursing, Pub. No. 20-1709, 1979. Reprinted with permission.

**Source: C. David Hughes, "Can Marketing Help Recruit and Retain Nurses?" Health Care Management Review, vol. 4, no. 3, © 1979 Aspen Publishers, Inc.

Table 30-1 Variables Influencing Employee Retention and Turnover

Job Dimension	Factors Encouraging Retention	Factors Encouraging Turnover
Career or job attitudes (employee motivation)	Organization provides a sense of respect for the work completed Pay equity exists with external labor markets Pay equity exists within the organization Jobs are structured to be challenging Employees perceive that their work units are allocated a fair share of total budgets, resources, and rewards	High salary expectations by employees Low utilization of employee skills relative to education and training Failure to integrate employee work goals with organizational goals
Environmental favorability (job situation)	Management gives employee relations a high priority Personnel receive periodic training and development Flexibility exists for defining work hours Task variety is high Performance is linked to objectives and periodic assessment Efforts are made to develop work teams Technology supporting tasks are periodically updated or replaced	Failure to acknowledge accomplishments; this pertains to personal attainments as well as organizational achievements Limited employee knowledge of organizational benefits Limited opportunities for employees to express dissatisfaction regarding their jobs Lack of a formal system for disseminating important information
Employee selection (employee capabilities)	Past performance is analyzed before employees join organization Mature employees and those with family responsibilities tend to be more stable	Inability to judge job candidates' motivation and goal sets Failure to involve peers of the candidates in the selection process

Source: Howard L. Smith and Richard Discenza, "Developing a Framework for Retaining Health Care Employees: A Challenge to Traditional Thinking," *Health Care Supervisor*, vol. 7, no. 1, © 1988 Aspen Publishers, Inc.

---

employment. Listed in order of importance they were as follows:

1. spouse working/studying in the area
2. assigned to the service of my choice
3. pay
4. responsibility consistent with my training
5. workload
6. fringe benefits
7. teaching hospital
8. social life
9. opportunity for university courses
10. reputation of the hospital
11. modern equipment
12. research hospital

The most important criterion was the fact that the spouse was in the area. This finding suggests that nurse recruiters will want to work with the personnel offices of local companies and graduate school admission officers to identify nurses whose spouses will be moving into the area.

The second most important dimension, and more important than pay, was the desire to be

Table 30-2 Where Newly Licensed Nurses Get Job Leads

Note: The data in this table is based on a survey of 6,000 newly licensed nurses conducted by the National League for Nursing and the Department of Health, Education, and Welfare.

Sources Utilized	Percentage of Nurses Who Used Source	Percentage of Job Leads That Produced Results		
		Total	Bacc.	A.D.
Faculty	82%	42%	46%	36%
Friends	76	51	61	47
Recruiters	73	12	19	12
Nurses' convention	59	3	3	3
State Nurses' Association placement service	48	2	2	2
State employment service	36	4	2	4
Commercial employment agency	35	3	2	3
Placement bureau of school	61	6	9	4
Professional journals	68	18	28	15
Civil service listings	50	5	6	5
Newspapers	54	23	22	24
Direct application	87	71	77	70

Source: P.M. Nash, Ph.D., "Evaluation of Employment Opportunities for Newly Licensed Nurses." Division of Research, National League for Nursing, published by Health Resources Administration of DHHS, May 1975.

assigned to the service of one's choice. Closely related to this dimension, and only slightly less important than pay, was the desire to have responsibility that is consistent with training. The career dimensions of the job are clearly important to the nurse during the *selection* of a hospital. They are also important considerations for *staying* with the hospital.

ABC's OF NURSE RECRUITMENT*

A—Acquire an effective nurse recruiter.

B—Budget to allow adequate funds for competitive recruitment programs carefully conceived and based on a realistic projection.

C—Convey a positive image in your ads and literature.

D—Develop strong internal recruitment resources.

E—Encourage promotion from within to fill leadership positions. Appoint the best-qualified candidate regardless of source.

F—Foster a climate of openness so that problems surface and are solved before they result in turn-over statistics.

G—Generate effective advertising that reflects not only high professional standards but an administrative philosophy that bespeaks concern for the individual.

H—Heed the advice of advertising experts concerning the selection of media, copy developing, timing, and general strategy for placing advertisements.

I—Immediately respond to employment inquiries with a personal letter; a well-prepared, informative, and persuasive brochure; details about specific opportunities available, salaries, benefits, housing, etc.; and a clear statement of qualifications expected. Send follow-up correspondence at regular intervals.

J—Judge the effectiveness of your nurse recruitment efforts in terms of the "average cost per hire." Use this index as a

*Source: Adapted from Edin Hoffman, "ABC's of Nurse Recruitment," *American Journal of Nursing*, April 1974, © 1974 American Journal of Nursing Company.

basis of comparison with previous results and with other employers' results.

K—Keep records of inquiries by origin (journal, newspaper, in-house, etc.) and by summary of their disposition (interviews, hires).

L—Learn which recruitment resources provide the greatest yield in quality as well as numbers of candidates.

M—Maximize the use of these resources.

N—Negotiate with other health care agencies to recommend qualified applicants for whom current vacancies do not exist.

O—Offer assistance to out-of-state applicants in finding convenient, reasonably priced housing. This is often essential in metropolitan areas.

P—Promote positive public relations by participating in and sponsoring events which involve potential candidates and present staff members.

Q—Query terminating staff members concerning reasons for resignation and consider their recommendations for improvement.

R—Reward exceptional performance by added responsibility and commensurate authority, compensation, and recognition.

S—Schedule regular performance reviews to assess individual progress, to identify problems, and to agree on appropriate job objectives.

T—Tell your nurse recruitment representatives and advertising agency about any changes or problems affecting your staffing situation so that suitable adjustments can be made in your recruitment campaign.

U—Understand the hidden costs of inadequate or inappropriate staffing.

V—Vitalize your orientation, in-service, and continuing education programs to provide the latest information.

W—Work with school and college guidance counselors and conduct "career day" programs.

X—X-ray your staffing and scheduling patterns to deploy your present nursing group most effectively.

Y—Yield to constructive criticism in the development of solutions to your recruitment problems and staffing patterns.

Z—Zero in on a unifying theme that distinguishes your hospital as a place to learn and to practice nursing. Promote this theme in all aspects of your recruitment program.

RECRUITMENT TECHNIQUES

How To Attract Nurses*

The first step in attracting nurses is to build the hospital's reputation as a good place to work. What are some of the marketing strategies to achieve this?

Typical marketing strategies to attain this objective would include the following: (1) specify your recruitment strategy (number and types of nurses needed), (2) appraise your marketing strategy (decide if bringing in more nurses is the answer and/or making your hospital as attractive to them as possible), (3) define the marketing target (where will you find people to fill your needs—nursing schools? dropouts? etc.), (4) develop and/or select your strategy (utilize a unified approach around a central theme and distribute your message through channels appropriate to reach your target), and (5) monitor results and modify them as necessary. Hospitals are just learning to appreciate the value of developing a market strategy, defining targets, and devising formal programs to resolve various problems. Marketing, at its best, will only bring in more nursing job applicants; it will not keep them from leaving. In fact, where marketing generates unrealistic expectations in nurses, it actually can accelerate turnover!

There is simply no sense in expending marketing efforts to increase the inflow of nurses if the institution's practices will just as quickly drive them away. The time and money would be better spent on improving nurses' autonomy and super-

---

Source: Phillip Decker, Rusti C. Moore, and Eleanor Sullivan, "How Hospitals Can Solve the Nursing Shortage," *Hospital and Health Services Administration*, November-December 1982. Reprinted with permission.

visory skills and providing day-care centers, continuing education opportunities, competitive pay and benefits, etc.

How To Attract the Inactive Nurse*

Some of the ways in which employers of nurses might assist the nurse who would like to resume working in her profession include the following:

- Opening in-service programs to inactive nurses and encouraging the use of library resources and teaching aids. In Wisconsin, hospitals made their telephone conference equipment available so that inactive nurses throughout the state were able to participate in twice-monthly programs sponsored by the University of Wisconsin's extension department of nursing.
- Offering refresher courses as part of an in-service program with pay while the enrollee is learning.
- Establishing child-care programs for employees on a cost-only basis.
- Offering six-hour days and six-month employment years.
- Offering substantial bonuses for weekend and holiday duty. If hospital policy requires rotation of weekend and night duty, the part-time worker should be expected to rotate only proportionately to the percentage of time he or she is working. For example, if full-time workers rotate every third weekend, the half-time worker should be expected to work only every sixth weekend.
- Offering fringe benefits that apply to the entire family rather than just to the worker: family outpatient services, group insurance and savings plans, and scholarships and job opportunities in health-related occupations for the children of workers.
- Chartering buses to provide more direct transportation to and from work for those who live in suburban areas.

*Source: Anne McKee, "Recruiting Inactive Nurses," Hospitals, Journal of the American Hospital Association, vol. 44, no. 17, September 1, 1970.

- Using part-time nurses in positions that do not demand continuity of care, such as in clinics, in the newborn nursery, and in recovery rooms.
- Offering supervised support to returnees until such time as they feel ready to assume responsibilities. A primary threat to returning nurses is the fear that they will be pushed into too much responsibility too soon.
- Grouping patients according to the nursing service they require rather than by strict medical or surgical classifications.
- Instituting 24-hour utilization of all departments, so that pharmacy, clerical, dietary, and other duties will not be thrust upon nurses because no one else is available to perform these functions.
- Developing more flexible personnel policies.

Sources

Hospitals often form recruitment committees for the purpose of establishing recruitment policies and procedures and developing an action program to recruit qualified nursing staff.

Among the sources and techniques used for recruitment are public employment agencies, private employment agencies, and advertising in newspapers, professional journals, and magazines. (See Tables 30-3 and 30-4.) Schools and colleges can be informed of job opportunities. The American Nurses' Association Professional Credentials and Placement Service supplies nationwide personnel services. State professional counseling and placement service offices, while offering nationwide services, tend to encourage filling of vacancies in the states in which they are located.

Management consulting firms or executive recruiters are best used for top positions in administration or management only. Also of growing importance are the annual conferences or meetings of professional associations, where you or your representative can meet job-seeking members of the association and discuss job opportunities. And, of course, there is internal

Table 30-3 Master List of Available Features and Benefits Used in Nurse Recruitment Advertising

The following is a master list of benefits noted in a survey of recruitment advertisements. Both career and financial benefits are included in this alphabetic list. Nurse administrators can use the list to identify items they want to include in contract negotiations or their own advertisements.

Advance to administration avenue
Affordable housing
Automatic pay raises
Career advancement
Career ladder
CE: Clinical specialty course
    Graduate degree program
    Nurse practitioner course
Certifications, increased pay
CEU Programs
Child-care subsidy
Clinical career mobility—an innovative career ladder
Competency-based orientation
Continuing education programs on all levels through staff development programs, seminars, and workshops
Continuous in-service and staff development programs to keep nurses up to date
Cost of living (example: 10 percent lower in Nashville)
Credit union
Differentials: intensive care, evenings, nights
Discounts on services
Educational assistance
Flexible fringe benefits package
Float pool—ability to pick one's shifts
Free covered parking
Free employee health insurance
Health care coverage, 100 percent employer paid
Health plan
Holidays, nine paid
Hospital discounts
ICU/CCU
Insurance: dental, life, health, individual health, family
Internal job bidding system
Internship programs
Interview reimbursement
Joint practice modality
Liberal sick leave benefits
Liberal vacation benefits
Management training

Medical and dental care
Modern diagnostic service
Modern equipment and technology
Modular nursing
No Social Security tax
No state or city income tax (examples: none in Tennessee, Florida, Texas)
Nuclear medicine
Nursing specialties, 12, with transfer into others
On-campus apartments
Opportunity for professional practice
Orientation program, in-depth, individualized
Paid days off
Pharmacy nurse program
Preceptorship program
Professional workshop program for RNs seeking advanced degrees (paying 100 percent of tuition and fees)
Recreation facilities
Relocation assistance
Retirement plan
Scheduling option 64/80 (work 64 hours and be paid for 80)
Seven on and seven off staffing
Sick leave conversion
Straight shifts
Subsidized apartments
Subsidized bus passes (half cost)
Tax-sheltered annuities
Teaching hospital
Team nursing
Time and a half for overtime
TLC package (travel lucrative compensation)
Tuition credits to $1,200
Tuition for studies leading to degrees in job-related fields
Tuition refunds
Tuition reimbursement (100 percent)
Unit management
Variable compensation plan
Weekend premium
Weekends, every one off
Weekends, every other off
Well pay (get paid for not being sick)

Source: Russell C. Swansburg and Phillip W. Swansburg, *Strategic Career Planning and Development for Nursing*, Aspen Publishers, Inc., © 1984.

Table 30-4 Advertising Placements

Employment Directories	Nursing Journals That Carry Employment Ads
Imprint's Annual Career Planning Guide Anthony J. Jannetti, Inc. North Woodbury Rd., Box 56 Pitman, NJ 08071 (609) 589-2319	*AANA Journal* (American Association of Nurse Anesthetists)
	American Journal of Maternal Child Nursing (American Journal of Nursing Company)
Nursing Career Directory Intermed Communications, Inc. 132 Welsh Rd. Horsham, PA 19044 (215) 657-4515	*American Journal of Nursing* (American Journal of Nursing Company)
	AORN Journal (Association of Operating Room Nurses, Inc.)
Nursing Job Guide Prime National Publishing Co. 470 Boston Post Rd. Weston, MA 02193 (617) 899-2702	*Heart & Lung* (American Association of Critical-Care Nurses)
	Imprint (Anthony J. Jannetti, Inc., Pitman, NJ)
	Journal of Nursing Administration (J.B. Lippincott, Philadelphia, PA)
Nursing Opportunities Medical Economics Company 680 Kinderkamack Rd. Oradell, NJ 07649 (201) 262-3030	*Nursing* (Intermed Communications, Inc.)
	Nursing Outlook (American Journal of Nursing Company)
AJN Guide American Journal of Nursing Company 555 West 57 St. New York, NY (212) 582-8820	*Pediatric Nursing* (Anthony J. Jannetti, Inc., Pitman, NJ)
	Perspectives in Psychiatric Care (Anthony J. Jannetti, Inc., Pitman, NJ)
	RN Magazine (Medical Economics Co.)

Source: Tina Filoromo and Dolores Ziff, *Nurse Recruitment: Strategies for Success*, Aspen Publishers, Inc., © 1980.

recruitment. Vacant positions can be posted on bulletin boards or announced at departmental meetings, and employees who feel qualified can be invited to apply. If the hospital has an official publication, it too could be used to announce job openings.

*Staff Members**

Staff members are a good source of new employees; they have friends and relatives. Involve your employees in the planning of internal programs, such as designing exhibits and brochures. But, most important of all, take a staff member along on your recruitment trips.

*Source: Tina Filoromo and Dolores Ziff, *Nurse Recruitment: Strategies for Success,* Aspen Publishers, Inc., © 1980.

For example, if you are traveling to a school career program and a recent graduate of that nursing program is on your staff, take that person with you. Your nurse will be a natural link to the graduating class and will encourage applications to your hospital.

Many health care facilities have tried bonus or bounty systems to encourage their own employees to assist in bringing nurses into the institutions. Some bonuses take the form of an amount of money paid to the employee on the day the new recruit begins work, followed by an additional bonus after the recruit completes a successful probation. In other bonus systems, employees who bring in recruits are rewarded by trips to popular vacation sites, extra time off, or large bonuses after they have recruited three or more nurses.

Student Nurses*

If your institution has a school of nursing or trains affiliating nursing students from local colleges and universities, do not neglect these students as a source of recruits. Make sure they know that you are interested in them for future employment. Entertain them at a dinner or a coffee and tea session either at the beginning or end of their affiliation.

In addition, encourage your staff members to put a special effort into making these students feel welcome and a true part of the health care team, whether they are there for only a week or for a full semester.

If your institution does not have affiliating students, but you do have nursing programs in your community, contact the directors of these programs to offer their students experiences at your hospital. Or if you have any special patient units or programs, offer tours to schools for their students.

Alumnae

Another source of prospects is the alumnae association of your hospital's school of nursing if you have one or had one in the recent past. Some alumnae who were at one time employed at the hospital may be interested in returning, at least on a part-time basis. Let them know such positions are available. Use the alumnae newsletter to reach alumnae with this information.

Yet another source of applicants is the hospital's personnel department, where there are files of past employees. Many nurses leave positions to further their educations or to raise families. It is possible that they are ready to return to work, in either full-time or part-time positions. But they need you to tell them that jobs are available and that your institution wants them back. A personal letter is a worthwhile investment for this group of people.

In this group, however, you may encounter some people who cannot make a regular part-time commitment, but who would like to become part of an on-call or per-diem list. Such

lists have worked quite well for some hospitals. People on the on-call list are called to duty whenever someone is needed to fill temporary openings due to vacations, sick days, or unexpected leaves of absence. The individual is under no obligation to accept work, and, at the same time, the hospital does not guarantee any specific amount of work to the individual.

There are some practical reasons for pursuing an on-call list for former employees. These people are already oriented to the hospital and have some understanding of its policies and procedures. They can reduce the use of nurses from temporary agencies, who have little, if any, orientation to the institution. And utilizing these people as part-time or on-call nurses may eventually lead to their full-time employment.

Recruitment Trips

Another important part of your recruitment program is travel to the major sources of professional nurse applicants.

These sources include career day programs at colleges, universities, and schools of nursing; nursing conventions; career conference programs; commercially sponsored job fairs; and hotel recruiting. They are often overlooked by traditional recruiting techniques. Be prepared to discuss your institution and its goals intelligently; know your future manpower needs in some detail; bring application forms and any available literature promoting your employment opportunities; and finally, do not overlook the potential of gentle gimmicks such as "smile" buttons, Chinese fortune cookies containing short messages about your hospital, and the like.

Target Areas

Before you begin to travel, you should first decide on your target area. A survey of your staff (and possibly of your competitors) will help you determine where your staff has come from in the past and suggest areas in which recruitment will be fruitful.

Once you have decided on the target area, start your travel program by contacting the nursing

*Source: Tina Filoromo and Dolores Ziff, *Nurse Recruitment: Strategies for Success,* Aspen Publishers, Inc., © 1980.

schools in that area. Advise them of your interest in visiting them, either at a planned career day program or at an on-campus interviewing session.

In addition, contact the organizations that produce various conventions and job fairs and ask to be placed on their mailing lists. They will keep you informed of any programs in your target area and, if you are doing national recruiting, of those being held on a national basis.

Collective Recruitment

There is another approach to recruitment travel. In many communities, two or more hospitals have merged their interests and sent one representative to major conventions and job fairs to promote the community as well as its health care institutions. Combined advertising campaigns have also been tried.

Collective travel and combined advertising can work. They are particularly effective in those parts of the country where selling the location is as much of a challenge as selling the hospitals. Recruiting as a group has a greater impact than individual efforts and can save money for the participating institutions. There is another advantage: Once nurses have been recruited to a specific geographic area, the chances of their staying in that area are good, even if job hopping occurs.

Ideally, each hospital participating in collective travel and advertising should have a different specialty. Heavy competition for each nurse is thereby reduced, as each hospital has something different to offer.

Employment Agencies and Headhunters*

Although they operate differently, search organizations and employment agencies offer several common advantages. They provide a measure of confidentiality and enable the employer to limit advertising expense and exposure. With good fortune and competence, the applicants ultimately interviewed by the

employer are restricted to those likely to be offered work.

Search organizations normally operate on a fixed fee to the employer or offer an estimate of cost based upon a daily charge plus out-of-pocket expenses. Often an hourly charge is made in addition to expenses and a placement fee. They will also provide some idea of how long the search should last. In most cases you can terminate the arrangement if you either decide not to fill the position or locate a suitable candidate from some other source. As is true with search firms, private employment agencies normally charge only the employer.

Agencies customarily operate on a contingency basis—no placement, no fee. As a rule, they screen a larger volume of candidates and tend to refer greater numbers of applicants for employer consideration.

Search firms bear the undignified sobriquet of "headhunters" because they do only minimal advertising and use their contacts to reach into competing organizations—including yours—for likely candidates. The ritual requires, among other things, that the candidate react first with surprise and then reluctance to change jobs. This is calculated to sweeten the compensation package, and if played with adroitness, does. Search firms have reached a level in recent years which has made them increasingly useful adjuncts in the difficult task of locating and recruiting scarce professional talent. Their charges have more than kept pace, however, and tend to run upwards of 25 percent of the successful candidate's first-year gross salary. Employment agency fees have also increased rapidly. They usually run 10 to 25 percent of the initial annual rate of pay and are contingent upon a successful placement. Some guarantee of satisfaction on the employer's part is customary.

Some questions to be asked in dealing with search firms and employment agencies are: What are the obligations of each party? How long has the firm been in business? Can the owners give you the names of client firms they now serve? Are the people you will be dealing with sensitive to the needs of the health field as well as the specialized jobs for which they will be asked to recruit? Do you and your people understand that by using an outside source for recruiting pur-

*Source: Martin E. Skoler, *Health Care Labor Manual,* Aspen Publishers, Inc.

poses you cannot abdicate your responsibility to critically examine the credentials and representations of all job candidates, however referred?

ORGANIZING FOR RECRUITMENT*

Nurse Recruiter

Selection of a nurse recruiter should be based on such qualifications as

- the ability to sell and persuade
- the ability to relate well to young applicants
- an affinity for administrative detail
- a knowledge of labor laws and general hiring and employment practices
- a ready knowledge of nursing or the ability to grasp job qualifications and licensure requirements
- complete honesty in presenting the facts to interested applicants
- freedom and willingess to travel

The basic job description offered in Table 30-5 should be helpful to a health care facility in establishing the new position or reevaluating the position as it currently exists.

A Recruitment Program

First, the hospital must decide where the recruiter will travel and where the advertising money will be placed.

One way to begin making these decisions is to research the hospital's past efforts and the results they produced (if there are records). Next, it may be helpful to survey your competitors, if they are willing to share information. Ask where they have placed ads, where they have traveled, and if they have profited from these activities. Finally, survey the nursing staff at your hospital.

Source: Tina Filoromo and Dolores Ziff, *Nurse Recruitment: Strategies for Success,* Aspen Publishers, Inc., © 1980.

A survey should include questions that will help you compile the information you will need to make decisions about your travel and advertising activities.

Recruitment Budget

Useful guideposts in budget planning are the surveys by the National Association of Nurse Recruiters (NANR). These surveys provide information on budgets allocated for recruitment by hospitals grouped according to size and geographical location.

Basic expense categories to consider when planning your recruitment budget and/or determining your average cost per hire at the end of the recruitment year are the following:

- salaries and fringe benefits for the recruiter and clerical support staff
- cost of office space and utilities
- telephone charges (including the flat rate as well as long distance and collect calls)
- postage for first class letters and recruitment packets
- printing costs for all recruitment materials
- exhibit costs
- travel costs to conventions and career programs for the recruiter and assistants
- booth fees at conventions and job fairs (including rental of furniture for the booth)
- advertising fees (local and national)
- advertising/public relations agency fees for brochures, advertisements, and other materials (if you hire an agency)
- staff time of the hospital's public relations department
- staff time for those involved in the interviewing process
- expenses incurred in interviewing
- entertainment of prospects, both in-house and on the road
- cost of preemployment physicals
- cost of orientation
- relocation expenses (if your institution offers them)

Table 30-5 Basic Job Description for Nurse Recruiter

Position Title: Nurse Recruiter
Department: Personnel or Nursing
Reports to: Director of Personnel or Director of
Nursing

JOB SUMMARY

Meets, screens, interviews, and refers RN applicants. Collects and keeps current listing of RN vacancies. Reviews RN applications and follows up on initial inquiries, interviews, and job offers. Works directly with department heads, supervisors, etc., in establishing rapport and cooperation with, offering jobs to, screening, and employing RN applicants. Periodically assists various members of the department and the director of the department in completing projects and research studies.

DUTIES AND RESPONSIBILITIES

1. Keeps in constant contact with department heads to maintain current records of their needs.
2. Responds to written inquiries about RN positions available; corresponds with RN applicants regarding interviews, openings, and any other questions applicants may have.
3. Greets and initially interviews RN applicants who come to the nurse recruitment office, fully explains hospital benefits, and sees that applicants have a chance to interview with a member of the department of their interest; provides information for callers in regard to RN vacancies; schedules appointments.
4. Acts as the coordinator between department heads and RN applicants for job openings and job offers.
5. Informs department heads when an RN applicant is acceptable or not acceptable by checking references and evaluating results; makes available the references to the department heads.
6. Informs the proper departments when an RN applicant does not accept a position.
7. Notifies RN applicants if they are unacceptable for employment.
8. Keeps a tally of the source of inquiries about RN vacancies and the number of job offers that can be traced back to each source.
9. Maintains other files and records as required.
10. Works directly with an advertising agency or the hospital's public relations department to coordinate recruitment materials; maintains the materials in up-to-date form.
11. Travels to annual RN and student nursing conventions, career days, and other career-related activities to recruit RNs; makes arrangements for, assembles materials for, attends, and is in charge of recruitment at these conventions.
12. Keeps the director of the department informed of any consistent problems and new developments in RN recruitment.
13. Performs additional tasks as assigned and requested by the director of the department.
14. Adheres to all organizational and personnel policies of the hospital.

NURSE RETENTION

Overview

Hospitals must redirect their energies and resources from short-term, stop-gap recruitment efforts to long-term retention efforts. Another way of putting this is that hospitals will have to learn to "recruit from within"—that is, to retain those productive nurses in whom the hospital has already invested time and money.

It is highly unlikely that a hospital can get a "quick fix" by adopting a single innovation, such as salary bonuses or primary nursing, to attract and keep nurses. In particular, changes that merely throw money at the problem are unlikely to work as retention devices. Many hospitals are now using such recruitment gimmicks as salary increments for baccalaureate nurses, bonuses for nurses who work weekends or nights on a regular basis, or bounties for recruited nurses. These methods may help a hospital compete with others in its locale or with temporary agencies to recruit more nurses in the short run, but they are unlikely to help retain nurses in the long run unless other job factors are also addressed. This is not to argue that competitive nursing salaries are not desirable and deserved, only that salary improvements must be combined with other strategies in a serious effort to retain nurses.*

Facts about Nursing Shortage

The American Hospital Association Report**

The key points of a 60-page AHA report on the nursing shortage are summarized below:

- In the average hospital, more than 60 days are required to recruit nurses for medical-surgical units, and almost 90 days are required to recruit nurses for critical care areas.
- Requirements for nurses with baccalaureate degrees are projected to be twice the projected supply by the year 2000.
- Combined enrollment figures for all three types of registered nurse (RN) education programs fell 13 percent between 1983 and 1985 and continue to decline.
- Federal funding for nursing education fell from $150 million in 1973 to $53 million in 1987.
- Currently, 68 percent of all employed RNs work in hospitals. However, the percentage working in alternate health care settings and outside clinical nursing continues to expand.
- Nurses perceive autonomy to be the strongest predictor of job satisfaction.
- Nurses believe that the key elements of their profession are technical expertise, information sharing and health teaching, patient

advocacy, a holistic view of the patient's needs, and patient empathy and support.

- Unless wages and benefits for nurses improve, expanding the supply of nurses by short-term strategies will not solve the long-term shortage.
- Central to any positive change in nurse recruitment is the need to recognize and accept the interdependence of nurse educators, nurse executives, hospital administrators, physicians, third-party payers, and health care consumers.

Supply and Demand*

- The Department of Labor projects that in the 1990s, the need for nurses will increase by 33 percent. "In 1984 there were 1.9 million registered nurses and 79 percent of them were working in nursing."
- There are 1.7 million licensed RNs, but only 1 million, or 80 percent, are actually practicing.
- The American Hospital Association (AHA) reports that 77 percent of hospitals are reporting a shortage of nurses.
- The women's movement has generated competition from many other fields.
- There has been an increase in competing worksites for nurses.
- Hospitals employ 800,000 registered nurses—a 30 percent increase since 1980. Yet, patient acuity, sophisticated technology, and lengthening of the lifespan have generated an increasing need for nurses that outstrips the 30 percent increase.

Other Contributing Factors**

- Because of *declining enrollments*, the available pool of students in general has become more limited. In addition, there has

*Source: Carol Weisman, "Recruit from Within: Hospital Nurse Retention in the 1980s," *The Journal of Nursing Administration*, May 1982. Reprinted with permission.

**Source: Karen Hawley Henry, *Nursing Administration and Law Manual*, Aspen Publishers, Inc., © 1986.

*Source: E. Dorsey Smith and Elizabeth C. Falter, "The Nursing Shortage: Coping through Cooperation," *Nursing Administration Quarterly*, vol. 13, no. 1, © 1988 Aspen Publishers, Inc.

**Source: "Executive Analysis: The Nursing 'Shortage' Is Probably Permanent," *Hospital Strategy Report*, vol. 1, no. 6, © 1989 Aspen Publishers, Inc.

Figure 30-1 Factors Contributing to Nurse Retention

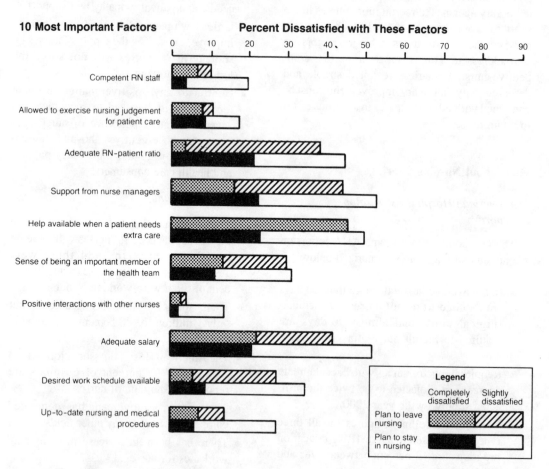

Note: Nurses who said they are not likely to stay in nursing three more years clearly do not have what they want—though they agree with the stayers on what is most important. Over 90 percent of all nurses rated the top four items as very important. Where leavers and stayers part company is on satisfaction with what they say is important: For each item, a higher percentage of leavers than stayers are dissatisfied.

Source: Reprinted from Florence L. Huey and Susan Hartley, "What Keeps Nurses in Nursing: 3,500 Nurses Tell Their Stories," *American Journal of Nursing*, February 1988. Copyright © by the American Journal of Nursing Company. Used with permission. All rights reserved.

been a substantial decline in enrollment in schools of nursing, particularly schools in the private sector.

- *A shift to medicine* from nursing is evident; more first-year women college students are now premed than are enrolled in nurse education, and 30 percent of medical students are now women.

- *Nurse vacancies* continue at a high level despite higher wages, dropping to 11.3 per-

cent in 1987 from an all-time high of 13.6 percent in 1986.

- *New technology* continues to push nurse skill levels higher; critical care nurses are among those in shortest supply today.

- The *aging of the population* is increasing the number of elderly patients with longer lengths of stay and greater care needs; Medicare covers 40–50 percent of the average hospital's patients.

- *Admission rates* are rising again, driven by the growing numbers of the elderly; older Americans will make up 13 percent of the population by 1990.
- *Prospective payment systems* contribute to higher levels of acuity and complexity of patients by shifting younger, healthier patients into ambulatory care settings.
- *Alternative career opportunities* for women are more lucrative and attractive; for a comparable educational investment, women can make 50–100 percent higher salaries in fields such as computer programming and engineering.

Finding Solutions

Redesigning Staff Nursing Jobs*

If we must direct retention efforts toward the redesign of staff nursing jobs, where do we target such efforts? One area is nurses' dissatisfaction with their degree of control over working conditions and the work process. (See Figure 30-1.) The other is the absence of incentives for staff nurses to build long-term careers in clinical nursing within the hospital.

Specific changes in nursing jobs that would enhance nursing control over the work process might include more flexible scheduling, higher nurse-patient ratios, and reduced substitution among RNs and between RNs and other personnel.

Both the research findings and the increasing popularity of temporary agencies attest to the importance of control over work schedules in nurses' job decisions. Hospitals need to be more creative in delegating responsibility to individual nurses and to groups of nurses for organizing schedules and ensuring 24-hour coverage of patients.

Career Development

Many staff nurses resign because there are no incentives to stay. Despite their considerable investments in recruitment and orientation of new nurses, hospitals generally do not tend to provide sufficient incentives to encourage their experienced nurses to remain with the organization, perhaps because hospitals don't expect nurses to stay. The need for career ladders in clinical hospital nursing—or "horizontal promotions" as some call them—has been recognized for some time, but the idea has not been implemented with uniform success. Currently, many hospitals designate several levels or ranks for staff nurses, but nurses typically advance through them within a few years and quickly attain the maximum salary level and degree of clinical responsibility they can expect. Clinical specialist positions typically require advanced degrees and therefore require nurses to leave the hospital in order to advance within it.

What we need is the concept of a long-term clinical career in hospital nursing, a concept that includes incentives for longevity. This would include ways to distinguish nurses on the basis of both length of service, which reflects on-the-job experience within the hospital, and functional levels of performance and responsibility within clinical nursing, much as the primary nursing model attempts to do. Within such a system, incentives for remaining in the hospital would include both increasing levels of pay and increasing amounts of control and responsibility in clinical nursing. Staff nurses might receive modest pay increments and an increasing ability to control their schedules with longer lengths of service in the hospital. In addition, promotions to higher levels of clinical responsibility and task complexity could be based on length of service and performance evaluations rather than on educational credentials. A performance-based promotion would also include a substantial pay increment.

Nurse Retention Guidelines*

What can hospitals do to retain nurses?

The following suggested procedures would remedy job factors that have been shown by research to be dissatisfying to nurses:

---

*Source: Carol Weisman, "Recruit from Within: Hospital Nurse Retention in the 1980s," *The Journal of Nursing Administration*, May 1982. Reprinted with permission.

*Source: Philip Decker, Rusti C. Moore, and Eleanor Sullivan, "How Hospitals Can Solve the Nursing Shortage," *Hospital and Health Services Administration*, November-December 1982. Reprinted with permission.

- Provide realistic job previews during the hiring process, emphasizing both the positive and the negative aspects of the job. Assessment center–type selection, especially for supervisory positions, is a good approach.

- Offer summer positions to BSN students to expose them to the variety of jobs in your hospital.

- Provide career planning for RNs. Develop a career ladder so that those who want to remain at the bedside can do so and yet progress. (An educational advisor in the staff of the education department can be a valuable adjunct in setting career goals.)

- Make certain that wages and benefits are comparable to other hospitals in the area.

- Establish a "retention position" and appoint a staff member to help personnel with such things as counseling, transfers, promotion, and relocation within the institution. This appointee should be a staff person, preferably not reporting directly to the director of nursing.

- Develop a nursing advisory committee as part of nursing administration and include staff RNs among its members.

- Consider centralized scheduling and post the results prominently and well in advance of work dates. As part of this process, institute a program to train those responsible for making such decisions.

- Introduce an incentive system with rewards for exceptionally good work. Consider, for example, a quality circle program or a financial reward system.

- Assess your orientation program to make certain it focuses on realistic expectations and encourage its presentation by your education services department. This step should be necessarily preceded by the recruitment of a departmental staff with full professional and educational credentials.

- Maintain communication with nurses, both upward and downward, through the use of conferences, quality circles, newsletters, etc.

- Enhance the status of head nurses and respect the influence you allow them.

- Institute sound behavior-based supervisory skills training for *all* supervisors, this to include coaching counseling, delegating, discipline, handling employee complaints, taking a problem to the boss, performance appraisal, on-the-job training, etc. These problems will best be resolved through the behavior-modeling process.

- Redesign nursing jobs so that nurses can adequately use all of their skills. This should be done to increase autonomy, feedback, skill variety, task significance, and task identity.

- Provide adequate staffing. Staffing needs to reflect a realistic pattern of nursing coverage. Allow for meeting time, downtime, sick time, vacation time, etc.

- Offer substantial opportunities for continuing education on the premises and provide the highest tuition reimbursement possible, especially for those aspiring to a BSN.

- Eliminate rotating shifts, if possible, and/or utilize a "flex-time" schedule.

- Approve RN hires at the unit level.

- Consider the establishment of quality day care and early childhood learning centers.

- Assess the possibility of a part-time float pool as an alternative to understaffing or the use of temporary agency RNs.

- Design a sabbatical/leave policy.

- Pay full-time hourly wages and benefits to those nurses willing to work weekends only.

- Educate the medical staff to cooperate and communicate better with the nursing staff.

Negotiating Terms: Fitting Jobs to Nurses*

Because there are many job vacancies, more employers are fitting jobs to nurses and creating opportunities for them. Nurses now can negotiate

---

*Source: Ellen M. Lewis and Joan Gygas Spicer, eds., *Human Resource Management Handbook: Contemporary Strategies for Nursing Managers*, Aspen Publishers, Inc., © 1987.

- the length of the shift, ranging from 4 to 16 hours
- the number of days worked: three on, four off; four on, three off; seven on, seven off; weekends only, etc.
- the shift they will work: days only, evenings only, nights only, or two-shift rotations (with weekends-only staffing and increased evening and night differentials, many nurses select those shifts, leaving day shifts and weekends off for others)
- benefits, including taking cash instead of benefits
- a patient load related to salary and payment per patient depending upon degree of illness
- a salary based on experience; nurses have stated that experience increases their ability to handle larger patient loads

- a staff organization for a more responsive administration (then they can join and participate in it)
- less paper work by volunteering to serve on a joint practice council
- more educational opportunities by helping to plan self-paying workshops that produce a profit to be used for staff development
- more opportunities for promotion by taking a job where clinical ladders exist or volunteering to serve on a committee to develop one

The job can be fitted to the nurse, when that individual becomes involved in the fitting. Nurses must do this in the spirit of tact and diplomacy so that they become part of the solution rather than part of the problem.

Chapter 31

Criticizing, Correcting, and Disciplining

CRITICIZING*

Criticism in its highest sense means trying to learn the best that is known and thought and measuring things by that standard.

Criticism can be used and met constructively or destructively. It can be the means by which people receiving it climb, or it can be used to bolster the critic's vanity. Captious criticism takes note of trivial faults; its author is usually unduly exacting or perversely hard to please. Carping criticism is a perverse picking of flaws. Cavilling criticism stresses the habit of raising petty objections. Censorious criticism means a tendency to be severely condemnatory of that which one does not like.

Ordinary faultfinding seems to indicate less background and experience than the art of criticism requires. It is wholly concerned with tearing down and scolding, whereas criticism is the art of analyzing and judging the quality of something.

Silence is sometimes the severest criticism.

What Is Fair Criticism?

Fair criticism does not judge without factual information. It considers the event on which it is

*Source: John R. Heron, "On Criticism," *Monthly Letter*, November 1977, Royal Bank of Canada. Reprinted with permission.

to pass judgment in the light of these factors: What was said or done? What did the person mean to say or do? What was his or her reason for saying or doing it? What is the effect of what he or she said or did? Why do I object to it?

Fair criticism does not exaggerate. All but a few careful and considerate persons seem to be urged either to overstate things by 100 percent or to understate them by 50 percent in order to criticize them with greater enjoyment.

Fair criticism does not include common gossip. Gossip may be merely friendly talking or useless chatter, but it too often degenerates into mischievous comment on neighbors or business associates.

The Ideal Critic

The ideal critic would know the topic, would be dispassionate in weighing the evidence, would have ability to see clearly what follows from the facts, would be willing to reconsider the facts if that seemed advisable, and would have courage to follow his or her thoughts through to the bitter end. The ideal critic would not, in all this process, brush aside the help of advisors. He or she would retain a keen and lively consciousness of truth.

In making his or her criticism known, the ideal critic would have regard for the feelings of the other person. Courtesy is easily the best single quality to raise one—even a critic—above the crowd.

Charming ways are quick winners. When an end is sought, why browbeat and shout and storm if one can persuade?

The good critic will not force the person being criticized too far. It is always good strategy to let the other person save face.

CORRECTING ERRORS*

The *purpose* of correcting errors is to help employees improve their work performance.

Correction must be focused on helping employees identify and understand their errors and learn how to avoid repeating them. They must know what the supervisor expects and feel confident that they can live up to these expectations.

There are three steps in correcting errors: (1) review the standards by which the job was to be done, (2) point out the error, and (3) indicate what must be done to correct it. These steps should be followed in sequence. Unfortunately, most supervisors start by pointing out the error. This usually results in defensiveness, excuses, or an attempt to focus on the things that the employee does do right. The employee tries to justify his or her poor performance rather than to correct it.

Reviewing Standards

The importance of reviewing standards as the first step in correcting errors cannot be over-emphasized, even though it is seldom done.

When an employee ignores step-by-step procedures for accomplishing a particular task, the supervisor should review the procedures with the employee and ensure that the latter understands the standards. But what about standards that govern certain behavior or practices but are not in writing? Often hospitals have no written policies, procedures, or rules about gossiping, pass-

*Source: Winborn E. Davis, "Correcting Errors in Work Performance," *Hospital Topics*, August 1973. Reprinted with permission.

ing along rumors, arguing with other employees, improper personal appearance, and so on.

Here one must fall back on broad policies of the organization, some of which may only be implied, not available in writing. The supervisor may even point out that management does not tolerate gossip and rumor because they waste time, affect morale, and reduce the quality and quantity of work.

Step-by-Step Guidelines

Effective guidelines have been developed for carrying out the three steps of correcting errors. Supervisors who follow these guidelines can make corrections far more objectively and are less likely to become involved in personalities and personal problems.

1. Correct the first error. No employee should be allowed to get by with a work error, even once. If he or she does, other employees will be encouraged to put forth less than their best effort.

2. Choose the proper time and place. Corrections should be made as soon after the error as feasible. Waiting a few days lessens the effectiveness of the correction. Correction interviews should be in private, never before fellow employees.

3. Be objective. To be objective, the supervisor must correct errors when not angry or irritated. Being objective means correcting the *situation*, not a personality. It is important not to criticize the employee as a person. Correction should be made for the sake of improvement.

4. Be specific. Never make general statements. General statements make employees defensive. They respond by pointing out the things they do correctly and believe can defend. Focus on specific errors.

5. Stick to the facts. Never base a correction on hearsay. Get all sides of a story before acting.

6. Do not react to excuses. Employees often try to justify their errors, to explain that errors were not their fault. Never let the listener divert attention from the specific work error under discussion, but stick to the three steps, saying, "These are the standards you agreed to follow, this is what you did wrong, and this is what must be done.''

7. Be serious. Avoid joking or teasing. If a work error is serious enough to call to an employee's attention, it is worthy of a serious approach.

8. Spell out the remedy. Be as specific about the remedy as about the error. Don't leave the employee uncertain of what is expected.

9. Allow employee questions. Let the employee ask questions. This gives immediate feedback on whether he or she understands the standards, the error, and the remedy.

10. Don't make excuses yourself. Supervisors often lessen the value of correction by being apologetic. Supervisors are paid to deal openly with errors in work performance. It is part of the job.

11. Individualize the employee. Sensitivities vary: approach employees differently, yet follow the same steps and guidelines.

12. Tie up loose ends. Get immediate feedback on whether the employee truly understands what went wrong and what is expected.

DISCIPLINING

Overview*

Over the years, discipline has had at least two meanings. Discipline first meant complete and total obedience to rules and regulations and to the directives and orders of superiors. Failure to comply resulted in punitive actions. Closer examination of discipline reveals that the most constructive and effective forms of discipline involve something more than mere obedience to authority. The second and higher discipline, then, involves self-control and a sense of personal responsibility for behavior and performance.

Traditional discipline is achieved through the authority of the individual in a supervisory

Source: Reprinted, by permission of the publisher, from *Managing Training and Developing Systems* by William Tracey, pp. 345–349, © 1974 by AMACOM, a division of American Management Associations, New York. All rights reserved.

capacity. The self-control form is achieved through the influence of a systematic frame of reference that is held in common by all individuals in the organization and that guides their actions.

Factors Influencing Discipline

There are several factors that influence the learning of self-discipline. They can be considered to be conditions that must be satisfied if discipline is to be developed and maintained within an organization.

Understanding of Requirements. Good discipline rests upon the security of understanding. Each individual in an organization must know and understand the ground rules, the limits, and the actions and behavior that are approved and disapproved. And those requirements must remain relatively consistent if subordinates are to learn them.

Atmosphere of Confidence. Good discipline rests on a foundation of mutual trust and confidence. That confidence includes the confidence of managers in their subordinates, of subordinates in the decisions and actions of their supervisors, and of everyone in the organization in his or her own ability to perform effectively.

Informal Sanctions. Good discipline is the result of the operation of informal sanctions— social pressures generated within a group or organization to enforce informal norms of performance and conduct. The extent to which norms allow a group to accept or resist organizational rules and principles plays an important part in the development and maintenance of discipline. The concept of group norm is comparable with such concepts as codes, customs, and traditions.

Formal Sanctions. When authority is used to enforce discipline, formal sanctions must play an important part in the process. But it is not just the sanctions themselves that exert an influence upon the development and maintenance of discipline. The way in which they are used to enforce compliance with decisions, rules, and principles is even more important. Two principles apply: First, justice and fairness to all concerned must

Analyzing Discipline Problems

Seriousness of Problem. How severe is the problem or infraction?

Time Span. Have there been other discipline problems in the past, and over how long a time span?

Frequency and Nature of Problems. Is the current problem part of an emerging or continuing pattern of discipline infractions?

Employee's Work History. How long has the employee worked for the organization, and what was the quality of performance?

Extenuating Factors. Are there extenuating circumstances related to the problem? For example, if there was a fight, was the employee provoked?

Degree of Orientation. To what extent has management made an earlier effort to educate the person causing the problem about the existing discipline rules and procedures and the consequences of violations?

History of Organization's Discipline Practices. How have similar infractions been dealt with in the past within the department? Within the entire organization? Has there been consistency in the application of discipline procedures?

Implications for Other Employees. What impact will your decision have on other workers in the unit?

Management Backing. If employees decide to take their case to higher management, do you have reasonable evidence to justify your decision?

be ensured and, second, the sanctions must be applied consistently. Subordinates must be confident that they will be treated fairly, and they must know that punishments come to them because of what they *do* and not because of how someone in authority *feels*.

Goals, Cohesion, and Morale. When individuals develop a strong commitment to the objectives of an organization, they are more likely to be highly motivated. Such motivation leads to acceptance of organizationally approved standards of conduct. Cohesion is related to identification with the organization and to the capacity of the unit to exert influence without the use of punitive measures. In general, cohesion results in greater conformity with the norms of conduct of the organization. Morale influences discipline because attitudes affect behavior. Poor morale and poor discipline are often partners in the disintegration of an organization.

Discipline Approaches*

The two most widespread problems in the administration of discipline are a broad managerial failure to act promptly in dealing with discipline problems as they occur and overreaction when a long-overdue action is finally taken. The basic foundation of any sound disciplinary program must be a set of procedures which are tailored to achieve the particular objectives of a given organization.

However, a well-written discipline policy is only as effective as its enforcement. And this is where most organizational efforts at effective discipline administration break down or are less than fully successful. Implementation is only successful when discipline is characterized by (1) promptness, (2) impartiality, (3) consistency, (4) nonpunitiveness, (5) fairness, (6) advance warning, and (7) follow-through.

The single efforts of a supervisor acting alone are quite insufficient to make an organizational discipline program effective. Any successful program must include the following elements: (1) an organizational set of discipline policies and procedures; (2) a uniform application of discipline rules; (3) supervisors who are trained in the knowledge and skills related to implementing a discipline policy; (4) an orientation program which informs all new employees about management's expectations of appropriate performance and behavior; and (5) a continuous management effort which communicates to employees all changes and revisions in person-

*Source: Wallace Wohlking, "Effective Discipline in Employee Relations," *Personnel Journal*, September 1975. Reprinted with the permission of *Personnel Journal*, Costa Mesa, California; all rights reserved.

nel and discipline policies—*before* changes are actually put into effect.

Problem Solving

A basic idea in contemporary management practice is that discipline should not be used as a substitute for effective supervision. The first approach to most employee-caused problems should be characterized by problem solving. Supervisors are expected to aid their employees in analyzing work problems, obtaining information not readily available to the employees, and in some cases serving as a counselor on personal problems affecting an employee's work problems.

In other words, the supervisor has an obligation to attempt to deal with the root cause of an employee's discipline problem. This approach does not preclude expressing management's concern over the employee's infraction; therefore, a problem-solving effort by the supervisor should be part of an oral warning discussion. In other cases, depending on the judgment of the supervisor, he or she may want to try a counseling problem-solving interview without resorting to a disciplinary action.

Disciplinary Action

While problem-solving efforts can eliminate or significantly minimize future employee discipline infractions, problem-solving will not always work. At this point, a disciplinary action should be taken. The typical sequence of steps under "progressive" or "corrective" discipline is as follows:

1. oral warning
2. written warning
3. suspension
4. dismissal

1. Oral Warning. As a rule, the oral warning should be conducted in an informal atmosphere. The purpose of this informality is to encourage the employee to relate his or her view of the problem with an opportunity for a reasonably complete statement of the facts as the employee sees them. The supervisor may expect to question the employee during the discussion, but normally the supervisor should avoid interrupting the employee. It is important to obtain all relevant facts.

After the supervisor knows the relevant facts, and after these facts have been analyzed and evaluated against the employee's past record, the employee should be informed of the supervisor's determination. This includes any expected improvement in future behavior; assistance, if appropriate, that the supervisor plans to give to the employee in correcting the problem; the disciplinary penalty being imposed (assuming there is one); and any follow-up action which will be taken.

2. Written Warning. The written warning is the second step. It is preceded by an interview similar to the oral warning–type discussion. Employees are told at the conclusion of the interview that a written warning will be issued. The key points that should be included in a written warning are a statement of the problem; identification of the rule which was violated; consequences of continued deviant behavior; the employee's commitment to make correction (if any); and any follow-up action to be taken.

3. Suspension. Suspensions can only occur for minor discipline violations after there has been a record of oral and written warnings established. Suspension, of course, can be applied without such a record if a major discipline infraction has occurred. Suspension rather than dismissal is used by management when it feels that there is still some hope for "rehabilitating" the employee. Or, because of a union presence, management may feel that it could not sustain a discharge if that discharge was taken to arbitration.

Suspension may be for a period of one day to several weeks. Disciplinary layoffs in excess of 30 days are rare.

4. Dismissal. The move to discharge a person should only be invoked when all other problem-solving and disciplinary efforts have failed. A word of warning. There should be an accurate documented record of the oral and written warnings (and suspensions, if any) received by the employee. If the employee primarily is being discharged for one violation, the supervisor should be very sure that the reason for the discharge conforms to the organization's criteria of a major discipline violation and that he or she can effectively support the case if it is reviewed by higher levels of management or if it should go to arbitration or before governmental agencies, such as the Human Rights and Equal Employment Opportunity Commissions.

Other Kinds of Steps

Through the sequence of oral and written warnings, suspension, and dismissal is considered to be the standard in the discipline process, some organizations have developed embellishments of the process by adding other elements to that sequence. For example, there is the "corrective" interview. This step is designed to precede any formal disciplining act. The corrective interview is used to instigate an improvement in behavior without having the interview necessarily go on the employee's personnel record.

Another device which is occasionally used in a progressive discipline policy is the "final warning." The final warning is a step inserted between the written warning and suspension. The effect of this extra step is to allow the employee additional and more gradual notification that he or she is approaching a point where severe punishment (suspension and/or dismissal) is about to be imposed.

The "Slide Rule" Approach*

Some organizations attempt to eliminate judgments that a supervisor is required to exercise in disciplinary cases by developing a "slide rule" set of discipline policies.

For example, discipline policy based on this concept might state, "The second time an employee is found smoking in the work area, he or she will be suspended for three days."

Slide rule policies remove much of the traditional considerations which must go into analyzing and assessing a determination in discipline cases. Factors normally considered in evaluating most discipline cases are ignored for a mechanistic, formularized approach.

Cautions in Disciplining*

An ill-advised decision to discipline an employee can invite serious legal complications and potentially costly backpay awards.

The discharge of an employee is sometimes necessary, and the corrective disciplining of an employee is often useful. However, given the growing number of antidiscrimination laws and collective bargaining agreements, the increasing number of cases brought by employees, and the substantial burden of proof placed on employers in such cases, it is prudent to review and revise disciplinary procedures to minimize the risks involved. Most employers who lose disciplinary cases before a government agency or before an arbitrator can usually trace their lack of success to one of three areas: inadequate or procedurally defective investigation; the existence of disparate treatment; or the lack of documented evidence.

Nothing torpedos a case faster than finding out an employer has discharged an employee for the same type of misconduct that it had previously only suspended employees. To avoid this, employers should have on file some type of reasonable disciplinary policy. Most employers segregate employee misconduct into two categories: (1) serious offenses for which immediate discharge is warranted and (2) less serious offenses for which discharge is warranted only after the imposition of progressive discipline. In the latter type of case, the employer usually establishes some progressive system involving the use of verbal and written warnings and/or suspensions, all of which culminate in eventual discharge for repeated offenses. See Table 31-1 for a checklist for progressive discipline and documentation.

---

*Source: Wallace. Ibid.

*Source: Martin E. Skoler, Health Care Labor Manual, Aspen Publishers, Inc., © 1981.

Table 31-1 Checklist of Progressive Discipline and Documentation

---

First: Always make sure that you already have provided your employees with group or other pertinent notice describing the rule, policy, procedure, or standard, as appropriate.

Then:

1. *Oral Reprimand* (if used by your facility)
   ____Do privately (not in the presence of other employees or supervisors).
   ____Reexplain rule/policy/procedure/standard and the need for compliance by the employee.
   ____Limit your documentation to a brief notation in your notes: Include the date, location, problem, what you told the employee, and retain any pertinent written materials.
   ____Conduct subsequent follow-up if required (e.g., to determine whether the employee has taken corrective action, to ascertain whether further disciplinary action is necessary, etc.), and document.
   ____Remember, an oral reprimand is not a written warning.

2. *Written Warning*
   ____Check prior disciplinary action, performance evaluations, etc., before you issue a written warning to ascertain whether these same problems have been discussed with the employee previously.
   ____Investigate before you decide to issue warning.
   ____Be prepared to defer, modify, or abandon the warning if you write it before asking the employee's version and the facts that emerge warrant such a step. Remember, it is better to change your mind when new facts are disclosed than to proceed with an inaccurate and unwarranted disciplinary action.
   ____Include the following in the warning:

   ____The facts to the warning: who, what, when, where, applicable employer policy, etc.
   ____The corrective action you expect from the employee and a restatement of the standard, if appropriate.
   ____The consequences to the employee if corrective action is not taken or if another incident occurs.
   ____References to prior counseling sessions, verbal reprimands, or other disciplinary action or discussions on the same issue (e.g., "Last week I told you that you must be at your duty station ready to work at 9 A.M.").
   ____Signatures of yourself and the employee (or a witness, if the employee refuses to sign) and the date.
   ____A copy for the employee.

3. *Disciplinary Suspension* (time off without pay)
   ____Investigate before you tentatively decide a suspension would be appropriate (this includes determining whether the employee had prior related written warnings if progressive discipline is appropriate, etc.).
   ____Talk to the employee before you make a final decision and double-check the individual's version, as appropriate.
   ____Make your decision, document it, and notify and discuss the decision with the employee.
   ____Keep your documentation (or written notice of suspension) similar to the written warning except that you will:

   ____Confirm the suspension (where you already have given the employee verbal notice of your decision, e.g., by telephone) but still include all points included in the written warning.
   ____Specify the workdays covered by the suspension and the date, day of the week, and shift of the employee's return to work.
   ____Notify employee that termination is the next probable step if there is a reoccurrence or no improvement.

continues

Table 31-1 *continued*

4. *Termination*
   ____Check and double-check: Has progressive discipline been followed? If not, does an exception exist and is termination warranted by the seriousness of the conduct?
   ____DO ALL INVESTIGATION PRIOR TO MAKING DECISION, INCLUDING TALKING TO EMPLOYEE AND VERIFYING/DISPROVING THAT PERSON'S VERSION, OBTAINING WRITTEN (IF POSSIBLE) WITNESS STATEMENTS FROM EMPLOYEES, PATIENTS, VISITORS, ETC.
   (Note: Your documentation of a termination will vary from that used for other disciplinary actions, depending on the circumstances.)

   ____Complete all investigatory documentation before the termination notice is prepared (but do not attach to termination paper; generally, you are not required to give—and should not give—this underlying documentation to the employee).
   ____Present statement of reasons; EXERCISE EXTREME CAUTION since the reasons you give are the reasons you must prove.
   ____Make sure the final paycheck is ready to give to the employee with the termination notice.
   ____Obtain any and all necessary approvals of your intended decision before it is communicated to the employee.

Source: Karen Hawley Henry, *The Health Care Supervisor's Legal Guide,* Aspen Publishers, Inc., © 1984.

Chapter 32

Troubled and Troublesome Employees

TROUBLED EMPLOYEES

Alcoholism, drug abuse, emotional illness, and family crisis are employees' personal problems that spill over into the environment of the health care organization and ultimately affect job performance. A personal crisis situation involving marital, family, financial, or legal troubles is considered the most prevalent problem among all employee groups.

Adopting the Proper Manner*

Employees with personal problems—those that people cannot help but bring to work with them—are rarely able to do their best work. As an administrator, you should be interested in the employee as a whole person, but the employee's private life and personal problems are none of your business; they represent an area you cannot enter without specific invitation.

In dealing with the apparently troubled employee, do not prod and do not push. Make yourself available to the employee, and make known your willingness to listen. You may have to go as far as to provide the time, the place, and the opportunity for the employee to talk with

you, without specifically asking the employee to "open up." Quite often, if your openness is evident, the troubled employee will turn to you.

In relating to the troubled employee:

Listen—but be aware at all times of the temptation to give advice. Some of the most useless statements you can make begin with, "If I were you. . . ." Also, although many troubled employees could use advice, it is usually advice that you are unqualified to deliver. The best you can do under most circumstances is gently to suggest that the employee seek help from qualified professionals.

Be patient—and show your concern for the employee as an individual. Although you should naturally be concerned with an individual's impairment as a productive employee, do not parade this before the troubled person. Rather, be patient and understanding. Perhaps, when possible, you can even be patient to the extent of easing off on tight deadlines and extra work requirements until the person is able to work through a problem.

Do not argue—and do not criticize an employee for holding certain feelings or reflecting certain attitudes. Avoid passing judgment on the employee based on what you are seeing and hearing.

---

*Source: Charles R. McConnell, *The Effective Health Care Supervisor*, Aspen Publishers, Inc., © 1988.

Be discreet—let nothing a troubled employee tells you go beyond you. Be extra cautious if an employee tends toward opening up to the extent of revealing much that is extremely personal and private. While it often does good for someone to be able to simply talk to someone else about a problem, a person often runs the risk of saying too much and might afterward feel extremely uncomfortable about having done so. If you can, try to demonstrate that you sympathize and understand without allowing the employee to go too far. Always provide assurance that what you have heard in such an exchange is safe with you.

Reassure—when you are honestly able to do so, provide the employee with reasonable assurance of things of importance, such as the security of the employee's job, the absence of undue pressure while problems get worked out, and the presence of a friendly and sympathetic ear when needed. You need not even know the nature of the employee's outside problem to supply very real assistance by reducing the job-related pressures on the individual.

In dealing with the troubled employee in general, listen honestly and sympathetically and do what can be done to reduce pressure on the employee, but leave the giving of specific advice related to the problem to persons qualified to deal with such matters.

How To Help*

There is a way of approaching troubled employees who may be in need of help through early diagnosis and intervention.

What may be most important is that the managers are aware of available resources and can encourage the employees to make an appointment. It is advisable for managers to follow up with the identified employees to ensure that they are obtaining the help needed. Organizations should make available for their managers lists of referrals and alternatives needed in dealing with problem employees.

If employees do not want this help, it should be made clear that their continued employment will depend on effective performance and the elimination of the problem, which is affecting the workers, the managers, and the organizational milieu.

Stress*

Managers typically react negatively to a discussion of organizational or job-related stress. They believe that stress is not a management but a personal problem. Individuals are expected to adapt as best they can; those meant to survive, will; those not meant to, won't.

Stressors. Typical interpersonal stressors include chronically angry or aggressive people with whom it is necessary to interact; passive aggressive individuals; ungrateful or demanding patients, bosses, doctors, nurses, administrators, board members, subordinates; those who have difficulty expressing their needs and leave others guessing; and those who have difficulty giving and receiving negative feedback. Differing perceptions and generally poor interpersonal communication are frequent sources of stress at this level.

Problems in Perception. Because people approach situations in terms of what makes sense to them in light of earlier experiences, problems in communicating with and understanding others occur, frequently leading to stress because "they just don't understand the way things ought to be." The way a person perceives something can be as important as what the situation actually is.

Problems in Communication. Interpersonal communication is probably the single most important aspect of management and is a contributor to organizational stress. Communication is the tool through which people discover the world and their relationship to it. They learn what are socially approved ways of behavior. They learn what others expect of them. They learn of others' intentions and how they react to

Source: Steven H. Appelbaum, *Stress Management for Health Care Professionals,* Aspen Publishers, Inc., © 1980.

Source: Rita E. Numerof, *Managing Stress: A Guide for Health Professionals,* Aspen Publishers, Inc., © 1983.

them—how the others appear to them through what they communicate.

Communication also is the means through which people get close to each other. It is the way they validate each other's experience. To be acknowledged and recognized suggests a person is worthwhile. There is perhaps nothing more devastating as not being recognized. It is for this reason that some people engage in destructive behavior in order to obtain a response from others on the theory that negative attention is better than none at all.

Burnout

Vulnerability to Burnout*

Personnel who deliver direct medical or nursing care are vulnerable to the burnout syndrome, in which their personal resources for coping with and managing stress are exhausted. Supervisory and administrative employees also become susceptible to burnout because of pressures to maintain an adequate support system for those who deliver direct health care services.

Some health care professionals attain burnout early in their careers because they experience physical and emotional exhaustion and no longer are able to deal with empathy, respect, or positive feelings for patients. They become extremely critical of patients and of the profession and deal with individuals in a demeaning and derogatory manner. They view their patients as being worthy of their illness since the burnout changes certain of their perceptions and makes it extremely difficult for them to practice their role in a humanistic, helping, positive manner.

One way in which health care personnel maintain their psychological equilibrium and at the same time attempt to keep stress at a minimum is to maintain a psychological distance from patients. They often behave in ways that justify patients' complaints about the care being received, since they are too impersonal and fail to give adequate explanations concerning the nature of the patients' problems and other pertinent factors.

Signs of Burnout*

Some of the signs of burnout are:

- when nurses' capacity to solve problems and satisfy cognitive requirements of the work are impaired by burnout and they consider job termination
- when nurses begin to perceive patients, families, and clients from a negative, judgmental perspective and label them as problems or troublemakers
- when nurses feel the administration is not supporting them or understanding their job performance and these feelings are directed through anger toward the work environment, peers, and administrators
- when interpersonal contact between the emotionally exhausted nurse and patient is affected adversely and the nurse experiences lower job satisfaction and self-esteem
- when perceptions of self-image begin to change drastically (negatively), accompanied by swings in emotional disposition
- when rigidity increases and the nurses' personal and social life changes via withdrawal and isolation
- when nurses have been trained to be aware of and sensitive to the needs of patients and then do not apply these skills
- when nurses increase self-imposed restrictions and experience stresses in their own lives such as marital and financial problems, parenting difficulties, social pressures, and other disruptive influences

Preventive Mechanisms

Preventive mechanisms include rap sessions, lectures on stress, management development, job restructuring, supervisory training, job discussion, variable work schedules, and health education and promotion.[1] See Figure 32-1 for a model for assessing burnout.

---

*Source: Steven H. Appelbaum, *Stress Management for Health Care Professionals*, Aspen Publishers, Inc., © 1980.

*Source: P.K.S. Patrick, "Job Hazard for Health Workers," *Hospitals*, November 15, 1979.

[1]Alice D. Seuntjens, "Burnout in Nursing," *Nursing Administration Quarterly*, vol. 7, no. 1, © 1982 Aspen Publishers, Inc.

Figure 32-1 A Model for Assessing Burnout

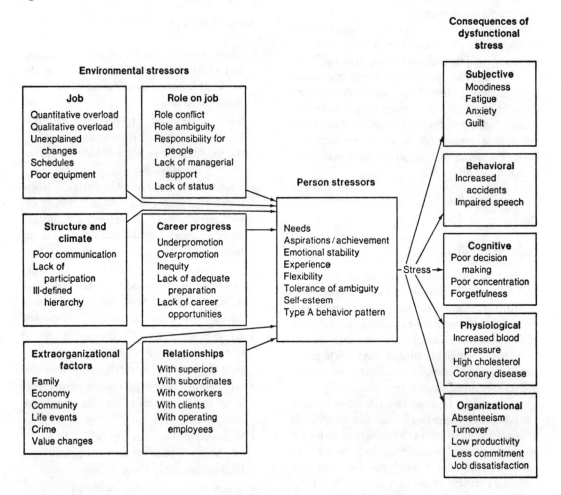

Source: Reprinted with permission from J. Ivancevich and M. Matteson, "Optimizing Human Resources: A Case for Preventive Health and Stress Management," *Organizational Dynamics*, Autumn 1980.

PROBLEM EMPLOYEES

Guidelines for Dealing with Problem Employees*

1. Listen. Make it clear that you are always available to hear what is bothering your employees. Display an open attitude, conscientiously avoiding the tendency to shut out possible unpleasantries because you "don't want to hear them." Many employees' doubts, fears, and complaints are created or magnified by a closed attitude on the part of the supervisor, so your obvious willingness to listen will go a long way toward putting some troubles to rest.

2. Always be patient, fair, and consistent, but retain sufficient latitude in your behavior to allow for individual differences among people. Use the rules of the organization as they were intended, stressing corrective aspects rather than punishment. Apply disciplinary action when truly deserved, but

Source: Charles R. McConnell, *The Effective Health Care Supervisor*, Aspen Publishers, Inc., © 1988.

do not use the threat of such action to attempt to force change by employees.

3. Recognize and respect individual feelings. Further, recognize that a feeling as such is neither right nor wrong—it is simply there. What a person *does* with a feeling may be right or wrong, but the feeling itself cannot be helped. Do not ever say, "You shouldn't feel that way." Respect people's feelings, and restrict your supervisory interest to what each employee does with those feelings.

4. Avoid arguments. Problem employees are frequently ready and willing to argue in defense of their feelings or beliefs. However, by arguing with an employee you simply solidify that person in a defensive position and reduce the chances of effective communication of any kind.

5. If possible, let your supposedly stubborn or resistant employees try something their own way. As a supervisor you are interested first in results and only secondarily in how those results are achieved (as long as they are achieved by reasonable methods). There is no better way to clear the air with the employee who "knows better" than to provide the flexibility for that person to try it that way and either succeed or fail. In other words, the employee who appears stubborn or resistant may not be so by nature but may rather be reacting to authoritarian leadership. More participative leadership might be the answer.

6. Pay special attention to the chronic complainers, those employees who seem to grouch and grumble all through the day and spread their gloom and doom to anyone who will listen. Chronic complaining is, of course, a sign of several potential problems and also breeds new problems of its own. The chronic complainer can affect departmental morale and drag down the entire work group. You should make every effort to find out what is behind the complaining and perhaps even consider altering assignments so that the complainer is semi-isolated or at least has limited opportunity to spread complaints.

7. Give each employee some special attention. The supervisor-employee relationship remains at the heart of the supervisor's job, and each employee deserves to be recognized as an individual as well as a producer of output. Honest recognition as individuals is all that some of our so-called problem employees really need to enable them to stop being problems.

The Turned-off Worker*

Alienation evidences itself in late arrivals and early departures, in the unduly protracted rest break, in the act of procrastination, and sometimes in the deliberate neglect of duty.

Frequently, students of alienation attribute it to the "meaninglessness" or the "purposelessness" of the worker. In the case of hospital employees, surely one would say there can be no uncertainty about meaning or purpose. The supervisor's job is to spell out the meaning and purpose of any specific task assigned by taking these necessary steps:

1. Explain the nature of the task so that there is no possible misunderstanding about what is expected. Always remember that an individual will not feel at home—that is, will be alienated—in doing something that seems strange to him or her. Lacking details, the subordinate is bound to feel anxious and uncomfortable. In giving an assignment, make sure the employee knows exactly what he or she is supposed to do. Time spent talking it over thoroughly is a good investment. Just think of the time you'll have to spend correcting the error! Worse yet—suppose the error, once committed, cannot be corrected!

2. Show how the task is related to the overall objective of the hospital. To you, it may be

---

Source: Aaron Levinstein, J.D., "Alienation in the Hospital," *Supervisor Nurse*, May 1975. Reprinted with permission.

crystal clear. With your sophistication as a professional, you know that no job performed in the hospital is unrelated to the ultimate purpose of patient care. You cannot expect others to appreciate this automatically. The challenge is to find fresh ways of saying it within the context of the kind of work you personally need done.

3. Give credit for the individual's contribution to the team effort. Precisely because each one does only a part, it is easy to forget the separate contributions. The stars are not likely to be your problem: It's the back-up team who must need your words of approval. A wit has said that the successful executive is the one who shares the credit with the person who has done all the work. Successful, perhaps, but not for long!

In providing preventive measures and a remedy for alienation, it pays to recall the words of John Ruskin: "In order that people may be happy in their work, these three things are needed: They must be fit for it; they must not do too much of it; and they must have a sense of success in it."

Dead-End Employees*

The dead-end employee is that employee who can go no further in the organization. Promotion to supervision may not be possible because basic qualifications are lacking; promotion to a higher level is not possible because the employee is already at the top of grade; pay raises are infrequent because the employee has reached the top of the scale and can move only when the scale itself is moved. In short, the dead-end employee is blocked from growth and advancement in all channels. Motivating this employee is a special problem because there are no more material rewards left with which to prevent creeping dissatisfaction from setting in and other rewards,

---

*Source: Charles R. McConnell, *The Effective Health Care Supervisor*, Aspen Publishers, Inc., © 1988.

the true motivators that should be inherent in the job, are limited.

It is unfortunate that many dead-end employees become problems because these employees very often have the most to offer to the organization. It falls to the supervisor to deal with the problem by appealing to the individual through true motivating forces that stress job factors rather than environmental factors.

In dealing with the dead-end employee, use these strategies:

- *Consult* the employee on various problems and aspects of the department's work. Ask for advice. It is possible that an employee with years of experience in the same capacity has a great deal to offer and will react favorably to the opportunity to offer it.

- Give the employee a bit of additional *responsibility* when possible, and let the person earn the opportunity to be more responsible. Some freedom and flexibility may be seen as recognition of a sort for the employee's past experience and contributions.

- *Delegate* special one-time assignments. Again, years of experience may have prepared the employee to handle special jobs above and beyond ordinary assignments.

- Use the dead-end employee as a *teacher*. The experienced employee may be quite valuable in one-on-one situations, helping to orient new employees or teaching present employees new and different tasks.

- Point the dead-end employee toward certain *prestige* assignments such as committee assignments, attendance at an occasional seminar or educational program, or the coordination of a social activity such as a retirement party or other gathering.

Note that all of the foregoing suggestions deal with ways of putting interest, challenge, variety, and responsibility into the work itself. In dealing with the dead-end employee, special attention must be given to true motivating forces, because the potential dissatisfiers, that is, the environmental factors such as wages and fringe benefits and working conditions, are present in force.

There are other potential solutions to the problem of the dead-end employee, conditions permitting. Maybe it is possible to transfer the person to a completely different assignment or perhaps set up a rotational scheme in which several employees trade assignments on a regular basis. Also, the dead-end employee may be cross-trained on several other jobs within the department and thus be given a chance to do a variety of work and become more valuable to the department.

The Impaired Nurse*

The Situation

Nurse managers must consistently and lawfully confront the problem of an alcohol- or drug-impaired nurse practicing in the hospital. The nurse must be identified and disciplined according to the hospital policy and state law. The appropriate action taken discreetly and promptly will protect the patients from being injured by a drug-impaired nurse and lessen the hospital's risk of liability for corporate negligence in continuing to employ a nurse it knew or should have known was impaired. In addition, it will eliminate the nurse's drug source and remove him or her from practice. It may also encourage the nurse to admit the problem and seek medical assistance.

Identification of the Problem

The proximity of drugs in a hospital facility makes the leap between temptation and addiction a very short step. Those health care professionals who take that step are people who are initially burdened with problems. The addiction— whether alcoholism or other substance abuse— then becomes the final feather.

Nurse administrators should be in a position to recognize the problem (see Table 32-1), prevent

---

Source: Carmelle Pellerin Cournoyer, *The Nurse Manager & The Law*, Aspen Publishers, Inc., © 1989.

The Drugs Most Often Diverted by Nurses

- Meperidine (Demerol), 25.7 percent
- Diazepam (Valium), 18.9 percent
- Codeine products, 9.6 percent
- Flurazepam, 6.6 percent
- Morphine, 6.5 percent
- Propoxyphene products, 5 percent
- Pentazocine, 4 percent
- Barbiturates, 3 percent
- Cocaine, 1 percent

Note: Most state nurse practice acts list a variety of drugs that may be involved in a disciplinary proceeding. Some states include the use or abuse of any drug as grounds for discipline.

---

access to the temptation, provide assistance where possible, and institute legal action when necessary. The recommended stance is to be alert, firm, and helpful. Nurses often seek treatment voluntarily, and there is an incentive in having a profession that they may return to after they have been rehabilitated.

Legal Approach

The most frequent legal proceeding involving alcohol- and drug-impaired nurses is an administrative hearing conducted by the state board of nursing for the purpose of determining whether there are grounds to suspend the nurse's license to practice nursing. The nurse has a right to due process and a fair hearing and in most states can obtain a judicial review of the board's final decision.

The board of nursing must prove the specific offence with which the nurse is charged. In most jurisdictions, the board's order to suspend a nurse's license must include a statement of law, a specific reference to the section of the nurse practice act or regulations that the nurse has violated, and a statement of fact, which is a citing of the evidence on which it based its decision.

Table 32-1 Chart for Identification of Chemical Dependency Behavior

Note: *There is increasing documentation that individuals are addicted to more than one chemical substance. The following list is not all-inclusive.*

	Alcoholic Nurses	*Drug-Addicted Nurses*
Personality/ Behavior Changes	• More irritable with patients and colleagues; withdrawn; mood swings • Social isolation: wants to work nights, lunches alone, avoids informal staff get-togethers • Elaborate excuses for behavior, such as being late for work; unkempt appearance • Blackouts: complete memory loss for events, conversations, phone calls to colleagues; euphoric or "glossed over" recall of events on floor (e.g., arguments or unpleasant events) • Frequent use of breath purifiers; drinks high volume of "sodas" • Flushed face, red or bleary eyes, unsteady gait, slurred speech • Signs of withdrawal: tremors, restlessness, diaphoresis • As disease progresses: jaundice, ascites, spider veins; cigarette burns and bruises caused by carelessness and clumsiness during intoxication, and gastritis from GI effects of alcohol	• Extreme and rapid mood swings: irritable with patients, then calm after taking drugs • Wears long sleeves all the time • Suspicious behavior concerning controlled drugs: —consistently signs out more controlled drugs than anyone else —frequently breaks and spills drugs —purposely waits until alone to open narcotics cabinet —constantly volunteers to be med nurse —disappears into bathroom directly after being in narcotic cabinet —vials/medications appear altered —incorrect narcotic count —discrepancies between his or her patient reports and others' patient reports on effect of medications, etc. —patient complaints that pain medications dispensed by him or her are ineffective —defensive when questioned about medical errors —abnormal number of syringes used, missing, or found in bathroom
Job Performance Changes	• Job shrinkage: does minimum work necessary • Difficulty meeting schedules and deadlines • Illogical or sloppy charting	• Too many medication errors • Too many controlled drugs broken or spilled • Illogical or sloppy charting
Time and Attendance Changes	• Increasingly absent from duty with inadequate explanation: long lunch hours, sick leave after days off • Calls in to request compensatory time at beginning of shift	• Frequently absent from unit • Comes to work early and stays late for no reason—hangs around • Uses sick leave lavishly

Source: Commission on Nursing Administration Ad Hoc Committee on Chemical Dependency, *WSNA Position on the Need for Employee Assistance Programs for Chemical Dependency*, Washington State Nurses Association, 1983.

Chapter 33

Staff Development

OVERVIEW

Role of Nursing Administration*

In a nursing-centered staff development program there is an interdependence between the chief nurse and the educational (staff development) director in the joint identification of teaching-learning needs.

The chief nurse administrator has the responsibility for staff development for nursing personnel, determines the scope of the program, and gives overall direction to the program. The chief nurse administrator is the *key* to current staff development practices and the roles and functions of present-day staff development directors.

The differentiation of educational duties within the nursing service organization is the prerogative of the chief nurse administrator. He or she must work out the most efficient and economical means for achieving the educational mission of nursing service. He or she selects

leadership, makes assignments, writes qualifications for positions, and outlines the duties of each position.

The chief nurse administrator gives positive and inspiring support to the staff development director by showing concern that the aims of the staff development program and those of the program of nursing service coincide, by demonstrating the belief that the educational function of nursing service is indispensable to administration, by actively participating in educational activities, and by dedicating him- or herself to the continuing improvement of nursing personnel.

That staff development is accepted by the administrator is evident in many ways, such as setting standards for jobs, providing on-the-job growth experiences, considering potential growth opportunities in all assignment planning, supervising and appraising performance proficiencies, and assuming responsibility for reparative or corrective training measures. The most important key is the system of promotions and rewards that recognize on-the-job growth. The more healthy, vital, and effective these administrative practices, the more certain will be the success of educational programs supporting staff development.

---

*Source: Drusilla Poole, "Roles and Functions of Staff Development Directors," *Proceedings of the 1976 National Conference on Continuing Education in Nursing*, 1977. Reprinted with permission of the American Nurses' Association.

Functions of Staff Development Department*

Following is a summary of the major functions of a representative, well-organized nursing-centered staff development department (The Nursing Service Division of Tucson Medical Center Department of Staff Development and Research).

Organized under the administrative leadership of a director, the educational functions of the medical center's staff development department include orientation as well as in-service and continuing education:

- Each level of nursing personnel receives *orientation* classes as well as skill delineation and clinical supervision. Clinical supervision runs from a minimum of four weeks up to as long as six months of individualized supervision for particular specialty skills. The Department of Staff Development and Research has a full-time staff of nurse clinicians. Each nurse clinician is a staff specialist responsible for the development needs of nursing personnel organized as follows: medical nursing, surgical nursing, urgent nursing, maternity, pediatrics, ostomy therapy, and cardiovascular nursing.
- *In-service* includes on-the-job training, counseling, and reviewing skills; introduction of new procedures, policies, and products is usually carried out at the unit or individual level of education or specialty area. Overall programs—such as a monthly nursing grand rounds and multidisciplinary patient care programs every three months—are also presented.
- *Continuing education* coordinates attendance at approved programs locally as well as in the state, helps in the presentation of appropriately approved programs within the facility, and furnishes opportunities for the sharing with other staff of things

gleaned from attendance at such programs. Unit and departmental programs are coordinated by the nurse clinicians through the head nurses, with both nursing and educational department staff actually presenting such programs. Educational needs are determined by directors, head nurses, and nursing staff in coordination with the nurse clinicians.

Using a Decentralized Staff Development Program*

In many nursing divisions, the task of staff development has been primarily delegated to a specific education/staff development department. The functional components of such a department include

- periodic needs assessment activity
- an orientation program (centralized and decentralized)
- an in-service and continuing education program
- a patient and community education program

However, as nursing units become more specialized, it is increasingly difficult for the staff development department to provide specific educational programs for individual staff members. Therefore, it is recommended that staff development activities be shared between the nurse manager and the staff development department.

Under such an arrangement, the staff development department retains primary responsibility for centralized orientation and community education while the nurse manager is responsible for decentralized orientation and patient education. Although assessment of educational needs is conducted jointly by the nurse manager and the staff development department, the nurse manager has primary responsibility for targeting which in-service and continuing education programs are needed by his or her staff. The nurse

Source: Adapted from ''Four Approaches to Staff Development,'' National League for Nursing, Pub. No. 20-15781. Reprinted with permission.

Source: Virginia K. Baillie, Louise Trygstad, and Tatiana Isaeff Cordoni, *Effective Nursing Leadership: A Practical Guide*, Aspen Publishers, Inc., © 1989.

manager continues to rely on the staff development department staff for material and human resources to help with planning, conducting, and evaluating the programs he or she designs for the unit staff. As staff developer, the nurse manager performs the following five key role functions: (1) sets staff development goals, (2) enhances and encourages decision making, (3) provides education and training opportunities, (4) monitors staff growth and development through the evaluation process, and (5) serves as a mentor to staff by facilitating career advancement and development.

Shared Services*

When staff development educators from several hospitals or health agencies in the community collaborate on their educational programs, it is sometimes called "shared services."

The idea is to combine and utilize their resources—in a formal or informal way—for their mutual benefit. Although one individual is responsible for the program, he or she is responsible to all participating hospitals equally.

Shared services is most applicable to small hospitals, which otherwise could not support education and training programs. By combining resources (manpower, money, facilities, existing programs, and so on), each can receive maximum benefits at minimum cost.

Shared services also can be effective in larger institutions when it provides one specific aspect of an educational program, such as management development, interpersonal skills training, or patient education, that is needed by several cooperating organizations.

A coordinating group of representatives from each agency is usually formed to identify learning needs and to select appropriate facilities and resource persons for the joint program.

Some of the benefits include: reduced costs, less duplication of effort, increased access to resources, and the ability to serve a larger number of needs.

Using Outside Resources

Some examples of how outside resources have been utilized include these:

1. Instructional personnel from a college nursing department were brought in to provide periodic in-service education programs—economical alternative to full-time staff educators.
2. Workshops developed by a medical center were offered to a number of small hospitals. Dartmouth Medical School provides programs on an interactive television network.
3. Listed topical programs viewed on two-way closed circuit television conserved instruction-time and teaching force.
4. Tele-lecture and radio lectures on a statewide basis (in Wisconsin) used the telephone for call-in conferences. Similar systems were tried out in Oklahoma and North Carolina.
5. Traveling university faculty have brought specialized programs to nurses in isolated regions.

IN-SERVICE EDUCATION

Steps in Planning an In-service Education Program*

Planning really takes place on *two levels*—the overall in-service education plan for a 6- or 12-month period, perhaps, usually developed by, or with the help of, a program planning committee and involving as many people as possible, and, on another level, the specific steps which the in-service education director needs to take to carry out the plan, to put together interesting and effective education programs. Following are the steps to be taken from the in-service education director's point of view.

Source: Adapted from "Four Approaches to Staff Development," National League for Nursing, Pub. No. 20-15781. Reprinted with permission.

Source: E.S. Popiel, "Educational Program Planning," *Problem Oriented Systems of Patient Care*, National League for Nursing, Pub. No. 21-1522, 1974. Reprinted with permission.

Assess Needs

In-service education directors need to realize the importance of early recognition of changes in nursing service, technology, legislation, research, economics, public demands, and the changing patient load within the institution, all of which affect what nursing personnel need to know to give effective and comprehensive nursing care.

Observations of the nursing care given on the units will assist in assessing needs. But a word of warning—if an in-service program is planned only in response to expressed interests, desires, and needs of nursing personnel, educational activities may prove to be limited in scope and remedial in nature, dealing with problems that are already deeply entrenched in the established system and are difficult of solution. Such educational offerings may be too little and too late, both to meet present needs and to forestall future problems. The director of in-service education is in a unique position and can view the total nursing situation in a manner detached from the immediate problems and pressures of the job of the nurse practitioner and with a degree of objectivity not available to most others. An education program planning committee and the nursing service administration may provide a great deal of assistance in outlining future, as well as present, needs for educational courses.

Set Goals and Define Specific Objectives

The program planning committee can also assist in setting the goals of a staff development or in-service education program. These objectives should express expected outcomes, because evaluation of the effectiveness of your overall program will be easier if your objectives are stated so they can be evaluated. Once the goals and objectives are formulated, they should be subjected to periodic scrutiny for the purpose of keeping them relevant.

Plan Courses and Design Learning Experiences

It is important to leave plans and schedules flexible enough that changes and additions can be made as short-range needs arise during the year. The planning and designing of learning experiences challenge the in-service coordinator to draw on the rich methodologies of adult education. Since the primary goal of in-service education is more than merely imparting information and is geared to changing the way a person performs, thinks, or feels, the plan calls for helping personnel to integrate the new knowledge or skill into their immediate experience and stimulating them to set future learning goals for themselves. Role-playing, simulated games, small group work, ''alone-time,'' lectures, independent study, pilot projects, and other methods facilitate the involvement and response of the total person to the learning situation.

Select Resource People

There are several attributes which should be kept in mind when selecting individuals as resource persons:

1. expertise and clinical competence in the area to be covered
2. ability to serve as a model for learners
3. knowledgeable about the concepts of adult learning
4. relates well with adult learners
5. knows how to communicate knowledge without a belittling or pompous manner
6. starts where the learners are and lets them progress at their own pace
7. willing to assist in evaluation process
8. an accepting, listening person who is willing to change the course in midstream if necessary to meet learner needs

Implement Plans

This phase centers around designing the curriculum. Content requirements, learning experiences, and expectations of the participants provide input for the program outline and schedule.

Once the year-long program has been projected, it is then time to decide how to implement the activities. Again, the planning committee can be very useful here. Some of the activities you may have planned would best be done on the supervisor, head nurse, or team leader level, that is, decentralized rather than institutionwide. When this is true, the task is to train, support, and assist the head nurses or team leaders in planning the decentralized activity. Everyone in the institution needs to be aware of the courses and educational activities scheduled so they can plan ahead to meet their own continuing education goals.

This is the time to ask the nursing personnel what courses or activities they would like to assist in planning and implementing. The committees for each educational activity can be selected at this time, getting more and more of the nursing personnel involved. The more personnel involved, the easier it will be to get good attendance at the activities and give the personnel the feeling that they have a responsibility to the program.

Evaluate Program

There are many ways of performing evaluation, and everyone should be involved—the director of the program, the planning committee, resource persons, the committees for each educational activity, the nursing personnel who attend the courses, their supervisors, and their peers. The most important questions to be answered are: Did this educational activity make a difference in the knowledge, skills, and attitudes of the participants? Was there a change in behavior so that better nursing care was given?

Having specific objectives for each activity which clearly delineate the desired outcomes will assist evaluation immensely.

Some evaluative methods include diaries; process recordings; tapes; reaction sheets; participant satisfaction ratings; personnel relations surveys; pre- and posttests of knowledge, skills, and attitudes; and specific rating of achievement of course objectives by the participants. Six-month or one-year postevaluations are helpful, as are interviews of peers and supervisors and observations of the nursing personnel at work.

Identification of Training Needs*

The process of identifying training needs is accomplished through the collection of evidence

---

*Source: E.S. Popiel, "Educational Program Planning," *Problem Oriented Systems of Patient Care*, National League for Nursing, Pub. No. 21-1522, 1974. Reprinted with permission.

Evaluate the Impact of Training on Job Performance

- Did training make a difference?
- Are individuals able to perform the tasks that formed the basis of training?
- Did training solve the problem or fill the need identified during the needs analysis process?
- Do supervisors, managers, and those receiving training feel that completion of the program by the employees made a difference?
- Did training affect the product produced by those completing training?

Note: If job performance has not improved, each phase of the training process must be examined through an internal evaluation. The internal evaluation process examines the instructional design, delivery, and evaluation phases of training. Even when job performance has improved, the evaluator may decide to monitor the training process in order to identify the strengths and address any concerns within the program.

Source: Richard L. Sullivan, Jerry L. Wircenski, Susan S. Arnold, and Michelle D. Sarkees, *The Trainer's Guide: A Practical Manual for the Design, Delivery, and Evaluation of Training*, Aspen Publishers, Inc., © 1990.

---

or data. Numerous methods are used, but the sources of information can be divided into two categories: staff input and focused observations.

Staff Input Methods

Involve a canvass of staff personnel, as individuals or as a group, to determine their own awareness of inadequacies. They may identify shortages of particular skills in their own background or on the unit in general. Among the methods used are

- individual interviews by in-service director
- self-evaluation checklists of required performance skills

- survey polls on specific functional areas
- establishment of a suggestion ''box'' system

Focused Observations

Involve the talents of a perceptive in-service educator who matches nursing care functions and standards to the priorities expressed by the hospital and nursing administration. Observations may be geared to uncovering problem areas on the unit, for example, in charting or in distribution of drugs or in determining trouble spots in a staff member's performance. Among the methods used are

- direct observation of unit/individual in performance
- inspection of incident reports
- review of previous performance evaluations of staff members
- checklist observations of specific functions

As the problem spots are revealed, the in-service educator should start to correlate needs with educational answers and be prepared to marshal available resources for effecting solutions to the problems presented.

Criteria for Evaluating Instructional Materials*

1. Are the materials appropriate for the training objectives? Materials selected must relate to the objectives. A trainer may use a set of existing materials to save development time, but learners may become confused and lose interest when there appears to be no relationship between the materials and the training objectives.

Source: Richard L. Sullivan, Jerry L. Wircenski, Susan S. Arnold, and Michelle D. Sarkees, *The Trainer's Guide: A Practical Manual for the Design, Delivery, and Evaluation of Training*, Aspen Publishers, Inc., © 1990.

2. Are the materials relevant to the organization? A commercially produced set of safety slides may show basic safety procedures, but if the equipment, products, and processes are not familiar to the learners, the effectiveness of the slides may be limited.
3. Are the materials compatible with existing media and media equipment? If not, programs must be returned or modified, or new equipment must be purchased.
4. Is the format of the materials consistent with that of existing materials? There are many sources of instructional materials appropriate for use in individualized training packets. The program designer may want to have all information sheets in the same format to ensure consistency.
5. Is the information contained within the instructional materials current? Dated content, photographs, and references limit the effectiveness of materials.
6. Is the information contained within the instructional materials factual? A subject matter expert should review the materials to ensure that the information presented is correct.
7. Is the information biased? The program designer must review materials to ensure that there is no job denigration bias, sex-role stereotyping, ethnic bias, racial bias, age discrimination, or religious bias.
8. Is the quality of the materials consistent with that of existing materials? Materials must be reviewed to ensure that the quality of sound, video, image, layout, and other factors meets the expectations of the organization.
9. Is the reading level of the materials appropriate for the learners? A procedure sheet written at a 12th-grade reading level may be inappropriate for learners reading at a 9th-grade level. The program designer may need to determine the approximate reading level of the learners in order to consider reading level in the selection of materials. There are standardized tests for determining the reading level of instructional materials.
10. Is the cost of the materials reasonable? A program designer may decide to use

interactive video as part of an individualized training program. The final decision to use this medium may be a budgetary decision that takes into account the cost of developing and delivering interactive video.

Guidelines for In-service Programs*

- Provision should be made for nurses to participate in the identification of their continuing education needs and in plans for meeting the needs.

- Programs of continuing and in-service education should be relevant to both the educational needs of professional nurse employees and the needs of the institution.

- Learning experiences of basic and higher degree programs in nursing should be monitored to determine the appropriateness of selected educational programs or learning activities for continuing education.

- The staff development program should be consistent with the overall goals and objectives of the institution.

- Objectives should be defined for each in-service education program and used as a basis for determining content, learning experiences, and evaluation. They should be stated in terms of the terminal overt behaviors which indicate successful achievement of desired outcomes. Plans for continuous and terminal evaluation should be made at the time objectives are identified.

- An interdisciplinary approach to sponsoring, planning, and implementing educational activities is encouraged. Close working relationships should be developed between the nursing service people and the staff development people.

- In-service education programs for nurses should be developed under the direction of nurses who, as well as being competent nurse practitioners, are skilled in planning and implementing educational programs.

- Faculty expertise in the content to be taught is essential.

- A variety of formats and teaching methodologies should be utilized, with selection based on the objectives.

- The time allotted to any in-service education activity should be sufficient to ensure achievement of the objectives. Provision should be made for nurses to have time available to devote to these educational activities.

- Facilities and resources appropriate to the educational program should be provided as follows: Instructional materials, libraries, learning laboratories, conference rooms, secretarial services, and consultants (if indicated).

- Adequate funds for planning, conducting, and evaluating the continuing education program should be included in the nursing services budget.

- Programs should be announced well in advance to enable all concerned to make personal and professional plans accordingly.

- Records of attendance should be maintained.

- Counseling and guidance should be offered so that staff will be informed about the range of continuing educational opportunities that may meet their intermediate and long-range career needs.

- Maximum opportunity should be provided for participants of continuing education programs to integrate new knowledge and skills into practice, share with others, and evaluate the effect on patient care.

CONTINUING EDUCATION— OUTSIDE THE HOSPITAL

Each nursing service should be constantly alert to available outside learning opportunities and the conceivable use which can be made of these in rounding out the program of development for its entire staff.

---

*Source: Guidelines for Continuing Education, Veterans Administration, 1977, #G-11, M2 Part V.

Included in this category are the following types of experiences:

1. institutes
2. short courses
3. conferences
4. workshops
5. clinical experiences in a civilian hospital or clinic
6. participation in a national professional meeting
7. tuition support for part-time university study
8. educational leave with or without tuition support for advanced study

Criteria for Selecting Individual Participants*

Planning *who* shall have *what* in terms of experiences outside the agency should be approached on a "first come, first served" basis. The selection of nurses for these experiences should depend to a large extent on the kinds of goals the nursing service has established for itself. The learning value to the individual and to the hospital should be considered. The ability of the nurse to make functional adaptation of the experience to the local situation should be a criterion for selection of both the individual and the experience. Matching experience with the individual is not easy; however, one question which always has to be examined is how closely related the experience is to the nurse's regularly assigned duties. The nurse who is able to state clearly his or her objectives in requesting such an educational experience is usually the one who can evaluate the experience in a way that has meaning for others. However, the position the nurse holds needs to be considered when projected plans include sharing this experience with many other persons. For example, a staff nurse may experience personal and professional development but is not in a position to readily implement new approaches or change existing

thinking of other persons in his or her unit, as is the head nurse or clinical supervisor.

Criteria for Funding*

In developing criteria for complete or partial defrayment of cost and/or authorizing absence and for an equitable allocation of time and funds for nursing personnel—consideration should be given to the

1. benefit to patient care
2. facility need for developing or updating staff skill and knowledge
3. degree to which the individual can assume responsibility for sharing and applying learning
4. preference for local continuing education activity over a distant equivalent offering
5. frequency of facility support of the individual's participation in a continuing education activity

Evaluating Program Quality**

In recommending standards for continuing education programs in nursing, the American Nurses' Association delineates a number of structural criteria which the prospective student can use as a guideline for measuring the acceptability of different offerings. When reading descriptive material, check and see whether these criteria are met:

1. The continuing education provider unit has an administrative organization which clearly delineates a system of authority, responsibility, communication, and fiscal accountability.
2. Criteria for selection of director, faculty, resource persons, and support staff are

---

*Source: Guideline for Continuing Education, Department of Medicine and Surgery, Veterans Administration, 1977.

*Source: Inservice Education Activities in Nursing Service, Department of Medicine and Surgery, Veterans Administration, 1963.

**Source: Standards for Continuing Education in Nursing, American Nurses' Association, Pub. No. COE-8 3M, 1984.

established. The person directly responsible for a continuing education provider unit is a nurse with the minimum of a master's degree.

3. There is a mechanism for learner input in planning continuing education activities.
4. An educational design based on adult learning principles is employed.
5. Physical facilities and material resources for each continuing education program are conducive to learning.
6. A system is in place which allows a provider to gather, record, and retrieve pertinent data for each program.
7. Quality assurance mechanisms are in place to monitor all continuing education programs and to determine the effectiveness of individual programs.

In addition, the credentials and past performance of the sponsor should be reviewed. If possible, obtain names of former participants to contact for references. And encourage participants to be fully prepared by requesting in advance the reading or activity list.

Continuing Education Units (CEUs)*

Requirements for Awarding CEUs

Any sponsor can award CEUs provided they

- have an identifiable educational arm that is administered by professional staff
- maintain administrative control of all of the continuing education activities they sponsor
- provide or arrange for appropriate educational facilities, including the locations in which programs are held, and related resources (materials or equipment)
- maintain individual records of participation on a permanent basis that participants can request if needed

---

*Source: Belinda E. Puetz and Faye L. Peters, *Continuing Education for Nurses: A Complete Guide to Effective Programs,* Aspen Publishers, Inc., © 1981.

The Council on the Continuing Education Unit established program criteria that must be met—among them that

- the activity is conducted under responsible sponsorship, capable direction, and qualified instruction
- the activity is planned on the basis of the needs of the target audience
- a clear statement of purpose and goals is prepared for each educational activity
- qualified instructors conduct the course
- there are specific performance requirements for participants to establish eligibility to earn CEUs
- registration forms contain enough information to permit permanent records to be kept
- records must be kept to verify completion by each participant who is awarded CEUs
- the course or workshop is evaluated in terms of its design and operation.

There are some events for which CEUs should not be awarded: courses for academic credit, committee meetings, entertainment or recreational activities such as travel groups, or high school equivalency programs. Another activity that does not qualify for CEUs is acting as a faculty member in an educational activity, even though this may involve considerable time preparing the material to be presented. CEUs are not awarded for the preparation, presentation, or publication of papers and reports, nor for work or on-the-job experience. Only individuals who participate in the courses are eligible to receive CEUs.

When calculating the CEUs to be awarded, only the time spent in the educational experience should be considered. Time spent in making announcements and introductions, going to lunch, or visiting exhibits, for example, is not included.

Proof of Completion

The council recommends that a CEU be awarded only upon proof of satisfactory completion of the course. That proof may be the passing of a posttest, an evaluation of the program, or whatever demonstration of completion is deemed appropriate by the director. Only individuals who complete the requirements satisfactorily should be awarded a CEU. If the award is based only on attendance, then prorating is appropriate, but the course objectives generally are not met if the nurse does not participate in the entire program. If a notice that attendance is necessary at all sessions to receive a CEU is included with the course publicity, participants will be forewarned that the unit will be awarded only at the conclusion of the entire program.

The approval of educational activities by an ANA-accredited SNA for which the sponsor awards a CEU indicates that the program meets the criteria established by the National Task Force and the Council on the Continuing Education Unit and the standards for quality continuing education as established by the professional organizations for nurses.

Many national nursing specialty organizations have systems for continuing education approval. Many of these have been accredited by the American Nurses' Association to provide approved continuing education activities and to approve those of their constituents. Some of the organizations accredited through the ANA mechanism are

- American Association of Nephrology Nurses and Technicians
- American Association of Occupational Health Nurses
- Association of Operating Room Nurses, Inc.
- Association of Rehabilitation Nurses
- Emergency Department Nurses Association
- Nurses' Association of the American College of Obstetricians and Gynecologists

Chapter 34

Evaluation: Performance Appraisal

OVERVIEW

Objectives of the Performance Appraisal System*

Objectives of a performance appraisal system fall into three broad categories: identifying and remediating problem behaviors, enhancing professional growth and development, and strengthening team efforts toward meeting departmental goals cooperatively.

Monitoring Work-related Behaviors

The first group of program objectives relates to monitoring, assessing, and remediating work performance. These are important as far as the ''control'' function of management is concerned. Without the ability and mechanisms to monitor carefully each individual employee's performance, the manager can neither identify nor help solve work problems stemming from unacceptable job-related behaviors.

To achieve effective monitoring, note the following requisite elements.

Assessing individual performance in relation to practice/work standards. Managers should

---

Source: Therese G. Lawler, ''The Objectives of Performance Appraisal—or 'Where Can We Go From Here?''' *Nursing Management*, vol. 19, no. 3, March 1988. Reprinted with permission.

use specific work standards as criterion measures for performance evaluation. It should be remembered that evaluation is a comparison of present work-related behaviors of an individual with defined and delineated standards, which are related to that individual's particular role or job category. In assessing individual performance one looks for compliance with those standards or an acceptable level of competence.

Providing incentives for the improvement and maximization of work-related behaviors. Various types of behavior reinforcement can come into play in evaluation systems. These reinforcements, whether positive or negative, provide incentives toward improved behaviors. Positive incentives may include something as obvious as a merit pay increase, but incentives which also motivate include praise and recognition; employee awards for outstanding evaluations; and increased job responsibility, which acts as an enriching factor. Negative reinforcers or disincentives may be as simple as supervisory displeasure or docking of pay for habitual tardiness.

Establishing a mechanism for the remediation of suboptimal performance. The manager builds into a performance evaluation system a ''due process'' system which can be used for dysfunctional staff problems. For instance, if a particular employee is habitually late for work, the established guidelines of the evaluation system or performance appraisal program would specify that after the second time the individual would be informally counseled. After the fourth incident, there would be a formal interview in which the discussion is noted and specific goals and objectives set. If the goals still are not realized in the specified time frame, the employee would be given an official warning and a final deadline for showing changes in behavior—that is, for being on time. Should additional infractions occur, due process would include, in sequential order, docking of pay, suspension, probation, and finally termination. The aim of the remedial mechanism always is to salvage the employee and to help direct him or her to an acceptable behavior pattern.

Maintaining documentation of problem areas and remedial action. Documentation itself is different from the establishment of a remediation mechanism. The process of recording dysfunctional behavior of a problem employee is vital; however, not only are the interactions between supervisor and subordinate noted but the mutually agreed upon solutions to the work-related problem are recorded and progress toward them is monitored. Documentation is not only important to ensure due process and equitable treatment of employee difficulty, but it also serves as an ongoing progress report to determine degrees and areas of improvement.

Documenting employee/supervisor interactions. Recordkeeping in this instance relates to keeping a log of what was said and what commitment to action was made. To accomplish this particular objective, as well as those previously mentioned, more than one conference yearly is necessary. Anecdotal records demand periodic dialogue and assessment, the foundations of any good appraisal program. Good behavior needs to be reinforced when it happens; likewise, suboptimal behavior needs to be confronted as soon as it occurs.

Stimulating Individual Growth and Development

The next group of expected outcomes or objectives of a performance appraisal system center on contributions to individual growth and development. An essential underlying assumption about staff evaluation is that it should be approached as a learning experience. In this context, both the employee and the manager should be learning from the process. If an evaluation system is to achieve this, it must allow for the following.

Recognition and/or rewards for performance. There are many creative ways in which recognition, a major positive reinforcer of behavior, can be built into a standards-based system. For example, monetary recompense is an obvious and tangible reward which has both real and symbolic value to an employee.

Identifying professional goals of the employee. An important function of the nurse manager's role is that of coach or director. A prime responsibility for anyone who supervises a group of employees is assisting with their personal and professional growth and development. To do this well the manager helps each person identify (1) personal and career goals and (2) strategies which will aid in their achievement.

Enhancing work performance through mutual goal setting. Goals can relate either to shoring up weak work behaviors or to increasing skill and learning new competencies. Managers must remember how important it is that people who *want* to be better at what they do be given as much supervisory attention and back-up as people who *need* to be better. Mutual goal setting between supervisor and subordinate and periodic tracking through a well-delineated evaluation system will allow for growth.

Enhancing Team Development

The last group of objectives are those which revolve around team development through the monitoring of *group* performance. Inherent in the definition of a manager as "one who gets things done through others" is a concept that individual employees band together under common direction to accomplish the unit's or agency's goals.

A performance evaluation system can assist the health care manager in the following ways:

Stimulating constructive communication through a formalized feedback system. The evaluation process provides a formalized channel for two-way communication and it is to the manager's advantage to use this channel productively and wisely. The manager is able to collect data on common problem areas seen by staff members and to identify better the strengths and weaknesses in the group as a whole.

Identifying training needs for both the individual and the group. If people are performing certain work behaviors poorly, there are many plausible explanations. One is that employees are not doing well simply because they do not know that their shortcomings are a result of a deficit in knowledge or skills.

Evaluating the quality of aggregate practice and productivity within a unit or department. In the role of controller or monitor, the manager is responsible for overseeing the quality assurance program of his or her nursing unit or department. A valuable methodology to ensure quality of care is (1) to set up practice or performance standards and then (2) to compare work-related behaviors of both the individual and the group to the standards. A broader application of the principle of quality assurance through an evaluation system can be illustrated through identification of particular competencies related to patient care which are not being carried out by the majority of a particular staff.

Providing a means for participation and staff input into job practice standards and departmental planning. Input by staff is a key factor. Becoming involved in evaluations, which provides mutual benefits both to employees and to the supervisor and ensures quality provision of care, can forestall many morale problems.

Benefits of Systematic Appraisal*

A formal evaluation system helps the manager consider these factors more carefully and reduces the chances that personal biases will distort the rating. It also forces the manager to observe and scrutinize the work of subordinates not only from the point of view of how well the employees are performing their jobs, but also from the standpoint of what can be done to improve performance. An employee's poor performance and failure to improve may be due in part to the manager's own inadequate supervision. A formal appraisal may serve to evaluate and improve the manager's own performance.

A formal appraisal system serves another important purpose. Every employee has the right to know how well he or she is doing and what can be done to improve work performance. Most employees want to know what their supervisors think of their work. An employee's desire to know how he or she stands can be interpreted as a need for assurance that he or she has a future in the organization.

Regular appraisals are an important incentive, particularly to the employees of a large organization. Many workers have the feeling that because of the great amount of job specialization, the individual worker's contributions are lost and forgotten. Regular appraisals provide some assurance that the employee is not overlooked by his or her superior and the entire organization.

Regular appraisals of all subordinates should be made by the manager at least once a year, normally considered a sufficiently long period of time. If an employee has just started in a new and more responsible position, it is advisable to make an appraisal within three to six months. In some organizations, appraisals are made according to the dates each employee started; in others, all appraisals are made once or twice a year on fixed dates. As time goes on, periodic appraisals become an important influence upon an employee's morale.

The Appraiser*

The ideal appraiser, one who observes and evaluates what is important and reports judg-

*Source: Jonathan S. Rakich, Beaufort B. Longest, and Thomas R. O'Donovan, *Managing Health Care Organizations*, W.B. Saunders Company, © 1977. Reprinted by permission of CBS College Publishing.

*Source: Marion G. Haynes, "Developing an Appraisal Program, Part I," *Personnel Journal,* January 1978. Reprinted with the permission of *Personnel Journal,* Costa Mesa, California; all rights reserved.

ments without bias or error, probably does not exist. But since human judgments must be used, several criteria have been developed to aid in determining an appropriate appraiser.

Qualities

1. An appraiser must have sufficient *opportunity to observe:* in other words, the appraiser must be in a position to collect relevant information about the person being evaluated. This can be accomplished through personal observation, reviewing records or talking with others who have direct knowledge of the person.
2. An appraiser's *ability to judge* depends on having a clear understanding of job requirements and standards of satisfactory performance. The objectives and procedures of the appraisal system must be understood as well. Research has shown that more competent supervisors give more valid appraisals, while less effective supervisors tend to reward the conservative, cooperative employee who does not represent a threat to the supervisor's position.
3. An appraiser's *point of view* needs to be appropriate for the purpose of the particular appraisal being prepared, because one's point of view usually influences which observed performance is considered desirable or undesirable. A clinical nurse supervisor and a head nurse might well have different perspectives on what constitutes excellence.

Position of Appraiser

The *position of an appraiser* helps determine opportunity to observe, ability to judge and the appropriateness of point of view.

Supervisors. By virtue of their position, supervisors have long been favored as appraisers. They have the necessary experience, knowledge, and ability, plus there is the fact that they represent the organization.

Peers. So far, peer appraisals have been used primarily for research purposes. It has not yet been determined how valid peer appraisals could be as a basis for administrative decisions.

Subordinates. Subordinate appraisals are considered to be deficient because the subordinate sees only a part of the supervisor's job. They have been successfully used, however, to gauge supervisor-subordinate relationships and in management development work where supervisors want feedback on how their subordinates experience them.

Self. Self-appraisals find their greatest use in performance discussions. When a person completes a self-appraisal prior to a performance discussion, the appraisal tends to be modest. Under most other circumstances, people tend to see themselves as better performers.

Reducing Individual Bias in Reviews

Appraisals by one individual can be influenced by personal bias. There are four ways to reduce this possibility:

Second-level Review. By having appraisals reviewed by a supervisor's superior, the chance of superficial or biased evaluations is reduced.

Group Appraisal. In a group appraisal, the judgment of a supervisor is supplemented by others who have an appropriate relationship with the employee being appraised (e.g., the functional supervisor or working leadman).

Multiple Appraisal. Here appropriate supervisors, in addition to an immediate supervisor, also appraise the subordinate. In selecting appropriate supervisors, the same criteria are used as in selecting appraisal groups.

Field Review Specialists. A field review specialist interviews a supervisor and prepares an appraisal form from the data obtained. With proper training, a specialist can contribute significantly to the quality of appraisals by maintaining consistency.

APPROACHES TO APPRAISAL

Analysis vs. Appraisal*

This approach to performance appraisal differs profoundly from the conventional one, for it shifts the emphasis from *appraisal* to *analysis*. This implies a more positive approach. No longer is the staff member being examined by the superior so that his or her weaknesses may be determined; rather, the staff member is examining him- or herself in order to define not only weaknesses but also strengths and potentials. The importance of this shift of emphasis should not be underestimated.

One of the main differences of this approach is that it rests on the assumption that the individual knows—or can learn—more than anyone else about his or her own capabilities, needs, strengths and weaknesses, and goals. In the end, only the individual can determine what is best for his or her development. The conventional approach, on the other hand, makes the assumption that the superior can know enough about the subordinate to decide what is best for him or her. In the discussions, the supervisor or evaluator can use his or her knowledge of the organization to help the staff member establish targets and methods for achieving them which will (1) lead to increased knowledge and skill, (2) contribute to organizational objectives, and (3) test the staff member's appraisal of him- or herself.

If the supervisor accepts this role, he or she need not become a judge of the staff member's personal worth. The supervisor is not telling, deciding, criticizing, or praising—not "playing God." The supervisor listens instead and uses his or her own knowledge of the organization and of professional competence as a basis for advising, guiding, encouraging staff members to develop their own potentialities.

Another significant difference is that the emphasis is on the future rather than the past.

The purpose of the plan is to establish realistic targets and to seek the most effective ways of reaching them. Appraisal thus becomes a means to a constructive end. Even the staff member who has failed can be helped to consider what moves will be best for him- or herself.

Finally, the accent is on *performance,* on actions relative to goals. There is less tendency for the personality of the staff member to become an issue.

Management by Objectives*

Peter Drucker's concept of "management by objectives" offers a novel approach to performance appraisal. His approach calls on the staff member to establish short-term performance goals *for him- or herself.* The supervisor enters the process actively only *after* the staff member has (1) done a good deal of thinking about his or her job, (2) made a careful self-assessment of strengths and weaknesses, and (3) formulated some specific plans to accomplish his or her goals. The supervisor's role is to help the person relate his or her self-appraisal, "targets," and plans for the ensuing period to the realities of the organization.

The first step in this process is to arrive at a clear statement of the major features of the job. Rather than a formal job description, this is a document drawn up *by the staff member* after studying the agency-approved statement. It defines the broad areas of the staff member's responsibility as they actually work out in practice. The evaluator and staff member discuss the draft jointly and modify it as may be necessary until both of them agree that it is adequate.

Working from this statement of responsibilities, the staff member then establishes goals or "targets" for a period of, say, six months. These targets are *specific actions* which the person proposes to take, for example, actively contributing to staff meetings concerned with patients' needs, keeping nursing care plans current, updating knowledge of specific methods of

Source: Reprinted by permission of the *Harvard Business Review*. Excerpted from "An Uneasy Look at Performance Appraisal" by Douglas McGregor, September-October 1972. Copyright © 1972 by the President and Fellows of Harvard College; all rights reserved.

Source: Ibid.

care relating to the staff member's area of practice. Thus they are explicitly stated and accompanied by a detailed account of the actions the staff member proposes to take to reach them. This document is in turn discussed with the evaluator and modified until both are satisfied with it.

At the conclusion of the six-month period, the staff member makes an appraisal of what he or she has accomplished relative to the targets set earlier. The staff member substantiates the appraisal with factual data wherever possible. The "interview" is an examination by evaluator and staff member together of the staff member's self-appraisal, and it culminates in a resetting of targets for the next six months.

Of course, the superior has veto power at each step of this process; in an organizational hierarchy anything else would be unacceptable. However, in practice the superior rarely needs to exercise it. Often staff members tend to underestimate both their potentialities and their achievements. A common problem is to resist a staff member's tendency to want the evaluator to say what to write down.

Evaluations by Subordinates*

Evaluations are almost always from the "top down." Nurses are evaluated by their superiors and even the director of nursing is evaluated by the administrative person to whom he or she reports. This type of review is vital but it is often not conducted adequately. As a result, it may be more damaging than positive to the subordinate's performance and the superior-subordinate relationship. Unfortunately, almost always the evaluation is one-sided.

A broader and more constructive type of evaluation is one which allows supervisors not only to learn how their superiors rate them, but also how their subordinates view their job performance.

This type of evaluation may be instituted by simply adopting an evaluation form which will allow subordinates objectively to evaluate their superiors in a confidential manner.

---

*Source: T. Moore and E. Simendinger, "Evaluating Is a Two-Way Street," *Supervisor Nurse,* June 1976. Reprinted with permission.

The Evaluation Form

Much of the success of a subordinate-supervisor evaluation depends on the type of form used and the way it is introduced. The form should be comprehensive, confidential, and easily interpreted by subordinates. It is vitally important that the identity of the employee completing the form be kept confidential. Very few individuals will be totally candid in evaluating their superiors if they believe that their identities will become known.

Prior to distributing the evaluation form, the supervisor should give an adequate orientation and emphasize the importance of objectivity in completing the form. Any questions which the subordinates have regarding the contents of the form should be explained at this time. The supervisor should also explain that the purpose of the form is to help improve performance; it should not be used either to "whitewash" or as a means to "even the score." Lastly, there should be a definite deadline for the completion of the form. A sample evaluation form is shown in Table 34-1.

Table 34-1 Sample Subordinate-Superior Rating Form

Please circle your answers.

1—Very Poor	4—Good
2—Poor	5—Excellent
3—Fair	

1. Cooperation	1	2	3	4	5
2. Responsibility	1	2	3	4	5
3. Honesty	1	2	3	4	5
4. Emotional Stability	1	2	3	4	5
5. Seriousness of Purpose	1	2	3	4	5
6. Leadership Ability	1	2	3	4	5
7. Job Achievement	1	2	3	4	5
8. Industry	1	2	3	4	5
9. Concern for Others	1	2	3	4	5
10. Appearance	1	2	3	4	5
11. Job Interest	1	2	3	4	5
12. Self Discipline	1	2	3	4	5
13. Desire to Learn	1	2	3	4	5
14. General Ability	1	2	3	4	5
15. Tardiness, Absenteeism	1	2	3	4	5

Benefits from a Subordinate-Superior Evaluation

There are numerous benefits to be derived from a formalized subordinate-superior evaluation. Among the more important are these:

- The evaluation enables the supervisor to learn how subordinates perceive his or her job performance. Both strengths and weaknesses should be documented if the form is completed properly.
- By being asked to complete the form, employees will usually believe that their superior values their opinion and is trying to improve.
- The form provides employees with a vehicle for giving their superior, in confidence, those comments which they might not discuss in person.

Supervisors should not expect to rate very high in all categories, nor should they rate very low. If properly completed, the form should allow them to gain a greater awareness of their strengths and weaknesses. If completed annually, the form should also provide a means for determining performance effectiveness and improvement.

Appraisal Methods*

The major approaches to performance appraisal are described below.

Rating Scales

Rating scales, the oldest and most widely used appraisal procedures, are of two general types.

In *continuous scales,* in reference to a particular evaluation characteristic, the evaluator places a mark somewhere along a continuous scale (Figure 34-1).

In *discrete scales,* each characteristic is associated with a number of descriptions covering the possible range of employee performance. The evaluator simply checks the box, or perhaps the column, accompanying the most appropriate description (Figure 34-2).

Rating scales are relatively easy to construct, and they permit ready comparison of scores among employees. However, rating scales have several severe disadvantages. Do total scores of 78 for Jane and 83 for Harriet *really* mean anything significant? If an employee scores low relative to quantity of work produced, can this

---

Source: Charles R. McConnell, *The Effective Health Care Supervisor,* Aspen Publishers, Inc., © 1988.

Figure 34-1 Continuous-type Rating Scale Excerpt

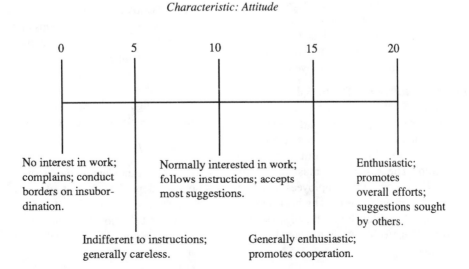

Characteristic: Attitude

Figure 34-2 Discrete-type Rating Scale Excerpt

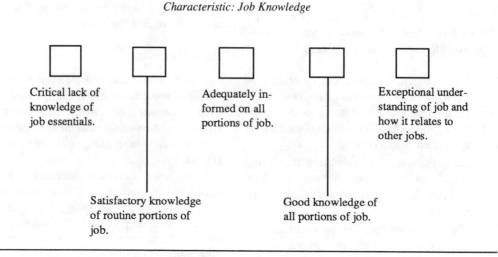

Characteristic: Job Knowledge

Critical lack of knowledge of job essentials.

Adequately informed on all portions of job.

Exceptional understanding of job and how it relates to other jobs.

Satisfactory knowledge of routine portions of job.

Good knowledge of all portions of job.

really be counterbalanced by high scores for attendance, attitude, and job knowledge?

Employee Comparison

Employee comparison methods were developed to overcome certain disadvantages of rating scales. Employee comparison may involve the ranking method or the forced distribution method.

Ranking. The ranking method forces the supervisor to rate all employees on an overall basis according to their job performance and value to the institution. One approach is to simply look at your work group and decide initially who is the best and who is the poorest performer and then to pick the second and next-to-last persons in your rank order by applying the same judgment to the remaining employees.

Forced Distribution. The forced distribution method prevents the supervisor from clustering all employees in any particular part of the scale. It requires the evaluator to distribute the ratings in a pattern conforming with a normal frequency distribution. The supervisor must place, for instance, 10 percent of the employees in the top category, 20 percent in the next higher category, 40 percent in the middle bracket, and so on. The objective of this technique is to spread out the evaluations.

Checklists

Weighted Checklist. The weighted checklist consists of a number of statements that describe various modes and levels of behavior for a particular job or category of jobs. Every statement has a weight or scale value associated with it, and when rating an employee the supervisor checks those statements that most closely describe the behavior exhibited by the individual. The completed rating sheet is then scored by averaging the weights of all the descriptive statements checked by the rater. Some evaluation characteristics are worth more or less than others.

Forced Choice. In the forced choice method, statements are arranged in groups of four or five each, and within each group the evaluator must check the one statement that is most descriptive of the performance of the employee and the one statement that is least descriptive. The actual value or weight of the statements is kept secret from the supervisor. (See Table 34-2.)

Critical Incident

The critical incident method requires a supervisor to adopt the practice of recording in a notebook all those significant incidents in each employee's behavior that indicate either effective or successful action or ineffective action or poor behavior.

Table 34-2 Illustrative Group of Statements from a Forced Choice Appraisal

Circle the letter for the statement that is *most* descriptive of the employee's performance *or the least* descriptive of the employee's performance.

Most	Least	
A	A	Makes mistakes only infrequently
B	B	Is respected by fellow employees
C	C	Fails to follow instructions completely
D	D	Feels own job is more important than other jobs
E	E	Does not exhibit self-reliance when expressing own views

However, supervisors are busy people and often everything that should be recorded does not reach the notebook. On the other hand, negative incidents, because of their "seriousness," are more likely to reach the pages of the book than are many occasions of positive performance. Also, this approach can lead to overly close supervision, with the employees feeling that the supervisor is watching over their shoulders and that everything they do will be written down in the "little black book."

Field Review

Under the field review appraisal method, the supervisor has no forms to fill out. Rather, the supervisor is interviewed by a representative of the personnel department who asks questions about the performance of each employee. The interviewer writes up the results of the interview in narrative form and reviews them with the supervisor for suggestions, modifications, and approval. No rating forms or factors or degrees or weights are involved; rather, simple overall ratings are obtained.

Free-Form Essay

This method simply requires the supervisor to write down impressions about the employee in essay fashion. If desired by the organization, comments can be grouped under headings such as job performance, job knowledge, and goals for future consideration. To do a creditable job under this method, the supervisor must devote considerable time and thought to the evaluation. On the plus side, this process encourages the supervisor to become more observant and analytical. On the other hand, the free-form essay approach generally demands more time than the average supervisor is willing or able to spend.

Group Appraisal

Under this approach an employee is evaluated at the same time by the immediate supervisor plus three or four other supervisors who have knowledge of that employee's work performance. The virtue of this method is its thoroughness. It is also possible for multiple evaluators to modify or cancel out bias displayed by the immediate supervisor.

EFFECTIVE PERFORMANCE APPRAISAL

Overview*

Setting the Climate

- Give employees advance notice to prepare for review.
- Provide employees with instructions on *how* to "self-assess" their performance for the review period and *how* to state their performance plans in terms of goals and objectives for the next review period.
- Review purpose of the performance and development review program with employees.

Supervisor/Reviewer Preparation

- Document expected job standards and responsibilities.   •

---

*Source: Unless otherwise noted, this section is from Sharon Meyers, *Procedural Instructions for the Performance and Development Review,* Evanston Hospital Corp., Illinois.

- Document past performance of employee.
- Document strengths and performance areas to be developed which will be discussed with employee.
- Develop and document developmental career plan with employee, which will assist in enhancing knowledge and skills required for present or potential position performance.

Conducting the Counseling Conference

How To Start

- Be friendly, relaxed, open to "listening" and receiving information from employee. Use reflective questions.
- Be direct, not vague and ambiguous. Begin conference with positive comments regarding employee's performance.
- Review time frame for the counseling conference (e.g., 60 minutes, 90 minutes, etc.) and state (if appropriate) that an additional conference may be necessary to cover in depth all aspects of the review process with the employee.

Assessing Present Performance

- Allow the employee to discuss his or her perspective first—the job description, job standards, present performance, and expectations for future performance and responsibilities.
- Supplement the employee's perspective with a supervisory assessment of present performance and career potential.
- *Mutually* clarify, amend, agree, and document present performance results and developmental career plans.

Productive Forward Planning

- Mutually plan the employee's goals and objectives and check their consistency with organizational goals and objectives of department, hospital, and corporation.
- Confirm mutual agreement by summarizing priority concerns at close of counseling

conference. Document agreements on the appropriate performance and development review form.

- Plan periodical conference sessions to review ongoing progress.

Writing Goals and Objectives

1. Start with the infinitive of an action verb (e.g., "to develop, to implement, to coordinate, to facilitate, to create).
2. Each objective should produce a single key result when accomplished.
3. Specify a target date for accomplishing each objective.
4. Specify maximum cost factors for each objective.
5. Be as specific and quantitative (and hence measurable and verifiable) as possible for each objective.
6. Specify only the "what" and "when"; avoid venturing into the "why" and "how" for each objective.
7. Relate directly to the accountable department head's goals and objectives and to the general goals and objectives of the organization.
8. Be realistic but still present the employee with a significant challenge for the review period—whether a short-term period, such as three to six months, or a long-term period, such as nine months to a year or more.
9. Be readily understandable by those who will be contributing to the attainment of the objective (e.g., peers, supervisors, employees supervised, etc.).
10. Provide maximum "payoff" on the required investment in time and resources, as compared with other objectives being considered. List objectives in priority of importance.
11. Be consistent with the resources available or anticipated.
12. Avoid or minimize dual accountability for achievement when joint effort is required.

13. Be consistent with basic hospital and organizational policies and practices.

14. Objectives should be willingly agreed to by both supervisor and employee without undue pressure or coercion.

15. List objectives on performance review form. Distribute to personnel department and employee and retain copy for departmental files. Periodically refer to established objectives with employee to determine if performance is on "target."

16. Select major objectives for listing during the performance review. Remember to be realistic and state the maximum number of objectives obtainable within the upcoming report period. Use "outline form" in listing your objectives for concise readibility and effective time management.

Mutual Goal Setting

Employees felt the following things were accomplished when mutual goal setting was used by their supervisors:

1. The amount of help the supervisor was giving them through day-to-day coaching was improving their job performance.

2. The supervisor appeared to be more receptive to new ideas and suggestions.

3. The supervisor's ability to plan appeared to improve.

4. The supervisor made greater use of their abilities and experience.

5. Employees felt the goals they were working for were what they should be.

6. The supervisor helped them plan for future job opportunities.

7. Employees valued discussions with their supervisor because these discussions opened communication and provided an exchange of information.

Source: Arthur X. Deegan II, *Management by Objectives for Hospitals*, Aspen Publishers, Inc., © 1977.

Performance Evaluation Interview Process

Take the following actions to ensure a positive interview process:*

- Schedule the appointment to ensure there are no unavoidable interruptions. Allow adequate time for the interview, and state the time frame at the beginning of the interview.

- Provide a private, comfortable setting for the interview.

- Allow time for the employee to analyze your written evaluation. Give the employee a copy of the evaluation the day before the interview. The employee should submit a self-evaluation to you 24 hours in advance of the interview using the same form and performance criteria and offering any additional documentation.

- Encourage a written response on the institutional evaluation form for the employee. Most evaluation forms have a "comments" section. Allowing the employee to write comments of agreement or disagreement reinforces the bidirectional nature of the evaluation process.

- Encourage free discussion in order to mutually identify problems and goals. Respect the employee's opinions and right to express them.

- Identify processes by which goals can be achieved and problems solved.

- Assist and counsel with humanity and compassion, as indicated.

- Inform the employee of recognition, as indicated. Reward achievement with an appropriate salary adjustment, merit award, or promotion. State the consequences of unacceptable performance.

- Summarize the interview in a succinct note for the personnel record.

- Establish a mutually agreed-upon time for reassessment of progress.

Source: Virginia K. Baillie, Louise Trygstad, and Tatiana Isaeff Cordoni, *Effective Nursing Leadership: A Practical Guide*, Aspen Publishers, Inc., © 1989.

A Step-by-Step Procedure*

1. Determine the nature of the conference, whether focused on a standard evaluation, specific problem, or administrative action.
2. Inform the employee of the purpose, time, and other arrangements made for the conference. Request that the employee prepare a self-assessment statement (as suggested above) for presentation at the meeting.
3. Check over notes on the employee's performance appraisal sheet against standards or duties of his or her job. List complimentary items as well as improvement items.
4. Focus the meeting on stimulating the employee's awareness of pertinent issues. Balance the employee's perception (review his or her statement orally) against the appraiser's evaluation and the performance standards required. Don't lecture—explore discrepancies together; don't give neat explanations—inquire about reasons.
5. Work toward the construction of improvement plans together, setting time limits if suitable. If administrative discipline action is intended, indicate expectations and consequences.
6. Review the main issues and decisions discussed and involve the employee in a feedback process.
7. File a written summary of the evaluation conference, substantiated by the subordinate's signature, in his or her personnel folder. At set intervals, check the employee's list of improvement goals to determine whether they have been achieved.

Employee Self-Appraisal. To eliminate the one-sided effect of the descending judgment and to maximize the employee's responsibility for performance improvement, some hospitals require a form of preliminary preparation from the employee before the conference. The employee is asked to provide a statement or

---

When an Employee is Resistant

Employee disagreement—If an employee disagrees with a rating or opinion, or with any of the comments or conclusions, the ratings and conclusions should be double-checked, even if this means further investigation to determine the accuracy of the individual's comments.

Employee's refusal to sign—If an employee refuses to sign an evaluation, supervisors should not force the issue. It should be explained that signing does not indicate the employee's agreement with the evaluation's contents, but is an acknowledgment that the employee saw it, reviewed it, and received a copy. If the employee continues to refuse to sign, the facts of refusal and the evaluation's review with the individual on a particular date should be noted. It also may be wise to have a second supervisor sign as a witness to the fact that the evaluation was reviewed with the employee (if applicable). A copy should then be given to the individual.

Source: Karen Hawley Henry, *Nursing Administration and Law Manual*, Aspen Publishers, Inc., © 1986.

---

answer a fill-out questionnaire indicating self-perceived work strengths and weaknesses on the job, current actions to correct noted deficiencies, and the types of assistance from supervisor levels which he or she would believe to be helpful. This self-assessment equips the employee for voluntary participation in the evaluation conference and paves the way for purposeful exchanges and feedback.

Developing Improvement Plans*

The key objective of any appraisal system should be positive change on the part of the employee being evaluated.

---

*Source: Sharon Meyers, *Procedural Instructions for the Performance and Development Review*, Evanston Hospital Corp., Illinois.

*Source: Len Schlesinger, "Performance Improvement: The Missing Element," *Personnel Journal*, June 1976. Reprinted with the permission of *Personnel Journal*, Costa Mesa, California; all rights reserved.

Given that an appraisal system has presented an employee with valid and meaningful performance data, how does he or she proceed to develop an improvement plan?

The improvement plan is a simple document which allows an individual to determine and document areas in which he or she would like to change and how the change could be accomplished. It focuses upon the priority of areas needing improvement as determined by the appraisors and employee and can serve as a commitment for improvement between those individuals. Once the priority areas for improvement have been determined, the following questions need to be answered by the employee.

1. Is it worth changing in this area? (What's in it for me?) This question is inserted because of a strong tendency for people to change behavior only when there is some tangible benefit for them to do so (e.g., career advancement, better boss-subordinate relationships, etc.).

2. How do I want to change? (What is the desired behavioral objective?) One can often change behaviors; however, productive change takes place only when a desired behavioral objective is well defined.

3. How will I change? It is important to be able to define the process to be used to reach the desired objective. Will the employee use outside courses, training, consulting assistance? Will the employee meet with supervisors more often or inform them more of his or her activities through written communications?

4. When will I do it? There is an innate tendency in all of us to procrastinate. Change is very often not an easy process and therefore tends to increase this tendency. Therefore, the establishment of a timetable is extremely important.

5. How will I know it got done? There needs to be some means of allowing the employee to know that the commitment to change has been met. It can be feedback from others, the completion of specific activities, etc.

To ensure that appraisers continue to give timely and valuable performance data, the employee should be certain to share this plan with each of them and continue to solicit feedback on his or her progress.

Finally, within the time frame of six months to one year, the employee should begin the full appraisal process once again.

What the Employee Needs to Know

In order to make behavioral changes, the employee must understand which behaviors are desired and which must be corrected. During this final phase of the interview the employee must[1]

- understand how he or she is going to change to the desired behavior and agree to do so
- understand the consequences of changing or not, identify desired behaviors, and participate in setting goals to change behavior
- develop an action plan on how the change will be accomplished, either at the interview or within one week of the interview
- establish a time frame in which the change will be accomplished
- ensure that the goal is measurable, achievable, and clear to the evaluator and to him or her
- understand that the nurse leader and other resource personnel are available to provide assistance as needed
- participate in setting ongoing checkpoints to receive feedback on how he or she is accomplishing specific goals

IMPLEMENTING A NEW PERFORMANCE APPRAISAL SYSTEM*

To implement a new performance appraisal system three steps should be taken.

Pilot Testing. A group should be selected which is large enough to provide a representative sampling. A measure of the effectiveness of that group's present appraisal program should be developed to serve as a base against which to evaluate the test program. (Such a measure might be an attitude survey. A less elaborate measure would be to identify problems with the present program.) After a reasonable time oper-

---

[1] Barbara A. Mark and Howard L. Smith, *Essentials of Finance in Nursing*, Aspen Publishers, Inc., © 1987.

Source: Marion G. Haynes, "Developing an Appraisal Program, Part II," *Personnel Journal*, February 1978. Reprinted with the permission of *Personnel Journal*, Costa Mesa, California; all rights reserved.

ating under the test program, an evaluation should be made to determine if it is better than the prior one and what changes, if any, should be made to improve it.

Announcing. When an acceptable program has been designed and tested, it needs to be announced to all involved by top location management. The announcement should include communication with employees who will be covered by the new program as well as supervisors who will be applying it. This announcement should be made in such a way as to confirm top management interest and confidence in the program and to foster this interest and confidence in its use.

Training. In order for a program to meet its objectives, the supervisors involved need to be trained in its use. In general, training would cover the basic procedures material and should concentrate on the actual preparation of appraisals using the forms involved. Such training experience can greatly improve supervisors' confidence in a program by giving them an opportunity to see it in action and to discuss any reservations or misconceptions they may have.

Maintaining the Program. Staff work is not complete with the implementation of a program. New concepts are continually being developed on appraisal methods, and departmental needs change. Therefore, in order to maintain a program which is current and meeting department needs some staff unit must assume responsibility for its maintenance. An important part of this function will be to provide channels for feedback from supervisors on problems encountered in working with the program. From this information, modifications can be made which will result in a program that meets department needs and is understood by both the supervisors and employees affected by it.

COMMON APPRAISAL PROBLEMS*

A common problem encountered in performance evaluation is the "halo effect." This refers

to the tendency of an evaluator to allow the rating assigned to one or more characteristics to excessively influence the rating on other performance characteristics. The rating scale methods are particularly susceptible to the halo effect. For instance, if you have declared an employee to be excellent in terms of "initiative" and "dependability," so might you be inclined to rate "judgment" and "adaptability" high. Since it is extremely difficult to completely separate the consideration of each performance factor from consideration of the others (many performance characteristics actually include shades of others), there is no guaranteed way of eliminating the halo effect.

Another common problem in most rating systems is the tendency of many supervisors to be liberal in their evaluations, that is, to give their employees consistently high ratings. Most approaches to rating are partially based on the assumption that the majority of the work force will be "average" performers. However, many people (supervisors included) do not like to be considered "only average."

Central tendency or clustering is another problem, one that some of the rating methods have attempted to overcome. Some supervisors are reluctant to evaluate people in terms of the outer ends of the scale. To many supervisors it is "safest" to evaluate all employees consistently. This often leads to a situation in which "everyone is average," contrary to the likelihood that in a work group of any considerable size there are, in fact, performers who are both better and worse than the so-called average.

Interpersonal relationships pose a considerable problem in performance evaluation. The supervisor cannot help but be influenced, even if only unconsciously, by personal likes and dislikes. Often a significant part of an evaluation will be based on how well the supervisor likes the employee rather than how well the employee actually performs.

APPRAISAL FORMS

In order to facilitate and simplify the appraisal process, most health care organizations find it advisable to use performance appraisal forms.

Source: Charles R. McConnell, *The Effective Health Care Supervisor*, Aspen Publishers, Inc., © 1988.

These forms stipulate various elements for appraisal in objective terms.

Although there are numerous types of forms for the evaluation or appraisal of workers, most include factors that serve as criteria for measuring job performance, intelligence, and personality. The following are some of the factors most frequently included in performance rating forms for workers: supervision required, attitude, conduct, cooperation, job knowledge, safety, housekeeping, adaptability, absenteeism, tardiness, judgment, quantity of work, and quality of performance. For each factor, the management may be provided with a number of choices or degrees of achievement. Some appraisal forms will use a series of descriptive sentences, phrases, or adjectives to assist the manager in understanding how to judge or evaluate the various rating factors. Many forms are of a "check the box" type and are relatively easy to complete.*

Designing Appraisal Forms**

The language on appraisal forms must be precise since appraisers tend to read each word very critically. The following thoughts will facilitate the design of forms which are clean, understandable, and relevant.

Express only one idea with each factor. If two thoughts are expressed, a person who is rated high on one and low on the other is difficult to appraise. For example, punctuality and atten-

Source: Jonathan S. Rakich, Beaufort B. Longest, and Thomas R. O'Donovan, *Managing Health Care Organizations*, W.B. Saunders Company, © 1977. Reprinted by permission of CBS College Publishing.

**Source*: Marion G. Haynes, "Developing an Appraisal Program, Part II," *Personnel Journal*, February 1978. Reprinted with the permission of *Personnel Journal*, Costa Mesa, California; all rights reserved.

dance often appear together. Does a low rating indicate the person is often late to work or often absent?

Use words the appraiser will understand. Be particularly careful to design the form for the supervisory group who will be working with it.

Have appraisers evaluate what they observe, not what is inferred. This is particularly appropriate in evaluating such things as knowledge. Without extensive testing, it cannot really be said how much knowledge a person has on a given subject. However, one can observe the extent to which an understanding of the job is demonstrated.

Avoid double negatives. A positive, declarative approach is easier to understand and respond to.

Express thoughts clearly and simply. Qualifying clauses, ponderous words, and complex expressions serve only to confuse the appraiser. Avoid long, wordy introductions and definitions.

Keep statements internally consistent. Occasionally, direct contradictions may creep into the appraisal form.

Avoid universal statements. Words such as "all," "always," and "never" lead to ambiguity. When "never" appears, most people interpret it as meaning "hardly ever"; yet no two people have exactly the same understanding of "hardly ever."

Concentrate on the present. Any attempt to go into the past for a rating will lead to distortion. Dramatic events in the past stand out in an appraiser's memory, while good daily work tends to be expected and therefore overlooked.

Avoid vague concepts. This is particularly apparent in attempts to appraise personality factors. The terms "honesty" and "integrity" frequently appear on forms; yet no one has a clear understanding of the two concepts.

Chapter 35

Promotions

CAREER LADDER MOBILITY

Multi-Role Promotional Ladder*

Most hospitals have traditionally awarded promotional opportunities only to those professional nurses who assumed administrative or teaching roles. To overcome the inflexibilities of the traditional promotion systems, a new classification system was developed by one hospital. Its design was based on the four major elements of professional nursing practice—clinical practice, administration, research, and education.

In terms of the institution's needs and the skill level brought to the job by an individual nurse, it was possible to classify all nurses within this basic system regardless of the job to be performed. Since the system depended not on job titles but rather on graduated levels of skill, an infinite number of job classifications could exist. (See Table 35-1.)

To accommodate new nurses, all position specifications for professional nursing classifications contained entry qualifications for each level above the beginning staff nurse position.

These minimum qualifications were graduated on the basis of educational background and experience in the specialty field. (See Table 35-2.)

Dual Career Pathway*

A dual career pathway allows the professional nurse to pursue a career in either clinical or administrative nursing and receive equal recognition for whichever option chosen. The clinical ladder concept rewards nurses for their role in staff orientation, inservice, and patient education by providing an opportunity for clinical promotion instead of the traditional administrative promotion. A professional role model within the unit is an additional benefit inherent in the concept of the clinical ladder.

In the past, skilled practitioners who were often better suited for clinical nursing found the administrative track to be the only mode of promotion and the only method of professional advancement. Frustration often resulted because the clinical nurse may have wished to remain in clinical nursing or lacked the skills and moti-

---

*Source: Harold MacKinnon and Lillian Eriksen, "C.A.R.E.—A Four Track Professional Nurse Classification and Performance Evaluation System," *Journal of Nursing Administration*, April 1977. Reprinted with permission.

---

*Source: Julie A. Wine and Sara J. Mapstone, "Clinical Advancement," *Nursing Administration Quarterly*, vol. 6, no. 1, © 1981 Aspen Publishers, Inc.

Table 35-1 Nurse Job Classifications

	NURSE I	NURSE II	NURSE III	NURSE IV	NURSE V
Clinical Practice	Assists in developing nursing care plans	Initiates, implements, and modifies nursing care plans	Develops care plans for complex patient problems	Makes innovative changes in care planning and practice	Analyzes clinical care problems and effects remedial modifications
Administration	Provides administrative support in the provision of nursing services in limited and specific areas of a nursing unit	Administers a nursing unit for part of a 24-hour period	Administers a nursing unit on a permanent round-the-clock basis	Administers several nursing units for either 8- or 24-hour periods	Provides administrative direction for a large nursing division on a 24-hour basis
Research	Assists in research which requires an unsophisticated approach to methodology	Does research which requires a moderate amount of sophistication in research methodology	Does research which requires sophisticated research methodology	Supervises research requiring complex and sophisticated research methodology	Plans and supervises research which requires highly sophisticated research methodology in a variety of areas of nursing and nursing administration
Education	Participates in nursing care conferences	Conducts pre- and post-patient-care conferences	Provides learning opportunities through in-service programs, unit conferences, and individual conferences	Plans and coordinates learning conferences and projects	Demonstrates expertise in curriculum development and a thorough knowledge of educational principles

Table 35-2 Job Classifications by Educational Background

	Degree	Non-degree
Nurse I	New graduate	
Nurse II	Baccalaureate with three years experience, one year in specialty, or master's in nursing with no experience	Three and a half years experience, one year in specialty
Nurse III	Baccalaureate with four years experience, two years in specialty, or master's in nursing with one and a half years experience	Five years experience, two years in specialty
Nurse IV	Baccalaureate with six years experience and two years in specialty, or master's in nursing with two years experience	Seven years experience, two years in specialty

vation to be an effective administrator. The organization of the traditional nursing service structure graphically demonstrated that clinical practice was not formally rewarded by a clinical ladder for professional advancement.

The lack of recognition for clinical expertise often leads to disillusionment with the nursing profession. Nurses may seek another career where they are better appreciated. Some nurses move into teaching or supervisory positions because of the traditional recognition these entail. Other nurses deal with their frustrations by maintaining the status quo and become passive and unmotivated. An increasingly large number of nurses pursue alternate career options or revert to an inactive status in the nursing profession.

Clinical Ladders

Characteristics of Clinical Ladders*

1. Clinical ladders have various levels and titles. There may be multiple tracks that combine clinical and career ladder concepts, or there may

---

*Source: Nursing Practices Committee, AORN, "Guidelines for Developing Clinical Ladders," *AORN Journal*, May 1983. Reprinted with permission.

be a single track related to direct patient care. The tracks provide for lateral mobility within defined position descriptions that contain more than one level. From level to level, there are requirements for increasingly complex skills and increasing use of the nursing process (assessment, planning, implementation, and evaluation).

2. The nurse initiates the advancement process, requesting promotion and review and gathering documents to support the claim of being able to perform at the next level. (See Figure 35-1.)

3. There must be a method of evaluation and periodic reviews and checkpoints to assess performance at that level based on established criteria. A mechanism must be included for advancing, staying at the same level, and being demoted.

4. There must be a reward system that offers incentives to enter the program and to remain in it. This may include titles, status, and benefits.

5. Each level must be defined by behaviors that are discrete, progressive, and stated as behavioral objectives. These behavioral objectives must be realistic and achievable. Performance is measured by established criteria rather than length of service or educational achievement. There may be formal or informal education requirements, however.

Figure 35-1 Credentials Validation Chart

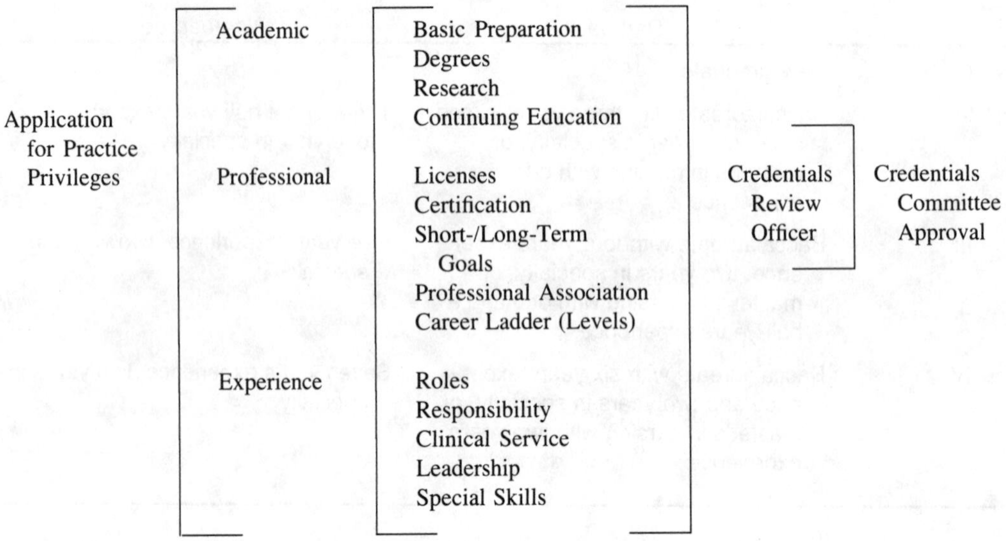

```
                 Academic        Basic Preparation
                                 Degrees
                                 Research
Application                      Continuing Education
  for Practice
  Privileges     Professional    Licenses            Credentials   Credentials
                                 Certification       Review        Committee
                                 Short-/Long-Term    Officer       Approval
                                   Goals
                                 Professional Association
                                 Career Ladder (Levels)

                 Experience      Roles
                                 Responsibility
                                 Clinical Service
                                 Leadership
                                 Special Skills
```

Mobility along the career ladder implies a structure for assessing standards, achievements, and the attainment of requisite credentials. The component items to be validated in a credential review process are outlined in the figure.

Source: Tim Porter-O'Grady, "Credentialing, Privileging, and Nursing Bylaws: Assuring Accountability," *Journal of Nursing Administration*, vol. 15, no. 12, December 1985.

---

6. Advance must be by choice and/or opportunity. A nurse must be allowed to remain at one level without penalty.

Benefits

Clinical ladders have a number of advantages. They

- have a positive or beneficial effect on patient care
- recognize the value of perioperative nursing practice
- provide a method for individual recognition of clinical expertise
- are a means of recognizing formal and informal educational achievement
- are a motivating force for individual growth and achievement
- provide advancement alternatives for nurses in direct patient care
- provide a reward system
- increase job satisfaction

- provide direction for increasing clinical expertise
- stimulate individual professional development
- aid in developing position descriptions
- provide criteria for developing performance evaluation tools.

Considerations

The following aspects need consideration before implementing a clinical ladder program.

The Need for a Clinical Ladder Program

- Does the existing evaluation system provide for the advancement of the individual nurse in the practice setting?
- Does the hospital recognize the need to reward the nurse who functions with advanced clinical expertise?
- Does the recognition provided for clinical expertise parallel the recognition provided to nurses for managerial or educational expertise?

- Does the nursing staff want a system that provides opportunities for advancement at a clinical level? Potential effects could be
  —pressure to compete for advanced clinical positions
  —perceived threat from change in the existing reward system
  —recognition based on performance rather than on length of service
  —changes in job security resulting in changes in status and potential changes in self-esteem (opportunity would be provided for increased accountability and responsibility and more comprehensive performance evaluations)

Impact on the Health Care Facility

- What are the economic implications of a clinical ladder program?
  —cost of developing and implementing program
  —salary and benefits related to clinical level
  —time and personnel to maintain the program
  —time for individual to fulfill role responsibilities
- What are the organizational changes that must occur to implement a clinical ladder program?
  —determination of the number of personnel in levels based upon hospital needs
  —effect of clinical levels on staffing patterns
  —necessity of redesigning organization chart related to distribution of authority, responsibility, and accountability
  —timing of implementation of clinical ladders program appropriate to organizational climate
- What are the potential effects on personnel?
  —changes in personnel policies, benefits, and salary (benefit changes and salary adjustments should not adversely affect personnel)
  —current contractual agreements
  —effects on other categories of hospital personnel
  —effects on retention of personnel

—restrictiveness caused by penalizing interdepartmental transfers with possible demotion if proficiency at previous level cannot be demonstrated within an established time period

- What are the potential effects on patient care?
  —greater patient satisfaction because care is provided by the most qualified professional nurse
  —improvement of consistency and efficiency of care throughout the health care facility because of appropriate matching of nursing expertise with patient care needs

Purposes of the Program

A clinical ladder program requires considerable deliberation and planning. A nursing unit cannot develop a clinical ladder program in isolation. The entire nursing department and hospital administration must be involved and committed to its development and implementation.

Specific purposes of the clinical ladder program should be identified:

1. Is this program for increased productivity?
2. Is it a reward system?
3. Is it a retention system?
4. What goals are to be achieved through the program?
5. Is this program to be a means of promotion on the individual clinical units, or is it to provide additional career opportunities in management and education?

*Implementation of the Program**

Experience with clinical ladder programs indicates that there are some general rules that can facilitate successful implementation.

Minimize quotas. Limiting the number of nurses that can advance can sap motivation and

---

*Source: Abby M. Heydman and Nancy Madsen, "Career Ladders for Nurse Retention," in *Managing the Nursing Shortage: A Guide to Recruitment and Retention*, Terence F. Moore and Earl A. Simendinger, eds., Aspen Publishers, Inc., © 1989.

discourage participation. Quotas limit the number of nurses who can be promoted, thus diminishing the impact of the clinical ladder system on nurse retention. The increasing acuity levels of patients and shortened hospital stays indicate that an investment in the highly skilled nurse will produce its own reward by reducing complications that create significant losses over reimbursement. In addition, the highly skilled nurse can far more readily manage the increasingly complex patients who have become the norm on most of the inpatient units.

Maximize staff nurse participation. Clinical ladder programs developed by nursing administration and educators do not always reflect the complexities of the staff nurse role at the bedside. Staff nurses are more inclined to participate if the expectations are realistic and match their perceptions of the clinical environment. The involvement of staff nurses in the steering committee that develops the clinical ladder proposal will alleviate this problem.

Differentiate between the levels through monetary reward. In many clinical ladders the incremental increase in monetary reimbursement is so small that it appears to the staff nurse to belittle the effort involved for progression. The clinical ladder system is one meaningful way to address the very real problem of salary compression within the field of nursing.

Make monetary rewards directly proportional to the need for retention. The fact remains that administrative advancement is still more lucrative than clinical advancement. If nursing is to be perceived as valuable and as a career worth having, financial rewards will have to reflect that value more directly.

Design the program so that the criteria are consistent with program goals. Sometimes clinical ladder programs are too idealistic and heavily weighted toward professional outcomes that are unrealistic for the practice setting (e.g., programs that emphasize research with a predominately diploma education–based work force). In other cases, the criteria are clinically based and do not adequately take into account professional development, as in the case where years of experience are more heavily weighted than educational preparation. In either case, staff nurse participation will not be as meaningful and the desired outcomes will not be achieved.

A NURSE PRIVILEGING SYSTEM*

The utilization of a privileging process for nurses has the potential for both improving nurses' professional competency and self-esteem and increasing the quality of patient care. Through privileging, nurses are required to meet specific established criteria in order to practice particular nursing skills. Criteria typically distinguish nurses according to their education and experience. Thus, the privileged nurse is recognized for his or her level of professional expertise and experience.

Privileging can be defined as a system for authorizing the performance of selected advanced nursing tasks through peer review of nurses' clinical expertise and education. The purpose of privileging is both to acknowledge nurses' education and skill level and to protect nurses from receiving assignments for which they are not prepared. The process of providing documented evidence of the nurse's qualifications is called credentialing.

The privileging procedure often requires each nurse to complete an application and present credentials and documents supporting the request for privileges (such as performance reports signed by training supervisors) to the nursing committee. At regular monthly meetings, the nursing committee reviews applications and verifies credentials from recognized licensing or certifying agencies such as the ANA, Nursing Registration and Licensure, or the state Board of Health. If approval is granted, the application is forwarded to the hospital privileging committee and the hospital chief executive officer (CEO).

Rejection of an application or of certain privileges requested by an applicant can be challenged by the applicant during a meeting with the committee. If the applicant disagrees with the committee's decision following this meeting, the decision can be challenged through the hospital's appeal process. A statement in the priv-

Source: Ruth Davidhizar and Robert Cosgray, "Developing a Privileging Process for the Psychiatric Nurse," *Quality Review Bulletin,* Vol. 13:8, August 1987. Copyright 1987 by the Joint Commission on Accreditation of Healthcare Organizations, Chicago. Reprinted with permission.

ileging application informs applicants that a nurse has 30 days in which to appeal an unfavorable decision.

Application of the System*

A privileging/credentialing system can simultaneously serve as a promotional tool and as a device to ensure quality standards for the nurse's ongoing nursing practice. For example, the following system uses credentialing to validate the competency of a newly hired nurse as well as to assess maintenance of skills and to advance the nurse based on the evidence of new 'credentials'. The systems used for maintenance and for advancement are both described below.

To Maintain

1. A nurse's credentials will be validated every two years in conjunction with the annual performance appraisal.
2. Six (6) months prior to his/her performance appraisal, the Nurse Manager will provide the nurse with the appropriate credentialing documents.
3. In collaboration with the Nurse Manager, the nurse will identify appropriate individuals to validate the applicant's competencies.
4. The professional nurse has six (6) months to obtain signatures validating competency. If the nurse does not meet the minimal and unit specific requirements of the current clinical position, a grace period of three (3) months will be extended to meet the requirements. If the credentialing requirements are not met during the grace period, the nurse will be reclassified to a lower position with a corresponding decrease in salary. No extensions beyond the three (3) months grace period will be granted without the recommendation of the Nurse Manager and Director of Nursing and the approval of the Vice President for Nursing. If a Primary Nurse III does

not meet the minimal requirements following the three (3) month grace period and an extension has been denied by the Vice President, the nurse will be terminated.
5. After approval signatures are obtained, the nurse will submit the credentialing documents to the Nurse Manager/Assistant Nurse Manager on the RN's unit who will review the document and send to Nursing QA for disposition and signature.

To Advance

1. When applying for promotion, the nurse submits credentials for the desired level.
2. Credentialing documents for the next promotional level are obtained from the Nurse Manager/Assistant Nurse Manager.
3. The applicant, in collaboration with the Nurse Manager/Assistant Nurse Manager, Clinical Specialist, and Clinician identifies individuals to validate clinical competencies.
4. The nurse demonstrates the required skills by direct and indirect patient care and professional activities.
5. After all signatures have been obtained, the nurse submits the credentialing documents to the Nurse Manager/Assistant Nurse Manager who reviews them for completeness and signature.

DEVELOPING MANAGERS

Overview*

Managerial development for positions such as supervisors, clinicians, and head nurses should be an integral part of the management process of any hospital nursing department.

Management Manpower Planning

A logical first step is management manpower planning. To be consistently effective, planning should not be occasional or haphazard, but

---

Source: Excerpt from "Nursing Service Credentialing Process," courtesy of Mt. Sinai Center, Miami Beach, Florida.

Source: Addison C. Bennet, "Towards More Effective Management," *Hospital Topics*, July 1973. Reprinted with permission.

should be done on a regularly scheduled basis, perhaps once a year. It is a process that embraces three distinct phases—analysis, forecasting, and inventory.

The analysis calls for the administrator and members of administrative staff to review and discuss internal conditions relating to the objectives, structure, and policies. The task of forecasting estimates the number of managers who will be required in the next three to five years, not only for new positions to be established, but as replacements for normal turnover. The forecast should also indicate the functions and levels and when the managers will be needed.

The inventory phase identifies those individuals with a good potential for filling existing or projected managerial vacancies.

Identification and Selection

If the selection of managers is made from within the organization, the criteria must go beyond the candidate's technical skills and capabilities and tenure history.

Much of the problem of building management teams has been created by hospitals themselves through their short-sighted pursuit of the best technicians at the first-hiring stage. It is the rare hospital that shows the wisdom to choose for its management team the person with less-than-the-best technical skills but with a clear promise of administrative and managerial ability.

Currently, the primary criteria being used for the selection of management personnel appear to be technical and professional competence, the ability to deal successfully with interpersonal relationships, and personal stability and maturity.

Offhand, these would appear to be excellent attributes, but they are unreliable in predicting whether the individual will be a good manager. A recent study identified these far more reliable indicators of effective management:[1]

- viewing the organization as a part of a larger system

- perceiving the organization as a patient-oriented system
- establishing goals and objectives
- handling interpersonal relationships
- utilizing manpower resources
- handling and imparting information
- implementating practices of financial administration

Promotions from Within

People are often the most visible yet overlooked resource within any health care organization. The heavy initial costs of recruiting, orienting, and training have already been borne, some degree of loyalty and stability has been demonstrated, and work appraisal, however informal, has at least begun. In short, you know much more about present employees and their potential than you will ever learn from a telephone call to an applicant's last employer. Furthermore, bringing in an outsider at the same or higher pay level than that paid to existing employees who are performing what they believe to be work of equal value can do violence to all of your progressive employee relations. Overlooked workers would do you a favor if they complained. More often they remain silent and vent their frustration upon patients, supervisors, new employees, and the institution itself.*

A Transfer/Promotion Program*

Opportunity for internal promotion and transfer should be an established and functioning privilege. It is normally the personnel department's responsibility to exercise leadership in articulating the policy and making it work. Managers will not ordinarily oppose interdepartmental transfers and promotions—so long as they themselves do not feel injured in the process. But there is a pervasive natural instinct to use such a policy to "unload bad apples" (without the pain of discharge) while keeping good ones.

[1]United Hospital Fund of New York: *Toward More Effective Management*, A Special Study in Management Problems and Practices, 1973.

Source: Martin E. Skoler, *Health Care Labor Manual*, Aspen Publishers, Inc., 1981.

The ingredients of a sound transfer/promotion program include the following:

1. an up-to-date skills inventory of your present work force
2. a fair, easily understood policy along with forms and procedures to make it work
3. a tuition assistance program together with on-site opportunities for skill improvement
4. personnel staff who can counsel employees who were considered for better things but were found unqualified
5. good statistics on the number and kinds of people who were transferred or promoted during each quarter of the year

*Encouraging Applications for
Promotions**

The traditional method of promoting staff to managerial levels relies on the astuteness of the nursing service director in perceiving the "best" choice. Often, length of service and reliability determine the selection. Occasionally favoritism by an immediate superior plays a significant part. Some critics of nursing service personnel practices have observed that when such decisions are made only at the topmost level of administration, upward mobility is often stymied.

One method for overcoming such problems is through a system whereby employees can apply for promotion. This procedure allows the nurse director to discover those employees who are interested in advancement and why they feel they are qualified. It also allows staff members to assess their own readiness for upper level positions.

To encourage applicants, notifications of job opportunities should be posted in a central location along with the specific qualifications for each position and the procedure for submitting the written application. A reasonable deadline should be set. A confirmation letter should be sent upon receipt of the application, setting up an interview appointment. Interviews should commence promptly after the application deadline. The interview should avoid becoming a performance evaluation. The focus should be on the applicant's concept of management, personal aspirations, assessment of the available position, and view of potential challenges, changes, or obstructions.

After the interview process, the nursing director would most likely discuss tentative choices with the supervisor under whom the successful applicant would work. The views of the immediate supervisor are of considerable importance, reflecting close experience with the demands of the job. Once the successful candidate has been selected, public announcement should be delayed till all nonappointees have received brief explanations of their shortcomings in terms of the position's requirements and have been offered guidance on developing needed strengths. This tone provides encouragement and gives direction for further preparation for promotion at a later date. These conferences should be scheduled within as short a time period as possible, preferably within one day, to prevent harmful news leakage. The helpful conference softens disappointment whereas whispered gossip might turn the rejected nurse into a resentful employee.

Don't overlook the selected candidate. Explain the exact requirements of her new position, indicate the associated salary and benefits, and set the date for transfer. Lastly, provide recognition of the promotion through a formal announcement or notice to the staff.

**Evaluating Subordinates for
Management Positions**

In evaluating applicants for top- and middle-level positions, various types of structural formats are employed, including performance appraisals and potential assessment centers; merit systems; psychological, intelligence, and

Source: Sigmund G. Ginsburg, "The 'I' Test—Evaluating Executive Talent and Potential," *Personnel Journal*, April 1976. Reprinted with the permission of *Personnel Journal*, Costa Mesa, California; all rights reserved.

Source: Sigmund G. Ginsburg, "The 'I' Test—Evaluating Executive Talent and Potential," *Personnel Journal*, April 1976. Reprinted with the permission of *Personnel Journal*, Costa Mesa, California; all rights reserved.

motivation tests; interviews; in-basket tests; managerial grid; transactional analysis; etc.

However, there are ten traits, skills, or attributes that distinguish the very successful manager from those who do not quite reach that level of performance. Thus, whatever selection or evaluation devices are used, the goal should be to identify those candidates who have a proven track record and/or high potential in regard to the items listed below.

To use this list as a scoring device, place different weights on each of these I factors. Some of the I s might have a weight of 1, others 1.25, and others 1.50. Thus, you could score individuals on a 1–10 scale, multiply by the weights involved, and then come up with a reasonably accurate differentiation among candidates.

The I-Factor Test: What To Look for in Managers

Intelligence. Demonstrates both broad and specific knowledge, understanding, and perception; quickly grasps the general as well as technical details; knows what information is needed and how to use it; demonstrates sharpness and clarity of thought and written and oral expression; comes up with creative solutions to difficult problems; shows flexibility in the face of changing times and needs; has ability to pose penetrating questions and deal with the main issues; has ability to learn from the past, deal with the present, anticipate the future; has ability to plan, organize resources to meet the plan, supervise and control.

Individual Confidence and Self-knowledge. Has trust and confidence in own ability to handle the ordinary as well as new, future, or extraordinary demands of the position without ending up as an egotist; understands own strengths and weaknesses and has ability to build on the strengths, improve on the weaknesses, or to shore up the weaknesses; has ability to know when he or she doesn't know enough or even anything about a problem and to take steps to acquire the knowledge either personally or through staff assistance; has ability to handle defeats and bounce back with confidence.

Intestinal Fortitude. Has ability and courage to make tough decisions, to be decisive, to stick his or her neck out to take sides if needed, to do the unpopular but necessary before the crisis stage is reached—yet at the same time is willing to reverse time-honored practices, precedents, and policies and his or her previous decisions; has courage to be bold, to take a chance, to be unpopular, to be wrong.

Integrity. Word and promises are good; is fair, trustworthy, and unbiased in action; holds to high standards of truth, conduct, honesty, ethics—and expects it of others.

Interpersonal Relations. Has ability to communicate and relate to people as well as problems; understands social and human dynamics, the effect of actions on individuals, and the various psychological, emotional, and ego needs of individuals at various levels; has ability to sympathize and empathize, to supervise and set high standards while earning respect and support.

Innovation. Has ability to think beyond the traditional or pedestrian, to see new opportunities and better approaches and ways of doing things, to "dream things that never were, and say, why not?"; possesses a healthy dissatisfaction with the status quo; is creative.

Intensity. Has ability to handle a wide variety of problems, both as to scope and magnitude, and to bear up under pressure; possesses the physical, mental, and emotional stamina to meet the everyday as well as crisis pressures of management responsibility; has ability to see the tough, often long, grinding tasks accomplished.

Implementation. Demonstrates a concern for seeing to it that plans, policies, and programs are carried through on a timely basis with modifications as necessary; demonstrates a concern for the details involved in bringing about successful implementation; has an ability to make things happen.

Identification. Has the willingness and ability to identify with the goals and aspirations of the department; to support and represent it with other departments; to identify with the hopes, aspirations, and needs of the staff of the organization; to be loyal to the organization and to supervisors, subordinates, and peers commensurate with integrity.

Influence-Inspire. Is able by word, action, interpersonal relations, achievements, standards of conduct, by how he or she carries out all the other 9 I s to influence all levels of the organization, inspire others to meet his or her high standards and expectations, and motivate others to develop fully their own potential.

Coworker Evaluations*

All organizations require leadership. In most cases, people are promoted from within an organization to positions of supervision. How should these people be chosen? An important rule is that a nurse should not be chosen for a position of leadership without obtaining some feedback from that nurse's coworkers. Indeed, coworkers, the people who work with the nurse on an equal basis, have an opportunity to develop a keener insight into the nurse's behavior than the higher echelons of management (see Table 35-3 for a useful tool for evaluating nurse managers). This is especially true at the level of interpersonal needs.

It follows that hospital administrators and nursing supervisors should seek feedback from a nurse's coworkers before selecting that nurse for a position of leadership. This information should play a significant role in the selection process. For example, answers to the following questions about a nurse's working conditions will indicate that nurse's future leadership behavior:

- Does the nurse attempt to see the other person's point of view? (This doesn't mean, does the nurse always agree with the other person?)
- Can the nurse disagree without being disagreeable?
- Does the nurse listen to and not just hear other people? (There is a real difference between listening and hearing; listening suggests that the nurse is at least trying to understand how the other person feels about things.)
- Is the nurse responsible? When given an assignment, does the nurse follow through?
- Can the nurse be trusted? When the nurse says something, can we believe it?
- Can I identify with the nurse in some way? Is the nurse one of us working toward a common goal?
- Does the nurse give others the opportunity to express their ideas?
- Is the nurse enthusiastic? Can the nurse transfer that enthusiasm to others?
- Does the nurse encourage coworkers and compliment them on a good job?
- Most important, is the nurse more interested in the welfare of other people and of the organization than in personal recognition?

MANAGEMENT TRAINING

Directors of nursing universally agree that a need exists for management training for nursing personnel. The professional background of nurses often does not include the pertinent knowledge to prepare the new graduate for first-line supervisory positions. Then, depending on each individual's employment situation, management skills may or may not be learned on the job. At best, one may assume that such learning experiences will be fragmented and inconclusive. Thus, a thorny problem facing nursing administrators is *how* to provide comprehensive training that will prepare nurses to function effectively as managers and administrators in the maelstrom of a rapidly changing environment—and yet be realistic in terms of time and cost.*

Source: Harry E. Munn, *The Nurse's Communication Handbook*, Aspen Publishers, Inc., © 1980.

Source: Virginia R. Eckvahl, "On-the-Job Management Training," *Journal of Nursing Administration*, March-April 1976. Reprinted with permission.

Table 35-3 Evaluation Tool—Competency Expectations of First-Level Nurse Manager

Unit Management

1. Staffs unit to meet patient care needs according to
   a. Classification system
   b. Staff level of responsibility/ability
   c. Contractual agreements
   d. Established patient care standards.
2. Determines priorities of unit activities based on
   a. Available resources
   b. Management principles
   c. Proven/commonly accepted practices.
3. Delegates responsibility/authority to those able to assume and implement them.
4. Proposes options for solving staffing problems that
   a. Are within legal parameters
   b. Utilize as few resources as possible.
5. Initiates methods for cost containment.
6. Submits on time written reports that communicate requested information accurately and succinctly.
7. Evaluates patient care given by staff for
   a. Achievement of intended outcomes
   b. Efficient use of resources
   c. Perceived satisfaction of patients/families.
8. Using hospital guidelines and format, participates in the development of unit budget.
9. Initiates staff conferences for solving patient care problems.
10. Makes management decisions that are
    a. Consistent with delegated authority
    b. Based on management principles
    c. Effective in achieving intended results.
11. Follows established lines of communication for
    a. Suggestions/complaints
    b. Reporting unresolved unit problems
    c. Reporting results of independent decisions.
12. Uses communication strategies with other departments and individuals that result in
    a. Achievement of intended results
    b. Perception of satisfaction/acceptance.

Staff Development

1. Evaluates staff, using reliable and objective criteria.
2. Gives feedback to staff on both acceptable and unacceptable performance.
3. Implements disciplinary action consistent with organization procedure and guidelines.
4. Sets goals with employees for improving/maintaining performance, including
   a. Measurable performance outcomes
   b. Action plan
   c. Time frame
   d. Consequences/rewards.
5. Holds staff accountable for achieving unit objectives.
6. Determines options for meeting identified learning needs of staff.
7. Using the established criteria and process, interviews prospective employees.
8. Participates in orientation plan for individual employees.

Professional Development

1. Participates in the development of departmental objectives.
2. With staff, determines patient care standards for the unit that are consistent with
   a. Organization philosophy
   b. Resource constraints
   c. Current nursing theory and practice.
3. Participates in nursing research projects.
4. Participates in activities that meet own identified learning needs.
5. Evaluates own performance against competency expectations.

Source: Donna R. Sheridan and Katherine Vivenzo, "Developing Prospective Managers: The Process, *Journal of Nursing Administration,* May 1984.

Learning Needs of Nurse Managers

In a survey of new nurse managers conducted by the American Society for Nursing Service Administrators the following were identified as among the most prominent learning needs in the area of *management skills*:

- how to identify, formulate, and write objectives
- how to prepare and monitor a budget
- how to classify patients
- how to improve documentation of nursing care
- how to be assertive
- how to contain costs and implement a cost-awareness program
- how to handle employee grievances
- how to implement primary nursing
- how to introduce and implement change

Among the most prominent learning needs identified in the area of *management knowledge* were:

- Management by objectives
- Primary nursing
- Synthesis of nursing and managerial roles
- Fiscal management
- Personnel management
- Cost-containment approaches
- Planning change and the change process
- Job satisfaction and enrichment
- Communication, counseling, conflict management, and motivation
- Labor relations
- Participative management
- Manager's accountability
- Staffing and scheduling innovations
- Managing small, rural hospitals
- Decentralization

Combined Academic-Clinical-Seminar Approach*

One such program to develop supervisory-level management personnel was initiated at Los Angeles County-University of Southern California Medical Center.

Selection of Trainees

The participants were nominated by the nursing directors from all clinical service areas. Basic guidelines for selection included

- a desire to manage combined with solid career objectives
- the demonstrated ability to work well with others
- an excellent, proven record of quality performance

- a potential for advancement and personal growth
- a stable, responsible approach to work assignments

Each nominee was interviewed by the director of nursing services, and the final selection was based on that interview, the employee's work record, and the stated career goals of the individual.

Program Design

The three-prong approach to the training program included academic preparation, related clinical experiences, and seminars.

The *academic preparation* included lectures by qualified persons from the nursing department as well as other hospital departments, workshops outside the medical center, reading and written assignments, and oral presentations. The subject areas covered were management

---

*Source: Ibid.

theory, organizational structure, interpersonal skills, techniques of evaluation, elements of research, communication expertise, current professional problems, and identification of institutional resources.

Clinical assignments, including both line and staff roles, were planned to provide the trainees with opportunities to observe different management styles and to develop expertise in problem identification, selection of alternative courses of action, decision making, and follow-up. The trainees were then given assignments of increasing complexity, which required not only observation but participation in all phases of problem solution. A member of the nursing management team was directly assigned to each trainee for each period of clinical experience and was responsible for planning, monitoring, and evaluating the individual's progress.

Each trainee, for example, was to observe and participate in nurse recruitment for an in-depth view of the process of interview techniques and employee selection.

The *weekly seminars,* ongoing throughout the program, provided opportunities for the coordinator and/or the director of nursing services to meet with the group. These seminars proved to be an effective method for helping the trainees to develop skill in the application of theory to the solution of actual problems. Wherever possible, the approach was twofold. The application of theory was considered specifically in the resolution of a particular problem and generally in the resolution of related problems with a common base.

Members were encouraged to bring actual encountered difficulties to the seminars for study. These problems were analyzed by the group using the standard approach of definition, identification of alternatives and constraints, and selection of the best solution. The group formulated recommendations for action, and the member returned to his or her clinical assignment to implement the suggestion. Each case was followed to resolution in terms of the success or failure of the advice. During the overall program approximately one-third of the time was spent in the classroom with seminars, lectures, and workshops and two-thirds in clinical assignments.

Development of Prospective Managers*

One program, Stanford University Hospital's Prospective Manager Project, has several unique and nontraditional features. Unlike most other programs, participation in this one takes place prior to actual placement in a management position. Also, the requirement of previous clinical experience is limited to a *maximum* of one year. This second feature, only one year of clinical experience, is not only unique but controversial. The managers' primary responsibility is *management* of patient care activities, not direct provision of patient care. Rewards are given to incumbents who are effective managers, not expert clinicians. Therefore, nurses with only one year of clinical experience should have less difficulty switching role orientation.

The trainee is not guaranteed a position as manager but rather is selected because of manager potential and is given the opportunity to learn the role. Once the program objectives are achieved, the trainee is then given the opportunity to compete with others for any available positions.

Potential benefits from such a program include

- greater availability of successful candidates
- increasing the ability to select successful candidates for management positions
- decreasing the frustration and anxiety of novice managers
- more competent manager performance
- providing a career track for nurses interested in management of patient care.

Source: Dorothy J. del Bueno and Duane D. Walker, "Developing Prospective Managers: A Unique Project," *Journal of Nursing Administration,* April 1984. Reprinted with permission.

Costs of implementing such a program include consultant fees, partial salaries for trainees, development of assessment/evaluation tools, acquisition or development of learning materials, time required of mentors, and promotional and recruitment expenses.

Developing Selection and Assessment Criteria

A task force of representatives from all nurse management levels identified the desired characteristics and skills in order of importance as follows:

1. interest and motivation
2. flexibility in use of management strategies and style
3. problem solving/priority setting skill
4. high self-esteem
5. ability to deal with frustration and anger
6. skill in written and oral communication
7. ability to set realistic, achievable goals
8. willingness to take risks
9. skill in group process
10. perseverance and tenacity

Any management experience would be considered a plus. Methods and tools to measure and assess the candidates according to the desired selection criteria included written case studies; videotape simulations; set-up situations (these are situations in which circumstances are purposely staged in order to find out what the individual will do under these conditions); questions; and use of the Hershey-Blanchard Leader Effectiveness and Adaptability Description Tool, a validated management-style self-assessment. A structured, scripted interview was developed and tested. Those who processed and scored candidates had practice sessions to make their evaluations consistent.

Flyers describing the Prospective Manager Project were sent to deans of schools of nursing and advertisements were placed in *Nursing Magazine* with the terms of the program stated: partial salary only, no guarantee of a management position, and no subsidy for travel or living expenses before or during the program.

The Management Assessment Center Concept*

The assessment center program is a means by which potential managers can be identified and helped to develop managerial skills.

An assessment program ideally takes potential candidates for promotion away from the workplace and exposes them to simulated situations designed to illustrate a specific managerial role. The simulation includes exercises in decision-making, management games, and leaderless discussion sessions. Standardized exercises provide an opportunity for evaluation of candidates under controlled conditions, which makes comparative judgments possible. The assessors typically are line managers trained to administer the program and to evaluate candidates on their managerial potential and growth needs. Assessors are usually two to three management levels above the people being assessed. The usual number of candidates taken at one time to an assessment program is 6 to 12, and the ratio of assessors to candidates varies from one to three to one to one. Two or three consecutive full-day programs are most common. Others are scheduled for five or six days and integrated with training activities. One-day programs also have been used successfully in some organizations.

Assessment Exercises

A program designed to help select a person for a specific position will be shorter than one designed to develop the participants' managerial strengths and diagnose any of their weaknesses. The organization's needs are of top priority, and the program should be specifically designed to identify the traits, abilities, and characteristics that will fit those needs. The American Management Association's Multimedia Supervisory Management Course is a resource that can be used to identify factors to be measured, for example, organizational ability, communication

---

*Source: Lynette Gerschefske, "Assessment and Development for Head Nurse Positions," *Supervisor Nurse*, February 1980. Reprinted with permission.

patterns, decision-making potential, ability to delegate, leadership potential, initiative, creativity, and flexibility. The exercises in an assessment program may include the following:

1. *A personal interview* based on background information supplied by each participant and conducted by an assessor.
2. *An in-basket exercise* that consists of 20 to 30 items simulating an in-basket in the managerial role. The items usually require the participant to respond by planning and scheduling, gathering facts, making decisions, and responding to others in writing. The items may be anything from a letter from the Executive Director to an anonymous letter from a hostile employee. The candidate is asked to prioritize items and record in writing the action to be taken. The participant's score is categorized according to predetermined areas and criteria. Following the completion of the exercise, the participant is interviewed and the way he or she handled each problem discussed.
3. *Leaderless group discussions* are held in which each participant is assigned a point of view to sell to the other group members. Candidates are observed for indications of emerging leadership, organizational ability, and the capacity to function under stress.
4. Another exercise involves *problem analysis*. This analysis is individual and

designed to assess the candidates' potential for making managerial recommendations by sifting through data to find pertinent information and developing logical and practical conclusions.

5. *Paper and pencil tests* include reading tests for self-development, reasonability tests, personality tests, and psychological tests.
6. Participants resolve issues, such as disciplinary action, in *group discussion*. Assessors note the time used to resolve problems, the candidates' appreciation of potential personnel problems, and their sensitivity to subordinates' views of events and actions.
7. A one-half hour *mock selection interview* of a person for a specified position is done. The candidate is questioned later to determine any insight gained during the interview.
8. *Oral presentations* regarding homework assignments on specified problems also are given. Following the oral presentations, the candidates meet in groups to reach a decision reconciling their recommendations.

Participants in assessment programs usually are nominated by their supervisors based on their performance and potential for advancement. Some organizations allow candidates to nominate themselves after they have reached a certain level in the organization.

Part VI

Opportunities for the Nursing Service and Administrator

Chapter 36

New Directions and Developments

RESPONDING TO CHANGING NEEDS

Requirements for Nurse Leaders*

Nurses must remember that nursing work is a part of a continuum that moves toward a future that is ever in transition. Both the nurse executive and staff nurse must be willing to take advantage of opportunities to create new frameworks for nursing service and be ready to accept challenges from others related to providing health care services in a broad variety of settings.

The nurse executive will always have to be alert to the impact of major social change on the management of the practice of nursing. The nurse executive will often be the front person on the road to assessing and evaluating both the nature and impact of change on the way health care services are provided and the nurse's role in their provision. As a leader, the nurse executive will have to be the visionary, conceiving as well as creating and facilitating the opportunity for nurses to assume roles that effectively move the nursing service into newer areas of opportunity.

Reading the signposts of change and reflecting on their meaning will be the first steps in creating models within which nursing services will be provided.

In his or her role as leader, the nurse executive will always be challenged to provide the milieu in which nurses will seek new ways of rendering services and new settings within which to offer nursing care. Often it will be the staff who have the best perspective on how nursing work is offered and the way in which it can unfold to best suit the community or constituency nurses seek to serve. Staff spend their professional lives on the front lines of service and are often positioned to identify opportunities for new services or different ways to provide existing services. The challenge for staff is to explore these options for service and undertake creative efforts to deliver health care services.

What is expected of the nurse executive is sensitivity not only to the opportunities that can be suggested by the nurse in practice but also to the changing milieu that provides the framework that will permit the practicing nurse to explore his or her options and opportunities and provide a plan and a strategy for making it live. Indeed, it is a part of the emerging role of the nurse executive to create and maintain an internal working environment that provides the expectation that

*Source: Tim Porter O'Grady, *Reorganization of Nursing Practice: Creating the Corporate Venture*, Aspen Publishers, Inc., © 1990.

newer staff roles will emerge as the new service opportunities are created.

The Limits of Diversification in Nursing

Diversification is a major direction for hospital organizations today. Diversification generally means moving into nonrelated businesses. The critical aspect of diversification which therefore needs examination is the relation of the new business to the mission. The critical questions are: What is our business? What should our business be?

Diversification in nursing is carefully weighed by considering the mission of the nursing department. First, it is unlikely that the nursing department will be creating a spinoff, non-health-related business. Second, if the diversification is not in line with the mission, it is likely to create an additional workload, driving up nursing costs and reducing profit margins.

The emphasis now is on the consumer as a purchaser and user of the product *health care*. Consequently, management efforts are shifting from decision making based on institutional needs to decision making based on customer research and careful matching of customer needs with the capabilities of the organization. In market-based management, customer wants and needs are best identified by those closest to the customer. This requires a participative process, with the manager being the knowledgeable facilitator. The management style, therefore, is participative.

Nursing, more than any other department, is for a longer period closer to the primary customers of the hospital: the patients, physicians, and RNs. Therefore, nursing is in a position to design, develop, implement, and market service programs effectively. Additionally, because of the competitive environment, the marketing model is an appropriate nursing management tool in developing and implementing objectives designed to meet customer needs.*

A Look at the Future*

Nurse executives will find themselves managing a far more diverse mixture of nursing and related clinical services. Roles and health care settings that nurses will find themselves in include the following:

- *Community-based practice*. Perhaps the greatest growth in health care will result from the shift of services outside of institutional models. As the cost of institutional care continues to rise, home health services will reflect a broader range of services— from well baby care to home births, from intensive home care (including ventilator support) to postsurgical care, and from medication treatments to stress testing and health assessment, as well as care for both the indigent and the underserved noninstitutionalized older adult.

- *Case management and clinical workloads*. This process will provide opportunities for nurses to follow patients/clients from entry into the health system to exit. If sickness serves as the base of entry into the system, the nurse will assess and identify long-term needs of the patient and develop the continuum of care and services throughout the chronology of care. If health is the point of entry, the nurse will assess and create models of health-maintaining practices and maintain the relationship, identifying the changing needs of the client, including the need for referral to other health providers within the economic parameters available for such services.

- *Specialized care providers*. Many services now considered a part of hospitalized care will be offered in decentralized settings in which the client may receive services without being hospitalized. The use of chemotherapy centers, dialysis centers, birthing centers, rehabilitation centers, dependency centers, and day therapy and/or clinical

---

*Source: Vi Kunkle, *Marketing Strategies for Nurse Managers: A Guide for Developing and Implementing a Nursing Marketing Plan*, Aspen Publishers, Inc., © 1990.

*Source: Tim Porter O'Grady, *Reorganization of Nursing Practice: Creating the Corporate Venture*, Aspen Publishers, Inc., © 1990.

service centers (diabetic, psychiatric, Alzheimers, etc.) will create places where nurses will work and provide services.

- *Multidisciplinary clinics and health service centers.* With nurses as primary providers, these will offer a range of services: assessment of health problems, triage of problem priorities, direct intervention in specified health or illness issues, referral to a variety of other services based on need and assessment, client teaching, therapeutic intervention, counseling, treatment plans, and protocols. The nurse will work with psychologists, physicians, therapists, clinical pharmacists, and other practitioners to meet both the preventive and the interventive needs of those who seek their services.

Nursing Intrapreneurship*

Nursing programs are now being asked to do more than just control costs. They are also encountering requests to enhance health facility revenues. This new mission is generally captured by the term *intrapreneurship*—the creation and implementation of new, creative, vibrant, and profit-oriented ideas that will instill renewed vigor in service delivery.

Intrapreneurship in nursing settings is commonly characterized by the following attributes:

- emphasis on creative efforts to control costs or to enhance profit generation
- reinforcement of innovative ideas through intrinsic and extrinsic rewards
- search for methods to generate revenues for nursing services and for the total organization
- enhanced financial viability of nursing programs, with expanded support (e.g., seed money) for new program efforts
- promotion of a supportive culture that retains nursing personnel and facilitates personal growth

- expansion of nursing business lines or products

In addition, intrapreneurship is a mechanism for increasing the power of nursing services. Instead of taking a traditional stance as a support service, nursing is allowed more freedom through intrapreneurship. Nurses can redefine what it means to offer nursing care. Intrapreneurship fosters a new way of looking at service delivery. It is an optimistic and constructive approach for improving nursing services and the return from the delivery process.

The way to think of intrapreneurship in nursing is in terms of the products or services delivered in nursing care. (See Table 36-1.) In many respects, nurse managers need to think in terms of marketing their product or service line. Once a nursing program has delineated its product or service line, it is in the position of being able to promote excellence in the services or products and to expand the services or products offered. At the heart of this issue is marketing nursing care as a profitable, cost-controlling, and valuable service.

Entrepreneurship: Decision-Making Process for Developing a New or Modified Service*

Current emerging trends of new service development, as well as new applications of delivery systems, accentuate the critical need for managerial resourcefulness and responsiveness to the swiftly evolving environment. Entrepreneurship exploits opportunities, optimizes what already exists, and obtains desired results. An entrepreneur continually searches for plausible and effective methods to respond to the market (the people served) and its shifts in preference.

Developing new services or significantly modifying existing services is an essential management pursuit in the process of adapting to a

*Source: Judith F. Garner, Howard L. Smith, and Neill F. Piland, *Strategic Nursing Management: Power and Responsibility in a New Era*, Aspen Publishers, Inc., © 1990.

*Source: Kenneth R. Emery, "Developing a New or Modified Service: Analysis for Decision Making," *Health Care Supervisor*, vol. 4, no. 2, © 1986 Aspen Publishers, Inc.

Table 36-1 An Inventory of Nursing Products

Operations management
Quality assurance plan for nursing
Absenteeism reporting system (Lotus)
Budget variance reporting system (Lotus)
Human resource use reports
Nursing research proposal critique tool
Guidelines for revenue-producing activities
Patient classification and charging system
Guidelines for university collaboration and
student placement
Policy, procedure, and protocol format

Consultation services
Hemodialysis skills—staff education and
training
How to open an oncology unit
Preoperative teaching program for open heart
patients, continuing education, and patient
education services
Primary nursing in the surgical intensive care
setting
Nursing administration and management

Publications
Discharge Teaching for Transplant Patients
*Infant Stimulation: Baby Learning—Baby
Play* (videotape)
*Leading a Balanced Life: Handbook for
Diabetics*
CenterNurse—A Nursing Newsletter

Education
Community education

- Food—facts and fallacies
- Focus on poison prevention
- Early cancer detection and preventing risks

- Drugs—not a dead issue
- Blood pressure screening

Patient education

- Medication care teaching tools
- Printed pamphlet series
  —Colonoscopy
  —Endoscopic retrograde choledocho-
   pancreatogram
  —Barium enema
  —Upper endoscopy
  —Upper gastrointestinal examination

Staff education

- Physical assessment
- Leadership
- Preceptorship
- IV therapy certification program
- Chemotherapy administration for registered
  nurses
- Self-learning modules—infection control
- A practical approach to 12-lead
  electrocardiogram interpretation
- Medical intensive care unit (ICU) course
  (university credit granted)
- Surgical ICU course (university credit
  granted)
- Neonatal ICU course (university credit
  granted)
- Perioperative course: basic operating room
  techniques (university credit granted)

Graduate nursing education

- Nursing administration course (area
  university)

Source: Reprinted from "Marketing Your Nursing Product Line: Reaping the Benefits" by J.E. Johnson, A.C. Arvidson, L.L. Costa, F.M. Heknuis, L.A. Lennox, S.B. Marshall, and M.J. Moran, *Journal of Nursing Administration*, vol. 17, no. 11, pp. 29–33, with permission of J.B. Lippincott Company, © November 1987.

changing environment. However, the development of a new service must stand the test of appropriateness and risk evaluation.

Developing new or modified services also requires considerable planning and cost analysis—including revenue projections and interfunctional cooperation and coordination. The more complete the information, the better the decision and the greater the ultimate level of success.

The format presented in Table 36-2 and discussed below addresses critical management issues for making effective and timely decisions. It is the responsibility of the new or modified

Table 36-2 Developing a New or Modified Service Analysis

Part 1: Service Description and Need

1. Describe the proposed new or modified service.
2. Describe the extent to which the service is compatible with the organization's philosophy and mission.
3. Identify the benefits of the service to the patients (community).
4. Describe how the need for the service was determined.
5. Fully explain the need for the service.
6. Identify the alternatives that exist to serve the need.

Part II: Market Information

7. Identify the segment of the community to be served: market (geographic) area, age group, sex, diagnosis, and other patient-origin information.
8. Describe how patients will be directed to the service.
9. Determine whether the location of the service will be convenient for patients: accessibility, parking, directions, and reception.
10. Identify who will provide the service.
11. Identify the hours of operation of the service and waiting time.
12. Describe the price structure for the service and how it was determined.
13. List the prices charged by primary competitors for the same or comparable services.
14. Describe the full scope of competition (name, location, range of service, and the strengths and weaknesses of the competitors).
15. Explain how the new or modified service would be better than each competitor's service.

Part III: Operational Information

16. Identify the persons who will be responsible for the management of the service.
17. Identify the persons who will be responsible for the medical direction of the service.

18. Attach job descriptions of any new positions to be created.
19. If there is a need for a medical director's contract, describe the suggested provisions of that contract.
20. If there is a need for malpractice insurance, explain why.
21. Indicate whether all necessary coordination with other functions has been completed.
22. Fully define and explain all legal ramifications (liability, contracts, regulatory restrictions, etc.).
23. If a certificate of need (CON) is required, explain why and provide details.
24. Identify any support resources required (personnel, material, space, facilities, equipment, etc.).

Part IV: Success Indicators

25. Describe the strengths of the service.
26. Describe the weaknesses of the service.
27. Identify all major areas of concern.
28. Describe all medical staff support that may be needed.
29. Describe how the necessary acceptance of the medical staff will be achieved.
30. Describe how the service will be promoted.
31. Outline the proposed buildup and implementation schedule (activities and dates).
32. Estimate the probability of success (rank success on a scale of 1 to 10, ten being high).

Part V: Financial Plan and Information Verification

33. Attach a complete three-year financial plan. Consider revenue, expense, labor and nonlabor costs, capital equipment, billing, collection, bad debts, indirect expenses, and renovation costs.
34. Calculate a three-year projected return on investment.
35. Ensure that all information is reviewed and verified: interdepartment, intradepartment, and fiscal services.

Source: Kenneth R. Emery, "Developing a New or Modified Service: Analysis for Decision Making," *Health Care Supervisor*, vol. 4, no. 2, © 1986 Aspen Publishers, Inc.

service sponsor (manager or supervisory manager) to respond thoroughly to each question or to request information from appropriate resource personnel.

Part I attempts to provide the reviewer of the proposal with a complete description of the service, the purpose of the service, and who is to benefit by the service and to identify duplicate or similar services that have already been established in the service area. This information lays an important foundation. Defining the need and the rationale supporting that need secures the underpinnings of the proposal. All service efforts should be market-oriented, responding to a special need for a defined market.

Part II provides important pieces of environmental information that will help in assembling the complex overall market puzzle. Every service should be associated with a specific market to be served. Each market consists of distinguishable segments that can be identified either geographically or demographically. If the employer conducts formal marketing surveys, the proposal could be augmented with information about consumer behavior, attitudes, and patronage.

With the use of the information contained in this section, promotional strategies can be developed and implemented once the program is approved. Therefore, all the effort expended to obtain the most complete information possible will lead to rewards not only in the decision-making process but also in the promotion process. Promotion strategies will be vital to the success of the service. The responses to items 10 through 15 supply the reviewer of the proposal with important supportive information and serve as a basis for the action that will be requested in item 30.

The operational information gathered in Part III is, in effect, the nuts and bolts of the proposal. Can the proposed service be successful given the realities of the internal and external environment? Health care organization managers are increasingly concerned with having the proper resources and the capabilities to capitalize on growth opportunities.

The success part of the analysis in Part IV provides the program reviewer with supportive information in order for the reviewing party to be able to gain a clear perspective on the possibilities for success. The service viability factor becomes more evident with the answers to these questions. Knowing constraints as well as opportunities provides decision makers with information vital in the decision-making process. Every service goes through a product cycle consisting of the introduction phase, the growth period, the maturity period, and the eventual decline of the product or service. An objective assessment of the product's strengths and weaknesses provides a reasonable means of assessing success during the initial and growth phases of a new or modified service.

Part IV also examines the proposed strategy for promoting the service. The approach for communicating the service to various groups of potential consumers begins to unify the entire proposal.

Once all the information in the analysis is reviewed, item 32 (the success scale) must be considered. This places the entire package in a nutshell—a simple and straightforward subjective assessment. Considering today's environment, if the answer is not an 8, 9, or 10, then it is suggested that the person who is making the proposal return to the drawing board and strengthen all supporting information.

Part V helps establish priorities based on reasonable risks and available resources. For an organization to remain financially viable, prudent decisions must be made. Therefore, a proposal should have complete financial data, including forecasts based on projected business volume and expenses. Without a thorough financial analysis and a clearly projected return on investment, it may be virtually impossible to obtain an informed decision. The final question of the analysis should not be overlooked. The information contained in the analysis should be accurate; therefore it is advisable to receive verification from all individuals who either contributed to the analysis by submitting information or who have reviewed the information for accuracy. This effort not only supports the validity of the information but it also expedites the decision process because there is no need for the final decision makers to request verification of the information.

PRODUCT LINE MANAGEMENT

Overview*

A pure product line structure is developed by organizing under customer services, not hospital departments. Traditional lines of authority are used, but the scope of responsibility includes cost centers for services identified by the hospital as major strength areas. The major areas of strength are the hospital's product mix. For example, in the box below each product item has a business plan identifying budgetary income and expense included in a cost center under rehabilitation services.

Each product item is a separate business within the hospital. Additionally, each product item has a product manager who develops a product team and reports to the vice president of rehabilitation services. Under this organizational structure, the vice president of nursing also manages a product line.

The emphasis in this organizational structure is service to customers, not operations or traditional departmental issues. The entire organization, staff to management, is brought into the product lines through participation in product teams. Administration and marketing are represented on the product teams, with the marketing representative being a facilitator and educator. The cost and revenue of nursing services, professional services, ancillary services, and support services are allocated appropriately to each product item cost center. This structure provides

- increased unity in implementing hospital objectives
- increased focus on customer service
- increased creativity in developing programs
- increased specialization and enhancement of expertise
- increased efficiency in defining the target market
- increased market attractiveness and competitiveness because of specialization

The disadvantages include the lack of attention to operations, policies, procedures, and detail as well as loss of some time-honored values of the organization. The matrix organizational structure addresses the disadvantages with the retention of traditional lines of authority but in the process creates confusing dual authority relationships.

Implications for Nurse Managers*

Product line management (PLM) has been successful in industries based on discrete and tangible products that can be mass produced. When the product is a clinical service that is provided by a team of health care professionals and does not lead to a discrete outcome, PLM faces inherent difficulties.

The basic premise of PLM is that one decision maker is responsible for all aspects of the product: design, development, production, market-

---

Source: Vi Kunkle, *Marketing Strategies for Nurse Managers: A Guide for Developing and Implementing a Nursing Marketing Plan*, Aspen Publishers, Inc., © 1990.

Source: Nancy Higgerson, "Product Line Management for Nurse Executives," *Aspen's Advisor for Nurse Executives*, vol. 4, no. 7, © 1989 Aspen Publishers, Inc.

Sample Rehabilitation Services Product Line

Rheumatology Center	Vocational Rehabilitation Center
Spinal Cord Injury Center	Developmental Pediatric Rehabilitation Center
Stroke Rehabilitation Center	Rehabilitation Inpatient Care
Head Trauma Center	Rehabilitation Outpatient Care

ing, sales, service evaluation, and profitability. This decision maker has the ultimate authority over the product. In the hospital setting, the product is patient care and services. This product is created by interdependent departmental systems. It is difficult to separate clearly clinical departments like nursing, laboratory, radiology, and special diagnostics and essential support departments such as food service, housekeeping, and materials management into distinct product lines.

If PLM addresses only those departments involved in the product of patient care, fewer departments are affected. The nursing department may become the primary focus for restructuring, as the nursing units are the essence and, in some product lines, the only component of the product. In this scheme, each nursing unit or service is responsible to a product manager or administrator who holds the ultimate decision-making authority. Consequently, this shift in the table of organization eradicates unified reporting to a central nursing department and fragments nursing with multiple reporting relationships to various product managers.

Fragmentation of nursing could mean a loss of power and influence, division of impact, and the eventual erosion of standards of patient care and nursing practice across an institution. Alliance to a product line as opposed to patient care stimulates interunit competition, rivalry, and dissonance.

The PLM structure does not usually view nursing as the primary product that it is for hospitals; rather, nursing is defined as a means to provide products such as cardiovascular services, oncology services, etc.

Questions To Ask about PLM

The following questions may be helpful in projecting the consequences of PLM:

- Given that nursing care is the primary product in a hospital, how does PLM support and enable the "nursing product"?
- How will PLM affect the hospital's reputation for nursing excellence, which, as studies demonstrate, affects physicians' and patients' selection of hospitals (market share)?

- What message does PLM convey about the position, influence, and importance of nursing?
- How will professional standards and quality assurance be established, maintained, and coordinated under PLM?
- How will PLM affect the recruitment and retention of professional nurses?
- How does PLM address the issues nurses identify as major contributors to nursing burnout and the growing shortage, such as participation in decision making and position within the institution?
- Will PLM increase or diminish nurses' participation in the organization's decison-making process?
- How does PLM affect the design and evolution of care delivery systems that are patient-focused, satisfying to professional practitioners, and cost-efficient?
- Under PLM, how will the hospital satisfy Joint Commission standards requiring a professionally qualified person to be accountable for nursing practice?
- What efficiencies will be gained or lost with PLM?
- How will nursing activities and systems among product lines and across the department be coordinated and integrated?
- How will nursing be represented on the board of trustees and at the executive level?
- How will the nursing department accomplish functions that are more efficient if centralized, such as core orientation and nurse recruitment?
- Where do nursing units that do not relate to a specific product fit in the organizational structure?

Structure for Product Line Management*

In a hospital setting, the ways in which product lines are differentiated are as many and as

---

*Source: Vi Kunkle, *Marketing Strategies for Nurse Managers: A Guide for Developing and Implementing a Nursing Marketing Plan*, Aspen Publishers, Inc., © 1990.

varied as the accompanying organizational structures. Traditionally, each product line has its own product manager, and the product line is treated as a business within the business.

Product Lines Defined

A *product line* is a group of products within a product mix that are closely related, either because they function in a similar manner, are made available to the same consumers, or are marketed through the same types of outlets. A product mix (width of consumer offerings) is defined, then each product line in the product mix is lengthened by the product items. The product line can be organized in several ways. Tables 36-3 and 36-4 show two options for presenting product lines in a university school of nursing. Table 36-3 shows product lines developed by product items that are similar in function. Table 36-4 shows a variation that defines product lines more progressively, and is organized by the similarities of consumers using the programs. Whereas the product lines in Table 36-3 are organized by similarities of the products, the product lines in Table 36-4 are organized by similarities of the consumers who use the product lines. The product lines in Table 36-3 are oriented toward the organization,

and the product lines in Table 36-4 are oriented toward the consumer.

A change in the way products or services are differentiated has major implications for the organization, one of which is a change in structure to facilitate the success of the product line. The other major implication is that product lines require product managers. For example, a product manager will cross departmental lines in developing and implementing the product items in the product line. That is, the product items in the health education product line will be developed from the offerings of other departments, such as psychiatry, pediatrics, sociology, nutrition, etc.

Selecting Product Lines

Various methods are used by hospitals to define appropriate product lines. Certainly, the driving force is the market-based planning process itself. Criteria, then, are

- recognized strength in the marketplace (includes clinical, educational, and research expertise)
- marketability in the area of strength (includes high profitability, high demand, and positive exchange relationships)

Table 36-3 Functional Product Mix and Product Lines

Science	Psychiatry	Humanities	Business	Practicum	Curriculum Development
SC 101	PSY 101	SOC 110	BUS 110	MS 110	Revision
SC 300	PSY 102	ENG 110	BUS 210	PED 110	New Courses
SC 310	PSY 200	SPN 110	COM 110	OB 110	Textbooks
SC 312	PSY 310	REL 110		RHB 110	Sequencing

Table 36-4 Consumer-Oriented Product Mix and Product Lines

Generic	Degree Completion	Master's	Health Ed	Continuing Ed	Marketing
Course A	Course A	Courses	Mental Hlth	Course A	Recruitment
Course B	Course B	Clinical	Child Dev	Course B	Planning
Course C	Course C	Thesis	Nutrition	Course C	Curriculum
Course D	Course D		Family Planning	Course D	Advertisement Promotions

- capability for expanding the area of strength
- compatibility with the mission
- consistency with the interest of the program experts

The market-based planning process identifies the five or six major areas that need development, and these can be used in defining the product lines. During the annual market-based planning process, the product mix is widened, the product lines are lengthened, and existing product lines are continued, dropped, or expanded.

Nursing uses the market-based planning model to identify product items and product lines. If product lines determine the organizational structure, only the most significant product lines are developed, product line managers are named, and separate cost centers are allocated.

Modified Approach

In the absence of a product line–oriented hospital model, integrating nursing product lines into cost centers is difficult. Matrix and project organizational structures are innovative approaches designed to change the organizational focus from departmental operations to services. This customer-oriented approach recognizes that services and programs are both more important and marketable than operations.

However, even if traditional lines of authority are retained, product lines and product items can be integrated under the already established structure. Table 36-5 shows an example of product lines and product items organized under traditional organizational structures. The nurse manager of pediatrics manages the inpatient and same-day surgery units as well as the various other programs. In this example, the unit staff nurses become the project managers for the various product items. Cost centers include only the inpatient units of routine care and intensive care. The same-day surgery income and expense are included in the routine care unit cost center. The costs of the various programs are written in a business plan format but are a part of the units' budget.

Table 36-5 Organizing Product Items or Product Lines Under Traditional Lines of Authority

Title	Preadmission Screening
Nurse Manager	*Parental Education*
	Child Development
Service	Pediatric Toxicology
Pediatrics	Pediatric Nutrition
	Support Groups
Product Line	Death and Dying
Children's Center	Diabetes Support
	Pediatric Emergencies
Product Items	Pediatric Newsletter
Inpatient Pediatrics	*Outreach Education*
Routine Care	Intensive Care Course
Intensive Care	Annual Seminar
Orthopedics	*Physician Relations*
Juvenile Diabetes	Office Nurse Seminar
Rehabilitation	Physician/Nurse
Leukemia	Mini-Grand Rounds
Same-Day Surgery	Primary Nurse Program
Unit Tours	*Nurse Retention/Recruitment Program*

Source: Vi Kunkle, *Marketing Strategies for Nurse Managers: A Guide for Developing and Implementing a Nursing Marketing Plan*, Aspen Publishers, Inc., © 1990.

Responsibilities of the Product Line Manager

Once a product line is established and a product line manager is placed in the position, the product manager becomes responsible for further development, implementation, and monitoring of the product lines against the objectives. A more detailed list of responsibilities includes

- fine-tuning the product line objectives and subobjectives
- organizing and leading an effective product line team
- implementing the product line objectives
- researching all aspects of the product line
- analyzing and preparing forecast reports based on research
- establishing a format for monitoring the objectives of the product line
- changing objectives based on new market information
- ensuring profitability of the product line
- coordinating team efforts with other departments
- developing periodic reports to go to the responsible administrator
- developing annual business plans

The Marketing Concept

1. The process of listening to consumers and the marketplace
2. The philosophy of organizing to satisfy needs of a group or groups of consumers
3. The satisfaction of these needs in a profitable fashion

Because hospitalized patients are too ill to coordinate their own plan of care, nurses also act on behalf of patients, representing patients to physicians and other professional disciplines. Although nursing at the organizational level works in close collaboration with the planning, marketing, and communications departments of the hospital, bedside nurses are key figures in micro-level nursing.

The nurse does marketing for the hospital in three ways. First, in the provision of excellence in patient care, nurses sell the hospital to physicians. Second, by their manner and approach to care delivery, nurses sell the hospital to patients. Third, by their positive attitudes and job satisfaction, nurses influence the retention of other nurses.

MARKETING PROCESS

The Role of the Nurse*

The product of the hospital and health care providers is health care. Nursing produces and delivers this health care. The outcome and purpose of patient care are patient compliance with the health care regimen and a resulting physical and mental state called *health*, restored at least to the previous level. In the process of producing and delivering health care, nursing is simultaneously selling an image of both nursing and the health care provider to the patient.

Nursing, by definition, is the primary interface between the hospital and its customers.

Planning vs. Marketing*

There is a great deal of confusion regarding the relationship of planning to marketing. Some believe a corporate plan should be established before a marketing plan is developed. For example, the organization establishes its mission and then develops its marketing plan within the context of its mission and goals. Although this is an interactive process, marketing can play a key first-step role by helping to determine which direction to go. However, most health care organizations that develop plans do not incorporate a market-based approach. The typical process begins with the wants and needs of people who

---

Source: Vi Kunkle, *Marketing Strategies for Nurse Managers: A Guide for Developing and Implementing a Nursing Marketing Plan*, Aspen Publishers, Inc., © 1990.

Source: Steven G. Hillstead and Eric N. Berkowitz, *Health Care Marketing Plans: From Strategy to Action*, ed. 2, Aspen Publishers, Inc., © 1991.

work in the hospital or own the clinic and their views of the marketplace. The market-based approach starts with customer wants and needs, and these become the basis for a program or service to address those needs.

An Overview of the Process*

A marketing plan begins with an analysis of the market. Most health care organizations think of their internal needs first and the marketplace second. This is a nonmarket-based approach. A market-oriented manager, however, begins with a determination of external needs and focuses internal actions on these external needs. This is a market-based approach. The two approaches vary in just a few instances (Figure 36-1), but

Source: Ibid.

the difference in the results obtained with these two planning approaches can be dramatic.

A market-based approach is not "right" and the nonmarket-based approach is not "wrong." Yet, as financial resources became more restricted, mistakes (in terms of programs that do not meet expectations) are more costly for the organization. A market-based approach helps improve the odds of success. It is easier to listen to buyers and provide the necessary programs than to attempt to divine what buyers may need.

Marketing Planning Sequence

The sequence of the market-based approach is relatively simple. It incorporates six steps:

1. setting the mission
2. performing an external/internal analysis
3. determining the strategy action match and marketing objectives

Figure 36-1 Diagram of Internal Planning vs. Marketing Planning

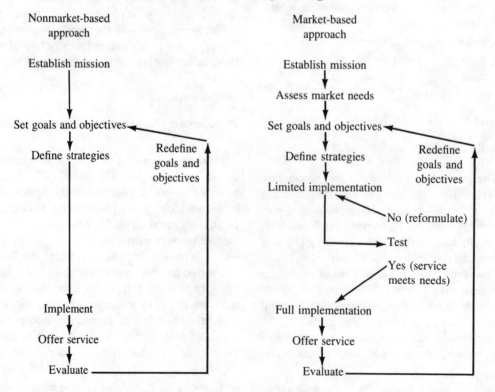

Source: Steven G. Hillstead and Eric N. Berkowitz, *Health Care Marketing Plans: From Strategy to Action*, ed. 2, Aspen Publishers, Inc., © 1991.

4. developing action strategies
5. integrating the plan and making revisions
6. providing appropriate control procedures, feedback, and integration of all plans into a unified effort

At each step, three types of activities are necessary for success:

1. the process of doing the staff work necessary to support decision making
2. the process of actually making decisions
3. the process of integrating the activities of all units or services to enhance coordination between the functional units, such as operations and finance

The collection of the details and data needed in the decision-making process constitutes the staff work. Here, marketing plans differ substantially from other planning approaches, because they require not only internal data, but also information on the attitudes, the opinions, and the environment of those outside the organization.

In the decision process, the actual steps of a marketing plan are charted. As the hospital or clinic or nurse executive assesses the external market data, it must decide how to react to external conditions in light of its internal capabilities.

The integration process involves the coordination of marketing plans with finance, personnel, operations, and resource allocation. Also included are the development of the organization's entire product or service portfolio and the sharing and coordination of plans with the other services within the health care organization.

The Marketing Plan

To establish an effective marketing plan, it is necessary to understand the first premise of marketing. Marketing is the process of determining customer wants and needs and then, to whatever extent possible, designing appropriate programs and services to meet those wants and needs in a timely, cost-effective, competitive fashion. It is the process of molding the organization to the customers rather than convincing customers that the organization provides what they need.

Table 36-6 Marketing Planning Questions

Who is the market?
Where is the market?
What are the needs and demands?
Where are you now?
- As an institution?
- As a department?
- As an individual?
- With respect to the environment and competition?
- With respect to capabilities and opportunities?

Where do you want to go?
- Assumptions/potentials.
- Objectives and goals.

How do you want to get there?
- Policies and procedures/levels of initiative.
- Strategies and programs.

When do you want to arrive?
- Priorities and schedules.

Who is responsible?
- Organization and delegation.

How much will it cost?
- Budgets and resource allocations.

How will you know if you did it?
- Feedback and review sessions.
- Continuous monitoring.

When completed, a marketing plan contains answers to the questions in Table 36-6. Answering these questions in sequence is the foundation for most marketing strategy sessions.

Key Questions for Conducting an Internal/External Analysis*

The internal/external analysis is a key component in developing the marketing plan, as it is the foundation from which the strategy action match is determined. It is also important in determining which specific action-oriented marketing tactics are appropriate. The following list is a reminder

---

Source: Steven G. Hillstead and Eric N. Berkowitz, *Health Care Marketing Plans: From Strategy to Action*, ed. 2, Aspen Publishers, Inc., © 1991.

as to which questions should be asked as part of the analysis.

The Environment and the Market

1. What kinds of external controls affect the organization?

   –Local?

   –State?

   –Federal?

   –Self-regulatory?

2. What are the trends in recent regulatory rulings?
3. What are the main developments with respect to demography, economy, technology, government, and culture that will affect the organization's situation?
4. What are the organization's major markets and publics?
5. How large is the service area covered by the market?
6. What are the major segments in each market?
7. What are the present and expected future profits and characteristics of each market or market segment?
8. What is the expected rate of growth of each segment?
9. How fast and far have markets expanded?
10. Where do the patients come from geographically?
11. What are the benefits that customers in different segments derive from the product (e.g., economics, better performance, displaceable cost)?
12. What are the reasons for buying the product in different segments (e.g., product features, awareness, price, advertising, promotion, packaging, display, sales assistance)?
13. What is the marketing standing with established customers in each segment (e.g., market share, pattern of repeat business, expansion of customers' product use)?
14. What are the requirements for success in each market?
15. What are the customer attitudes in different segments (e.g., brand awareness, brand image mapping)?
16. What is the overall reputation of the product in each segment?
17. What reinforces the customer's faith in the company and product?
18. What reasons force customers to turn elsewhere for help in using the product?
19. What is the life cycle status of the product?
20. What product research and improvements are planned?
21. Are there deficiencies in servicing or assisting customers in using the product?

The Competitive Environment

1. How many competitors are in the industry?

   –How are competitors defined?

   –Has the number increased or decreased in the last four years?

2. What is the organization's position in the market (size and strength) relative to competitors?
3. Who are the organization's major competitors?
4. What trends can be foreseen in competition?
5. Are there other companies that may be enticed to serve the organization's customers or markets? This should include conglomerates or diversified companies that may be attracted by the growth, size, or profitability of these markets.
6. What about companies on the periphery—those that serve the same customers with different but related products? This may include related pieces of equipment. It is impossible to list all related items, but those closest should be included.
7. What other products or services provide the same or similar function? What percentage of total market sales does each substitute product have?
8. What product innovations could replace or reduce the sales of the organization's products? When will these products be commercially feasible? (*Note:* Information about potentially competitive products can be found by searching the U.S. Patent Office or foreign patent offices.)

9. What are the choices afforded patients?
   –In services?
   –In payment?
10. Is competition on a price or nonprice basis?
11. How do competitors (segment/price) advertise?
12. Are there competitors in other geographical regions or other segments who do not currently compete in the organization's markets or segments, but may decide to?
13. Who are the customers served by the industry? Are there any who may want to move backwards?
14. Who are the suppliers to the industry? Are they moving? Why?

The Internal Assessment

1. What has been the historical purpose of the clinic?
2. How has the hospital changed over the past decade?
3. When and how was it organized?
4. What has been the nature of its growth?
5. What is the basic policy of the organization? Is it health care or profit?
6. What has been the financial history of the organization?
7. How has it been capitalized?
8. Have there been any accounts receivable problems?
9. What is the inventory investment?
10. How successful has the organization been with the various services promoted?
11. Is the total volume (gross revenue, utilization) increasing or decreasing?
12. Have there been any fluctuations in revenue? If so, what caused them?
13. What are the organization's present strengths and weaknesses in
    - management capabilities?
    - medical staff?
    - technical facilities?
    - reputation?
    - financial capabilities?
    - image?
    - medical facilities?

The Marketing Function and Programs

1. Are there specialized training programs for key personnel that emphasize the marketing concept?
2. Do the administrator and other key personnel have marketing experience?
3. Does the marketing department have a key role in the planning activities of the organization?
4. Does the person with marketing responsibility report directly to the chief executive officer or top administrator?
5. Is marketing research appreciated as an ongoing task necessary for the development of effective marketing plans?
6. Are policies and procedures in place to coordinate the marketing activities with the other ongoing activities of the organization?
7. Does the organization have a high-level marketing officer to analyze, plan, and implement its marketing work?
8. Are the other persons who are directly involved in marketing activities competent people? Do they need more training, incentives, or supervision?
9. Are the marketing responsibilities optimally structured to serve the needs of different activities, products, markets, and territories?
10. What is the organization's core strategy for achieving its objectives, and is it likely to succeed?
11. Is the organization allocating enough resources (or too many) to accomplish its marketing tasks?
12. Are the marketing resources allocated optimally to the various markets, territories, and products of the organization?
13. Are the marketing resources allocated optimally to the major elements of the marketing mix (i.e., product quality, personal contact, promotion, and distribution)?
14. Does the organization develop an annual marketing plan? Is the planning procedure effective?
15. Does the organization implement control procedures (e.g., monthly, quarterly) to

ensure that its annual plan objectives are being achieved?

16. Does the organization carry out periodic studies to determine the contribution and effectiveness of various marketing activities?

17. Does the organization have an adequate marketing information system to service the needs of managers in planning and controlling various markets?

Products/Services

1. What are the organization's products and services, both present and proposed?

2. What are the general outstanding characteristics of each product or service?

3. How are the organization's products or services superior to or distinct from those of competing organizations?

   –What are the weaknesses?
   –Should any product be phased out?
   –Should any product be added?

4. What is the total cost per service (in use)? Is service over- or underutilized?

5. Which services are most heavily used? Why?

   –Are there distinct groups of users?
   –What is the profile of patients/physicians who use the services?

6. What are the organization's policies regarding

   –number and types of services to offer?
   –needs assessment for service addition/deletion?

7. What is the history of the organization's major products and services?

   –How many did the organization originally have?
   –How many have been added or dropped?
   –What important changes have taken place in services during the last ten years?
   –Has demand for the services increased or decreased?
   –What are the most common complaints against the services?

–What services could be added to make the organization more attractive to patients, medical staff, and nonmedical personnel?
–What are the strongest points of services to patients, medical staff, and nonmedical personnel?

8. Does the organization have any other features that individualize its services or give it an advantage over competitors?

Pricing Strategy

1. What is the pricing strategy of the organization?

   –Cost plus?
   –Return on investment?
   –Stabilization?
   –Demand?

2. How are prices for services determined?

   –How often are prices reviewed?
   –What factors contribute to a price increase/decrease?

3. What have been the price trends for the past five years?

4. How are the organization's policies viewed by

   –patients?
   –physicians?
   –third-party payers?
   –competitors?
   –regulators?

5. How are price promotions used?

6. What would be the impact of demand on a higher or lower price?

Promotional Strategy

1. Is the sales force large enough to accomplish the organization's objectives?

2. Is the sales force organized along the proper principles of specialization (e.g., territory, market, product)?

3. Does the sales force show high morale, ability, and effort? Is it sufficiently trained and motivated?

4. Are the procedures adequate for setting quotas and evaluating performance?

5. What is the purpose of the organization's present promotional activities (including advertising)?
   –Protection?
   –Education?
   –Search for new markets?
   –Development of all markets?
   –Establishment of a new service?
6. Has this purpose undergone any change in recent years?
7. To whom has advertising been largely directed?
   –Donors?
   –Patients?
   —Former?
   —Current?
   —Prospective?
   –Physicians?
   —On staff?
   —Potential?
8. Is the cost per thousand still favorable?
9. Is it delivering the desired audience?
10. What media have been used?
11. Are the media still effective in reaching the intended audience?
12. Are the objectives being met?
13. What copy appeals have had the most favorable response?
14. What methods have been used for measuring advertising effectiveness?

Public Relations

1. What is the role of public relations?
   –Is it a separate function/department?
   –What is its scope of responsibilities?
2. Has the public relations effort led to regular coverage?
3. Are the public relations objectives integrated with the overall promotional plan?
4. Are procedures established and used to measure the results from the public relations program?

Distribution Strategies

1. What are the distribution trends in the industry?

–What services are being performed on an outpatient basis?
–What services are being performed on an at-home basis?
–Are satellite facilities being used?
2. What factors are considered in location decisions?
3. How important is distribution in establishing a competitive advantage for a particular service?
4. Where does the hospital or clinic stand on this component?

SELLING THE NURSING SERVICE

Monitoring the Pulse of Nursing's Customers*

The concept of monitoring the pulse of the customer is a strategy requiring continuous feedback concerning the perceptions of nursing care in the mind of its customers. Responsive nurse managers devise and implement ongoing systems for continuous feedback.

Patients' Perceptions

Patients are the primary customers of the nursing department, and as such, their satisfaction with care is of paramount value to the providers. With so many classifications of personnel coming in contact with patients, it is difficult to control and standardize approaches to patient care. One of the best methods of obtaining immediate feedback concerning patient perceptions of care is to simply ask patients about the care received.

Administrative Welcome Rounds. A positive and high-visibility program to determine the efficiency of the admission process is the administrative welcome rounds. The nurse administrator, accompanied by the manager or staff nurse, chats briefly with each patient admitted the night before, giving a welcome and leaving a

Source: Vi Kunkle, *Marketing Strategies for Nurse Managers: A Guide for Developing and Implementing a Nursing Marketing Plan*, Aspen Publishers, Inc., © 1990.

business card for future use by the patient in contacting the nurse administrator. This program sets a positive tone for the admission and leaves the patient with an accessible person's name if problems should occur later.

Postdischarge Follow-Up Calls. Primary nurses call the discharged patient within three days postdischarge to reinforce patient compliance with the treatment regimen, express concern about the patient's condition and health status after discharge, and inquire about satisfaction with care. The telephone call in and of itself is a powerful marketing strategy for nursing. It shows that the nursing organization cares about the customers.

Physicians' Perceptions

The responsive nurse manager keeps a constant pulse on the perceptions and attitudes of physicians. A physician questionnaire is developed and administered to physicians monthly to monitor perceptions. Discussions on patient-physician problems can be initiated. Using a patient-oriented questionnaire as supportive evidence avoids the evaluation of nursing based on subjective criteria such as likes and dislikes of a particular unit, nurse manager, or nurse. A more informal method is face-to-face discussions with physicians about items on the questionnaire. The feedback is used to assess physicians' satisfaction level, and immediate action is taken where appropriate.

Nurses' Perceptions

Responsive nurse managers continuously monitor not only the supply of nurses but nurse vacancy rates and the reasons for the vacancies. Analyzing the reasons for resignations requires an accurate monitoring system of the attitudes and beliefs of the resigning nurses and those who are still employed. Continuous feedback strategies for nurses include termination, or exit, interviews, an attitude questionnaire, and a nurse ombudsman program.

Termination, or Exit, Interview. The termination interview is used to determine why nurses leave the hospital. A systematic format is devel-

oped for the interview so that the data can be summarized and analyzed for patterns. Each nurse manager receives a monthly report of the termination data. Nurse administrators analyze the data for evidence of generalized problems or problems with a specific unit or issue.

Nursing Ombudsman. In order to implement the nursing ombudsman program, a position is created or responsibility added to another position. In some hospitals, a similar position is called patient advocate or patient representative with responsibilities for patient satisfaction. Often, the incumbent is not a nurse, and the position does not report to nursing. The nursing ombudsman is concerned with customer relations with and satisfaction levels of all of nursing's customers: patients, nurses, and physicians. The position is filled by an RN who reports to nursing. Responsibilities include visiting patients, following up with orientees, and visiting physicians. The primary purpose of the follow ups and visits is to monitor attitudes and perceptions, keeping the nursing department informed of what is satisfying to customers as well as problems and dissatisfaction levels.

Ideas for Patient Promotional Programs*

Promotional programs designed to attract or retain patients are based on programs or services that are already developed but that need special promotions in order to compete. These strategies are primarily based on augmented services rather than on price, although, occasionally, price competition is one of the strategies. Highly competitive areas or services design special promotional services to link current patients and potential patients to the institution. This is especially common in obstetrics and pediatrics but can also occur when there is more than one of any specialized program in the community such as oncology, rehabilitation, home, emergency, and ambulatory care. Although these promotions are often designed by the marketing and promotions departments, staff at the unit level

---

*Source: Ibid.

are indeed creative in generating ideas for the promotion of their specific services. Examples include

- birthday cards for newborn nursery infants
- free pictures for newborns at birth and ages one and two
- videotapes of infants receiving the first bath by their mother
- exercise classes for obstetric patients (designed with physician input)
- child development classes for parents of young children
- quarterly health update newsletters for cardiac patients
- reunions for rehabilitation patients
- support groups for relatives who have lost loved ones
- hotlines for obstetric, emergency, and psychiatric patients with qualified response staff
- follow-up telephone calls to the patient from the primary nurse
- unit tours for elective patients
- unit tours and receptions for the public
- CPR certifications for the public

Promotions such as these are topics of controversy in health care and are often labeled *gimmicks* by critics. Actually, they are augmentations of already developed services and programs. Although they are designed to attract patients, these augmentations also improve services to the customer. Additionally, such promotions provide increased top-of-mind name awareness of the hospital among customers.

Physician Bonding*

The changing environment of health care requires nurse executives to examine more closely the physician as customer. Faced with declining admissions and reimbursements, health care agencies are competing to attract and

retain physicians. Nurse executives know the significant contributions physicians make to patient care revenues. Health care agencies are in fierce competition to attract and retain physicians.

The nurse executive must include physician relations and satisfaction with the agency and services provided in the long-range planning for service excellence. The development of a program to ''bond'' physicians to the nursing department will greatly assist in meeting the agency's overall objective of long-term survival through enhanced revenues and the delivery of quality care.

The nurse executive plays a key role in developing a successful physician bonding program. Physicians are most attentive to patient care and the quality of services offered to produce favorable outcomes. As administrators of patient care, the nurse executive can facilitate successful bonding strategies to enhance the quality of patient care as well as foster loyalty and bonding of physicians to the nursing department and ultimately the health care institution. For the variety of strategies available, see Table 36-7.

Perhaps the greatest challenge to the nurse executive is selling the concept of the bonding program to the chief executive officer and governing body. When selling the program, the nurse executive should focus on the overall benefits to the agency. Two major benefits are as follows:

1. Physician bonding programs lead to increased physician commitment to the agency and thus increased utilization of services and patient admissions. The end result is a real increase in patient-generated revenues and stronger, more secure operating margins.
2. Bonding programs have a positive effect on the entire morale of the institution: Staff members and physicians gain a better understanding of each other's priorities and agendas; communication and cooperation increase, thus providing a more professional and satisfying work environment; and nurse and physician retention and recruitment are enhanced. This results

---

*Source: Dominick L. Flarey, '' Physician Bonding: The Role of the Nurse Executive,'' *Journal of Nursing Administration,* vol. 20, no. 12, December 1990.

Table 36-7 Strategies to Promote Physician Bonding

1. *Nurse–physician liaison committees* promote collaborative problem solving and program planning.
2. *Joint nurse–physician question and answer programs* enhance professional working relationships and ensure mutual goal setting and direction.
3. *Physician lecture series* allow participation of physicians in the continuing education of nurses.
4. *Patient teaching programs* position nursing as a primary deliverer of preventative and restorative care and assist physicians in overall patient management.
5. *Patient screening programs* assist physicians in overall patient care and preventative health care (e.g., breast exams, cholesterol screening).
6. *Nurse–physician team conferences* bridge the gap between medical practice and professional nursing practice, foster collaboration, increase communications, and facilitate quality care planning.
7. *Collaborative practice models* enhance mutual goal setting for quality care, enhance communications, increase bonding and physician commitment to the nursing department and the delivery of nursing care, and position nursing as an integral and primary component of patient care.
8. *Physician office training programs* assist physicians in the continuing education of their office staffs and position nursing as an important resource for medical practices.

Source: Dominick L. Flarey, "Physician Bonding: The Role of the Nurse Executive," *Journal of Nursing Administration,* vol. 20, no. 12, December 1990.

in considerable cost savings and increased profit margins for the institution.

Follow-up interviews after implementation of the bonding program will ascertain physicians' perceptions and feelings about the program as well as verifiable evidence of increasing satisfaction with care services offered, the nursing department, and the institution. The degree of customer satisfaction by the physician is an important indicator of program success or failure.

Chapter 37

Grant Programs and Research

PLANNING FOR GRANTS*

Literally billions of dollars are available through grants and contracts from government agencies and private foundations and individuals. Although religious and related charities are the most popular recipients of such donations, health-related programs usually receive the second largest sum.

The dollar amounts fluctuate from year to year, but large sums of money are available each year and often go unclaimed. Grant writers must start with the assumption that the dollars are there and must continue to be optimistic and enthusiastic.

Agencies and institutions usually have mission statements, goals and objectives, and long-range plans to implement the goals and objectives and fulfill the mission statement. Possible grants should be reviewed and discussed in this context. Most important, grant applications should be prepared only for tasks that an agency would like to undertake, even if external money were not available.

Rational planning is also essential in development of the proposal. Grant reviewers look for a proposal that is stated clearly and convincingly.

*Source: Donald J. Breckon, John R. Harvey, and R. Brick Lancaster, *Community Health Education: Settings, Roles, and Skills*, ed. 2, Aspen Publishers, Inc., © 1989.

They look for documentation that a problem exists and for a plan that will help alleviate the problem. They look for measurable objectives that are feasible. They look at the credibility of the agency and the credentials of the staff. They look for the probability of success and how such a project will be evaluated.

Stated differently, agency personnel who review and act on grant applications are concerned that their money is being spent wisely and that full value will be received. Rational planning and sound administrative practices are therefore essential parts of the grant preparation process and the program that is proposed.

The committee approach is recommended for grant development, although one person usually needs to do the actual writing for the proposal to be coherent. The value of having several people involved in generating ideas and in reviewing drafts cannot be overstated. If a proposal represents the best thinking of several people, it will be better than if it represents the good thinking of only one person.

Proposal Development for State or Federal Agencies

A proposal is a positive statement that sets forth a program or a set of activities. It requires two parties. It is a statement of what an individual or agency intends to do. It is made to another agency or institution and should be uniquely suited to that agency. It is written for presentation to another party in order to gain its acceptance.

Several types of proposals can be developed, the most common of which is a program proposal that offers a specific set of services to individual families, groups, or communities. Technical assistance is a feature of many grant applications. Some planning proposals detail a set of planning and coordinating activities, which usually result in a program proposal. Similarly, there are research proposals to study a specific problem, evaluate a service, and so on.

Proposals can be solicited or unsolicited. A solicited proposal is prepared in response to a formal, written "request for proposal," called an RFP. RFPs are prepared and sent to prospective agencies and operations. Similarly, program announcements and guidelines are described in various publications. The *Catalog of Federal Domestic Assistance* and the *Federal Register* are helpful in locating grant money and are available in most libraries. There are also grant-oriented newsletters, some of which are free. Potential grant writers need only request that their names be placed on an agency mailing list. A number of commercial organizations also prepare and sell subscriptions that describe currently available grant money. Although such subscriptions are expensive, they can pay for themselves quickly in terms of time saved and dollars garnered.

Unsolicited proposals are also received and reviewed regularly. It is important in both cases to ascertain if a project is a priority in the agency that is being solicited. A telephone call to the agency will usually result in the needed information.

Once one or more potential sources of grant money have been developed, the agency (or agencies) should be contacted for available guidelines and application forms. Further, it is recommended that prospective grant writers telephone or visit a contact person in the agency and describe the essence of what will be proposed. Such firsthand information and advice is readily available, and staff members prefer to provide it before the project is fully developed, rather than after. Seeking and using such advice can save a lot of time and energy, but more importantly, it can increase the probability of a project being funded.

Each funding agency has its own application forms and guidelines. It is imperative that the forms be filled out completely and accurately. Writing a grant is more complicated than filling in the blanks, but ability and willingness to follow directions completely is an important part of the process.

Foundations

A foundation is a nongovernmental, nonprofit organization. It has funds and programs managed by its own board of directors. With few exceptions, they make grants only to other tax-exempt, nonprofit agencies.

A foundation may have either a narrow range or a wide range of problems it is interested in funding. Smaller foundations prefer to fund projects in their own geographical locale, whereas larger foundations may prefer projects that are state, regional, or national in scope. In either case it is important to locate one or two foundations whose interests somewhat match the interests addressed in the proposal.

The Foundation Directory is a good reference to use in identifying interested foundations. It describes the purpose and activities of specific foundations, the locale in which they make grants, and the general size of the grants they make.

An important follow-up step is to contact the foundation and ask for an annual report or material that describes the major thrust of the foundation. A careful review of such material usually reveals whether the foundation would be interested in funding the project. A program officer's first question usually is, "Is this the kind of activity that fits within our foundation's interests?" A second related question is, "Is the request for support the kind and amount that our foundation usually gives?" If proposal writers can anticipate these questions and submit to foundations that have "a good fit," the probability of funding increases.

Proposals for foundations are essentially the same as those for state and federal agencies, only smaller. Most foundations do not want a fully developed proposal as their first point of contact. Some small foundations prefer personal contact before any written proposal is submitted, and others prefer a letter and a summary. In some instances an expanded letter is preferred, whereas in the case of large foundations, application forms may be used. A five-page concept paper is somewhat typical for a first submission to a foundation; a more detailed submission will be required after the first screening. The first submission should be short, clear, and persuasive; it should state at the outset what is to be accomplished, who expects to accomplish it, how much it will cost, and how long it will take.

Guide to Nursing Research Grants

Those in search of research and project grants in nursing can find funding sources quickly in a new comprehensive directory edited by the American Association of Colleges of Nursing (AACN). The 298-page guide, *The Complete Grants Sourcebook for Nursing and Health*, is a single-source reference designed specifically to help nursing and other health professionals develop effective grant-seeking strategies and find the best sources of funding for a variety of research, practice, and educational programs.

The AACN *Sourcebook* provides information on 300 corporate, foundation, and federal sources that either have funded nursing- and health-related research and projects or whose interests match those of the nursing and health professions. Listings include details on eligibility and application requirements, deadlines, financial data, contact persons, and the funds each has contributed to nursing and health activities.

Source: Holly A. De Groot, "Patient Classification System Evaluation, Part I: Essential System Elements," *Journal of Nursing Administration*, vol. 19, no. 6, June 1989.

THE GRANT PROPOSAL

The Steps in Development of Grant Proposals*

Grant writing is no longer limited to securing funds for research purposes. Major changes in the allocation of health care funds require that administrators develop and seek more funds. Unfortunately, the amount of grant funds available is often limited and competition for the funds intense. Therefore, the ability to develop a successful grant proposal is crucial.

Step 1: Identify a Funding Source. Funding sources include government agencies (at the federal, state, and city or county levels), private foundations, corporations, and associations, and academic institutions. Each funding source has different policies, missions, and application forms. To determine the best funding source, familiarize yourself with each funding source's history, dollar limitations, objectives, and areas of interest. A guide like the *Complete Grants Sourcebook for Nursing and Health*, which contains in-depth profiles of 300 corporate, foundation, and government sources, could be of great help.

Grant applications should be tailored to meet the priorities of the funding source. One of the most inefficient methods of developing a grant application is to write the proposal and then look for a funding source. A thorough library search to analyze funding sources before developing the proposal will save countless hours of revising the proposal to fit the funding source.

Step 2: Obtain Application Materials from the Funding Source. Thoroughly read the application materials before you begin to write the proposal. This is very important and often ignored. These materials provide instructions on content and format of the application and are often developed by the same individuals who will review the application. The instructions will assist you in preparing a complete application

---

*Source: Deidre Richards, "Ten Steps to Successful Grant Writing," *Journal of Nursing Administration*, vol. 20, no. 1, January 1990. © 1990 J.B. Lippincott Company.

that meets all requirements of the funding source.

Step 3: Identify Content Essential to Developing the Proposal and Note Areas in Which You Need Clarification. Underline the content essential to the actual writing of the proposal, for example, application format, required signatures, number of copies. Take special note of proposal deadlines. Missing a deadline in all likelihood will disqualify your proposal. Contact the funding source to clarify points of confusion such as questions relating to the forms, budget, or instructions.

Step 4: Follow the Application Instructions Precisely. It is very important to strictly adhere to proposal page limits. Do not include information that is not requested. If you think additional information is essential to the reviewers' understanding of how the project will operate, then place the information in an appendix and reference it in the proposal narrative. Reviewers appreciate a proposal that is easy to read and includes only what must be known.

However, do not omit requested information because it is not readily available to you. Keep in mind, the grant reviewers will definitely notice if requested information is omitted or unrelated information is added. These practices will jeopardize the success of your proposal.

Step 5: Clearly Describe Project Goals, Objectives, Implementation Strategies, and Evaluation Criteria. Identifying the need for grant funds, explicitly describing what will be done with the grant funds, and evaluating the project are extremely important parts of the grant proposal. Most funding agencies adhere to a general grant format.

Step 6: Proofread the Proposal. Carefully proofread the final draft of the typed proposal. Proof for typographical errors and to determine that all of the required information is included, the application forms provided by the funding source are completed correctly and signed when necessary, and the application is arranged in the order requested by the funding source.

Step 7: Complete a Presubmission Review of the Finished Proposal. Give a copy of the application instructions and the completed proposal to a colleague who is knowledgeable about the project but not directly associated with developing the proposal. Your colleague should read the proposal for required content and critique each section for clarity, specificity, and overall "flow" of the proposal from assessment of need to evaluation.

Step 8: Revise the Proposal Based on the Presubmission Review. Frequently, grant writers do not allow sufficient preparation time to permit the presubmission review and subsequent revision. "The uninitiated seldom appreciate the number of revisions and the amount of time consumed in preparing a sound proposal."

Step 9: Avoid Common Mistakes. These mistakes reflect a rushed and disorganized grant writer. Common mistakes to avoid include submitting the proposal after the deadline; omitting literature citations that support the needs assessment or implementation strategies; incorrectly completing the application forms; omitting required signatures; mathematical errors in the budget; inconsistent budget figures throughout the application; goals, objectives, or implementation strategies that do not pertain to the identified need; evaluation criteria that do not include project outcomes; padding the application with unnecessary information; and using a format that does not conform to the application instructions. For the grant reviewer's convenience, include a table of contents and number all of the pages.

Step 10: Submit the Proposal to the Funding Source. The application should be sent by certified mail, return receipt requested. Occasionally, applications have been lost in the mail or delivered to the wrong person. If certified, you have documentation when you sent it and who received it. This documentation may mean the difference between a review or a disqualification.

Elements in a Grant Proposal*

Letter of Transmittal. The letter of transmittal, or cover sheet, is the first page of a grant but

---

Source: Donald J. Breckon, John R. Harvey, and R. Brick Lancaster, *Community Health Education: Settings, Roles, and Skills,* ed. 2, Aspen Publishers, Inc., © 1989.

may, in fact, be the last part of the application to be prepared. It provides, at minimum, the name and address of the organization submitting the proposal, a concise summary of the problem, and the proposed program. In an initial attempt to establish credibility, it often includes a statement of the organization's interest, capability, and experience in the area. It must contain the contact person's name, address, and telephone number and an authorized signature from a chief administrative officer. The authorized signature is necessary because the proposal is offering to use agency space, equipment, and staff to do specific tasks. Grant reviewers want to know that the agency is committed to such tasks. When funded, such a project has the effect of a contract.

Table of Contents. If the application is large, a table of contents usually follows the letter of transmittal. Use of headings in the body of the proposal facilitates development of a table of contents. Headings also make it easier for reviewers to follow the organization of the project and should be used even if a table of contents is not needed.

Introduction. An introductory statement that puts the proposal in context is appropriate. The statement may or may not include a description of the problem; the description can be a separate section. In either case, it is important to establish that there is a problem and that it has serious consequences to the citizenry. Documentation is usually necessary at this point and, even if not necessary, is helpful.

Target Group. The target group should be described in detail and put in the context of the geographical area in which the program will take place. The number and kind of clients is valuable information. A description of how the client group has been involved in the project planning process is also important.

Objectives. The specific objectives should be included in measurable form. Although behavioral objectives are not necessarily required, they lend themselves well to grant application specifications. A timetable for accomplishing the objectives should also be included.

Procedures. The procedures that will be used should be detailed. A logical, sequential timeta-

ble for the work plan is helpful. Specific methods and materials should be identified, with emphasis given to the innovative features of the program.

Evaluation. A plan for evaluation should also be included and is often a key part of the proposal. The tools and methodology to be used should be described in enough detail to ensure funding agencies that the results of the program will be summarized accurately.

Budget. A budget sheet is usually included in the application form. Because this varies from agency to agency, the forms of the grant agency should be used when possible. However, grant budgets have some commonality. Usually they list salaries, by position. Salary schedules of the applicant agency should be used in calculations. Fringe benefits are ordinarily figured on a percentage of salary. They include employer contributions to Social Security, health insurance, unemployment compensation, workers' compensation, and so on. The figures vary from agency to agency and from year to year but are usually about 25 percent of the total salary costs.

If consultants are needed on technical projects, a realistic per diem fee should be used in a separate section of the budget. Consultants are not entitled to fringe benefits.

Supplies and materials should also be described in a separate section. They should be itemized by major types, such as office supplies, mail, telephone, duplication costs, printing.

Equipment is usually itemized in a separate category, giving such specifics as model number and vendor.

Travel should be categorized (e.g., in country/out of country, in state/out of state); it can be divided by personnel or by program function. Reviewers usually want to know how travel allowances are going to be used.

Indirect costs include such items as utilities, space, procurement, and accounting staffs. Governmental funding agencies usually have a maximum allowable indirect rate. The rate is often negotiated; it may approach 50 percent of salaries and wages for the project.

Matching Funds. If matching funds are being used, they should be described. They represent the portion of the project cost that the institution is providing. In some instances, in-kind contributions have been used for this purpose. Institutions may agree to provide space, office furniture, and so on, and place a monetary value on that. In other instances, matching funds are required. In any case the larger the amount of matching funds or in-kind contributions, the more attractive the application will be.

Assurances. When applying to government agencies it is also necessary to provide assurance compliances. There are a number of such assurances and they change from time to time. They might include such items as treatment of human subjects, following affirmative action procedures when hiring, handicapped accessibility, and accounting practices. Again, funding agencies can readily provide copies of such required assurances.

Appendices. As in other written documents, the appendices are used to include material that, if included in the body of the proposal, would interrupt the flow. Curricula vitae of key personnel in the project and supporting letters of other agencies are usually appended. Brochures, flow charts, diagrams, and other supporting material may be included.

RESEARCH IN THE NURSING SERVICE SETTING

Scope*

To establish a successful research section within a practice setting requires a commitment to the value of research in terms of guiding decision making as well as allocating and generating resources. The consistent pressure in practice settings for accurate information to guide administrative and clinical decisions and long-term policies stimulates the endeavors for integrating research. However, the integration process is not without its challenges. For example, not all problems confronting nurse admin-

Source: Ada Sue Hinshaw and Carolyn H. Smeltzer, "Research Challenges and Programs for Practice Settings," *Journal of Nursing Administration*, vol. 17, nos. 7 and 8, July-August 1987.

istrators and clinicians are researchable. Some are more amenable to immediate problem-solving techniques than to research strategies. Experience, however, suggests that clinical and administrative problems with the following characteristics are researchable:

1. The problems or issues are repetitive.
2. The problems or issues occur across multiple clinical settings.
3. The problems or issues are testable empirically and are not philosophical stances representing values such as "should" or "ought."
4. The problems or issues represent long-term practices and/or policies for which accurate information or data will be necessary for decision making.

Defining researchable problems in this manner requires that the department of nursing's long-term strategic plans outline the type of information that will be needed for policy decisions.

Setting Limits and Guidelines

It is important when research is integrated in the clinical setting that realistic guidelines are set for each individual investigation, either clinical or administrative, in terms of the time frame that the project can be expected to require. Establishing such a time frame in the early stages of the research process allows personnel in the practice setting to understand what can be expected in terms of feedback about the results or involvement in different stages of the research project. Ongoing team meetings about the project allow for all parties to remain involved with the research decisions and to be realistic about the time frame in which the project is progressing.

Where information is available at several key points in the research process, data can be reported as long as it does not bias further data collected within the project. This strategy allows the practice personnel, as well as the researcher, to be aware of the progress of the research findings and to be involved in their interpretation at appropriate points. Finally, it is useful for administrators/clinicians and researchers in the service setting to have negotiated together a set of explicit guidelines for when investigative results will be considered appropriate for utilization in the practice arena. This strategy curbs the researcher's natural inclination to hedge as well as the practitioner's premature push for the use of inappropriate findings.

Conducting Research

One of the major research programs in a clinical agency, just as in an academic setting, is the actual conduct of scientific investigations. In a clinical setting, purposes for these investigations are usually twofold: the provision of information for long-term practice decisions and policies as well as the generation of knowledge for the discipline.

The investigations are generally multiphased in nature, that is, they consist of a number of phases in the same content area. Two types of substantive research investigations tend to be prominent in clinical settings: health services research and clinical nursing research. Health services or nursing administration research consists of investigations targeted at providing information for administrative decisions and policies. These investigations are often initiated by nurse administrators or head nurses with the intent to study structural or system type of variables that impact heavily on the delivery of nursing care.

Investigations that focus on the study of clinical nursing phenomena often reflect questions about the efficacy of nursing interventions and are cost-efficient in terms of producing certain kinds of desired patient outcomes. Nurse managers and staff nurses generally initiate these types of investigations because of recurring clinical issues on their particular units for which there does not seem to be a standardized set of interventions or a well-understood set of alternatives.

The various types of research projects cited are conducted within a collaborative model. A collaborative model involves merging the expertise of the clinician or nurse administrator with the research expertise of the nurse scientist. Staff nurses and nurse administrators are not expected to conduct independent research, but neither is the nurse scientist expected to have the detailed clinical knowledge, although they need to be sensitive to the clinical issues of the project. Integrating the expertise of these various types of people, however, provides a very strong base from which to conduct nursing research and allows for both the protection of the scientific rigor of the project and the clinical or practice integrity of the investigations.

Utilizing Research

Research findings may be generated by investigations that have been conducted by the agency itself or may be gathered from the research literature of the discipline. The primary focus of research utilization programs is to put into practice, in terms of nursing activities and policies, those findings that meet the criteria that were cited earlier, that is, they have been replicated and the findings substantiated.

Because of the tailoring that must occur with research findings in order for them to be fully effective within any given clinical agency, the nurse scientist can carry the application of research findings only so far and does have responsibility for making research findings available, understandable, and generalizable across numerous settings. It then becomes the responsibility of nursing administrators and clinicians in practice settings to actually utilize the results within specific agencies. Nurse researchers can serve as consultants in such a process, but it is the nurse administrators and clinicians who have the practice knowledge, resources, and understanding of the clinical setting that completes the utilization process.

Role of the Nurse Administrator: Initiator, Facilitator, and Utilizer of Nursing Research*

As an *initiator*, the nurse administrator participates in or may originate research. As a *facilitator*, the nurse administrator is responsible

---

Source: Mary E. Conway, "Knowledge Generation and Transmission: A Role for the Nurse Administrator," in *Nursing Education: Practical Methods and Models*, Barbara J. Brown and Peggy J. Chinn, eds., Aspen Publishers, Inc., © 1982.

for supplying resources and encouraging research to take place. As a *utilizer*, the nurse administrator operationalizes research findings.

The role in each of these areas of nursing research may vary depending upon the setting, contextual management, organizational control, extent of collegial relationships, and preparation and expectation of nurse administrators. The nurse administrator is expected to maximize research to the greatest extent possible regardless of the setting and situation.

Associated Activities*

As an initiator, the nurse administrator generates research proposals in nursing practice and nursing administration, including such activities as

- writing grants
- preserving data for research
- organizing studies of both an experimental and nonexperimental nature
- initiating interdisciplinary and intra-disciplinary proposals and studies

As a facilitator, the nurse administrator develops an organizational design, including philosophy and structure, in which scientific inquiry is the norm rather than the exception. This includes such activities as

- providing support for personnel for research, including the generation of grant proposals
- ensuring control in the case of both inter- and intradisciplinary efforts and intervening as necessary
- ensuring nursing's access to and share of technological resources such as computers
- providing time for nursing staff to explore problems needing research as well as for application discussions

- promoting placement of graduate students on human subject review committees
- promoting or creating new coalitions of individuals in practice and education to facilitate research and research application

As a utilizer, the nurse administrator evaluates and applies research findings to the practice of nursing. Activities may include

- keeping up to date with published research
- evaluating research findings
- functioning as part of a network to identify research in process as well as forming coalitions of nurses to promote research utilization
- promoting research colloquia to explore research findings and their application
- modifying administrative and organizational systems to promote utilization of findings
- applying change theories in the promotion of research findings

Potential Administrative Research Issues*

Examples of priority research questions for nursing administration include the following:

- What are the philosophies, nursing care models, and administrative behaviors used by head nurses on units that deliver high quality care?
- What environmental, organizational, technological, and individual criteria are best used to evaluate the overall effectiveness of nursing departments?
- What organizational and individual factors support or impede interdisciplinary collaboration and coordination among nurse administrators, physicians, and other organizational members?

Source: Mary E. Conway, "Knowledge Generation and Transmission: A Role for the Nurse Administrator," in *Nursing Education: Practical Methods and Models*, Barbara J. Brown and Peggy J. Chinn, eds., Aspen Publishers, Inc., © 1982.

Source: Barbara Brown and Beverly Henry, "Nursing Education Administration, Practice, and Research," in *Health Care Administration: Principles and Practice*, Lawrence F. Wolper and Jesus J. Pena, eds., Aspen Publishers, Inc., © 1987.

- What computer technologies are used in nursing, and what is the cost benefit of these technologies for nursing practice and nursing administration?
- What impact will the increase in outpatient services have on nursing employment and management?
- What are the foremost ethical issues confronting nurse administrators and staff?
- How are masters and doctorally prepared nurse specialists and practitioners effectively incorporated into health care organizations?
- How do inservice and patient education programs affect the quality of patient care, length of patients' hospital stay, need for health services, and health care costs?
- How do interdepartmental relationships hinder or enhance the productivity of nursing department employees?
- What education and skill mix of nurses provide the highest quality care and is the most cost effective in health care agencies of varying size, purpose, organization, and location?

PREPARATION FOR NURSING RESEARCH

The Nursing Research Committee*

Through the establishment and support of a nursing research committee, the nurse executive creates an important vehicle to assist staff in developing an appreciation for the merits of nursing research while providing a climate conducive to fostering nursing research.

Specifically, the development of an NRC within a clinical agency serves several important purposes for nurse executives. First, research findings generated from well-developed projects can be instrumental in formulating new solutions and approaches in practice to unsolved or persistent problematic situations. Instituting ideas that have been grounded in research can offer new and validated ways for handling difficult and time-consuming problems. Second, the establishment of an NRC dictates the implementation of a systematic process of inquiry to test out hypotheses and questions using a logical, analytic, and clearly defined method of investigation. Therefore, results generated through this approach have greater validity and application across clinical disciplines.

Last and most important, the formation of a functioning NRC acts as a device that enables nurse administrators and executives to present information and make administrative decisions based upon facts and clinical findings. Decisions made on the basis of well-substantiated information are more likely to be accepted by clinicians because they have a history of success as demonstrated in clinical trials. This allows administrators to

- become increasingly more comfortable with decisions that they make
- decrease judgments primarily grounded in tradition or ritualistic behaviors
- generate facts that support ideas as demonstrated on smaller projects and pilot studies before general implementation
- use facts together with intuition to guide the development and modification of policies and procedures used within the nursing department

Specific Functions

The NRC within the clinical agency functions to strengthen and facilitate clinical nursing research. The NRC can support nursing research in three major ways:

1. It establishes a mechanism to assist the researcher and reviewers in preparing and critiquing proposals.
2. It contributes to the positive climate of nursing research within the department and throughout the hospital by encouraging and soliciting proposals.
3. It reviews nursing research proposals for scientific merit and protection of human

Source: Helene J. Krouse and Suzanne Diffley Holloran, "The Nursing Research Committee," *Journal of Nursing Administration*, vol. 18, no. 12, December 1988. © 1988 J.B. Lippincott Company.

subjects' rights as well as for feasibility in the hospital.

An NRC review should occur in relation to the facility's mandated institutional review process. Once reviewed and changed as recommended, the proposal is approved. An approved proposal receives the support of nursing administration within the agency and is then sent to the institutional review board (IRB). The major thrust of the IRB review is the evaluation of scientific merit and protection of human subjects. Once approved by the IRB, steps are taken to implement the study.

A nursing review process serves to complement the IRB process. The researcher contacts the nursing and protocol or research offices at the agency and obtains information and guidelines for preparing the research proposal. The researcher has the responsibility of initiating contact with hospitals and agencies being considered as data collection sites early in the process. Because time is a critical factor, speaking to nursing administration can be helpful before contacting the IRB. Carefully following the guidelines as an initial step facilitates review and passage of the proposal.

If a facility has an NRC, researchers can request information, preferably written about the necessary process and forms that must be submitted to institute review boards. In preparing the proposal for review, the researcher should consider (1) professionally preparing the proposal; (2) what reviewers will be looking for in terms of study design and procedure, subjects' time involved, use of staff, and information to be obtained; (3) solicitation of subjects; (4) weaknesses in study design; (5) procedures and implementation of the study; and (6) how the study will enhance nursing's current or future practice and professional development.

The principal role of the reviewer is to give careful and thoughtful review to the researcher's proposal. The reviewer should be allowed approximately three weeks to read the proposal before the scheduled meeting. In reviewing the proposal, the committee member should pay close attention to guidelines or review criteria established by the NRC.

In general, the points and concerns raised by reviewers and nursing administration often help to clarify and strengthen the proposal. Issues raised at the initial review will frequently be brought up later at the IRB if not properly resolved by the researcher. Used properly, members of the NRC can be catalysts for initiation and maintenance of research in the clinical area. The concept of peer review by other clinicians, administrators, educators, and researchers will permit the profession to influence its own destiny regarding research and theory development.

The Institutional Review Board and Human Subjects Review*

Human subjects review refers to the required review process for any research proposal involving the use of human subjects. Over the years the United States Public Health Service (USPHS), the Department of Health, Education, and Welfare (DHEW), the National Research Act and its Commission for the Protection of Human Subjects of Biomedical and Behavioral Research, and the Department of Health and Human Services (DHHS) have issued reports and guidelines for protecting the rights of human subjects in research. Federal guidelines requiring review of funded studies came in 1966. This development spurred research-conducting institutions to acknowledge their ethical responsibility to protect the rights of human research subjects.

Current Federal Guidelines

Since most nursing studies involve human subjects, nurse researchers need to know that there are federal regulations protecting the rights of human subjects in research. Furthermore, nurses must anticipate that any proposed study will be reviewed according to federal guidelines to ensure that subjects are respected as persons and will have the freedom to participate or not participate, to receive no harm if at all possible, and to be treated fairly.

*Source: Daniel W. Tetting, "Preparing for the Human Subjects Review," Critical Care Nursing Quarterly, vol. 12, no. 4, © 1990 Aspen Publishers, Inc.

Basic Requirements for Studies Involving Human Subjects

For local IRBs to approve research involving human subjects, a proposal must ensure that seven major requirements are met.

The study will minimize risks to subjects by using procedures that are consistent with established research designs. Whenever possible, procedures are used that are already being performed on subjects for diagnostic or treatment purposes.

The risks to subjects will be reasonably outweighed by the anticipated benefits and the importance of the knowledge that may reasonably be expected to result. Categories of risks identified in the past include no risks, temporary or minimal discomfort, unusual levels of temporary discomfort, risk of permanent damage, and certainty of permanent damage. Proposals undergoing full IRB review will be closely scrutinized to determine the risk-benefit or cost-to-benefit ratio.

Selection of subjects will be equitable. Ensuring equity of subject selection requires taken into consideration the purpose and setting of the research. The most desirable method of selecting subjects to ensure fairness or equity is, of course, random selection; however, random selection is not always possible. Some populations—prisoners, mentally handicapped, persons of all ages with rare diseases and conditions, pregnant women, and fetuses—have been more heavily studied than others. This has caused a lack of consideration and equity in many circumstances.

Informed consent will be documented according to requirements and records will be maintained.

Informed consent will be obtained from each potential subject or the subject's legal authorized representative.

The research plan will include provisions for monitoring the data collected to ensure the safety of subjects.

There should be plans to protect the privacy of subjects, to maintain confidentiality of information given by subjects and obtained during the course of the study. The Privacy Act of 1974 gives subjects the right to anonymity and confidentiality. Anonymity means that even the researcher should not be able to link the subject with the data gathered. Although anonymity is the ideal, it may not be practical for all types of research. When anonymity is not feasible, confidentiality must be achieved. Confidentiality applies to the handling of private information given by the subject and implies that the researcher will not make public such information without the subject's authorization. In many instances researchers maintain confidentiality by reporting group data, which prevents there being a link made between individual subjects and their responses.

Source: Protection of Human Subjects (45 CFR 46) *Code of Federal Regulations*. Washington, D.C.: U.S. Dept of Health and Human Services publication 0-406-756, 1983.

How To Prepare for the Human Subjects Review*

- Obtain from your local departmental review committee (DRC) or institutional review board (IRB) a copy of their procedures or guidelines for human subjects review.

- If possible, obtain a copy of the federal guidelines for protection of human subjects.

- To ensure that you have included all essential elements or requirements, consult local and federal guidelines as you write the methodology section and develop the consent form of your proposal.

- If you intend to apply to an organization other than your own for funding of the project, or if you plan to collect data at multiple sites, each of which requires its own DRC or IRB review, contact those agencies and ask for their procedures and guidelines for human subjects review. Use these guidelines in developing your proposal.

- Find out specifically if your proposed project must undergo a total or an expedited review. Obtain a list of research categories that are exempted. This information should be included in your institution's procedures

*Source: Daniel W. Tetting, ''Preparing for the Human Subjects Review,'' *Critical Care Nursing Quarterly*, vol. 12, no. 4, © 1990 Aspen Publishers, Inc.

or guidelines. If it is not, ask for it from the chairperson of the DRC or IRB that will be reviewing your proposal.

- Obtain copies of previously approved projects and look at their sections on human subjects and consent forms. Use these as examples or models to follow.

- Locate other successful researchers; seek their advice.

- Ask local DRC or IRB committee members for assistance or advice.

- Prepare your materials according to federal guidelines. If you do, you can be reasonably confident that you have included everything, and local approval should therefore be easily obtained.

- If total review (nonexempt) is anticipated, offer or request to attend the DRC or IRB committee meeting at which your proposal will be discussed so that you can provide clarifying information.

- When you have successfully negotiated the human subjects review, offer to share your work and experiences with others.

- Last, offer to serve on a DRC or IRB as a member; it will be an excellent learning experience.

Misconduct and Fraud*

The potential for misconduct and fraud is always present during research activities. Data may be fabricated (a practice known as "drylabbing"), or manipulated ("trimming"), or interpreted so that one hypothesis is favored over others (a process called "cooking"). If the researcher enrolls ineligible subjects in a study, false data may result. If research data are misappropriated, their ownership misrepresented, or interpretations improperly reported and acknowledged, charges of plagiarism may be levelled. All of these activities are considered scientific misconduct or fraud because they are deviations from accepted practices in proposing, carrying out, or reporting results from research.

To ensure the integrity of nursing research, the community of nurse researchers must

1. carry out funded studies with accuracy and with an adequate "audit trail"
2. closely supervise graduate students, postdoctoral students, and other faculty associated with funded studies
3. remain knowledgeable about misconduct policies in their schools and institutions
4. teach the ethical requirements of research activities to the next generation of nurse researchers through course content and by example

Data fabrication, plagiarism, falsification of data, and deviation from accepted research practices are clear indications of scientific misconduct. However, sloppy recordkeeping, duplicate or selective reporting of research results, honorary authorship of publications, and the underreporting of research results are equally serious and may qualify as scientific misconduct in some instances. Nurse researchers will need to conduct research activities very carefully in order to meet their moral obligation to contribute to patient well-being. They also need to carefully consider their obligations to report reliable research results and to conduct research according to acceptable standards recognized by the community of nurse researchers.

*Source: Sara T. Fry, "Outlook on Ethics—Ethical Issues in Research: Scientific Misconduct and Fraud," *Nursing Outlook*, November-December 1990.

Chapter 38

Career Advancement

INTRODUCTION*

In nursing there are steps to be taken for advancement, including maintaining a wide set of career options by getting experience in more than one area. Nurses who choose a clinical area should not become narrow specialists.

For example, if they elect to pursue pediatric oncologic nursing, they should learn every possible aspect of it: clinical nursing related to chemotherapy; radiation therapy; surgery; home and hospital care; management aspects of oncology nursing, particularly those related to finances; research and how to write proposals for grants; writing for publications; and clinical and classroom teaching related to oncology nursing. Those are but a few of the wide number of career options.

Two qualities that will be noticed by an organization's leadership are the ability to add to income and an effort to reduce expenses. Nurses who aspire to climb the promotion ladder should give careful consideration to these two qualities. Nurses can examine their present jobs for what they can do right now to save on expenses. They should do a walkaround survey; talk with col-

leagues; and look at routines, procedures, records, reports, and other activities. They can make themselves candidates for promotion by increasing the income and decreasing the expenses of their unit (or any other unit for that matter).

See Table 38-1 for a guide for planning to move up.

MOVING UP: EXAMINATION OF PROSPECTIVE POSITIONS*

If you are planning to schedule an interview, do not hesitate to request reading materials in advance that may provide you with some basic understanding about the organization, its purpose, goals, and structure. When reviewing the information sent, organize a list of issues which are significant to you and keep these in mind during the interview process. Some of the issues worth investigating are indicated below.

You should expect to be interviewed by the chief executive officer, chief of medical staff,

---

*Source: Russell C. Swansburg and Philip W. Swansburg, *Strategic Career Planning and Development for Nurses,* Aspen Publishers, Inc., © 1984.

---

*Source: American Nurses' Association, Commission on Nursing Services, "A Guide for Nurses Considering a Career Move in Nursing Administration," Copyright © American Nurses' Association, Pub. No. NS-26 3M, 1979. Reprinted with permission.

Table 38-1 Guide for Planning To Move Up

Activity	Time Frame
1. Learn about new reimbursement procedures of Medicare, Medicaid, other third-party payers.	
2. Learn about systems for rating patients' acuity of illness.	
3. Learn about methods of staffing related to patients' acuity of illness.	
4. Learn techniques of marketing and make a plan for marketing nursing services in your unit or department.	
5. Learn about nursing research in your area of specialty and make a plan for applying it in your practice.	
6. Identify problems of nursing services that could be developed into research protocols.	
7. Identify areas that will be the focus of organizational efforts during the next five years.	
8. Identify community and professional organizations you want to move up in. Make a plan for doing this and do it.	
9. Identify activities you will do to promote nursing.	
10. Read the mission, philosophy, objectives, and bylaws statements of your organization, department, and unit. Make a plan of activities to support them.	
11. Identify committees and work groups in which you want visibility within the organization and join them.	
12. Identify the problems and interests of your CEO and other top officials and make plans to support them. Do so without fanfare.	

executive committees or board of trustees, key representatives in nursing, and other departments you feel significant.

Questions about Organizational Climate and Philosophy

- On the organizational chart, where is the director of nursing in relation to the chief executive officer and in relation to other top management level personnel, departments, and governing body?

- What are the expectations regarding the participation of the director of nursing in professional association activities? In community activities? In teaching?

- What is the impact of state and local health laws in the day-to-day operations of the facility?

- What is administration's commitment to supporting the status of nursing, and what is the importance of consumers and their needs?

- What is the operational budget of the organization? Give special attention to the nursing portion, the dollar amount, the percentage of total budget, the preparation process, and the budgetary control by nursing.

- What is the extent of organized, professional, and ancillary services? Are the new programs being developed and will nursing be involved in the decision making?
- Where and how does nursing have input and participation in medical staff and organizationwide committees?
- Does long-range planning exist to give evidence of further direction of the organization?
- Does the organization have a history of innovative programs?
- What is the current status of labor-management relations within the institution? Any recent strikes? How many grievances have gone to arbitration?
- What is the status of the institution with regard to Joint Commission accreditation?
- Does the administration have working knowledge of federal laws, rules, and regulations?
- What is the participation of the institution in educational programs for nursing and medicine?
- What state or community nursing education programs exist from which staff can be recruited?
- What is the philosophy of administration regarding nursing continuing education and staff development?
- What is the composition of the board of trustees?

Questions about Nursing's Status within the Organization

- What is the nurse administrator's authority and role in policymaking for the organization and for nursing?
- How much freedom does the nurse administrator have to make decisions?
- Is someone else's approval necessary before the nurse administrator can hire, fire, promote, or discharge an employee?

- Why is the position available? Does this influence what you would hope to accomplish as goals for the nursing department?
- What are the perceptions of power for nursing? What is the level of nursing care provided?
- What does the formal nursing organization reflect? Attempt to identify its strengths and weaknesses.
- What is the attitude of the community and consumer toward nursing?
- What is the attitude of administration, medical staff, and other departments regarding nursing?
- What is the level of morale and the attitude of the nursing staff?
- What would be the approval mechanism for institution of new programs, such as primary nursing?
- What does the person interviewing you see as problems in nursing? This may provide a clue to the institution's philosophies and biases.

LOCATING A JOB

Sources of Job Information*

Job information can be obtained from a variety of sources. One of the best is the library, primarily in publications devoted to nurse recruitment.

Clinical career opportunities are listed in such periodicals as the *American Journal of Nursing, Nursing,* and *RN.* Managerial career opportunities are identified in such periodicals as the *Journal of Nursing Administration* and the *American Nurse.* Educational career opportunities appear in such periodicals as the *Chronicle of Higher Education* and *Nurse Educator.* Research career opportunities are listed in such periodicals as *Research in Nursing and Health*

Source: Russell C. Swansburg and Philip W. Swansburg, *Strategic Career Planning and Development for Nurses,* Aspen Publishers, Inc., © 1984.

and *Nursing Research*. Above all are local newspapers, particularly the Sunday editions.

To conduct an extensive job search nurses will need to do several things.

First, get a list of area hospitals and write to all of them. Hospitals are listed in *The American Hospital Association Guide to the Health Care Field*. Letters should receive prompt replies and provide specific information needed in narrowing down the list. It gives the institutions an opportunity to identify available opportunities that coincide with the desired move. Many prime positions are filled by the time they appear in advertisements. Once the field has been narrowed, telephone contact can be made.

Second, get local newspapers from the area of interest. These may be found in the library, at newsstands, or by subscription for a month or two. The papers will provide news of area institutions that employ nurses.

Third, write to nurses and nurses organizations such as the state nurses association and the district nurses association. These are the best sources of information about job opportunities in any area. They are accurate and unbiased. The names and addresses of presidents of district nurses associations are available from the state nurses association. Names and addresses of the latter are listed in *Nursing Job News Directory Edition* or *Nursingworld Journal Annual Career Directory*.

Fourth, write to the state board of nursing for information and an application for licensure. The process takes several months in some states, although most will issue a temporary license if a nurse already has a current one in another state.

Using Headhunters*

The rules are basically the same whether you are hiring or looking for a position. Interview the headhunter. Be sure that he or she does not distribute your resumé without your authorization.

Don't be reluctant to share information with the recruiter. He or she knows what you consider to be confidential. If you want to relocate, it helps to know why, even if it is because of a "romantic interest."

There are some situations that will make you less marketable, especially with top management or administrative positions. Don't quit your present position until you have a new one. Your being unemployed can raise doubts in the minds of those hiring. It also puts an enormous pressure on the headhunter to find a position, often not the best one for your career growth. Being fired from your previous position is not an insurmountable obstacle for the headhunter, although it may be devastating for you. The risks of upper management positions are many and being fired is just one of them. A legitimate reason for being unemployed is relocation of your spouse. Educational leave is valid if you have finished your degree.

Another impediment is an extended start date. A facility looking for a qualified individual does not want to wait more than four to six weeks for the new person to be on board. One month's notice is standard across the nation for nursing administration and management positions.

Networking*

Networking is building relationships. *Focused* networking is being able to know and to influence key people who can accelerate your career. Some tips follow.

- Know how to communicate with people. Ask open-ended questions and listen attentively. Avoid asking stupid questions by finding out things beforehand. Respond promptly and enthusiastically.
- Be selective. Focus on those who can enhance your chances of reaching your goals, but do not neglect old friends.
- Keep relationships businesslike.

Source: Gilda Taylor, "How To USE A Headhunter," *Journal of Nursing Administration*, July-August 1984. Reprinted with permission.

Source: William Umiker, "Networking: A Vital Activity for Health Care Professionals," *Health Care Supervisor*, vol. 7, no. 3, © 1989 Aspen Publishers, Inc.

- Keep in touch with your contacts.
- Express appreciation for favors.
- Regularly attend major professional meetings.
- Circulate at parties and at meetings. Introduce yourself rather than wait for someone else to do the honors.
- Be involved and try to attend the meetings of your organizations.
- Be cordial and courteous to everyone, but be somewhat selective about the people with whom you develop special rapport.
- Volunteer for committees and task forces. Agree to give lectures and workshops.
- Share clippings, reports, articles, and information derived from seminars.
- Establish relationships with newcomers. Volunteer to help with indoctrination and job training.
- Do not take unfair advantage of fellow networkers. Do not abuse other people's time, but do not pass up opportunities. Do not be afraid to ask for what you need.
- Do not rely on only one or two people.
- Do not let networking interfere with your work responsibilities.

The Resumé*

The resumé should communicate the best possible professional self-portrait without seeming to brag. It should be concise and highlight career objectives, strengths, particular experiences, and educational preparation. It gives prospective employers a quick, precise idea about the applicant and the applicant's talents and qualifications.

If possible, keep the basic resumé to a single page. The following areas should be included.

Name, address, and telephone number. This should be at the head of the page and unless the

person does not want to be called at work, should include home as well as work numbers. Before including the work number, one should be able to answer yes to three questions: ''Do I mind if others know I'm job hunting?'' ''Does my employer allow me to receive phone calls at work?'' ''Do I want to be available at all possible times?''

List of professional objectives. These should be specific enough for a job that requires a special interest and general enough to apply to several areas that interest the applicant. Some experts recommend they be put in the cover letter rather than in the resumé.

List of schools attended. To be consistent, the most recent should be put first. The list should include names, addresses, dates attended, and credentials or degrees received at technical schools, colleges, and universities.

List of work experiences. Again, the current or last one should be put first. This should include the job title and dates of employment plus a one- or two-sentence function statement that summarizes responsibilities while working at each job.

List of states in which licensed, license numbers, and expiration dates. It may be desirable to list related activities such as professional certification in any area of nursing.

The names and address of three persons who are willing to give references. It is important that they be successful professional or business people who will provide good references. Prospective employers often call previous employers. References can be matched to jobs. The statement ''references available on request'' can be used. If a file is on record at a college or university placement office, the resumé should state ''professional file available at'' and indicate the name, address, and phone number of the school.

List of honors received and professional societies, fraternities, and activities participated in. Graduation with honors, honor societies, offices held, and special awards should be included.

List of works published. A specific format should be followed.

List of special lectures, papers, and workshops presented.

List of special committees served on.

---

*Source: Russell C. Swansburg and Philip W. Swansburg, *Strategic Career Planning and Development for Nurses*, Aspen Publishers, Inc., © 1984.

What Not To Include

- Don't include any disadvantageous information such as age, marital status, sex, personal opinions, or health status. These may be addressed in the personal interview only if appropriate to the job and its requirements, so the detail should be limited here.
- Don't bring attention to negatives regarding your background—poor grades, time spent out of nursing, etc.
- Don't distinguish between paid and voluntary work.
- Don't include dates if they are not to your advantage.
- Don't list every job ever held; those in or related to nursing and part-time work while in college (especially if related to career) are all that are appropriate.
- Don't include hobbies or interests not associated with nursing. If they serve as rational reasons for changing location, such as interest

- in skiing or water sports, consideration should be given as to whether there is an advantage in listing them.
- Don't give salary history, since many employers may use it to their advantage.
- Don't supply references; simply state that they are available on request and make sure there are at least three reliable ones.
- Don't fabricate any information; lies will always be detected.
- Don't appear to brag but at the same time don't be timid; be assertive with the facts.
- Don't be too specific in stating the kind of job you are looking for.
- Don't state any reasons for looking for a job.
- Don't use buzz words such as *tolerated, creative, enthusiastic,* or *decision maker* that prove nothing.
- Don't start paragraphs with the words, I, me, mine, and my.

Community service. This is another area that could be important in certain jobs, such as a position at a university or company whose officers want to have it visible in the community.

The Cover Letter

Any resumé, no matter which format is used, should include a cover letter. It should consist of only two or three paragraphs stating the specific job being sought and a brief summarization of qualifications and skills pertinent to the employer's needs. It should be clear, interesting, and to the point, personally typed, and, when possible, addressed to a specific individual. A form letter should not be used. Finally, the cover letter should contain the present address and phone numbers where the candidate can be contacted at all times.

THE SEARCH COMMITTEE INTERVIEW*

The interview can be the most traumatic process in the entire search procedure. To consider it anything less will leave applicants ill prepared for the goring they could take. To begin with, nurses will not be subjected to a one-on-one or even a one-on-two or one-on-three series of interviews. Instead, they will face the full search committee of diverse backgrounds at one setting. Sometimes there will be a standard set of questions designed to obtain comparative answers from candidates. At other times, committee members will conduct free-for-all questioning that can be intimidating. It certainly is often subjective, and candidates may even get the feeling that they were brought in to legitimize

---

Source: Ibid.

the principle of equal opportunity, the decision on selection having been made already.

There is no way to prepare absolutely for the ordeal. One method, however, is to anticipate some questions to which answers can be prepared beforehand. (See Table 38-2.) Answers should be brief. If the answer is not known, say, "I don't know. Would you like me to answer the question in writing after this meeting?" This also can be done for a question for which the applicant would like to think through the answer. The applicant should not be undone if a member appears antagonistic; the appropriate reaction is to answer in a cooperative and friendly manner.

Most search committees follow a standard procedure for interviewing. They consider the interview to be a two-way evaluation. One or more members are assigned to take each candidate to meals. Introductory questions on non-threatening topics are constructed to set the applicants at ease. Specific questions are pre-determined by the committee but are inter-spersed with spontaneous ones during the interviews. Some committees will supply candidates with their predetermined questions.

It can be worthwhile to get the committee members to do some of the talking by asking them questions related to the topics they introduce in their questions. Nurses should try to discuss their background, accomplishments, and other qualifications during this process.

It is very important to stay away from contro-versial subjects such as religion, abortion, pol-itics, and confidential matters.

Some of the questions will relate to career goals. Is this a short-term job or does the plan provide for a longer stay? Employers do not want short-term employees in strategic positions. The applicant should tell the employer about his or her skills and experiences and how those relate to the job at hand. The applicant should show that he or she has an inquiring and analytical mind that will be used to help the organization. The goal is to present the image of a person whom the employer will be able to work with, will like and trust, and will find capable of doing the job. The applicant must be careful not to brag but simply present his or her good points in a straightfor-ward manner, giving examples of skills that the job requires.

Table 38-2   Preparatory Questions for Search Committee

1. What style of management do you follow?
2. What are your personal weaknesses and strengths?
3. What are your perceptions of the role this person will perform?
4. What are your ideas of what the relationships should be between nurses and physicians?
5. What job in nursing would you most like to have?
6. What do you view as the role of nursing in this organization?
7. What do you view as the role of nursing in the community?
8. What do you think of collective bargaining?
9. How would you go about determining that your department operates effectively and efficiently?
10. Why should I (we) hire you?
11. How would you go about meeting the goals of the organization?
12. How will your family adapt to this area?
13. What other jobs are you interviewing for?
14. What are your career goals?

Preparation for the Interview

While it is best not to speculate on the course of a job interview, it is possible to prepare for it in such a way that success will be most likely.

The nurse's objective at the outset of an inter-view is to create a positive, amicable rela-tionship with the employer to the end that a job offer emerges. The interview is the most impor-tant factor in gaining the desired position, as it allows expression of personal ideas, abilities, and accomplishments. It adds individual person-ality to a resumé. To prepare for a job interview nurses should do the following.

1. Decide beforehand that they want the interview to culminate in a job offer. They want this even though they might not want the job, because it strengthens their ego, telling them they are desirable candidates.

2. Know the specific qualifications needed by the organization. The nurses then will be able to relate them to their own abilities.

3. Decide to make the interviewer like them. They should prepare to come across as persons who will support the executive and the organization in accomplishing their goals. Reasons for changing a job should be based on a desire to acquire a new opportunity. It is important to be self-confident and exude the personal chemistry of optimism, good manners and etiquette, charm, and enthusiasm.

4. Gain a feeling for the values of the interviewer. Nurses should stay on the conservative side of behavior.

5. Be prepared to deal with certain questions that are illegal but may be asked. These refer to age, marital status, children (existing or planned), whether they have ever had wages garnisheed, military discharge, bankruptcy, religion, and racial ethnic group. Nurses may choose to answer such questions honestly but evasively. Refusing to answer them, even though they are illegal, may give the interviewer a reason to dislike the applicants and not make a job offer. This asking of illegal questions may be a tip-off about employer attitudes and policies. It will make the decision about jobs easier.

6. Be positive about themselves. This can be done by acting maturely and being emotionally stable, sweet-tempered, cooperative, tactful, adaptable, assertive, self-disciplined, self-confident, conscientious, reliable, honest, sincere, and industrious. Nurses also can demonstrate they have good business sense and can relate to people to obtain the best results for the hospital.

7. Be mentally prepared by being aware of the following tactics. The interviewer's pause: a tactic some interviewers use to retrieve additional information. Nurses should not ramble on when answering a question but should keep answers concise and pause occasionally.

The sympathetic interviewer: this is the tactic of sympathizing with the negative comments applicants make about their abilities (weaknesses) or former employment. Most interviewers will not disagree with candidates but

may label them prospective problem employees. It also is wise to be aware of vague questions such as, "Tell me about yourself." This is not asking for a personal answer and should be dealt with by discussing only previous experience and education pertinent to the position sought.

Hidden-agenda questions: "What are your future plans?" might mean "How long do you intend to remain in this position?" "What did you like best about your previous position?" might mean "Will you be satisfied with this position?"

Why questions: "Why aren't you earning more at your age?" and "Why do you feel you have potential for this job?" It is important to show competence, ability, and decisiveness in responding to questions concerning job, career, and goals.

8. Dress well. Attire for an interview cannot be overstressed. Conservatism is never out of order, and casual garb will not contribute to one's getting the job.

9. Be on time. The schedule should provide for arrival at the interview 10 to 15 minutes early. Nurses should appear calm and unhurried and have time to collect their thoughts about important points they want to bring up during the interview. When invited in, they should shake hands, introduce themselves with their full name, wear a smile, and not sit down until asked. It is important to be casual and pleasant and not introduce controversial topics of any kind. It is valuable to appear interested in the interviewer's conversation, to sit up straight, look directly at the person when the interviewer is talking, and speak clearly and confidently.

10. Convey the mannerisms of a person the interviewer would welcome as a colleague. This means coming across as a thoroughly pleasant, cooperative, and competent person, an applicant who can deal with the most difficult people problems tactfully, objectively, and successfully and is not blustering or flamboyant, mouselike or servile. Many questions will be asked about information on the application or resumé. If a member of the panel expresses disagreement, the applicant must not change stances but should stick to the expressed opinion in a courteous manner.

Suggestions

- Maintain honesty and be conservative in manner, opinion, and dress; avoid all attention-getting ruses.
- Be prepared to discuss current trends in the sphere of the post for which you are applying.
- Say you do not know if asked about a subject of which you do not possess adequate knowledge. You should not try to bluff your way through or suggest that the interviewer has asked a question in a way that is misunderstood.
- Be specific in responses; the panel will be more interested in what candidates are saying than in how they are saying it, so consistency and factuality need to be maintained.
- Be prepared not to hide embarrassing incidents of prior employment; they should be discussed matter-of-factly if the panel brings them up.

THE EMPLOYMENT CONTRACT*

From the individual nurse administrator's perspective, it is good business practice to have a written document that covers in detail his or her relationship with the institution.

Content of Contract

If an employment contract is needed, its content must be established. Employment agreements vary widely in context and format. Every nurse administrator who is confronted with an agreement should therefore consider obtaining the assistance of qualified legal counsel to assist the nurse administrator in properly evaluating the contract. Employment agreements usually discuss at least the following general points.

Source: Darlene M. Trandel-Korenchuk and Keith M. Trandel-Korenchuk, "Legal Forum," *Nursing Administration Quarterly*, vol. 13, no. 4, © 1989 Aspen Publishers, Inc.

General Statement of Employment

Each contract contains a general statement that the nurse administrator and the institution create an employment relationship based on the terms and conditions set forth in the employment agreement. This general paragraph forms the basis of defining the rights and parameters of the parties and specifically references the other provisions of the agreement.

Duties

An employment agreement also contains a provision that describes the duties the nurse administrator provides. Generally, the nurse administrator is obliged to perform those specified duties within the policies, rules, and procedures of the hospital or health care facility that are established from time to time. A description of the nurse administrator's duties should be found in this section. From the employer's perspective, it is important to have the nurse administrator agree to faithfully serve the institution and to devote such time as may be necessary for the adequate performance of duties. From the nurse executive's viewpoint, this provision should clearly specify what is expected of the nurse administrator. A general job description in addition to the reporting responsibilities of the administrator should be included.

Other Activities

Employment contracts usually contain a provision that prohibits an employee from engaging in activities that are determined to be detrimental to the institution or from devoting less than his or her full time to the business of the institution. From the institution's perspective, it is important to establish that the nurse administrator is devoting his or her full time to the business of the health care facility. It is also important for the institution to obtain agreement from the nurse executive that he or she will not engage in other work for other institutions without the prior written consent of the employer. To the extent that the nurse administrator desires to engage in other community activities or independent teaching or research, specific reference should be made to these activities so that no questions arise in the future regarding the proper authorization for such activities.

Compensation

Another major feature of an employment contract, both from the institutional and nurse perspective, is a statement concerning compensation. The contract should set forth the amount of the compensation along with a method for annual or periodic reviews. To the extent that the nurse administrator is able to secure the inclusion of a clause that allows automatic increases in compensation over a period of years, the contract will be more favorable to the nurse executive. Additional items found in executive contracts in business and industry, such as bonuses and other incentive bases for performance, are likely to be new concepts for nurse administrators, but it is likely that as concepts of business develop further in the health care setting such arrangements will become more common.

Vacation and Sick Leave

For most institutions, accrual of vacation and sick leave is a matter of personnel policy. From the institution's perspective, therefore, no further obligations with respect to additional vacation or sick leave are likely to be made. On the other hand, depending on the bargaining position of the nurse, additional vacation, sick leave, or an express reference to time for meetings or professional continuing education should be negotiated. The nurse administrator should especially set forth the right to meetings, because institutional policy does not generally allow for meeting time.

Fringe Benefits

Most employment contracts contain a provision about fringe benefits. From the perspective of the institution, the provision would likely state that the employee can participate in the usual employee benefits provided by the institution but that no special fringe benefits are provided for the nurse executive. If the nurse administrator is able to negotiate other fringe benefits such as a car allowance, additional life insurance, or different professional education reimbursement allowances, those provisions should be recorded in this fringe benefit provision. Whether the nurse administrator is able to negotiate these particular provisions will depend on his or her bargaining position and on the extent to which the institution needs his or her particular set of skills and abilities.

Term of Contract

The term of a contract is one of the most important provisions of any employment agreement. To the extent that a long-term contract is entered into, the institution is obligated to pay for services rendered and the nurse is obligated to render services for that stated period of time. Thus, a multiple-year contract such as a three- or five-year agreement would obligate the nurse to provide services and the institution to pay for them over a long period of time. Generally, the longer the term of a contract, the more favorable it is for the employee. The rationale for this conclusion is that it is difficult for an institution to specifically require an employee to work if the employee does not want to perform. Employees who desire to leave a situation are in most instances of little use to the employer, and the employer has little to be gained in seeking redress for the breach of the obligation. From the nurse administrator's perspective, longer employment agreements provide great protection. If an employer decides to terminate the services of a nurse executive in the first year of a three-year agreement, the employer will be obligated (unless it has cause to terminate the agreement) to pay the employee for the full term of the agreement. While the employee has an obligation to seek out new work to lessen the damages, the employer is required to pay. This position is favorable to an employee, since it provides a safety net during the job-hunting phase and also provides an established minimum salary during the remainder of the term of the contract.

Termination

An equally critical provision in an employment contract is how it may be terminated prior to the expiration of the term of the agreement. If a nurse administrator has an employee contract that states it has a two-year term, but the contract can be terminated on 30 days' notice, the contract is really a 30-day contract rather than a two-year contract.

An employment contract provision that allows a contract to be terminated by either party without reason is called a provision for termination "without cause." Thus, it is in the institution's interest for its employment contracts to contain a termination without cause provision with a very short notice period. Nurse administrators or other executives often argue that a contract should run for its stated term and should be terminated only if one of the parties fails to fulfill its obligations under the agreement (in other words, "for cause"). How these issues are resolved depends on the bargaining positions of the parties.

A more difficult area is raised in the termination sections of employment contracts regarding what circumstances permit agreement termination with cause. The phrase "with cause" means that the contract can be terminated if there is some good reason that allows the nonbreaching party to terminate the agreement. Cause provisions that specify how the institution has failed to live up to its obligations in the contract are relatively straightforward.

Typically, employment agreements define cause as chronic absenteeism, willful or repeated failure of the employee to comply with the reasonable directives of his or her supervisors, willful misconduct resulting in damage to the institution, or alcoholism or addiction of the employee to habit-forming drugs. These types of reasons can be expanded or narrowed depending on the bargaining positions of the parties. In any event, the institution will require that the nurse executive, at the very least, continue to provide services under the agreement and to comply with the reasonable directives of his or her superiors.

Appendix 1

A Guide to Federal Policy and Health Care Delivery Systems*

Health care is one of the largest industries in the United States, both in size of expenditures and persons employed. Recent annual expenditures on health care totaled $500.3 billion, or 11.1 percent of the gross national product (GNP). Expenditures for hospital care alone totaled $194.7 billion. The industry is rapidly changing in response to legal, cultural, technological, and economic developments within its environment. Terms commonly used to describe the environment include "turbulent," "unstable," and "complex."

1901–1945

The period 1901 to roughly 1945 included remarkable medical advances, the expansion of state and federal subsidies for health services, the revamping of medical education, and the emergence of the framework for the health care system as it currently exists. During this period, the focus of health care shifted from epidemics to individual episodes of acute disease. Support for medical research was greatly expanded, and advances were made in diagnosis, treatment, and prevention of disease.

Medical education was revolutionized as a result of the efforts of the American Medical Association, the advances in medical science, and the publication of the Flexner Report in 1910. During this period, many of the medical specialties developed. Only 1 specialty existed in 1920; by 1940 there were 16.

Government involvement at both the state and federal level increased. At the federal level, the Pure Food and Drug Act was passed in 1906. The Sheppard-Towner Act of 1921 made small federal grants available to state and local governments for maternal and child health programs and for the development and strengthening of local health departments. Other federal action included the 1935 Social Security Act. Title V of this act increased federal assistance to maternal and child health programs and greatly expanded assistance to state and local health departments. Another outcome of this legislation was the growth in proprietary nursing homes. Finally, the 1944 Public Health Service Act brought all the federal public health programs together under one agency.

The Committee on the Costs of Medical Care was created in 1927 through the support of private foundations. A series of 27 field studies were conducted and a total of 28 reports published. The last report, published in 1932, recommended that health services be delivered through organized groups. Restructuring of the

*Source: Janet Thompson Reagan, "Health Care Delivery Systems," in Handbook of Medical Staff Management, Cindy A. Orsund-Gassiot and Sharon Lindsey, eds., Aspen Publishers, Inc., © 1990.

health care system was proposed as a means of addressing economic inefficiency and reducing preventable pain and needless deaths.

It was during this period that the third-party pay system emerged as an important source of financing for health services. During the Depression, the Blue Cross and Blue Shield plans were developed to ensure that individuals would have access to hospital and physician services. The first commercial insurers also entered the marketplace, and the first prepaid group, the Ross-Loos Plan, was established.

1946–1965

The role of the federal government in health services was greatly expanded. With the passage of the Hill-Burton Act (Hospital Survey and Construction Act) in 1946, the federal government began to subsidize the construction of hospitals. Between 1947 and 1971, Hill-Burton funds helped to build 345,000 hospital beds. Through amendments to the original legislation, funds were later used for hospital renovations and for the construction of ambulatory clinics and nursing homes. Mental health services were supported through the 1946 Mental Health Act and later through the 1963 Mental Retardation Facilities and Community Mental Health Centers Construction Act.

The federal government also subsidized the development of human resources through a variety of programs, including the Vocational Education Act of 1946, the Grants-in-Aid to Schools of Public Health in 1958, and the Health Professions Education Assistance Act of 1963. New occupations emerged in response to the introduction of new technology and advances in medical practice.

1966–Present

The mid-sixties are considered by many to be a turning point in the health care industry. The predominant health care focus shifted from individual episodes of acute disease to chronic health conditions, partly as a result of an aging popula-

tion and partly as a result of medicine's success in preventing and treating acute disease.

The federal government began to play an even larger role in health services. With the implementation of Medicare and Medicaid in 1966, the federal government became a major source for financing of health services. Expenditures for Medicare, a federal insurance program for those qualifying for Social Security benefits, and Medicaid, a federal-state assistance program for the indigent, soon far exceeded projected levels. For Medicaid, the federal response was to allow states to reduce covered services, restrict the eligible population, and modify reimbursement methods to control expenditures. For Medicare, the federal government sought to control expenditures through regulation and reimbursement, for example, through the introduction of professional standards review organizations (PSROs) in 1972 and the prospective payment system (PPS) in 1983.

Federal policy in the 1970s was one of reorganization and regulation. Reorganization was seen as a way of increasing system efficiency and controlling expenditures. The Health Maintenance Organization (HMO) Act of 1973 is an example of action in this area. Additionally, Title XIX of the Social Security Act was amended to encourage the enrollment of persons covered by Medicaid in alternative delivery systems, usually prepaid groups.

The federal government sought to regulate the system through the health planning legislation. The Social Security Amendments of 1972 authorized PSROs, whose function was to monitor the appropriateness and quality of care rendered under the Medicaid and Medicare programs. PSROs were replaced by professional review organizations (PROs) in 1982 with the passage of the Tax Equity and Fiscal Responsibility Act (TEFRA). TEFRA also modified the method of reimbursement under Medicare. A prospective payment system based on diagnosis-related groups (DRGs) replaced the retrospective cost-based system.

In the 1980s the health care industry continued to evolve. Innovations included the development of new alternative delivery systems, the introduction of new financing mechanisms, and the first attempts by states (Hawaii and Massachusetts) to provide universal health insurance coverage.

As the 1990s continue, it is anticipated that the retrenchment of health care expansion, the restructuring and reorganizing of institutions, and the experimentation with alternate health care delivery services will help contain the escalation of costs. New attitudes toward productivity, efficiency, and quality will be the underlying motif in hospital actions. Those who pay for services—the government, the health care insurers, and the consumers—all have more sophisticated expectations about health care and a shortened pocket for paying for them.

The Nation's Health Objectives for 2000*

On September 6, 1990, the U.S. Department of Health and Human Services released the report *Healthy People 2000*, the national public health goals and objectives for the 1990s. *Healthy People 2000* outlines three broad goals for public health over the next ten years: (1) to increase the span of healthy life, (2) to reduce disparities in health status among different populations, and (3) to provide access to preventive health care services for all persons. To help meet these goals, 298 specific objectives have been identified in 22 priority areas.

At least two themes distinguish the year 2000 objectives from the 1990 objectives. First, greater emphasis is placed on quality of life. This emphasis is evident through the parallel targets of (1) preventing morbidity and disability and (2) preserving functional capacity. Second, the year 2000 health objectives place greater emphasis on targeting high-risk groups. Separate targets have been established to improve the risk and health profile of population groups (e.g., minorities, persons with low incomes, and persons in certain age groups) who have a disproportionate share of illness, injury, disability, and premature death.

Formation of a National AIDS Information Clearinghouse

The National AIDS Information Clearinghouse is a comprehensive information service for persons working with human immunodeficiency virus (HIV) and acquired immunodeficiency syndrome (AIDS). As a service of the U.S. Department of Health and Human Services, Public Health Service, CDC, the Clearinghouse collects, classifies, and distributes up-to-date information and provides expert reference assistance to HIV- and AIDS-prevention professionals.

The Clearinghouse maintains information data bases that are accessed by reference specialists on request. The data bases contain descriptions of more than 12,000 organizations that provide HIV- and AIDS-related services and resources and more than 6000 AIDS-related educational materials.

Source: *Healthy People 2000: National Health Promotion and Disease Prevention Objectives for the Year 2000*, Office of Disease Prevention and Health Promotion, Office of the Assistant Secretary for Health, U.S. Department of Health and Human Services, 1990.

Health Objectives

Priority Area	Lead Federal Agency
Health Promotion	
1. Physical Activity and Fitness	President's Council on Physical Fitness and Sports
2. Nutrition	National Institutes of Health
	Food and Drug Administration
3. Tobacco	Centers for Disease Control
4. Alcohol and Other Drugs	Alcohol, Drug Abuse, and Mental Health Administration
5. Family Planning	Office of Population Affairs
6. Mental Health and Mental Disorders	Alcohol, Drug Abuse, and Mental Health Administration
7. Violent and Abusive Behavior	Centers for Disease Control
8. Educational and Community-based Programs	Centers for Disease Control
	Health Resources and Services Administration
Health Protection	
9. Unintentional Injuries	Centers for Disease Control
10. Occupational Safety and Health	Centers for Disease Control
11. Environmental Health	National Institutes of Health
	Centers for Disease Control
12. Food and Drug Safety	Food and Drug Administration
13. Oral Health	National Institutes of Health
	Centers for Disease Control
Preventive Services	
14. Maternal and Infant Health	Health Resources and Services Administration
15. Heart Disease and Stroke	National Institutes of Health
16. Cancer	National Institutes of Health
17. Diabetes and Chronic Disabling Conditions	National Institutes of Health
	Centers for Disease Control
18. HIV Infection	National AIDS Program Office
19. Sexually Transmitted Diseases	Centers for Disease Control
20. Immunization and Infectious Diseases	Centers for Disease Control
21. Clinical Preventive Services	Health Resources and Services Administration
	Centers for Disease Control
Surveillance	
22. Surveillance and Data Systems	Centers for Disease Control

Appendix 3

Statistical Terms and Formulas*

Terms	Formulas

ADMISSION

Hospital patient
An individual receiving, in person, hospital-based or coordinated medical services for which the hospital is responsible.

Inpatient admission
The formal acceptance by a hospital of a patient who is to be provided with room, board, and continuous nursing service in an area of the hospital where patients generally stay at least overnight.

> Number of patients in the hospital
> at midnight April 29 535
> Plus ...... Number of patients admitted
> April 30 .... +30
> 565

Hospital inpatient
A hospital patient who is provided with room, board, and continuous general nursing service in an area of the hospital where patients generally stay at least overnight.

Inpatient census
The number of inpatients present at any one time.

> Minus ..... Patients discharged (including
> deaths) April 30 .... −18
> Patients in hospital at 12 P.M.
> (midnight) April 30 547
> Plus ...... Patients both admitted and discharged (including deaths) on
> April 30 .... +3

Daily inpatient census
The number of inpatients present at the census-taking time each day, plus any inpatients who were both admitted and discharged after the census-taking time the previous day.

> Inpatient census (inpatient service
> days) April 30 550

*Source: Kathleen A. Waters and Gretchen F. Murphy, *Medical Records in Health Information*, Aspen Publishers, Inc., 1979. The information has been adapted from Edna K. Huffman, *Medical Records Management*, Physicians Record Company Publisher, 1972; *Glossary of Medical Terms*, American Medical Record Association, 1974; and Candace Dillman, RRA, who designed the section on "Psychiatric Survival Rates" for use in the Alaska Psychiatric Institute.

Terms	Formulas

Inpatient service day (also called census day)
A unit of measure denoting the services received by one inpatient in one 24-hour period.

Example of Care Unit Breakdown: Intensive Care Unit
Inpatient Service Days

Census .... Patients remaining midnight
April 29 8
Plus ...... Patients admitted April 30 ...... +1
Plus ...... Patients transferred on unit from
another unit in hospital .... +1
Minus ..... Patients discharged .... −0
Minus ..... Patients died .... −2
Minus ..... Patients transferred off unit to
another unit in hospital .... −1
Midnight census April 30 7
Plus ...... Patients both admitted and dis-
charged on April 30 .... +1
(These patients have already been counted as admission and discharges or deaths. However, since their patient days have been canceled out by adding them as admissions and subtracting them as discharges, they must be added again to determine the inpatient service days on this unit.)

Total inpatient service days (also called census days)
The sum of all inpatient service days for each of the days in the period under consideration. Notice it is the numerator in the formula.

The formula to obtain the average daily inpatient census for a whole hospital is:

$$\frac{\text{Total inpatient service days for a period}}{\text{Total number of days in the period}}$$

Average daily inpatient census
Average number of inpatients present each day for a given period of time. This is always calculated by a formula such as indicated in the example.

The average daily inpatient census (average daily census) for newborn inpatients is generally reported separately. When it is, the following formula is used to determine the average daily inpatient census excluding newborns:

Inpatient bed occupancy ratio
The proportion of inpatient beds occupied, defined as the ratio of inpatient service days to inpatient bed count days in the period under consideration.

Synonymous terms: percent occupancy, occupancy percent, percentage of occupancy, occupancy ratio

$$\frac{\text{Total inpatient service days (excluding newborns)}}{\text{Total number of days in the period}}$$

$$\frac{\text{Total inpatient service days for a period} \times 100}{\text{Total inpatient bed count days} \times \text{number of days in the period}}$$

Example: A hospital has an inpatient bed count (bed complement) of 150 (excluding the newborn bassinet count of 15). During April, the hospital rendered 3,650 inpatient service days to adults and children. April has 30 days. According to the formula, this is $3,650 \times 100 \div 150 \times 30 = 365,000 \div 4,500 = 81.11\%$. Therefore, the inpatient bed occupancy percentage for April was 81.1%, or 81%.

Terms	Formulas

EVENTS DURING HOSPITAL STAY

Transfer (intrahospital)
A change in medical care unit, medical staff unit, or responsible physician of an inpatient during hospitalization.

Not applicable

Adjunct diagnostic or therapeutic unit
  (ancillary unit)
An organized unit of a hospital, other than an operating room, delivery room, or medical care unit, with facilities and personnel to aid physicians in the diagnosis and treatment of patients through the performance of diagnostic or therapeutic procedures.

Not applicable

Consultations may be viewed from two perspectives.

Medical consultation
The response by one member of the medical staff to a request for consultation by another member of the medical staff, characterized by review of the patient's history, examination of the patient, and completion of a consultation report giving recommendations and/or opinions.

1. Total consultations rendered. This may be used to show specialty activity, such as the total number of psychiatric consultations rendered by the psychiatric service.

2. The percentage of consultations rendered per patients treated in the hospital. The formula for this would be:

$$\frac{\text{Total number of patients receiving consultations} \times 100}{\text{Total number of patients discharged and died for the period}}$$

Surgical operation
One or more surgical procedures performed at one time for one patient via a common approach or for a common purpose.

The formula approved by the Joint Commission on Accreditation of Healthcare organizations for computing the postoperative infection rate is:

Complication
An additional diagnosis that describes a condition arising after the beginning of hospital observation and treatment and modifying the course of the patient's illness or the medical care required.

$$\frac{\text{Number of infections in clean surgical cases for a period} \times 100}{\text{Number of surgical operations for the period}}$$

Usually calculated in a rate only in infection cases, since the formula above clearly assigns the source of the complication.

Hospital live birth
The complete expulsion or extraction from the mother, in a hospital facility, of a product of conception, irrespective of the duration of pregnancy, which after such separation breathes or shows any other evidence of life such as beating of the heart, pulsation of the umbilical cord, or definite movement of voluntary muscles, whether or not the umbilical cord has been cut or the placenta is attached; each product of such a birth is considered live born.

Live births may be classified according to the birth weight:
  1,000 grams (2 pounds, 3 ounces) or less;
  1,001 grams to 2,500 grams (5 pounds, 8 ounces);
  over 2,500 grams.

Hospital cesarean section rate
Hospital cesarean section rate is the ratio of cesarean sections performed to deliveries. For statistical purposes, when a delivery results in a multiple birth, it is counted as one delivery.

Formula:

$$\frac{\text{Total number of cesarean sections performed in a period} \times 100}{\text{Total number of deliveries in the period}}$$

Terms	Formulas

Inpatient discharge
The termination of a period of inpatient hospitalization through the formal release of the inpatient by the hospital.

Discharge transfer
The disposition of an inpatient to another health care institution at the time of discharge.

Length of stay (for one inpatient)
The number of calendar days from admission to discharge.

Admit Jan 20   Calculation:
Disch Jan 24
                                          24
                                        -20
                      Disch days $= 4$
                    or
Admit Jan 20   Total days in
                      Jan   31
Disch Feb 14 -20
                      days in Jan $=11$
                      days in Feb $+14$
                      Disch days $=25$

The length of an inpatient's hospitalization is considered to be one day if he or she is admitted and discharged the same day and also if he or she is admitted one day and discharged the next day.

Total length of stay (for all inpatients)
The sum-of-the-days stay of any group of inpatients discharged during a specified period of time.

Total duration (discharge days) of inpatient hospitalization (including deaths; excluding newborns)

Average length of stay
The average length of hospitalization of inpatients discharged during the period under consideration.

$$\frac{\text{Total duration (discharge days) of inpatient hospitalization (including deaths; excluding newborns)}}{\text{Total discharges (including deaths; excluding newborns)}}$$

Gross death rate

$$\frac{\text{Total number of deaths (including newborns) for a period} \times 100}{\text{Total number of discharges (including deaths and newborn deaths) for the period}}$$

Net death rate (also called institutional death rate)

$$\frac{\text{Total number of deaths (including newborns) minus those under 48 hours for a period} \times 100}{\text{Total number of discharges (including deaths and newborns) minus deaths under 48 hours for the period}}$$

Postoperative death rate

$$\frac{\text{Total number of deaths within 10 days postoperative for a period} \times 100}{\text{Total number of patients operated on for the period}}$$

Maternal death rate

$$\frac{\text{Total number of maternal deaths for a period} \times 100}{\text{Total number of maternal (obstetrical) discharges (including deaths) for the period}}$$

Anesthesia death rate

$$\frac{\text{Total number of deaths caused by anesthetic agents for a period} \times 100}{\text{Total number of anesthetics administered for the period}}$$

Hospital fetal death
Death prior to the complete expulsion or extraction from its mother, in a hospital facility, of a product of conception, irrespective of the duration of pregnancy; death is indicated by the fact that after such separation, the fetus does not breath or show any other evidence of life such as beating of the heart, pulsation of the umbilical cord, or definite movement of voluntary muscles.

Early: Less than 20 complete weeks of gestation (500 grams or less)
Intermediate: 20 completed weeks of gestation, but less than 28 (501 to 1,000 grams)
Late: 28 completed weeks of gestation and over (1,001 grams and over)

Usually only intermediate and late fetal deaths are included.

Terms	**Formulas**

Abortion

Abortion is the expulsion or extraction of all (complete) or any part (incomplete) of the placenta or membranes, without an identifiable fetus or with a live-born infant or a stillborn infant weighing less than 500 grams. In the absence of known weight, an estimated length of gestation of less than 20 completed weeks (139 days) is calculated from the first day of the last normal menstrual period.

$$\frac{\text{Total number of intermediate and/or late fetal deaths for a period} \times 100}{\text{Total number of births (including intermediate and late fetal deaths) for the period}}$$

Gross autopsy rate
The ratio during any given period of time of all inpatient autopsies of all inpatient deaths.

$$\frac{\text{Total inpatient autopsies for a given period} \times 100}{\text{Total inpatient deaths for the period}}$$

Net autopsy rate
The ratio during any given period of time of all inpatient autopsies to all inpatient deaths minus unautopsied coroner's or medical examiner's cases.

$$\frac{\text{Total inpatient autopsies for a given period} \times 100}{\text{Total inpatient deaths minus unautopsied coroner's or medical examiner's cases}}$$

Hospital autopsy rate (adjusted)
The proportion of deaths of hospital patients following which the bodies of the deceased persons are available for autopsy and hospital autopsies are performed.

$$\frac{\text{Total hospital autopsies} \times 100}{\text{Number of deaths of hospital patients whose bodies are available for hospital autopsy}}$$

SPECIAL NEEDS

Psychiatric survival rates
The monthly statistics provided to staff gave no information as to how long a patient was able to function independently.

Admission date − discharge date
of last visit = survival time

This formula was created when it became evident that staff was being discouraged by the high reported readmission rate, in spite of additions to staff and improved therapy programs.

The use of survival time statistics demonstrated two factors to administration that were then used to revise procedures:

- The survival time for which patients were functioning without support was increased with each discharge.
- There was no evidence that outpatient visits increased the survival time between hospitalizations. (Patients were returning due to attachments to staff.)

A program was developed to introduce outpatient clinic staff to patients and create attachments to the appropriate staff prior to discharge to reduce dependency on the patient facility.

$$\frac{\text{Cumulative survival time for all patients for the period utilizing outpatient clinics}}{\text{Total number of admissions for the period}} = \begin{array}{l}\text{Average survival} \\ \text{rate of patients} \\ \text{utilizing clinics}\end{array}$$

$$\frac{\text{Cumulative survival time for all patients for the period not utilizing outpatient clinics}}{\text{Total number of admissions for the period}} = \begin{array}{l}\text{Average survival} \\ \text{rate of patients} \\ \textit{not} \text{ utilizing clinics}\end{array}$$

Appendix 4

Nursing Administration Certification Programs*

The certification programs in nursing administration are available to nurse administrators, consultants, and educators engaged in nursing service administration at the middle management or executive level on a full- or part-time basis. Administrators and educators may apply for certification in either nursing administration or nursing administration, advanced.

Consultants may apply for certification in nursing administration, advanced, if they currently provide consultation services in executive level nursing administration, i.e., within the last calendar year.

Educators may meet the position and experience requirements through such arrangements as joint appointments, or continued or periodic part-time employment. Their experience must be in middle management or executive level nursing service administration.

PROGRAM FOR NURSING ADMINISTRATION

Application

You may apply for certification in nursing administration if you

*Source: American Nurses' Association, The Measure of Distinction among Professionals: Certification, © 1985. Reprinted with permission.

1. are currently licensed as a registered nurse in the United States or its territories
2. hold a baccalaureate or higher degree from an accredited institution (for nurses licensed after 1990, the degree must be in nursing)
3. currently hold a middle management or executive nursing administrative position, as described in the chart on Characteristics of Nursing Administrative Levels (see below)
4. have been in a verified middle- or executive-level nursing administrative position at least 24 months within the past five years and provide documentation of your administrative responsibilities and experience on the application blank

Examination

The examination for certification in nursing administration will cover such topics as

- Nursing Organization (24%)
  —Philosophy of Nursing Management
  —Organizational Structure
  —Policy and Procedures
  —Delivery System
  —Interprofessional Relationships

—Governing Boards
—Regulatory Commissions

- Nursing Service Delivery Systems (31%)
  —Standards
  —Contractual Agreement
  —Evaluation
  —Application of Research Findings

- Resources (33%)
  —Interrelationships
  —Budget
  —Acquire Human Resources
  —Acquire Material and Support Resources
  —Allocate Resources
  —Management of Human Resources

- Issues (12%)
  —Legal/Ethical Concerns
  —Political
  —Research and Development
  —Professional Leadership

PROGRAM FOR NURSING ADMINISTRATION, ADVANCED

Application

You may apply for certification in nursing administration, advanced, if you

1. are currently licensed as a registered nurse in the United States or its territories
2. hold a baccalaureate or higher degree from an accredited institution (for nurses licensed after 1990, the degree must be in nursing)
3. hold a master's or higher degree in any field
4. currently hold an executive-level nursing administration position, or currently provide consultation services in executive-level nursing administration as outlined in the chart on Characteristics of Nursing Administrative Levels (see below)
5. have worked in a verified executive-level nursing administrative position *or* have provided executive-level consultation services for at least 36 months within the past five years

---

Characteristics of Nursing Administrative Levels

Middle Management–Level Nursing Responsibilities:

- Participate in nursing department program planning, goal setting, and policy formulation.
- Direct the operation of one or more nursing department units through coordination of nursing personnel activities.
- Evaluate and supervise nursing personnel performances.
- Evaluate and supervise nursing care given.
- Recruit and select nursing staff, and provide for their orientation and continuing education.
- Coordinate nursing unit operation with the operation of other agency departments.

Executive-Level Nursing Management Responsibilities:

- Participate in activities related to the total health care agency's organizational programming, goal setting, and policy development.
- Determine clinical and managerial goals and direction of the nursing department.
- Establish and/or revise nursing department structure, functions, and activities to achieve goals.
- Acquire and allocate human and material resources for nursing department operation.
- Evaluate nursing department operation and goal attainment, and provide for a planned change to attain current or new goals.
- Provide direction and programs that assure the development and productive performance of nursing department personnel.

---

6. provide documentation of your administrative responsibilities and experience on the application blank, and if you are a consultant, verify services provided to a current or recent client

Examination

The exam for certification in nursing administration, advanced, will cover such topics as

- Nursing Organization
- Nursing Service Delivery Systems
- Resources
- Issues
- Personnel Management
- Planning and Evaluation
- Total Health Care Organizations
- Professional and Societal Concerns

To apply for certification in nursing administration or nursing administration, advanced, you must complete an application form available from:

American Nurses' Association
2420 Pershing Road
Kansas City, Missouri 64108

Appendix 5

State Nursing Boards*

For application forms and answers to questions about fees, licensing requirements, and continuing education, contact the nursing board in the state where you plan to work.

ALABAMA. State Board of Nursing, One East Office Building, 500 East Blvd., Suite 203, Montgomery, AL 36117. (205) 261-4060.

ALASKA. Board of Nursing, Division of Occupational Licensing, Frontier Building, 3601 C St., Suite 722, Anchorage, AK 99503. (907) 561-2878.

ARIZONA. State Board of Nursing, 5050 N. 19th Ave., Suite 103, Phoenix, AZ 85015. (602) 255-5092.

ARKANSAS. State Board of Nursing, Westmark Building, 4120 W. Markham, Suite 308, Little Rock, AR 72205. (501) 371-2751.

CALIFORNIA. Board of Registered Nursing, 1030 13th St., Room 200, Sacramento, CA 95814. (916) 322-3350.

COLORADO. State Board of Nursing, State Services Building, 1525 Sherman St., Room 132, Denver, CO 80203. (303) 866-2871.

CONNECTICUT. Board of Examiners for Nursing, 150 Washington St., Hartford, CT 06106. (203) 566-1032.

DELAWARE. Board of Nursing, Margaret O'Neill Building, Box 1401, Dover, DE 19901. (302) 736-4522.

DISTRICT OF COLUMBIA. Board of Nursing, 614 H St. N.W., Room 904, Washington, DC 20001. (202) 727-7455 or 7456.

FLORIDA. Board of Nursing, 111 Coast Line Drive E., Suite 504, Jacksonville, FL 32202. (904) 359-6331.

GEORGIA. Board of Nursing, 166 Pryor St. S.W., Atlanta, GA 30303. (404) 656-3943.

HAWAII. Board of Nursing, Box 3469, Honolulu, HI 96801. (808) 548-4100.

IDAHO. State Board of Nursing, 700 W. State St., 2nd Floor, Boise, ID 83720. (208) 334-3110.

ILLINOIS. Department of Registration and Education, 320 W. Washington St., 3rd Floor, Springfield, IL 62786. (217) 785-0800.

INDIANA. State Board of Nursing, Health Professions Bureau, 964 N. Pennsylvania St., Indianapolis, IN 46204. (317) 232-2960.

*Source: "Finding Your Way through the Licensing Maze," *RN Nursing Opportunities*, Supplement, 1987.

IOWA. Board of Nursing, Executive Hills East, 1223 E. Court Ave., Des Moines, IA 50319. (515) 281-3255.

KANSAS. State Board of Nursing, 503 Kansas Ave., Suite 330, Box 1098, Topeka, KS 66601. (913) 296-4929.

KENTUCKY. Board of Nursing, 4010 Dupont Circle, Suite 430, Louisville, KY 40207. (502) 897-5143.

LOUISIANA. State Board of Nursing, 150 Baronne St., Room 907, New Orleans, LA 70112. (504) 568-5464.

MAINE. State Board of Nursing, 295 Water St., Augusta, ME 04330. (207) 289-5324.

MARYLAND. Board of Examiners of Nurses, 201 W. Preston St., Baltimore, MD 21201. (410) 225-5880.

MASSACHUSETTS. Board of Registration in Nursing, 100 Cambridge St., Room 1509, Boston, MA 02202. (617) 727-9961.

MICHIGAN. Board of Nursing, Department of Licensing and Regulation, Ottawa Towers North, 611 W. Ottawa, Box 30018, Lansing, MI 48909. (517) 373-1600.

MINNESOTA. Board of Nursing, 2700 University Ave. W., #108, St. Paul, MN 55114. (612) 642-0567.

MISSISSIPPI. Board of Nursing, 135 Bounds St., Suite 101, Jackson, MS 39206. (601) 354-7349.

MISSOURI. State Board of Nursing, P.O. Box 656, Jefferson City, MO 65102. (314) 751-2334.

MONTANA. Board of Nursing, Department of Commerce, Division of Business and Professional Licensing, 1424 Ninth Ave., Helena, MT 59620. (406) 444-4740.

NEBRASKA. Board of Nursing, Department of Health, Bureau of Examining Boards, P.O. Box 95007, Lincoln, NE 68509. (402) 471-2115.

NEVADA. Board of Nursing, 1281 Terminal Way, Suite 116, Reno, NV 89502. (702) 786-2778.

NEW HAMPSHIRE. Board of Nursing, State Office Park South, 101 Pleasant St., Concord NH 03301. (603) 271-2323.

NEW JERSEY. Board of Nursing, 1100 Raymond Blvd., Room 319, Newark, NJ 07102. (201) 648-2490.

NEW MEXICO. Board of Nursing, 4125 Carlisle N.E., Albuquerque, NM 87107. (505) 841-4620.

NEW YORK. State Education Department, Division of Professional Licensing Services, Cultural Education Center, Empire State Plaza, Albany, NY 12230. (518) 474-3817.

NORTH CAROLINA. Board of Nursing, P.O. Box 2129, Raleigh, NC 27602. (919) 828-0740.

NORTH DAKOTA. Board of Nursing, Suite 504, Kirkwood Office Tower, 7th Street & Arbor Avenue, Bismarck, ND 58501. (701) 224-2974.

OHIO. Board of Nursing Education and Nurse Registration, 65 S. Front St., Suite 509, Columbus, OH 43266-0316. (614) 466-3947.

OKLAHOMA. Board of Nurse Registration and Nursing Education, 2915 N. Classen Blvd., Suite 524, Oklahoma City, OK 73106. (405) 525-2076.

OREGON. State Board of Nursing, 1400 S.W. Fifth Ave., Room 904, Portland, OR 97201. (503) 229-5653.

PENNSYLVANIA. State Board of Nursing, Department of State, Box 2649, Harrisburg, PA 17105-2649. (717) 783-7142.

PUERTO RICO. Board of Nurse Examiners, Call Box 10200, Santurce, PR 00908. (809) 725-8161.

RHODE ISLAND. Board of Nurse Registration and Nursing Education, Health Department Building, 75 Davis St., Room 104, Providence, RI 02908. (401) 277-2827.

SOUTH CAROLINA. State Board of Nursing, 1777 St. Julian Place, Suite 102, Columbia, SC 29204. (803) 758-2611.

SOUTH DAKOTA. Board of Nursing, 304 S. Phillips Ave., Suite 205, Sioux Falls, SD 57102. (605) 334-1243.

TENNESSEE. Board of Nursing, 283 Plus Park Blvd., Nashville, TN 37219. (615) 367-6232.

TEXAS. Board of Nursing Examiners, 1300 E. Anderson Lane, Building C, Suite 225, Austin, TX 78752. (512) 835-4880.

UTAH. Division of Occupational and Professional Licensing, Board of Nursing, 160 E. 300 South, P.O. Box 45802, Salt Lake City, UT 84145. (801) 530-6628.

VERMONT. Secretary of State, Board of Nursing, Pavilion Office Building, 109 State St., Montpelier, VT 05602. (802) 828-2363.

VIRGINIA. Board of Nursing, Department of Health Regulatory Boards, P.O. Box 27708, Richmond, VA 23261. (804) 786-0377.

WASHINGTON. Board of Nursing, Health Care Licensing, Box 9649, Olympia, WA 98504. (206) 753-3726.

WEST VIRGINIA. Board of Examiners for Registered Nurses, Embleton Building, 922 Quarrier St., Suite 309, Charleston, WV 25301. (304) 348-3596.

WISCONSIN. State Bureau of Nursing, Box 8935, Madison, WI 53708. (608) 266-3735.

WYOMING. Board of Nursing, Cheyenne, WY 82002. (307) 777-7601.

Index

UNIVERSITY OF RHODE ISLAND

3 1222 00652 1754

DISCARDED
URI LIBRARY

DATE DUE	
JUL 2 9 2010	

DEMCO, INC. 38-2931